COMING OF *Age*

READINGS IN
CANADIAN HISTORY
SINCE WORLD WAR II

Donald Avery
Roger Hall
UNIVERSITY OF WESTERN ONTARIO

HARCOURT
BRACE
CANADA

Harcourt Brace & Company, Canada

Toronto Montreal Orlando Fort Worth San Diego
Philadelphia London Sydney Tokyo

Copyright © 1996
Harcourt Brace & Company Canada, Ltd.
All rights reserved

No part of this publication may be reproduced or transmitted in any form or by any means, electronic or mechanical, including photocopy, recording, or any information storage and retrieval system, without permission in writing from the publisher.

Requests for permission to make copies of any part of the work should be mailed to: Permissions, College Division, Harcourt Brace & Company, Canada, 55 Horner Avenue, Toronto, Ontario M8Z 4X6.

Every reasonable effort has been made to acquire permission for copyright material used in this text, and to acknowledge all such indebtedness accurately. Any errors and omissions called to the publisher's attention will be corrected in future printings.

Canadian Cataloguing in Publication Data

Main entry under title:

Coming of age : readings in Canadian history
  since World War II

ISBN 0-7747-3372-1

1. Canada – History – 1939–   . I. Avery,
Donald, 1938–   . II. Hall, Roger, 1945–   .

FC600.C65 1996   971.064   C95–930853–9
F1034.2.C65 1996

Publisher: Heather McWhinney
Senior Acquisitions Editor: Christopher Carson
Projects Manager: Liz Radojkovic
Developmental Editor: Laura Paterson Pratt
Director of Publishing Services: Jean Davies
Editorial Manager: Marcel Chiera
Supervising Editor: Semareh Al-Hillal
Production Manager: Sue-Ann Becker
Production Co-ordinator: Sheila Barry
Copy Editor: Claudia Kutchukian
Cover Design: Opus House
Typesetting and Assembly: True to Type Inc.
Printing and Binding: Best Book Manufacturers, Inc.

Cover Art: Greg Curnoe, *April, May, London, Toronto, Montreal* (1964). Private collection, Toronto. Reproduced with permission.

This book was printed in Canada.

1   2   3   4   5   00   99   98   97   96

COMING OF *Age*

Preface

Coming of Age: Readings in Canadian History since World War II is an innovative and useful source for those interested in the recent past. Unlike most other anthologies, which give only cursory treatment to the modern period, *Coming of Age* provides a comprehensive analysis of the major political and social issues that have influenced Canadian society since the outbreak of the Second World War. The topics are wide-ranging and reflect the interdisciplinary approach of this book: immigration and ethnicity, class and cultural identity, gender and family issues, civil liberties and the security state, political parties and political leadership, social inequality and the welfare state, science and health care, popular and elitist culture, national and regional loyalties, federalism and separatism, multiculturalism and aboriginal rights.

The anthology is organized into five thematic parts. Part One discusses the different symbols and perceptions of the Canadian identity. Part Two, "The Second World War: A Nation in Arms, 1939–1945," provides an examination of the war years through a series of articles that deal with Canada's political leadership during those years, its military contribution to the war, and civil liberties and the changing role of women in the country during that period. Part Three, "Postwar Canada: National and Regional Trends," explores important social trends and conditions such as the development of the postwar welfare state; the growth of suburbia; the expansion of the trade union movement; cultural changes in Quebec, as exemplified by changes at Laval University; and the experience of black women in Nova Scotia. Part Four, "The Turbulent Sixties and Seventies," is concerned with the issues that emerged in Canadian society after the conservative fifties, as revealed in the career of Lester B. Pearson and the writings of George Grant, the October Crisis of 1970, the debate over Big Science, and the tribulations of aboriginal peoples as exemplified by the Alberta Lubicon band. Part Five, "Foreign Policy and National Security," traces Canada's role in the United Nations, its involvement in and response to the 1962 Cuban Missile Crisis, and its commitment to peacekeeping and foreign aid. Part Six, "Contemporary Issues and Debates," explores the ongoing debates over Quebec's role in Canada, the health-care system and controlling health-care expenditures, multicultural policies, constitutional change and the media's influence with respect to such change, and the need to protect cultural industries while embracing free trade.

Acknowledgements

Foremost, we would like to thank the many authors and publishers who permitted us to reproduce the articles included in this volume. Thanks go, as well, to the editorial/production team at Harcourt Brace Canada for their hard work and commitment to this project, especially Chris Carson, Laura Paterson Pratt, and Semareh Al-Hillal. We are indebted, too, to our anonymous reviewers for their many helpful observations and comments. Special gratitude is reserved, as always, for those closest to the writers (those who always learn more than they wanted to know): Irmgard Steinisch and Sandra Martin.

A NOTE FROM THE PUBLISHER

Thank you for selecting *Coming of Age: Readings in Canadian History since World War II*, by Donald Avery and Roger Hall. The authors and publisher have devoted considerable time to the careful development of this book. We appreciate your recognition of this effort and accomplishment.

We want to hear what you think about *Coming of Age: Readings in Canadian History since World War II*. Please take a few minutes to fill in the stamped reader reply card at the back of the book. Your comments and suggestions will be valuable to us as we prepare new editions and other books.

Contents

Introduction

Students are frequently called upon to answer the question "What is history?" An equally intriguing query, and one asked less often, is "When is history?" These have always been tough questions, and for contemporary students they are even tougher. Cynics might argue that history is whatever it is that historians do. In our postmodern world, poor old objective history with a capital "H," the way it appears in university calendars, has frequently been dismissed as something of a minor intellectual inquiry.

Lately, national histories have come in for a particularly severe drubbing. For many years, Canadian history was dominated by grand themes concerning the relentless development of the nation-state, a political entity fashioned largely by business-minded white males. A quarter-century ago, the apogee of historical scholarship was the so-called synthesis, an impressionistic rendering of social, economic, and political forces usually filtered through a single mind and wedged between two book-covers. What characterized historical writing was a high level of *certainty*, a largely agreed-upon way of looking at the Canadian experience. Happily, our history is now viewed as much more multifaceted and complex. We have practitioners in dozens of new fields of inquiry, from women's history to sports history to legal history to immigration studies. What we have gained is a much more representative story; what we have lost is a sense of certainty and consensus.

Along the way, we might also have seen the degradation of objective scholarly inquiry. The discipline of history is not the only victim — in the last twenty years, the study of science has seen its objective status exploded as researchers have revealed its corporate connections, its environmental ignorance, and its gender biases. So, too, has the literary canon — the "great books" — come under attack for excluding women, homosexuals, and ethnic and other groups. Objective analysis is an impossible dream for postmodern scholars, since "texts," the raw stuff of any inquiry, are open to multiple interpretations. Who is to say which interpretation is correct? For those involved in this deconstruction, there is not one truth, but many — or perhaps none at all. Basically, the differences between cause and effect, the very stuff of the "old history," have become blurred, and "truth" has become a relative concept at best.

1

So the question "What is history?" is more complicated than ever. Our view, however, is that somewhere between the galloping nihilism of postmodernism and the stodgy consensus of dead certainties there is still a vital role for historians and even for "national" history. Past realities can never really be reconstructed, but they can be replicated. Language can be a barrier, but it can also be a bridge to understanding, after hidden meanings and contradictions are exposed. Every generation writes its own history, and contemporary Canadians will replicate new Canadian realities. For our recent past — what this book is concerned with — the new historical reality is one in which our diversity becomes the chief narrative theme.

What about the "when" of history? The questions "What?" and "When?" are interrelated. The simplest, and most serviceable, definition of history remains that it is the story of the past as told through surviving records in chronicle, document, and material form. When does yesterday's hockey game or last week's municipal election become history? The usual, rather glib, answer is that events pass into history when enough time has passed that they can be seen "in perspective." That's clear enough concerning something finite, like a war or an election. Obviously, one must wait until the tumult and shouting are over before one can overview events and circumstances. The situation is much less clear when dealing with social and cultural events whose evolution may be long-term, or even ongoing. And what constitutes "the past" becomes murkier still when one remembers that those who really "make" history are the historians — they are the people who choose the events that chronicle and interpret the past. These historians themselves are, as postmodernists remind us, inescapable products of their own contemporary social and cultural milieus.

We hope that all of this will help to explain the "why" of this book, with its focus on Canada since the outbreak of the Second World War. Other Canadian historical compilations have studiedly avoided isolating our contemporary Canadian past, or given it notoriously short consideration. Our view is that a definable era came to an end not long ago with the international conclusion of the Cold War, nuclear disarmament, and Canada's entry into the North American Free Trade Agreement. That era had its clear beginnings with the outbreak of the Second World War and may roughly be considered to have lasted about half a century. This is scarcely an original thought, but it seems clear that the implications of the war for this country, as for most of the world, were profound by every definition — socially, economically, politically, and culturally. Certainly, no credible explanation of Canada's role in the postwar world is possible without understanding the nation's evolution during the war. Postwar Canada is the precise product of the national maturation that Canada experienced during the war. "Big government" as we know it had its beginnings in wartime, as did such Canadian institutions as the welfare state, the particular character of our labour movement, and our dependence on the United States in military and defensive terms. Arguably, certain of the racial and linguistic divisions that exist in this country were exacerbated by the war. Not least, our peculiar and obsessive concern with social and cultural identity emerged as a fit subject for national debate.

In short, we believe that it was during this war and postwar period that Canada came of age. We further consider that enough time has passed to put the events of that half-century in perspective, to try to give some coherence to the whole period and provide some definition of the Canadian experience of it.

We have searched a vast number of journals in a wide variety of disciplines to achieve a balance of articles that address the varieties of recent Canadian experience. We have tried not to be swayed by fashions and trends, especially those in historical writing. If politics once dominated historiography in Canada, it may now be said that social history rules — particularly "bottom-up" social history that emphasizes the identification and assessment of the roles of ordinary people in Canada's past. Indeed, most current historical anthologies and texts reflect this social interest. Our selection necessarily reflects this current enthusiasm and we make no apology for it, since it has produced much helpful thought and good writing. But not all of these contributions have been produced by historians, and so we include many scholars from other disciplines: sociology, geography, anthropology, medicine, and literature, to name a few. We have also unashamedly resurrected politics, so long unfashionable in Canadian historical writing, but, it seems, of irresistible interest to average Canadians. Increasingly, we argue, the study of the political and economic context for social history occupies serious scholarly inquiry. So much social change is a result of political public policy initiative or economic ideology or enthusiasm. Our experience as teachers has also suggested that students find this contextualized approach more rewarding, since so much of the recent dominant social emphasis has been methodologically driven and is therefore correspondingly narrow in focus.

It has been remarked that the past is a "foreign country," an observation that applies as much to the recent past as to that of centuries ago. Our view is that this book will function as a passport, and we hope readers will have as profitable a journey in reading it as we had in its preparation.

Part One

Images of the Canadian Identity

Part One is intentionally emblematic. Canadians in the half-century after the Second World War spent a great deal of time looking for a place called Canada. This self-appointed task was sometimes aided and definitely abetted by academics, was usually financed by government, and was made doubly difficult because satisfactory definitions for Canada kept changing. Canada remained unswervingly a product of its past, but the dynamism of its present dominated how that past was interpreted and presented. In 1939, a high school class of young Canadians would have had little trouble establishing their collective identity — the answers were as clear as the Union Jack on the wall or the impending visit of the King and Queen. Five decades later, a similar class could point to no such convenient icons — they knew they were Canadians still, but they couldn't precisely or automatically tell you what this meant.

Our first chapter chronicles and reflects some of this confusion with a selection from *Survival*, novelist Margaret Atwood's immensely popular and influential 1972 definition of the Canadian identity. Atwood was building on work suggested by one of her teachers, the distinguished literary critic Northrop Frye, with whom she shared the belief that every culture contains an essential core of ideas, images, and beliefs that functions as a central symbol. She examines Canadian literature to unlock the country's unifying symbol, and concludes that it is that of a victim struggling for survival. Atwood argues that these twin ideas of victimization and survival characterize our national experience, and that they are largely the result of, on the one hand, having had to confront a hostile natural environment on a grand scale and, on the other, having experienced the degradations of being a servant to imperial masters: French, British, and now American.

Atwood's book is part criticism and part polemic, and it acted as something of a rallying cry for then-nascent Canadian literature. Critics have suggested that her definition of nationalism and identity is too monolithic (like the American definition, ironically) and that her own success gives the lie to many of her observations. Nevertheless, the book remains a landmark for defining Canadian interests in the postwar period.

In some ways, post-Confederation Canada has always performed a balancing act between Mother England and Uncle Sam. Canadians now like to think of themselves as being beyond that barbed dependence and influence. Much of Canada's contemporary and self-congratulatory view of itself relies upon its commitment to internationalism, to peacekeeping, and to a major world profile through the United Nations. Canadians only occasionally bask in international praise, however. One such international arena has been science, particularly the role of Canadian Nobel laureates. In an important and reflective piece, prize-winner John Polanyi considers the role of the pure scientist in contemporary society, and in another short article journalist Barry Came tells us about the tribulations of doing advanced scientific research in a country as small as Canada.

A number of symbolic issues come together in an article by the distinguished critic Robert Fulford that addresses the life and work of celebrated painter Emily Carr. Carr's work, thought by many to be a pure expression of Native life on the west coast, has come under intense postmodern scrutiny. To what extent did Carr really understand Native culture? Was she guilty of the politically incorrect crime of "appropriation"? Should the past ever be judged by the standards and interests of the present? Fulford assesses all of these questions in the context of postmodern criticism of Carr's work.

The final article in this introductory section deals with another theme that Canadians consider an essential part of their identity — the role and contribution of the immigrant. Drawing partly on her own experience, Didi Khayatt effectively shows much of the contemporary complexion of this important issue, particularly the roles of race, class, and gender. She reminds us of the usefulness of fluid, dynamic definitions in assessing both individuals and societies.

Further Reading

Carl Berger, *The Writing of Canadian History: Aspects of English-Canadian Historical Writing since 1900*, 2nd ed. Toronto: University of Toronto Press, 1986.

Northrop Frye, *The Bush Garden: Essays on the Canadian Imagination*. Toronto: Anansi, 1971.

Serge Gagnon, *Quebec and Its Historians: The Twentieth Century*. Montreal: Harvest House, 1988.

R. Cole Harris, "Regionalism and the Canadian Archipelago." In L.D. McCann, ed., *Heartland and Hinterland: A Geography of Canada*, 460–84. Scarborough, ON: Prentice-Hall, 1982.

Linda Hutcheon, *As Canadian as . . . possible . . . under the circumstances!* Toronto: York University/ECW Press, 1990.

Seymour Martin Lipset, *Continental Divide: The Values and Institutions of the United States and Canada*. London: Routledge, 1990.

Mordecai Richler, *Oh Canada! Oh Quebec! Requiem for a Divided Country*. Toronto: Penguin, 1992.

Maria Tippett, *Making Culture: English-Canadian Institutions and the Arts before the Massey Commission*. Toronto: University of Toronto Press, 1990.

Survival: A Thematic Guide to Canadian Literature

MARGARET ATWOOD

I started reading Canadian literature when I was young, though I didn't know it was that; in fact I wasn't aware that I lived in a country with any distinct existence of its own. At school we were being taught to sing "Rule, Britannia" and to draw the Union Jack; after hours we read stacks of Captain Marvel, Plastic Man and Batman comic books, an activity delightfully enhanced by the disapproval of our elders. However, someone had given us Charles G. D. Roberts' *Kings in Exile* for Christmas, and I snivelled my way quickly through these heart-wrenching stories of animals caged, trapped and tormented. That was followed by Ernest Thompson Seton's *Wild Animals I Have Known*, if anything more upsetting because the animals were more actual — they lived in forests, not circuses — and their deaths more mundane: the deaths, not of tigers, but of rabbits.

No one called these stories Canadian literature, and I wouldn't have paid any attention if they had; as far as I was concerned they were just something else to read, along with Walter Scott, Edgar Allan Poe and Donald Duck. I wasn't discriminating in my reading, and I'm still not. I read then primarily to be entertained, as I do now. And I'm not saying that apologetically: I feel that if you remove the initial gut response from reading — the delight or excitement or simply the enjoyment of being told a story — and try to concentrate on the meaning or the shape or the "message" first, you might as well give up, it's too much like all work and no play.

But then as now there were different levels of entertainment. I read the backs of Shredded Wheat boxes as an idle pastime, Captain Marvel and Walter Scott as fantasy escape — I knew, even then, that wherever I lived it wasn't *there*, since I'd never seen a castle and the Popsicle Pete prizes advertised on the comic book covers either weren't available

SOURCE: Excerpted from *Survival: A Thematic Guide to Canadian Literature* (Toronto: Anansi Press, 1972), pp. 29–36, 237–46. Reprinted with permission of Stoddart Publishing Co. Limited.

in Canada, or cost more — and Seton and Roberts as, believe it or not, something closer to real life. I *had* seen animals, quite a few of them; a dying porcupine was more real to me than a knight in armour or Clark Kent's Metropolis. Old mossy dungeons and Kryptonite were hard to come by where I lived, though I was quite willing to believe they existed somewhere else; but the materials for Seton's stick-and-stone artefacts and live-off-the-land recipes in *Wildwood Wisdom* were readily available, and we could make them quite easily, which we did. Most of the recipes were somewhat inedible, as you'll see if you try Cat-tail Root Stew or Pollen Pancakes, but the raw ingredients can be collected around any Canadian summer cottage.

However, it wasn't just the content of these books that felt more real to me; it was their shapes, their patterns. The animal stories were about the struggle to survive, and Seton's practical handbook was in fact a survival manual: it laid much stress on the dangers of getting lost, eating the wrong root or berry, or angering a moose in season. Though it was full of helpful hints, the world it depicted was one riddled with pitfalls, just as the animal stories were thickly strewn with traps and snares. In this world, no Superman would come swooping out of the sky at the last minute to rescue you from the catastrophe; no rider would arrive post-haste with a pardon from the King. The main thing was to avoid dying, and only by a mixture of cunning, experience and narrow escapes could the animal — or the human relying on his own resources — manage that. And, in the animal stories at any rate, there were no final happy endings or ultimate solutions; if the animal happened to escape from the particular crisis in the story, you knew there would be another one later on from which it wouldn't escape.

I wasn't making these analytical judgments at the time, of course. I was just learning what to expect: in comic books and things like *Alice in Wonderland* or Conan Doyle's *The Lost World*, you got rescued or you returned from the world of dangers to a cozy safe domestic one; in Seton and Roberts, because the world of dangers was *the same* as the real world, you didn't. But when in high school I encountered — again as a Christmas present — something labelled more explicitly as Canadian Literature, the Robert Weaver and Helen James anthology, *Canadian Short Stories*, I wasn't surprised. There they were again, those animals on the run, most of them in human clothing this time, and those humans up against it; here was the slight mistake that led to disaster, here was the fatal accident; this was a world of frozen corpses, dead gophers, snow, dead children, and the ever-present feeling of menace, not from an enemy set over against you but from everything surrounding you. The familiar peril lurked behind every bush, and *I knew the names of the bushes*. Again, I wasn't reading this as Canlit, I was just reading it; I remember being elated by some stories (notably James Reany's "The Bully") and not very interested in others. But these stories felt real to me in a way that Charles Dickens, much as I enjoyed him, did not.

I've talked about these early experiences not because I think that they were typical but because I think that — significantly — they weren't: I doubt that many people my age had even this much contact, minimal and accidental though it was, with their own literature. (Talking about this now makes me feel about 102, because quite a lot has changed since then. But though new curricula are being invented here and there across the country, I'm not convinced that the *average* Canadian child or high school student is likely to run across much more Canadian literature than I did. *Why* this is true is of course one of our problems.)

Still, although I didn't read much Canadian writing, what I did read had a shape of its own that felt different from the shapes of the other things I was reading. What that shape turned out to be, and what I felt it meant in terms of this country, became clearer to me the more I read; it is, of course, the subject of this book.

★　★　★

I'd like to begin with a sweeping generalization and argue that every country or culture has a single unifying and informing symbol at its core. (Please don't take any of my oversimplifications as articles of dogma which allow of no exceptions; they are proposed simply to create vantage points from which the literature may be viewed.) The symbol, then — be it word, phrase, idea, image, or all of these — functions like a system of beliefs (it *is* a system of beliefs, though not always a formal one) which holds the country together and helps the people in it to co-operate for common ends. Possibly the symbol for America is The Frontier, a flexible idea that contains many elements dear to the American heart: it suggests a place that is *new*, where the old order can be discarded (as it was when America was instituted by a crop of disaffected Protestants, and later at the time of the Revolution); a line that is always expanding, taking in or "conquering" ever-fresh virgin territory (be it The West, the rest of the world, outer space, Poverty or the Regions of the Mind); it holds out a hope, never fulfilled but always promised, of Utopia, the perfect human society. Most twentieth century American literature is about the gap between the promise and the actuality, between the imagined ideal Golden West or City Upon a Hill, the model for all the world postulated by the Puritans, and the actual squalid materialism, dotty small town, nasty city, or redneck-filled outback. Some Americans have even confused the actuality with the promise: in that case Heaven is a Hilton hotel with a Coke machine in it.

The corresponding symbol for England is perhaps The Island, convenient for obvious reasons. In the seventeenth century a poet called Phineas Fletcher wrote a long poem called *The Purple Island*, which is based on an extended body-as-island metaphor, and, dreadful though the poem is, that's the kind of island I mean: island-as-body, self-contained, a Body Politic, evolving organically, with a hierarchical structure in which the King is the Head, the statesmen the hands, the peasants or farmers or workers the feet, and so on. The Englishman's home as his castle is the popular form of this symbol, the feudal castle being not only an insular structure but a self-contained microcosm of the entire Body Politic.

The central symbol for Canada — and this is based on numerous instances of its occurrence in both English and French Canadian literature — is undoubtedly Survival, *la Survivance*. Like The Frontier and The Island, it is a multi-faceted and adaptable idea. For early explorers and settlers, it meant bare survival in the face of "hostile" elements and/or natives: carving out a place and a way of keeping alive. But the word can also suggest survival of a crisis or disaster, like a hurricane or a wreck, and many Canadian poems have this kind of survival as a theme; what you might call "grim" survival as opposed to "bare" survival. For French Canada after the English took over it became cultural survival, hanging on as a people, retaining a religion and a language under an alien government. And in English Canada now while the Americans are taking over it is acquiring a similar meaning. There is another use of the word as well: a survival can be a vestige of a vanished order which has managed to persist after its time is past, like a primitive reptile. This version crops up in Canadian thinking too, usually among those who believe that Canada is obsolete.

But the main idea is the first one: hanging on, staying alive. Canadians are forever taking the national pulse like doctors at a sickbed: the aim is not to see whether the patient will live well but simply whether he will live at all. Our central idea is one which generates, not the excitement and sense of adventure or danger which The Frontier holds out, not the smugness and/or sense of security, of everything in its place, which The Island can offer, but an almost intolerable anxiety. Our stories are likely to be tales not of those who made it but of those who made it back, from the awful experience — the North, the snowstorm, the sinking ship — that killed everyone else. The survivor has no triumph or victory but the fact of his survival; he has little after his ordeal that he did not have before, except gratitude for having escaped with his life.

A preoccupation with one's survival is necessarily also a preoccupation with the obstacles to that survival. In earlier writers these obstacles are external — the land, the climate, and so forth. In later writers the obstacles tend to become both harder to identify and more internal; they are no longer obstacles to physical survival but obstacles to what we may call spiritual survival, to life as anything more than a minimally human being. Sometimes fear of these obstacles becomes itself the obstacle, and a character is paralyzed by terror (either of what he thinks is threatening him from the outside, or of elements in his own nature that threaten him from within). It may even be life itself that he fears; and when life becomes a threat to life, you have a moderately vicious circle. If a man feels he can survive only by amputating himself, turning himself into a cripple or a eunuch, what price survival?

Just to give you a quick sample of what I'm talking about, here are a few capsule Canadian plots. Some contain attempts to survive which fail. Some contain bare survivals. Some contain crippled successes (the character does more than survive, but is mutilated in the process).

Pratt: *The Titanic:* Ship crashes into iceberg. Most passengers drown.

Pratt: *Brébeuf and His Brethren:* After crushing ordeals, priests survive briefly and are massacred by Indians.

Laurence: *The Stone Angel:* Old woman hangs on grimly to life and dies at the end.

Carrier: *Is It the Sun, Philibert?* Hero escapes incredible rural poverty and horrid urban conditions, almost makes it financially, dies when he wrecks his car.

Marlyn: *Under the Ribs of Death:* Hero amputates himself spiritually in order to make it financially, fails anyway.

Ross: *As for Me and My House:* Prairie minister who hates his job and has crippled himself artistically by sticking with it is offered a dubious chance of escape at the end.

Buckler: *The Mountain and the Valley:* Writer who has been unable to write has vision of possibility at the end but dies before he can implement it.

Gibson: *Communion:* Man who can no longer make human contact tries to save sick dog, fails, and is burned up at the end.

And just to round things out, we might add that the two English Canadian feature films (apart from Allan King's documentaries) to have had much success so far, *Goin' Down the Road* and *The Rowdyman*, are both dramatizations of failure. The heroes survive, but just barely; they are born losers, and their failure to do anything but keep alive has nothing to do with the Maritime Provinces or "regionalism." It's pure Canadian, from sea to sea.

My sample plots are taken from both prose and poetry, and from regions all across Canada; they span four decades, from the thirties to the early seventies. And they hint at another facet of Survivalism: at some point the failure to survive, or the failure to achieve anything beyond survival, becomes not a necessity imposed by a hostile outside world but a choice made from within. Pushed far enough, the obsession with surviving can become the will *not* to survive.

Certainly Canadian authors spend a disproportionate amount of time making sure that their heroes die or fail. Much Canadian writing suggests that failure is required because it is felt — consciously or unconsciously

— to be the only "right" ending, the only thing that will support the characters' (or their authors') view of the universe. When such endings are well-handled and consistent with the whole book, one can't quarrel with them on aesthetic grounds. But when Canadian writers are writing clumsy or manipulated endings, they are much less likely to manipulate in a positive than they are in a negative direction: that is, the author is less likely to produce a sudden inheritance from a rich old uncle or the surprising news that his hero is really the son of a Count than he is to conjure up an unexpected natural disaster or an out-of-control car, tree or minor character so that the protagonist may achieve a satisfactory *failure*. Why should this be so? Could it be that Canadians have a will to lose which is as strong and pervasive as the Americans' will to win?

It might be argued that, since most Canlit has been written in the twentieth century and since the twentieth century has produced a generally pessimistic or "ironic" literature, Canada has simply been reflecting a trend. Also, though it's possible to write a short lyric poem about joy and glee, no novel of any length can exclude all but these elements. A novel about unalloyed happiness would have to be either very short or very boring: "Once upon a time John and Mary lived happily ever after, The End." Both of these arguments have some validity, but surely the Canadian gloom is more unrelieved than most and the death and failure toll out of proportion. Given a choice of the negative or positive aspects of any symbol — sea as life-giving Mother, sea as what your ship goes down in; tree as symbol of growth, tree as what falls on your head — Canadians show a marked preference for the negative.

You might decide at this point that most Canadian authors with any pretensions to seriousness are neurotic or morbid, and settle down instead for a good read with *Anne of Green Gables* (though it's about an orphan . . .). But if the coincidence intrigues you — so many writers in such a small country, and *all with the same neurosis* — then I will offer you a theory. Like any theory it won't explain everything, but it may give you some points of departure.

*   *   *

Let us suppose, for the sake of argument, that Canada as a whole is a victim, or an "oppressed minority," or "exploited." Let us suppose in short that Canada is a colony. A partial definition of a colony is that it is a place from which a profit is made, but *not by the people who live there:* the major profit from a colony is made in the centre of the empire. That's what colonies are for, to make money for the "mother country," and that's what — since the days of Rome and, more recently, of the Thirteen Colonies — they have always been for. Of course there are cultural side-effects which are often identified as "the colonial mentality," and it is these which are examined here; but the root cause for them is economic.

It came as a shock to me to discover that my country's literature was not just British literature imported or American literature with something missing, that instead it had a distinct tradition and shape of its own. The shock was partly exhilarating, partly depressing — I'll explore both reactions later — and partly a kind of outraged surprise: why hadn't I been told? Our writers, apparently, had been working within this tradition for some time; but what they'd been writing had often been confused with — or compared for put-down purposes with — the products of other traditions. Canadian writers have not been trying to write American or English literature and failing; they've been writing Canadian literature. The general invisibility of this fact suggests that what we need now is not so much a way of writing Canadian literature as a way of reading it.

As I've tried to make clear, Canadian literature is not equivalent with "Canadian Content." Boy wearing Mountie suit meets Rose Marie with a maple-leaf in her hair is more likely to be an American musical comedy than a Canadian novel. But there's no reason why boy can't meet girl in Canadian literature; Canadian literature does not exclude the universals, it just handles them in a characteristic way. It's not necessarily the "subject matter" — families, Indians, and so forth — that constitutes the Canadian signature, but the attitudes to that subject matter, and through the attitudes the kinds of images and the outcomes of stories. But you can't read that signature (nor decide whether the book that incorporates it is well or badly written) if you've been looking all along for a different name.

The question, then, is not whether boy should meet girl in Winnipeg or in New York; instead it is, What happens in Canadian literature when boy meets girl? And what sort of boy, and what sort of girl? If you've got this far, you may predict that when boy meets girl she gets cancer and he gets hit by a meteorite. . . .

That wasn't just a bad joke; it indicates the dangers of cliché writing once there's a defined tradition, and that in turn raises an important question: What do you do with a tradition once you discover you have one? The answers in terms of the Canadian tradition can get rather complicated, but I'll make two simple initial suggestions:

• If you're a writer, you need not discard the tradition, nor do you have to succumb to it. That is, you don't have to say, "The Canadian tradition is all about victims and failures, so I won't have anything to do with it"; nor need you decide that in order to be truly Canadian you have to give in and squash your hero under a tree. Instead, you can explore the tradition — which is not the same as merely reflecting it — and in the course of the exploration you may find some new ways of writing.

• If you're a reader, you can learn to read the products of the tradition *in terms of the tradition itself*. You don't knock Faulkner for not being

Jane Austen, and those who do reveal nothing but their own obtuseness; the terms of reference are completely different. Recognizing your own tradition won't make you less critical; on the contrary, it ought to make you a better critic. (I'm not suggesting that you pretend bad writing is good, or fall into the trap of praising something just because it's Canadian.)

I'd like to explore these two areas — writing and reading — in a little more depth. I'll begin as usual with writing. There are two recent short stories which indicate one possible direction in which the tradition can be explored, as well as pulling together our central themes in some interesting ways. Their exploration consists of making explicit the experience of being a victim in a colonial culture — rendering it self-conscious as a literary theme.

The first story, by Ray Smith, is called "Cape Breton Is the Thought-Control Centre of Canada." Using a form Smith terms "compiled fiction," it juxtaposes snatches of prose which follow three main threads: a dialogue between a married couple; a fantasy about the Americans invading Canada and the guerilla resistance movement which fights them; and the fictitious history of one Count Z., a Pole who is loath to cede Poland to either the Germans or the Russians. The married couple, when they are not lukewarmly discussing whether or not they love each other, are debating whether they should move to the States; the resistance movement material is done as movie and thriller cliché; and poor Count Z. gets cut down leading a cavalry charge in the war that ensues when he will not sell his country to either contender — after which the Germans and the Russians sit down at the bargaining table and divide Poland.

Smith's story is an illustration of what can result in literature when the Canada-as-collective-victim theme surfaces or becomes conscious, instead of remaining submerged as it is in much of our literature. Calvinism and Colonialism have always fed each other, and their interaction is circular: Calvinism gives rise to the "I am doomed" attitude, which fits into the Colonial "I am powerless" one. But in much of our earlier literature, the Calvinism is in the foreground, and the Colonialism, with all the feelings of cultural self-deprecation and insignificance that go with it, in the background. In Smith's story these positions are reversed. The story approaches the Colonial predicament from three different angles: the indistinctness and, finally, the *unreality* of the national situation viewed from the cosy domestic nest; the fantasy nature of possible resistance against imperialism (without an actual resistance movement, the individual's dreams of standing up to the "enemy" can remain only Walter Mitty dreams); and the spectacle of what happens, historically, to small nations caught between big ones when the former try to preserve their own identity. Poland is the place where the others fight it out. "Polish history is very simple in this way," Smith comments. "The Poles also are simple: they love Poland." Smith's story not only points the finger at "the enemy" (identified as America); it suggests too that resistance is absolutely necessary, though possibly futile and perhaps even ludicrous, as his parting joke indicates: "For Centennial Year, send President Johnson a gift: an American tourist's ear in a matchbox. Even better, don't bother with the postage."

The second story, by David Godfrey, is called "The Hard-Headed Collector," and it too uses the technique of intercut story lines. The main plot concerns the epic journey of seven men from West to East across a mythologized Canada, on their way to an important goal. They appear to be artists: singers, poets, carvers. One by one they are lured away from their quest by various temptations — material comforts such as food and sex, demands by other groups that they be leaders or priest-figures, calls to battle — or captured by hostile elements — one becomes a slave in a whorehouse to pay debts incurred there, another is tortured and castrated by the Town Fathers and discovers he likes it. Only one man makes it to the end of the journey, and it is there that we discover what the quest was about: the men were to have forged a magic axe, cut down a giant tree with it, and then presumably — since despite their diverse ethnic names they were all from the Queen Charlotte Islands — made a totem pole, symbol of unity, ancestry and identity. But the last survivor is too late: all the trees have either been ruined by flooding or turned into the produce of a lumberyard. He is given a menial job and dies shortly afterwards. A ship comes for his body, suggesting that he is a figure of heroic stature, like King Arthur, though a failed one.

This piece of myth-making is interspersed with scraps of documentary, from the *New York Times*, about an aggressive American capitalist of the rugged individualist school, the "hard-headed collector" of the title, who has used his stock-market and investment earnings to compile a valuable art collection. He is donating his collection to the United States, because "I couldn't do what I did in any other country." The art is to be put in a Washington museum. The money that bought it has been made from Canadian oil and uranium.

If we read the myth part of the story alone, it would appear that opposition to the artists and to their task comes only from elements within the society: the bourgeoisie who offer bread and security in return for being entertained, the credit-system whores who enslave through debt, the factionalism that makes battles, the religious fanatics who convert artistic vision to their own uses, the Town Fathers who are petty politicians and amputation experts. But when the "collector" sections are added the meaning shifts. The collector lives in the centre of the Empire but makes his money on its fringes; the ultimate end of his activities is to reduce both art and the environment to a commodity. "You have forsworn me," says the remaining artist to the manager of the lumberyard; to which the latter replies "Forsworn you, my ass. Terms is terms." The lumberyard is part of the Empire; it acknowledges only money; in fact, it exists to convert the environment into money, whereas the artists wish to convert it into art. At the centre of the Empire art is a thing to be gathered and exchanged, easily and without pain. On its fringes it is a thing that cannot even be produced. In the vain attempt much blood is spilled, but the country has been sold before its identity can be forged. Though elements within the society have co-operated against the full expression of that society, it is the "collector" and his like who have created the conditions for that co-operation.

Both these stories are firmly within the tradition we've been examining; but both break new ground in an important way. They are stories about failure and victimization; but they are naming real causes of victimization, not displacing the causes onto Fate or the Cosmos. And unlike most other books, they include political realities — the United States as an imperial master — among the causes of victimization which can be explored. As in Hubert Aquin's *Prochain Episode*, successful action against these causes can as yet be taken only in fantasies, or projected into the future: Smith's characters remain powerless and trapped, Godfrey's fail in their quest and die. But here, we feel, failure occurs not because the author's literary tradition demands a failure but because failure is consistent with the conditions depicted in the stories. A successful revolution in the present is not imaginable. And it's at points like these — when literature names situations we can recognize — that writer and reader connect in an area we call real life: it's *our* situation that's being talked about (which is not to deny that readers of, say, MacLennan and Garner had the same feeling). A friend of mine has two phrases he falls back on when literature or reality get rough: "It's only a book" and "It's only my life." Sometimes the two can be used interchangeably.

I chose these two stories because they're short, they're experimental, and they deal with traditional Canadian themes in new ways. What is new about the approach is its consciousness, the making explicit of something that was hitherto implicit: Smith's analytical investigation of what it is to be a colony of the American Empire, Godfrey's mythological dramatization of the same fact of life. There are other books that approach different areas of our tradition in an equally conscious way . . . (such as Cohen's *Beautiful Losers* and Blais's *A Season in the Life of Emmanuel*). . . . What such works suggest is that a writer does not have to repeat his tradition unaltered. He can explore it further, dig out all its implications; or he can play variations on it, even make departures from it which will gain their impact from their measurement against the basic ground of the main tradition.

*   *   *

When I started thinking about whether or not anyone had attempted in poetry what Godfrey and Smith had done in prose — the mythologizing or analyzing of the country's predicament as a political victim —

I found myself remembering a number of individual poems, but not very many books of poetry. Also, the tendency in English Canada has been to connect one's social protest not with the Canadian predicament specifically but with some other group or movement: the workers in the thirties, persecuted minority groups such as the Japanese uprooted during the war. English Canadians have identified themselves with Ban the Bombers, Communists, the F.L.Q., and so forth, but not often with each other — after all, the point of identifying with those other groups was at least partly to distinguish oneself from all the grey WASP Canadians you were afraid you might turn into.

But four books stand out: Dorothy Livesay's *Collected Poems* (especially "The Documentaries" and "The Thirties"), Milton Acorn's *I've Tasted My Blood*, Bill Bisset's *Nobody Owns th Earth*, and Dennis Lee's *Civil Elegies*. These are four extremely different poets, but all have two things in common: they connect individual oppression with group oppression and individual liberation with group liberation, and they connect social liberation with sexual liberation; or, to put it another way, social liberation means Nature no longer has to be dead or a monster. Especially in Acorn and Bissett, this liberation extends to a liberation of the language, which includes the use of four-letter words and, in Bissett, phonetic spelling. In the work of all four, liberation means roughly the same thing: the freedom to live a life which realizes to the full its available human possibilities, and to live that life by participating joyfully in one's "own" place. For Livesay and Acorn one's "own" place (in their poetry, at least) tends to be The World; for Bissett and Lee this place is emphatically Canada. Since the subject of this book is Canada I will concentrate on the two later poets, though anyone writing poems of social concern and action in this country must acknowledge a debt to the earlier ones.

The amazing thing about Bissett's book is that it juxtaposes visions of Edenic happiness and peace with angry political poems like "Th Canadian" and "Love of Life, th 49th Parallel," the latter being probably the most all-inclusive poem on American takeover to appear so far. And yet it isn't, finally, amazing: anger and the desire for change depend on the assumption that change will be for the better, that it is in fact possible to achieve not only individual but social freedom. The title, *Nobody Owns th Earth*, predicts a world that will be not "international" but post-national, in which people will live on the earth with love both for it and for each other, and some of the individual poems give us glimpses of this world. The angry "political" poems, however, recognize the fact that we do not yet live in this world, and if we assume too soon that the millennium has arrived we will simply end up as victims again, owned by people who do not even admit the possibility of a non-"owned" Earth. These Bissett identifies as "th Americans." . . . Like Blake, Bissett is a kind of social visionary, and for such a visionary there must always be Songs of Experience as well as Songs of Innocence. Paradise here and now is individual and sexual, Hell here and now is social and mechanical; but the potential for social redemption is present, as witness the strength of the image at the beginning of "Nobody Owns th Earth," in which "a whole peopul" is seen "moving / together."

Bissett can make images of the two poles of Hell and Paradise, but he isn't sure how we can get from one to the other. Dennis Lee's *Civil Elegies* contains the same two poles, Hell which is a condition of servitude, being "owned," and Paradise which would be a form of freedom; but instead of simply presenting the images Lee investigates them, and investigates also the process of transition, the choices that would have to be made before reaching the potential Paradise. One important difference between the two books is that Bissett places himself to some extent "outside" the society, as a rebel against "straight" Canada as well as the United States, and thus for him sexual freedom and ecstatic vision are possible; while Lee is "inside," he makes himself a representative of his society. He embodies its plight, and since domination by an empire involves both cultural castration and stunting of vision, he is blocked off to a greater extent from the sources of light.

Civil Elegies leads off with a quote from George Grant: "Man is by nature a political animal, and to know that citizenship is an impossibility is to be cut off from one of the highest forms of life." It is the impossibility, or near-impossibility of "citizenship" in Canada that the poem deals with, tracing the historical roots of the predicament and exposing its results. Because Canada was never claimed by and for the people who live there — there were, after all, foreign flags on those historic flagpoles — the citizens dwell in a kind of limbo, a state of unreal suspension. What must happen is a claiming, a "will to be" in this country. Lee does not make explicit which comes first, rebellion against the dominating Empire or the individual and group self-confidence (call it faith) required to sustain such a rebellion. But both, it appears, are necessary if we are not to live forever on "occupied soil."

Part of *Civil Elegies* is concerned with the relationship to the land, as are many of the poems in *Nobody Owns th Earth*. For both poets Nature is no longer a monster but a potential home; both protest the kind of attitude towards the land that results in its exploitation, men taking with their own machines what there is to take. Both urge us to control our own space, physical as well as cultural. But that space must be controlled with love or it will be the control typical of a tyranny: there will not be that much difference between Canadian ownership and the absentee-landlord draining of the land we already live under. (Exploitation without representation wasn't good for Ireland either.) If choices destructive towards the land are made it doesn't much matter finally who makes them. But there is more chance of destructive choices being made by outsiders than by people who will have to endure the effects of these choices because they actually inhabit the country.

I'm not saying that all writing should be "experimental," or that all writing should be "political." But the fact that English Canadian writers are beginning to voice their own predicament consciously, as French Canadian writers have been doing for a decade, is worth mentioning. For both groups, this "voicing" is both an exploratory plunge into their own tradition and a departure from it; and for both groups the voicing would have been unimaginable twenty years ago.

*   *   *

These then, are some of the directions writers are now moving in. What about readers? I said earlier that readers could learn to read the works of their tradition in terms of the tradition itself; and this act would seem to involve a double perspective or vision. Imagine a picture of a landscape in which everything is dark grey — sky, lake, shore — except for a few points of light — a red flower, or a small fire, or a human figure. (Except for the colour scheme — blue, green and white are preferred to dark grey — this could in fact be a description of an actual Canadian painting, since many of them employ the same composition.) You can look at the picture with two attitudes. You can decide that the grey landscape is so large and overpowering that the points of light are totally dominated by it, rendered insignificant. Or you can see the points of light in contrast to their surroundings: their dark background sets them off and gives them meaning in a way that a bright one would not.

The tone of Canadian literature as a whole is, of course, the dark background: a reader must face the fact that Canadian literature is undeniably sombre and negative, and that this to a large extent is both a reflection and a chosen definition of the national sensibility. (That is, the artist takes his colouring from his environment, though he may intensify it by adding a little murk of his own.) But in that literature there are elements which, although they are rooted in this negativity, transcend it — the collective hero, the halting but authentic breakthroughs made by characters who are almost hopelessly trapped, the moments of affirmation that neither deny the negative ground nor succumb to it. These elements are not numerous, but they gain their significance from their very scarcity: thus, in Canadian literature, a character who does much more than survive stands out almost as an anomaly, whereas in other literatures (those in which European Princes are common, for instance) his presence would be unremarkable.

I said at the beginning of this chapter that when I discovered the shape of the national tradition I was depressed, and it's obvious why: it's a fairly tough tradition to be saddled with, to have to come to terms with. But I was exhilarated too: having bleak ground under your feet is better than having no ground at all. Any map is better than no map as long as it is accurate, and knowing your starting points and your frame of reference is better than being suspended in a void. A tradition doesn't necessarily exist to bury you: it can also be used as material for new departures.

The title of this chapter [Jail-Breaks and Re-Creations] comes from a poem by Margaret Avison, which begins:

Nobody stuffs the world in at your eyes.
The optic heart must venture: a jail-break
and re-creation . . .

What these three lines suggest is that in none of our acts — even the act of looking — are we passive. Even the things we look at demand our participation, and our commitment: if this participation and commitment are given, what can result is a "jail-break," an escape from our old habits of looking at things, and a "re-creation," a new way of seeing, experiencing and imaging — or imagining — which we ourselves have helped to shape.

I'll leave you with two questions which someone asked me while reading the manuscript of this book:

Have we survived?
If so, what happens *after* Survival?

The Scientist as Citizen: Freedom and Responsibility in Science

JOHN C. POLANYI

A major landmark in the appreciation of our obligations as citizens came with the dawn of the nuclear age. As scientists, we can take pride in those of our colleagues who, before there had been any demonstration of nuclear explosions, were drawing attention to the fact that the nature of warfare, and consequently the nature of relations between nations, would be transformed by the advent of nuclear weapons. They made it clear that the future of the world depended as never before upon global co-operation, since no other future was possible.

Those were farsighted individuals from within the scientific community, and we salute them. We would wish to emulate them. They were, however, an exceedingly small group. In addition, human imagination being limited, their focus (and mine too) proved to be too narrow.

Their concern with the arms race led to an organization of scientists that deserves mention: the Pugwash Group. It spawned other organ-

SOURCE: Excerpted from "The Scientist as Citizen: Freedom and Responsibility in Science," *Queen's Quarterly* 99, no. 1 (Spring 1992): 125, 132–33. Reprinted with permission.

izations of concerned scientists and physicians. Pugwash was, and remains, the prime international organization of scientists to address the problems posed by modern weapons of mass-destruction. Those problems assuredly remain with us despite the ending of the Cold War.

What we now realize, however, is that the power of modern science has transformed the world in a much more extensive way than is represented by the emergence of weapons of mass destruction. There is another highly explosive situation, namely the intolerable and increasing inequities deriving from the expanding population of the world (one more China per decade gives a measure of the rate of increase), escalating energy consumption, and depleted resources. Hidden in that statement is the fear that we may now be doing irreversible damage to our habitat — and the certain knowledge that we must act without delay if we are to stand a chance of avoiding irreversible damage in the future.

These profound problems require our active attention as citizens educated in science, even though it will be at the sacrifice of some of our lives in science.

The Renaissance represented a modest transformation compared with that which science and technology have brought about in recent decades. We scientists, being in the centre of the cultural stream that is presently reshaping the global landscape, have an obligation to offer our services, not as Messiahs but as interpreters between the language of science and that of society.

Ours is a powerful language but, let it be admitted, a narrow one. We have much to teach and more to learn. Striking the balance between these activities will constitute a creative act of the first order, with fateful consequences for mankind. We can be hopeful of the outcome only so long as we accord human imagination the freedom that it needs in order to flourish.

Tale of Two Nobels

BARRY CAME

In 1956, when he was 17 years old, Sidney Altman embarked upon his still unfulfilled quest. Armed with a passion for science and a diploma from Montreal's West Hill High School, he left Canada to pursue university-level studies at the prestigious Massachusetts Institute of Technology in Cambridge. Recalled Altman, now 52: "I was determined to succeed — and I was also determined to return home." By any measure,

SOURCE: "Tale of Two Nobels," *Maclean's*, October 21, 1991, pp. 32–33. Reprinted with permission.

he has accomplished the first of those objectives. Altman crowned a long and distinguished career as scientist and educator by winning a share of the 1989 Nobel Prize for chemistry. But despite this success, he has yet to find a path home. And for that, he blames the authorities in the land of his birth, who rebuffed repeated attempts to secure funding for his postgraduate studies and his early work. "The reception was not very friendly," he told *Maclean's* earlier this month, leaning across his littered desk in a cramped office at Yale University in New Haven, Conn., where he has taught biochemistry and genetics since 1971. "I found to my dismay that Canada had a very narrow attitude towards Canadian researchers who had earned degrees abroad."

The situation may well have changed in the quarter-century that has elapsed since Altman searched for Canadian financing to launch his career. Indeed, there are some in Canada's academic community who fault Altman for failing to explore fully the avenues that existed even then. "I think that he may have been misinformed," suggested the University of Toronto's John Polanyi, whose experience is in many ways a mirror image of Altman's. German-born and British-educated, the 62-year-old Polanyi, currently a professor of chemistry at U of T, moved from Europe to Canada in 1952 precisely because of the available opportunities for research. His inquiries into what he has described as "the molecular dance underlying chemical reactions" won him a share of the 1986 Nobel Prize in chemistry.

But no matter what the disagreement about the adequacy of Canadian policies, few dispute that the future of advanced Canadian research will depend on the ability to attract — and hold on to — individuals very much like Sidney Altman. "People like him should be our prime target," says Polanyi. "If we cannot get bright scientists with roots in Canada to throw in their lot with this country, then we are lost."

Both Nobel laureates agree that nurturing and retaining the kind of scientific talent capable of operating along the cutting edge of human knowledge has never been an easy task in Canada. "I'm afraid that it all boils down to money," says Altman. "I know several Canadians here in the United States, outstanding people, who would go home if they could match the conditions they have here — money for facilities, money for students and postdoctoral fellows, money for the next several years for their research."

Polanyi's view is similar. "Where do bright young Canadian scientists go to get a job?" he asked a visitor in the tidy suite of offices he occupies at the University of Toronto's downtown campus. "They can look for it in the Canadian academic world, where employment is scarce because universities are trying to shrink their faculties. They can look for it in Canadian government laboratories, where exactly the same situation prevails. Or they can look for it in Canadian industry, which, as is well known, has yet to commit itself to high technology."

Indeed, in 1988, the National Advisory Board on Science and Technology, a federal advisory committee composed of leading members of the political, business and academic communities, recommended that Ottawa double the amount of money allocated to Canadian university research funding over a three-year period. The recommendation is still awaiting action. Earlier this year [1991], the parliamentary standing committee on science and technology arrived at exactly the same conclusion. That committee's report, as well, is awaiting a response from the federal government.

In addition to the scarcity of funds, advanced Canadian research also suffers from another, subtler handicap. "There is always pressure in this country to try to make fundamental science responsive to the marketplace," claimed Polanyi. He mentioned by way of example the fact that both the Ontario and federal governments have attempted to justify the recent creation of networks of university-based "centres of excellence" on the grounds of industrial spin-offs. In the view of Polanyi and Altman, that is a dangerous rationale. "If basic science is being sacrificed for applied science, it is a huge mistake," says Altman, underlining the vast differences in time pressures in the two approaches. Polanyi voiced the same opinion. "To do well in basic science, you have to look for a payoff that is 10 or 15 or 20 years hence," he explained. "Industry wants results in two or three years. In Japan, even the big companies understand the need for patience."

Both laureates point to their own prize-winning research to illustrate the necessity of forbearance. It took nearly two decades before Polanyi's early observations about molecular excitation during chemical reactions eventually led to the creation of a marketable chemical laser. Similarly, while Altman's discoveries concerning the catalytic nature of the genetic material ribonucleic acid opened the door to the development of new methods to prevent viral diseases, those methods remain possibilities rather than realities.

Polanyi and Altman agree on another point, as well, but their views run counter to some long-standing Canadian ideals. "Canada has always been constrained by the notion that everybody across the country should get a little bit of the pie so that everybody feels part of the country," explained Altman. "But for a country with limited resources, the best strategy is to create a few outstanding centres and try to put the best talent you have in those centres." To some Canadian ears, Altman's suggestion may sound alarmingly elitist. But as Polanyi, leaping to the defence of his fellow Nobel laureate, argued, "Elitism in academe is no more vicious that elitism in, say, hockey. And in hockey I'll bet there are not many Canadians who think that all teams should be roughly equal."

In any case, there are some clear moves in the direction suggested by the two Nobel laureates: the Ontario government has established seven centres of research excellence, and Ottawa has subsequently decided to develop 14 networks of research centres involving 30 universities from across Canada. Despite some skepticism, Polanyi greets those measures as largely positive. He says that the twinned Ontario-Ottawa initiatives have increased Canadian funding for research by about 10 per cent. "It's far less than the doubling that has been repeatedly recommended," he says, "but it is, at least, a hopeful development."

Altman, too, is encouraged. "It's a sign that Canada is drifting very, very slowly towards adopting the kind of policies needed to create the proper environment for first-class research," he said. But the Yale scientist is still not completely convinced: "I think that there's a lot more that has to be done." Has there been enough progress to persuade him that it might be time finally to come home? "I've never given up the hope that I might one day return to Canada," he replied non-committally, before pausing to add with a smile: "And I still have my Canadian passport."

The Trouble with Emily

ROBERT FULFORD

In the summer of 1990, a wall text accompanying an Emily Carr exhibition at the National Gallery declared that Carr "forged a deep bond with the native heritage" of British Columbia, and developed a "profound understanding of the meaning of that heritage." That's not a new notion: it's a point often made about Carr by those who write earnest schoolbooks, and anyone who has read even a little about Canadian art will be familiar with it. But what does it mean? The answer involves a controversy that has been gathering around Carr in recent years, nibbling at the pedestal on which she has stood for two generations, drawing her into the midst of racial politics and postmodern theory, and challenging her place of high honour in Canadian art and women's history.

How profound, exactly, *was* the understanding to which the wall text pays tribute? Did Emily Carr understand native culture in the way she understood, say, the British-colonial Victoria in which she grew up? Or did she understand it in the way a diligent scholar may come to know a single foreign culture after years of study? Could she have explained the subtleties of belief by which coastal natives lived their lives and made their art? Or could she have described the differences between the Haida she encountered at Skidegate and the Tsimshian she met on

SOURCE: "The Trouble with Emily," *Canadian Art* 10, no. 4 (Winter 1993): 33–39. Reprinted with permission of the author.

the Skeena River in a way that either the Haida or the Tsimshian would recognize? Or does the word "profound," which springs so easily to our lips, mean something vaguer in this case, something like a mystical leap of imagination and empathy by which Carr miraculously found her way, through otherwise impenetrable forests of exotic belief and custom, into the very heart of native life?

Perhaps the wall text was no more than a pious tribute to one of the saints of Canadian culture, a saint whose story has nourished nationalists, feminists, British Columbians, and many other admirers of her work. Judith Mastai, who runs public programs at the Vancouver Art Gallery, has noticed how Carr enthusiasts love to burnish this story and "stand in its warmth," a beautiful phrase for one of the familiar uses of the cultural past. By now just about everyone knows the two dramas that make up Carr's myth. One is the standard modernist saga of the solitary artist whose talent and courage triumph over obscurity, neglect, poverty, and depression, making each painting into a personal victory that later generations adopt as part of their national heritage. In this case the sex of the protagonist heightens the narrative and places it firmly in women's history as well as in the history of Canadian painting. The other drama, equally powerful, involves her encounter with the great wooden sculpture of the coastal villages of British Columbia, sculpture which was largely created in the nineteenth century and allowed to rot through much of the twentieth, neglected both by the descendants of those who made it and by the white authorities who were governing the province and making every effort to obliterate the native cultures.

Carr began visiting those villages in 1907, fell in love with them, and soon (to use a phrase that seemed quite innocent only a few years ago) "made them her own." She found them dying and determined to give them life in her paintings, a project that involved much arduous travel; it turned her into one of those artist-adventurers whose work involves going long distances to find their subjects.

She succeeded so well that even today many of us, when we think of those villages, think first of Carr's paintings. We understand that her work was stylized, sometimes caricatured, that she added her own distortions to the native art that she saw. We know that sometimes it's impossible to say for certain which distortions are Carr's own and which belonged to the objects she sketched, sometimes in haste. She was, after all, an artist, not a reporter. We have far more precise visual accounts from photographers and filmmakers who have made their way up and down the B.C. coast. And yet it is Carr's version that first springs to mind, partly because of her undoubted talent and partly because she was seeing it freshly, discovering for herself a miracle of cultural history in her own part of the world. She was far from the first outsider to see the poles of the coastal and river villages, but she was the first to focus on them with the eye of an outstanding artist in the European tradition. She was equipped to do for them what Picasso did for the African sculpture he encountered around the same time, and what Gauguin earlier did for Tahitian art: she could take them imaginatively out of their own milieu and exhibit their virtues within another culture, a service that artists have been performing for other art at least since the time when ancient Romans copied Greek sculpture and thereby spread Hellenic influence through the empire. The idea that her eloquent tributes to native B.C. carving would one day be resented, and even perhaps labelled "appropriation," could not have occurred to her, any more than it could have occurred to Picasso or Gauguin or the Romans.

Carr was also something of an amateur anthropologist, which has lately turned out to be another source of trouble. In 1935, aged sixty-four, with her travels to the coastal villages and her paintings of native art now well in the past, she discussed the life of the natives with great confidence as well as obvious affection. Lecturing in Victoria, she implied that native B.C. art could be ranked alongside the greatest known, an idea that must have seemed radical at the time and is by no means universally acknowledged even today. She discussed, as equivalents, "the old masters of Europe, the Chinese and Japanese, the Greeks, the Byzantines, the Assyrians, the African negroes, the Indians of America. . . ." She argued that the source of the greatness of the coastal art could be found in the natives' relationship with nature, a relationship she believed she understood. She particularly focused on the simplicity of native life, which in her view made their art possible. The natives were obliged to work directly from nature: "They saw, heard, smelled, felt, tasted her," drawing knowledge from intimate contact rather than theory. "They looked upon animals (through which they mostly expressed their art) as their own kindred. Certain of the animals were more than that: they were their totems and were regarded by them with superstitious reverence and awe." She described the use of animal symbols by the chiefs, and the pride a carver took in representing these creatures: "His heart and soul were in his work; he desired not only to uphold the greatness of his people but to propitiate the totem creature." The Indian's art became great "because it was produced with intensity. He believed in what he was expressing and he believed in himself."

When she described this accomplishment, every verb she used was in the past tense. Finally she mentioned the artists of the present, 1935. She acknowledged that some still carved well, "but the objective and desire has gone out of their work." They no longer believed in the power of the totem. "The greatness of their art has died with their belief in these things." Reading, writing, and "modern ways" had irreparably broken their concentration on art. By the end of her talk it was clear that she was speaking a lament for a dead culture, one which she had been fortunate enough to glimpse and portray in its dying moments before the last great poles collapsed of their own weight and were reclaimed by the rain forests.

* * *

For much of her life, Carr was personally isolated, but she nevertheless painted, thought, and wrote from inside the heart of an empire of taste that ruled the world by what it regarded as natural right. She proceeded from the European tradition (somewhat, but not radically, modified by Canadian experience), and looked at the world, including the coastal natives, as a European. For that reason, her reputation is now under attack. Her legacy has become a battlefield in the culture wars, the subject of postmodern revisionism combined with retroactive racial justice. Just as she used native culture as a way of expressing herself, now natives (and others sympathetic to the present situation of natives) are using her as a way of exhibiting and analyzing the imperialism of white Canadian culture, in her time and ours.

To understand what has happened we need to understand that postmodernism represents the triumph of context over art. This kind of criticism began as a way of demonstrating the importance of the environment in which art is produced and used. It arose specifically to deny the work of the New Critics of the 1940s and 1950s, whose "close reading" of poetry excluded biography and history and searched for meaning within the poem itself. It also opposed formalist art criticism, which depicted the development of art as proceeding from an inner logic rather than as a part of its society. Twenty or thirty years ago, enemies of the New Critics and the formalists believed they were righting the balance, introducing realism into a too-rarefied criticism by insisting on the importance of social and political influences. But since then, postmodern thought has reversed the old emphasis rather than adjusting it; in fact, criticism now habitually uses art as an illustration of its context rather than using the context to illuminate the art. Art has become criticism's tool. In many a literature class across western Europe and North America, theory has superseded poetry itself, reducing Wallace Stevens or Sylvia Plath or Shakespeare to the level of "examples," evidence to prove academic theories about race, sex, and imperialism.

Within this world, it seems natural to focus on what we can now properly say on the subject of Emily Carr, and what that in turn says about her time, our time, and the relationship of culture to social justice. Marcia Crosby, a Haida/Tsimshian student of art and history, has a firm response to that National Gallery wall-text's assertion about Carr's "profound understanding." She states it in her essay, "Construction of the Imaginary Indian," published in 1991 in *Vancouver Anthology: The Institutional Politics of Art*, edited by Stan Douglas. Put plainly, she doesn't believe a word of it. In her view Carr could not possibly have had a profound understanding of the many nations inhabiting British Columbia. Crosby names sixteen distinct nations, from Nisga'a to Sto:lo, and that's the short list — she doesn't mention any of the nations of the interior. It would be impossible for anyone to develop, as a part-

time interest over a couple of decades, a deep understanding of so endlessly complicated a world. What Carr did was form an emotional bond
with it: it deeply touched her imagination, and she felt for it. But even
that bond (Crosby argues persuasively) was not with the nations themselves but with something that never existed: a homogeneous civilization,
Carr's own mental construct, a kind of generic native civilization, what
Crosby calls "the Imaginary Indian."

This was a fantasy vessel that Carr, like other whites, created. Into
it she poured her longing for a Canadian culture and her ideals about
nature. Believing she understood this "Indianness," she naturally felt
qualified to judge it, and even to write its obituary. Like the European
writers who enjoyed their own melancholy feelings about the dead cities
of the Middle East (the theme of Rose Macaulay's *The Pleasure of Ruins*),
Carr saw the sweet poetry of death in the fallen totems of the Northwest.
As Crosby says, her paintings of the last poles "intimate that the authentic Indians who made them existed only in the past, and that all
the changes that occurred afterwards provide evidence of racial contam-
ination, and cultural and moral deterioration. These works also imply
that native culture . . . may be measured in degrees of 'Indianness'
against defined forms of authenticity," which were also located in the
past. "Emily Carr loved the same Indians Victorian society rejected, and
whether they were embraced or rejected does not change the fact that
they were Imaginary Indians."

This is why (as Judith Mastai wrote in a paper given in November,
1992 at the University of Essex) "Today Carr's images are perceived
as part of the problem" rather than as the act of tribute that Carr believed
they were. Mastai argued that "paternalistic, white artists" romanticized
the idea of dying races and claimed to salvage the remains of these
doomed civilizations while at the same time, "consciously or unconsciously" supporting the federal government's development of a nation
that ignored aboriginal rights. These artists also, and Carr in particular,
"appropriated the imagery of the First Nations' peoples."

The word "appropriation," bearing the implication that people of
one culture do not have the moral right to depict other cultures in fiction
or painting, has lately become a rhetorical weapon in the hands of intellectuals claiming to speak for minority rights. Its power derives, oddly,
from its very irrationality. In my experience, people hearing of it for
the first time cannot believe that anyone could put forward so ludicrous
an idea: even the most modest education in cultural history teaches us
that art of all kinds has always depended on the mixing of cultures.
But just because the concept of "appropriation" stands so far outside
the realm of common sense, it has acquired the charm of the exotically
radical and attracted an exceptional amount of attention. It depends heavily on another idea, which has no name but has nevertheless become
widely popular: I call it "ethnic possession." According to this doctrine,

I hold a form of ownership in the culture produced by members of my race, even if I myself actively produced none of that culture. More than that, I am, by virtue of my race, inherently more knowledgeable about "my" heritage than people of other races can ever be.

"Ethnic possession" applies, so far, only to races and cultures oppressed by the majority. If someone of English background said "I automatically understand Chaucer better than any Pakistani who has studied him daily for ten years — and those who argue otherwise are both insensitive and insulting," that statement would be seen as almost insanely racist. But if an intellectual speaking for a minority sets forth precisely the same formulation, it is not only given a fair hearing but may sometimes be applauded and even taken seriously by institutions such as the Canada Council. The burden of historic guilt created by racism has so distorted the perceptions of western intellectuals that frequently we cannot see support for this notion as the act of condescension that it surely is.

Robert Linsley, a teacher at the Emily Carr College of Art and Design, carries the critique of Carr to another level: he attacks her not only for what she did but also for what she failed, in his view, to do. In *Vancouver Anthology* he writes: "Carr's empathy with the natives partly depends on her distance from them. The glamour of the noble savage that surrounds the Haida and other northern tribes in her work could not belong to the natives of the Songhees reserve in Victoria." He goes on to note the absence of figures in her mature work: "People are replaced entirely by their artifacts." Linsley implies that it was Carr's duty to paint the living Songhees rather than the villages left by dead Haida. Apparently Carr should have looked ahead to the 1990s, when she would be judged by Linsley and similar critics; then she might have made some small contribution to the understanding of the situation of natives in the twentieth century. True, she could still have been accused of appropriation, but she could have consoled herself with the thought that it was done in a good cause. Instead, poor fool, she acted like an artist: she saw a magnificent subject, unknown to the world but within her reach, and, hardly able to believe her luck, joyfully painted it.

Scott Watson of the UBC Fine Arts Gallery has convicted Emily Carr of another sin: she didn't keep up with public affairs. "She seemed to have little knowledge of the real legislative oppressions of her First Nations friends," he announces in an essay that appeared in *Eye of Nature*, published by the Walter Phillips Gallery at Banff in 1991. Watson can't forgive Carr for painting what she saw, in this case, magnificent villages that were on the point of disappearing: "Carr's ruins are carcass-like; there's a sense of something violated, a body disinterred, of something brought wrongly into the corrosive light and air. This morbidity in her was stimulated and fueled by the idea of cultural extinction and annihilation. . . . " Watson seems to be saying that there was something unhealthy ("morbidity") in Carr's fascination with the dying villages. Unlike her critics of the 1990s, she lacked the power of positive thinking. She should have turned away from this amazing spectacle and focused her attention instead on the problems of native rights and the difficulty of maintaining native cultures in the twentieth century. If she had been truly healthy she might have avoided art altogether, and perhaps have found work as a social worker, a politician, or even a professor. Postmodern criticism could have saved her from herself.

A far more thoughtful and sympathetic account of Carr's relationship with the natives can be found in "Northwest Coast Native Culture and the Early Indian Paintings of Emily Carr, 1899–1913," a recently completed doctoral thesis by Gerta Moray of the University of Guelph. Unlike Carr's other contemporary critics, Moray has gone far beyond the usual sources: her research encompasses the written record, contemporary newspaper coverage of Carr's activities, oral-history material, and, most important, the many paintings and sketches that Carr made in the years she spent studying native art. Moray understands the postmodern critique of Carr, and has read these arguments with care. Yet her thesis is an eloquent defence of Carr, her work, and her motives. In the end she persuasively refutes just about every point made by Carr's critics.

For Moray, the notion that Carr appropriated Indian art for the use of whites, and ignored the native culture of her own time, entirely misses the point. As Moray shows, she was not an artist seizing on Indian art for purely formalist reasons; all to the contrary, her art was a public, political act, owing as much to her civic conscience as to her artistic sensibility. She specifically opposed the white authorities, whether missionaries or government employees, who were urging natives to change their way of life, and she saw the totem poles as part of "an integrated and complex native culture. . . ." In writing about her travels to native villages "she took pains to acknowledge that these places belonged to her guides and it was they, not she, who understood them."

Carr's goal was to vindicate the natives against the negative views of whites, "asserting their honour, dignity, and the coherence of their traditional way of life and beliefs." Far from ignoring contemporary natives, she took care to show them her work, and took pride in the fact that they accepted it. Moray quotes George Clutesi, an Indian artist who knew Carr and visited her studio: "She made it so very simple for me to see how important it was to remain myself, and to not change my style. . . . It was largely because of her counselling that I kept the style that I began with." Carr understood that some natives, in their desire to assimilate, were ignoring or destroying the evidence of their cultural past, and she wanted to persuade them that this art was worth saving.

Unfortunately, she didn't have the effect on the white community that she hoped to have. In her dealings with provincial museums and in her Vancouver exhibition of 1913, she discovered that few of her fellow whites could be persuaded to share her esteem for native art. As Moray says, "Carr's espousal of native art forms was not acceptable for her own local audience until . . . the message of her art's significance came from Ottawa." But that doesn't reduce the fact that her documentary project was what she called it: an "homage" to the art of the coastal Indians.

The past can be a great burden for the living, if one's present life is seen as no more than a melancholy epilogue to vanished greatness. But this is not a unique problem for natives, and should not be discussed in isolation. Egyptians, Greeks, and Italians have known about it for millennia; the English are beginning to understand it, and the Americans think they can see it just ahead. Its implications for those who live with it are far more complicated than the formulations of postmodern criticism might suggest. It is a gross insult to any group of people to say that they have no future. But avoiding that insult should not involve distorting the past.

Marcia Crosby, in dealing with another work of art, George Bowering's novel, *Burning Water*, objects to the depiction of bad-smelling, drunken, promiscuous Indians, even though she acknowledges that Bowering's intention is to criticize white, Western ideology. Good authorial intentions aren't enough, she says: "There is a difference between using a theoretical critique and being used by it." Emily Carr, if she could speak from the grave, might well make precisely the same point.

The Boundaries of Identity at the Intersection of Race, Class and Gender

DIDI KHAYATT

Moment One

The year was 1981. A graduate student at the Ontario Institute for Studies in Education, I was working on my Ph.D., I was a novice feminist, listening to the words of my professors and of my fellow students, and absorbing the ideas that were changing my life and my thoughts. We were being taught to attend to the words of other women, and to locate ourselves in our research. That day, in class, the discussion centred on immigrant women. Students were attempting to grapple with the new (to us) sociological methodology which began from the standpoint of

SOURCE: "The Boundaries of Identity at the Intersection of Race, Class and Gender," *Canadian Women's Studies* 14, no. 2 (Spring 1994): 6–12. Reprinted with permission.

the oppressed, in this case, "immigrant women," and not from a defined sociological category. The debate was raging for close to an hour when finally the Professor was asked to give her opinion regarding what constituted an "immigrant woman." The Professor smiled, looked in my direction, and said: "We have an immigrant woman in our midst, why do we not ask *her* what she thinks?" Following the Professor's example, the whole class focused on the space where I was seated, and, likewise, I, too, glanced behind me, trying to find the "immigrant woman" to whom the Professor was referring. In my astonishment at being included in that category, I was rendered speechless. It had never occurred to me that I could be perceived as an "immigrant woman," a category which, to be precise, did include me because I had emigrated from Egypt in 1967, but one which did not fit me any more than it did our "immigrant" British Professor.

Why did I reject being included in the category "immigrant woman?" Why did I feel the label did not fit? We had just been told that people who originated from white, western, industrialized countries were not considered "immigrant." I came from Egypt. Why did I think I did not qualify?

The term "immigrant" technically refers to any individual who has a legal status in Canada of "landed immigrant" or "permanent resident" as opposed to being a "citizen." It is a temporary category intended as a period of adjustment, but also an interval during which those who are being considered as potential citizens are being evaluated. Individuals are given the rights and privileges in areas of work and education but are not yet able to vote or to carry Canadian passports. Indeed, historically, immigration policies were traditionally tied to labour needs and the political and economic imperative of populating certain areas of Canada with various skilled and unskilled labour. However, currently, as Roxana Ng suggests, the term is used in government documents to suggest all persons who are "foreign-born," regardless of their citizenship status. She continues:

> In common sense usage, however, not all foreign-born persons are actually *seen* as immigrants; nor do they see *themselves* as "immigrants." The common sense usage of "immigrant women" generally refers to women of colour, women from Third World countries, women who do not speak English well, and women who occupy lower positions in the occupational hierarchy (29).

I agree with Roxana Ng that there is a disjunction between the legal government definition and the common sense notion of what comprises an "immigrant woman."

Moment Two

I was recently going up the elevator with one of the cleaning staff of my building. Since I often saw her, smiled, and always greeted her previously, it was appropriate that in the time we had to go up nineteen floors we would engage in a short conversation. I asked her where she was from. She answered: "Me from Korea." I informed her that I was from Egypt. She smiled at me and said: "No, you Canadian, me Korean." I laughed and insisted that I was from Egypt. She was adamant. She kept shaking her head and repeating: "You Canadian, me Korean" right up to the floor where I got off.

What had this woman seen in me that was Canadian, that denied my assurance to her that I came from Egypt? Evidently, she perceived me as assimilated, as having power, and, in her eyes, as undifferentiated from those people who fit her notion of "Canadian." Although not all immigrant women are "visible minorities"[1] (another state originated term) like this Korean woman, and neither are all "visible minorities" foreign-born, often both categories are *perceived* as almost interchangeable. Frequently, as Roxana Ng points out, the situation of Canadian-born "visible minorities" and that of "immigrants" are similar in many respects because of the race and class biases inherent in the social structure (29).

In her analysis of theories of race and class oppression, Caroline Ramazanaglu argued against the notion that racism can often be reduced to class. She rightly points out that black women and, I add, women of colour, "are not uniformly oppressed and they can have contradictory interests in which race, class, ethnicity, and nationality cut across each other." Furthermore, she asserts that colour "is not a static or universal category of disadvantage that transcends all other sources of social difference which determine the quality of people's lives" (134). Although I agree with Ramazanaglu's position, I suggest that colour is *perceived* to be a category of disadvantage, as are other labels, such as "immigrant," "visible minority," "refugee," "person from a developing or Third World country," and so on. This perception does not just stem from bigotry, but is in keeping with official government ideology which currently has designated individuals who fit into state categories of gender and/or of multiculturalism[2] as disadvantaged minorities who should be protected from discrimination and assisted in maintaining equal access to Canadian standards of living. The state, for the most part, has defined these categories, and as such, they have entered the currency of institutional language. They each have a state produced definition which is designed to signal difference, but, at the same time, to protect those included in these classifications from social and economic discrimination in this society. It is precisely because of the perception that these categories are of disadvantage that I am concerned with indiscriminate labelling of individuals. To call me an "immigrant woman" or a "woman of colour" is to trivialize the very real oppressions of those who are within these categories and who are disadvantaged. Moreover, those "benign" categories themselves, although useful for state supported policies of affirmative action or legal bases for human rights complaints, are not as effective for the individuals themselves who are named within them. They often do not locate themselves in that manner precisely because the categories emphasize what seems to be an inalienable difference between themselves and the rest of the population. Where these classifications are significant is when they are appropriated to provide a feeling of belonging to a community, where this self-labelling may develop into an accepted identity, or whenever these terms are taken up by the women so identified and transformed into a political identity. For instance, being referred to as a "woman of colour" because a person merely belongs to a particular ethnic group, regardless of whether this individual shares any common concerns, becomes more a means of slotting people to force containment, rather than self-labelling, where, even if the same term is applied, it is used by the people themselves to achieve a cohesive community of support based on shared concerns or political perspectives.

In this article, I want to use my own experience to discuss the intersections of sex, race, class, and ethnicity. I am interested in examining how, in the process of assimilating into a new culture, one finds the self definitions which will eventually comprise one's identity. I shall also investigate the distinctions made between the various expressions of dominant white culture and minority groups within the social contexts of Canada. Finally, I shall demonstrate how the categories used to describe race and ethnicity operate differently to keep certain groups oppressed when particular elements are present. These include such factors as sex, religion, sexuality, class, language, financial situation, education, relative darkness of skin, combined with an individual's particular history.

I came to Canada in the late sixties to do graduate work. At the end of my first year in this country, I decided I wanted to stay and I applied for immigration status. At that time, the process included an application form, a set fee, and, most important, an appointment with an immigration officer who would assess, based on a predetermined point system, whether I, as a candidate, was suitable to become a landed immigrant. According to Alma Estable, this hurdle consisted of assigning points to different categories, the most significant of which were employment skills and professional qualifications. Immigrants were also "assessed on the basis of their personal characteristics (such as age, and professional qualifications), education, possession of a skill in demand"[3] (28). Because it was quantifiable, this system was supposed to be neutral and equitable. However, it should be noted that the linking of citizenship with occupation points to a system which is located within the dynamics of capitalism. Canada needed (and still needs) young, skilled immigrants, therefore practical training and work experience comprised the category which yielded the highest points. For my appointment with the immigration officer, I dressed up and made a special effort to look "good," not that I had any idea what would really make a difference. I presented myself at the appointed time, and we proceeded with the interview. On the one hand, my age, my very fluent English, my education, as well as my knowledge of Canada's second official language, French, gave me a certain number of points. On the other hand, my chosen field of anthropology did not rate at all on the priority list of needed skills, neither did I gain any points because of professional capacity. I had never worked in my life, not even at a summer job. The education officer questioned me regarding sponsorship by a relative, an organization or a company. I had none. Did I presently have a job? No. What kind of work was I capable of doing? I was a cultural anthropologist, my choices were limited. The poor man obviously wanted to give me the points, but I was clearly ten short of the required number and no amount of prodding into my professional experience could produce one single point more. Finally, he just looked at me, smiled, and said: "I know. I shall give you ten points for charm."

Would I have obtained these points had I spoken English haltingly? Would he have had the same measure of patience with my lack of skills and work experience had he perceived me as a "visible minority?" The accredited "charm" that the education officer appreciated relied on a combination of social relations which are not quantifiable, nor were they meant to be. Points were based on very practical state-defined occupational categories as well as potential characteristics which would eventually lead to job proficiency. I was assigned ten points based on nothing more functional than class and gender. I was located as a woman with no colour. My different-ness was invisible. I was perceived as posing no threat to the ruling white system. As a woman, my potential for work was trivial when compared with my youthfulness, and thus my procreational capacity. Therefore, I would suggest, what he saw was a woman of the right age and class to marry well, after which my assimilation would eventually be complete.

The assumptions implicit in the categories of "immigrant woman," "woman of colour," and "visible minority" conceal real differences in experience and do not account for nor distinguish between the various levels of oppression. They assume a homogeneity of background amongst all people who fall into those various groupings. As Linda Carty and Dionne Brand point out, these terms are "void of any race or class recognition and, more importantly, of class struggle or struggle against racism" (39). Who is entitled to determine who we are? How are those labels made to apply to various people? What do the labels really signify and how does that translate itself in the experiences of the individuals to whom they are applied? The question becomes, not who we are, but who we are perceived to be. It is not my identity which is of concern but the appropriate label that can be attached to me and which can decipher what I represent. The labels are applied by those in power to differentiate between themselves and those they want to exclude, and they accomplish this on the basis of race, class, ethnicity, and other factors. Or, as Linda Carty and Dionne Brand suggest: "State policy around issues of race, class, or sex can be characterized as policy of containment and control" (39).

Moment Three

Several years after I obtained my landed immigrant status, I was finally granted citizenship. By that time I had qualified as a secondary school teacher and had been gainfully employed by a northern Ontario Board. The day I was supposed to be sworn in was finally at hand and I presented myself at the local courthouse. The judge had to come all the way from Toronto for just this occasion, to oversee the transition from immigrant to citizen of several people. There were only five of us: a Chinese family of three, an Italian man, and myself. After the ceremony, we were all invited to attend a tea given by the I.O.D.E. (the Imperial Order of Daughters of the Empire) where they were to present us with a few mementoes, a Bible and a Canadian flag, to commemorate the occasion. I crossed the street from the courthouse to the church basement and found myself surrounded by older women bent on making me feel "welcome to Canada," my new land. Since the other four people had great difficulty with English, I became the centre of attraction, the one queried about conditions of my "old" country. The gist of the conversation was to make me articulate how I had left behind a dreadful situation to come to this land of plenty. The questions revolved around how we dress in Egypt, what and how we eat, do we have cars or is our public transportation based on camel power. I thought they were joking. I believed that they spoke in stereotypes on purpose and I played along. I laughed at their references and exaggerated differences, all in the name of fun, until the moment I left. Since I was the only Egyptian for miles around in that northern Ontario town, people often made humorous allusions to pyramids and camels in order to tease me. It never occurred to me that these women were deadly serious. I did not take offence at the conversation.

I did not translate the exchanges as a level of racism. I knew my background and therefore I did not perceive their presumptions about Egypt as anything more than lack of information. It was many years later, when I understood the language of racism, that this incident fell into place, that I recognized their benevolent attention not as welcoming me, but as relegating me to my "proper" place as grateful immigrant. Racism is not about colour, it is about power. Racism is power. It is not only a recognition of difference, but is the explicit emphasis on difference to mediate hierarchy based on colour, ethnicity, language, and race. Those women would probably not have seen me as particularly distinctive if

I had met them socially without mention of my cultural background. Within the framework of my class, they had no power over me, which is why I took no offence at their words. I was neither destitute, nor was I essentially dependent on Canada for my well-being. I had emigrated for personal reasons which had more to do with the necessity of finding myself than the urgency of earning my living.

In a recurrent discussion with my friend Marian McMahon (where she plays devil's advocate), she suggests that just because I am not conscious of racism does not mean that I am not the brunt of racist attitudes and remarks. When I interject that racism serves to place an individual in a vulnerable position, that, like sexism, it is flagged as a fundamental difference to highlight hierarchy and therefore justify discrimination, she agrees, but argues that as with those women who say they are not oppressed, my inability to feel oppressed is a denial of my status as a woman of colour, indeed, is in itself a form of internalized racism on my part. I take up her discourse seriously. However, I see that because of my privileged background, I can hardly qualify as "a woman of colour" and it would be inconsistent with the spirit of the common sense usage of the word for me to assume that label when I have never been submitted to the anguish of discrimination, the alienation of being slotted without my consent, or the experience of being silenced.

Moment Four

In 1967 I came to Canada to do graduate work at the University of Alberta, Edmonton. I was 23. My entire formal education had been in English up to this point, and I spoke French and Arabic as well. Shortly after my arrival, the Chair of the department in which I was enrolled invited all new graduate students and faculty to a party at his house to meet the rest of the department. I attended. I mingled. I exchanged pleasantries with many people. I answered innumerable questions about my country, our traditions, our ways of eating and dressing. When I thought it was appropriate to leave, I went to my host who promptly accompanied me to find my coat and boots, scarf and gloves. It was late October in Edmonton. At the front door, in full view of a room full of his guests, after he turned around and winked at them in collusion, he offered me his hand to wish me goodnight. Since I was already dressed to go out, I tended my gloved hand toward him, and following the rules of formal social conventions I had been taught, I said, with all the dignity of youth: "Please excuse my gloves." At which point, the entire room full of people who had been watching our exchange burst into laughter. I looked at them in surprise, and left without bothering to give or receive any explanation. To my youthful naive eyes, these people proved to be boors without redemption. Not for a single second did it occur to me that my behaviour was inappropriate, or that I needed to feel self-conscious. To me, they were simply amiss in their manners.

Laughter and humour, when aimed at a certain person or is at the expense of someone, when the individual is not "in the know" because she is new to a culture, when she is different from the rest of the group in some way(s), is a method of ridicule or mockery. It is particularly so when the person being laughed at is not included in the jocularity. If I had not the assurance of privilege, the knowledge that my manners were impeccable, the assumption that my class background transcends most western cultures, I would have withered in shame, wondered at my possible "faux pas," and wilted from the insensitivity of these, perhaps, well meaning strangers. However, I did not give them a second thought. Consequently, in the same way that, in the first account, I knew that the term "immigrant woman" did not quite apply to me, I did not experience this incident as humiliating nor as a negative comment on my race or ethnicity. Even though I had just arrived from Egypt, a country considered "Third World," even though as a new graduate student I was at the bottom of the intellectual hierarchy within the context of that department, and even though I was probably perceived as non-white, I had the composure of class and the confidence of privilege to protect me from the exclusion to which I may have otherwise been subjected and of which I may have been made an object.

From a very young age I was taught that I was the daughter of such a family, from a certain class, from a particular city in the south of Egypt. Managing class is not just the knowledge that one is born to privilege, but the understanding that this privilege may transcend different social and cultural changes. For instance, it did not come as a surprise to me when one day, as I was shopping for a sofa-bed in Eaton's department store in Toronto, the salesman recognized my family name. He came from Egypt and asked me the inevitable question to verify whether I came from that certain city in Upper Egypt and whether I was a Copt. Even though I was living on the limited means of a graduate student, he was immediately deferential. It was not me personally that he recognized, but how class operated in Egypt. The major discount he gave me was, perhaps, a reflection of his acknowledgment that, even in this new country, he had not forgotten the conventions of our past lives, that we both belonged — if differently — to a distant past, that in the vast sea of Canadian foreignness, we shared a common history.

The formation of my identity includes my class, my colour, my ethnicity, my sex, my sexuality, and my religion. These factors seem constant since I have been old enough to identify myself. They are my location. However, other elements which are as important are variable, their relevance modified by changes in personal politics, circumstances, age, career, current ideologies, the general political climate.

I came to this country over two decades ago. I could speak both official languages very fluently and with minimum accent. The relative lightness of my skin colour combined with my privileged class background have spared me from experiences of discrimination or prejudice. At best, I intimidated people around me, at worst, they found me exotic. Even though "exotic" is, broadly speaking, a form of racist categorization, the word is often used to imply a kind of difference which is coveted rather than scorned.

Although I claim not to have suffered racism, I am often made to feel aware of my different-ness. Strangers regularly mispronounce my name but then people in North America often stumble over most names which are not simply spelt or are uncommon. When I refuse to use my first name, Madiha, it is because of the way it is frequently butchered, and because it is seldom remembered (even when people comment on "what a pretty name" it is). As a result of its foreignness, if my name is being called out to take my turn at being served, it is often presumed that I do not understand English (especially if I hesitate before answering), therefore, I am addressed in that loud, over-enunciated diction which assumes that volume will make up for language. But it only takes a moment to set people straight.

I would maintain that those incidents are very minor, that if they constitute racism they, essentially, do not have any recognizable consequence on my life. I have been assimilated well. I do not stand out. I have had to adjust to Canadian cultural significations, not to prevent discrimination against me, but to avert feelings of inadequacy which may spring from lack of communication. I have had to alter my British accent, to tone down my formal manners, to adapt to many Canadian customs and traditions. I have learned to use cultural referents to project the messages I want to convey. Consequently, I become visible because I am recognizable. What is concealed is my history, what is hidden is my Egyptianness. However, I am in a position to produce my history when it suits me, when it adds a new dimension to my qualities, and certainly not when it can be held against me.

Can it be said that my very insistence on assimilating is itself a response to levels of internalized racism? Is the invisibility of my foreignness precisely an indication of racism? I have argued that I do not suffer racism because of class and skin colour. This does not deny that racism exists, but it does suggest that, given certain other factors, I am not touched by its virulence. My assertions contain elements of contradiction because they stem from an issue which is complicated. The fact remains that I am spared, that in the ability to define my own identity, to convey a specific persona, to contain these contradictions, I can manage to control how I am perceived. I choose to make myself invisible only in that I want to blend; I do not want to stand out. Consequently, although I can be heard, a part of me is silenced.

Rigid definitions of race and ethnicity which do not account for the fluidity of the categories are not useful in that they mask the differences of class and location. They fail to respect individual identities or to take into account lived experiences. Conversely, gender as a category, when considered a basis for discrimination without accounting for class or race, conceals distinct and intelligible levels of oppression within the category. And yet, Catharine MacKinnon reminds us, "to argue that oppression 'as a woman' negates rather than encompasses recognition of the oppression of women on other bases, is to say that there is no such thing as the practice of sex inequality" (20). It is also difficult to forget an early comment by Audre Lorde who informs us succinctly that: "Black feminists speak as women because we are women" (60). Feminism transcends yet recognizes difference. As a feminist, I bring to the discussion of race and gender the specificities of colour and class. Unless the boundaries of race, gender, class, and sexuality intersect to make visible the various nuances of each category, the usefulness of each becomes lost in a hierarchicalization of oppressions. In other words, if we isolate each characteristic in an attempt to make it visible without taking the whole framework into consideration, we are, in effect, rendering invisible the significant factors which combine to produce situations of oppression and discrimination. We are reduced to piling one oppression on another to show the extent of discrimination, or we attempt to debate which form of oppression, race or gender or class or sexuality, is more potent. Gender, race, class, sexuality have to be considered together and at the same time. They must each convey specific location without denying the distinctiveness of individual experiences.

Finally, if I have personally ever felt the alienation of national identity, it is not in Canada but in Egypt. Egypt, situated in what the Europeans called "the Orient," is anchored in people's minds as "a place of romance, exotic beings, haunting memories and landscapes," but, as Edward Said continues: "The Orient was almost a European invention" (79). In Egypt where colonization by French and English has reworked class structures to incorporate western notions of "culture" and "education," upper class society demands an understanding and consideration of and an affinity with the conquerors, with their locus of power. Some of the questions Said addresses in his book are appropriate:

> What . . . sorts of intellectual, aesthetic, scholarly, and cultural energies went into the making of an imperialist tradition . . .? What is the meaning of originality, of continuity, of individuality, in this context? How does Orientalism transmit or reproduce itself from one epoch to another? (15)

I am a product of his problematic. Despite my pure Coptic origins, each one of my family sports a European name, my father Andrew, my uncles Albert, Maurice, Robert, and my aunts Edna, Margaret, Dora. My generation was defiantly christened with Arabic names, another conqueror, but closer in geography and culture. It is in Egypt where I have never properly learned my native tongue that I feel like a foreigner.

I have never read Egyptian literature except in translation. The imagery that filled my formation is that of distant lands. I recited poems on daffodils when I had never set eyes on one. I described fields, streams, and forests while living in a land of intensive agriculture and wasted deserts. I knew of snow but had never experienced it. I enjoyed western toys, bought real estate in London playing British *Monopoly*, and donned clothes made in Europe. I attended French and English schools, and an American university. I walked the streets of Cairo and felt I did not belong because I spoke my own language with the exaggerated enunciation of one who is not using it continually; my idioms are outdated, my expression forgotten. When I return to my native land, I stand as foreign, am perceived as alien. I was never assimilated because class demanded a perceived difference from the masses. In Canada I am integrated because my survival depends on my being like everybody else.

NOTES

I gratefully acknowledge the support and ideas of Marian McMahon, Frieda Forman, Linda Carty, Peggy Bristow and Dina Khayatt. They should get the credit of refining my thinking, although I take the responsibility for my words.

1. "Visible minority" is a comprehensive term which describes any person who is non-white, including South Asians, Blacks, Chinese, but also, broadly speaking, Native Canadians. The term is not currently utilized because its use has proven limited.
2. "Multiculturalism" is a term which expresses the varied ethnic heritages of Canadians. *The Collins Dictionary of Canadian History, 1867 to the Present* (by David J. Bercuson and J.L. Granatstein), states that the term was first heard in the 1960s "as a counter to the emphasis on Bilingualism and Biculturalism that characterized the Liberal Government." The authors explain that the "ethos of multiculturalism is that every Canadian, whatever his or her origin, has the right to honour his or her heritage in Canada." However, the dictionary also notes that government policies of multiculturalism were subsequently perceived to be a political tool to remove francophone concerns from the limelight by introducing those of other rapidly growing ethnicities. This strategy promoted politics of divide and rule by using federal funds. Marjorie Bowker distinguishes between two versions of multiculturalism, in the first of which "all cultures are allowed to prosper and flourish amongst their followers; that nothing in the law be allowed to impede the personal enjoyment and enrichment to be derived from one's ethnic heritage." The other version, like the above, "concerns government funding for ethnic programs which tend to divide rather than unite, resulting in a loss of cohesiveness and eventually a fragmented Canadian culture" (87).
3. Alma Estable mentions that the Immigration Act was revised considerably although the point system continues in effect, and where practical training and experience continue to be assigned the greatest number of points.

REFERENCES

Bercuson, David J., and J.L. Granatstein, eds. *The Collins Dictionary of Canadian History, 1867 to the Present.* Toronto: Collins, 1988.

Bowker, Marjorie. *Canada's Constitutional Crisis: Making Sense of It All.* Edmonton, Alta.: Lone Pine Publishing, 1991.

Carty, Linda, and Dionne Brand. "'Visible Minority' Women — A Creation of the Canadian State." *RFR/DRF* 17(3) (1988).

Estable, Alma. "Immigration Policy and Regulations." *RFR/DRF* 16(1) (1987).

Lorde, Audre. "Sexism: An American Disease in Blackface." *Sister Outsider*. Freedom, Ca: The Crossing Press, 1984.

MacKinnon, Catharine. "From Practice to Theory, or What Is a White Woman Anyway?" *Yale Journal of Law and Feminism* (Fall 1991).

Ng, Roxana. "Immigrant Women in the Labour Force: An Overview of Present Knowledge and Research Gaps." *RFR/DRF* 16(1) (1987).

Ramazanaglu, Caroline. *Feminism and the Contradictions of Oppression*. London and New York: Routledge, 1989.

Said, Edward. *Orientalism*. New York: Vintage Books, 1979.

Part Two

The Second World War: A Nation in Arms, 1939–1945

The Second World War marked an important transition in the development of Canada. Under the pressures of this desperate conflict, the Liberal government of William Lyon Mackenzie King mobilized the country's military, economic, and scientific resources to support the war effort. By 1945, Canada was truly a nation in arms: it had the world's fourth-largest air force, its fifth-largest navy, and a well-equipped army of about half a million men and women. The Canadian economy also performed admirably: by 1945 it was fourth in war production among the Allied powers.

During the war years, control of the Canadian economy was determined largely by federal authorities. Clarence Dectaur Howe, Minister of Munitions and Supply, was particularly effective in using the talents and resources of Canada's major corporations for manufacturing explosives, tanks, warships, and airplanes. And when the private sector could not provide the necessary facilities or expertise, Howe was prepared to create Crown corporations to meet wartime requirements. The talents of Canadian universities were likewise commandeered, especially their scientists, engineers, and medical researchers, who became involved in developing a wide range of weapons, including the atomic bomb.

Never before in Canada's history had the government asked so much of its citizens. All able-bodied men were eligible for compulsory military service, many skilled workers and professionals were assigned war-related tasks, and the government recruited thousands of women for work in war plants. To fulfil its side of the social contract, Ottawa implemented a variety of social measures, including unemployment insurance, and new federal guidelines for collective bargaining. By 1944, the King government had substantially expanded Canada's welfare state through the introduction of the family allowance, the housing act, and the creation of two new social departments, Health and Welfare and Veterans Affairs. Many of these programs were drawn from the comprehensive Marsh Report on postwar reconstruction. These changes also reflected the growing influence of the federal bureaucracy on government policy and the ability of Ottawa to launch new social programs through its expanded access to tax revenues.

The articles in Part Two reflect the many ways in which Canadians were affected by the war. This section also deals with a number of scholarly debates about the direction and character of Canada's war effort. Robert Keyserlingk starts off with an intriguing assessment of the leadership qualities of Prime Minister William Lyon Mackenzie King, his spiritualism, and his view of Adolph Hitler prior to 1939. Brereton Greenhous and the historical team at the Department of National Defence join the bitter controversy surrounding the CBC series *The Valour and the Horror* with an "insider's" perspective on Canada's role in the air war over Germany. The excerpt from Terry Copp and Bill McAndrew's *Battle Exhaustion: Soldiers and Psychiatrists in the Canadian Army, 1939-1945* is an astute blend of military and medical history; the authors' observations provide new insights into the physical and psychological realities of combat.

The domestic aspects of the Second World War are explored in two articles. Ann Gomer Sunahara provides a provocative interpretation of why the Canadian government was determined to deport most of the Japanese Canadians who had been interned in February 1942, and why this policy was defeated. Excerpts from Ruth Roach Pierson's *"They're Still Women After All": The Second World War and Canadian Womanhood* demonstrate how the war affected the occupational focus and lifestyle of Canadian women and the importance of gender issues during these years.

These five articles demonstrate the complexities of trying to understand the impact of the Second World War on Canadian society. Most could be categorized as social history, but only in a broad and comprehensive way that does not exclude political or military history. Together, they pose a number of important questions about the tumultuous war years. To what extent did Mackenzie King's personal views influence Canada's defence and foreign policies prior to 1939? Did Canadian political and military leaders commit serious blunders that cost thousands of Canadian soldiers and airmen their lives? How did the Canadian military and its doctors respond to the problems of battle exhaustion? Why were there differing degrees of severity in the Canadian government's response to people of Japanese, Italian, and German background? What real gains, if any, did Canadian women achieve during the war years?

Further Reading

Ken Adachi, *The Enemy That Never Was: A History of the Japanese Canadians*. Toronto: McClelland & Stewart, 1976.

Robert Arcand, "Petain et De Gaulle dans la Presse Québécoise entre Juin 1940 et Novembre 1942." *La Revue d'histoire de l'Amérique française* 44, no. 3 (1991): 363-95.

David Bercuson and Syd Wise, *The Valour and the Horror Revisited*. Mont-real/Kingston: McGill-Queen's University Press, 1994.

Robert Bothwell, *C.D. Howe: A Biography*. Toronto: McClelland & Ste-wart, 1979.

J.L. Granatstein, *Canada's War: The Politics of the Mackenzie King Gov-ernment, 1939-1945*, 2nd ed. Toronto: University of Toronto Press, 1990.

J.L. Granatstein, *The Generals: The Canadian Army's Senior Commanders in the Second World War*. Toronto: Stoddart, 1993.

Norman Hillmer et al., *On Guard for Thee: War, Ethnicity and the Ca-nadian State, 1939-1945*. Ottawa: Canadian Committee for the History of the Second World War, 1988.

Marc Milner, *North Atlantic Run: The Royal Canadian Navy and the Battle for the Convoys*. Toronto: University of Toronto Press, 1985.

Allan Moscovitch and Jim Albert, eds., *The "Benevolent" State: The Growth of Welfare in Canada*. Toronto: Garamond Press, 1987.

Doug Owram, *The Government Generation: Canadian Intellectuals and the State, 1900-1945*. Toronto: University of Toronto Press, 1986.

C.P. Stacey, *Arms, Men and Government: The War Policies of Canada, 1939-1945*. Ottawa: Queen's Printer, 1970.

David Stafford, *Camp X: Canada's School for Secret Agents, 1941-45*. Toronto: Lester & Orpen Dennys, 1986.

Mackenzie King's Spiritualism and His View of Hitler in 1939

ROBERT H. KEYSERLINGK

Prime Minister Mackenzie King of Canada exhibited a strange ambiv-alence towards Adolph Hitler before the Second World War. He refused to criticize him in public, and persisted in his belief that Hitler was basically a man of peace. Only three days before the outbreak of war in September 1939, King confided proudly to his diary that no one could count him among those who had antagonized the German leader: "I never let myself declare . . . against Hitler," he wrote.[1] One scholar has gone so far as to label King's feelings for Hitler "an unrequited love

SOURCE: "Mackenzie King's Spiritualism and His View of Hitler in 1939," *Journal of Canadian Studies* 20, no. 4 (Winter 1985-86): 26-44. Reprinted with permission.

affair from afar."[2] In a recent book, C.P. Stacey hinted that King's spiritualism influenced strongly his view of Hitler. "King's curious relationship with Hitler can only be understood as an episode in the Prime Minister's mystical life."[3] However, these rather terse if insightful statements about King's spiritualism and relationship to Hitler hang tantalizingly in the air, isolated from the more conventional discussion of King's political ideas and activity.

King's reluctance to take a strong public stance against Hitler or to prepare Canada for the eventuality of war is usually attributed to his innate caution and wise statesmanship. Keen to avoid imperial and European entanglements and deeply concerned with preserving his country's fragile domestic unity, King operated quietly behind the scenes to guarantee that, when war broke out, Canada could enter it as a strong rather than damaged actor. By declaring Canada's alliance with Britain before outside circumstances forced the country to this decision, he could drive a rift between the French and English.[4] Thus when cabinet met on 24 August 1939 for the first time formally to discuss the issue of war, it did so behind a veil of secrecy. At that time cabinet agreed in principle to go to war with Britain if war actually occurred, to call Parliament to bless this decision, and to order warplanes. Although the British High Commissioner and the German Consul General were informed confidentially of these momentous conclusions, King decided against telling the Canadian public. Instead, a soothing statement was issued which spoke vaguely of strong cabinet solidarity at this moment of heightening international tension.[5]

Without wishing to call into question King's pragmatic political instincts, the problem of his curious lack of private as well as public anti-Hitler sentiments remains. This article will look at this intriguing question from the point of view of King's passionate interest in spiritualism. Behind King's dry, secretive, bachelor exterior was a warm, romantic spirit seeking a higher meaning in life and interpreting the world through poetic and occult symbolism. Many have remarked upon this trait in his character, but few have cared to follow it up. On the whole, King's spiritualism has been a deep source of embarrassment for most scholars, little more than a sad indication of his personal, social, or psychological weaknesses. As a result, this part of King's life has been hived-off to a private realm.

In order to understand King's view of Hitler in the period immediately before World War Two, it is necessary to bring King's private and public lives closer together again. His spiritualism, which developed strongly in the early 1930s, influenced his view of Hitler and of the international tensions in Europe. Nevertheless, scholars have experienced enormous difficulties in facing the issue of King's spiritualism and consequently have denigrated it. In order to counter such responses, it is important to consider King's deeply religious search for meaning in the larger framework of similar motives which have fueled other religious men and women, mystics, ideologues, and even scientists through the ages. More specifically, spiritualist beliefs were fairly widespread among members of King's generation, many of whom also held positions of trust and responsibility in public life.[6] As King himself often wrote in his diary, his own spiritualism was the central cement of his life, inseparable from his public role: "Private life cannot be separated from public . . . and the highest good comes from the purest life."[7] By this, King meant that man must develop his higher spiritual side in order to understand better the mysterious directives for activity in this world from the Beyond, as he called the world of guiding spirits. Finally, King's spiritualist frame of reference exerted great influence over his view of Hitler in 1939. The divine directives pointed him to pagan and Christian legends and symbols, especially those popularized by Wagner, through which he interpreted Hitler. Although King did not always approve of the guidance the spirits gave his fellow medium, Hitler, he hoped to help him avoid evil and remained convinced that good would triumph in the end. This mystical approach skewed his view for it explained the Fuehrer less in terms of practical politics than in poetical and mythical categories. In this vein, King was quite capable of comparing Hitler's *Mein Kampf* to Bunyan's *Pilgrim's Progress*, for both were written in jail and delineated a cosmic wrestling between the forces of good and evil.[8]

The occult in King's life has not received a favourable press. As an adept himself in the secrets of the Beyond, King no doubt would have been the first to appreciate others' difficulties in understanding his inner life. Not attuned to, or initiated into, these mysteries as he felt he was, others would not be able to appreciate their importance or discover their meaning as he could. During his own lifetime, King's preoccupation with privacy allowed no hint of his personal beliefs to become public knowledge. His extensive personal diaries, which he hoped would be destroyed after his death, were eventually preserved by his executors and gradually opened to research because of their crucial importance for the interpretation of Canadian politics of the period and of King's long political career.[9] Readers of this massive self-reflective labyrinth have learned a good deal about King's political leadership and motives, and in this sense have proven the executors correct in their decision to preserve the diaries. But the occult side of King revealed in his private papers has baffled scholars, who either have not comprehended his insights or could not forgive such quackery. On the one hand, these voluminous diaries and papers constitute perhaps the single most valuable collection of political documentation of modern Canadian history. On the other hand, it became evident that they were written by a man who was not only for twenty-two years a successful prime minister of Canada, but at the same time a shy, reflective, and deeply religious bachelor. The diaries have not helped to explain the enigma of an eminently able and practical politician possessed by wildly romantic personal beliefs. They have merely compounded it by rendering King unsuitable to be fitted into the respectable categories ordained by worldly historians. Sound secular academics not normally given to occult introspection have chosen to focus their attention on King's public political life, leaving his strange spiritual activities aside as an embarrassing eccentricity or alarming weakness.

Once King's executors arrived at the decision to preserve the diaries and to open them in stages to research, his spiritualistic writings continued to nag them. Unable to see anything but damaging scandal in his occultist beliefs, his executors early considered censorship or suppression of this side of his life. In 1977 they finally took the drastic and dramatic decision to burn King's spiritualistic notebooks and to close the remainder of his spiritualistic collection of clippings and letters, evidence of what they saw to be his unbalanced private indulgence, until the year 2001.[10] Despite these quite extraordinary precautions, King's secret interior life, his quest for complete spiritualist explanations of human history, and his interest in clairvoyance leaked out, for his regular diaries still contained a good deal of information on these topics. However, his mystical side has not attracted scholars, having been firmly relegated to the status of irrelevant anecdote or personality flaw.

The first professional historian to investigate King's private life through his diaries was C.P. Stacey, whose *A Very Double Life* (1976) exposed its thesis in its title. Stacey closely examined the personal and public records, but emerged offended by the subject of spiritualism. He launched a few very suggestive rockets about King's growing interest in the occult spirit world, his attendance at seances after 1931, his discovery two years later of his own direct route of "conversations" with the departed, and his ferocious concentration upon everyday signs, symbols, and coincidences as messages from Beyond. Yet, in the final analysis, Stacey judged this spiritualism to be marginal to an understanding of the public figure. At best it was evidence of a private egotism, loneliness, or character weakness. There was, therefore, no need to consider this area of King's life too seriously. His inner fears, even his need for entertainment, explained away these secret lusts of his spirit. In this way, King's rather morbid private life and his resolutely highminded public career remained mercifully divorced from each other. Besides, Stacey argued, these bubbling visions and "conversations" quickly died down again after 1935 when, because of his return to political power and the consequent need to concentrate on matters of state, King was unable to find much private time for esoteric ruminations. Thus, his spiritualist beliefs and practices could have had absolutely no effect upon his public life after that. As confirmation for his position, Stacey referred to interviews held after King's death with mediums and long-time spiritualist friends such as Joan Patteson of Kingsmere.[11]

However, to anyone familiar with the intricate veil of protective secrecy drawn by spiritualists over their sacred knowledge and mysteries, confirmation by these friends of the purely private nature of King's spiritualism is hardly surprising. The true believers told down-to-earth skeptics such as Blair Fraser and others what they wished to hear. But it is the nature of spiritualist knowledge that only those attuned to and initiated into it will be permitted to partake of it. Nor was the year 1935 a cut-off date in King's spiritualist career, although the practical considerations of his position as prime minister clearly began to dominate his daily activities after his return to power. His 1939 diary still reflects concentrated spiritualist reading, discussion, and activity, especially at his residence in Kingsmere in the company of his friend, Joan Patteson.

Stacey's dualist character analysis has been followed by others hoping to protect the image of King the great liberal politician from that of King the secretive religious eccentric. In the same year that Stacey published his sprightly book, another scholar wrote of his horror upon discovering for himself such overwhelming evidence of "ghostly ravings" in King's diaries. Reginald Whitaker amusingly described how he "staggered shell-shocked and blinking from the Public Archives" after his "descent into delirium."[12] By contrast, Whitaker demonstrated elsewhere a sensitive understanding of the basic religious-moral motivation behind King's political reformism. Whitaker's need to see King's spiritual values coincide with social reality led him to the eclectic spiritualist approach:

> Nor is it surprising that in later life he [King] should have fallen into outright occultism. Not content to be a mystic at night and practical politician by day . . . it is perhaps inevitable that . . . he would end by finding "evidence" of the penetration of the material by the spiritual.[13]

Yet, in the end, Whitaker too did not integrate King's private and public lives in satisfactory fashion, preferring to discuss him under normal, secular scholarly headings. Unable or unwilling to link his strange views with his public life, Whitaker concluded that King's private personality and public achievements were spectacularly at odds with each other. His occult beliefs became a savage if unconscious self-indictment. They indicated a serious bifurcation of personality, which King never seemed to notice or care about. To resolve this "schizophrenic dualism," Whitaker reached back to his own ideological framework of explanation. Looked at in social terms, King's private and public division of character reflected the unresolved social divisions and tensions within the bourgeois order of Canada. His schizophrenia mirrored the ambiguities of the middle class's social position and ideals. Thus King's private beliefs became a type of mental escape or "defence mechanism of the bourgeois order." His "vulgar Hegelianism" turned easily into "right-minded Babbitry." It reflected his failed attempt to cross the unbridgeable chasm between his ideals and the stubborn social reality through a leap into spiritualism. For a time, Whitaker notes, King's "Panglossian liberal faith that all was for the best" even accommodated Hitler within its wide embrace.[14]

Thus, in Whitaker's analysis of King's interior life, the esoteric and political remained separate. Only someone as basically tough-minded as King could have dared to exhibit such comic, cosmic self-knowledge in his diaries and still have functioned so well on the level of practical political ideas and activity. In this way his spiritualism was disarmed. "If the inner King had become the outer King, what a hallucinatory politics Canada would have had. The mind boggles, the heart quails."[15] In a similar vein, the most recent book on this topic, ironically entitled *Knight of the Holy Spirit*, filters the diary evidence to King's spiritualism through Freudian categories. As a result of this trip to the psychiatrist, King emerges as an even more hopelessly neurotic, egotistical, hypocritical, and self-deluded shell than has usually been assumed.[16]

Yet it should be remembered that King's religious yearning for direct insight into the hidden mysteries of human life and the universe were not so unique or strange. The same search has motivated many other men and women. Nor was his spiritualism so unusual. Despite its apparent demise in Europe following the end of the Renaissance and Reformation, spiritualism re-entered western thought again in the romantic movement of the nineteenth and early twentieth centuries, and has enjoyed another, more familiar third wave since the 1960s. King's own amalgam of liberal Protestant Christianity and ancient mystery myths emerged as a type of western cultural pessimism common in the late Victorian and First World War eras, when a rejection of modern materialism and the confusions of rapid social and political change caused men and women to sense a loss of traditional religious and social roots. Convinced that modern scientific and industrial society was shallow, coarse, and directionless, they hoped to follow new (or not so new) spiritualist paths which promised to pierce through the heavy veil of life to truth. They looked for hidden, deeper truths and missions in life through pagan and Christian legends, personal intuition and art, dreams and imagination. This new poetic and imaginative romance aimed to release true human creativity, freedom, and energy. At the same time, they were children of their time deeply affected by scientism and evolutionary thought. The human race was capable of higher evolution through ancient wisdom and intuition which appeared superior, or at least supplementary, to traditional Judeo-Christian beliefs. Christianity itself became merely one of the great, poetic books of human wisdom. The older the message and the more hidden the meaning in symbol, fable, and myth, the truer it was for those few able to unravel the deep directives. Great interest was rekindled in Druidic and Egyptian cults, Arthurian and Teutonic legends, eastern philosophies, and a poeticized Christianity as vessels of ancient, lost truths.[17]

This rejection of flat industrial and money motives in human affairs for initiation into ancient, secret mysteries and personal illumination produced many different cults, which together comprised a sort of international, western fellowship sharing many basic common beliefs. Chief among these was the spiritual evolution of the universe and the human spirit through stages of history as a result of struggle between good and evil spirits. Believers easily united eastern reincarnation myths with a typically western optimism in human progress.[18] They saw in the Holy Grail and in promises of Christ's Last Supper metaphors for universal brotherhood, social welfare, or sexual equality; many became inspired social or political reformers. The direct intervention of spiritual forces into human affairs would, if heeded, lead to higher stages of human consciousness and social existence by training imaginative reason to step beyond the purely rational in the traditional sense. Theosophy, "the science of the secret doctrine of the universe," was founded by Madame Blavatsky about 1870 and introduced in Canada in the 1890s by Conn Smythe's Irish journalist father.[19] Theosophists saw the evolution of the universe through seven historical "root races." Humanity since Christ represented the fifth or aryan race; a concept common to, if differently applied by, spiritualists and Nazis. According to Madame Blavatsky, a sixth and higher race would be born through the white races' mixture in North America. All human entities, individuals, groups, races, nations, or cultures played particular and valid roles in this cosmic evolution.[20] The various spiritualist groups often disagreed with each other and developed their own special practices and beliefs. Most dedicated themselves to "white" or good secrets, some to "black" evil mysteries. Some were more pagan, others more Christian. But they shared certain common spiritualistic assumptions about the direction of human affairs through spiritual forces, and reflected a common disillusionment with industrial western society and its religious-cultural traditions.

Each spiritualist group nurtured its own special truths, practices, and initiates behind a veil of secrecy. As a result, it is difficult to document these groups in detail except through their own writings, or to judge the influence of their shared beliefs on the public lives of their members. Madame Blavatsky's influence on social reformers such as the founders of the British Labour Party has been noted.[21] German Field Marshal von Moltke's lack of energy during his failed 1914 attack on France has been blamed on his fatalistic belief in anthroposophy. Hitler's surprisingly rapid rise in 1919 Munich has been credited to a local group of secret middle-class spiritualists of both Christian and Jewish background united in the Thule Society. These wealthy and influential burghers picked him as a mystical leader, funded his party, bought him his party newspaper, the *Völkischer Beobachter*, and passed him around to similarly-inclined salons across Germany. Hess's flight to England in 1941 has been attributed to the esoteric links he forged during the 1936 Berlin Olympic games with the Duke of Hamilton, a leading British spiritualist, whom Mackenzie King also visited during his trip to Britain in 1936.[22] Theosophy in Canada exercised a crucial influence in the aesthetics of Lawren Harris, the feminism of Emily Stowe, the politics of Philipps Thompson, and the nationalism of William Arthur Deacon.[23] It is therefore reasonable to conclude that King was not unique in his beliefs. Like many others, he functioned perfectly well in public while maintaining a perhaps bizarre, but not necessarily insane or schizophrenic, spiritualistic belief.

King's personal creed was deeply affected by both his Scottish Calvinism and his spiritualism. From the former he inherited a scepticism about the nature of the human condition, subjected as it was to coarse lusts, drives for power and money, and the brute force of selfishness. This view of Calvinist Providence ensured such a flux of earthly experience as to undermine any purely human emotion or motive beyond the moment, except among those chosen and elected by God. At the same time, he was critical about certain fundamental aspects of Presbyterianism. He refused to accept traditional notions of predestination or hell. "Perfectly hideous," he termed them, seeing them as quite in conflict with his idea of a loving God. He rejected communion as a sort of "anthropomorphic cannibalism."[24] Seeking deeper answers to life's mystery than his traditional religious roots gave him, and rejecting modern atheism, socialism, and materialism as possible solutions, King turned to an improving spiritualism. He came to believe that the world as our torment and mystery could be understood and transcended not only after death, but here and now by attuning oneself to the guidance of the universe and the spirits from the Other World, whether pagan or Christian. On this last issue he was ambivalent, claiming sometimes that the Christian would vanquish the pagan, while at other times seeing the pagan too as part of the divine plan. Like many other educated people of his time, King was steeped in the works of Greek, Anglo-Saxon, and Germanic mythology, easily falling into poetic interpretations of reality. Both non-Christian and Christian legends were therefore doors to deeper truths and secular harmony, if only their keys could be found. Visible nature was merely a mask behind which the real spiritual forces of the universe struggled for supremacy.

Imaginative myth and ancient wisdom as well as everyday signs and coincidences hid spiritual directives for those attuned souls called upon by destiny to lead humanity upwards and onwards to the light of the Holy Grail, the universal brotherhood of man. There is little doubt that this vision inspired a good deal of King's social reformism.[25] Thus, he could move easily in his diaries from the mystical to the political and back again, from the sentimental to the serious, and from the realistic to the almost farcically mysterious in a manner which has displeased scholars in search of more traditional secular or political motivation. The following excerpt about his interior struggles and a planned 1939 campaign is a typical example:

... the [spiritual] conflict that has been mine all the way, — but with God's help must be ended if possible from now on — that the note may be clear forever — while living and before death comes, — that mankind may be helped — to prepare for the campaign of 1939 in this spirit and with this purpose is from now on my express aim.[26]

Or again, regarding the guidance he received from the spirits during the glorious Royal Visit to Canada of the summer of 1939, King triumphantly wrote in his diary: "I know that the voices of goodwill have guided me, used me as an instrument, e.g., Royal Visit."[27] For him, spiritualism was at once an escape from the narrow limits set by modern civilization on the human spirit, a pilgrimage to self-knowledge and control, and a mission to struggle for all humanity against evil forces seeking to crush the good in the human spirit.[28] This mixture of the mystical and of the real was, for King, the very centre from which he viewed the rest of his life and activity.

King was prepared to admit that as a practicing politician he did not have as much time as he might have liked to spend on the interpretation of his dreams; for speculating and learning about the Other World's "principles of conduct"; for investigation of his cloud, mirror, or numerical symbols; or for his "conversations" with his departed spiritual guides. After all, destiny had called him to be Canadian prime minister, to become what he called a "practical medium" like a Cromwell or a Hitler.[29] Man's struggle to evolve higher could no longer be led by traditional, but degenerate, aristocracies of birth and inherited social position, the "smart set" as he deprecatingly labelled them. Now a new, hidden group of aristocrats of the spirit would take over, leaders who emerged from and grew up unknown among the people, embued with a deep sense of their cosmic and public responsibilities, men like King himself, Hitler, and others.[30] Like other spiritualists, King did not keep his belief in or attitude to the spirit world secret because he felt there was anything shameful or ridiculous about it, but because it was a secret insight to be shared only with other initiates, especially his neighbour, Joan Patteson.[31] The artificial temple and ruins that King constructed at his farm in Kingsmere assisted his spiritual contemplation and "conversations" with the departed spirits. Only if the spiritually-advanced like himself fought hard against evil in conjunction with the good spirits of the Other World would the supernatural higher good defeat the brutal, material, and instinctual principle in the world. The goal of both King and the "forces unseen" in the Beyond was the same — "peace on earth and good will to men."[32]

King kept copious records in his diaries, liberally interspersed among his political records, of the direct verbal guidance he received from the departed spirits "who [have] been guiding me in the search for the Holy Grail." He conversed with many of the illustrious dead, including his dear departed parents, Gladstone, Lord Byng, and Joan of Arc, and he kept detailed scripts of their advice and comments. He regarded Joan Patteson, who shared his mystic revelations at Kingsmere, as another guide sent by fate to direct him to the highest good. His small dog, Pat, was not only the beloved companion of a lonely bachelor, but more importantly a symbol of his dead mother's continuing love, devotion, and promise of guidance. Mrs. Dowden, his medium in London, had given him as a very special spiritual guide the long-dead priest-king and German Knight Templar Johannes, who figured prominently in his 1939 "conversations."[33] With the help of his personal galaxy of spirits King hoped to move towards the Holy Grail, which represented not merely a higher level of human consciousness but also a higher and better state of social existence for all men. He believed in a classical spiritualist mixture of modern evolutionism, the Christian legend of battle by King Arthur, the story of the Holy Grail, and eastern reincarnation myths. It is therefore not surprising that these same mystical insights and voices would also guide him in his response to the greatest international problems of that time attendant upon the rise of Hitler and Nazi Germany.

Nazi philosophers and leaders propounded a harsher mystical belief in racial history and evolution and the aryan myth than did other spiritualists of the time. Hitler gave these mystical influences a particular aggressive and political direction not acceptable to most other spiritualists, who suspected a certain evil aura around him.[34] King too was attracted by, and suspicious of, aspects of German culture and Nazism. He appreciated their deep spiritual basis but worried about the question of their final good or bad results. He recognized in them many similarities to his own beliefs: the theory of spiritual and racial evolution, the aryan race, the ancient myths of struggle, the continuing secret influence of the warring Knights Templar disbanded in the 1300s for their esoteric beliefs, Wagner's and Nietzsche's supermen and heroes railing against a debasing materialistic civilization, and salvation sought beyond the traditional.[35]

It is well known that during King's 1937 visit to Germany he gained the conviction that Hitler was a mystic and a man of the people like himself, dedicated to the good of his people and free of the traditional ruling class's selfishness and corruption. In August 1939 he still fondly remembered this momentous visit: "I left Hitler not with a curse, but a blessing . . . meaning may God's blessing guide you (not bless his wrongful acts) but his strivings for Humanity."[36] Although time soon raised new questions about his peaceful aims, King continued to respect the spiritual war besieging the Fuehrer's soul and remained convinced that good forces would win out in the end. Upon Hitler's Anschluss of Austria in early 1938, King recorded in his diary both his uncertainties and hopes:

> I am convinced he is a spiritualist — that he has a vision to which he is being
> true . . . his devotion to his mother — that Mother's spirit I am certain is his
> guide . . . I believe the world will yet come to see a very great man — a mystic,
> in Hitler . . . much I cannot abide in Nazism — the regimentation — cruelty and
> oppression of Jews . . . but Hitler him[self], the peasant — will rank some day
> with Joan of Arc among the deliverers of his people, and if he is only careful
> may yet be the deliverer of Europe.[37]

Until September 1939, King kept faith that the good would win and
that it was his duty to aid in this victory of the good in Hitler.

The most important stimulus to King's own inner development and
to his understanding of Hitler in the summer of 1939 was his discovery —
by divine guidance — of the nineteenth-century German dramatist-
composer Richard Wagner as a guide.[38] By chance, in June 1939 he came
upon a neglected Christmas present, a book on Richard Wagner. At random he opened the book first at the spot where a voice spoke to the
agnostic Wagner on Good Friday, thereby leading him to sketch out
his Christian opera of Parsifal and the Holy Grail. King's enthusiasm
knew no bounds. There could be no doubt that this book and Wagner
had been sent him by his divine guides:

> May it be so with me — the Parsifal motive from today on, more certain and
> clear than ever. (How I recall going with dear Mother to see Parsifal and how
> like her white head one of the characters in the play.) She is guiding me, I
> know, like Elizabeth in Tannhauser, like the highest and noblest influence in
> Parsifal.[39]

Reading this biography, King immediately became deeply impressed by
Wagner's own interior struggles and by his mythical amalgam of chivalry,
paganism, reincarnation, and Christianity as the route towards man's
higher and better future.

King had long had an interest in Wagner's operas, having seen Parsifal at the New York Metropolitan Opera in 1922. From June to September 1939, this book constituted King's main inspiration:

> The Wagner book has come by divine aid. I can see that it will help me in
> my inner life — in my political life, — the dramatization of the [1939 election]
> campaign on right lines — the understanding of Hitler and Germany, — and the
> world situation — Life's journey — I was interested in seeing Wagner's concept
> of mercy and pity for the poor — vs. self-satisfaction in selfishness, sensuality,
> etc.[40]

As he read aloud to her from the book, he told Joan Patteson in July
1939 that it "is the very thing I have been thirsting for. . . . Something
urges me to read Wagner's life as helping to understand Hitler, also
myself." Together they "picked out Wagner — because of getting a better
understanding of Hitler this summer."[41]

The author of this romantic biography approached his subject in a manner which fit easily into King's mode of thought. Count Guy de Pourtalès was a German-born aristocrat who had picked Switzerland as his home after World War I and rejected his native German language for French. From his adopted home and in his adopted language, de Pourtalès wrote a series of extremely popular salon books idealizing the restless and rebellious artistic spirits of the period 1830–80. They railed against the flat materialism and directionlessness of modern life, and called for men to rediscover their own creative spirit and divine mission. In his biographies of Liszt, Chopin, Berlioz, Wagner, and Nietzsche, de Pourtalès praised those poetic ideals which had, unfortunately, "floundered in the sea of History" because of modern falsehoods and hypocrisies. In his flowery language, he attacked materialistic greed and power seeking; he aimed at "reawakening, in the hearts of those who read these pages, some woodland melody, some distant trumpet call, or tragic dissonance, such as even our humble longings are adorned withal." These themes struck a deeply responsive chord in King.[42]

According to de Pourtalès, Wagner preached the optimistic doctrine that the day would return when a hero such as Siegfried would tear down the sensual god Wotan and his demeaning material desires so that a new human order governed by love and brotherhood could arise on the ruins of the gods. Through strife, love, and creative spirit, men would enact great deeds, escape from contemporary restrictive bonds, and create a true cult of humanity. They could escape their loneliness and sensuality and assuage their longing for things of the spirit if they aimed at these noble goals. Acts of Providence and direct spiritual intervention into human affairs would be guides in this great adventure. King agreed with much of this already, although he felt that de Pourtalès somewhat underestimated Wagner's basic optimism and religiosity. If, in Wagner's *Ring*, Siegfried could bring down the evil gods, the pure Christian hero Parsifal could rescue the Holy Grail.[43]

Seen by means of Wagnerian images Hitler became a mythical Germanic Hero-warrior struggling to redeem his people and to lead them to a harmonious, uplifting future. In July 1939, King wrote of his conviction that Hitler's similarity to the Wagnerian heroes was proof of his peaceful intentions, a conviction King felt his mother had sent him:

> Can it be that Parsifal is to be again associated with Munich and that under dear Mother's guidance before life is over, I may yet come to hear the triumphal chorus of victory for Christ's sacrifice upon the Cross and its helping to save mankind, of the spiritual reality, should it be possible to avert war, by having the spiritual triumph over the pagan — though finding the good in the pagan as well, it being a part of God's creation and His loving all things He has made — I believe I am writing inspired words, and that time will see this prophecy fulfilled.[44]

Both pagan and Christian insights led to the conclusion that Hitler was a man of peace. On 27 August 1939 in the midst of the Polish crisis King wrote:

> I believe Hitler to be like Wagner in his beliefs on reincarnation, also that like Wagner, under the influence of Schopenhauer and others he is agnostic regarding Christ like Nietzsche and some other German philosophers in believing in Christianity and the Gospels for the weak and as perpetuating weakness but like Wagner believing in compassion, — pity as the thing to aim at, also ultimate perfection in purity of living. This may cause him in the end not to yield to force . . . Wagner's revolutionary side has been greatly stressed — Hitler was also a revolutionary. — Like Wagner, he may become, or strive to become, Siegfried — Amfortus — Parsifal. I believe to understand Hitler one should become saturated with Wagner. Wagner's music has possessed Germany, — and his philosophy with it. Hitler loves his music to the exclusion of much else, and doubtless had imbibed his philosophy. Is a mystic, a spiritualist, believes I am sure in reincarnation, and thus his life becomes intelligible. It is that which makes this appeal to his good, his spiritual side, important.[45]

That day was also the anniversary of the signing of the Kellogg Pact against war which, together with a correspondence between the cross-like Nazi symbol and Christ's cross, promised well:

> Good Friday moment — cruxification of Christ (on green hill far away) — which caused Wagner to sketch out Parsifal so I believe Hitler will feel compassion for mankind, pity is holding the sword for today — time is being given. — It will be Christ who will win in the end. *In hoc signo vinces.* That I truly believe. (Buchan spoke of the Zwastica (Swastika?) [sic] as the crooked cross.) It is a sort of jagged cross, — any cross is a true symbol of suffering and sacrifice — they are bearing it unbeknown.[46]

Wagnerian insights helped King see the crisis in an optimistic light. Reading of Wagner's personal struggles led King to write that this story "bore out my feeling re Wagner and his belief in the ultimate triumph of good, thro' suffering and sacrifice — conquest of self — purity over senses."[47]

Seen through poetic lenses, Hitler became for King in 1939 a Wagnerian hero within whom good and evil struggled and who was guided by voices of uncertain provenance. Were the evil voices "gaining over those of concentration on his own people, and goodwill which I am perfectly sure have him in large part?" King asked. He was convinced that he better understood Hitler now that they "were 'communicating' with each other thro' the world of thought," and that his mysterious role was to help the good win in Hitler's divided soul.[48] Earlier, in February 1939, the "squire of Kingsmere" wrote the "squire of Berchtesgaden," as Stacey labelled them, a personal letter indicating their shared relationship. King informed Hitler that the letter was "an expression of the faith I have in the purpose you have at heart, and of the friendship with yourself, which you have been so kind as to permit me to share."[49]

One evening in August 1939, amid the ruins at Kingsmere, he reverentially read Joan Patteson Hitler's personal response asking for a Canadian delegation to visit him. King was so moved by the great mystical meaning of the moment that he asked Joan to "take off her shoes for the place whereon she stood was holy ground."[50]

The good in Hitler, King was certain, would defeat the evil, just as Siegfried had beaten down Wotan. Joan Patteson reminded King of this when she pointed out that Hitler had not named his western defence line the "Hitler line" but the "Siegfried line." King recorded that "I believe he believes in reincarnation and probably believes himself to be Siegfried reincarnated. If so," he wrote in his diary four days before the outbreak of war, "he must also believe in Parsifal as a further reincarnation and will be guided in the end by pity, by compassion."[51] The day before Britain and France declared war, he still thought that Hitler desired peace. Upon learning from the German Consul General to Ottawa, Erich Windels, that the "Berchtes" in the name of Hitler's mountain retreat Berchtesgaden was the name of an old Germanic deity, King concluded joyfully:

> . . . that bears out my view of Hitler — his believing he is a reincarnated spirit and dwelling with the gods on the highest — obliged to come into humble circumstances into the world, and win his way as an unknown — sort of outcast — to greatest heights of mankind. The German Knights — Siegfried — Parsifal etc., were not "milk and water" men, they were fighters or ready to fight if need be. Their higher natures overcame their lower. It is the supernatural — the spiritual that counts.[52]

King, with his Wagnerian views of the ultimate triumph of spiritual good, could not see Hitler in a negative light.

Partly through his spiritualist sympathies for Hitler and partly through his political antipathies for the 1919 Versailles Treaty, King blamed the old powers (were France and England Wotan?) for refusing since 1933 to negotiate with Hitler over his justified national demands. Such continual rejection encouraged the victory of the evil in Hitler. Had not even Lloyd George himself as early as 1919 spoken strongly against the national injustices contained in the Polish settlement, prophesying that they were likely to cause problems later? These chickens were now coming home to roost. Little wonder that Hitler, in frustration, had turned to force.[53] On 20 August 1939, King re-read to the Pattesons a 1935 Reichstag speech of Hitler and concluded again with regret that Britain and France were largely the authors of the present Polish crisis:

> It seemed to me an admirable speech, and a true one, — that the British and French governments had been wholly in the wrong in not seizing the moment to come to a real settlement with Germany. From what Hitler said to me in 1937 I have every reason to believe that conferences even at that date would have led with very slight concessions (based on justice) to disarmament and peace in Europe. I keep coming back and back to the failure of England to try to make friends with Germany, — postponing and postponing conferences.[54]

Consequently it was not with disappointment but with an immense sense of relief that King heard in late August 1939 that Russia and Germany had signed a pact of friendship. Whatever the difficulties thereby created for Britain and France, it would finally bring them "to their senses in the matter of pledges made without knowledge of what others are prepared to do — also, I believe, it has just come in time to save them becoming involved in a war." If Hitler wished to gain world domination, this would be the moment to strike. But, concluded King at this late date, "I have never felt this to be his aim."[55]

King's passionate interest in Germanic culture and in Hitler as a reincarnation of a Wagnerian hero also helps to explain why he developed such a warm, intimate relationship with Erich Windels and his wife. For King, the French minister in Ottawa was a distant and ill-informed official, the Governor General too formal, and the British High Commissioner too superior and imperial. But King got on famously with the Windelses and, uncharacteristically, visited their house without invitation. He also spent surprisingly friendly moments with them at Kingsmere, to which other diplomats were not normally invited, and discussed with them his favourite topics of Germanic culture and Hitler.[56] No doubt this unusual relationship between the Canadian prime minister and the German representative to Canada was reported with some satisfaction to Berlin, but the friendship between King and the Windelses seems to have been quite sincere on both sides. King told Windels several times during 1939 that Canada would stand by Britain in case of war, thus showing a greater openness towards the German representative than he revealed to his own countrymen. The two men worked together on King's letters to Hitler, apparently in the same spirit of hope that war could be avoided. When Hitler offered in August 1939 to meet a Canadian delegation, King was delighted with the idea which seemed to confirm his special relationship with Hitler. However, he decided to postpone the meeting for political reasons until November so that the visit would not become an issue in the election he was planning.[57] He spoke to the Windelses of his own joyful feelings that the two leaders understood each other so well and appreciated the need for peace:

> I said to both Windels and his wife that the three of us would have to work together for all we were worth and see what has been begun in this way should succeed as a real means of effecting peace, if that were possible, and to bring together into friendly relationship and understanding, the German and British people . . . I said that (if Hitler approved) deliberately believing that it would reach Hitler — let him see I might be able to come, and so help — *as he will know* as a conciliator in the event of his not wishing to go to war himself but to get more in the way of understanding arranged between the different countries.[58]

Their common mission to help Hitler avoid war remained clear.

To this end, King hoped that together with Windels he could still help to assure the general peace. Two days before Britain and France declared war, the lonely bachelor prime minister again invited the Windelses for a late summer's afternoon at Kingsmere. King and the Windelses, and perhaps Hitler too in spirit, appeared united in the search for peace. As they rocked together on King's big wooden swing, this goal seemed to them to be both possible and necessary. Not a word of criticism against Windels or his leader can be found in the diary's full recital of that last visit.[59] The outbreak of war did not change King's mind about the Windelses, who still remained "fine people." King ordered police harassment of the couple to cease and personally visited them alone three times before they left. King told Mrs. Windels he would like to make public her husband's helpfulness as regards their common attempts to influence Hitler for peace, but thought that the time might not be propitious. On his last visit, Mr. Windels broke down and began to cry holding King's hands in his own, to which King responded with great emotion. He sadly told Windels that he had tried to keep faith with Hitler, but that the ruthless invasion of Poland had opened his eyes. However, he hastened to add, this was in no way Windels's fault nor did it affect his warm feelings for him. The spiritual struggle within Hitler was resolved for evil.[60]

King's disappointment in Hitler and in his own lack of initiative for not having tried harder to push Hitler to peace now became evident in his diary. On 6 September he awoke to another vision. "All things focused," he wrote in his diary, and he began feverishly to work out his speech to the House of Commons on the need for a Canadian declaration of war against Hitler. He wrote out of his anger and sense of deception:

> I wanted to expose all his [Hitler's] appalling deception. One hardly knows whether to think he was sincere at the time of speaking or not . . . having made the astounding coups he has, he evidently turned in a completely opposite direction, and is prepared to do things which, two years ago, he was still saying would occasion the most appalling catastrophe to the world.[61]

King did not begin to question his spiritualism. Rather, he blamed himself for not having risen to the challenge offered and for having neglected to employ his spiritual insights in an appropriately realistic manner. He regretted that he had not spent more time studying the actual European situation rather than reading Wagner. "I have kept reproaching myself for not having given to the European situation practically all the time I have devoted to reading in other directions." At the same time, he felt keenly his own failure as conciliator and guide for Hitler. "I keep feeling, however, that had I had more faith in my own powers I might have been very strong in the present situation. The strength may yet come," he added in the expectation that peace negotiations might still be possible. But his spectacles remained Wagnerian. It seemed to him that Hitler had finally been pushed or had chosen the way of evil fate like an ancient pagan hero. "I believe that Hitler like Siegfried has gone out to court death hoping for Valhalla — an immortality to be joined by death," he wrote on 2 September 1939. "I think Hitler's belief in reincarnation, and believing himself to be a certain mystical personality, accounts pretty much for his last desperate act."[62] To the end, King's poetic spiritualism and search for a higher mission shone through.

This paper has not tried to claim that King's tolerance for the Fuehrer did not have political roots within the appeasement tradition. But his fascination with the mystical in German culture, and especially in the summer of 1939 with Wagnerian myth as a divinely-sent tool for understanding and influencing Hitler, should be added to this account. King saw no tension or dichotomy between his own spiritualist and political activity; the former informed the latter. This outwardly dull politician lived at one and the same time in a world of mundane politics and in a secret romance of knightly and spiritual struggles of good against evil. As a result, he viewed Hitler in more than purely political terms, as a mystic like himself, struggling within the cosmic plan and guided from the Beyond to overcome evil for good. They both "conversed" in the same way together and with the spirit world, and they both could be great forces for good. Because of their spiritualist affinities, King believed that he was called upon to help lead Hitler towards peace. This hopeful, esoteric view severely tempered his criticism of Hitler and his fear of war, while it promised him a major, if secret, role in world affairs. The outbreak of war was a great blow to his hopes. The evil in Hitler had won. Once war began, spiritualist speculations seem to have almost disappeared from his diary to be replaced by the more hectic discussions of wartime politics.

NOTES

The author is not a spiritualist, but has tried to illuminate some of the motives of this historical personality. Thanks for encouragement to Susan Mann Trofimenkoff and Joe Levitt of the University of Ottawa, and Donald Page of the historical section of the Department of External Affairs.

1. William Lyon Mackenzie King Diaries (hereafter Diary), Public Archives of Canada, MG26 J13, 28 August 1939. References here are to the diary's second copy.
2. R. Whitaker, "Mackenzie King and the Dominion of the Dead," *Canadian Forum*, February 1976, 11.
3. C.P. Stacey, *Canada in the Age of Conflict*, vol. 2, *1921-1948: The Mackenzie King Era* (Toronto, 1981), 249.
4. "The overriding consideration which guided Mr. Mackenzie King in his conduct of Canada's foreign policy was that the maintenance and strengthening of internal unity was the indispensable condition of its successful application." N. Mansergh, *Survey of British Commonwealth Affairs: Problems of External Policy, 1931-1939* (London, 1952), 136; H. Blair Neatby, *William Lyon Mackenzie King, 1932-1939: The Prism of Unity* (Toronto, 1976), 5ff, 278, 292.
5. Diary, 24 and 25 August 1939.
6. For a fascinating view of the theosophy group's spread and influence in Canada after 1890, see M. Lacombe, "Theosophy and the Canadian Idealist Tradition: A Preliminary Exploration," *Journal of Canadian Studies*, 17 (Summer 1982), 100ff.

7. Diary, 18 June 1939.

8. *Ibid.*, 27 August 1929.

9. C.P. Stacey, *A Very Double Life: The Private Life of Mackenzie King* (Toronto, 1976), 9–10.

10. Jean E. Dryden, "The Mackenzie King Papers: An Archival Odyssey," *Archivaria*, 6 (Summer 1978), 40–69. The closed King Spiritualist writings are in King's Papers, MG26 J9. *Ibid.*, 58 and 66.

11. Stacey, *A Very Double Life*, 9–10, 172ff, 185. Stacey wrote: "Did he [King] conduct the affairs of Canada in accordance with what he believed to be advice from Beyond? And the answer is quite clearly No." This appeared to be confirmed by his friend and fellow spiritualist, Joan Patteson of Kingsmere, who said that "*never* did he allow his belief to enter into his public life" (*Ibid.* 198). Mrs. Patteson's statement is patently protective.

12. Whitaker, "Mackenzie King," 8 and 11.

13. R. Whitaker, "The Liberal Corporatist Ideas of Mackenzie King," *Labour* (1977), 146. See also his "Political Thought and Political Action in Mackenzie King," *Journal of Canadian Studies*, 13 (Winter 1978–79), 40ff, in which he pleads for a tighter linkage between King's ideas and his political actions.

14. Whitaker, "Mackenzie King," 8, 11; also his "Political Thought and Political Action" 43–44.

15. Whitaker, "Mackenzie King," 11. Stacey's judgement of King's opinion that he was chosen by God to lead and help his fellow men is that "the combination of single-mindedness and egotism required to produce this result leaves one slightly breathless" (*A Very Double Life*, 175).

16. J. Esberrry, *Knight of the Holy Spirit: A Study of William Lyon Mackenzie King* (Toronto, 1980). For an insightful review of this book, see D. Swainson, "Neurosis and Causality in Canadian History," *Queen's Quarterly*, 89 (Autumn 1982), 611–17. Swainson rejects Esberry's "causally simplistic" Freudian and psychological categories, arguing instead for more complex motivations. However, among these motives, he too does not take King's spiritualism seriously.

17. There exists a massive literature on the history and types of modern spiritualism, only a few of which can be noted here: W. James, *The Varieties of Religious Experience* (New York, 1929); R.M. Burke, *Cosmic Consciousness: A Study in the Evolution of the Human Mind* (New York, 1901); M.A. Stobart, *Torchbearers of Spiritualism* (New York, 1925); Rudolf Steiner, *The Occult Movement of the Nineteenth Century and Its Relationship to Modern Culture* (London, 1973); F. Podmore, *Modern Spiritualism: A History and Criticism* (London, 1902); M.F. Bednarowski, "Nineteenth Century American Spiritualism," Ph.D. thesis, University of Minnesota, 1973; R. Otto, *Mysticism East and West: A Comparative Analysis* (New York, 1962).

18. For instance, Rudolf Steiner, founder of Anthroposophy, wrote books such as *Christianity as a Mystical Fact and the Mysteries of Antiquity* (London, 1972); *The Lord's Prayer: An Esoteric Study* (London, 1958); *The Mysteries of the East and Christianity* (London, 1972). See also L. Pauwels, *Monsieur Gurdjieff* (Paris, 1954). One might also include metaphysical idealists such as Nietzsche in Germany, Bergson in France, and Marinetti in Italy.

19. Lacombe, "Theosophy," 102; Conn Smythe, *If You Can't Beat 'Em in the Alley* (Toronto, 1981), 8–9.

20. H.P. Blavatsky, *The Secret Doctrine: The Synthesis of Science, Religion and Philosophy* (Pasadena, 1963); C.J. Ryan, *H.P. Blavatsky and the Theosophical Society: A Brief Historical Sketch* (Pasadena, 1975); B.F. Campbell, *Ancient Wisdom Revived: A History of the Theosophic Society* (Berkeley, 1980); M. Meade, *Madame Blavatsky: The Woman Behind the Myth* (New York, 1980).

21. Concerning the Fellowship of the New Life, Annie Besant, and Frank Podmore, see H. Pelling, *The Origins of the Labour Party, 1880–1900* (Oxford, 1965), 33–37, 45, 49ff.

22. Diary, 3 October 1936. See also G.L. Mosse, "The Mystical Origins of National Socialism," *Journal of the History of Ideas*, 22 (1961), 81ff; A. Brissaud, *Hitler et l'Ordre Noir: Histoire secrète du national-socialisme* (Paris, 1969); W. Gerson, *Le nazisme société secrète* (Paris, 1969); R.H. Phelps, "Before Hitler Came: Thule Society and German Order," *Journal of Modern History* (1963); R. Cecil, *The Myth of the Master Race: Alfred Rosenberg and Nazi Ideology* (London, 1972).

23. Lacombe, "Theosophy," 100.

24. "I was glad to hear Ferguson [Minister at St. Andrew's Church, Ottawa] stress strongly that the old Calvinist tradition of predestination and eternal perdition was all wrong . . . the thought of eternal damnation instead of illimitable love of God is perfectly hideous" (Diary, 8 January 1939, 11 June 1933); Whitaker, "Political Thought and Political Action," 43–44.

25. Diary, 17 and 18 June, 28 August 1939; Whitaker, "Political Thought and Political Action," 42–49.
26. Diary, 23 June 1939.
27. *Ibid.*, 1 July 1939.
28. His goal for the summer of 1939 was to study the "triumph of spiritual forces, Liberalism in Canada — Peace between Nations" (*Ibid.*, 18 June 1939).
29. *Ibid.*, 23 June 1939.
30. *Ibid.*, 18 June 1939. King believed that because of his similarity, as he saw it, to Hitler, he was best suited to get on with him: "That those who were concerned about titles or looking for social recognition were bound hand and foot in a situation of the kind. That even those given to wearing top hats, taking in races, etc., were not cut out for work of the kind that needs to be done with a man of Hitler's temperament and with others who come up, as it is said, from the masses" (*Ibid.*, 11 August 1939).
31. Almost daily King met with Joan alone or together with her husband Godfroy in the evening at Kingsmere to read spiritualist books together or hold "conversations" with the departed. This was very much the case during the summer of 1939; e.g., *Ibid.*, 20 August 1939.
32. *Ibid.*, 18 June, 21 July 1939.
33. His "conversations," like movie scripts of dialogue, have been left untyped in his original, crabbed handwriting in his diary, which makes these photostats almost — and perhaps conveniently — illegible. See *Ibid.*, 16 August 1939, for instance; also *Ibid.*, 28 and 30 August 1939. Hester Dowden was well known in spiritualist circles, especially for books such as *Talks with Elizabethans Revealing the Mystery of William Shakespeare* (New York and London, 1947).
34. The Nazis persecuted spiritualists including theosophists and anthroposophists, despite individual Nazis' somewhat similar or astrological beliefs in a World Beyond. See Mosse, "The Mystical Origins of National Socialism," 81ff.
35. Diary, 27 August 1939.
36. *Ibid.*, 26 August 1939. See also J. Eayrs, *In Defence of Canada: Appeasement and Rearmament* (Toronto, 1965), 43–44; Stacey, *Canada in the Age of Conflict*, 2, 210ff.
37. Diary, 27 March 1938.
38. Comte Guy de Pourtalès, *Richard Wagner: The Story of an Artist* (New York, 1932, 1972 in translation from French). King Diary, 23 June 1939.
39. Diary, 23 June 1939; Pourtalès, *Wagner*, 203.
40. Diary, 24 June 1939. King complained in 1922 that his seat at Parsifal was too close, "but we enjoyed Parsifal immensely. It made me feel sad in parts and it seemed more full of meaning that [sic] at any previous time. . . ." *Ibid.*, 14 April 1922.
41. *Ibid.*, 21 July 1939; Stacey, *A Very Double Life*, 192, footnote.
42. De Pourtalès, *Wagner*, vi, xii, 1, 130, 150; Diary, 23 June 1939. "I believe to understand Hitler one should become saturated with Wagner" (*Ibid.*, 27 August 1939).
43. De Pourtalès, *Wagner*, 112, 121, 150, 164, 184–85; Diary, 27 and 29 August 1939.
44. Diary, 23 July 1939.
45. *Ibid.*, 27 August 1939.
46. *Ibid.*
47. *Ibid.*
48. *Ibid.*, 1 July, 23 June, 21 July, and 19 August 1939.
49. Canada, Department of External Affairs, *Documents on Canadian External Relations*, vol. 6 (Ottawa, 1972), 1122–23, King *Persönlich* to Hitler, 1 February 1939; also Stacey, *Canada in the Age of Conflict*, vol. 2, 248.
50. Diary, 20 August 1939.
51. *Ibid.*, 28 August 1939.
52. *Ibid.*, 30 August 1939.
53. *Ibid.*, 26 August 1939.
54. *Ibid.*, 20 August 1939.
55. *Ibid.*, 22 August 1939.
56. *Ibid.*, 30 July and 26 August, 19, 20, 22 July and 11 August 1939.
57. *Ibid.*, 20 August 1939. The fact that British Prime Minister Chamberlain's telegram agreeing that King accept Hitler's invitation was dated August 7 (the number 7 being of great spiritual significance) greatly impressed King and convinced him that the proposed visit was a divinely-arranged one. *Ibid.*, 10 and 11 August 1939.
58. *Ibid.*, 11 August 1939. King's emphasis here denotes the mystical bond between the two men.

59. "Nothing between us but friendship and gladness to be meeting in my little 'upper room' —
my chapel — quiet room." As they swung together, King spoke to Windels of the folly of
the white races fighting among themselves, leaving "the Brown, Yellow and Black in control."
Ibid., 29 August 1939.
60. *Ibid.*, 10, 11 and 12 September 1939.
61. *Ibid.*, 6 September 1939.
62. *Ibid.*, 2 September 1939.

The RCAF, Bomber Command, and Armageddon over Germany, 1941–1945

BRERETON GREENHOUS, STEPHEN HARRIS,
WILLIAM JOHNSTON, and WILLIAM RAWLING

Since the strategic bomber offensive was, by 1941, the only way to strike directly at Germany, regardless of its shortcomings the build-up of Bomber Command won broad — though not universal — support. Canada was quick to join in, and the Royal Canadian Air Force (RCAF) eventually mustered fifteen bomber squadrons overseas. All of them were formed in the United Kingdom, largely from British Commonwealth Air Training Program (BCATP) graduates, with the first, No. 405, being formed in April 1941.

By 1942 the nature of the strategic bombing offensive was changing radically. The Butt Report of August 1941 had revealed that on most nights only a minority of crews bombed within three miles of their aiming point — five miles over the smog-ridden Ruhr — an effort that was demonstrably of little use if their goal was the destruction of specific objectives. Since the British War Cabinet considered it to be of the utmost importance to continue carrying the war directly to Germany, however, over the next nine months Bomber Command was projected into an "area" offensive — what Adolf Hitler (quickly) and Winston Churchill (eventually) dubbed "terror" bombing. Sir Arthur Harris, who was appointed air officer commanding-in-chief of Bomber Command in February 1942, became the premier advocate and exponent of that approach, sarcastically labelling those who still thought in terms of precision attacks, "panacea-mongers."

What Bomber Command lacked in precision it would now make up with numbers. If one hundred machines could not shut down a particular factory in Essen, perhaps five hundred (or a thousand) could de-

SOURCE: Excerpted from *The Crucible of War, 1939-1945: The Official History of the Royal Canadian Air Force*, Vol. III (Ottawa: Ministry of Supply and Services, Department of National Defence; Toronto: University of Toronto Press, 1994), pp. 523, 524, 526, 829, 830-31, 854-55, 856-57, 863-64. Reproduced with the permission of the Minister of Supply and Services Canada, 1995.

stroy the whole city — if not in one raid, then in ten. Yet accuracy could not be entirely dispensed with, even if it was measured in terms of thousands (rather than hundreds) of yards from the aiming point. In an attempt to improve the record, work on a number of electronic navigation aids was accelerated; a specialist target-marking force (the Pathfinders of No. 8 Group) was created; and renewed emphasis was placed on the production of more and better bombers able to carry bigger loads of high explosive and incendiary bombs. Accuracy might be slow in developing, but in the meantime more damage would be done.

More and more, the air war over Germany revolved about electronics, as counter-measure was met by counter-counter-measure, ad infinitum. Tactical innovations accompanied the technological breakthroughs, and the advantage swayed back and forth as bomber, night-fighter, and Flak struggled to find and maintain an edge in what was certainly the most sophisticated campaign of the Second World War.

An average casualty rate of 5 per cent per mission was considered to be the most that bomber crews could bear without faltering over any prolonged length of time. Losses on that scale occurred between 1 January and 31 March 1944 when, on twenty large raids to Germany, 754 of 13,259 sorties failed to return — a missing rate of 5.6 per cent. Over the same period No. 6 Group's loss rate was higher still, standing at 7 per cent. If morale within Bomber Command should ever have cracked, it was in the first few months of 1944. It did not, and the number of airmen who became neuro-psychiatric casualties was infinitesimal.

In the five RCAF squadrons flying Halifax IIs and Vs, 10 per cent of sorties failed to return from just six major raids between 14 January and 20 February 1944. Withdrawn immediately from operations over Germany, they were employed for the next two months on minelaying duties. Their transfer to Gardening operations in order to save them from intolerable losses was not a new policy. Harris had done the same thing with his last Wellington squadrons when, also because of the performance of their aircraft, they could no longer survive over the Reich. The significance of Gardening went far beyond the number of enemy ships sunk or damaged: it not only interfered with German coastal shipping, but also impeded U-boat training in the Baltic.

If their shift to minelaying "saved" the Halifax II and V squadrons, the rest of Bomber Command was similarly saved in April 1944 when Harris brought the assault on Berlin to a halt. His bombers were needed to prepare the way for the invasion of Europe — Operation Overlord. Placed under the ultimate control of Supreme Headquarters, Allied Expeditionary Forces, in mid-April, Bomber Command's effort was split for the next six months between transportation targets in France and the Low Countries — intended to isolate the Normandy battlefield — and the continuing attempt to destroy the industrial centres of northern and western Germany, especially the Ruhr heartland.

★   ★   ★

Although it had taken longer than anticipated for the Allies to break out of Normandy, victory seemed to be in sight by mid-September 1944. In the west, most of France had been liberated, British and Canadian forces were deep inside Belgium, and the Americans had arrived on the German frontier near Aachen. In Italy, Anglo-American armies (including a Canadian corps) had broken through the Gothic Line and were approaching Ravenna. On the Eastern front, the Red Army had taken Romania in the south and was poised to debouch onto the Hungarian plain; further north, having reached an armistice with Finland, the Soviets were preparing to clear their Baltic flank and push through Poland into East Prussia.

Yet, from a Luftwaffe perspective, the situation was not entirely hopeless. Most nights at least one radio channel was open for the running commentary. Similarly, although Allied jamming of AI [radar] was often very effective, so that fighter crews knew they were in the bomber stream "only . . . from the air disturbance caused by the slipstreams of the bombers"[1] — the same clue that had helped the pioneers of German night-fighting three years before — Naxos and Flensburg enabled them to track and intercept bombers through their H2S and Monica emissions. In fact, "hair-raising" accounts about the efficiency of Naxos would soon produce "great disquiet" at High Wycombe, especially when linked to the "unpleasant potentialities" of Schräge Musik's upward-firing guns.[2] Even after tactical countermeasures had been devised and instructions laid down to restrict the use of H2S until the bomber stream was well inside Germany, the morale problem in Bomber Command was "not . . . readily redeemable." Many crews remained convinced that, for all its value as a navigation aid, H2S was also a potential danger even when used judiciously, and they conveniently forgot to turn it off.[3]

It was difficult, then, to say that the tide of war had necessarily or inevitably turned in Bomber Command's favour. Indeed, persuaded there were few holes left to exploit in the enemy's air-defence system, and beginning to see the electronic war as something of a stalemate, Sir Arthur Harris feared that his crews might again suffer "prohibitive losses." "Like the U-boat," he told Winston Churchill on 30 September, "the heavy bomber . . . will meet its counter in the end," and it was therefore essential to "get going while the going is good."[4]

In fact, the going would remain better than Harris anticipated for quite some time. Although senior Luftwaffe officers spoke wistfully about new radars able to withstand jamming and the commitment of jet-powered aircraft in large numbers to the night-fighter role, it was expecting too much of an economy under siege to produce such technologically advanced and sophisticated equipment quickly and in quantity.

As for active defence, Adolf Hitler still insisted that Flak should have first priority, and until November 1944 he was determined that the jet-engined Me 262 should not be employed defensively.[5]

While German aircraft production had finally begun to drop, between them the U.S. Eighth and Fifteenth air forces could now call upon an average of just over 3000 heavy bombers and perhaps a thousand fighters every day. The sixty-seven main-force squadrons of Bomber Command (forty-two Lancaster, twenty-five Halifax) added another 1300–1400 to the total. (No. 6 Group's fourteen squadrons — eleven Halifax, three Lancaster — accounted for just under three hundred.) In Bomber Command alone, the monthly average number of sorties had risen from 5400 in 1943 to 14,000 in 1944, while average payload per sortie had nearly doubled.[6] Beyond that, there were about 1000 medium bombers in the Allied tactical air forces, along with another 3100 fighters and fighter-bombers — most of them now the equal or better than their German counterparts and their pilots far better trained.[7]

★　★　★

[Early in 1945] the idea of launching a series of punishment and demonstration raids . . . against a variety of targets was being resurrected. These included Clarion, the American plan to disrupt communications and morale by widespread bombing and fighter attacks; Thunderclap, the British plan to deliver a catastrophic blow on Berlin, first adumbrated by Harris in June 1944 and subsequently put forward by Portal and Bufton in August 1944; and Bugle, a continuation of the concentrated offensive against the Ruhr meant to prepare the way for the British, Canadian, and American crossings of the Rhine. With an eye to assisting the Russian winter offensive just under way, Bufton was inclined to substitute Breslau and Munich for the German capital in Thunderclap. For his part, Harris, who had already compiled his own list of cities needing to be finished off, added Chemnitz, Dresden, and Leipzig, as they would "equally share with Berlin the task of housing German evacuees from the East." Like Bufton, Portal now questioned whether decisive results would result from attacking Berlin, but neither he nor the Air Staff had any qualms about Thunderclap's purpose. Since it was to have "primarily . . . morale and psychological effect" it must not be dissipated by concurrent attempts to knock out "tank production . . . jet engine factories etc." The prime minister was thinking along roughly the same lines, asking "whether Berlin, and no doubt other large cities in East Germany should not now be considered especially attractive targets?"[8]

. . . In due course, Halle, Plauen, Dessau, Potsdam, Erfurt, and Magdeburg were also added to the Thunderclap list. Thus was set in motion the chain of events that would produce Bomber Command's most controversial operation of the war, the attack on Dresden of 13/14 February 1945. It had the wholehearted support of everyone who mattered in the chain of command and, as we have seen, the city had been singled out for attack by Harris and others long before there was any consultation with the Red Army. Indeed, when (during the Yalta conference) the Soviets were asked whether the bombing of east German cities would assist them, only Berlin and Leipzig fitted the bill. Dresden, Vienna, and Zagreb were mentioned only as reference points along a general bombline east of which the Western Allies should not bomb.[9]

★   ★   ★

"That the bombing of Dresden was a great tragedy none can deny," Harris's deputy admitted after the war. "That it was really a military necessity . . . few will believe. It was one of those terrible things that sometimes happen in wartime, brought about by an unfortunate combination of circumstances." There were, as we have seen, no industrial objectives of immediate importance in Dresden — an abrasives plant and Zeiss lens factories were probably the most significant — but the aiming point, a large sports stadium, was chosen because it could be seen easily, not in order to lead the bomber stream to either of those installations. Similarly the railway yards, given as the objective to some squadrons and also easily seen, did not serve as an aiming point until the last few waves flew over the city.[10]

The possibility of raising a firestorm had been incorporated in the operational plan from the beginning; carrying a bombload largely made up of incendiaries, the main force (guided by the flames from No. 5 Group's preparatory attack) was able to do just that. The glow was perfectly visible to those returning from Böhlen, over a hundred miles to the northwest. The old city centre was "almost completely wiped out," and at least 25,000 were killed and an additional 35,000 missing.[11] As at Hamburg, German eye-witnesses had lurid tales to tell.

In 1948 Margret Freyer, a twenty-four-year-old with an undoubted will to live at the time, recalled her experience on the edge of the fire storm.

> I stumbled on towards where it was dark. Suddenly, I saw people again, right in front of me. They scream and gesticulate with their hands, and then — to my utter horror and amazement — I see how one after the other they simply seem to let themselves drop to the ground. I had a feeling they were being shot, but my mind could not understand what was happening. Today I know that these unfortunate people were the victims of lack of oxygen. They fainted and then burnt to cinders. I fall then, stumbling over a fallen woman, and as I lie right next to her I see how her clothes are burning away. Insane fear grips me and from then on I repeat one simple sentence to myself continuously: "I don't want to burn to death — no, no burning — I don't want to burn!" . . .
>
> Twenty-four hours later, I asked for a mirror and did not recognise myself any more. My face was a mass of blisters and so were my hands. My eyes were narrow slits and puffed up, my whole body was covered in little black, pitted marks. . . . Possibly the fire-sparks ate their way through my clothing.[12]

Mounting only twenty-nine sorties, the Luftwaffe was scarcely to be seen, and only six bombers were lost to enemy action, less than 1 per cent of those dispatched.

On 8 May 1945 Canadians knew a good deal about what Bomber Command had been doing to Germany for the past five years. Along with stories filed by journalists who accompanied the Allied armies into western Germany, there were photographs and newsreel films that bore witness to almost unbelievable devastation. From what could be seen, they seemed to prove every claim Sir Arthur Harris had ever made for the bombing offensive. "City after city has been systematically shattered," General Eisenhower had declared earlier that spring, and the German war economy had all but ceased to function.[13]

Taking its cue from Eisenhower's remarks, Toronto's *Globe and Mail* rendered its verdict on the strategic air offensive on 23 March 1945. Not doubting for one moment that bombing had ruined the German economy, the *Globe* nevertheless did not view "the real victory of Allied air power" in that light. Rather its "great achievement" was likely "a thing of the mind — a lesson so terrible as never to be forgotten." "This time," the *Globe* observed, comparing the situation in Europe to that which existed at the end of the First World War, "Germany is being conquered and occupied, rubble-heap by rubble-heap. But this time the German people will not need the presence of Allied armies to persuade them that they lost this war. The storm which is sweeping them from the air . . . is convincing them that they have suffered the most terrible defeat ever inflicted on a people in all history." Perhaps, the editorial continued, the Germans would learn from their defeat, and discover a new way of life which would allow them to exist "constructively and compatibly alongside the neighbors they have made [into] enemies."[14]

If that were the case, then the long casualty lists the *Globe* had published over the last five years would have some meaning. Bomber Command had mounted 364,514 operational sorties during the course of the war, of which 8,325, 2.3 per cent, failed to return. Well over a thousand more were lost in crashes. No. 6 Group flew 40,822 of these sorties, of which 814, 1.9 per cent, failed to return, while more than a hundred crashed in England.[15] In his memoirs (but not his official report), Sir Arthur Harris stated that 125,000 aircrew flew at least one operational or training sortie in Bomber Command.[16] How and where he obtained this figure has never been explained — what kind of Second World War personnel records system would be geared to extracting that sort of information? — but so far as can be determined there is no alternative to his estimate and it will therefore have to serve as our best guess — however erroneous — as to the total cumulative aircrew strength of Bomber Command.

Casualties, of course, are easier to account for — systems *are* geared to record that kind of information — and 47,268 were killed in action or died as prisoners of war, and 8195 in flying or ground accidents. A further 9838 became prisoners of war; 4200 were wounded on operations but returned to base; and 4203 were injured in flying or ground accidents. If Harris was right, then 44 per cent of those who flew with Bomber Command died on operations or during training, while total casualties (including prisoners) amounted to 58.9 per cent. Total RCAF fatal battle casualties during the Second World War numbered 13,498, of which 9919, almost three-quarters, came in Bomber Command. No. 6 Group lost 4272 dead — the vast majority, but not all of them, being Canadian — almost a third of the Canadian total.[17]

NOTES

1. Bomber Command ADI(K) report No. 599/1944, 2 Nov. 1944, DHist 181.009 (D4398).
2. The director of air tactics had produced a reasonably accurate analysis of Schräge Musik in August 1944. His estimates were confirmed in December 1944 when a Do 117 equipped with upward-firing guns landed at Zürich, Switzerland. Before destroying the aircraft (in exchange for ten Me 109 fighters), the Swiss made a thorough investigation of the equipment, and their findings found their way to the Air Ministry.
3. See minutes of 5th meeting Bomber Command Tactical Planning Committee 30 Sept. 1944, Public Record Office (PRO), G.B. Air Ministry (Air) 14/1453; McBurney (No. 64 Base) to stations, squadrons, 13 Oct. 1944, DHist 181.009 (D2365); Bomber Command, "Report on the use of NAXOS by GAF night fighters to home on to H2S aircraft," 25 Oct. 1944, DHist 181.009 (D1606); Telecommunications Research Establishment (TRE) to Bomber Command, 9 Jan. 1945, PRO Air 14/1297; SASO No. 6 Group to bases, stations, 13 Nov. 1944, DHist 181.009 (D5050); SASO No. 6 Group to station radar officers, 6 Dec. 1944, DHist 181.009 (D1606); Bomber Command, ADI(K) report No. 599/1944, 2 Nov. 1944, DHist 181.009 (D4398); DGMS to DAT, 23 Dec. 1944, PRO Air 2/5604; BDU report No. 61, part III, "Defence of bombers against upward-firing guns in enemy fighters," 31 March 1945, PRO Air 14/1798.
4. TRE, "Aids to the bomber offensive during the winter of 1944-1945," 23 June 1944, PRO Air 14/1764; Arthur Harris to Winston Churchill, 30 Sept. 1944, PRO Air 14/3507; R.V. Jones, Most Secret War (London, 1978), 469.
5. "Generalnachtrichtenführer Kriegstagebuch Nr. 2, 1944, 3 Abteilung" [War diary No. 2, 3rd Section, Chief of Communications], 26 Aug. and 8 Dec. 1945. DHist SGR II 320, folder 38; Grabmann, "German air defense," DHist 86/451, frames 1685-97; USAFE, AI 12, "Interrogation of Director of GAF Signals, Martini, on radar and aircraft reporting service," 9 Nov. 1945, DHist 181.009 (D292); Sir Charles Webster and Noble Frankland, The Strategic Air Offensive against Germany, III (London, 1961), 272.
6. Striking power depended on payload as well as numbers. The range of an American Boeing B-17 — the workhorse of the U.S. Eighth Air Force — carrying 4000 lbs. of bombs was about 2000 miles. The Avro Lancaster could carry an internal bomb load of 18,000 lbs. without modification to the standard bomb bay, while specially modified machines could carry the 22,000-lb. "Grand Slam" over a range of 1500 miles. Even the maligned Halifax III could carry an 8000-lb. "Blockbuster" to Berlin.
7. Wesley Craven and James Cate, The Army Air Forces in World War II, III (Chicago, 1949), 596; Air Ministry, Air Historical Branch, Bomber Command narrative, VI, 127, 273, DHist 82/286.
8. Webster and Frankland, SAO, III, 97-104, 111, 255; Richard G. Davis, "Operation THUNDERCLAP: The US Army Air Forces and the bombing of Berlin," Journal of Strategic Studies 14, 1 (1990): 90-111; Bottomley to Portal, 26 Jan. 1945, Portal to Bottomley, 26 Jan. 1945, and Air Staff, "Strategic bombing in relation to the present Russian offensive," 26 Jan. 1945, PRO Air 20/3361.
9. Bottomley to ACAS and to Harris, 27 Jan. 1945, PRO Air 20/3361; AHB, Bomber Command narrative, VI, 196-202, DHist 86/286; Webster and Frankland, SAO, III, 106-8.
10. Sir Robert Saundby's foreword to David Irving, The Destruction of Dresden (London, 1963), 5.

11. Irving, *The Destruction of Dresden*, 96-146; John Terraine, *A Time for Courage* (New York, 1985), 678; Spencer Dunsmore and William Carter, *Reap the Whirlwind* (Toronto, 1991), 347ff.
12. Alexander McKee, *Dresden 1945* (London and Toronto, 1982), 173-5.
13. *Globe and Mail*, 23 March 1945.
14. Ibid.
15. Webster and Frankland, *SAO*, IV, 439; Martin Middlebrook and Lewis Everitt, *The Bomber Command War Diaries: An Operational Reference Book, 1939-1945* (New York, 1985), 782ff; No. 6 Group historical review, DHist 181.003 (D4720).
16. Sir Arthur Harris, *Bomber Offensive* (London, 1947), 247.
17. Ibid., 267; Middlebrook and Everitt, *BCWD*, 708-11; No. 6 Group historical review, DHist 181.003 (D4720).

Battle Exhaustion: Soldiers and Psychiatrists in the Canadian Army, 1939-1945

TERRY COPP and BILL McANDREW

"Sergeant! . . . W.A.T. for Private Turvey . . . And send the others away, can't see them this morning."

Turvey went along, baring his arm for another inoc, but he found that W.A.T. was only a very amusing game called the Word Association Test . . .

When it was over there was a wait . . . The sergeant filled in the time with sedate chatter about the captain.

"He's really going to enjoy talking with you, Turvey. Isn't often he takes time to lay on a W.A.T., poor fellow. Generally he interviews twenty in a morning and has to write out a diagnosis and recommendations on all of them by 1500 hours so I can type them in time for the Medical Board."

"Gosh, are there that many nuts around here every day?"

"Well, of course" — the sergeant coughed good-humoredly — "we don't use the word 'nut.' Not in psychiatry. We have all sorts of *cases* though, you'd be surprised. Psychopaths, aggressive or inadequate," the sergeant rolled the words fondly, "suspected epileptics, schizoid personalities, manics. And scads of neurotics — compulsives, depressives. But battle fatigues mainly. Anxiety states, you know."

"What're they all in a state about?"

"O, about getting killed, mostly . . ."

"Course, it's all very hard on the captain. He's very young, you know . . . Had a sheltered home life, then went direct from interning into the army. Hasn't had much of a chance to develop himself as a clinician. Sent straight over here a month ago. Now he gets enough material in one day to last him a year on Civvy Street, and no time to analyze it. Some of it really shocks him, too. He's kind of a shy type really. Has personality problems himself. All these psychiatrists have."

— Earle Birney[1]

SOURCE: Excerpted from *Battle Exhaustion: Soldiers and Psychiatrists in the Canadian Army, 1939-1945* (Montreal/Kingston: McGill-Queen's University Press, 1990), pp. 1, 11-13, 18-19, 63-71, 74-77. Reprinted with permission of McGill-Queen's University Press.

The Canadian Army mobilized for war in the late summer of 1939 with a national call to arms. Just after noon on 1 September Army Headquarters alerted military districts, which in turn spread the word to local militia units. Commanding officers paraded their soldiers, called for active service volunteers, then filled vacancies with other recruits from nearby communities. Enthusiasm varied regionally and from unit to unit. The Chief of the General Staff noted that the "infantry was not coming along as well as might be desired."[2] Infantry soldiering was not the most appealing life, particularly for those who considered it somewhat redundant in an age of modern mechanized warfare. Nonetheless, more than 58,000 joined up in the first weeks. Most formed the cores of the 1st and 2nd Canadian Infantry Divisions. The 1st shipped to the United Kingdom in December 1939 and the 2nd several months later. In due course the 3rd Infantry, 4th and 5th Armoured Divisions, and 1 and 2 Armoured Brigades followed to compose the First Canadian Army. These fighting elements of the overseas army numbered about 100,000. A like number were employed in bases and support facilities.

The Royal Canadian Army Medical Corps (RCAMC), like all other branches of the Canadian Armed Forces, was magnificently unprepared for rapid mobilization. As late as November 1939 there were only 42 medical officers and 11 nursing sisters in the permanent army.[3] But unlike other branches of the armed services, which would have to train most of their recruits in the elementary arts of war, the RCAMC could draw upon its militia units and upon the medical community at large with the certain knowledge that its key volunteers had been professionally trained.

Initially there was little evidence that the medical corps was capable of organizing these recruits to serve effectively. The system of medical examination for recruits had changed little since World War I and, despite representations from the medical community, no provisions were made for routine chest x-rays, urinalyses, or Wassermann tests. It was also decided that it would not be necessary to employ specialists on medical boards because "In any instance where a specialist's report is considered necessary to establish a candidate's fitness, the individual should be rejected by the board."[4]

Criticism of the army's methods of examining volunteers came from all directions and before the end of 1939 re-examination of all recruits was ordered. It was to include a chest x-ray, chemical urinalysis, and a more detailed physical.[5] Psychological testing for the selection and classification of army personnel was also considered. A conference on "The Use of Psychological Methods in Wartime" held in Ottawa on 2 October 1939 concluded that "it would be advisable to introduce into the recruiting examinations, intelligence and aptitude tests"[6] and urged that the Director General of Medical Services (DGMS) be asked to cooperate with the Canadian Psychiatric Association (CPA), which had offered to devise and implement the tests.

The chairman of the conference was Canada's most distinguished scientist, Sir Frederick Banting, the co-discoverer of insulin. Prominent among the advocates of testing at the meeting was Major-General A.L.G. McNaughton, President of the National Research Council. McNaughton had been Chief of the General Staff from 1929 until 1935 and in early October he was anxiously awaiting the call to return to the colours. When the call came it was to the post of Inspector-General of the units of the 1st Canadian Division with a view to commanding the Red Patch Division when it was sent overseas, not to the post of Chief of the General Staff, the senior position in the military.

Without McNaughton's direct involvement psychological testing stood little chance of being accepted. The Chief of the General Staff, Major-General T.V. Anderson and the Adjutant-General, Major-General H.H. Matthews showed no interest in the idea. Neither the senior medical officer Colonel J.L. Potter nor his successor as DGMS, Brigadier B.M. Gorssline, would voluntarily have anything to do with "psychological methods." Indeed a meeting of psychiatrists called to discuss approaches to psychiatric problems in the army was flatly told that "there would be no testing and no psychiatric screen at enlistment."[7] The examining boards were to "reject obvious misfits, subsequently unit medical officers were to make their diagnosis and refer difficult cases to regional consultants for disposal."[8] When new instructions to medical boards were issued in early 1940 doctors were told to establish "that the recruit is sufficiently intelligent" by questioning him. Obvious misfits were defined as those "with a history of nervous breakdown . . . residence in an institution . . . drug addiction . . . or a family history indicating nervous instability such as migraine, eccentricity etc."[9]

The lack of concern for intelligence testing, not to mention any form of personality evaluation, reflected the attitude of the Canadian medical profession toward psychology and psychiatry. The overwhelming majority of doctors inside or outside the army sincerely believed that well trained physicians, particularly those who had served as medical officers in World War I, could evaluate an individual's ability or stability as well as any psychiatrist and better than any psychologist. If the medical board had doubts about an individual's mental fitness its job was to reject him, not to diagnose him.

There is a good case to be made for this point of view, but during the early fall of 1939, when more than 50,000 Canadians enlisted in the army, some overworked medical boards did not take the time to evaluate carefully all of the volunteers. A number of recruits with a history of mental illness[10] and many more who were mentally deficient were enrolled in the army as category A or B personnel, the two classifications that placed no limitations on military service.

The attitude of the RCAMC towards intelligence testing and psychiatric screening was clear enough, but what did it intend to do with psychiatric casualties produced by the stress of war? The Canadian Army had admitted to 15,500 "neuropsychiatric disabilities" in World War I — 9,000 of them diagnosed as "shell shock and neurosis."[11] It had to be assumed that similar casualties would occur again.

The number of reboardings, which reclassified soldiers as unfit for military service, was causing the Canadian military authorities some concern by 1941. Between February 1940 and March 1941, 2,135 troops of all ranks were returned to Canada for discharge and 21 per cent of these were classified as mental cases — "chiefly anxiety neuroses, chronic alcoholism or mental deficiency."[12] In addition to these, hundreds of other Canadian soldiers were, or had been, neuropsychiatric patients at No. 1 Neurological Hospital or No. 15 General Hospital. The problem began to reach epidemic proportions in the winter of 1941 and Luton appointed a "committee on cases of anxiety neurosis"[13] to study the matter.

The committee met at Basingstoke on 13 January 1941 and the first order of business was to change the name of the committee and the scope of its investigation. Since the whole range of mental illness was to be examined, the title Functional Nervous Diseases was adopted and the Official Nomenclature of Diseases 1931 was used to enumerate the five diagnostic categories: 1. Mental deficiency; 2. Chronic alcoholism and drug addiction; 3. Functional psychoses; 4. Psychopathic personalities; 5. Psychoneuroses.

The Committee decided that the "higher grade of defectives . . . would be able to perform routine tasks quite efficiently"[14] and should only be discharged if they had behaviour problems that did not respond to army discipline. Drug addicts, chronic alcoholics, and functional psychotics were to be returned to Canada forthwith.

The broad category of psychopathic personalities was also easily disposed of.[15] Generally neuropsychiatrists used this term to encompass a variety of chronic social misfits who had been arrested for burglary, larceny, petty theft, robbery with violence, homosexual activity, or absence without leave. These patients were referred to Basingstoke from various prisons and detention barracks. They were to be returned to Canada and discharged from the service unless there was clear evidence that they would respond to military discipline.

This left the largest category, the psychoneuroses. In 1940 psychoneurosis was a catch-all term for a variety of personality disorders that made it difficult, or impossible, for an individual to function adequately. Major Hyland, as the senior neuropsychiatrist (Colin Russel was absent due to illness), presented the case for the retention and treatment of all anxiety and hysteria cases. At Basingstoke a good deal of attention was paid to each patient[16] with treatment "initiated by a careful evaluation of physical, psychological and sociological components." A detailed case history with "questioning about childhood environmental influences, parental attitudes and relationships, phobias, school and work record, disposition towards sports and physical dangers, sexual habits, adaption to difficulties, mood changes, details of army experiences, etc." followed a thorough physical. Then came a systematic mental examination "surveying intellect as well as emotion" and a detailed discussion of the factors "causing the immediate mental conflict and tension." Hyland believed in repeated talks with patients so that "repressed fears and conflicts" could be aired again and again. The immediate problems that had caused or at least precipitated the neurosis were to be dealt with where possible, but when the problem was insoluble Hyland urged a "philosophical outlook" and the avoidance of continued "emotional thinking." In selected cases "hypnosis, sodium pentathol, suggestion by use of faradism and occasionally prolonged narcosis" were tried.[17]

★   ★   ★

One of the paradoxes of military affairs is that a unit needs battle experience to complete its training, but the inherent strain of operations begins a wearing-down process, which if not arrested, leaves the unit impotent. Accumulating casualties can easily shift the boundary between battle worthiness and ineffectiveness. Eventually the unit can become, as it were, a collective neuropsychiatric casualty. The 1st Division was on the brink in the weeks after Ortona. Heavy losses in rifle companies, especially of junior leaders, seriously strained battalions. "I am compelled to bring to your attention, therefore," the divisional commander, Major-General Christopher Vokes, informed his British Corps Commander, "that in my opinion the infantry units of this division will not be in fit condition to undertake further offensive operations until they have had a period of rest, free of operational commitments, during which they can carry out intensive training."[18]

In the circumstances the division could not be pulled out of line. The primary focus of the Italian fighting had moved to the west coast where the United States Fifth Army was similarly stalemated before Cassino some 100 kilometres south of Rome. In fighting as bitter as that at Ortona, the Americans, reinforced by the New Zealand Corps, battered fruitlessly against the Germans' Gustav Line. The front stabilized for the winter across the shin of the Italian boot and except in local situations divisions could not be spared for major refit. They adjusted as they might.[19]

Generals may propose but their soldiers ultimately dispose — not always in intended fashion. Some were reluctant to risk their lives for little apparent purpose and "wanted to know their sacrifices really counted."[20] The full range of soldiers' reactions and behaviour on any battle field is impossible to recapture. Soldiers have always found ways to relieve stress by avoiding the stressful circumstances. For example, if the need for patrolling was not readily perceived and accepted, it was a simple matter for soldiers to lay up short of the objective so as not to provoke a reaction. . . . In none was an enemy ambushed or prisoner taken. It seems likely that prudence tempered an ill-conceived patrol policy, making life less stressful for some soldiers, if not for higher staffs.

Other soldiers took more direct action to avoid or escape their surroundings. Between December and February sixty-seven cases were categorized as self-inflicted wounds; an unknown number went undetected.[21] Soldiers deserted, went absent without leave, or otherwise breached military discipline and ended up in rigorous confinement. The 1st Division opened its own field punishment camp in the Ortona Castle in February 1944 for offenders serving up to twenty-eight days detention. In a few weeks it had two hundred prisoners. Soldiers serving longer sentences were incarcerated in Canadian and British military prisons that had been opened in Italy. They operated on the fundamental detention barracks premise that conditions should be sufficiently unpleasant to deter soldiers from casually choosing to endure them. The camp's War Diary remarks that: "of necessity initiation must be tough, or the whole camp would fail in its purpose, that of instilling a sense of discipline in soldiers who 'fall out of line.' It is hard to describe it — the soldier under sentence is not touched in any way, but he is kept so busy doing things, and being constantly shouted at by four or five sergeants, that he doesn't know whether he is coming or going, and soon he doesn't care." All movements in camp were at the double. There was a daily half-hour talking period and a one-hour Sunday reading period when prisoners would read mail and write one letter. They might also at this time eat one issue chocolate bar.[22] While conditions were undoubtedly tough, it must be kept in mind that prisoners were not being shot at by Germans.

In this period of shaken morale the arrival in Italy of 1 Canadian Corps Headquarters marked a significant change for Canadians in the theatre. Neither the headquarters nor its commander, Lieutenant-General Harry Crerar, were welcome. Responding to Canadian representations for the need to give their senior commanders high level command and staff experience, the War Office belatedly agreed to send the Corps and the 5th Armoured Division to Italy. Unfortunately they neglected to consult either General Alexander or General Montgomery. The latter, especially, made it quite clear that he did not want another Corps headquarters, particularly one commanded by an inexperienced Canadian, and had no need for an armoured division in the Italian mountains. Montgomery snubbed Crerar who, although underwhelmed by British assumptions of natural military omniscience, was placed in a difficult position. He had a mandate to command Canadian formations in the theatre and he had to tread a very fine line between his national and his operational responsibilities. These were not always compatible and differences compounded already tenuous morale problems.[23]

If the Eighth Army was less than hospitable to the newcomers many 1st Division veterans equally resented their arrival. The old Desert Army was by then a comfortable informal club under Montgomery's paternalistic guidance and General Vokes and others had taken kindly to its casual professional ways. Belying stereotypes of breezy Canadians and stuffy Brits, Crerar's Headquarters displayed a jarring concern for disciplinary forms. For instance the Eighth Army had cultivated an image of casual dress that appeared very unmilitary to the uninitiated. An apocryphal story circulated that Montgomery issued just one injunction on proper dress. After encountering a driver in baked Sicily naked except for a liberated top hat he ordered that in future top hats would not be worn in the Eighth Army.[24] In contrast Crerar insisted on more conventional dress and other restrictions that annoyed at least some veterans.

Crerar and his senior staff had developed their attitudes about soldierly behaviour in a simpler, less equivocal World War I setting. Times had changed, however, with behavioural nuances more freely acknowledged. As General Burns recalled: "Psychiatrists and psychologists in their attempts to explain human behaviour have made . . . distinctions far less clear, insofar as the Army is concerned than they were, or seemed to be, in 1914–18. At that time a man did what he was told, encouraged by the kindly admonitions of his sergeant or sergeant-major — or else. If he reported to the medical officer with nothing visibly the matter with him, he was malingering, a crime under the Army Act."[25] In that war, it may also be observed, it seems plausible that at least some of the 25 Canadians and 246 British soldiers executed for cowardice or desertion were dysfunctional psychoneurotics.[26]

Crerar and his senior doctor, Brigadier E.A. McCusker, were taken aback when they learned about the manifestations of declining morale. "The pride that I have in our Canadian troops makes me hesitate to discuss openly such problems as the high incidences of SIW [self-inflicted wounds] and of neuropsychiatric casualties during the past winter," McCusker wrote when the immediate crisis had passed.[27] Earlier he had relieved Colonel Playfair, the 1st Division's Assistant Director Medical Services, for a time and had experienced the difficulties at first hand. Enemy resistance and bad weather had made things go poorly, he recorded, and "this has been the first real test of the stamina of officers and men and consequently the weaklings are being weeded out. The psychiatrists say that all, or nearly all cases are genuine. The Officers in Command (OCs) feel that they are a bad influence and must be gotten rid of as they upset their companies. The problem is what to do with them."[28]

However, McCusker was not fully persuaded that soldiers were not faking or malingering. Doyle found him upset, "ascribing [the NP casualties] to everything from poor leadership to the presence of a psychiatrist."[29] Doyle and Colonel Playfair had three long discussions with him, reviewing patient records and finally persuading McCusker to examine a group of patients himself. Doyle thought that he seemed convinced when he remarked, "There's not one who could make a soldier; the Corps Commander must see these men so that he will understand."[30]

McCusker was caught uneasily between his medical and his soldierly convictions. A short time later they came into direct collision when an administrative officer in his own Corps broke down under shellfire. A very awkward situation developed when McCusker "was extremely harsh with this officer, asserting that he would be given two alternatives (1) that of reverting to rank of private and going to Pioneer Company as labourer, and (2) to go with the section in forward Field Ambulance."[31] Doyle intervened and found the officer other employment, but the rift widened between some 1st Division veterans, who by this time accepted the phenomenon of NP casualties as fatalistically as they did the weather, and the newcomers who viewed the matter as an affront to their beliefs about proper soldierly behaviour.

It would be instructive to have a full record of the consultations between General Crerar and his medical staff at this time. Despite scanty documentation, however, it is possible to trace some aspects of their attitudes and policies. For example, conserving manpower was a compelling imperative, especially as planning for the Normandy landings matured in 1944, leaving Italy a neglected theatre. Reinforcements arrived, but for the most part the Corps had to regenerate itself from its internal resources. This meant severely limiting evacuations from the theatre for any reason. Wounded soldiers went back into trenches after the briefest convalescence. Crerar concluded that the "general problem concerns the natural but, in the circumstances of war, reprehensible objection of a small proportion of other ranks of 1 Cdn Corps to risk death, or serious injury, for their country. The 'angles' include such things as desertion, self-inflicted wounds, attempts to be diagnosed as 'exhaustion cases,' VD re-infection and so on."[32]

His solution was to tighten discipline, with rapid response to infractions and exemplary punishments. "By 'education' all ranks should be brought increasingly to the view that 'escapism' is a shameful thing." Unit leadership was the key. Crerar observed that "there is a general tendency amongst forward units and formations to take the easy way out of this difficult problem. If a man shows himself to be unreliable under fire, he is left behind in the case of a fighting patrol and left out of battle in the case of a unit action."[33] This was a natural reaction by those actually fighting under trying circumstances, but it established a natural selection process that separated reliable and willing soldiers from those incapable or unwilling.

The residue of unwilling and/or incapable soldiers presented the fundamental problem. Crerar thought not all of them were genuine medical cases: "Undoubtedly, a pretty high proportion of the cases which get back to General Hospital are real nervous breakdowns on the part of the unstable mental characters. On the other hand, as it is not considered any disgrace to be an 'exhaustion case' it is becoming increasingly tempting to 'lead swingers' and others, whose hearts are not in the war to seek this way out. While, therefore, the real 'shell-shock' must be regarded and treated as a casualty, I consider it very important that the mesh of the administrative sieve should be so close that the fake exhaustion case should be detected and held . . . suitably punished and not allowed to get away with it."[34]

Doyle was also concerned with conserving manpower but his views were closer to those of combatant officers than to those of higher commanders. He fully sympathized with platoon and company commanders who wanted to be rid of unreliable soldiers. He discounted malingering as a serious problem, noting that "OCs and other officers of combatant units are almost unanimous in the opinion that the soldier hides his fear and his complaints rather than parades them. They rarely have any reason to suspect malingering." Those of suspicious minds, he thought, "surely have some psychological weakness in themselves," and cited a recent incident in one unit where "the only officer who was afraid of malingering in his company was one about whom his medical and his commanding officer had asked professional advice. His own weakness was betrayed by his lack of confidence in his men."[35]

Undoubtedly some soldiers malingered. Their numbers are debatable. Doubts about the endurance of fighting troops varied proportionally with the observer's distance from the front. Brigadier Rees has remarked that the "fighting soldier was in no doubt at all as to what kind of man he wants to have with him. The further you get away from the front line the tougher become the comments, the more hints there are that everyone is trying to evade the service, and that is a common experience of armies."[36] One much-decorated Canadian battalion commander cautioned that "persons who are not exposed to the bullets and shells in a slit trench situation or having to advance over open ground against a determined enemy should be very careful of using the words 'cowardice,' 'yellow,' and 'malingerer.' Sooner or later, in those circumstances, we would all break down, some sooner than others."[37] Doyle was possibly disappointed but not surprised at the response when he spoke to the 5th Division Medical Society just before the battle for Rome began in May 1944. His first questioner asked: "Should some demoralized, malingering cases, cropping up whilst in action, be shot on the spot as an example?" Doyle replied that it was "purely a disciplinary problem.

If we were to adopt this, we would be well advised to start our disciplinary measures from the bottom rung rather than off the top one."[38] He also might have pointed out that shooting men was hardly a means of conserving manpower.

Traditional attitudes about proper soldierly behaviour defined the problem in one way, professional psychiatric opinion in another. The premise that any individual regardless of character or circumstance could be made an effective soldier was not self evident. The timid might be motivated and the recalcitrant disciplined up to a point, but, as General Burns acknowledged after the war, "it is difficult to fix the point beyond which disciplinary measures can have no good result, either exemplary, or in producing a reasonably useful soldier from indifferent material."[39] Burns noted larger implications:

> The psychologists point out, and the Army must agree, that it is of no use training a man as an infantryman or for one of the more hazardous military postings if, in the first hours of stress, in combat, his weakness of nerve and brain will render him useless and, what is more, a bad example for others who do not have his excuse.
>
> The difficulty is that it seems somewhat unjust that the brave and steadfast must be sacrificed, while the poor spirited are allowed to avoid hardship and to preserve their lives . . .
>
> It is obviously unfair that well-behaved and valuable citizens should have to risk their lives and submit to the restraints of life in the forces if criminals and psychopaths are allowed to be discharged to civil life. Furthermore, soldiers who are bored would be tempted to procure their discharge by bad behaviour.[40]

Unpalatable as it may have been, an increasing number of neuropsychiatric cases were accumulating around base hospitals and holding units where, left idle, they demoralized incoming replacements as well as themselves. Combatant units did not want them back, the psychiatrists said they should not go back, and command policy dictated they were not to be evacuated from Italy. One group of evacuees was removed from a ship about to sail for the United Kingdom. The solution to their disposal was to form them into a pioneer company for general labouring duties. Within a few months two more units were formed and their name was changed to Special Employment Companies (SECs). Each had a different function. Nos. 16 and 17 were located in the Corps area, the former acting as a reception centre for cases whose prognosis promised a quick return to the units, the latter for others who remained SEC labourers. No. 18 SEC was a base facility adjacent to holding units receiving soldiers discharged from hospitals. An NCO's school was attached to the base to evaluate the potential of NCO cases. The SECs were a Canadian innovation. Their soldiers loaded ammunition and fuel, worked as medical orderlies, and performed other useful work. They were freed from idleness and morale improved. The SECs were viewed as being something between a penal battalion and a rehabilitation centre. Doyle believed that these soldiers were treated harshly.[41] General Burns, however, then commanding 1 Corps, considered that he had to make a distinction between them and regular units: "It was felt that if troops were allowed to believe that evacuation because of nervous or emotional conditions was a passport for the United Kingdom or Canada, the weak and the wavering would be encouraged to let their pride go and take the easy way out. Whether or not it got to be known that instead of a ticket to Blighty, an evacuation only meant hard labour at the base, I do not know; but I imagine it did, and it may have encouraged some men to hang on, who otherwise might have given up. In any case, I never heard the frontline men complain that the special companies were being treated harshly or unreasonably."[42]

Officer psychiatric casualties presented the most difficult problem of all. They were a danger to their men when they broke, but it was difficult to decide what to do with them. General Crerar had decreed earlier that officers judged unfit for service in the field should not be employed on staff, administrative, or instructional duties. With evacuation ruled out because it set a bad example, not many alternatives remained. If an officer became inefficient he could be given a customary adverse report and sent away for other employment. However, if he acquired a psychiatric tag as well he was in limbo. Doyle described one case: "I have just examined an officer who is anxious to lead his men. He is just not a leader though he could render good service elsewhere. I hesitate to label him with a psychiatric diagnosis but will do so rather than allow men to be entrusted to him in battle. He has done his best in a situation to which he was not suited and I fear that psychiatric diagnosis will prejudice his chances of getting a fair opportunity of success in other work . . . There is no sense recommending a rest or treatment and return to duty because the man, put back into the same situation will again develop symptoms of stress."[43]

Officers with lowered S categories were ostracized — not only those who were unable to accommodate themselves to battle stress when they first met it but also those worn out through long and perhaps distinguished combat service. Moreover the S factor was an all-encompassing one, another psychiatrist recorded, "used for a great many widely differing types of personality disorder and psychiatric illness." He continued: "Under the same label are included such serious reactions as insanity, drug addicts, sexual abnormalities, psychiatric criminal tendencies, and also such mild abnormalities as tendencies to general nervous tension under stress, marked swings of mood, symptoms related to over-meticulous rigid thinking, mild depressions, etc. States of anxiety, depression and fatigue developing with battle stress are graded under the S but the grading often doesn't differentiate between the timid immature officer who had broken down with little battle experience and the steady mature leader who has developed disabling psychiatric symptoms only after very prolonged severe stress."[44]

Rank did not immunize an individual from breakdown. An inexperienced officer might well panic when introduced to the chaos of battle. Many did, although the challenge of leadership doubtless helped some control their fear, at least outwardly. As a British subaltern recalled of his experience in North Africa:

> We were all afraid now. Before an attack fear is universal. The popular belief that in battle there are two kinds of person — the sensitive, who suffers torment, and the unimaginative few who know no fear and go blithely on — is a fallacy. Everyone was as scared as the next man, for no imagination was needed to foresee the possibility of death or mutilation. It was just that some managed to conceal their fear better than others. Officers could not afford to show their feelings as openly as the men; they had more need to dissemble. In a big battle a subaltern had little or no influence over the fate of his platoon — it was the plaything of the gods. His role was essentially histrionic. He had to feign a casual and cheerful optimism to create an illusion of normality and make it seem as if there was nothing in the least strange about the outrageous things one was asked to do. Only in this way could he ease the tension, quell any panic and convince his men that everything would come out right in the end.[45]

Burn out from long exposure was almost inevitable, although timings varied. One very experienced Canadian battalion commander has remarked that it was the accumulated stress of responsibility in command as much as battle itself that wore commanders out.[46] A young man in the last months of the war in Germany found himself commanding his company, after eight months of combat during which his platoon had been shot out five times. He had to report to his commanding officer, but "instead of furnishing a coherent account, I simply stood in front of him weeping inarticulately, unable to construct a sentence, even to force a single word out of my mouth. He approved my release from front-line platoon-leading, which I had requested of him three weeks before, when it had really begun to break me . . . I am too tired out to care."[47]

Not only combat commanders were seriously affected. One of the most trying jobs was that of conscientious chaplains who had to mind the "aftermath of battle . . . sorting the personal effects of the dead, making burial returns, writing letters to next-of-kin."[48] One padre who was evacuated as an exhaustion case described how his reactions evolved when he returned to a front line unit:

> During my first afternoon with the forward infantry I had to harden myself to battle over again. Jerry was putting some shells down around a house four hundred yards away. I had intended going over to it but was deterred, and, telling myself that they were not expecting me anyway, I actually turned to go the other way. Then I realized what had happened to me and I was ashamed. In the months of summer fallow I had begun to count on surviving the war and now here I was taking care of myself. I went over. When I was a hundred yards or so from the house a shell hit it and sent a cloud of dust with pieces of rubble into the air. There were two casualties, one wounded and one mental. The first was sent back on a stretcher. The lieutenant in charge was a recent

reinforcement and asked me what to do with the mental. I advised him to put him in a sheltered place and send him back with another on the next carrying job.[49]

He acknowledged his foreshortened stamina and limited his forward visiting. "As long as I was not tired out the shelling did not bother me; the brain analyzed the noise quickly enough for the nerves to be controlled. When I was tired, though, the process was slowed down and I found myself wincing before the rational faculty took control."[50] Even more difficult than willing himself to go forward when rational calculation told him not to was the increasing strain of trying to comfort the afflicted. "Now come the interviews. In England a considerable number of these had concerned girls. Now it was trouble at home, lost love, ill health, death, financial difficulties, children becoming a problem, and through it all the heartache of separation, the emotions of the soldier mangled and raw by battle tension, death and weariness . . . Listening to these men [the chaplain] must in his own way bear their griefs and carry their sorrows. I now found one interview more wearing than a day's shelling at Cassino. I never had any serious carry-over from shell fire, I am thankful to say, but interviews produced tensions that stayed day and night."[51]

These honest officers recorded experiences that might have happened to anyone in such circumstances. The chaplain was very concerned to have the "gratifying assurance that no marks to my detriment would be put on my medical record," and thus avoid the stigma of psychiatric disability. A formal psychiatric label would have left him, like others, with the lingering stigma of a lowered S category. One must be very careful when treading the minefield of battlefield behaviour lest underlying nuances explode.

NOTES

1. Earle Birney, *Turvey* (Toronto, 1976), 207.
2. Quoted in C.P. Stacey, *Six Years of War* (Ottawa: Queen's Printer, 1955), 54.
3. W.R. Feasby, *Organization and Campaigns*, vol. 1, *Official History of the Canadian Medical Services, 1939–45* (Ottawa: Queen's Printer, 1956), 8.
4. Ibid., 34.
5. Ibid., 51.
6. W.R. Feasby, *Clinical Subjects*, vol. 2, *Official History of the Canadian Medical Services, 1939–45* (Ottawa, 1956), 100.
7. Dr. Jack Griffin, interview with Terry Copp, Toronto, 25 Oct. 1982.
8. Feasby, vol. 2, *Clinical Subjects*, 56.
9. *General Instructions for the Medical Examination of Recruits for the CASF and SPAM* (Ottawa: King's Printer, 1940).
10. Report of Selection of Personnel and Mental Disease in the Canadian Army Overseas 18 July 1941, National Archives of Canada (NA), Record Group (RG) 14, vol. 12,620, File 31.
11. J.P.S. Cathcart, "The Neuro-Psychiatric Branch of the Department of Soldiers' Civil Re-Establishment," *The Ontario Journal of Neuro-Psychiatry* 8 (1928): 46.
12. J.M. Hitsman, *The Problem of Personnel Selection in the Canadian Army Overseas, 1939–46*, report no. 64, Historical Section, Canadian Military Headquarters (CMHQ), U.K. (1946), typescript, DHIST, Dept. of National Defence, 28, 4.

13. Minutes of Meeting, Committee on Cases of Anxiety Neurosis, Canadian Active Service Force (CASF), 3 Feb. 1941, Russel Papers, vol. 4.
14. Ibid.
15. Ibid.
16. Hyland and Richardson, "Psychoneurosis," 20-1. All quotations in the paragraph are from this account of treatment at Basingstoke.
17. Minutes, Committee on Cases of Anxiety Neurosis, 3 Feb. 1941.
18. Major-General C. Vokes to General Officer in Command (GOC) V Corps, 3 January 1944, DHIST, CMHQ Report 165, appendix.
19. For the most comprehensive recent history of the Italian campaign see D. Graham and S. Bodwell, *Tug of War: The Battle for Italy* (New York: St. Martin's Press, 1986).
20. Stevens, *Royal Canadian Regiment*, 130. For powerful historical evocations of soldiers in battle see John Keegan, *The Face of Battle* (New York: Vintage, 1977); D. Winter, *Death's Men: Soldiers of the Great War* (London: Penguin, 1979); G.F. Linderman, *Embattled Courage: The Experience of Combat in the American Civil War* (New York: Free Press, 1987); John Ellis, *The Sharp End of War* (London: David and Charles, 1980).
21. War Diary, DDMS, I Corps, NA, RG 24, vol. 15,651. Officially diagnosed self-inflicted wounds rates for 1944 (per 1,000 strength) were British 0.21, Canadian 2.40, New Zealand 0.10. W.F. Mellor, *Casualties and Medical Statistics* (London: Her Majesty's Stationery Office [HMSO], 1972).
22. War Diary, Field Punishment Camp, February-April 1944, NA, RG 24, vol. 16,516. The film *The Hill* offers an unexcelled portrayal of the finely turned tension of military detention.
23. Nicholson, *Canadians in Italy*, 340-62; Lieutenant-General E.L.M. Burns, *General Mud* (Toronto: Clarke Irwin, 1970), 120-37.
24. See the version in K. Beattie, *Dileas: History of the 48th Highlanders of Canada, 1929-1956* (Toronto: 48th Highlanders, 1957).
25. E.L.M. Burns, *Manpower in the Canadian Army, 1939-1945* (Toronto: Clarke Irwin, 1956), 106.
26. See Babington, *For the Sake of Example*; also Desmond Morton, "The Supreme Penalty; Canadian Deaths by Firing Squad in the First World War," *Queen's Quarterly* (Autumn 1972): 345-52.
27. Brigadier E.A. McCusker to Major-General R.M. Luton, Director of Medical Services (DMS) CMHQ, 22 April 1944, War Diary, DDMS, I Canadian Corps, April 1944, NA, RG 24, vol. 15,651.
28. Ibid., January 1944.
29. A.M. Doyle, "The History and Development of Canadian Neuropsychiatric Service in the CMF," unpublished typescript, n.d., NA, RG 24, vol. 12,630.
30. Ibid.
31. War Diary, No. 2 Canadian Exhaustion Unit, June 1944, NA, RG 24, vol. 15,951.
32. Crerar to Lieutenant-General G.G. Simonds, 15 July 1944 (quoting from a letter Crerar had written earlier to General Burns on turning over command of the Corps). NA, Manuscript Group (MG) 30 E157, Crerar Papers, vol. 3.
33. Ibid.
34. Ibid.
35. Doyle, "Report 10 July - 10 November 1943," NA, RG 24, vol. 15,951.
36. J.R. Rees, *The Shaping of Psychiatry by War* (New York: Norton, 1945), 27.
37. Personal communication.
38. 5 CAD Medical Society, minutes of meeting, 11 May 1944. War Diary, ADMS, 5 CAD, May 1944, appendix 6, NA, RG 24, vol. 15,664. The death penalty as deterrent is discussed in R.H. Ahrenfeldt, *Psychiatry in the British Army in the Second World War* (London: Routledge and Kegan Paul, 1958), 271-5.
39. Burns, *Manpower*, 107, 110.
40. Ibid.
41. Doyle, "History and Development CMF."
42. Burns, *Manpower*, 108.
43. A.M. Doyle to ADMS, 1st Division, "Stress Reactions in Officers," 19 December 1943, NA, RG 24, vol. 10,924.
44. Memorandum, "Battle Weary Officers," 28 November 1944, DHIST 147.98009 (D4).
45. Norman Craig, *The Broken Plume* (London: Imperial War Museum, 1982), 75.
46. Personal communication.

47. D. Pearce, *Journal of a War* (Toronto: Macmillan, 1965), 165.
48. W. Smith, *What Time the Tempest* (Toronto: Ryerson, 1953), 278. The lack of reference to clergymen in the documents on handling psychiatric casualties is as striking as the lack of reference to Freud.
49. Ibid.
50. Ibid.
51. Ibid.

Deportation: The Final Solution to Canada's "Japanese Problem"

ANN GOMER SUNAHARA

When British Columbia's legislators successively disenfranchised Chinese, Japanese and East Indians, they created politically impotent targets for the rhetoric of self-seeking politicians. They also set a precedent for political behaviour toward Asian Canadians. Henceforth the politically castrated Asian minorities would be used as scapegoats for British Columbia's political, social and economic ills. The exploitation of the despised Asians as a salve for public discontent in British Columbia remained a legitimate and unquestioned political tactic throughout most of the first half of the twentieth century. Defenceless, the Asian minorities became victims of laws and regulations designed to prevent further Asian immigration, and to discourage Asians already in British Columbia by restricting them to a permanent second-class status.

With the outbreak of the Pacific War in December 1941, public anger and insecurity in British Columbia focussed on the twenty-two thousand Japanese Canadians resident there. Conditioned by fifty years of anti-Japanese propaganda, B.C. politicians, press and public readily perceived Japanese Canadians as an enemy within. Content to continue fifty years of proven political tactics, the federal government elected to salve British Columbia's unwarranted hysteria at the expense of the innocent and defenceless Japanese minority. Beginning in February 1942, 20,881 Japanese Canadians were uprooted from their homes, stripped of all real and personal property, and confined, at their own expense, in government detention camps.

In December 1945, three months after the armistice with Japan, the federal government chose to impose a final solution on Canada's "Japanese problem": deportation. Employing the immense powers of the War Measures Act a scant two weeks before it expired, the federal government

SOURCE: Excerpted from "Deportation: The Final Solution to Canada's 'Japanese Problem,'" in Jorgen Dahlie and Tissa Fernando, eds., *Ethnicity, Power and Politics in Canada* (Toronto: Methuen, 1981), pp. 254–76. Reprinted with permission.

ordered the deportation to a starving Japan of over ten thousand Japanese Canadians. This paper traces the evolution of that deportation policy from its origins in the rhetoric of B.C. politicians, through its maturation within the wartime government of Prime Minister William Lyon Mackenzie King, to its promulgation by the federal Cabinet against the will of Parliament.

This paper also traces the defeat of those deportation orders by Japanese Canadian associations allied with Caucasian activists. Their victory, significantly, was not a legal victory, but a political one. Although libelled as traitors and stripped of their civil liberties, Japanese Canadians with their Caucasian allies succeeded in delaying the implementation of the deportation orders long enough to generate strong opposition to them from outside apparently antiJapanese British Columbia, making the deportation of Japanese Canadians not only politically unnecessary but politically unwise.

*   *   *

Deportation as a solution to the "problem" of Asian minorities in British Columbia had been part of antiAsian rhetoric since the late nineteenth century. Previously, however, attempts to deport Asians from British Columbia had failed because of opposition from the federal government, in whose jurisdiction deportation lay. That opposition by the federal government, however, was not rooted in concern for the rights of the Asian minorities, but rather in diplomatic considerations. As long as the Asian nations remained valuable trade partners and allies of Canada and Great Britain, diplomatic relations prohibited the deportation of Asian nationals and their descendants.[1] The outbreak of the Pacific War, however, nullified all diplomatic protection for Japanese Canadians, a fact readily apparent in their subsequent uprooting and dispossession. Moreover, at the outbreak of the War there was a man in Cabinet willing and able to promote deportation as a solution to the "Japanese problem": Ian Alistair Mackenzie, Member of Parliament for Vancouver Centre and Minister of Pensions and Health.

At the time of the uprooting of the Japanese minority in 1942, Ian Alistair Mackenzie was the only British Columbian in the federal Cabinet. A seasoned politician, Mackenzie had a reputation as a personable bachelor, a liberal champion of workers' and veterans' rights, a first class parliamentarian and, most importantly, an expert in retaining political power. Mackenzie was also virulently antiAsian and the impetus behind the Liberal Party's antiAsian campaigns in British Columbia. He sincerely believed that Asians polluted British Columbian society and, importantly, that most other British Columbians shared his feelings. As a politician, he was convinced that strong measures against Asians could win the Liberal party "every seat in British Columbia."[2]

A major force behind the decision to uproot and dispossess Japanese Canadians, Mackenzie gave notice of his desire to see them deported as early as April 1942. The uprooting of the Japanese "for reasons of national security," Mackenzie and his supporters declared, proved that Japanese Canadians were dangerous. If they were a danger in time of war, they were a danger in time of peace. British Columbia, therefore, would never be secure as long as any Japanese Canadian, citizen or alien, remained within its boundaries.[3] On the west coast where the public readily accepted Mackenzie's contention that Japanese Canadians were dangerous traitors, deportation quickly became a popular cause. Such enthusiasm however, was less easily aroused in Ottawa where, Mackenzie acknowledged, there would be "a great many bad days ahead of us all before we can get [deportation] implemented."[4]

In fact, the possibility of deporting any Japanese Canadians was not even considered in Ottawa until August 1943. At that time officials at the Department of External Affairs were primarily concerned with setting up the machinery to enable the voluntary "repatriation"[5] of any Japanese Canadian who wished to go to Japan after the armistice. Any "disloyal" Japanese Canadians, they assumed, would be deported.

The main problem lay in defining the term "disloyal." By 1943, Norman A. Robertson, the Under-Secretary of State for External Affairs and one of Prime Minister MacKenzie King's principal advisors, favoured regarding as disloyal all Japanese Canadians who had been interned at Angler, Ontario or who had at any time placed themselves under the protection of the Spanish Consul.[6] Since simply applying to see the Spanish Consul in order to place a complaint before him was sufficient to put a Japanese Canadian into this category, almost all the wartime leaders in the camps in British Columbia and the sugar beet fields of Alberta and Manitoba would be deported, as would those Nisei[7] who had been interned for protesting their uprooting.[8]

Other civil servants[9] favoured a loyalty survey similar to that undertaken in the American concentration camps in early 1943.[10] The Canadian survey, it was suggested, should require all Japanese nationals to swear to abide by Canadian laws and to refrain from interfering with the war effort. The naturalized and the Nisei should be required to swear allegiance to Canada and to deny their loyalty to Japan. Those who refused, along with their families, should then be segregated into special camps and deported along with the interned men and any Japanese Canadian whose behaviour was deemed "disloyal." The last category would include anyone who broke Canadian laws or incited others to disobey Canadian authorities. Deportation, the senior civil servants contended, was justified on the grounds that it was necessary to get the provinces to accept Japanese as permanent residents. Deporting a few to secure permanent resettlement for the majority, they hoped, would result in postwar policies "not too flagrantly unjust" to those "who have been blameless."[11] In their estimation, the end justified the means.

Although approved by the Cabinet War Committee in April 1944, the loyalty survey and the segregation of "loyal" and "disloyal" Japanese

Canadians was delayed because of uncertainties about American policy. Canadian officials were anxious to develop postwar policies consistent with those that would be adopted by the United States. A joint policy, Robertson felt, would stabilize internal political opinion on the "Japanese question."[12] Strong objections from either liberals or racists could be blunted by pointing out the need for international consistency. Consequently, the Americans had been approached in November 1943 for information on their plans for deporting Japanese Americans. They had replied that the matter was under consideration. In fact "the far larger part of official sentiment" in the United States was "to get rid of" the Japanese Americans when the war ended.[13] The Constitution of the United States, however, prohibited the deportation of citizens. In order to circumvent the Constitution, the American authorities were in the process of obtaining legislation which would make the renunciation of American citizenship in time of war relatively easy. The new law, they reasoned, would be used by Japanese American dissidents to continue protesting their uprooting by renouncing their citizenship. Once having denied their citizenship, they could be deported as aliens.[14] In the spring of 1944 when the Denaturalization Act was before Congress, however, the Americans could not commit themselves to a joint policy with Canada. The matter was accordingly shelved in Ottawa.

★   ★   ★

While Ottawa procrastinated, B.C.'s racists demanded the deportation of Canada's Japanese minority. In the week preceding the Allied invasion of Normandy, the annual convention of the B.C. Canadian Legion and Vancouver's Mayor J.W. Cornett demanded that the "Japanese and their children be shipped to Japan after the war and never be allowed to return here."[15] Applauded by Ian Mackenzie, Legion representatives from Lillooet and Rossland resurrected the usual racist lies, arguing that Japanese Canadians "had betrayed the trust placed in them by the Canadian government," and were "a serious threat to the existence of other Canadians" because of their low standard of living and high birthrate. Endorsing the antiJapanese resolutions, Mayor Cornett pledged his wholehearted support and lamented that some of his fellow council members felt that the Nisei should be allowed to stay in Canada. "But I say," he informed the enthusiastic crowd, "they have Japanese nationals for wives and how are you going to split them up?"[16]

Contrary to the headlines in the press, however, the Legion lacked solidarity on the deportation question. Some of the newly returned veterans saw the resolution as a denial of everything they had fought for and said so. One such soldier, Eric S. Flowerdew of Langley Prairie, publicly protested the resolution, pleading to no avail that the Nisei were loyal.[17]

While rejected by most of his fellow Legionnaires, Flowerdew's opinions, in fact, conformed with the majority of British Columbians. In

February 1944 a Gallup poll had indicated that while 80 per cent of Canadians favoured the deportation of Japanese aliens, only 33 per cent favoured the deportation of the Canadian-born and the naturalized. Opinion in British Columbia did not differ significantly from the national opinion.[18] While some public figures like Ian Mackenzie ignored this poll and clung tenaciously to their antiJapanese prejudices, others had begun to adjust their stance. Among these were the majority of Vancouver's aldermen, who rejected Mayor Cornett's mass deportation resolution on June 5, 1944.[19]

The civil rights of Japanese Canadians were also being debated in the House of Commons in June 1944. The occasion was the introduction of the Soldiers' Vote Bill, setting up the machinery under which Canadian soldiers serving overseas were to vote in the forthcoming general election. After the bill had passed the Commons, it was discovered that it disenfranchised "any person whose racial origin [was] that of a country at war with Canada."[20] Since the overlooked clause would disenfranchise considerable numbers of German and Italian Canadians, opposition to the bill rapidly escalated. Amid charges that the clause embodied Nazi principles of racial hatred, Senators J.J. Bench and Norman Lambert of Ontario attempted to have it deleted, but only succeeded in changing the wording so that it applied only to Japanese Canadians. Returned to the Commons for approval as amended, the offending clause was further modified amid heated and well-publicized debate to leave disenfranchised only those Japanese Canadians who had previously been without the franchise by virtue of their residence in British Columbia in 1940. This meant that Japanese Canadians who had already moved east of the Rocky Mountains remained disenfranchised. The bill was just, Prime Minister King argued, because it avoided the racial discrimination of disenfranchising those few Japanese Canadians who had previously enjoyed the franchise, while also avoiding the "racial favouritism" of granting Pacific Coast Japanese privileges they had not previously enjoyed.[21] King did not acknowledge, however, that the bill also prevented the uprooted Japanese from showing their anger by voting against the Liberal government, and voting for the only party which had publicly defended them, the CCF.

King's "racial favouritism" rationalization was promptly ridiculed by the CCF MPs, who continued to ask pointed questions about the postwar fate of Japanese Canadians. Thus pressured, Prime Minister King finally acknowledged on August 4, 1944, that no acts of sabotage had been committed by any Japanese Canadian. Despite this unblemished record, the government had decided that Japanese Canadians could remain in Canada after the war only if they were judged loyal by a Loyalty Commission, and if they dispersed themselves across Canada. Those judged to be disloyal, King informed the Commons, would be "deported to Japan as soon as that is physically possible," and any Canadian nationals among them would be stripped of their citizenship. In addition,

Japanese Canadians who wanted to go to Japan after the war would be "encouraged" to do so, while postwar immigration from Japan was to be prohibited.[22] Although King acknowledged that to do other than "deal justly with those who are guilty of no crime or even of ill intention" would be to accept "the standards of our enemies,"[23] the policies he outlined were clearly based on the assumption that the only people in Canada who were to be considered guilty until they had proved their innocence were people with Japanese faces.

The overt discrimination in the Soldiers' Vote Bill, followed one month later by King's public acknowledgment that no Japanese Canadian had committed any disloyal act, publicized the plight of Japanese Canadians. The press in central and eastern Canada, which until 1944 had largely ignored the Japanese "question," began to realize and to publicize what had been done, and was still being done, to Japanese Canadians. While presenting the facts, however, few magazines or newspapers were prepared to take a strong editorial stand. There was a war to be won. The "Japanese question" could wait.[24]

For Ian Mackenzie and the Liberal members of parliament from British Columbia, however, the "Japanese question" could definitely not wait. The policy outlined by Prime Minister King in 1944 was, in their opinion, far too liberal. Having vowed publicly that he would not remain part of a government which allowed Japanese Canadians to return to the Pacific Coast, Mackenzie, along with Tom Reid and George Cruickshank, took the question of deportation to the people of British Columbia in an attempt to convince Ottawa to take a harder line. Campaigning under the slogan "Not a Japanese from the Rockies to the sea," Mackenzie fanned the dying embers of racial hatred and called on his audiences to "serve notice on the rest of Canada that we will not have Japanese in this fair province."[25] His success, however, was minimal. Over the next eleven months, Prime Minister King received only nineteen submissions favouring the mass deportation of Japanese Canadians, while receiving eighty-five submissions urging a moderate policy.[26] In late 1944, it appeared that moderation might well prevail.

★   ★   ★

In December 1944, however, the federal government panicked. At that time the American authorities announced that Japanese Americans could return to their homes on the Pacific Coast. Afraid to allow Japanese Canadians the same freedom of movement, the federal government hurriedly set its own "Japanese" policies. The policy makers'[27] objectives were twofold: to "repatriate" or deport as many Japanese Canadians as possible and to disperse the rest across Canada. In their haste, they decided that a "repatriation survey" would be the quickest way to separate those who wished to go to Japan from those who wished to stay in Canada. Anyone selecting Japan would be considered "disloyal," while the loyalty of those selecting Canada was to be further tested by the proposed Loyalty Commission.

The survey was presented in the spring of 1945 in a manner calculated to induce the bitter and confused inmates of the detention camps in British Columbia to choose Japan. Repatriates, the inmates were told, could continue to live and work in British Columbia until transportation to Japan was arranged, and could receive relief without first using up their assets on deposit with the Custodian of Enemy Property. Upon reaching Japan, they would receive, in addition to their free passage, funds equivalent to the value of their assets in Canada. Those lacking property would receive $200 per adult and $50 per child to sustain them until established in Japan. In addition, the inmates at the Tashme camp were told "there was no suggestion of disloyalty because of signing the forms" for repatriation.[28]

In contrast, those who stayed in Canada could expect considerable difficulty. Firstly they were to be moved to the camp at Kaslo, British Columbia from where they would be shipped at some future date to any place east of the Rocky Mountains designated by the government. The failure to take the government-assigned employment, the inmates were warned, would be "looked upon as evidence of a lack of willingness to cooperate,"[29] and presumably would be noted on an individual's file for the attention of the proposed Loyalty Commission. Refusal would also disqualify the inmate and his family from receiving relief benefits. In addition, the placement allowance for rescuers was only $60 per couple and $12 per child, a paltry sum the federal government considered adequate because the resettlers were being sent from the camps to "definite employment."[30]

The federal government, however, could not guarantee that that "definite employment" would last longer than a few weeks. Nor could it guarantee adequate housing. In fact, the inmates at the Lemon Creek Camp were warned, veterans would undoubtedly receive preference in housing and employment. The government could not even guarantee the resettlers that their resettlement would be permanent. The original contract with the province of Alberta had specified that the federal government would remove the resettled Japanese from Alberta after the war, and a similar verbal understanding existed with Ontario, Quebec and Saskatchewan. While new contracts were under negotiation, only Saskatchewan's CCF government had expressed any willingness to accept Japanese Canadians as permanent residents.[31] That is why, Japanese Canadians were told, the government was offering such generous terms "to those who come to the conclusion that conditions might be too difficult for them in Canada and the opportunity might be better . . . in Japan."[32]

The manner in which the survey was presented only reinforced what Japanese Canadians already knew. Everyone knew of someone who had gone east and met with difficulty. They knew that the eastern cities were overcrowded with war workers and that housing was often poor, very expensive, and very difficult for Japanese to obtain. They knew that many of the Nisei who had gone east were working in dirty, low-paying jobs, and that they had met with discrimination in public places and even in some churches. They knew also of the hostility and violence the Japanese Americans were experiencing on their return to the Pacific Coast, and feared that similar violence might erupt in Canada once the war in Europe was over and Canada's full attention was focussed on the war with Japan.[33]

The manner in which the survey was presented also reinforced the apathy of the demoralized camp inmates, and aggravated tensions within the camps. In the spring of 1945, morale in the detention camps was at an all-time low. Battered by the triple shocks of uprooting, dispossession and destitution, many inmates had become apathetic and ripe to be manipulated by anyone with strong views. In the detention camps, the strongest views were held by the proJapan patriots. The patriots firmly believed that Japan must inevitably defeat the Allied nations. Relying on shortwave Japanese language broadcasts from Tokyo, they had formed very unrealistic ideas about the progress of the war. They dismissed the victories reported in the Canadian press as "propaganda," and countered that Japan's apparent retreat was a strategic move "to draw her enemies into one spot and defeat them."[34] Bolstered by their belief in Japan's imminent victory, the proJapan element in the detention camps welcomed the repatriation survey and attacked any who leaned toward resettlement.[35] By coercing friends, neighbours and family members into signing for "repatriation," the proJapan element unwittingly helped the Canadian government.

The government knew of the stresses and strains dividing the camps and influencing the "repatriation" decisions, but chose to ignore them. Privately officials admitted that loyal Japanese Canadians who would prefer to remain in Canada would probably sign for repatriation out of "discouragement" with their wartime experiences, or to avoid family separation. Publicly, however, they firmly stated that signing for repatriation was "strictly voluntary" and that "no pressure whatsoever was being exerted" on Japanese Canadians to do so.[36] The repatriation survey, they rationalized, was "reasonably fair in terms of what is politically feasible at the moment."[37]

Politically, the results of the survey looked very good, at least to Ian Mackenzie and the antiJapanese B.C. members of parliament. Some 6884 Japanese Canadians over sixteen years of age had signed for "repatriation" by the beginning of August 1945. With their 3503 dependants they represented almost 43 per cent of the Japanese population of Canada. More importantly, 86 per cent of those 10,347 potential "repatriates" resided in British Columbia. Should they all go to Japan after the war, British Columbia would be left with less than 4200 Japanese Canadians, a number which would be further reduced by the resettlement program.[38] To antiJapanese British Columbians, the survey results must have been heartening. They now had only to ensure that the "voluntary repatriates" actually "repatriated," and the "Japanese problem" would be virtually obliterated in British Columbia.

★   ★   ★

When choosing to use a biased survey to maximize the number of deportable Japanese Canadians, the federal government made two important errors. It had failed to realize that the fate of Japanese Canadians was no longer just a British Columbian concern. They also failed to realize that the position of the Japanese minority in 1945 was very different from that of 1942 when Japanese Canadians were uprooted, and of 1943 when they were dispossessed. In 1942 and 1943, Japanese Canadians had been alone and friendless, pariahs libelled as traitors. By 1945, however, they had made some very determined friends, friends who lived outside antiJapanese British Columbia.

While King and his Cabinet were aware of the most vocal of those friends, the twenty-eight CCF MPs, they underestimated the quieter proJapanese Canadian lobby, a lobby which had grown rapidly since the spring of 1944. At that time, the publicity accompanying the Soldiers' Vote Bill debate had alerted liberal Canadians to the ongoing abuse of Japanese Canadians under the rubric of "national security." Reinforced by the publicity efforts of two tiny groups in Toronto and Vancouver, opposition to that abuse began coalescing. By the spring of 1945, the groundwork had been laid. Ten thousand copies of a pamphlet, *A Challenge to Patriotism and Statesmanship*,[39] had been printed and distributed across Canada in an attempt to get the truth about Japanese Canadians before the public. Informal contacts had been established between the church and social organizations working with Japanese Canadians, and the Ontario and B.C. civil liberties associations. The press had grown suspicious of the government's explanations. Perhaps most importantly, Japanese Canadians outside the B.C. camps had regained their self-confidence and had begun to organize. In Winnipeg, Hamilton and Toronto, Japanese Canadians had formed organizations and had allied themselves with sympathetic Caucasians. In British Columbia, the Japanese Committee at the Tashme Camp, near Hope, had formed similar links with a Vancouver group. By 1945 Japanese Canadians and their Caucasian allies were ready to protest.

When the truth about the "repatriation" survey leaked out in the spring of 1945, the growing proJapanese Canadian lobby quickly organized. In late May 1945 the representatives of twenty Caucasian organizations in Toronto met with the Japanese Canadian Committee for Democracy (JCCD), a Nisei organization, to form a Cooperative Committee on Japanese Canadians. Officially incorporated on June 19th, the Co-operative Committee quickly grew to include representatives from over thirty organizations, including the major churches, labour unions, civil liberties and professional associations, the National Council of Women and the Canadian Jewish Congress.[40] Chaired by Reverend James Finlay of Carleton Street United Church, the Cooperative Committee sought to demonstrate that all Canadians were not antiJapanese and that many were very disturbed by the wartime treatment of Japanese Canadians. They circulated a petition deploring the "repatriation" survey and the continuing restrictions on Japanese Canadians. In July, they sent a delegation to Ottawa to try to persuade the government to change its stance on deportation, and to allow Japanese Canadians to again buy property. They accelerated their public education campaign with the distribution of fifty thousand copies of a pamphlet *From Citizens to Refugees — It's Happening Here*. They established contact with similar groups scattered across Canada, groups who tried to use the local media to get the truth about Japanese Canadians before the Canadian public.[41]

On its own the JCCD organized the Japanese minority. Working through Japanese Committees in the camps and on the prairies, the JCCD began to collect sworn statements from the unwilling signers, statements which detailed why they had felt compelled to sign for repatriation.[42] At the same time it founded a magazine, *Nisei Affairs*, to link Nisei across Canada and to discuss Japanese Canadian issues in a more forthright manner than was possible in *The New Canadian*.

The JCCD was not the only active group. In the Slocan Valley of British Columbia, the Japanese Committees of the five camps in that area (New Denver, Bay Farm, Lemon Creek, Slocan City and Popoff) united to attack the repatriation issue on their own by authorizing Vancouver lawyer Dennis Murphy to contest the validity of the repatriation survey in the Supreme Court of British Columbia. Apparently unfamiliar with the plethora of Orders-in-Council affecting Japanese Canadians, Murphy chose to sue the British Columbia Security Commission, arguing that the repatriation survey was beyond its powers. Once in court, however, he was rudely awakened to the fact that the BCSC had not existed since February 1943, when its duties were taken over by the Department of Labour. The case, accordingly, was dismissed since the defendant did not exist.[43]

Although disappointed by the failure of the court case, the Japanese Canadians forged ahead. In Winnipeg, the Japanese Committees concentrated on organizing petitions. They were undoubtedly helped by the strong antideportation stance of the influential *Winnipeg Free Press*. In Toronto, where the press took a weaker but still generally favourable antideportation stance, a committee of both Issei and Nisei was created to coordinate fund-raising activities.

The sudden end of the Pacific War in August 1945 surprised both the federal government and the "voluntary repatriates." With Japan's capitulation came the realization of the potential seriousness of those "repatriation" applications. Japan's defeat also totally undermined the power of the proJapan patriots over their relatives and neighbours. People who had signed for repatriation under family, religious or neighbourhood pressure, in anger, or to keep their jobs, soon sought to revoke their signatures. By April 1946, 4527 of the 6844 adult "repatriates" had applied to remain in Canada.[44]

Beginning in September 1945, however, the federal government sought to make those signatures binding. On September 5th, the Minister of Labour, Humphrey Mitchell, called a meeting of the Cabinet Committee on the Japanese Question, now retitled the Special Cabinet Committee on Repatriation and Relocation. At that meeting, Mitchell submitted the most repressive deportation program yet proposed. His new plan called for the deportation of all Japanese nationals, except a few who would be allowed to remain on compassionate grounds; of all naturalized Japanese Canadians who had signed repatriation requests; and all Nisei who had not revoked their "repatriation" requests before the official surrender of Japan three days previously. To implement his program, Mitchell asked for the Committee's support for three Orders-in-Council under the War Measures Act: one declaring the "repatriation" requests binding on the persons signing them and their dependants; a second stripping the "repatriates" of their status as Canadian nationals; and a third setting up a Loyalty Commission to decide which Japanese nationals could remain on compassionate grounds.[45]

If Mitchell had expected the Special Cabinet Committee on Repatriation and Relocation to rubber stamp his proposals as the old Cabinet Committee on Japanese Questions had, he was in for a rude surprise, for more than the name of the committee had changed. While still chaired by Mitchell, dominated by Ian Mackenzie, and advised by Norman Robertson, the new committee had gained three more members: Douglas G. Abbott, the Minister of National Defence, Joseph Jean, the Solicitor General, and Colin Gibson, the Minister of National Defence for Air. Abbott, Jean and Gibson did not have the strongly antiJapanese bias of Mitchell and Mackenzie. They were far less willing to use racism for political gains. In addition, their Ministries placed them in daily contact with Canada's senior military and police officers, men who had remained convinced of the loyalty and innocence of Japanese Canadians. In addition to the presence of these more broad-minded MPs, Norman Robertson was becoming less willing to go quietly along with repressive measures against Japanese Canadians. Robertson explained his feelings to Prime Minister King a few months later.

We do discriminate against the Japanese, against the Chinese, and against the British Indians, in our immigration laws and indirectly in our electoral laws, but until my native province of British Columbia achieves some change of heart,

I do not see what we can do about it except to strive to limit and lessen the discriminations every time an opportunity offers.[46]

September 5, 1945, proved to be just such an opportunity as the new committee members rejected the idea that all Japanese nationals should be summarily deported.[47]

Because of the division within the Special Cabinet Committee, it was almost two weeks before they could make any recommendations to Cabinet. The compromise they reached, however, was only marginally less repressive than Mitchell's original proposal. The Special Cabinet Committee had agreed to recommend that everyone who had requested repatriation, except the Nisei and naturalized who had revoked their requests before the surrender of Japan, should be deported along with all Japanese Canadians interned during the war. In addition they recommended that no action be taken until General Douglas MacArthur, Supreme Allied Commander in Occupied Japan, had indicated when the "repatriation" of Canadian Japanese could begin.[48]

MacArthur's approval, the Special Cabinet Committee was aware, was not likely to be immediate. Conditions in Japan were desperate. In the fall of 1945, disease, malnutrition and even starvation were commonplace. Faced with the problem of feeding Japan, MacArthur was understandably reluctant to increase the number of hungry mouths.[49] It was soon clear that the deportations would have to wait until 1946.

The delay was a considerable inconvenience to the federal government. Mitchell had intended using the all-encompassing powers of the War Measures Act to make the deportations legal. The War Measures Act, however, was due to expire on January 1, 1946, when it would be replaced by the National Emergency Powers Act of 1945, commonly called Bill 15. Bill 15 was intended only as a transitional measure allowing for the gradual removal of wartime economic controls. While Parliament had been unable to censor Orders-in-Council passed under the War Measures Act, Parliament could annul Orders-in-Council passed under Bill 15. Aware that the deportation of Japanese Canadians would become a sensitive issue in Parliament, where the CCF would certainly seek to annul any deportation Orders, King and his Cabinet wanted the power to deport Japanese Canadians without the danger of a confrontation in Parliament. In October 1945, they took steps to assure that power.

The method used reflected the Cabinet's mastery of parliamentary techniques. Accordingly, the federal government quietly inserted a clause into Bill 15 which gave the Governor-in-Council (in fact the Cabinet) power over "entry into Canada, exclusion and deportation, and revocation of nationality." As written, clause 3(g) would give the federal cabinet a year in which to revoke the Canadian nationality of and to deport any resident of Canada. Further, the deportations could not be challenged by Parliament since no Orders-in-Council would be involved. Rather the deportation could be effected by the simple ministerial order.

The announcement of the deportation Orders-in-Council shocked but did not surprise the Cooperative Committee on Japanese Canadians. They had been expecting the worst since their July meeting with Humphrey Mitchell, when he made it very clear that the government intended to follow the demands of public opinion in British Columbia in Japanese matters.[50] Aware that the first shipment of deportees was scheduled for midJanuary, the antideportation groups knew they must act quickly if they were to stop those deportations. Their first impulse was to challenge the deportation Orders in the Supreme Court of Canada. A reference to the Supreme Court, however, carried with it two major problems: it required the consent of the federal government, and it did not prevent the government from deporting Japanese Canadians while the case was in progress.[51] What the antideportation lobby needed was a means of forcing the government to cooperate.

It was quickly apparent that far from cooperating, the federal government had every intention of making the work of the antideportation lobby very difficult. In the week following the deportation announcement, the Commissioner of Japanese Placement, T.B. Pickersgill, denied entry into the Tashme camp at Hope, British Columbia to anyone attempting to help the unwilling repatriates, including Robert J. MacMaster, counsel for Vancouver's Consultative Council for Cooperation in Problems of Wartime Citizenship. Angered by Pickersgill's obstruction, MacMaster threatened to inform the press that Japanese Canadians were being denied the right to legal counsel. That threat prompted a quick consultation between Pickersgill and the Department of Labour in Ottawa, where it was decided that MacMaster must be allowed to see his clients, but only under conditions which cost MacMaster two precious days of the short time he had to stop the deportation of the unwilling "repatriates."[52]

In the end, MacMaster had the last laugh. On December 31st, he discovered the legal means to bring the government to heel. Deportation, MacMaster noted, was a two-step process: first the deportee was detained in legal custody, then he was deported. While the second part of the process, actual deportation, could not be challenged without the consent of the government, the first step could be. The War Measures Act permitted detention in legal custody without recourse to the courts only in time of war. The war was now over, which meant that the detention which preceded deportation could be challenged by a simple writ of habeas corpus.[53] Moreover, even if unsuccessful, habeas corpus proceedings could delay the sailing of the deportees. Since deportation depended heavily on using scarce shipping space, a habeas corpus proceedings for each unwilling deportee could completely disrupt the deportation program.

Faced with the threat of hundreds of habeas corpus proceedings, the federal government agreed to negotiate with the antideportation lobby through Toronto's Cooperative Committee on Japanese Canadians.

Meeting with Justice Minister Louis St. Laurent on January 4th, lawyer Andrew Brewin outlined the Committee's position. The deportation Orders-in-Council, he told St. Laurent, were a threat to civil liberties in Canada and an anathema to the organizations allied with the Co-operative Committee. Further, the Committee was of the opinion that the deportation Order was unconstitutional, since they felt that the power of the federal government was limited to the deportation of aliens. Reminding St. Laurent that the deportation of citizens was not only contrary to international law but had recently been declared a war crime by the newly formed United Nations, Brewin requested that the Orders-in-Council be referred to the Supreme Court of Canada for a ruling as to their validity.[54]

While MacMaster, Brewin and Cartwright used the law to try to halt the deportations, the Cooperative Committee and its allies used the press and the pulpit. Recognizing that the deportation issue was basically a political issue, the antideportation lobby worked through January and February 1946 to create an antideportation clamour which would make the shouts of Ian Mackenzie and the B.C. racists seem like whispers. Across Canada a myriad of organizations raised money, distributed pamphlets, organized public meetings, delivered sermons, talked to any individual or group who would listen, wrote Prime Minister King and their MPs, and sought and received the wholehearted support of the Canadian press. Their message was simple. The deportation of Canadian citizens of Japanese ancestry was an assault on Canadian democracy and must not be allowed to occur.[55] The Canadian public, they discovered, agreed. In an outburst of public opinion stronger than any previous outburst in the long career of Prime Minister King, the Canadian public told its government to leave Japanese Canadians alone.[56]

On February 20th, as Mackenzie's influence declined and the antideportation forces grew, the Supreme Court justices handed down a badly divided decision. The deportation of Japanese nationals and naturalized Japanese Canadians was declared legal unanimously. The justices, however, were split five to two in favour of deporting the Canadian-born and, importantly, four to three against deporting the unwilling dependants of the male deportees.[57]

The judicial division embarrassed the government. They were now in the position to legally deport the 6844 adults who had signed "repatriation" requests, but not their 3500 dependants.

By April 1946, the divisions in the Cabinet on the deportation question were marked. Mackenzie and Mitchell still promoted a hard line, but the public posture of the Cabinet was changing quickly. Prime Minister King set the new tone in a meeting with a delegation from the Cooperative Committee on March 26th, when he publicly scolded Mitchell for calling Japanese Canadians "yellow bastards."[58] King blamed Ian Mackenzie and the "silent majority" for the deportation fiasco.

Reprieve for the potential deportees, however, was not immediately forthcoming. King wanted the "Japanese problem" solved. To do so, he returned to the policies he had outlined in August 1944. Japanese Canadians would be "encouraged" to "voluntarily repatriate" to Japan and to disperse themselves across Canada under an accelerated resettlement program.

* * *

There is often a fine line between "encouragement" and "coercion" in government programs. The second uprooting of Japanese Canadians in the summer of 1946 contained elements of both. New policies setting up hostels east of Alberta, raising the resettlement allowances, making it easier to buy property outside British Columbia, and permitting "deportable" Japanese nationals to move east with their Canadian-born children encouraged resettlement by easing the practical problems and the fear of family separation. Nonetheless, resettlement was not voluntary. Only the sick, the unemployable, the veterans and their families, and those who lived in self-supporting communities were "free to remain in B.C."[59] The rest, the so-called "relocateables," were forced to leave. Denied the right to employment in British Columbia, the "relocateables" who chose not to go to Japan were required to choose a hostel east of Alberta from which they could be channeled into employment and housing, or have one chosen for them by the Commissioner of Japanese Placement T.B. Pickersgill.[60]

For the most part, Japanese Canadians cooperated with this second uprooting. While a few individuals continued to protest the wartime treatment of Japanese Canadians by refusing to leave the detention camps and later the hostel at Moose Jaw, Saskatchewan, most recognized the futility of resistance.[61] Some resettlers saw their second uprooting as an acceptable solution to the problems they had experienced in British Columbia. Others saw it as an alternative to deportation, and dared not object. Still others saw dispersal as the price of their freedom, a price they were willing to pay to return to a normal life. Slipping quietly into their new jobs and communities, the resettlers were often pleasantly surprised and reassured by the indifference toward them in most of those new communities.[62]

While the resettlers moved through the hostels into new jobs and communities, five ships left for Japan. The 3965 people on those ships ostensibly went voluntarily. In fact, most went because they felt they had no alternative. The elderly who had lost everything during the war and who despaired of re-establishing themselves left hoping their families in Japan would support them in their old age, or at least until their dependent children were old enough to assume that responsibility. Those whose parents, children or spouses had been trapped in Japan by the advent of the Pacific War had no alternative except to go to Japan if they wished to be reunited with them. In 1946, the Canadian government was repatriating to Canada only the Caucasians among the Canadians trapped in Japan during the war. Canadian citizens of Japanese ancestry in Japan were ignored by Ottawa until 1947, when they were finally allowed to obtain documentation of their Canadian birth, but were allowed no other assistance, not even a passport.[63] The despair of many of the repatriates was evident in the comment of one repatriating Angler internee who when asked why he was repatriating replied: "The white people hate us and we have no other place to go."[64]

★   ★   ★

By December 1946 the camps were virtually empty. Only a residue of nine hundred sick and elderly and their families remained in New Denver in the Slocan Valley. Over thirteen thousand Japanese Canadians had resettled east of British Columbia, 4700 in 1946 alone. In addition almost 4000 Japanese Canadians, despairing of re-establishing themselves in Canada, or seeking reunion with family members trapped in Japan by the war, had chosen to go to Japan on the five ships the government made available for that purpose. By January 1947, only 6776 Japanese Canadians remained in British Columbia, less than one-third of the 1942 population.[65]

★   ★   ★

In the end, Japanese Canadians were not deported. Nevertheless, that fact does not diminish the implications of the event. The record shows that the Canadian government attempted to commit the same crime for which Nazi officials were tried and executed — the deportation of citizens. The Canadian government was deterred from that crime not for moral or constitutional reasons, but for political reasons. Only when faced with strong political considerations did the government abandon its repressive course of action and turn to one which conformed with the wishes of the majority of Canadians. While it is heartening to learn that our system has successfully pulled back from the brink of repressive governments in the past, it is disturbing to recognize the massive effort that about-face required, and how easily it could have failed. The attempted deportation of ten thousand Japanese Canadians should serve as a reminder of how easily in our imperfect system the rights of a minority — be it ethnic, religious, linguistic or political — can be abused by a government responding to misinformed prejudices.

NOTES

1. For a history of antiAsian movements in British Columbia see W. Peter Ward, *White Canada Forever* (Montreal, 1978).
2. *Maclean's Magazine*, April 15, 1946, p. 66.

3. See the Vancouver *Sun*, April 3 and 6, 1942; Minutes of a meeting on July 21, 1942, of the British Columbian Members of Parliament with the Minister of Labour, Humphrey Mitchell, Department of Labour Papers, RG27, Vol. 175, Public Archives of Canada (hereafter P.A.C.); Cornett Resolution, *New Canadian*, September 5, 1942, p. 1; Ian A. Mackenzie to Wm. Douglas, Secretary Saanich Branch, Canadian Legion, October 19, 1942, and Ian A. Mackenzie to F. Howlett, City Clerk, Vancouver City Council, October 26, 1942, Ian A. Mackenzie Papers, Vol. 25, 70-25(3), P.A.C.

4. Ian A. Mackenzie to Wm. Douglas, October 19, 1942, *op. cit.*

5. Sic. "Repatriation" is an erroneous term reflecting Robertson's tendency to think of Japanese Canadians solely in terms of Japan. The "patria" of the Canadian-born Japanese was Canada. Norman A. Robertson to Wm. Lyon Mackenzie King, August 20, 1943, W.L.M. King Papers, MG26J4, Vol. 283, C194881–C194883.

6. *Ibid.* Spain was the neutral power designated under the Geneva Convention to police the treatment of Japanese nationals in Allied nations during the war.

7. Nisei, from the Japanese for "second" and "generation," are Canadian-born Japanese. Their parents, the immigrant generation, are called Issei.

8. BCSC Papers, RG36/27, Vol. 16, P.A.C.

9. The interdepartmental committee studying deportation was composed of the Under-Secretary of State, the Under-Secretary of State for External Affairs, the Deputy Ministers of Justice and Labour, the Director of Immigration, and the Deputy Commissioner of the RCMP. R.G. Robertson to the Cabinet War Committee, April 18, 1944, External Affairs Papers, 104(5)-1, E.A.A.

10. See Roger Daniels, *Concentration Camps U.S.A.: Japanese Americans in World War II* (New York, 1971), pp. 104–129.

11. R.G. Robertson to Norman Robertson, March 20, 1944, A.R. Menzies to Norman Robertson, March 22, 1944, Norman Robertson to W.L.M. King, March 27, 1944, R.G. Robertson to Cabinet War Committee, April 18, 1944, External Affairs Papers, 104(5)-1, E.A.A.; Memorandum, unsigned and unaddressed, August 3, 1945, Labour Papers, RG27, Vol. 658, P.A.C.

12. Memorandum, Norman Robertson to W.L.M. King, August 20, 1943, *op. cit.*

13. Memorandum, Beckenridge Long, Assistant Secretary of State to Cordell Hull, Secretary of State, December 17, 1943, Department of State Files, 740.00115 PW/2170, National Archives, Washington, D.C. The American authorities were to be frustrated in their ambitions as the U.S. Supreme Court later ruled that the renunciations had been made under duress and therefore were invalid. See Roger Daniels, *op. cit.*, pp. 155–157.

14. Roger Daniels, *op. cit.*, pp. 112–116.

15. Vancouver *Sun*, June 1, 1944, p. 13.

16. *Ibid*, and June 2, 1944, p. 1.

17. Vancouver *Sun*, June 3, 1944, p. 13. The bigots rebutted Flowerdew with the charge that the best-educated Nisei were serving in the Japanese army. This charge arose from the fact that a few of the educated Nisei who had been unable to find employment in Canada in their field of training had accepted employment in Japan or in Japanese-occupied Asia. Some Japanese Canadians and Japanese Americans who were in Japan at the outbreak of the Pacific War were subsequently conscripted into the Japanese army. See J. Yoshida and W. Hosakawa, *The Two Worlds of Jim Yoshida* (New York, 1972).

18. See Forrest E. La Violette, *The Canadian Japanese and World War II* (Toronto, 1948), p. 154.

19. Vancouver *Sun*, June 5, 1944, p. 19.

20. As quoted in Carol F. Lee, "The Road to Enfranchisement: Chinese and Japanese in British Columbia," *B.C. Studies* No. 30, Summer 1976, p. 52.

21. *Ibid*, p. 54.

22. Canada, House of Commons, *Debates*, August 4, 1944, p. 6062.

23. *Ibid.*

24. *Saturday Night* and *Maclean's* magazines both printed articles on the situation of the Japanese Canadians. The former was openly proJapanese Canadian, while the latter gave space to both liberals and racists.

25. Carol F. Lee, *op. cit.*, pp. 55–56.

26. Memorandum, R.G. Robertson to H.H. Wrong, October 24, 1945, W.L.M. King Papers, MG26J4, Vol. 361, C249600–C249606, P.A.C.

27. The major "policy makers" were Prime Minister W.L.M. King and the Cabinet Committee on the Japanese Question, consisting of Humphrey Mitchell, the Minister of Labour, Ian

Mackenzie, the Minister of Veterans Affairs, and Norman McLarty, the Secretary of State. They were assisted by Norman Robertson, the Under-Secretary of State for External Affairs; Arthur Macnamara, Deputy Minister of Labour; and R.G. Robertson, Office of the Prime Minister.

28. Transcript of an interview between T.B. Pickersgill, Commissioner of Japanese Placement, and the Japanese Committee, Tashme, B.C., March 31, 1945, Japanese Canadian Citizens' Association (hereafter JCCA) Papers, MG28V7, File D278, P.A.C.; Memorandum, Norman Robertson to W.L.M. King February 21, 1945, King Papers MG26J4, Vol. 361, C249584, P.A.C.

29. Memorandum, Norman Robertson to W.L.M. King, February 21, 1945, op. cit.

30. T.B. Pickersgill to R. Shirakawa, Chairman, Japanese Committee, Tashme, B.C., April 10, 1945, JCCA Papers, MG28V7, D278, P.A.C.

31. Only the agreement with the Province of Alberta actually contained the clause calling for the removal of the B.C. Japanese after the war. Because this clause had been mentioned in all negotiations with the provinces and only explicitly refused by Manitoba, the federal government considered itself bound by it until new contracts could be renegotiated. See the BCSC Papers, RG 36/27 for contract negotiations.

32. T.B. Pickersgill as quoted in Memorandum, R.G. Robertson to W.L.M. King, April 23, 1945, W.L.M. King Papers, MG26J4, Vol. 361, C249590, P.A.C.

33. See the Department of Labour Papers, RG27, Vols. 1527 to 1529 for the perceptions of Japanese Canadians in 1944 and 1945.

34. Ibid; Barry Broadfoot, Years of Sorrow, Years of Shame (Toronto, 1977), pp. 194–197, 201–206, 223–224. See Diasuke Kitagawa, Issei and Nisei: The Internment Years (New York, 1967) for the parallel American case.

35. Rolf Knight and Maya Koizumi, A Man of Our Times (Vancouver, 1976), p. 81. See also the Department of Labour Papers, RG27, Vols. 1527–1529, P.A.C.

36. Memoranda, N.A. Robertson to W.L.M. King, February 21, 1945, op. cit., and R.G. Robertson to W.L.M. King, April 23, 1945, op. cit.

37. Memorandum, N.A. Robertson to W.L.M. King, February 21, 1945, op. cit.

38. See Appendix A for statistics on the "repatriation" requests.

39. Norman Black, A Challenge to Patriotism and Statesmanship (Toronto, 1944). For details of the evolution of the proJapanese Canadian groups see Edith Fowke, They Made Democracy Work: The Story of the Cooperative Committee on Japanese Canadians (Toronto, 1951), pp. 1–10.

40. For a complete list of the supporting bodies see Appendix B.

41. Edith Fowke, op. cit., pp. 10–13.

42. Ibid, p. 14. For copies of some of these statements see the Japanese Canadian Citizens' Association (hereafter JCCA) Papers, File D273, P.A.C.

43. The New Canadian, July 19, August 8 and 18, and September 19, 1945. The Department of Labour took over the administration of the camps under P.C. 946, February 5, 1943. Both the camp administrators and the inmates, however, continued to use the expressions "the Commission" or "the BCSC" throughout the war, hence Murphy's confusion.

44. Statistics from Memorandum, Department of Labour Papers, RG27, Vol. 658, 23-3-17-1(pt 4), P.A.C.

45. Memorandum, Department of Labour, RG27, Vol. 658, P.A.C. Mitchell felt that restrictions on Japanese remaining in Canada should not be lifted until the "repatriates" had been deported.

46. N.A. Robertson to W.L.M. King, January 5, 1945, W.L.M. King Papers, MG26J4, Vol. 283, C194932, P.A.C.

47. Cabinet Conclusions, September 5, 1945, Privy Council Office Records, RG2/16, Vol. 2, P.A.C.

48. Cabinet Conclusions, September 19, 1945, Privy Council Office Records, RG2/16, Vol. 3, P.A.C.

49. MacArthur's affirmative reply was not received until the end of October 1945, Cabinet Conclusions, October 31, 1945, Privy Council Office Records, RG 2/16, Vol. 3, P.A.C.

50. Nisei Affairs, Vol. 1, No. 2, August 28, 1945.

51. Ibid, Vol. 1, No. 5, December 15, 1945.

52. Ibid, Vol. 1, No. 6, January 19, 1946. R.J. MacMaster to F.A. Brewin, December 28, 1945, Andrew Brewin Papers, MG32C26, Vol. 1, P.A.C.

53. R.J. MacMaster to F.A. Brewin, December 31, 1945, Andrew Brewin Papers, MG32C26, P.A.C.

54. Memorandum, F.P. Varcoe, Deputy Minister of Justice, to Norman Robertson, Under-Secretary of State for External Affairs, January 4, 1946, W.L.M. King Papers, MG26J4, Vol. 283, File 2965, P.A.C.

55. See Edith Fowke, *op. cit.*, p. 20, and *The New Canadian*, January and February 1946; *Nisei Affairs* Vol. 1, No. 6, January 19, 1946, and No. 7, February 9, 1946.

56. Interview with F. Andrew Brewin, September 1976. Memorandum, R.G. Robertson to Prime Minister W.L.M. King, March 4, 1946, W.L.M. King Papers, MG26J4, Vol. 283, File 2965, P.A.C. Robertson notes that the Prime Minister received seven hundred to one thousand letters on the subject of the deportation of Japanese Canadians between December 1945 and March 1946.

57. In the Supreme Court of Canada, *In the Matter of a Reference as to the Validity of Orders in Council of the 15th Day of December, 1945 (P.C. 7355, 7356, 7357), in Relation to Persons of the Japanese Race* (Ottawa, 1946), House of Commons, Sessional Paper 133, 1946.

58. Interview with F. Andrew Brewin, September 1946.

59. Memorandum, T.B. Pickersgill to A.H. Brown, Assistant to the Deputy Minister of Labour, August 5, 1946, Department of Labour Papers, RG27, Vol. 647, 23-2-3-17, P.A.C.

60. *Ibid.*

61. For details see Ken Adachi, *The Enemy That Never Was* (Toronto, 1976), pp. 340–343.

62. Interviews with resettlers.

63. Memorandum to the Cabinet Committee on Japanese Problems, Reference Document JAP 3, April 16, 1947, Department of External Affairs Papers, Vol. 1868, 263-38, PtIV, P.A.C.

64. As quoted in Ken Adachi, *op. cit.*, p. 317.

65. Department of Labour, *Report on the Re-establishment of Japanese in Canada, 1944–1946* (Ottawa, January 1947), p. 15. Of the 3965 Japanese Canadians who "repatriated" to Japan, 34 per cent were Japanese nationals, 15 per cent were naturalized Japanese Canadians, and 51 per cent were Canadian-born. Over 1300 of the "repatriates," and most of the Canadian-born, were under sixteen years of age.

"They're Still Women After All": The Second World War and Canadian Womanhood

RUTH ROACH PIERSON

"They're Still Women After All" was the title given, with an audible sigh of relief, by L.S.B. Shapiro, Canadian foreign correspondent and future novelist, to a piece he did for *Saturday Night* in September, 1942. In a light, jocular vein, the article expressed one man's fears, aroused by the British wartime sight of so many women stepping into formerly male jobs, that women might cease to be women, that is "feminine individuals," synonymous terms in Shapiro's vocabulary. Although closer observation convinced Shapiro that his fears were unfounded, similar fears continued to plague many other Canadians, male and female, as they viewed women entering the munitions plants and, what in the eyes of some was even worse, joining the armed forces.[1]

SOURCE: Excerpted from *"They're Still Women After All": The Second World War and Canadian Womanhood* (Toronto: McClelland & Stewart, 1990), pp. 129–40, 158–68, 215–20. Used by permission of the Canadian Publishers, McClelland & Stewart.

As the primary purpose of the services is the provision of the armed might of the state, their male exclusivity had been in keeping with a deeply rooted division of labour by sex that relegated women to nurture, men to combat, women to the creation and preservation of life, men, when necessary, to its destruction. Closely connected to the sexual division between arms bearers and non-arms bearers was a gendered dichotomy of attributes that identified as masculine the military traits of hardness, toughness, action, and brute force and as feminine the non-military traits of softness, fragility, passivity, and gentleness. Hence, the very entrance of women into the Army, Navy, and Air Force sharply challenged conventions respecting women's nature and place in Canadian society.

Two specific sets of circumstances induced the Department of National Defence to admit women into the armed services: manpower shortages, felt first by the Canadian Army and the Royal Canadian Air Force, and a reserve of womanpower embodied in a Canada-wide paramilitary movement of women eager to serve. For the men in charge of Canada's military, efficient prosecution of the war was the reason for putting women in uniform and under service discipline. They had no desire to tamper with existing gender relations by altering the sexual division of labour or the male-over-female hierarchy of authority. Obviously the members of the women's volunteer corps eager to become part of Canada's official forces wanted to end the male exclusivity of the military. But even they gave no indication of a desire to erase the demarcation line between male and female spheres. There was thus a tension inherent in the admission of women to the armed services: the tension between the Canadian state's wartime need for female labour within those preeminently masculine institutions and Canadian society's longer-term commitment to a masculine–feminine division of traits as well as separation of tasks. This tension was also apparent, albeit to a lesser degree, in the entrance of women into non-traditional trades in war industry. In both cases, under the pressure of the war emergency, women appeared to be breaking sex barriers on an alarming scale.

Reactions to women's admission to the forces, similar to but more pronounced than those to women's mobilization for war industry, provide a good index of the social attitudes toward women prevailing in Canada at the time of the Second World War. And the records of the Department of National Defence provide a good source for those reactions. The department had to be sensitive to the values of the larger civilian society: its dependence on women volunteers, not conscripts, made it especially so. To inform itself of those attitudes it made use of opinion surveys and to influence public opinion it made use of the media. Also, as a part of the established order, the Department of National Defence itself incorporated and acted on widely held unexamined notions of women's nature and capabilities. The dilemma facing the department thus brought the current social attitudes toward women into high relief: by admitting women to the services it had violated the convention that the armed forces were no place for a woman; in seeking volunteers, it had to advertise its conformity with as many other received notions of proper womanhood as possible.

What were the reactions to women's entrance into the armed forces (as well as into non-traditional trades in war industry)? One was that the war was opening up for women a world of opportunity unrestricted by sexual inequalities. The ceremonial launching of a ship that women workers had helped to build "from the first bolts and staves to the final slap of paint and piece of polished brass" moved journalist Lotta Dempsey to suggest that the event symbolized the launching of women as well: "the great and final stage of the movement of women into industry . . . on a complete equality with men."[2] The office of the Directorate of Army Recruiting suggested in February, 1943, that recruiting officers should speak of the war's having "finally brought about complete emancipation of women."[3] Evidence for this was to be found in women's admission to the forces and to an ever-increasing number of jobs within the forces. News stories designed to promote interest in and support for the women's services often played up the achievements of individual women. And women were racking up many firsts. "First woman in the history of the R.C.A.F. to take the officers' administrative course at Trenton . . ." read the caption of a photograph in the *Globe and Mail* December 24, 1942; "First Class of Airwomen Graduated from RCAF Photography School" was the headline of an article in the same newspaper later that same month.[4] The 1944 article in *Saturday Night* celebrating the expanding number of trades open to [members of the Canadian Women's Army Corps (CWAC)] singled out in illustration the first "qualified girl armourer in the CWAC" and the first CWAC to operate "a Telecord recording machine."[5]

This perception of the war's having fully emancipated women and of the war's having made it possible for women to "Achieve Heights Hitherto Undreamed Of"[6] meshed with the view that women were participating in the war effort on an equal footing with men. "Shoulder to Shoulder," which was an Army motto adopted by the Canadian Women's Army Corps and made the title of their official marching song, epitomized that sense of the equality of women's and men's service. When the Corps was celebrating its second anniversary in August, 1943, Headquarters of Military District No. 12 (Regina) dedicated its regular monthly bulletin to the CWAC and placed under the bulletin's title, *Shoulder to Shoulder*, an illustration of a CWAC marching shoulder to shoulder with two army men, all three wearing steel helmets on their heads and gas mask bags on their chests (but only the men shouldering rifles).[7] This image was also used on a recruitment poster for the Corps.

Of a piece with the celebration of equality and emancipation was a kind of wartime advertisement that proclaimed the end of women's confinement to the domestic sphere. Many companies advertising in the Canadian press between 1939-1945, especially those trying to hold on to post-war markets, sought to give a patriotic cast to their messages. One such series of advertisements run by General Motors of Canada in the special 1943 issues of *Mayfair* on "Women at War" took as its theme women's movement into the wide open spaces of the public domain. Running for five pages, the ad was set up so that a reader would encounter in bold print on a right-hand page "Woman's place . . ." and then turn to find not "is in the home" but "is Everywhere . . ." followed on the fourth and fifth pages by the qualifier "with Victory as Their Business" and a brief description of the many fields in which women were serving the nation at war.

Canada's mobilization of women for the war effort necessitated violation of the social ideal of the woman dedicated to home and family. Even without challenging established patterns of work and behaviour considered appropriate to each sex, war cruelly disrupted and dislocated human lives. To contain the disruptive and destructive forces of war as far as would be compatible with its efficient prosecution seems to have been a goal tacitly agreed upon by those in charge of the war effort and by many in the media. Thus, with respect to women's participation in the armed forces, alongside the talk of emancipation, equality, and the overcoming of tradition, recruitment propaganda and wartime advertising also sought to minimize the degree of change required and to hint at and occasionally even stress the expectation of a rapid return to normalcy once the war was over.

So, at the same time recruiting officers were led to speak to NSS officials of the war's "complete emancipation of women," they were also instructed to stress that women's employment in the armed forces was "an emergency measure" and that "After this war they will go back to their place in civil life; they will retake their positions in the household and in the office or anywhere else where they originally came from."[8] For *Mayfair*'s 1943 celebration of women's contribution to the war effort, Westinghouse of Canada provided a more graphic statement of the expectation that at war's end women would return to motherhood and child-rearing as their principal life's work. A large two-page ad headed "These Are Tomorrow's Yesterdays" showed the pride the future son of the female war worker would take in his mother's war service. Looking through a book on *Women at War* in the school library in 1955, the boy was surprised by a picture of his mom, taken in a war plant in 1943. Overcome with emotion, the child has sat down to write his mom to say how proud of her he is. The ad carried not only a tribute to Canadian women's role in Canada's struggle, but also the projection that in ten or twelve years' time the women would all be back where they belonged, taking care of the home and rearing Canada's future generation.

Recruitment propaganda, promotional newspaper stories, and patriotic advertising, then, reveal a deep ambivalence toward women's joining the armed forces. On the one hand was the celebration of the trailblazing and achievement of women in the services and, on the other, the assurance that joining the forces changed nothing in women's nature and place in Canadian society. In 1943 the ambivalence intensified as more and more women were needed but recruitment met resistance and monthly enlistment figures dropped. From the first enrolments in September, 1941, to July, 1942, 3,800 women had "stepped forward to serve" and been accepted into the Canadian Women's Army Corps.[9] Many of these came from the women's volunteer corps.[10] By March, 1943, the strength of the Canadian Women's Army Corps had risen to just over 10,000.[11] Although the CWAC's peak strength in 1945 would not exceed 14,000 (636 officers plus 13,326 other ranks totalling 13,962, on April 25, 1945),[12] military authorities in 1943 geared up for a considerable expansion of the women's forces on the assumption that "the Army, Navy and the Air Force urgently need 65,000 more service women to release men for combat duty."[13]

In February, National Selective Service began participating "in the recruiting of women for the Navy, the Army, and the Air Force" by providing information to interested applicants and referring them to recruiting offices.[14] In March the Defence Council concurred in the recommendation of the National Campaign Committee for an intensive tri-service campaign to recruit women for the three armed services.[15] A Combined Services Committee was established to co-ordinate joint promotional and publicity endeavours for the CWAC, the WRCNS, and the RCAF (WD). The recruitment push coincided with the growing signs of opposition to women in the military.

The monthly enlistment figures for the women's services in late 1942 and early 1943 were disappointing. Faced with this slowdown, the National Campaign Committee granted authorization to two opinion surveys in the first half of 1943.[16] The Combined Services Committee charged with joint recruitment endeavours for the three women's services proposed that a commercial market research agency conduct a general survey of public opinion. The firm of Elliott-Haynes Limited of Montreal and Toronto was retained to determine: (a) public awareness of the need for women in the armed forces; (b) factors believed to influence women in favour of joining the forces; (c) factors believed to influence women to avoid joining the forces. The survey, which collected the opinions of 7,283 civilian adults from "56 Canadian centres and their surrounding areas," claimed to have covered "both sexes, all races, all geographical regions, all age levels, all economic levels, all occupations and all classes of conjugal condition."[17] Conducted in March and April of 1943, the results appeared under the title *Report: An Inquiry into the Attitude of the Canadian Civilian Public Towards the Women's Armed Forces.*

In April and May the Directorate of Army Recruiting carried out the second survey: a study of CWAC opinion. Based in part on the results of the first study insofar as they pertained to the CWAC, the in-house inquiry drew primarily on the "written answers to a questionnaire prepared by NDHQ in both English and French" and administered to a cross-section of 1,100 CWAC other ranks from all CWAC units, 18 per cent of whom were non-commissioned officers and 10 per cent French-Canadian women.[18] The secret and confidential report of the second inquiry, "Canadian Women's Army Corps: Why Women Join and How They Like It," was ready for limited distribution in July.

Both surveys revealed that there was widespread disapproval of women's joining the armed forces. The public opinion survey disclosed that few Canadians in the spring of 1943 gave high priority to enlistment in the armed forces as a way for women to contribute to the prosecution of the war. In answer to the question "How can women best serve Canada's war effort?" only 7 per cent replied "by joining the women's forces." Five other categories of work took precedence. "Maintaining home life" ranked first in importance for the highest proportion of Canadians (26 per cent), followed by "doing war work in factories" (23 per cent), "part-time voluntary relief work" (13 per cent), "conserving food, rationing" (11 per cent), and "buying war bonds, stamps" (8 per cent).[19] The ranking remained the same when the answers from French Canada were treated separately, the main difference being that an even higher proportion of French Canadians (40 per cent) thought "maintaining home life" was the most important job for women in wartime while only 18 per cent thought working in war industry was; a minuscule 3 per cent thought "joining women's forces" was most important. Separating out the answers from parents and from young men did not change the ranking either. Only the answers from young women showed a different order of priority: "maintaining home life" switched places with "doing war work in factories."[20] But the young women also placed ahead of "joining the forces" the same five kinds of war service as mentioned above. Furthermore, as "part-time voluntary relief work," "conserving food, rationing," and "buying war bonds, stamps" were all compatible with "maintaining home life," the inescapable conclusion is that an overwhelming majority of Canadians in 1943 saw women's place to be in the home, wartime or not.

Furthermore, according to the public opinion survey, among friends and relatives of young eligible women disapproval of their joining the forces ran higher than disapproval of their taking jobs in war industry. Of parents, husbands, boyfriends, and brothers, 39 per cent disapproved of their daughters, wives, girlfriends, and sisters joining the armed forces (43 per cent approved, and 18 per cent didn't know), while only 27 per cent disapproved of their female friends and relatives entering munitions factories (59 per cent approved and 14 per cent didn't know).[21] When the data for English and French Canada were segregated, the level of disapproval of women in the forces was found to be significantly higher in French Canada.[22] If one took the "don't know" as indifference or neutrality, a more negative construction could be put on the data, as was done in the report of the CWAC survey. "When pressed," it submitted, "57% of the public stated that they would not give open approval to their friends and relatives enrolling in the women's forces."[23] The public opinion survey highlighted another noteworthy contrast in level of disapproval. By separating mothers and fathers from boyfriends and brothers, it revealed that a higher proportion of young men objected to their girlfriends' and sisters' joining the forces than parents did to their daughters'.[24]

Young eligible women were aware of this disapproval among relatives and friends. When asked about expected responses to their joining up, 46 per cent of the women eligible for enlistment assumed their parents' attitude would be unfavourable and 51 per cent expected an unfavourable response from their brothers and boyfriends.[25] The only group from which support was expected to any significant degree was that of young women friends already in the forces: from that quarter 59 per cent of the eligible women responding assumed they would receive encouragement.[26] According to the CWAC survey, even the women who had ended up joining the Canadian Women's Army Corps had "received about as much discouragement as encouragement" from the friends and relatives whose advice the women had sought.[27] The CWAC survey and the public opinion survey led to the same conclusion: "Women friends already in the forces were the only people which [sic] gave outspoken approval and encouragement."[28]

Given the extent of the disapproval, it is not surprising that 61 per cent of the eligible women (56 per cent in English Canada, 72 per cent in French Canada) responded that they had never considered joining the armed forces.[29] Nor is it surprising that of the 39 per cent who did consider joining, about one-half finally abandoned the idea.[30] There was a connection between the disapproval of family and friends and the reluctance of eligible women to join. Of those who entertained the idea of joining but ended up rejecting it, 33 per cent gave as their reason that the family objected (24 per cent of the English Canadians, 54 per cent of the French Canadians).[31] Of the members of the Canadian Women's Army Corps who remembered hesitating before they joined, the largest proportion (35 per cent) reported that "disapproval of family and friends" was what had given them pause.[32]

In light of that sentiment, it is no wonder that those in charge of women's recruitment for the three services saw their task as essentially one of educating the public. The big push to recruit women for the armed forces, initially planned for March 15 to June 15, 1943, was actually mounted between June 15 and September 15. In late summer 1943 the Combined Services Committee was given the go-ahead to continue its operation from October 1 to December 31. In its proposal to continue the campaign to recruit women for a second three-month period, the working committee of the Combined Services Committee observed that "overcoming established tradition and developing acceptance of a new idea is obviously a long-term educational proposition." The proposal went on to define as the primary object of the campaign and the essential task of the Committee: "overcoming the tradition that women's place is exclusively in the home . . . or at least not in military uniform."[33]

Both the inquiry into public opinion and the investigation of CWAC opinion played an important part in the educational campaign. The results of these surveys were studied and analysed and the analyses pored over by members of the working and policy committees of the Combined Services Committee and officials in the Directorate of Army Recruiting. From the CWACs' answers to the question "How did you first learn of the CWAC?" DAR analysts concluded that recruitment advertising had been woefully inadequate. The more conspicuous "news items, feature stories and pictures about the Women's Services" in newspapers and magazines had been interesting but had not carried sufficient "sell" copy, and radio had "been used extensively and effectively only on the Prairies."[34]

The tri-service campaigns of the second half of 1943 represented a massive increase in promotion of the women's services. The Combined Services Committee paid for 1,000-line recruitment advertisements to be run in all daily newspapers across Canada and for full-page ads to appear in magazines and in the rotogravure sections of the metropolitan weekend papers. It contacted newspaper editors and arranged for them to sell recruiting ads "on a sponsored basis to local advertisers," providing the ad design in mat form and suggesting the pitch to the local businessmen: "a convenient, direct way for him to help along the war effort."[35] At the committee's bidding the National Film Board produced two women's recruitment films: *Proudly She Marches* and *Canada's Women March to the Colours*. Five-minute radio spots and "flash" announcements were scheduled on the CBC national and regional networks and on local radio stations across Canada. Stores and other commercial establishments were persuaded to donate some of their window space to displays promoting women's recruitment. In co-operation with others, "special events," such as conventions held by national organizations, were used to publicize the women's services. Finally, recruitment posters and streetcar signs were displayed as widely as possible.[36] In this intensification of recruitment for the women's forces, the Combined Services Committee and the Army's Directorate of Recruiting aimed to apply the lessons learned from the results of the two surveys. They sought to play up any features that had elicited a positive response and to play down, deny, disguise, or reinterpret the sources of disapproval.

One source of disapproval was a fear, similar to that expressed in L.S.B. Shapiro's *Saturday Night* piece, that the woman who joined the forces did so at the risk of her femininity. Although neither survey posed the question in so many words — is fear of loss of femininity a reason why their family and friends are reluctant to see them join the forces? — other questions carried much the same meaning, such as, is the reason for objection that military life is considered unsuitable for young women? According to the Elliott-Haynes survey, 20 per cent of the "young eligible women reported that they thought their parents, husbands, brothers, sisters," and male and female "friends would object to their joining the forces" on the grounds that "army life" was "unsuitable."[37]

In the hopes of dispelling that notion, speeches of recruitment officers, recruitment literature, sponsored advertising, and promotional news stories, even before but especially after the surveys, were full of assurances that membership in the CWAC — or RCAF (WD) or the Women's Royal Canadian Navy Service (WRCNS) — was not incompatible with femininity. "Our women in the Canadian Armed Forces are nothing if not thoroughly feminine in manner and appearance," recruiting officers instructed National Selective Service personnel being trained to help with servicewomen's recruitment in February, 1943.[38] Clearly, while the armed forces could persuade a male potential recruit that military service would make a man of him, they felt they had to do the reverse with a female prospective volunteer, that is, convince her that military life would not make her less of a woman.

From the start Army authorities assumed women in the services would be concerned about their appearance. Opposition to wearing a uniform *per se* was not anticipated from the women in the volunteer service corps (as many such corps sported their own uniforms), only opposition to a poorly designed one. In general, the planners of the CWAC calculated they would have a better chance of attracting volunteers the more attractive the uniform. The basic costume "underwent a considerable evolution before it settled into" the two-piece khaki suit identifiable as the CWAC uniform of World War II.[39] After National Defence Minister Colonel Ralston, his wife, the Master-General of the Ordnance, and a Toronto dress designer had all had a hand in the design, a committee at NDHQ produced the final model: the two-piece khaki ensemble of gored, slightly flared skirt and single-breasted tunic with hip pockets and one breast pocket, brown epaulets and brown CWAC and Canada badges, khaki shirt and brown tie, khaki peaked cap, and khaki hose and brown oxfords. According to the Director-General's preliminary history of the Corps, the CWAC uniform was "voted in some American and Canadian quarters to be the smartest of all women's service uniforms on this continent."[40] CWAC recruitment literature used this reputation to sell the Corps. The 1942 brochure *Women in Khaki* boasted: "C.W.A.C. uniforms have been acknowledged by leading dress designers to be the smartest in the world."[41]

                ★ ★ ★

The survey of CWAC other rank opinion had revealed that, after patriotism and the urge to travel, the third strongest motive for joining the service had been the desire "to be near family, friends in the forces." While 68 per cent had been influenced by having women friends in the forces, a larger proportion (77 per cent) had followed men friends into the military.[42] Recruitment propaganda, capitalizing on this information, came up with the poster: "Are you the girl he left behind?" In Army photo stories on life in the CWAC, public relations made a point of including material on dances and dates and boyfriends. The first photo in a series on Kildare Barracks showed three CWAC sergeants "with plans for a big evening ahead" approaching the company sergeant-major in the orderly room "on the subject of late passes." The caption to a later photo in the same series read: "There is no place for 'shop talk' in C.W.A.C. barracks after duty hours. Girls go typically feminine." Depicted as "typically feminine" was the one CWAC sergeant writing to a boyfriend in the RCAF while the two other CWAC sergeants looked "admiringly" (if not enviously) at his framed photograph. In the series' last photo the letter-writing sergeant had paused, pen in hand, to gaze dreamily at the photograph, which shows an Air Force officer clenching a pipe between his teeth and looking, even with the trim mustache, a lot like Henry Fonda.[43]

The message of one Army photo in a series on CWACs in Washington, D.C., was that members of the Canadian Women's Army Corps stationed outside Canada could find dates in the armed forces of Canada's allies. It showed two CWAC privates stepping out with a soldier and a sailor of the United States forces.[44] Attached to a similar photo in a later series on the same subject was the caption: "Carrying out the 'Good Neighbour Policy' to a 'T', Private (X) of the U.S. Engineers shows Private (Y), C.W.A.C. of Toronto, Ontario, a few of the scenic highlights of Washington, D.C."[45]

Servicewomen were also shown as not having lost the ability to be pleasing to men. "The Quickest Way to a Man's Heart — Even a Sergeant's Heart" appeared below a photograph publicizing the parties held in honour of the fourth anniversary of the Canadian Women's Army Corps (August 14, 1945). The sergeant is identified as a guest at the CWAC's birthday party at Kildare Barracks; the CWAC corporal, as the one who "is seeing that the guest is satisfied."[46]

Indeed, the concern whether life in the armed forces made a woman more or less attractive boiled down to a concern whether enlistment made a woman more or less marriageable. The public opinion questionnaire contained the question: "Do you think the wearing of a uniform interferes with a girl's chances of marriage?" While 58 per cent of those polled answered "no" (68 per cent in English Canada, but only 43 per cent in French Canada), a remaining 42 per cent either thought the wearing of a uniform did restrict "a girl's chances of marriage" (22 per cent) or were not sure (20 per cent didn't know).[47] Thus, dispelling the fear that enlistment would scare away dates was not enough. Recruitment literature had to give the further assurance that membership in the women's services would not reduce one's marriageability.

The 1944 CWAC recruitment pamphlet assured the prospective volunteer that "yes" she could get married while she was in the service, provided she had her commanding officer's permission.[48] The Army's Department of Public Relations encouraged news coverage of marriages between servicemen and servicewomen. The *Globe and Mail* of December 2, 1942, reported "the first marriage of a member of the C.W.A.C. to a member of the Army" (it had taken place the day before in Halifax between a CWAC private and a corporal of the Provost Corps of a Highland regiment) and thereafter announcements of such military weddings became a regular feature of the women's activities columns of Canadian newspapers.[49] Official Army, Navy, and Air Force photographers took pictures of such weddings for release to the press.[50] In the *C.W.A.C. News Letter* announcements of "military alliances," as weddings of armed forces personnel were sometimes called, took precedence over announcements of military promotions. Early issues carried only a few mentions but by the end of 1944 whole pages were devoted to marriage news. "The Bride Wore Khaki," a full-page item in the November, 1944, issue, told the romantic story of a Canadian Army sergeant and a CWAC corporal exchanging vows in a bombed-out church in Italy.

One of the least examined and most unshakable notions of the time about women was that subordination and subservience to men were inherently female characteristics that dictated women's role and place in society. This assumption converged with the real position of CWACs in relation to Army men, for in jobs, pay and benefits, and place in the command structure of the Army, the servicewomen were in general subordinate. As reflected in mottoes and enlistment slogans, the very function of the women's services was to subserve the primary purpose of the armed forces: the provision of an armed and fighting force. Having been excluded/exempted from combat, the women of the Canadian armed forces could adopt as their motto: "We Serve That Men May Fight."[51] That general motto had been adapted from the airwomen's "We Serve That Men May Fly." Even more expressive of the secondary status and supportive role assigned to Army women was a slogan used on enlistment ads: "The C.W.A.C. Girls — The Girls behind the Boys behind the Guns."[52]

In preserving the male monopoly on armed service, the Department of National Defence was acting in harmony with social convention and conviction. The only evidence of women strongly desiring admission to jobs classified as operational came from the handful of women in Canada with pilots' licences who were eager to put their flying skill at the service of their country, and who were to be denied that opportunity. A few joined the British civilian Air Transport Auxiliary, formed to ferry aircraft from "anywhere to anywhere" and open after 1940 to women pilots.[53] The prevailing view was that men were by nature suited to dangerous, life-risking jobs while women were naturally adapted to monotony and behind-the-scenes support work. This view was reflected in the remarks of one Air Force officer on the suitability of airwomen for the trade of parachute rigger.

> Take parachute packing. To a man it's a dull, routine job. He doesn't want to pack parachutes. He wants to be up there with one strapped to his back. But to a woman it's an exciting job. She can imagine that someday a flier's life will be saved because she packed that parachute well. Maybe it will be her own husband's life or her boy-friend's. That makes parachute packing pretty exciting for her and she does a much more efficient and speedy job than an unhappy airman would.[54]

Deeply entrenched as the assumption was that the female was the second sex, there still surfaced from time to time the fear that women who were serving with the Army would lose their deference toward men and become "bossy." Mainly, it was the prospect of female officers that seems to have aroused this fear. When Jean Knox, Director of the British Army's Auxiliary Territorial Service, toured Canada in the fall of 1942, newspaper coverage showed a preoccupation with the fact that she, the first female Major-General in the British Army, outranked her husband. As if looking for qualities to counter-balance her high military rank, news stories invariably described Knox as the "petite and pretty general" or "petite and completely feminine." Speaking of the women of the British Auxiliary Territorial Service and the Canadian Women's Army Corps, she herself remarked: "They're not an Army of Amazons doing men's work — they're still women. . . . " In her view, "All women should share with men the experience of this war — but I would be violently displeased if in so doing, women lost their femininity."[55]

Similarly, when Lionel Shapiro covered Major Alice Sorby's arrival in London, England, to command the CWACs overseas, he approved of the fact that she was "pretty" and had "graciously submitted" to the press conference. But at the perception that she was also "a woman full of the barbed-wire quality of a colonel in the Indian service," Shapiro confessed, "my man's world was beginning to totter before my eyes." But a question of his that "penetrated her military facade and revealed her in all her feminine vulnerability" saved the day for Shapiro. "'Major Sorby,'" he asked, "'your husband is a lieutenant and you are a major. I assume he will have to salute you when you meet. Is that not so?'" After a moment's thought, Major Sorby replied that, yes, she supposed that would be regulations, but as she had not seen her husband for more than a year, she doubted whether they'd "'bother about salutes.'" Missing the irony of Major Sorby's retort, Shapiro was jubilant. "Moment triumphant!" he exclaimed. "My man's world returned in full flower. Major Sorby was really only Mrs. Sorby with a King's crown on her epaulettes, and Mr. Sorby, though a mere lieutenant, was still master of the Sorby household."[56]

Female other ranks also expressed uneasiness at having women in command over them. The CWAC other ranks surveyed in 1943 registered a lot of complaints against their CWAC commanding officers. The survey revealed that in general female other ranks "disliked taking orders from women" and that "some felt men administrative officers would be better."[57] However large that "some" was (unfortunately not measured by the survey), the existence of such a feeling among female other ranks in a women's corps speaks for the pervasiveness of the association of male with authority and command. One suspects that the charge of "playing soldier"[58] leveled against some female officers was a criticism that such women were putting on "masculine airs" of commanding authority. The apprehension that women serving in the forces would lose their femininity included the fear that the male-over-female hierarchy of authority might be upset.

Just as importantly, the public had to be assured that the work women in the forces were asked to perform was suitable to women. With an ambivalence typical of the promotion of the women's services, speeches or publications in one sentence applauded women's breakthrough into positions theretofore dominated by men and in the next denied that servicewomen were being asked to do anything inimical to their feminine nature. The *CWAC Digest: Facts about the C.W.A.C.*, a 1943 recruiting booklet, is a case in point. The middle pages were given over to photographs with captions of women performing tasks conventionally identified as male: one showed a CWAC fitter working on a lathe; another a class of CWACs at a motor mechanics' school. But the inside cover contained "A Tribute to the Canadian Women's Army Corps" from the Governor General of Canada, stating: "In a modern army women are a necessity, not in order to replace men in men's jobs, but to take over from men jobs which," while previously done by men, were really women's work and hence more suitably performed by women anyway. "If a woman can drive the family car, she can drive a staff car" is another example of the recruitment line that sought to reassure the public that military jobs for female personnel, although performed in new settings and under different conditions, remained essentially "women's work."[59] Thus the contradiction between the armed services' need for women in uniform and the ideology of woman's place being in the home (or in a paid job long sex-typed as female) was reconciled through the redefinition of certain military jobs as womanly.[60]

In actual fact, as we have seen, the overwhelming majority of uniformed women employed by the Army were assigned to jobs that had already become female niches in the civilian labour market or could be regarded as extensions of mothering or housework. In propaganda and practice, a "woman's place" was created within the wartime armed services. Nonetheless, the very association of women with the military touched off fear of an impending breakdown of the sexual division of labour, akin to that triggered by the entrance of women on a massive scale into waged work. Under the anxiety over the changed appearance of women lay a more profound but less often articulated fear that women were invading male territory and becoming too independent. Humour of various sorts provided an outlet for these fears. In a 1942 article on "Woman Power" in *Maclean's*, for instance, Thelma LeCocq jokingly proposed a number of possibilities "that make strong men break out in a lather." What if, at war's end, she speculated, the thousands of war working women

> refuse to be stripped of the pants and deprived of the pay envelopes? What if they start looking round for some nice little chap who can cook and who'll meet them lovingly at the door with their slippers in hand? What if industry has to reorganize to give these women sabbatical years for having babies?[61]

These fears survived till the end of the war. In September, 1945, despite the fact that approximately 80,000 women war workers had already been laid off by then, *Maclean's* ran a cartoon by Vic Herman that derived its humour from the preposterous yet feared possibility of a reversal of the sexual division of labour between male breadwinner and dependent female domestic. A husband wearing an apron and standing with a mop in his hand and a bucket at his feet frowns in annoyance at his overalls- and bandana-clad wife who, home from the factory, has headed straight for the refrigerator, tracking muddy footprints across his nice, clean floor.[62]

After studying the results of the CWAC survey, the Director of Army Recruiting requested discontinuance of the recruitment pitch "You Can Free a Man to Fight." While the strongest reason CWACs had given for enlisting was "patriotism, help win the war," a significant proportion, as already noted, had cited the desire to be near family and friends, a category including fathers and brothers as well as sweethearts. To emphasize releasing men for combat, the Director of Army Recruiting argued, was thus in conflict with the real interest of the women to keep their loved ones alive, as well as contrary to his conception of the eternally feminine — woman's nurturant and preservative nature:

> In reality, women have joined up to be near, help and protect their boy friends and brothers overseas. It is woman's natural tendency to protect her loved ones from danger, not force them into the line of battle.

He inferred from the report also that too many members of the CWAC were not convinced their jobs were essential. He therefore recommended a new line of appeal that would both stress the vital importance of women's work in the forces and identify it as an essential part of the "intricate web of supporting services and pre-battle planning" whose purpose was "to protect their boy friends and brothers from unnecessary battle dangers."[63]

The *CWAC Digest* of 1943 apparently went to press before the analyses of the CWAC survey took effect, for it still stressed the noncombatant servicewoman's part in releasing servicemen for combat. "Would you deprive a fighting man of his opportunity to fight?" it asked. "Do you want some fighting man to do *your* job? . . . Don't let a man take your place if you can help it." Other new recruitment material, however, reflected the spirit of the suggestions from the Director of Army Recruiting. In one Combined Services leaflet of 1943, for instance, emphasis was taken off the need for women to release men for combat and put on the vital importance of women's work in the service *per se*: joining the forces was sold as "The Most Important Job Ever Offered Women."[64] And some enlistment ads designed for sponsorship by patriotic businesses took up the theme of women's respect for life. Under the heading "YOUR TALENT may save a life," one asked the prospective volunteer to reflect on "what it would mean to you in long years ahead, if you carried in your heart the knowledge that some talent of yours — great or small — had saved a life in a battlefront — perhaps even dozens of lives." Another interpreted the slogan "This is a Woman's War, too" to mean enlistment was a way of hastening the return of loved ones. "THIS IS *OUR* WAR, TOO," said the pretty CWAC in the drawing, " — our homes are upset, sons, brothers, husbands away defending *us*. Help bring them home sooner!"[65]

Here the military was no longer seeking only to mollify a public fearful that women in uniforms would lose their femininity. The military had turned inward and was re-examining its own policies for fear they were not attending sufficiently to important components of the feminine nature of women. This was occasioned by the knowledge of a deterrent to women's recruitment more serious than the fear that servicewomen would cease to be women: the fear/suspicion that they would become "loose" women. The preoccupation with preserving women's sexual respectability, like the preoccupation with preserving women's femininity, was triggered by war's destabilization of gender relations and both reflected and reinforced prevailing definitions of womanhood.

★   ★   ★

We women of the so-called second wave of feminism sometimes look back nostalgically to the Second World War as a period of women's emancipation. The temptation to do so is great, especially in the face of certain kinds of visual evidence. Photographs show female munitions workers operating lathes with smiling confidence and uniformed servicewomen marching in formation with disciplined precision. But such images do not give the whole picture. One needs to place them alongside other, more conventional representations, for even at the peak of the war effort, mobilization propaganda and wartime advertising were delivering another message, less subversive of pre-war gender relations. The self-reliant woman, performing competently in a traditionally male sphere of activity, was all right, these other images said, as long as she remembered that "THERE'LL COME A DAY"[66] when the men would return to reclaim their rightful place — of privileged access to the public world of paid work and of lordly authority within the private domain of home and family.

And that day did come. Women's participation in the paid work force, which had risen from 24.4 per cent in 1939 to a high of 33.5 per cent in 1944, began to slide in 1945 and then, in 1946, to plummet. It reached its post-war nadir of 23.6 per cent in 1954 and would not climb back to its 1945 level until 1966.[67] Post-war restrictions on women's gainful employment coupled with inducements to return to the home took effect.

So also did a post-war atmosphere conducive to more, and earlier, marriages. Studies revealed that more women were marrying, and they were marrying at a younger age. The rate of marriage for women twenty to twenty-four years old rose from 75 per 1,000 in 1937 to 100 per 1,000 in 1954, and for younger women aged fifteen to nineteen, from 30 per 1,000 in 1937 to 62 per 1,000 in 1954.[68] This had consequences for the marital status of women in the work force. In 1931 a bare 10 per cent of women in gainful employment were married; in 1941, only 12.7 per cent. Then, as war production gathered momentum, the proportion of working women who were married rose- to an estimated 35 per cent in 1944. By 1951 it had dropped back only slightly to 30 per cent. Thus, even though only 11.2 per cent of married women were working outside the home for pay in the early 1950s, the fact that 30 per cent of Canada's waged and salaried women in 1951 were married indicated that one wartime trend was not reversed: married women continued to make up a large proportion of the female labour force, however reduced in overall size that force was.[69]

The mere fact, however, of a growing tendency for gainfully employed women to combine marriage and job was not in itself liberating. Instead, it heralded the establishment of a pattern that would prove immensely oppressive to women, that of the double day of labour. The war, after all, had not upset the sexual division of domestic labour whereby home exists as a place of leisure for men but of work and service for women. Furthermore, post-war reconstruction had rescinded the wartime accommodations made to the special needs of the working woman burdened with home responsibilities.

Moreover, while the war effort necessitated minor adjustments to sexual demarcation lines in the world of paid work, it did not offer a fundamental challenge to the male-dominated sex/gender system. And the post-war years witnessed a return to unquestioning acceptance of the principles of male economic primacy in the public sphere and male leadership in the private. Research on organized women in the post-war era, particularly women's union activities, would help give us more of a sense of the extent to which some women resisted the pressures to vacate non-traditional jobs and to put marriage and family at the centre of their lives. Some evidence of resistance made it into the popular press. An ex-servicewoman from Winnipeg, writing for the *Canadian Home Journal* in April, 1945, expressed rage at the idea that women whom the war had turned into competent, skilled workers were to be cast aside at war's end. Sending women back home was, in her view, "like putting a chick back in the shell — it cannot be done without destroying spirit, heart or mind." On the other hand, the winner of the *National Home Monthly*'s contest in 1945 for the best letter on the subject, "If there's a job in industry for you after the war, do you want it?" registered a definite preference for domesticity. "One thing I would like to make clear," she wrote, "I do not feel I am sacrificing myself for housekeeping. The thing I wanted most was a husband and home of my own."[70] And if that meant on patriarchal terms, so be it.

As recent scholarship has demonstrated, whether in wars or revolutions, if feminist demands have not been on the agenda, feminist gains have been unlikely to survive into post-war or post-revolutionary society.[71] Dorothy Johnson, socialist feminist and member of the Co-operative Commonwealth Federation, recognized this in 1943. She began an article in the *Canadian Forum* by listing a number of wartime developments affecting women:

> Women are gainfully employed again. The cry of patriotism is urging women into all the work they've been trying to get into since World War I ceased. American states which were busy passing acts actually to stop married women from working outside their homes have quietly dropped the matter. School boards are imploring married teachers to return to the fold; hospitals are employing married nurses; aircraft factories are astonished to find women capable of operating simple machines, and even governments are taking a hand in the business of caring for children while mothers work.

She noted, however that "The feminist movement" could "claim none of the gains" and went on to predict that women "will rush to work now, and they will give up their work to men after the war as soon as they are asked to."[72] While she exaggerated the willingness with which women would retreat to domesticity, Johnson was right about the non-feminist basis and consequent short-lived nature of Canadian women's wartime gains.

Reviewing a recent conference convened at Harvard "to re-examine the effect of the two world wars on women's lives," one scholar commented that the debate over whether war liberates women "must necessarily remain . . . inconclusive."[73] On an individual basis that statement is indisputable. Some women without doubt derived experience from their war service that improved their post-war opportunities, particularly exceptional women like CWAC veteran Judy LaMarsh who used her rehabilitation benefits to acquire the education that would launch her on a career as lawyer and politician.[74] One could also point to individuals whom the post-war anti-feminist backlash helped to propel two decades or more later into the front ranks of the reborn women's movement. In *Rough Layout*, Doris Anderson describes the disillusioning effect on a young girl of seeing her strong and self-determining mother transformed into a deferential and "feminine" wife on the return of "the Man" at war's end.[75] Furthermore, life in the armed forces and munitions plants of the United States during the war has been interpreted as liberating for lesbian women in the sense that living and working away from home and in same-sex communities provided a better opportunity for discovery and/or expression of their sexual preference.[76] The research to test that hypothesis for Canadian military life is yet to be conducted.

Beyond its arguably inconclusive nature, one should take note of the limitations inherent in the very question of whether war has a liberating effect on women. Obviously, the question is wholly inappropriate in the face of war's destructiveness and the devastating experience of the loss or physical or psychological maiming of loved ones. Nor does this line of inquiry speak to the experience of the victims of national and racial hatreds fanned by war. The question of war's possible emancipating effect on women takes on an obscene quality, for example, in relation to the forced evacuation, incarceration, and dispersal that Japanese-Canadian women suffered together with Japanese-Canadian men at the hands of the Canadian government during and after the Second World War.[77] And clearly principled pacifist women for whom the resort to armed force as a solution to conflict is a violation of their belief in the sacredness of human life have difficulty conceiving of wars as liberating.

The concern in this [study] has been both narrower and more general. The foregoing [text has] not attempted to capture Canadian women's experience of the Second World War in its full range and diversity. Instead, the focus has been on the larger patterns in government policy and gender ideology that map the determinants to women's social existence. As we have seen, while the war effort necessitated shifts in sexual boundaries in the public workplace and the reformulation of proper womanhood to accommodate those shifts, the seeds of backlash were already present during the war itself, in expressions of the fear of loss of femininity and in the contradictory messages of recruitment literature. The CWAC of the promotion photo wears a helmet and a respirator, but tilts her head to the side in a "pin-up" pose. The congratulations for breaking into non-traditional fields, which the media and officials gave out to women one moment, were taken back in the next in the assurances and predictions of women's post-war return to hearth and home. To bridge the contradiction between the cult of domesticity and Canada's wartime need for women in munitions plants, doing housework was "militarized" and assembling explosives was "domesticated."

The tension between woman as wife/mother/homemaker and woman as paid worker was eased on only a limited scale and only for the duration of the war, mainly through the Dominion-Provincial Wartime Day Nurseries Agreements implemented in Ontario and Quebec. Furthermore, shifts in sex/gender lines of demarcation took place exclusively in the public sphere. The subject of reorganizing the household division of labour was broached only in jokes and cartoons about male/female role reversal. Women could don military uniforms, but not even for the war emergency were husbands/fathers to don aprons. Moreover, the war intensified the traditional demands on women to be emotionally supportive of men. . . . Finally, as the chapter . . . [has] shown, the immediate legacy of the Second World War was an indisputable reaction against war's upheaval, including the unsettling extent to which women had crossed former sex/gender boundaries. The war's slight yet disquieting reconstruction of womanhood in the direction of equality with men was scrapped for a full-skirted and redomesticated post-war model, and for more than a decade feminism was once again sacrificed to femininity.

NOTES

1. *Saturday Night*, September 26, 1942, p. 10.
2. Lotta Dempsey, "Women Working on Ships and Aircraft," *Mayfair*, June 1943, p. 74.
3. Notes for the Assistance of Speakers at School for NSS Employment Office Personnel, February, 1943, PAC, RG 24, reel no. C-5303, file HQS 8984-2.
4. *Globe and Mail*, December 24, 1942, p. 8; December 31, 1942, p. 13.
5. " 'Jill' Canuck Has Become CWAC of All Trades," *Saturday Night*, March 4, 1944, p. 4.
6. Margaret Ecker, *Globe and Mail*, December 26, 1942, p. 8.
7. Copies in PAC, RG 24, Vol. 2256, file HQ 54-27-111-144, vol. 1 .
8. "Suggested Notes for the Guidance of Speakers at the N.S.S. Schools," "Further Suggested Notes . . .," February, 1943, PAC, RG 24, reel no. C-5303, file HQS 8984-2.
9. *Women in Khaki*, n.d., but internal evidence places publication in second half of 1942, DND, DH, 164.069 (D1).
10. According to the nationwide survey of CWAC other ranks carried out in April–May, 1943, "about 20% of CWAC women belonged to a volunteer women's part-time service organization prior to enrolling in the CWAC. Most of these belonged to one of the unofficial uniformed women's corps or the Red Cross." *Report of Enquiry — Canadian Women's Army Corps: Why Women Join and How They Like It*, April–May, 1943, p. 23, copy at DND, DH, 168.009 (D91).
11. "Strength — Canadian Women's Army Corps as at 27 March 1943" was 354 officers plus 9,741 other ranks, totalling 10,095. PAC, RG 24, reel no. C-5303, file HQS 8984-2.
12. Weekly Strength Returns by D. Org. DND, DH, 113.3C1065 (D3) CWAC.
13. Letter of October 1, 1943, to newspaper editors from Captain T.H. Johnstone, Combined Services Committee, PAC, RG 24, reel no. C-5303, file HQS 8984-2. By July 1, 1943, 28,000 women had been accepted by the three services, 13,000 by the CWAC. *Report — C.W.A.C: Why Women Join and How They Like It* (hereafter *C.W.A.C. Report*), p. 11.

14. Communication of January 30, 1943, to all regional superintendents, from R.G. Barclay, Assistant Director, Employment Service and Unemployment Insurance Branch, PAC, RG 24, reel no. C-5303, file HQS 8984-2.
15. Memorandum of March, 1943, to the Minister from Major-General H.F.G. Letson, PAC, RG 24, reel no. C-5303, file HQS 8984-2.
16. Minutes of the 89th Meeting of the National Campaign Committee, February 22, 1943, PAC, RG 24, reel no. C-5303, file HQS 8984-2.
17. *Report: An Enquiry into the Attitude of the Canadian Civilian Public Towards the Women's Armed Forces* (Montreal/Toronto: Elliott-Haynes Limited, 1943), p. 3, hereafter cited as Elliott-Haynes, *An Enquiry*.
18. *C.W.A.C. Report*, pp. 3–4.
19. Elliott-Haynes, *An Enquiry*, p. 8.
20. *Ibid.*, p. 9.
21. *Ibid.*, p. 12.
22. *Ibid.*, p. 13.
23. *C.W.A.C. Report*, p. 28.
24. Elliott-Haynes, *An Enquiry*, p. 14.
25. *Ibid.*
26. *Ibid.*, p. 32.
27. *C.W.A.C. Report*, p. 28.
28. *Ibid.*
29. Elliott-Haynes, *An Enquiry*, p. 15.
30. *Ibid.*
31. *Ibid.*, p. 25.
32. *C.W.A.C. Report*, p. 26.
33. PAC, RG 24, Vol. 2252, file HQ 54-27-111-1, vol. 2.
34. *C.W.A.C. Report*, p. 12.
35. Letter of July 26, 1943, to Gentlemen from T.H. Johnstone, Captain, Combined Services Committee, PAC, RG 24, reel no. C-5303, file HQS 8984-2.
36. PAC, RG 24, Vol. 2252, file HQ 54-27-111-1, vol. 2; reel no. C-5303, file HQS 8984-2, *passim*.
37. Elliott-Haynes, *An Enquiry*, p. 24.
38. Notes for the Assistance of Speakers for NSS Employment Personnel, February, 1943, PAC, RG 24, reel no. C-5303, file HQS 8984-2; NSS Representatives Conference, London, Ontario, February 15-17, 1943, PAC, RG 24, reel no. C-5322, file HQS 9011-11-5.
39. Director-General, CWAC, presumably Col. Margaret C. Eaton, "Preliminary Historical Narrative, History of the CWAC & Appendices" (n.d., but internal evidence suggests ca. mid-1945), p. 33, copy at DH, DND, 113.3C1 (D1).
40. *Ibid.*, p. 34.
41. *Women in Khaki*, p. 20.
42. *C.W.A.C. Report*, pp. 18, 24.
43. PAC, National Photography Collection, Army photos "In Barracks," negatives Z-1765-(1-9), July 7, 1943.
44. PAC, National Photography Collection, Army photo, negative Z-1885-17, August 11, 1943.
45. PAC, National Photography Collection, Army photos, negatives Z-2544-23 and 24, February 16, 1944.
46. PAC, National Photography Collection, Z-4037-2.
47. Elliott-Haynes, *An Enquiry*, p. 27.
48. *50 Questions and Answers About CWAC*, p. 11.
49. "Private of C.W.A.C. Weds Army Corporal," *Globe and Mail*, December 2, 1942, p. 11.
50. PAC, National Photography Collection, Army photos "C.W.A.C. Wedding," negatives Z-2586-(1-9), March 1, 1944; "C.W.A.C.-Navy Wedding at Kildare Barracks," negatives Z-3796-(1-4), April, 1945.
51. NSS Representatives Conference re Recruitment of Women for Armed Services, London, Ontario, February 15, 16, 17, 1943, PAC, RG 24, reel no. C-5303, file HQS 8984-2.
52. CWAC Recruiting Pamphlet used in Military District No. 4 in January–March, 1943, campaign, DH, DND, 164.069 (D1).
53. Godfrey Winn, "Through Fair Weather and Foul, Britain's . . . Women Ferry Pilots Fly that Men May Fight," *Saturday Night*, November 28, 1942, pp. 4–5; D.K. Findlay, "Anywhere to Anywhere," *Maclean's*, April 15, 1943, pp. 12-13, 57, 61.

54. Mary Ziegler, *We Serve That Men May Fly: The Story of Women's Division Royal Canadian Air Force* (Hamilton, Ontario: R.C.A.F. (W.D.) Association, 1973), pp. 66–67.

55. *Globe and Mail*, September 9, 1942, p. 9; October 10, 1942, p. 11. Discussed in Marie T. Wadden, "Newspaper Response to Female War Employment: *The Globe and Mail* and *Le Devoir* May–October 1942" (History honours dissertation, Memorial University of Newfoundland, May, 1976), pp. 13–14. Statement of Major-General Knox quoted in Conrod, *Athene, Goddess of War*, p. 96.

56. L.S.B. Shapiro, "They're Still Women After All," *Saturday Night*, September 26, 1942, p. 10.

57. *C.W.A.C. Report*, p. 15.

58. Memorandum of July 22, 1943, to DAG(C) from Director of Army Recruiting, PAC, RG 24, reel no. C-5303, file HQS 8984-2.

59. "Suggested Notes for the Guidance of Speakers at the National Selective Service Schools," February 9, 1943, sent out from the Office of Director of Army Recruiting, PAC, RG 24, reel no. C-5303, file HQS 8984-2.

60. See Ruth Milkman, "Redefining 'Women's Work': The Sexual Division of Labor in the Auto Industry During World War II," *Feminist Studies* 8, 2 (Summer, 1982), pp. 336–72.

61. Thelma LeCocq, "Woman Power," *Maclean's*, June 15, 1942, pp. 10–11, 40.

62. Drawn for *Maclean's* by Vic Herman, September 15, 1945, p. 32.

63. Memorandum of July 22, 1943, to DAG(C) from Director of Army Recruiting, PAC, RG 24, reel no. C-5303, file HQS 8984-2.

64. Copy at DH, DND, 164.069 (D1).

65. Sponsored CWAC advertising, summer/autumn 1943, DH, DND, 164.069 (D1).

66. Community Silverplate ads, *Maclean's*, November 1, 1943, back cover, December 1, 1943, back cover.

67. Pat and Hugh Armstrong, *The Double Ghetto: Canadian Women and Their Segregated Work* (Toronto: McClelland and Stewart, 1978), p. 19; Hugh and Pat Armstrong, "The Segregated Participation of Women in the Canadian Labour Force, 1941-1971," *Canadian Review of Sociology and Anthropology*, 12, 4, part 1 (November, 1975), pp. 370–71.

68. Richard L. Edsall, "This Changing Canada — Postwar trend: more marriages among younger set/more weddings later in the year," *Canadian Business*, March, 1957, pp. 44, 46.

69. "Wartime History of Employment of Women and Day-Care of Children," Part 1, p. 75; Canada, Department of Labour, *Women at Work in Canada: A Fact Book on the Female Labour Force* (Ottawa: The Queen's Printer, 1959), pp. 14–24.

70. *Canadian Home Journal*, April, 1945, p. 1972; *National Home Monthly*, May, 1945, pp. 58–59.

71. See, for example, Carol R. Berkin and Clara M. Lovett, eds., *Women, War & Revolution* (New York: Holmes & Meier, 1980).

72. Dorothy Johnson, "Feminism, 1943," *Canadian Forum*, XXI, 266 (March, 1943), pp. 352–53.

73. Persis Charles, "Women and the Two World Wars: Report on Conference at Harvard," *Women's Studies Quarterly*, XII, 2 (Summer, 1984), p. 7.

74. Judy LaMarsh, *Memoirs of a Bird in a Gilded Cage* (Toronto: McClelland and Stewart, 1968), pp. 2, 3.

75. Doris Anderson, *Rough Layout* (Toronto: Seal Books, 1982), pp. 93–100, 116–19.

76. Allan Bérubé, "Coming Out Under Fire: The untold story of the World War II soldiers who fought on the front lines of gay and lesbian liberation," *Mother Jones*, VIII, 2 (February/March, 1983) pp. 23–29, 45.

77. Joy Kogawa, *Obasan* (Toronto: Lester and Orpen Dennys, 1981); Ann Gomer Sunahara, *The Politics of Racism: The Uprooting of Japanese Canadians During the Second World War* (Toronto: James Lorimer, 1981).

Part Three

Postwar Canada: National and Regional Trends

The affluence brought on by the Second World War was a welcome contrast to the grim days of the Great Depression. Between 1945 and 1960, Canadians enjoyed a new quality of life made possible by constantly rising wages and the welfare state. As growing numbers of people satisfied their basic needs for food and shelter, the manufacture of attractive but nonessential goods actively competed for the consumer's dollar. And these goods found a ready market — with their newfound wealth, Canadians increasingly indulged in automobiles, television sets, films, music, fashion, and commercial sports.

After the war, the birthrate in Canada soared. This "baby boom," along with a generally increased emphasis on education, caused a major surge in school enrollment. At the same time, schools were being asked to do all sorts of new things: to provide instruction in everything from athletics and music to how to drive a car, and even to develop in their students "correct" attitudes toward alcohol and sex. University enrollment also increased dramatically during these years, partly as a result of the return of thousands of wartime veterans, and then, by the 1960s, the baby boomers.

Concentration of economic power in business was another characteristic of this period, especially in the manufacturing heartland of central Canada and in resource-rich provinces such as Alberta and British Columbia. Many of these powerful corporations were foreign-owned, as the Royal Commission on Canada's Economic Prospects documented in 1957. The Canadian trade union movement was also strongly continentalist through affiliation with U.S.-based craft and industrial unions, although this trend was much weaker in Quebec.

Politically, most of the postwar era was dominated by the Liberal Party of Louis St. Laurent. This all changed in 1957 when John Diefenbaker's Progressive Conservative Party gained power for a brief but eventful term of office (1957–63). Although Diefenbaker is often remembered more for his rather erratic personality than for his reform record, during these years the welfare state was expanded, the 1960 Bill of Rights was passed, and attempts were made to reform the Immigration Act.

The 1950s were a decade of strong provincial premiers who were determined to protect their constitutional powers and their political hegemony. Alberta and British Columbia were dominated by the populist Social Credit Party, while the democratic socialists (CCF/NDP) prevailed in Saskatchewan. Politically, Ontario belonged to the Progressive Conservatives, while Atlantic Canada was Liberal country, at least until the mid-1950s. In Quebec, Maurice Duplessis maintained his own special form of control through the Union Nationale party and an often uneasy relationship with Ottawa.

Part Three begins with Brigitte Kitchen's reassessment of the Marsh Report of 1943, one of the foundations of Canada's postwar welfare state. J.M. Bumsted, in his article "Home Sweet Suburb: The Great Post-War Migration," provides a lively and informative account of the emergence and characteristics of Canadian suburban culture. The growth and influence of organized labour after 1945 is the primary focus of Christopher Huxley, David Kettler, and James Struthers' article, reprinted here under the title "Trade Unions in North America since 1945: A Comparison." The authors show important differences between the Canadian and American trade union experiences.

Distinctive regional, economic, and cultural developments also characterized the postwar years, and these are the focus of the last two articles in Part Three. Michael Behiels evaluates the role of educators such as Father Georges-Henri Lévesque in providing an intellectual climate that would foster many of the ideas that would flourish in Quebec during the Quiet Revolution of the 1960s. The final article, "Triple Jeopardy: Assessing Life Experiences of Black Nova Scotian Women from a Social Work and Historical Perspective," provides a sensitive and personal account of how ethnic, class, and gender disadvantages have affected African Canadians in Nova Scotia.

All of these articles raise a number of questions about the character of Canadian society during the postwar years. What were the direction and the goal of the welfare state? How did the culture of suburbia reflect the values of the 1950s? Were Canadian workers able to improve their standard of living and their bargaining-power rights? What was the national and regional influence of the intellectual elite? In what ways did minorities change the country's ethnic character? Were gender relations different from those of the war years? Does Canada have a problem with racism?

Further Reading

Irving Abella, *Nationalism, Communism, and Canadian Labour: The CIO, the Communist Party, and the Canadian Congress of Labour, 1935-1956*. Toronto: University of Toronto Press, 1973.

Donald Avery, *Reluctant Host: Canada's Response to Immigrant Workers, 1896-1994*. Toronto: McClelland & Stewart, 1995.

Robert Bothwell, *Nucleus: The History of Atomic Energy of Canada Limited*. Toronto: University of Toronto Press, 1988.

Richard Cavanagh, "The Development of Canadian Sports Broadcasting, 1920-1978." *Canadian Journal of Communications* (1992): 301-17.

Alvin Finkel, *The Social Credit Phenomenon in Alberta*. Toronto: University of Toronto Press, 1989.

Gerald Friesen, *The Canadian Prairies: A History*. Toronto: University of Toronto Press, 1984.

Warren Gill, "Region, Agency and Popular Music: The Northwest Sound, 1958-1966." *The Canadian Geographer* 37, no. 2 (1993): 1-12.

Roger Hall, William Westfall, and Laurel Sefton MacDowell, eds., *Patterns of the Past: Interpreting Ontario's History*. Toronto: Dundurn Press, 1988.

Franca Iacovetta, *"Such Hardworking People"*: *Italian Immigrants in Postwar Toronto*. Montreal/Kingston: McGill-Queen's University Press, 1992.

Paul-Andre Linteau et al., *Quebec since 1930: A History*. Toronto: James Lorimer, 1991.

R. Ogmundson and J. McLaughlin, "Changes in an Intellectual Elite, 1960-1990: The Royal Society Revisited." *Canadian Review of Sociology and Anthropology* 31, no. 1 (1994): 1-13.

James Pitsula, "The Saskatchewan CCF Government and Treaty Indians, 1944-1964." *Canadian Historical Review* 75, no. 1 (1994): 21-52.

John Porter, *The Vertical Mosaic: An Analysis of Social Class and Power in Canada*. Toronto: University of Toronto Press, 1965.

Larry Pratt and John Richards, *Prairie Capitalism: Power and Influence in the New West*. Toronto: McClelland & Stewart, 1988.

Alison Prentice et al., *Canadian Women: A History*, 2nd ed. Toronto: Harcourt Brace, 1996.

Susan Trofimenkoff, *The Dream of Nation: A Social and Intellectual History of Quebec*. Toronto: Gage, 1983.

R.A. Young, "'and the people will sink into despair': Reconstruction in New Brunswick, 1942-52," *Canadian Historical Review* 69, no. 2 (June 1988): 127-66.

The Marsh Report Revisited

BRIGITTE KITCHEN

In December 1939, only a few months after the outbreak of war, a special committee of the Cabinet on Demobilization and Re-establishment was constituted under Order-in-Council P.C. 4068-1/2 to begin post-war planning for the demobilization and reintegration of members of the armed forces into civilian life.[1] After a year of work it became apparent that the problems of demobilization could not be assessed without reference to the total post-war economic situation. The best medical care, vocational training, and education for discharged veterans could prepare them for employment, but could not guarantee that jobs in sufficient quantities would be available. In recognition of this fact a further Order-in-Council, P.C. 1218 on 17 February 1941, broadened the terms of reference of the Cabinet Committee to include *all phases* of reconstruction.[2] The Committee's chairman, Minister of Pensions and Health Ian Mackenzie, invited representatives from agriculture, business, and labour, along with two civil servants and three academic economists, to explore with him how this broadened mandate could be met.[3] So emerged what would become one of Canada's foremost attempts at national social and economic planning, the Advisory Committee on Reconstruction, chaired by McGill University principal Dr. F. Cyril James.

This paper will examine the most well-known product of the James Committee, the *Report on Social Security for Canada*, authored by its principal research advisor, Dr. Leonard Marsh, who had been director of the McGill Social Science Research Programme since 1930. This report represented the crowning achievement of Leonard Marsh's career as a pioneer in Canadian social research and social policy and still remains one of the most coherent statements on the purpose and potential scope of the welfare state ever made in Canada. At a time when the future of social security and welfare programmes in this country remains clouded by uncertainty and confusion, and basic principles such as universality and redistribution are now under attack, a reexamination of Marsh's 1943 vision of the Canadian welfare state is well worth making.

Leonard Marsh, The Social Scientist

Leonard Marsh was eminently qualified for his position with the Advisory Committee in Ottawa. Before taking up his position at McGill University

SOURCE: "The Marsh Report Revisited," *Journal of Canadian Studies* 21, no. 2 (Summer 1986): 38–48. Reprinted with permission.

he had worked as a research assistant for Sir William Beveridge, later to become Lord Beveridge, on a project researching unemployment in Britain. Beveridge had recommended him for the position at McGill. It is important to recognize Marsh's connection with Beveridge in view of later claims that his work on social security was simply a transplantation of Beveridge's work into Canadian soil. Marsh certainly held Beveridge in great esteem, was impressed by his accomplishments, and had learned from his experience of working with him. Comparisons with Beveridge were embarrassing to Marsh. "I wouldn't want to be compared with Sir William I have too much respect for him," he was reported as saying in an interview with the *Globe and Mail* on 18 March 1943. Marsh certainly did not need to rely on Beveridge to carry out his work for the Advisory Committee. His social science research at McGill had provided him with sufficient experience to meet the tasks that were awaiting him in Ottawa.

During the 1930s Marsh and Harry Cassidy, a University of Toronto social work professor and later British Columbia civil servant, were Canada's foremost academic researchers into social welfare questions.[4] Marsh's undergraduate education at the London School of Economics had left him with a commitment to social justice and social equality steeped in British pragmatism. He strongly believed that practical solutions to social problems could be found, and that these solutions depended on a combination of sound social planning informed by rigorous social research methods borrowed from the natural sciences. Social facts uncovered by research, he insisted, would speak for themselves and convince reasonable people that reform was both necessary and inevitable. Although he held a Ph.D. in economics from McGill, he preferred to consider himself a social scientist rather than an economist. Economics for him was indeed "a dismal science." Main-stream economics, he felt, devoted much time and thought to questions of allocative efficiency while largely ignoring questions of personal income distribution that involved making explicit ethical judgements. Poverty, and other social security issues which were so important to Marsh, generally received little attention from the economics profession. It was therefore hardly surprising that he turned to the social welfare field in order to find both an intellectual as well as an emotional home.[5]

The Importance of Post-War Planning

Leonard Marsh was undoubtedly excited about the opportunity provided by the reconstruction planning of the Advisory Committee to have a part in shaping Canada's future in the post-war years and beyond. Working with the Advisory Committee gave him a chance to combine his enthusiasm for social improvement and reform with his belief and commitment to the planning of social and economic affairs. His work during the next two-and-a-half years with the Advisory Committee has to be placed in the context of the whirl of post-war planning that occupied Canadians at the time. "Reconstruction was in the air," he wrote in the introduction to the 1975 edition of his *Report on Social Security for Canada*.[6] Planning became a primary concern for all levels of government in Canada while Canadians watched eagerly for some assurance that the mass unemployment of the 1930s would not repeat itself.

In Ottawa, committees of both the Senate and the House of Commons were accepting briefs aimed at influencing government post-war policies. Within the federal civil service the Cabinet's Economic Advisory Committee, chaired by Deputy Finance Minister W.C. Clark, played a powerful role in post-war planning. The provinces established their own reconstruction commissions in order to prepare for the post-war world, and in a number of cities special committees were set up to study urban problems likely to emerge once hostilities ended. In addition, three reports were prepared by outstanding individuals within the Canadian social welfare field. The first, published in February 1943, was Harry Cassidy's *Social Security and Reconstruction in Canada*, an independent scholarly analysis of the nation's prospects after the war. This was followed by Marsh's report for the Advisory Committee, and a few months later came Charlotte Whitton's *The Dawn of an Ampler Life* which the prominent Ottawa social worker wrote at the request of John Bracken, federal leader of the Progressive Conservative party. Whitton's book was both a direct attack on Marsh's proposals and an alternative conservative vision of Canada's social welfare future. Of the three 1943 blueprints for change, Marsh's report arguably has best stood the test of time. His proposals, if implemented during the 1940s, would have transformed Canada from one of the most backward into one of the most advanced English-speaking nations in the field of social security.[7]

The Marsh Report

The Advisory Committee, along with Leonard Marsh and his small staff, worked at a hectic pace in order to develop their plans for the post-war world, a quest made all the more urgent by the December 1942 publication of the path-breaking British *Report on Social Insurance and Allied Services*, authored by Marsh's mentor, Sir William Beveridge. The Beveridge Report, as it came to be known, with its blueprint for a cradle-to-grave welfare state, garnered enormous publicity throughout the English-speaking world and increased the political pressure within Canada for a similar statement of the federal government's post-war social security objectives. As a result, after six weeks of work in a Chateau Laurier hotel suite in Ottawa, and with the help of only a few civil servants and outside consultants, Marsh completed his *Report on Social Security* which was released to the public on 18 March 1943. It received generous coverage from newspapers and professional social work and policy journals throughout Canada. Given the limits of his time frame, the "magnitude of [Marsh's] single-handed achievement," Canadian Welfare Council director George Davidson commented, was "all the more impressive."[8]

Marsh conceded that his report was written under pressure. But he defended himself against criticism that it was hasty either in "conception or [in the] material assembled." It should not be forgotten, he later pointed out, that he "had been lecturing on these subjects for more than ten years previously at McGill University, that he had been employed on a series of related research topics, all concerned at one point or another with employment, housing, education, and social welfare services in Canada."[9] In the *Report* Marsh was able to bring together his knowledge about social problems from his research work of a decade and offer operational solutions. These were of the foremost importance if Canadians were to be protected against the large and complicated problems of the insecurities of working and family life. When Marsh's *Report* was published there were only six social security programmes in place in Canada. The federal government exclusively was responsible for unemployment insurance, while vocational training, old age pensions, and pensions for the blind were joint cost-shared federal–provincial programmes administered by the provinces. Workmen's Compensation and Mothers' Allowances were provincial programmes financed and administered by the provinces alone.

The Importance of Social Security Provisions

For Marsh social security signaled the prospect of a better future. "It is one of the concrete expressions of a better world which is particularly real to those who knew unemployment, destitution, inadequate medical care and the like in the depression periods before the war." The starting-point of all social security discussion in his judgement was the level of family income.[10] The Dependents' Allowance payable to enlisted men and their families during the duration of the war represented to him an example of a form of social security provision. Families receiving them had become accustomed to the fact that the state could step in to protect their income if there was a need for it. A failure to introduce social security programmes after the war to protect family income, he argued in the *Report*, would inevitably lead to revealing "in more marked contrast than any other, differences in respect of social provisions for Canadian citizens when they are in army . . . and when in ordinary civilian life."[11] Furthermore, there were the services and income maintenance programmes which the state normally provides to reintegrate members of the armed forces and their families into consumer production. These services, together with the Dependents' Allowance, Marsh considered to be a model for the extension of social security provisions for all Canadians. Marsh certainly did not ascribe to the view that soldiers and their families were more deserving than civilian families.

The Interdependence of Social and Economic Policy

Marsh took a broad view of social security. Clearly thinking on Keynesian lines, he considered social spending as a strategic factor in economic policy planning and only indirectly as a welfare issue. Social security expenditures would stimulate consumption and therefore production which would contribute to economic growth and provide jobs. He described the cyclical relationship between social security expenditure, consumption and production as follows:

> One of the necessities for economic stability is the maintenance of the flow of purchasing-power at the time when munitions and other factories are closing down and war activity in many other spheres is being liquidated. Sound social insurance, which is a form of investment in physical health, morale, educational opportunities for children, and family stability, is a desirable and a comparatively easy vehicle for expenditure. It is not only an eminently appropriate peacetime alternative for expenditures now being used devoted to destruction: it is also a form of using some of the deferred backlog of consumer expenditure to which reference is so often made only in terms of radios, frigidaires and other tangible consumer goods.[12]

Marsh realized that social and economic problems could not be addressed separately. Thus he emphatically stressed that it was essential to recognize the point "that social security legislation in the post-war context has no firm foundation without special employment measures for the transition period."[13] Marsh attempted to reflect his awareness of the interdependence of the insecurities of working and family life in his proposals for an integrated social security system. On the one hand, he firmly believed that the best solution for loss of employment was not unemployment insurance but a job, but he was equally aware that not all jobs pay an adequate wage to meet the need of economic security for families of different sizes. He argued, therefore, that organized provisions would have to be made "in the post-war world for the risks and contingencies of family life that are beyond the capacity of most of them to finance adequately from their own resources." "Economic planning," wrote George Davidson, "produces economic security, which is part of, but not all of social security."[14] Leonard Marsh shared this view. For him the key to social planning for the protection of people's income needs was to be found in employment policies. Nevertheless, a strong social security system was equally important.

A National Employment Programme

Because the social welfare issues of his *Report* were given so much prominence, it is sometimes forgotten that Marsh grounded his social security proposals within the operation of a national employment programme. His proposals for a public investment and development programme never gained the same kind of interest with the public as his income security proposals. Yet both are equally important since they were intended to complement one another. It was against the background of full employment policies and extensive public expenditures that Leonard Marsh developed his comprehensive system of social security programmes ranging from unemployment and health insurance, disability and old age pensions to family allowances and funeral expenses.

The war economy had provided employment for some 1,890,000 people, whose participation in the work force would end with the conclusion of hostilities.[15] In addition, the men and women who had enlisted in the armed forces had to be reintegrated into civilian life and civilian production. The volume of wartime expenditure that was producing full employment in Canada at that time was in the realm of two or three billion dollars a year. Marsh thought that a minimum of one billion dollars was required in government anti-depression expenditures to finance his proposed investment and development programme during the first post-war year to maintain employment levels.[16]

Marsh argued that the availability of jobs paying reasonable wages in reasonably satisfactory working conditions was an essential key to the overall improvement of working people's lives. Social security provisions could not achieve that by themselves, any more than could employment without social security provisions. "The first positive measure in providing social security, therefore, is a programme which makes work available, or, in other words, which will offer wages rather than subsistence maintenance to the farthest extent to which it is possible."[17]

The kind of work and the quality of working conditions were as important to him as the availability. As a result he stressed that "useful public work projects and developmental expenditures . . . need to be undertaken, not merely as stop gap expedients but as desirable social and economic improvements."[18] Government work programmes, however, had acquired a bad reputation in Canada in the 1930s. This did not deter Marsh. He was quick to point out that these programmes had not worked because of the Depression emphasis on employing the maximum number of people instead of organizing them on principles of efficiency.[19] The kinds of projects he had in mind were those which almost certainly would be carried out only through public initiative. He listed the removal of wastes and eyesores, and the replacement of slum dwellings as possible enterprises that provide desirable social as well as economic benefits.

The Social Minimum

The Beveridge Report had defined "freedom from want" as the guiding principle for its network of social security provisions. Marsh used the concept of the "social minimum" to describe the objectives of his social security programmes: "social security systems are primarily designed to lay the foundation of a social minimum. What this minimum should be is a matter of definition. Certainly, however, it means the direct elimination of poverty."[20] To overcome poverty he proposed a two-tier system made up of, on the one hand, social insurance programmes and, on the other, for those who for some reason or other could not be covered by a social insurance programme, social assistance as a secondary but largely exceptional line of defence. He firmly believed that with the stabilization of the labour market progressively more Canadians would be covered by social insurance programmes, and the need for social assistance, along with humiliating and degrading means tests to establish eligibility, would be greatly reduced.

Social Insurance

Marsh's *Report* proposed a comprehensive social insurance scheme to protect Canadians against a range of both predictable and unpredictable risks "which may be met in hit and miss fashion by individual families or . . . by forms of collective provisions." There were many whose incomes were inadequate to cope with these risks. He dismissed the argument that higher wages alone were the answer by pointing out that: "It is impossible to establish a wage which will allow every worker and every family to meet the heavy disabilities of serious illness, prolonged unemployment, accident and premature death." Protection against such risks, he believed, could be effectively found through social insurance, that is, the collective pooling of resources. "The basic soundness of social insurance is that it is underwritten by the community as a whole."[21] Because social insurance was concerned with the equitable administration of contributions made to a common pool, and not with the claims of each individual to receive back in benefits exactly the amount of previous payments, it reinforced the solidarity of citizenship.

The Basic Social Insurance Unit

Marsh went to a great deal of trouble to identify, on as equitable a basis as possible, whether the individual or the married couple should be considered as the basic social insurance unit. Once society had defined a desirable social minimum, he pointed out, the next step was to determine how many people it should encompass. He opposed the rigid determination of social insurance benefits by market forces. For the purpose of social insurance planning, Marsh argued, the basic or unskilled wage level should not be confused with a desirable social minimum for families. Instead, Marsh decided that the contributions of an individual man should also cover his actual or potential wife. He did not think that this two-person basic insurance unit was unfair to those who chose not to marry, since they could be expected, in their capacity as citizens of the country, to make somewhat larger contributions than married people whose responsibilities were greater. In order to minimize the gap between minimum wage levels and social insurance contributions and benefits, however, Marsh argued that "the normal coverage of an adult worker, if it is to be extended at all beyond the individual, should not go further than his marital partner." This did not solve the problem of coverage for children. With unemployment insurance, for instance, serious anomalies could occur if the state attempted to stretch monetary benefits to cover all members of the family. This could lead to situations where benefits would exceed earnings during work.[22] In order to provide social insurance coverage for children, Marsh recommended the payment of children's allowances which, strictly speaking, could not be considered as part of a social insurance plan, yet were an essential complement to it.

Children's Allowances

Income security for children occupied a central position within Marsh's proposed social security system. Children presented a special need in terms of family spending. "The need of income sufficient to give them health, proper food, and clothing and desirable conditions of family life is not an unpredictable risk or contingency in the same way as unemployment, sickness or the death of a husband."[23] Rather it was a continuous requirement in times of prosperity and in times of depression. Children's allowances, therefore, should be paid whether the main breadwinner was in or out of work. To illustrate how children's allowances would supplement the benefits of an unemployed insured couple, Marsh gave the following example:

> A married man under insurance, with two children, who becomes permanently disabled or who retires on account of age, would receive his old age benefit of $30, a supplementary benefit for his wife of $15, and a continuation of the children's allowance in respect of each child which he had received during his working years.[24]

Furthermore, children's allowances played a specific role in Marsh's attempt to demonstrate how existing social welfare legislation could be integrated or transformed into social insurance legislation. If children's allowances were introduced, there no longer would be a need for a particular form of public assistance to mothers and children such as Mothers' Allowances. The needs of children would be met through allowances set at the social minimum level. At the same time, the existence of this scheme would also draw attention to the plight of widows who required assistance.[25]

Separating the needs of the parent(s) from those of the children was the most distinctive feature of Marsh's approach to social security provisions. This made his conceptualization of social programmes different from that of Beveridge and other social security planners. Marsh advocated children's allowances as a specific social security measure justified in its own right but also geared into other programmes in the social security system. The benefits a family would receive would thus be made up of two components: social insurance benefits based on the two-person insurance principle, and children's allowances. Acceptance of this principle would mean that married women were automatically included in their husbands' social insurance coverage. He suggested that married men be paid higher insurance benefits than single persons so that a couple would receive at least the "assistance minimum" for two people. He did not consider that married women outside the labour market living with their husbands had an independent claim on the state and the community for their maintenance. The case for children was different. They had a special claim on the community because of the "inflexibility of wages or earnings (no matter what the level of skills)" compared to the needs of families of varying sizes, particularly large families. Children's allowances were the logical complement to other social insurance programmes which would be welcomed by all mothers for two reasons. First, they would assure children at least a minimum provision of welfare and, second, they would contribute towards treating a mother as an individual in her own right by clearly setting the needs of parent(s) apart from those of the children.[26]

The Needs of Women

Marsh's treatment of women for social insurance purposes can only be understood in the context of his structure for an integrated social security system. For women who were wage-earners in full-time employment, he did not see any special social insurance problems. They would be covered by unemployment and sickness insurance on the same terms as male workers in comparable income groups. He dismissed the argument that wage-related social insurance benefits would affect women more than men by pointing out that women, as newcomers to the labour market, shared the problems of low pay and short-term attachment to the labour market with younger, part-time, or inexperienced male workers.

Social insurance eligibility criteria were free from any sex biases. As far as he was concerned, the purpose of social insurance programmes was not to compensate for the structural inequalities of the labour market, but rather to protect people against the insecurities of income loss or reduction. His emphasis on equality of the sexes for social insurance purposes led him to present maternity cash benefits for working women as a desirable corollary to sickness cash benefits for men.[27]

As we have seen, Marsh considered married women outside the labour market to have social insurance coverage through their husbands. For women who continued as wage-earners after marriage, he proposed certain modifications in social insurance coverage that would be different from men's. Marsh clearly considered men as the main breadwinners responsible for the maintenance of their families. He argued, for instance, that different standards in unemployment insurance coverage were justified for a woman: "Because she has other definite sources of support . . . her registration [for benefits] must be attested by strict interpretation of [her] genuine availability for employment." He did not propose a lower benefit for married women as Beveridge had done in Britain, since Canadian benefit scales would operate on a graduated rather than the British flat-rate scale. Instead he suggested that their benefits be governed by a ceiling. In a further modification, which also discriminated against married women, Marsh recommended lower pension rates for women workers if both husband and wife were pensionable and living together. However, he did contemplate a tentative step towards pensions for housewives by advocating the payment of a double pension to married couples, regardless of the age of the wife, once the husband had reached a pensionable age.[28]

Conclusion

The Marsh *Report* has been called "the most important single document in the history of the development of the welfare state in Canada."[29] However, the reality of the slow and piecemeal growth of social programmes over the past four decades tells a different story. The demand for comprehensiveness, as set out in the Marsh *Report*, was ignored[30] as governments in Ottawa and the provinces added disjointed pieces of incrementalist social security provisions to construct a version of the Canadian social security system that certainly was not Leonard Marsh's. The result, in the recent words of the Macdonald Commission report, is a welfare state "so complex and inextricably intertwined" that it is "impossible to make coherent moral sense of the present incoherent system by more *ad hoc* intervention."[31]

Marsh had said as much forty-three years ago. As he warned in his *Report*, when all had been said and the time for action had come:

It is finally necessary to recognize the essential unities of social security — to fit together, in other words, all the branches of social insurance and social provisions in such a way that they support each other, and work together as a coherent administration. . . . There is abundant evidence to show the obstacles which will be left on the path of progress if a piecemeal approach is adopted. In a federal state the warning is all the more necessary.[32]

His caution went unheard. Today, the *Report on Social Security* still remains the most important single document attesting to the failure of Canadian governments to build a comprehensive social security system. The Marsh *Report* is a record of what could have been. The reasons for that failure require another story.

NOTES

1. Advisory Committee on Reconstruction, *Report* (Ottawa: Queen's Printer, 24 September 1943), p. 1.
2. Leonard Marsh, *Report on Social Security for Canada*, 1943 (Toronto: University of Toronto Press, 1975), p. xviii; Advisory Committee on Reconstruction, *Report*, p. 1.
3. Advisory Committee on Reconstruction, *Report*, p. 4.
4. Allan Irving, "Canadian Fabians: The Work and Thought of Harry Cassidy and Leonard Marsh, 1930–1940," *Canadian Journal of Social Work Eduction*, 7:1 (1981), p. 9.
5. A statement of Marsh's orientation to social science research can be found in his *Employment Research: An Introduction to the McGill Programme of Research in the Social Sciences* (Toronto: Oxford University Press, 1935).
6. Marsh, *Social Security for Canada*, p. xiii.
7. For a lucid contemporary comparison of the three studies, see Harry Cassidy, "Three Social Security Plans for Canada," *Public Affairs*, 7 (1945), p. 69.
8. Kevin Collins, "Three Decades of Social Security in Canada," *Canadian Welfare*, 5:7 (1976), p. 5; George Davidson, "Improving the Social Services," *Public Affairs*, 7 (1945), p. 74; Davidson, "The Marsh Report on Social Security for Canada," *Canadian Welfare*, 69 (1943), p. 3.
9. Marsh, *Social Security for Canada*, pp. xx, 9.
10. *Ibid.*, pp. 15, 29.
11. *Ibid.*, p. 16.
12. *Ibid.*
13. *Ibid.*, p. 2, Marsh's letter of transmittal of the Report.
14. *Ibid.*, p. 7; Davidson, "Improving the Social Services," p. 6.
15. *Globe and Mail*, 5 December 1942, p. 2.
16. Marsh, *Social Security for Canada*, p. 78.
17. *Ibid.*, p. 76.
18. *Ibid.*, p. 77.
19. *Ibid.*, p. 79.
20. *Ibid.*, p. 30.
21. *Ibid.*, pp. 9–11.
22. *Ibid.*, pp. 58, 64, 66.
23. *Ibid.*, p. 196.
24. *Ibid.*, p. 224.
25. *Ibid.*, p. 223.
26. *Ibid.*, pp. 23, 200, 210, 212.
27. *Ibid.*, pp. 68, 211.
28. *Ibid.*, pp. 213–14. For an excellent discussion of the treatment of women's issues by another sub-committee of the Advisory Committee on Reconstruction, see Gail Cuthbert Brandt, "Pigeon-Holed and Forgotten: the Report of the Advisory Committee on Reconstruction's Sub-Committee on Women," Histoire Sociale/Social History, 15:39 (1982).
29. Collins, "Three Decades of Social Security in Canada," p. 5.

30. For the reasons behind the political eclipse of the Advisory Committee on Reconstruction within the Mackenzie King government, see Robert A. Young, "Reining in James: the Limits of the Task Force," *Canadian Public Administration*, 24:4 (Winter 1981), pp. 596–611; and J.L. Granatstein, *Canada's War: The Politics of the Mackenzie King Government, 1939–1945* (Toronto: Oxford University Press, 1975), pp. 254–64.
31. *Report of the Royal Commission on the Economic Union and Development Prospects for Canada, volume I* (Ottawa: Minister of Supply and Services, 1985), p. 49.
32. Marsh, *Social Security for Canada*, p. 28.

Home Sweet Suburb: The Great Post-War Migration

J.M. BUMSTED

In September 1952 the Canadian Broadcasting Corporation opened Canada's first two television stations in Toronto and Montreal, and over the next two years extended its television coverage into seven other major metropolitan areas. Television was hardly a new technology. The British and Americans both had experimental television stations operating before the war, and the Americans had begun introducing comprehensive television broadcasting, with national network organization, in 1946. By 1952 *I Love Lucy*, American television's first nationally popular hit show, had been running for over a year. At the time of the introduction of television broadcasting in Canada only 146,000 Canadians owned television receivers (or "sets" as they were usually called), tuning to American border stations and using increasingly elaborate antenna systems to draw in distant signals. Most Canadians thus missed entirely the first generation of American television programming, broadcast almost exclusively live from the studio, and were able to tune in only as U.S. television moved from live to filmed programs and from New York to Hollywood. But if Canada got a slightly late start into life with the tube, it rapidly caught up. By December 1954 there were nine stations and 1,200,000 sets; by June 1955 there were twenty-six stations and 1,400,000 sets; and by December 1957 there were forty-four stations and nearly three million sets. The rate of set proliferation had been almost twice that of the United States, and the market for new ones was virtually saturated within five years.

Perhaps more than the automobile, or even the detached bungalow on its carefully manicured plot of green grass, television symbolized the aspirations and lifestyle of the new suburban generation of Canadians.

SOURCE: "Home Sweet Suburb: The Great Post-War Migration," *The Beaver* (October–November 1992): 26–34, which is an excerpt from "The New Suburban Society, 1946–1972," in *The Peoples of Canada: A Post-Confederation History*, by J.M. Bumsted. Copyright © Oxford University Press 1992. Used by permission of Oxford University Press Canada.

Unlike other leisure-time activities that required leaving the home, it was a completely domesticated entertainment package that drew Canadian families *into* the home. Until the late 1960s most Canadian television sets were located in the living room. Particularly on weekend evenings in the winter, the only sign of life on entire blocks of residential neighbourhoods was the flickering dull glow of black-and-white television sets coming from otherwise darkened houses. The family could even entertain friends who were interested in the same popular programs. Some of what people watched was Canadian-produced, but most of it came from the Hollywood Dream Factory. Despite the Saturday-evening popularity of *Hockey Night in Canada*, which was first telecast in 1952, television drew Canadians into the seductive world of American popular culture. Everyone watched television, but perhaps none were more influenced by it than the young, whose perceptions and reading abilities were greatly affected by their being transfixed by an endless array of images.

After the war the serious housing shortage — there had been little new domestic building since the 1920s — and a spate of young couples starting their lives together led the government, through the Canada Mortgage and Housing Corporation (CMHC), to promote suburban development, offering very cheap mortgages. The suburbs were built quickly by companies that had gained expertise during the war, and were often developed around a school. The municipalities then had to link these new communities to each other, and to the city, through roads and infrastructures. Suburbia was a physical place of detached and semi-detached houses with yards and lawns around the outskirts of a city, but it was also a rather complex constellation of expectations and values centred on the home, the family, and continued economic affluence.

In overall terms the trends for urban and rural residency established in the early years of the century continued through the period 1946 to 1972. Urban population steadily increased, both absolutely and as a proportion of the total, while the numbers of rural inhabitants remained relatively constant. Within the rural population, however, there occurred a massive decrease in the number of farm residents, from 3,117,000 in 1941 to 1,420,000 in 1971. Declining numbers of farmers was a national trend, most evident in these years in provinces still dominated by agriculture: Prince Edward Island, Manitoba, and Saskatchewan. On PEI for example, the number of farms declined from 12,230 in 1941 to 4,543 in 1971. Farm depopulation was caused by no single factor. The continued inability of the farmer to make a decent financial return on labour and investment was undoubtedly one of the prime factors. Canadian farms got bigger and more mechanized in an attempt to compensate for low rates of return per acre, and many farm families gave up and got out when the older generation still left on the farm died. Farm land anywhere near cities became uneconomic to retain for farming, and most of Canada's finest agricultural land — in the Fraser Valley in British

Columbia and in southwestern Ontario — had been sold to speculators by 1971 or cut into hobby farm plots. Many former farm families discovered they did not have to move to enjoy brighter lights, for the outskirts of cities expanded in all directions into rural areas.

While Canadian cities grew significantly in size, little of that population growth occurred in the downtown areas or the traditional residential sections. The trend in the downtown core was just the reverse. Rising land prices made it uneconomic for land there to be used residentially except for high-rise apartment blocks, which were less profitable uses of space than comparable office blocks and thus emerged only on the fringes of the downtown. Building upwards, the core of the business district produced those breathtaking skylines we have come to associate with the modern city. Gradually, beginning in the 1960s, they came to be dominated by buildings that showed vast expanses of tinted plate glass to the world, as the International Style of architecture made its way to Canada. One of the country's most famous monuments in this style is a complex of rectangular towers of black steel and dark bronze-tinted glass, the Toronto-Dominion Centre (1963–9) in Toronto, designed by the German-American architect Mies van der Rohe. Within the world of faceless skyscrapers would come two fascinating developments. One was the virtual evacuation of the downtown area by human inhabitants after working hours. The other was the tendency of these working-hour inhabitants to turn inwards on the building complexes themselves, which were maintained at constant levels of temperature and humidity throughout the year, and contained below ground an extensive shopping mall, provision for all necessary services, and parking.

As might have been expected, the only real development strategies for Canadian cities in this period were those dominated by greed, the market, and some unspecified and almost wistful belief that progress was inevitable and would triumph in the end. City development, like most aspects of Canadian life, had been put on hold by the Depression and the war. There was a pent-up sense within local groups of architects, planners, and developers that making new things happen was positive, even at the cost of losing links with the city's (mostly Victorian) past. The result was the destruction of many wonderful old buildings in order to make way for new ones that were often undistinguished. Such a trade-off was made in Toronto when the city's first skyscraper, the majestic Temple Building of 1895 at Richmond and Bay Streets, was demolished in 1970 to be replaced by two bland towers without any public character at all. (One such threatened demolition, that of Toronto's Old City Hall, was stopped in the 1960s as a result of a public outcry.) In Montreal there was much more indiscriminate destruction. For example, the handsome Georgian-style Prince of Wales Terrace of eight attached dwellings — commissioned by Sir George Simpson and finished in 1860 — was demolished in 1971, to be replaced by the ungainly juxtaposition of a tall hotel and a banal six-storey building to house a department of McGill University. Canadian cities, however, did not go so far with their bulldozers as the urban renewals of the United States and Great Britain, where hundreds of square miles of slum dwellings were razed with little idea of sensitive replacement. Canadian destruction on the whole was piecemeal rather than wholesale. One entire community, however, *was* demolished: Africville, an old working-class black community in Halifax, was razed in 1965.

After World War II urban development in the Western world was dominated everywhere by an impatience to demolish (and relocate) old slums and ghettos, and in North America by a recognition that much of the desirable residential activity was in the suburbs. Many of the slum tenements of older cities were dreadful eyesores of deterioration, inhabited by recent immigrants and the poor; brand-new blocks of apartments, or bungalows, seemed a considerable improvement. Not until the early 1960s — perhaps beginning with the publication of Jane Jacobs' influential *The Death and Life of Great American Cities* (1961) — was the case made publicly that any urban renewal that destroyed existing organic neighbourhoods and communities in the process was retrogressive. Academics joined politicians, young professionals, and citizens' groups in insisting that any city planning that ignored the needs of people and neighbourhoods invited unforeseen damaging consequences.

Toronto probably went furthest in its rush to modernize because of the extent of its metropolitan growth. The model planned suburb of Don Mills was developed in the early 1950s; the city was associated with twelve suburban municipalities in 1953 to form Metropolitan Toronto. In 1954 the Yonge Street subway was opened; in 1964 it was extended by the east-west Bloor line. Toronto also built a series of bypass highways — the 401, the Gardiner Expressway, the Don Valley Parkway — to enable people to get quickly from one end of the metropolitan area to another. While not quite in the same league with Los Angeles, Toronto nevertheless was thinking in the same direction in terms of a freeway culture. With the ring-roads done, the developers moved to the inevitable inner-city connectors, such as the Spadina Expressway, which would give every resident ready access to the freeway system. But there were two problems. One was that superhighways created new traffic as much as they relieved old bottlenecks; by 1972 bypass highways like the 401 were multi-laned traffic jams of bumper-to-bumper vehicles at first during rush hours and eventually for almost the entire day. Improving connections between the city and its outskirts only prompted more people to move away or use the roads more frequently. The other problem was that freeways constructed in populated areas could be built only by tearing down existing housing and devastating neighbourhoods. An extended period of Toronto opposition finally managed to stop construction of a projected expressway in 1971, which brought to a symbolic end the period of unrestricted and unplanned expansion in the city. In Vancouver at about the same time, proposals to extend the Trans-Canada Highway into the city's centre, virtually demolishing many neighbourhoods — including the traditional Chinatown district — were fought to a standstill. By the later 1960s citizens' coalitions were at work in every Canadian city, attempting to control the developers who influenced most city councils and most city departments.

Urban development was orderly by comparison with what happened beyond existing settlement. New suburbs were created — usually well beyond zoning bylaws — by fast-talking developers who managed to convince rural municipal councils that population growth meant jobs (rather than new taxes and a totally changed community character). The principal attraction of the new suburbs was lower cost per square foot of house, which meant that land costs were kept down by not providing amenities (especially costly sewers) in advance. The ubiquitous septic tank (and the exceptionally green grass that grew above it) became the symbol of the true suburban bungalow. Leaving trees up in a developing subdivision cost more in building costs than knocking them down. So down came trees, although a few developers were willing to keep them around in return for a premium price for the lot. But in most suburban developments, planting new trees and shrubs (often in areas that had only recently been heavily forested) was the first outdoor task of the new homeowner. Drawing up for any new block only a handful of floor-plans — with roughly an identical number of bedrooms, floor area, and maximum mortgageable value — also saved money and made marketing easier. The number of amenities depended on price, and most builders were interested in the mass market at the lower end of the scale. The result was residential segregation based not on race or ethnicity but on number of children and ability to make mortgage payments.

No developer regarded the suburban creation of infrastructure — schools, hospitals, shopping centres, connecting roads — as part of his responsibility, and many buyers of the 1950s and 1960s would have shied away from any development whose community structure was predetermined. The trick was to sell houses to recent parents or the newly affluent — often the same people. The typical first-time suburban buyer was a young couple with two children, partly attracted to the suburb by the Canadian love of green grass, but mostly by cost. Marketing techniques tried to attract buyers by giving fantasy names to the developments themselves (Richmond Acres, Wilcox Lake, Beverly Hills) or to street names (Shady Lane, Sanctuary Drive, Paradise Crescent), but most newspaper advertisements concentrated on the price and down-payment required. Few buyers did much research into the surrounding amenities, most being influenced chiefly by internal house space and price.

Few suburbanites had any idea that they were the advance guard of a new Canadian lifestyle. Fewer still had had any real experience of suburbia, particularly those who were moving to developments well beyond the reach of sewers, libraries, cultural facilities, shopping, and urban transit. They had not deliberately abandoned the amenities of the city so much as they had been forced by the need for space to move beyond them. Their adjustment to new conditions became part of the major socio-cultural movement of the time.

The suburbs of the post-war period have acquired more than a bit of bad press, becoming exemplars of a vast identa-kit wasteland of intellectual vacuity, cultural sterility, and social conformity — Pete Seeger's "little boxes." They could be and sometimes were all those things, of course; but they were also the spawning ground of much of the revolt and rebellion of the 1960s.

The beginnings of the modern suburb can be found in eighteenth-century London, evolving gradually as "the collective creation of the bourgeois elite." Suburbanization began as an English phenomenon, extending to North America in the nineteenth century. Europe and Latin America remained committed to their central cities, as any visitor to Paris or Buenos Aires quickly realizes. By the twentieth century the United States had become the international centre of suburbanization. Canada lagged behind the Americans, as in so many other matters, and at least before 1945 had never previously pursued the middle-class suburb with the singlemindedness of its southern neighbours. Although there were many examples of Canadian suburbs before World War II — such as Lawrence Park in Toronto, Westmount in Montreal, Crescentwood in Winnipeg, and Shaughnessy Heights in Vancouver — they were not normally as autonomously divorced from the urban centre as their American counterparts.

As might be expected, a resurgence of traditional domestic values after World War II was accompanied by a revival of Christian commitment, at least in terms of formal church membership and attendance. All the usual indices of revival, from attendance figures to enrolment in seminaries, increased in Canada after the war for both Protestants and Catholics. There was no evidence that the deep-rooted problems of modern Christianity — including its identification with an outmoded morality and its reliance upon belief systems that were being challenged by secular thought — profoundly influenced increased church membership and attendance. The religious upturn of post-war Canada, like the Baby Boom, was a temporary and largely cosmetic aberrant blip in long-term trends. Not surprisingly, much of the vitality of Christianity appeared to be in the prospering suburbs. As one observer has commented, " . . . between 1945 and 1966 the United Church erected 1,500 new churches and church halls, and 600 new manses — many of them handsome rambling broadloomed ranch houses."

Suburban houses became "homes," easily the most expensive physical object possessed by their owners. For most Canadian suburbanites, so much time and emotional energy was devoted to their house that it often seemed to possess those who occupied it. The house focused the life of the nuclear family at the same time that it permitted individual members to have their own private space. The kitchen, for example, was seldom large enough to serve as a family room, although children of each sex were entitled to his or her own bedroom. Basement recreation rooms were developed to provide "space" for growing children. Technology increasingly turned the home into a self-regulating cocoon of constant temperature and convenience. Most consumer investments added new furnishings and appliances, not all of which were immediately visible to the stranger. The replacement of coal with oil and gas furnaces governed by thermostats, the introduction of automatic hot water heating, even the beginning of domestic air-conditioning, all insulated the inhabitants from an earlier world in which domesticity required hard work and constant vigilance. Now air temperature could almost be taken for granted — no mean accomplishment in the harsh Canadian climate. Those suburbanites who worried about "getting soft" assuaged their concerns with summer camping-trips and roughing it at the cottage.

Life in suburbia depended on a clear understanding of family roles. Husbands were the breadwinners, often working far away from the home, while their wives were actually responsible for its daily functioning. Most Canadian women had chosen — at least at war's end — to remain out of the work-force in order to enjoy marriage and child-rearing. They were reinforced in their decisions by articles in the women's journals exalting the roles of housewife and mother, and by advertising that appealed to their domesticity. At the same time that many women made "careers" as housewives and mothers, the sociologists of *Crestwood Heights: A North American Suburb* (1956) — a study based on Forest Hill Village, a wealthy residential area in Toronto — found a good deal of ambivalence over this decision and the values underlying it:

> The career of the woman in Crestwood Heights, compared with that of the man, contains many anomalies. Ideally, the man follows a continuous, if looping, spiral of development; the woman must pursue two goals and integrate them into one. The first goal has to do with a job, the second with matrimony and motherhood. The second, for the woman, is realized at the expense of the first; the man's two goals combine, since matrimony is expected to strengthen him for his work, and at it.

Even younger women away at university were confused. One confessed to an interviewer:

> Why I want to work — because I hope to express my personality through struggle and achievement. Why I want to get married — because my real role in society is that of wife and mother. If I don't get married, I will feel insecure — I will have no clearly defined role in society. I will probably sacrifice career to marriage if the opportunity comes because the rewards of marriage are obvious, those

of a career uncertain. In a way I envy those girls who only want to get married. They don't have to equate two conflicting desires.

For the female, suburbia was often little more than an arena in which this conflict was continually acted out.

Central to any suburban household were its children, around whose upbringing the lives of the parents increasingly revolved. The baby-boom generation of children were brought up in a child-centred environment, particularly in the home. Older standards of discipline and toughness in the parent–child relationship were replaced by permissiveness. New childrearing attitudes were influenced by all sorts of factors, but found their popular expression in *The Pocket Book of Baby and Child Care* by Benjamin Spock, M.D., which outsold the *Bible* in Canada in the years after the war. Many Canadian and American mothers referred to Spock as "God." Canada had its own semi-official child-care manual, *The Canadian Mother and Child*, by Ernest Couture, M.D. — director of the Division of Child and Maternal Health of the Department of National Health and Welfare — which was distributed free by doctors to pregnant women. It was a forbidding and austere grey-covered book, filled with slightly out-of-date photographs and a prim, no-nonsense style. Couture's advice to fathers was typical. They needed to accompany their wives on first visits to the doctor at the beginning of pregnancy; to understand what prenatal and postnatal care meant; and to adopt an attitude that was "patient, kind, and forebearing" during pregnancy, for women suffered from mood changes they were "quite unable to control." He also stressed cleanliness and good sanitation for the home: "Plumbing and drainage should be kept in good condition. Nothing is more destructive to a home, and to health, than leaky pipes and drains." Small wonder Canadian parents, at least in English-speaking Canada, preferred the folksy conversational approach of the American expert to the bleak advice of the Canadian.

The triumph in Anglo-Canada of Dr. Spock over Dr. Couture says a good deal about Canadian versus American style in the realm of culture. The Canadian approach was firmly élitist, with useful information produced at the top and trickled down to the potential "client." The American approach was frankly democratic and commercial, with useful information mass-marketed to the "consumer." Spock's book was one of the earliest mass-marketed paperbacks and sold over the counter at drug stores and supermarkets. In its pages the reader could find continual reassurance. Use your common sense, said Doctor Spock, for almost anything reasonable is okay. "Trust Yourself" was his first injunction. The good doctor came down fairly hard against coercion and forcing of the child, however. He was against early toilet training, for example, arguing, "Practically all those children who regularly go on soiling after 2 are those whose mothers have made a big issue about it and those who have become frightened by painful movements." While Spock seldom was this categorical about any child-rearing strategy — adopting a non-prescriptive position on breast-feeding versus bottle-feeding, for example — he was certainly not, in early editions, enthusiastic about working mothers:

> The important thing for a mother to realize is that the younger the child the more necessary it is for him to have a steady, loving person taking care of him. In most cases, the mother is the best one to give him this feeling of "belonging," safely and surely. She doesn't quit on the job, she doesn't turn against him, she isn't indifferent to him, she takes care of him always in the same familiar house. If the mother realizes clearly how vital this kind of care is to a small child, it may make it easier for her to decide that the extra money she might earn, or the satisfaction she might receive from an outside job, is not so important after all.

At the same time, Spock had more encouraging words for fathers than Dr. Couture, emphasizing that "You can be a warm father and a real man at the same time" while adding that it was "fine" for Dad to give bottles or change diapers "occasionally."

In opposing over-structured child-rearing practices, Spock may well have gone too far. But the post-war Canadian mother came to rely on his commonsensical advice. He saw that children passed through stages, and that once parents recognized what stage their child had reached, they could appreciate that seemingly incomprehensible behaviour and problems were quite common.

Spock's chapter on the adolescent, "Puberty Development," dealt with the sexual maturing of children, emphasized their awkwardness, and pointed out that most girls reached puberty two years ahead of boys. A full page was devoted to "Skin troubles in adolescence," particularly the pimples that the patent medicine folks labelled "teen-age acne." Spock was for washing the skin and against squeezing, which probably helps explain the folk wisdom of the era about those ubiquitous pimples. For suburbia, however, the adolescent was more than merely a creation of puberty. The "teenager" represented the emergence of a new generation that coincided with the maturing of the baby-boomers.

Both the elongation of the adolescent stage and its general significance took on new meaning in the two decades after the war. A general extension of the school-leaving age (and the expectation of suburbia's parents that children would continue their education beyond legal requirements) combined with the new affluence and permissiveness to produce large numbers of adolescents with considerable spending power. In English-speaking Canada teenagers became avid consumers — a recognizable market for fast food, popular music, acne medicine, and clothing fads.

For the new term "teenager," an English-language neologism, there is no equivalent in French. Obviously "adolescence" — the word is the same in both languages — does not carry the same cultural freight.

French Canada has never had a "teenage problem," but rather a *"problème de jeune,"* a quite different matter. It has also tended to view the suburb in physical rather than in cultural terms. In the autobiographical *Nègres blancs d'Amérique* (1968)/ *White Niggers of America* (1971), the radical Québécois Pierre Vallières (b. 1938) — who was jailed on charges connected with his FLQ activities and wrote his book in prison — suggests that men like his father had their own suburban fantasies:

> If only Madeleine [Vallières's mother] can agree to it, he said to himself. . . . We'll be at peace. The children will have all the room they need to play. We'll be masters in our own house. There will be no more stairs to go up and down. . . . Pierre won't hang around the alleys and sheds any more. . . . The owner was prepared to stretch the payments out over many years. . . . Life would become easier. . . . He would enlarge the house. A few years from now, Madeleine and the "little ones" would have peace and comfort.

And so in 1945 the Vallières family moved to Longueuil-Annexe: "the largest of an infinite number of little islands of houses springing up here, there, and everywhere out of the immense fields which in the space of a few years were to be transformed into a vast mushroom city."

Trade Unions in North America since 1945: A Comparison

CHRISTOPHER HUXLEY, DAVID KETTLER, and
JAMES STRUTHERS

In its labor relations as in many things, Canada has often been considered, since the Second World War, little more than an appendage to the United States. Patterns of union organization, collective bargaining, and labor law appear essentially similar in both countries, and, indeed, many of the unions and large employers are the same. The Americans have provided models and, often, the leadership. But the past few years have brought about some interesting changes. Starting in the late 1950s, the extent of unionization in the United States first stagnated and then started to decline, while all measures of union involvement in labor relations in Canada began a steady increase, which continues. Not surprisingly, a number of American unionists and academic specialists have become curious about differences between the two situations.

The AFL-CIO Committee on the Evolution of Work, in a widely publicized report on the causes and possible remedies for the failure

SOURCE: "Is Canada's Experience 'Especially Instructive'?" in Seymour Martin Lipset, ed., *Unions in Transition* (San Francisco: ICS Press, 1986), pp. 113–32. Reprinted with permission.

of the American trade union movement to keep up with the expansion of the work force, well illustrates this interest. "The Canadian experience is especially instructive," the Committee remarks. With "roughly the same kind of economy," "many similar employers," and comparable changes affecting the labor market, "the percentage of the civilian labor force that is organized increased in the period 1963–1983 from roughly 30 percent to 40 percent, at the same time that the percentage of organized workers declined in the United States from 30 percent to 20 percent."[1] Following an analysis developed by several of its most influential economic advisers, the Committee saw differences in public labor policy as the principal cause for the divergence. "In Canada, unlike in the United States," it maintains, "the government has not defaulted in its obligation to protect the rights of self-organization."[2]

The AFL-CIO Committee refers, here, mainly to legal and administrative policies concerning certification of unions as bargaining agents and to sanctions against unfair labor practices by employers. There is no doubt that differences in these respects are important. But a statement by a different union organization on another occasion suggests a complementary approach to the differences between American and Canadian developments.

At the end of 1984, the Canadian section of the United Auto Workers (UAW), the sixth largest union in Canada, comprising about 10 percent of the parent international union, made demands for autonomy that were so sweeping that they led to separation. In explaining and justifying his proposals, the Canadian UAW Director, Robert White, repeatedly stressed that the Canadian union had to gain the freedom to pursue its "separate program." And this program was said to include not only a distinct set of bargaining priorities for the automobile industry but also a "Canadian labour movement program" in which the UAW had "a responsibility to play a lead role."[3]

White stressed the rejection by the Canadian UAW and the Canadian Labour Congress of the "concession era" in collective bargaining and their determination to "address the issue of jobs through political action" and through collective bargaining efforts to shorten the working day.[4] His union had already parted company with the international in the 1982 auto industry negotiations, refusing to accept profit sharing in lieu of regular increases, and in 1984 it had carried its disagreement to the point of a strike against General Motors rather than accepting the lump sum increases negotiated in Detroit.

It would be a journalistic oversimplification to trace differences that also involve pragmatic readings of distinctive market situations to a contrast between "business unionists" at the head of the American union, and the Canadian "social democrats." Yet, White and the Canadian UAW do represent a conception of the relationship between collective bargaining and broader political aims, as well as of strategies, which is more prevalent and influential in the Canadian labor movement than it has been in the American, especially during the past two decades.[5]

We suggest that the differences in governmental policies and practices noted by the AFL-CIO Committee, in its brief allusion to Canada, must be seen in conjunction with differences in the outlook and activities of unions, epitomized by the Canadian UAW's reasons for separation. Some commentators have spoken of the greater "militancy" of Canadian auto workers. Indeed, more generally, Rose and Chaison's study of the contrasting contemporary states of American and Canadian unions has suggested that the greater militancy of many Canadian unions — as measured, for example, by major indicators of overall strike activity during the years of growing divergence in density rates — cannot be ignored as a possible factor in the divergence itself.[6]

We relate American and Canadian union membership patterns to differences between the two labor regimes, defining the latter term as the "principles, norms, rules and decision-making processes around which actor-expectations converge in a given issue-area,"[7] along with the constellation of power upon which the arrangement rests.

Canada maintains adversarial collective bargaining within legal constraints that limit but also normalize the pattern. In the U.S., by contrast, the adversarial relationship within the labor regime has been moved back a step, in the direction of struggle over the legitimacy and normality of the collective bargaining pattern itself. This does not imply a "pro-labor policy" in Canada. Like other modern states, Canada is conditioned by public economic policies to manage the labor market in the interests of economic growth. Compared to the U.S., however, this management has proceeded more frequently through negotiations at the highest level or through *ad hoc* interventions that regulate or supersede collective bargaining, especially in the public sector, rather than through a weakening of the competitive position of organized labor within the adversarial system.[8]

Employers in America are more apt in general to pursue the goal of "union-free organizations," especially in new and growing sectors, and unions accept limitations imposed by employer resistance. Canadian employers and unions are both more willing to accept one another, and commit themselves more directly and blindingly to political parties. Although the labor-funded, socialist New Democratic Party (NDP) has never threatened the preponderant electoral position of the other two parties (Liberals and Progressive Conservatives) in federal elections, it has occupied a strategic "balance-of-power" position during periods of minority government, and it has been the governing or official opposition party in several of the more important provinces, whose governments in Canada control the bulk of labor policy. Unlike the American trade union movement, which has been divided from an important segment of its historical political support since the 1960s, the NDP has remained intact.

In short, the stronger position of Canadian unions has nothing to do with "mutualism" or long-term cooperation, which some have urged upon American unions as a new direction.[9] It seems doubtful that the lessons of this experience — if any can be transferred — are compatible with the American unions' preference for alternatives to the "adversarial collective bargaining relationship" or to the extreme caution with regard to political alliances implied in the AFL-CIO report.

Union Density in Canada and the U.S.

Data on unionization in Canada and the U.S. have been available since the early 1920s.[10] Table 1 shows changes in union density for each country for selected years between 1920 and 1984.

For more than half of the past sixty years, union membership density in Canada has exceeded that of the U.S. The major exception occurred in the long period of rapid union growth in the U.S. beginning in 1933. A corresponding breakthrough in union organization in Canada was not achieved until the end of World War II. This illustrates the uneven patterns of union growth in the two countries and raises a question about the most recent developments.

The most dramatic periods of union growth in the U.S. and Canada have taken place at different times, with different durations. Bain and Price note that over the years 1921–1977 the annual rate of change in union density fluctuated considerably more widely in the U.S. (ranging between –16.1 percent and +38.8 percent) than in Canada (where the range was between –13.8 percent and +19.0).[11] But if allowance is made for this difference in the amplitude of fluctuations in union growth, the similarity between the general trends in union density in the two countries for the first two-thirds of the period since the early 1920s becomes apparent. This similarity came to an end by the early 1960s. Since then, as noted by the AFL-CIO committee, the two patterns of union growth have diverged sharply.

The question nevertheless arises whether this continuing and increasing difference in union densities represents another expression of unevenness, and this question leads us to look carefully for signs of a return to similarity. Comparison between the two countries reveals no other instance of opposing tendencies at work for so long a period. For almost twenty-five years now, the two labor movements have been progressing along quite different trajectories. The longest period of sustained union growth in the U.S. extends from 1933 to 1947, although, as we shall show later, this is more correctly viewed as two distinct phases, the New Deal and World War II, with the union growth of the latter being followed shortly in Canada. Most other periods of union growth in the U.S. comprise gains over relatively short periods of time. For the years covered by our comparisons, Derber points to the periods 1950–1953 and

TABLE 1   Canadian and American Union Densities,[a] Selected Years, 1921–1984

	Canada (Labour Canada)	United States (BLS)	
	(percent)		
1921	16.0	18.3	
1924	12.2	11.9	
1927	12.1	11.3	
1930	13.1	11.6	
1933	16.7	11.3	
1936	16.2	13.7	
1939	17.3	28.6	
1942	20.6	25.9	
1945	24.2	35.5	
1948	30.3	31.9	
1951	28.4	33.3	
1954	33.8	34.7	
1957	32.4	32.8	
1960	32.3	31.4	
1963	29.8	29.1	
1966	30.7	28.1	
1969	32.5	27.0	(29.5)[b]
1972	34.6	26.4	(29.4)
1975	36.9	25.3	(28.9)
1978	39.0	23.6	(26.2)
1980	37.6	N/A[c]	(24.6)
1981	37.4	N/A[d]	
1982	39.0	N/A[e]	
1983	40.0	20.7[e]	
1984	39.6	19.5[e]	

[a]Union membership as a percentage of nonagricultural work force.
[b]Starting in 1968, the BLS statistics add data on both unions and employee associations. Figures in parentheses include members of both types of organizations.
[c]Separate statistics for union members were unavailable in the 1980 survey.
[d]Data have not been collected by the BLS since 1981.
[e]Data supplied by Troy (see his chapter 3 in [Seymour Martin Lipset, ed., *Unions in Transition* (San Francisco: ICS Press, 1986)]) are drawn from a different series from that of the BLS and are not strictly comparable. They are, however, indicative, and correspond to the figures which the AFL-CIO Committee appears to have available.

Sources: Canadian union density: G.N. Chaison, "Unions: Growth, Structure, and Internal Dynamics," in John Anderson and Morley Gunderson, eds., *Union-Management Relations in Canada* (Don Mills, Ontario: Addison-Wesley, 1982), p. 149, for the years 1921–1980. Minister of Labour (Labour Canada), *Directory of Labour Organizations in Canada, 1984* (Ottawa: Minister of Supply and Services Canada, 1984), p. xxvi, for the years 1981–1984. United States union density: G.S. Bain and R. Price, *Profiles of Union Growth* (Oxford: Blackwell, 1981), pp. 88–89 for the years 1921–1975. J.B. Rose and G.N. Chaison, "The State of the Unions: United States and Canada," *Journal of Labor Research 6:1* (Winter 1985), p. 99 for the years 1976–1980. L. Troy, "The Rise and Fall of American Trade Unions: The Labor Movement from FDR to RR" (see chapter 3 in [Seymour Martin Lipset, ed., *Unions in Transition* (San Francisco: ICS Press, 1986)]) for the years 1983–1984.

1965–1970 (although the latter spurt in membership did not suffice to interrupt the decline in union density, since the nonagricultural work force grew faster).[12] In Canada, comparable periods of abrupt union expansion occurred during both world wars. In contrast to continuing union decline in the U.S. since the late 1950s, the Canadian upturn in the early 1960s has been sustained and represents a longer-term phenomenon deserving explanation.

Divergences in union growth in the U.S. and Canada might be understood by looking at the overall industrial distribution of employment in the two countries. Meltz finds, however, that this will not explain matters. He reports that if the pattern of employment in Canada in 1980 had been the same in the U.S., and if existing Canadian rates of union organization had pertained, the overall level of union density for Canada would have been about 10 percent higher than its actual figure. In sum, he writes, "if Canada were more like the United States in its employment distribution there would be a greater difference in the overall rates of organization."[13]

A related argument, which Meltz also considers, is that particular occupational groups can account for most of the difference in union densities. More extensive unionization of the public sector in Canada, for example, might provide an explanation. While this is an important factor, it does not stand alone. Meltz reports that by 1980 — in contrast to the mid-1960s, when industry groups such as construction, transportation, communications, and public utilities, for example, were more unionized in the U.S. — all broad occupational sectors were more highly unionized in Canada than in the U.S. Weiler concludes that "Developments in the public sectors of the two countries . . . cannot explain the divergent . . . union density in the two countries."[14] An indicator of private sector union growth in Canada noted by Rose and Chaison is that Canadian sections of "international" unions have been increasing as a proportion of the overall membership, while American memberships have fallen or at best held steady.[15]

Structural changes in the composition of the labor force in both the U.S. and Canada since World War II have been well documented, with a similar relative decline in the manufacturing sector and a relative growth of government and service related sectors. But the patterns of unionization in the two countries still reveal a sharp contrast. As Meltz observes:

> In both countries, had there been no other changes, the shift in employment towards trade, finance, and service employees would have lowered overall rates of unionization. A decrease did not occur in Canada because membership rates grew in these industries and remained unchanged in the others. A net decline occurred in the United States because the growth of unionization in trade, finance, service and government was not sufficient to offset the declining rates of organization in the other sectors.[16]

The data are strong and consistent. Like the other observers who have considered them, we do not see any promising purely economic explanations. We believe, rather, that the historical differences between the labor regimes provide the most promising starting point.[17]

Disparate Developments toward Similarity: Canadian and American Unionism, 1935–1964

During and for the three decades immediately following World War II, the relations among labor, business, and the state stabilized within the U.S. and Canada. In both nations this "settlement" was supported by similar legal frameworks, deriving from the design of the U.S. National Labor Relations (Wagner) Act of 1935. In return for government recognition of workers' rights to collective bargaining, trade unions in both countries agreed to institutionalize labor conflict within conditioned terms of entry, collective agreements, and tactics. The corresponding agreement by business groups seems more reluctant, qualified, and by no means universally accepted; and the history of settlements has been marked by efforts by some parts of the business community — and intermittent efforts by many — to undo it. The labor regimes, accordingly, are characterized by political conflicts, notwithstanding their settled appearance.

Despite similarities in the shape of the labor "settlements" in Canada and the U.S., the process by which they were achieved and their subsequent durability differed significantly. In the U.S., the evolution of a *more regulatory* labor regime took place in three distinct stages between 1935 and 1952. During the first stage, lasting from 1935 through 1937, industrial unionism achieved its initial breakthroughs in America's mass production industries. After 1937, however, this initial organizing impetus was stalled by a new recession and employer resistance. Only the onset of World War II completed the dramatic recovery of American trade unionism. By virtue of full employment, expanding business profits, effective organization, and vigorous regulatory protection by the National War Labor Board, mass production unionism broke through the last barrier of "open shop" resistance. CIO membership more than doubled, and by the war's end approximately 35 percent of the American nonagricultural work force were union members.[18]

The years 1946–52 marked the third stage of the American labor settlement. The postwar strike wave of 1945–47, combined with a political reaction against wartime controls associated with labor's political allies, fostered legislative responsiveness to business campaigns against union power. The 80th Congress passed the Taft-Hartley Act, placing substantial new limits on trade unions — including restrictions on the closed shop, a ban on secondary boycotts and sympathy strikes, the provision of sweeping new federal labor injunctions, the prohibition of strikes in cases of national emergency — and granting state governments the authority to outlaw union shops for employees otherwise under federal jurisdiction.[19]

Despite a concerted campaign, the American labor movement was unable to secure the repeal of Taft-Hartley. Union membership grew modestly during the early 1950s, but organized labor, in an increasingly unfriendly political environment, was unable to recover the organizing momentum of the 1941-46 era. Reaching a postwar peak in 1953-54 of nearly 35 percent of the nonagricultural work force, union density in the U.S. began a slow decline, which continues to the present.

Within Canada, a broadly similar labor settlement emerged during the 1940s, but the process was telescoped within a much shorter time period and did not come up against as sweeping a legislative backlash as Taft-Hartley. Canada's labor situation is also conditioned by a difference in constitutional doctrine. Under a 1925 decision, Canadian federalism was interpreted to place labor law jurisdiction over 90 percent of the work force in the provinces. During the 1930s, Canadian trade unions enjoyed no legislative protection. Federal labor legislation remained oriented towards the avoidance of work stoppages, not union recognition. The Industrial Disputes Investigation Act of 1907 provided elaborate procedures for conciliation, including compulsory "cooling-off" periods before strikes could lawfully occur. Although this legislation ceased to apply to cases placed under provincial jurisdiction after 1925, it continued to set the tone. As a consequence, Canadian unions, for the most part, failed to achieve major breakthroughs equivalent to the 1937 recognition drives of the CIO in the U.S. On the eve of World War II, unionization in Canada was making gradual headway, compared to the American experience of a steady steep climb.

World War II transformed Canadian, as well as U.S., labor. During the first three years of Canadian involvement, the federal government attempted to manage the war effort without significant reform in labor legislation. Through the legislative authority of the War Measures Act, which superseded provincial jurisdictions, it enforced compulsory conciliation, wage controls, and compulsory allocation of essential labor. However, it refused to establish compulsory union recognition or collective bargaining.[20] The gains of Canadian unions during much of the war were less dramatic and more uncertain as collective bargaining relationships than in the U.S.

Yet there was a breakthrough. It was directly linked to labor unrest, unprecedented until that time. Denied legislative protection, Canadian unions refused to agree to a wartime no-strike pledge, unlike many American unions to which some were affiliated. By 1943, a larger proportion of workers was on strike than in any years since 1919. Equally important was the growth in support for the socialist Co-operative Commonwealth

Federation (CCF) — the electoral organization that would later, with official labor backing, become the NDP — outside of its prairie heartland in Saskatchewan. A 1943 Gallup Poll revealed that it was Canada's most popular party, and during the same year, the CCF came within four seats of forming the government of Ontario, Canada's most industrialized province.

Faced with evidence of working-class militancy, Canada's provincial and federal governments rushed to implement a new labor settlement. In 1943, Ontario passed a collective bargaining act which closely duplicated the main provisions of the American Wagner Act. Quebec followed suit a year later. But because of the sweep of wartime powers, temporarily shifting jurisdiction to the center, the framework for Canada's postwar labor settlement was laid down by Mackenzie King's government through federal Privy Council Order-in-Council 1003. Borrowing heavily from the Wagner Act, P.C. 1003 established procedures for union certification and a modest conception of unfair labor practices, as well as national regulation. Under P.C. 1003, key industries such as steel were successfully organized for the first time, and "recognition" strikes ebbed for the remainder of the war. In some contrast with the U.S., legislative protection for trade unions was extracted from a reluctant state through a combination of strike activity and the growth of a socialist party.

During 1945–47, Canada experienced a postwar strike wave similar to that in the U.S.: unions fought for security clauses and substantial wage increases once wartime controls were lifted. In contrast to the U.S., however, the postwar strike wave did not provoke an immediate backlash against the power of trade unions. In 1948, the Industrial Relations and Disputes Investigation Act put into statute form the wartime provisions of P.C. 1003 by grafting American Wagner Act certification and recognition onto Canada's procedures for strike avoidance. More importantly, the provinces had regained primary jurisdiction over labor relations, and all nine provinces moved to duplicate P.C. 1003.

In Canada, as in the U.S. during the 1950s, organized labor appeared to approach a high-water mark. Trade unionism continued to make modest gains in existing sources of strength, reaching a peak in 1956 similar to that achieved in the U.S. two or three years earlier. Despite this growth, Jamieson observes that by 1956, "virtually all the workers that were organizable in terms of prevailing union techniques, finances, ideologies and policies, had been enrolled."[21]

After 1956, escalating unemployment and anti-union provincial legislation frustrated union hopes for expansion. Unemployment in Canada between 1957 and 1962, which was more prolonged and severe than in the U.S., increased the pressure for restrictive legislation and facilitated its passage. Unemployment also took its toll. Despite an outburst of strikes in 1958, unrest had ebbed by 1960 to its lowest point since the war.

Economic recovery combined with new political leverage for labor, thanks to the reorganization of the old CCF with official labor support as the NDP, to reverse dramatically this pattern of union decline during the remainder of the decade. From 1961 onward, Canada experienced a cycle of union growth and militancy, culminating in strikes during 1965-66 far beyond any level of unrest in the U.S. Rank-and-file frustration with contracts negotiated during the 1958-62 recession, which failed to keep pace with inflation, and anger at attacks on union rights, particularly injunctions against strikes and picketing, produced bitter disputes across Canada. During 1965-66 large extra-legal walkouts by Sudbury nickel miners, Hamilton steelworkers, Montreal longshoremen, and railway and postal workers across Canada, suggested that Canada's postwar settlement was coming apart.[22]

Out of 617 Canadian strikes in 1966, involving 411,459 workers, almost one-third were "wildcats."[23] A number of these, including the longshore, railway, and postal disputes, were only settled by legislative intervention, as the minority federal government of the time, under pressure from the New Democrats, conceded annual wage increases in excess of 18 percent. Mass picketing in the 1960s and early 1970s ended use of *ex parte* injunctions, as provincial governments, in the face of such widespread unrest and rising support for the NDP, adopted conciliatory approaches. Under these new conditions, unionization in the private sector began a sustained new growth.

Public Sector Unionism

Between 1956 and the early 1960s, there was a parallel decline in union density in Canada and the U.S., although the Canadian level did not drop as steeply. In both countries, public sector unionization during the 1960s and 1970s provided the main impetus for revitalization. But public sector unionism in Canada and the U.S. has differed significantly, with impact upon the shape of the labor movement in each. While the decline in union density continued in the U.S. after 1964, with new gains failing to compensate either for losses or the growth of the nonagricultural labor force, the Canadian curve moved sharply upward, surpassing all previous peaks by the early 1970s. Public sector unionism made a greater quantitative difference in Canada than in the U.S., and it also appears to have made a greater qualitative difference, strengthening the elements of aggressiveness and competitiveness in the movement. The Canadian labor mobilization of the mid-1960s, which changed the condition of private sector unionism as well, is unthinkable without the activities of employees in the public sector.

In both countries, the rapid expansion of public sector employment, particularly at the provincial or state and local levels, in the two decades following World War II, provided a major impetus to public sector unionization. By the mid-1970s, one in every five U.S. wage and salary earners worked for some level of government; and in Canada, the proportion reached one in four.[24]

In both Canada and the U.S., the conditions of closely contested political changes during the 1960s provided organized labor with opportunities for extending bargaining rights into the public sector. During the closely fought presidential election of 1960, organized labor's support of John F. Kennedy proved decisive. In 1961, federal employees gained the right to unionize but not to strike or to bargain collectively over wages and benefits, which remained within the exclusive purview of Congress. As a result, federal public sector unionism in large measure remains confined to "the development of a grievance and advisory arbitration procedure,"[25] keeping unions cut off from many aspects of the employment relationship, especially compensation issues. A majority of state governments followed the federal lead. By 1977, thirty-eight states had extended collective bargaining rights to their employees; however, many state and local governments also extensively restricted the scope and conditions of collective bargaining.

Despite these limitations, the result of these reforms was that American public sector unionism achieved considerable growth in the 1960s and 1970s, particularly at the state, county, and local levels, which had a later start and vast numbers. By 1978, 23.5 percent of America's total public work force belonged to unions and 39 percent belonged to unions and employee associations combined.[26] The AFL-CIO Committee on the Evolution of Work claimed in 1985 that "approximately 50 percent of full-time state and local government employees are organized."[27]

In Canada, public sector unionism also achieved major breakthroughs in the 1960s, but the extent of unionization and scope of bargaining rights moved far beyond that of U.S. public workers. Indeed, it seems plausible that the greater unionization, militancy, and bargaining rights of Canadian public employees, by virtue of their indirect effects on the union movement as well as by their direct effects on membership figures, account for at least some present-day differences between the two countries. Public sector bargaining in Canada has a longer history than in the U.S. More importantly, as was also the case with collective bargaining in the private sphere, public sector unionism burgeoned in Canada during the 1960s through a more contentious process of political confrontation and engagement at both the provincial and federal level. By the late 1950s, the growing intrusion of federal and provincial governments into labor disputes was unintentionally paving the way for public sector unionization. As Jamieson argues:

> Where governments were directly or indirectly recommending standards and influencing rates of pay, hours and conditions of work and fringe benefits in industries operating under "free enterprise" and "free" collective bargaining,

via compulsory conciliation procedures, they provided a strong and growing inducement for employees of public utilities or publicly regulated enterprises and of governments themselves to seek comparable gains through collective bargaining and, if need be, by strike action.[28]

During the early 1960s, the politics of Quebec's "Quiet Revolution" took this process even further. Throughout the late 1950s, Quebec's national trade union movement, led by Jean Marchand, had backed the provincial Liberal Party in its efforts to overthrow the quasi-authoritarian, clericalist "anti-labor" Union Nationale government of Maurice Duplessis. When the Liberals successfully took power in 1960, Marchand's influence was soon apparent. In 1965, as part of its concessions to labor in the period leading up to a new election, the Liberal government enacted a new labor code granting full collective bargaining rights, including the right to strike, to almost all public employees in the province.

During the summer of 1965, postal workers in most major Canadian cities staged an illegal "wildcat" strike demanding pay and benefit increases. The Quebec developments, postal walkout, and the parliamentary position of the NDP convinced the minority Liberal federal government to extend collective bargaining to its own employees. Under the Public Service Staff Relations Act of 1967, federal employees were given not only the right to bargain collectively over wages and benefits and most other aspects of the employment relationship but also the right to choose between two bargaining routes: one leading to compulsory arbitration and the other to the strike option.[29] Within a decade, other Canadian jurisdictions once again followed the federal lead. Between 1962 and 1977, government employee unionism had grown by 150 percent, accounting for a large proportion of Canada's overall union growth.[30] Coincident with the legal transformation of the collective bargaining status of public employees, restrictions on private sector unionization were eased. The new wave of organization brought heightened influence and energy, strengthening the more socially minded and political elements of labor.

It is arguable that the greater extent, scope, centralization, and militancy of Canadian public sector unionism provoked [a] cycle of exceptional legislation in Canada, notably temporary "emergency" wage controls, beginning in 1975, and more recently [early 1980s], comparatively frequent back-to-work legislation to end strikes. If the pre-1962 interventionism of the Canadian state played a major role in stimulating the growth of public sector unionism, so too, paradoxically, has labor's very success since the 1960s provoked an even higher level of interventionism during the 1970s and 1980s, as Canadian governments at all levels attempt to contain public sector spending.[31] Public sector unionism may have rounded out the postwar labor settlement, while at the same time putting it in jeopardy.

Conclusion: Law and Politics

The cumulative effect of the differences between the Canadian and American labor regimes, overall, is to give the adversarial system of collective bargaining greater weight in Canada, and this difference helps importantly to account for the declining membership and coverage of American trade unions. Paradoxical as it may seem, collective bargaining is not losing ground in the United States because unions are less attractive, but unions are less attractive because collective bargaining is losing ground.

A brief summary of the differences between the current state of the two regulative schemes, so similar in basic features, will substantiate this contention. It will also show why the AFL-CIO Committee on the Evolution of Work stressed legal policy and administration in its analysis. First, Canadian jurisdictions have a more categorical prohibition on strikes during the life of a collective agreement than most American law, and they back this up with legislative provision for mandatory grievance arbitration, whether the agreement includes it or not (and recently, in several key jurisdictions, with provision for quick and comparatively inexpensive arbitration). Unions commonly cannot legally strike after an impasse has been reached in negotiations until there has been an attempt at conciliation by a public official and a finding by the minister that further conciliation efforts will not bear fruit. As a practical matter, this means above all that there must be considerable notice given before there can be a legal strike or lockout. In addition, the strike must be supported by a majority vote of the entire bargaining unit in a secret ballot (and recent legislation in some jurisdictions also allows the employer to demand one secret ballot on his last offer at any time before or during a strike). But there is some reason for believing that these requirements may do more to establish a bargaining ritual, involving mutually supportive interplay between union negotiators and members and culminating in a solemn strike authorization, than they do to deter strikes. In any case, many negotiations go to the conciliation stage, and settlements that wait for the last minute or brief strikes are common. On the whole, the adversarial style of the Canadian trade union movement appears to be reinforced by this regulation of the strike decision.[32]

A second significant difference between Canadian and American labor law during recent decades, as noted earlier, concerns the collective bargaining rights of employees in the public sector. Since the mid-1960s, most jurisdictions provide these employees with rights and procedures that approximate those of workers in private employment, especially with regard to the forms of organization and the scope of permissible collective bargaining. Not all jurisdictions allow public employees the right to strike, and none allows that right to all categories, but even where alternative modes of impasse resolution are mandated, arbitrators usually have been given a much freer hand to adjudicate interest issues than is possible under comparable American law.[33] Expansion of collective bargaining in this sector has also been a prominent feature of American developments during the past two decades, but the extent, scope, and conflictual character of public sector unionization in Canada make the legal differences worth underlining.

The third important area of difference concerns the divergent legislative, administrative, and judicial implementations of the shared principles of voluntary choice, certification of exclusive bargaining agents, and good faith bargaining, as well as the remedies provided. These are different enough to be seen by several observers as the principal cause of the differences in unionization trends.[34] In no Canadian jurisdiction is it the case at the time of this writing, as in the United States, that all certification applications which are not voluntarily consented to by employers must be approved by majority decision in a secret ballot of everyone in the bargaining unit, with the elections preceded by a campaign that may last months, during which time the employer enjoys guaranteed privileges of "free speech" regarding the choice to be made. The most common rule in Canadian jurisdictions is automatic certification where more than 55 or 60 percent of the bargaining unit are shown to have signaled their adhesion to the union by the signing of membership cards and the payment of a nominal sum for dues. Where certification elections are required (including in Nova Scotia, which has been exceptional in requiring elections in all cases), they occur within a few days of the formal request for certification and, in many jurisdictions, interventions by employers are restrained by express legislative provisions for automatic certification where employee preferences cannot be clearly ascertained because of employer action.[35] Canada has seen nothing like the dramatic expansion of active management opposition to unionization that is indicated by the growth in the United States of consultancies specializing in preventing certification, the rise of discriminatory dismissals of union supporters during organizing campaigns, the decline of consent certifications, and the consistent failure of unions to win more than half of the certification elections.[36] In contrast to the existence of numerous states with "right-to-work" laws outlawing important forms of union security, the most important Canadian jurisdictions now eliminate free-riding by nonunion members of certified bargaining units by making the agency shop universal.[37] Although the policy is not universal, there have been well-noted labor board decisions limiting the power of companies to shift operations away from unionized sites.[38] Canadian law is moving toward increased backing for the actual establishment of a collective bargaining relationship after the preliminary step of certification. Four jurisdictions already have legislation allowing the imposition of a binding first agreement by governmental action if negotiations fail, and there is a strong likelihood that several others will follow suit.[39] In sum, it is fair to say that the Canadian legal design overall serves in greater measure to encourage, as the Ontario legislation purposes, "the practice and procedure of collective bargaining between the employers and trade unions as the freely designated representatives of employees," and that it is prepared to limit some of the otherwise preponderant power of employers in order to achieve this, without interfering with the effects of the power disparity, especially in a weak economy, *within* the collective bargaining relationship. While the similar language in the preamble of the National Labor Relations Act has never been repealed, it would be more accurate to say that the American legal scheme now *allows* rather than *encourages* such bargaining, and that it also allows comparatively free play to the very considerable forces opposed to it.

But the most striking difference between the Canadian and American movements during the [1970s and 1980s] is the increasing importance of more adversarial and political unionism in Canada, marked above all by the interdependence and effective mutual aid between key unions and the New Democratic Party in English Canada, and analogous developments in Quebec involving a more electorally amorphous and even an extra-parliamentary left. This occurred at a time when American unions found their distinctive concerns only intermittently of interest to the presidential and much of the congressional Democratic Party, notwithstanding AFL-CIO attempts to broaden legitimacy by attempting to represent all socially-disadvantaged or even "consumer-class interests" in general.[40] In view of the differences between the two political cultures and institutional frameworks, and in some major social values, as well, it is not clear whether the Canadian experience can be of much help to American unionists and others who are troubled by the decline of American unionism.

NOTES

1. *The Changing Situation of Workers and Their Unions*, A Report by the AFL-CIO Committee on the Evolution of Work (Washington, D.C.: AFL-CIO, February, 1985), p. 15.
2. Ibid.; Richard B. Freeman, "Why Are Unions Faring Poorly in NLRB Representation Elections," in Thomas Kochan, ed., *Challenges and Choices Facing American Labor* (Cambridge, Mass.: MIT Press, 1986); Paul Weiler, "Promises to Keep: Securing Workers' Rights to Self-Organization under the NLRA," *Harvard Law Review* 96 (June 1983), pp. 1769-1827. Himself a Canadian, a prominent labor arbitrator, and former Chairman of the Labour Relations Board in British Columbia, Weiler is not embarrassed to speak of "the Canadian model," in both senses of the latter term; for a more publicistic use of the same comparison, see Bob Kuttner, "Can Labor Lead?" *The New Republic*, March 12, 1984.
3. Robert White, "Report of UAW Director for Canada and International Vice President Robert White," December 1 and 2, 1984, unpublished document, p. 33.
4. UAW Canada, *Building a New Union in Canada*, p. 11.
5. For illustrative contrasting journalistic assessments, see James Bagnall, "UAW's White Takes Next Step in Independence Fight," *Financial Post*, December 15, 1984, p. 12 and Wilfred List, "Little Change in Store for Independent Canadian UAW," *Globe and Mail*, April 15, 1985, p. B5. The head of the Canadian Labour Congress, himself a member of the UAW,

welcomed White's move with the following statement: "The facts are that we are not clones of Americans. We do have a different society, and a different culture, a different political system and a different judicial system. As workers, our economic and social goals in the collective bargaining system are distinctly different . . . " *Canadian Labour*, January, 1985, p. 7. But this brought a quick warning against overstatement from a meeting of Directors of other Canadian international industrial unions, assembled by the Canadian director of the United Steel Workers. See Wilfred List, "Autonomy Issue Creates a Stir on the Labour Scene," *Globe and Mail*, February 18, 1985, p. B8. For background on recent developments in relations between Canadian unionists and international unions, see Mark Thompson and Albert A. Blum, "International Unionism in Canada: The Move to Local Control," *Industrial Relations* 22 (Winter 1983). Additional sources of internal conflict, undermining the capacity of the CLC to speak for all Canadian unions, are illustrated in Joseph B. Rose, "Some Notes on the Building Trades–Canadian Labour Congress Dispute," *Industrial Relations* 22 (Winter 1983), pp. 97–111. The actions taken by the UAW and the support for them from the head of the CLC (as well as the head of the Ontario Federation of Labour, another UAW member) are indicative of something very important, but they are not representative for the complex movement in any simple sense.

6. Joseph B. Rose and Gary N. Chaison, "The State of the Unions: United States and Canada," *Journal of Labor Research* 6 (Winter 1985), pp. 97–111, at p. 108. In average annual totals of days lost per thousand workers, Canada was second only to Italy among major industrial nations during 1960–1970 as well as 1971–1982. But it should be noted that there has been a dramatic decline, with 1983 totals only 50% of the 1981 figure and 28% of the 1982 one. Bradley M. Dow, "The Labour Movement and Trade Unionism: Summary Outline (June 1984)" in W.D. Wood and Pradeep Kumar, eds., *The Current Industrial Relations Scene in Canada, 1984* (Kingston: Queen's University Industrial Relations Centre, 1984). Rose and Chaison naturally weigh economic as well as other legal and political factors, as does another respected Canadian specialist, who has also published a recent valuable analysis and comparison. See also Noah M. Meltz, "Labor Movements in Canada and the United States," in Kochan, op. cit. We are greatly indebted to both of these earlier publications.

7. Stephen D. Krasner, "Structural causes and regime consequences: regimes as intervening variables," *International Organization* 36 (Spring 1982), p. 185.

8. Leo Panitch and Donald Swartz, "Towards Permanent Exceptionalism: Coercion and Consent in Canadian Industrial Relations," *Labour/Le Travail* 13 (Spring 1984), pp. 133–57. Recent changes and proposals in British Columbia, Alberta, and Quebec may indicate some shift towards the American design, but this is by no means clear, and the force of the resistance makes these exceptions, which on the whole prove the rule. David McMurray, "Labour and Policy: Summary Outline," in Wood and Kumar, op. cit., pp. 93ff. More characteristic of the longer-term pattern is the fact that the Ontario legislation, which for a time replaced all negotiated salary settlements of public employees (very broadly defined) with a standard increment, constructively interpreted a considerable variety of arrangements as if they were collective agreements, and expressly put those who could not be said to be under such agreements at a possible disadvantage. It is arguable of course that such a design, since it binds unions to discipline its members to comply with the settlements imposed in the guise of collective agreements, is eventually more damaging to the integrity of the labor movement than almost anything else. The question plays an important part in debates about the failure of the German trade union movement to resist Hitler, since very similar legislation was a recurrent feature of Chancellor Bruening's policy between 1930 and 1932. See Hans-Hermann Hartwich, *Arbeitsmarkt, Verbaende und Staat, 1918–1933* (Berlin: Walter de Gruyter, 1967); Andreas Kaiser, "Probleme gewerkschaftliche Politik in der Endphaese der Weimarer Republik," *Blaetter fuer deutsche und Internationale Politik* 9 (September 1980), pp. 1099–114.

9. An astute introduction to the American debate is provided in James A. Craft, "Post-Recession Bargaining: Mutualism or Adversarial Relations?" *Labor Law Journal* 34 (July 1983), pp. 431–39. See also Jean Mayer, "Workers' Well-Being and Productivity: The Role of Bargaining," *International Labour Review* 122 (May–June 1983), pp. 343–53 and somewhat surprisingly, Bob Kuttner, "Can Labor Lead?" *The New Republic*, March 12, 1984. During the decline of the 1920s, confronted with anti-union "welfare capitalism," the American Federation of Labor proclaimed the "American Plan" as a non-adversarial strategy for survival. Except for some of the railway unions, Canadian organizations were little influenced by this conception.

10. The total union density series used for Canada is based on official data provided by Labour Canada. This series includes all unions and employee associations that engage in collective bargaining. It is calculated on the basis of labor force data for the total number of non-agricultural paid workers, which includes all full- and part-time wage and salary earners in nonagricultural employment. The total union density series used for the U.S. are those published by the Bureau of Labor Statistics (BLS), giving union membership as a percentage of nonagricultural employment. A number of problems have been identified with the accuracy of the union membership figures used by the BLS, especially between 1936 and 1952, when the rivalry between the AFL and the CIO resulted in inflated membership claims. Further problems have been found with the concept of union membership. For example, see George Sayers Bain and Robert Price, *Profiles of Union Growth* (Oxford: Blackwell, 1980), p. 81. The procedure adopted here of comparing union densities for the two countries on the basis of the Labour Canada and the BLS series follows the approach of Weiler, op. cit., and others. In addition to the BLS aggregate union membership series for the U.S., there exists one compiled by the National Bureau of Economic Research. It was begun by Leo Wolman, extended by Leo Troy, and most recently revised and updated through 1984 by Leo Troy and Neil Sheflin, *Union Sourcebook* (West Orange: Irdis, 1985) . This most up-to-date series was unavailable to us at the time of writing, except for the total density figures for 1983 and 1984, which we have included, notwithstanding the differences between the BLS series and that of Troy and Sheflin. See further Troy's contribution in chapter 3 [of Seymour Martin Lipset, ed., *Unions in Transition* (San Francisco: ICS Press, 1986)].
11. Bain and Price, op. cit., p. 163.
12. Milton Derber, "Comment," on A. Rees, "The Size of Union Membership in Manufacturing in the 1980s," in H.A. Juris and M. Roomkin, eds., *The Shrinking Perimeter* (Lexington, Mass.: Lexington Books, 1980), pp. 55–58.
13. Meltz, op. cit., p. 322.
14. Weiler, op. cit., p. 1818, n. 171.
15. Rose and Chaison, op. cit., pp. 98–100.
16. Meltz, op. cit., p. 321–22. As noted by Bain and Price, op. cit., p. 168, comparisons of changes in the level of union density in particular sectors "are made difficult by variations between countries in the way in which trade unions, trade union members, potential union members, and industries are defined." Nevertheless, comparisons of disaggregated data for Canada and the U.S. have been attempted by Bain and Price, op. cit.; Weiler, op. cit.; Meltz, op. cit.; and, most recently, Rose and Chaison, op. cit.
17. A major emphasis in much recent research on trade union growth has been on the influence of economic variables, such as employment growth, the rate of unemployment, price changes, and the level or rate of profits. Interestingly, an influential initial contributor to this body of research did suggest the value of testing for political variables based on political representation in government. See Orley Ashenfelter and John H. Pencavel, "American Trade Union Growth: 1900–1960," *Quarterly Journal of Economics* 83 (1969), pp. 434–48. And this has been taken up in a few attempts in Canada. See Dennis R. Maki, "Political Parties and Trade Union Growth in Canada," *Industrial Relations/Industrielles* 37 (1982) pp. 876–85. The comparative questions asked by this paper appear to us to require comparative historical research.
18. David Brody, *Workers in Industrial America: Essays on the Twentieth Century Struggle* (New York: Oxford University Press, 1980) and David Brody, "The Expansion of the American Labor Movement: Institutional Sources of Stimulus and Restraint," in David Brody, ed., *The American Labor Movement* (New York: Harper & Row, 1971).
19. Joseph Rayback, *A History of American Labor* (New York: The Free Press, Collier-Macmillan Ltd., 1966), pp. 396–400.
20. Laurel Sefton MacDowell, "The Formation of the Canadian Industrial Labour Relations System during World War Two," *Labour/Le Travail* 3 (1978). The consequence of Ottawa's refusal to enact compulsory union recognition and collective bargaining during the war became evident during the Kirkland Lake gold miners' strike of 1941 in northern Ontario. Despite the recommendation of a government-appointed conciliation board, mine owners in Kirkland Lake refused to recognize or bargain with the Mine, Mill, and Smelter Workers Union. Forced into a strike position during the worst months of winter by lengthy government conciliation procedure, the miners eventually lost a bitterly fought three month strike. This conflict almost bankrupted the fledgling CIO organization in Canada and proved to be a turning-point in mobilizing organized labor's resistance against the King administration's war labor policy.

For an excellent analysis of the strike and its significance, see Laurel Sefton MacDowell, *"Remember Kirkland Lake"*: *The History and Effects of the Kirkland Lake Gold Miners' Strike, 1941-42* (Toronto: University of Toronto Press, 1983).

21. Stuart Jamieson, "Times of Trouble: Labour Unrest and Industrial Conflict in Canada, 1900-1966," Study No. 22, *Task Force on Labour Relations* (Ottawa: Information Canada, 1968), p. 348.

22. Convincing evidence that the federal government shared this concern came from the appointment in 1966 of a major Task Force on Labour Relations, chaired by one of the leading Canadian authorities in industrial relations, McGill University dean, H.D. Woods. The 23 background studies of the task force subsequently published between 1966-69 constitute the most comprehensive analysis of labor relations yet undertaken in Canada. The task force concluded that "signs of . . . rebellions have been unmistakable. They include increasing turnover among senior union leaders, especially at the international level, a number of cases in which workers have refused to ratify collective agreements, a spate of wildcat strikes, and seemingly greater willingness on the part of workers to change their union allegiance." Although recognizing that Canada's "adversarial system" of industrial relations was undoubtedly flawed, the task force concluded that it was nonetheless well suited to the country's political culture and consequently did not recommend major changes in government policy. Michael R. Smith, "Industrial Conflict in Post-War Ontario or One Cheer for the Woods Report," *Canadian Review of Sociology and Anthropology* 18 (August 1981), p. 371; Morton, op. cit., p. 362.

23. For strike data, see Jamieson, op. cit., p. 371.

24. Lewin and Goldenberg, op. cit., pp. 243, 246; Mary Lou Gillis, "Trade Unionism: Summary Outline," in *The Current Industrial Relations Scene 1980* (Kingston: Industrial Relations Centre, 1981), p. 219.

25. Kenneth P. Swan, "Public Bargaining in Canada and the U.S.: A Legal View," *Industrial Relations* 19 (Fall 1980), pp. 276-78; George Hildebrand, *American Unionism: An Historical and Analytical Survey* (Reading, Mass.: Addison-Wesley, 1978), pp. 91-93.

26. Lewin and Goldenberg, ibid., pp. 239-40.

27. AFL-CIO Committee on the Evolution of Work, op. cit.

28. Jamieson, op. cit., pp. 391-92.

29. Desmond Morton, op. cit., p. 258.

30. Lewin and Goldenberg, op. cit., p. 242.

31. Panitch and Swartz, op. cit.

32. Compare Christopher Huxley, "The State, Collective Bargaining, and the Shape of Strikes in Canada," *Canadian Journal of Sociology/Cahiers Canadiens de Sociologie* 4:3 (1979); Panitch and Swartz, op. cit.; and James B. Atleson, *Values and Assumptions in American Labor Law* (Amherst: University of Massachusetts Press, 1983).

33. Swan, op. cit.

34. Weiler, op. cit.; Freeman, op. cit.; AFL-CIO, op. cit.; compare Meltz, op. cit. and Rose and Chaison, op. cit.

35. McMurray, op. cit.; Weiler, op. cit.; Jeffrey Gandz and Darryl Slywchuck, "The Implications of Developments in the Legal-Administrative Framework of Canadian Industrial Relations," *Business Quarterly* 46 (Summer 1981), pp. 64-75.

36. Weiler, op. cit.; Rose and Chaison, op. cit.; Jules Bernstein, "Union-Busting: From Benign Neglect to Malignant Growth," *U.C.D. Law Review* 14 (Fall 1980), pp. 3-77. A measure of the most recent American development is the trend in the ratios between employees newly covered by certifications granted and decertifications granted. The indices were as follows: for 1978, 8.9; for 1980, 8.98; for 1981, 8.2; for 1982, 3.9; for 1983 (first half), 2.97. Ratios computed from data in Dow, op. cit., p. 226. Despite some downward fluctuations in certifications in Canada, there are no signs of anything resembling such a turn.

37. McMurray, op. cit.; Gandz and Slywchuck, op. cit.; Trevor Bain and Allan D. Spritzer, "Private Sector Industrial Relations in the South," Proceedings of the 1981 IRRA Spring Meeting, *Labor Law Journal* (August 1981), pp. 536-44; Joseph Krislov and J. Lew Silver, "Union Bargaining Power in the 1980s," in ibid., pp. 480-84.

38. Canada Limited v. UE Local 504 (1980) OLRB Repr. Apr. 577, see Gandz and Slywchuck, op. cit.

39. McMurray, op. cit.; Gandz and Slywchuck, op. cit.; Rose and Chaison, op. cit.

40. J. David Greenstone, *Labor in American Politics*, Phoenix edition (Chicago: University of Chicago Press, 1977); Vernon Coleman, "Labor Power and Social Equality: Union Politics in a Changing Economy," Mimeo, American Political Science Association, 1984.

Father Georges-Henri Lévesque and the Introduction of Social Sciences at Laval, 1938–1955

MICHAEL BEHIELS

> If we do not allow scholars, at their own best speed and in full academic freedom, to carry on their research aimed at extending human knowledge and ultimately improving the quality of human life, the result will be to make science sterile and to dry up the main source of human progress.[1]
>
> — Georges-Henri Lévesque

The teaching of the social sciences took root in the francophone universities of Quebec at the beginning of a crucial period of socio-economic change stimulated by the Second World War. This process of change would contribute to the renewal of conflict between clerico-nationalist and liberal ideologies. Before the 1940s the Catholic church in Quebec — and the great majority of its clerics — supported the clerico-nationalist ideology, which had as its principal goal the "sacralization" of the institutions, customs, and values associated with the new industrialized urban society. The creation of the School of Social, Economic, and Political Sciences at Laval University in 1938 under the direction of Father Georges-Henri Lévesque would permit the preaching of liberal principles by a small minority of clerics and lay people. Ultimately, a new definition of the collective character of Quebec society would emerge, pervaded by secular values, by individualism and rationalism. Thus the liberal values and beliefs that were long established in Quebec society at a more popular level, as the work of Yves Roby has shown, would receive the open encouragement of a new elite trained in the social sciences.[2] Also, a wider and deeper understanding of the problems facing French Canada would prompt Father Lévesque and his early colleagues to abandon French Canadian nationalism in favour of "clear-sighted integration into a new Canadian federation." The professors of the next generation, however, would reject what they considered to be a false set of options and instead would gradually develop a new nationalism, reflecting the beliefs and aspirations of a new technocratic and bureaucratic class.

At Laval the introduction of the social sciences was not accomplished without difficulty. For fifteen years, there was strong and tenacious op-

SOURCE: "Father Georges-Henri Lévesque and the Introduction of Social Sciences at Laval, 1938–1955," in Paul Axelrod and John G. Reid, eds., *Youth, University and Canadian Society* (Montreal/Kingston: McGill-Queen's University Press, 1986), pp. 320–41. Translated from the French by John G. Reid. Reprinted with permission of McGill-Queen's University Press.

position both inside and outside the university. The sociologist Marcel Fournier, in his study of the institutionalization of social science in Quebec, argues that the essential cause of these problems can be found in the efforts of social-science professors to obtain social recognition for and institutionalization of their new disciplines. Teaching and research in social science represented, at that time, a threat to established elites and to the power base of the Duplessis government. If the Laval Faculty of Social Sciences wished to preserve and extend its autonomy, it had no choice but to oppose the Union Nationale and the complex of interest groups that kept the party in power. Had it not been for this vigorous resistance, the Duplessis government would have continued its policy of reducing the faculty's subsidies and would have refused to employ social-science graduates of Laval. According to Marcel Fournier,

> [Their professors and their dean] could not hope, in view of all the evidence, to gain recognition in society or a higher status in the university except by contributing to the defeat of the government. This implied an alliance, on the one hand, with the trade union and co-operative movements and, on the other hand, with the Liberal party. That party drew inspiration from the faculty's research and reflections, and committed itself to administer affairs of the state "with expertise," that is, by making use of whatever expertise was available. In effect, it was by supplying expertise to these diverse opposition movements and in return receiving their support that the social-science professors were able to redefine their mission outside the university and to take advantage of opportunities for accomplishing their internal goals of building up an accumulation of specialized knowledge, forming an integrated "scientific community," and providing coherent and well-focused education.[3]

There is no doubt that the pressures associated with institutionalization, and conflicts between the interests of social classes, formed part of the explanation for this opposition to the established order both outside and inside Laval. However, an ideological dimension must also be considered in order to explain fully and satisfactorily the social and political action of the dean and his colleagues between 1938 and 1954. It was largely thanks to the skill, determination, and ingenuity of Father Lévesque that the young Faculty of Social Sciences was able to survive this difficult period. Under the aegis of Catholic social doctrine, which they interpreted liberally, the dean and the professors advocated a dualistic concept of the social sciences. The faculty's program of studies reflected this duality: "normative" courses on the social doctrine of the church were accompanied by "positive" courses on the methodologies and scientific theories of the various social sciences. In a society still officially Catholic, with its universities church-controlled, this dualistic approach was absolutely necessary if teaching of the social sciences was to be introduced in Quebec. Had the dean not been a cleric, preaching this dualism with evident conviction, the attacks on the new faculty might well have been successful.

The dualist approach had been inspired by the liberal and socially oriented Catholicism preached by Lévesque and his colleagues. Their ideological convictions had led them to adopt a policy of social action. Imbued with social passion, this first generation of social-science professors intended to turn their new forms of knowledge to the cause of reforming the *mentalité* and the institutions of Quebec society. Thereby, they believed, the Catholic Church could remain as a vital and dynamic force in the daily lives of all French-Canadians. This social movement within Catholicism arrived too late, however, to be successfully established in Quebec. The secularizing process had attained such momentum by the 1950s that this second attempt at "sacralization" — this time involving a more liberal form of Catholicism — was destined for virtually inevitable failure. It is this reality that explains why, when the future of the faculty finally became secure during the decade, it became possible for a second generation of professors, all lay people, to abandon dualism and dedicate themselves solely to teaching the methods and secular theories of social-science fields that were constantly becoming more specialized.

The Advent of the Social Sciences at Laval

An essential precondition for the renewal of liberal ideology in Quebec and for its successful confrontation with clerico-nationalism was a profound transformation of francophone university education. The ground had been well prepared by the conjuncture of socio-economic forces in the interwar period. The economic growth of the 1920s, largely based on exploitation of natural resources, had accelerated the urbanization and the secularization of Quebec. After the Depression of the 1930s the double process of urbanization and economic growth began again and eventually destroyed the foundations and the frameworks of traditional society. The number of French Canadians living on farms fell from 41 per cent in 1941 to 13 per cent in 1961. At the same time the number of francophone males working in the tertiary sector of the economy rose from 28 per cent in 1941 to 45 per cent in 1961. These changes, and many others in the same period, contributed to the changing of the occupational structure and — little by little — to the secularization of the customs and values, the *mentalité*, of francophone Quebec.[4] Francophone elites no longer formed a solid bloc, and their socio-political discourses ceased to present a unified image of society. Increasingly, new members of the elites, trained in the social or the natural sciences, preached a liberal ideology and defined a new identity for the Québécois collectivity, one that was rationalistic, individualistic, and secularized.

With the creation in 1920 of the Faculty of Science at the University of Montreal and of the School of Chemistry at Laval, the process of transformation was implanted. It was symbolized in 1923 in the foundation of the *Association canadienne-française pour l'avancement des sciences* (ACFAS), which prompted a vigorous debate on the need to introduce the teaching of natural and physical sciences into the classical colleges.[5] Most professors were opposed to this, for, as Jean-Charles Falardeau has shown, the transformation amounted to nothing less than a radical reorientation of the entire character of university and secondary education by redefining some of the fundamental goals. The classical college, traditionally the cornerstone of Quebec education, had justifiably based its curriculum on the Greek and Latin humanities but for historical reasons had limited its role to directing students towards the liberal professions and in its teaching had emphasized the abstract and other-worldliness.[6]

The introduction of the natural sciences having provoked a major debate, that of the social sciences — involving the study of human beings, and infused with value judgments — generated a second one. It would be longer and more agitated than the first, because the ascendancy of the traditional elites in Quebec society would be called into serious question.[7]

The systematic teaching of the social sciences at Laval began in the fall of 1938. Cardinal J.-M. Rodrigue Villeneuve, eminent theologian and sociologist, archbishop of Quebec (1931–47), and apostolic chancellor of Laval, announced on 1 April 1938 the establishment of a School of Social, Economic, and Political Sciences at Laval, leading to the baccalaureate and to the *licence ès lettres*.[8] Part-time instruction in social science had been available since 1920 at the University of Montreal and since 1932 at Laval. Most of the students had been clerics; the courses had led to no diploma and offered no prospect of professional employment. The purpose of these programs, according to the church hierarchy, had been to provide academic facilities for teaching and propagating the social doctrine of the church, as embodied in the relevant papal encyclicals. The economic crisis that enveloped Canada and the rest of the industrialized world after 1929 made the hierarchy, along with the professional elites and the politicians, extremely nervous. Cardinal Villeneuve believed that if the church were to survive and prosper in Quebec it would need a more elaborate strategy, and a structure, for teaching social doctrine. Moreover, the church also needed more lay workers to assist in such areas as in teaching, in social work, and in the Catholic trade unions.[9] Thus, the creation of the School of Social Sciences at Laval in 1938 represented in part a further step towards the "sacralization" of society, a strategy pursued by the Quebec episcopate since the early twentieth century. Villeneuve and his advisers hoped that Catholic education in the social sciences would dissuade the Québécois from adopting the relativistic philosophy of the "objective" social sciences or the atheistic collectivism of Marxism.[10]

To meet this challenge, Villeneuve chose Father Georges-Henri Lévesque as director. A member of the Dominican order, Lévesque had been a professor of economic philosophy in the Faculty of Philosophy at Laval since 1936. With previous experience teaching at the Dominican College in Ottawa from 1933 to 1935 and at the School of Social Sciences at the University of Montreal in 1935, Lévesque was well qualified for his new position. He also showed himself to be a skilled administrator as the new school grew in its number of personnel. Born at Roberval in 1903, Lévesque had his earliest education from the Marist brothers. He obtained his baccalaureate from the seminary at Chicoutimi, where he decided to become a Dominican. After spending a year of his noviciate at St-Hyacinthe, he attended the Dominican College in Ottawa to complete his studies in philosophy and theology. With the general economic crisis fully evident, his superiors sent him to Europe to specialize in the social sciences at the Catholic University of Lille. Between 1931 and 1933 Lévesque made a number of research trips to Geneva, where he studied the League of Nations and the International Labour Organization. He also visited Belgium to meet with the renowned Father Ceslas Rutten, a militant advocate of Catholic social action who had taken a leading role in the creation of trade unions, co-operatives, and youth movements for Catholic action in his country. Lévesque returned to Canada even more convinced than heretofore that Catholic social doctrine could be successfully applied to the social and economic problems of a crisis-ridden Quebec society.

In February 1933 J.S. Woodsworth rose in the House of Commons to announce the impending establishment of a new political party, the Cooperative Commonwealth Federation (CCF). The CCF advocated democratic socialism for Canada, and fear of socialism prompted the Catholic church in Quebec to oppose it. Father Lévesque, as a teacher of Catholic social doctrine who also sought to put that doctrine into effect, was chosen as one of a team made up of clerics and lay people and charged with drafting the church's response to the menace of the CCF. He was one of thirteen ecclesiastics who were convened in Montreal on 9 March 1933 under the auspices of the École sociale populaire to study the CCF program from the perspective of church social doctrine. Lévesque himself wrote the critique of the new party.[11] He concluded that the CCF had espoused "the three great vices which characterize the pure socialism condemned by the church: violent class struggle, suppression of private property through excessive socialization of assets, and finally a materialistic concept of society."[12] Following the directives in the encyclical *Quadragesimo anno* of Pope Pius XI, Lévesque believed that it was impossible at the same time to be a loyal Catholic and a thoroughgoing socialist. Only if the CCF were to abandon the three "great vices" would it be open to Catholics to support the party.[13]

Gradually, however, Lévesque realized that the socialism of the CCF had virtually nothing in common with the anti-Catholic and materialistic socialism of continental Europe. He began to understand the social and intellectual context of the CCF program, which drew its inspiration from

British Fabian socialism. It had been adapted to Canadian needs by the League for Social Reconstruction, led by F.R. Scott, Frank Underhill, and other professors of McGill University and the University of Toronto. Lévesque also came to accept that the CCF had a spiritual and moral dimension that sprang from the social-gospel movement in the Protestant denominations. In 1939 he changed his opinion of the CCF and began to teach in his courses that, given a liberal interpretation of Catholic social doctrines, church censure of the party was neither necessary nor useful. It was Lévesque, in fact, who persuaded Cardinal Villeneuve to join in October 1943 in the signing of a declaration of Canadian bishops giving permission to Catholics to vote for the CCF. Nevertheless, in spite of the efforts of Lévesque, Archbishop Charbonneau of Montreal, and a small group of other priests and lay people to set forth the affinities between Catholic social doctrines and the democratic socialism of the CCF, most ecclesiastical leaders in Quebec continued to adhere to a narrow interpretation of doctrine and rejected socialism in any form.[14] This majority attitude largely explains the conflict between the church and Lévesque's new Faculty of Social Sciences.

At first the progress of the School of Social Sciences was slow. It continued to be affiliated with the Faculty of Philosophy, and its mandate was "to give a higher education on social questions based on Christian principles and adapted to the particular conditions and needs of our country," with a view to the training of "the teachers, proselytizers, and leaders without whom it would be hopeless to aspire to a Christian social order."[15] According to Father Gonzalve Poulin, then a member of the school, the program of study was strongly oriented towards the teaching of social and political philosophy, and gave "an over-riding importance to the social doctrine of the papal encyclicals."[16] As director of the school Father Lévesque firmly maintained this Catholic approach to the social sciences, and as a priest it was natural that he should regard "God as the greatest of all sociologists."[17] Yet his experiences since 1933 had brought him to recognize that modern scientific methodology could not properly be taught solely through a didactic consideration of the encyclicals. In 1974, he wrote: "Nevertheless, all my diverse experiences, all the courses, all the meetings, all the travel, had brought me to see clearly that we had an enormous and urgent need for sociologists, economists, political scientists, and industrial relations experts, and that all the evidence showed that to train these specialists we absolutely needed to organize genuine teaching of the social sciences in Quebec."[18]

Lévesque declared in 1940 that the school must be upgraded to become a faculty, with autonomous departments of economics, sociology and social ethics, industrial relations, and social service, along with an institute of social research. This transformation was accomplished in 1943 and inaugurated a new era for the social sciences in Quebec. Even if it is true, as put by Jean-Charles Falardeau, that "it was only little by little that new wine was poured into the old bottle," nobody else could have accomplished the modernization of social science at Laval with the same skill, diplomacy, and tenacity as did Lévesque.[19]

His first challenge was to deal with the near-total lack of French Canadian specialists in social science. In 1943 most professors of the school were clerics with degrees in philosophy and theology. The dean of the faculty dealt with this problem in two ways. First, he recruited well-qualified professors from diverse backgrounds, such as Father I. Eschmann, of German origin (1940–42), Father J. Thomas Delos of France (1940–44), and the renowned University of Chicago sociologist Everett C. Hughes (1942–45). Secondly, he encouraged — often with financial aid — a number of the faculty's most gifted graduates to go to the United States, and after the war to Europe, to undertake doctoral study in sociology, political science, and economics.[20]

This strategy soon bore fruit. Within a few years the new faculty had at its disposal young Québécois who were specialists in the various social-science disciplines. Jean-Charles Falardeau, at the suggestion of Everett Hughes, went to Chicago in 1941 for doctoral work in sociology. He returned to Laval as a professor in 1943 and became director of the Sociology Department ten years later.[21] Maurice Lamontagne and Maurice Tremblay obtained doctorates at Harvard, in economics and political science respectively, and were then employed by Laval. Roger Marier chose the Catholic University in Washington and returned to establish at Laval a school of social service.[22]

Following the end of the war other graduates of the Faculty of Social Sciences were free to pursue their studies in Europe. Léon Dion taught sociology in the faculty before attending the London School of Economics and eventually obtaining in Germany a doctorate in political science. His colleague Gérard Bergeron, with a professional interest in international affairs and the role of the United Nations, spent the year 1947 at the Institut universitaire des Hautes Études internationales in Geneva; he later enrolled for two years at the Faculty of Law of the University of Paris, where in the late 1950s he gained a doctorate for his study of the role of the state in the modern world.[23] Dion and Bergeron returned to Laval to teach in the Faculty of Social Sciences, and made the Department of Political Science a dynamic and progressive centre of study. Two other graduates of the faculty, Guy Rocher and Fernand Dumont, completed their post-graduate studies at Harvard and at Paris respectively. They also returned to Laval and were largely responsible for the complete secularization of the methodology and the curriculum of the faculty.[24]

Most of these candidates were personally selected by Lévesque, and the majority came from similar social and regional backgrounds. Lamontagne, Tremblay, and Dion came from the economically underdeveloped regions of Lac Saint-Jean and the lower St Lawrence Valley, and they had received their classical education at the seminaries of Chicoutimi and Rimouski. Furthermore, this first generation of true social scientists shared common goals: the development of a methodology for objective research, ideological pluralism, dynamic social action, and the political and social modernization of Quebec society.[25]

The Faculty and Its Adversaries

The first decade of the new Faculty of Social Sciences was a turbulent and demanding time for Father Lévesque and his colleagues. The faculty encountered stiff opposition, as interpreted by Léon Dion, from "groups, including the provincial political leadership and certain ecclesiastics, who — whether through self-interest or through sincere conviction — wanted the faculty to commit itself firmly to the defence of the traditional social order, which is to say that the human sciences would be turned to the service of national mythology and the interests of the wealthy."[26] Apart from the national and Catholic trade unions, it was the Faculty of Social Sciences at Laval that was in the 1940s the main centre of opposition to the policies of the Duplessis regime, to traditional French-Canadian nationalism, and to the supremacy of the church in education and social services.[27] During the 1950s several members of the faculty identified themselves with other opposition groups, such as the *Cité libre* group led by Pierre-Elliott Trudeau and Gérard Pelletier, or the Institut canadien des affaires publiques, through which those on the left developed and publicized a systematic critique of Quebec society and especially of the traditional nationalist ideology.[28]

At first the opposition to Father Lévesque and the faculty came from ecclesiastics, both inside and outside the university. The dean had to deal with the accusation that, simply put, the faculty was producing specialists with radical ideas who would do no more than swell the ranks of the unemployed. The critics argued that the faculty's program of study was too empirical, too positivistic, too secular, too much on the left, that the original function of the social sciences was being neglected — namely, to teach the social doctrine of the church.[29] Much time and energy had to be expended in rebutting these accusations and in asserting the practical importance of the social sciences for Quebec.

Foreseeing in 1938 the allegation that social-science graduates would end up unemployed, Lévesque moved to associate the Faculty of Social Sciences with certain practical programs that he saw as a means of putting Catholic social doctrine into practice. The dean was convinced that the extreme individualism and the pre-eminence of personal gain, which he saw as characteristic of North American capitalism, could induce Quebec workers to leave the church, which they would see as incapable of serving the needs of an industrial society.[30] To forestall this possibility, Quebec must develop an extended co-operative network and must have dynamic Catholic trade unions, fully able to respond to the needs of the workers. To this end, Lévesque founded in 1939 the Conseil supérieur de la coopération, and also established a co-operative journal, *Ensemble*. Until 1944 he was president of the council and editor of *Ensemble*. The council functioned as a federated body, encompassing the Coopérative fédérée, the Alliance des Coopératives de consommation, the Pêcheurs units, the caisses populaires, the Union catholique des cultivateurs, and the Confédération des travailleurs catholiques du Canada (CTCC). *Ensemble* supported and publicized the socio-economic and cultural advantages of the co-operative movement. It campaigned for the improvement of legislation affecting co-operatives at both federal and provincial levels.[31]

The Department of Industrial Relations and the School of Social Service stressed the study of both practical and theoretical problems. Professors and students took part in programs of outreach to urban and rural communities. The Department of Industrial Relations published a bilingual journal, *Relations industrielles/Industrial Relations*, and from 1946 onwards it organized annual conferences for all those in the province who were interested in this field. The school of social work was responsible for the establishment of the Service familial de Québec, a centre of social rehabilitation for delinquents and former prison inmates, of several recreation centres, and of a Social Service Council to co-ordinate the activities of these organizations.[32] In effect the School of Social Service was successful in creating employment for its students. Father Lévesque made many further efforts to offset the public image of the university as an ivory tower. The Faculty of Social Sciences published a series of *cahiers* on major current issues, established a Centre de culture populaire to provide community education on social subjects and especially to offer courses on family life, urban development, economic problems, and the co-operative movement.[33] The principal goal of the Centre de culture populaire was to democratize higher education by widening the participation of Québécois in the programs of the faculty.[34]

Paradoxically, it was the very success of the new faculty that precipitated a stormy debate that embroiled the faculty with the École sociale populaire, with the Jesuits, and with two-thirds of the Quebec bishops, mainly those from rural dioceses. Lévesque had to offer a public justification of the need for the School of Social Work and for the Department of Industrial Relations. Critics were proclaiming that the social-work specialists and the new centres of social services would soon replace the traditional charitable agencies; Lévesque's response was that modern social services simply represented a rational and systematic way of organizing charitable work. They were, in short, the modern version of "our ancient forms of bodily and spiritual mercy," new techniques put at the service of charity. The methods, but not the goals, had been modernized for the benefit of society in Quebec.[35] These remarks may have helped to turn aside criticism. Nevertheless, the modernization of social services was going to have much more dramatic effect than the dean was willing to admit. Over time the School of Social Work and its graduates would be responsible for the complete secularization of the traditional system of church-administered charities.

Many priests and politicians felt deep anxiety when faced by the challenge of the trade unions during and after the Second World War and were especially disturbed by increased militancy in the Catholic unions. Some among them held that a Catholic university such as Laval should not be encouraging the radicalization of the union movement by establishing a Department of Industrial Relations and organizing annual conferences to discuss labour–management problems. Father Lévesque and Gérard Dion, professor in the Department of Industrial Relations, believed that a society such as Quebec — in the grip of profound changes arising from industrialization and urbanization — desperately needed an institution independent of church, state, business, or unions, where specialized researchers could probe the difficulties created by the new socioeconomic structures and try to find solutions. Furthermore, a department of industrial relations could train experts with the leadership qualities and sense of social responsibility needed to administer trade unions, employers' organizations, and government departments. These specialists would play an essential part in ensuring economic progress and continuing social stability in Quebec.[36] Lévesque put up a convincing defence of the need for the social sciences, but for all that his critics were not likely to be persuaded only by theoretical arguments.

In 1946 several Jesuits associated with the École sociale populaire and several bishops, encouraged by Archbishop Georges Courchesnes of Rimouski, tried to discredit Lévesque and his faculty. They forwarded to the Vatican a report accusing Lévesque of writing an article in *Ensemble* in December 1945 arguing that the co-operative movement wished to become officially non-confessional. In 1940 Cardinal Villeneuve and Bishop Charbonneau, by approving the Manifeste du Conseil supérieur de la coopération, approved this policy of deconfessionalization. Lévesque had convinced them that only through this strategy could co-operation be assured between francophone and anglophone co-operative associations in Quebec and throughout Canada. The co-operatives, Lévesque maintained, were essentially economic, not religious, organizations, and the church had no right to insist on a confessional structure. If it did so, it would only destroy the unity of the co-operative movement and risk compromising the church's integrity in certain cases.[37]

The accusation against Lévesque was serious. The combined power and influence of the Jesuits and the bishops was sufficient to ensure that a canonical trial would be held before the Congregation of the Holy Office in Rome. Fortunately for the dean, he was strongly supported by Father Gaudrault, superior of the Dominicans in Canada, and by

Father Suarez, director of the order in Rome. Lévesque's adversaries were unable to convince the Congregation of the Holy Office that he had advocated secularization, and the Congregation in fact gave its approval to the policy of deconfessionalization of the co-operative movement in Quebec.[38] Whether thanks to Lévesque or not, this decision would have the effect of encouraging the secularization of the co-operative movement and of the CTCC. The old strategy of the church, to "sacralize" worldly institutions, simply would not work any more. Seen from this perspective, the concerns of Lévesque's detractors were well justified, though also anachronistic.

Shortly afterwards, a group of priests from Laval, and some others, sent a critical report on the Faculty of Social Sciences to the Congregation on Seminaries and Universities in Rome. They alleged that the faculty was teaching socialist and Marxist theories that were heretical at a Catholic university. Even more pointedly, they accused the dean of hiring too many lay professors who — in their teaching and in their research — neglected almost entirely the social doctrine of the church in favour of propagating socialist theories of class conflict and a methodology based on materialism.[39] This time Lévesque responded directly and aggressively. At the Learned Societies meeting in Quebec in May 1947, and before the general council of Laval University in December, he expounded his dualistic concept of the role of the social sciences.[40]

Lévesque postulated a subtle — perhaps a "jesuitical" — explanation for the importance and necessity of the social sciences. The human being, by nature a social animal, needed knowledge of the various forms of social interaction and of the related pre-conditions and demands. There was, he argued, "a science of life in society, and human progress is contingent on its laws being known and its imperatives heeded." Because life in society could be studied in two essential ways, both of them scientifically valid, two distinct methodologies were needed:

1. The *positive* element: this involves life in society as lived in the past and the present, in other words, the *social facts*.
2. The *normative* element: this is concerned with life in society in the future, which men must necessarily carry on and which, because they are rational beings, they must organize rationally according to rules of conduct that we call *social duties*.[41]

Thus, human progress would require that the human being have a rational and scientific understanding of the laws governing modern society. The role of the social sciences was to discover and clarify those laws. When the laws of human behaviour were made known, it would then be up to the value-loaded normative sciences — philosophy and theology — to determine the proper norms and the goals of social activity. This dualistic approach was not only good strategy in Lévesque's efforts to turn aside criticism; it was also an accurate exposition of the outlook of the first generation of social scientists at Laval.[42] It was a view that could not be acceptable to traditionalists who believed that social-science methodology should be solely determined by Catholic values and by the social doctrine of the church.[43] Nevertheless, it was essential for the Laval social scientists that they be able to specialize in their discipline without rejecting the role of their religious faith in guiding the uses to which their research would be put. Lévesque put the point concisely:

> This double approach to knowledge is very important to us, for everyday experience of society shows us that to have scholars without social principles is hardly more desirable than to have philosophers with no knowledge of facts; the narrow authoritarianism of theoreticians who cultivate principles in isolation from factual knowledge is just as unrealistic, and just as harmful to the human spirit, as the excessive relativism of the positivists who wish only to consider the facts without considering the guiding principles of life in society.[44]

In reality, the conflict over the social sciences at Laval was a power struggle between socially oriented Catholics and traditional Catholics, the prize being to determine which of the two groups would dominate the development of the new human sciences in the modern university.

The outcome of this fight would affect the evolution in Quebec both of higher education and of Catholicism in society. At Laval the conservatives were in the majority. Lévesque knew that one mistake could cost him his position. Nevertheless, he took a firm stand in declaring that his faculty would continue to be a faculty of social sciences, not a faculty of philosophy and theology. He took precautions to ensure that his professors would enjoy full academic freedom in their research, so that their scholarly inquiries would always take priority over value-judgments. It was essential, the dean believed, that sociology and economics graduates of Laval should be able to compete effectively with their counterparts throughout the world. At the same time, aware of the power of the critics, Lévesque continued to offer reassurance that the social doctrines of the church had a secure place in the courses and programs of the faculty. Speaking to the general council at Laval, he identified ten "normative" courses in which social problems were studied from the perspective of the social doctrine of the church as embodied in the *Summa theologia* of Aquinas and in papal encyclicals.[45] Finally, he appealed to the faculty's detractors to be tolerant and to understand the pressures under which his professors were working:

> Is it not too often forgotten that the faculty is working in one of the most difficult and delicate fields of service: that of human relations, where the danger of making mistakes is surely greater than in other fields, where one works on inert material such as statistics or literary tests? Is enough consideration given to the entrenched prejudices and easily offended interest groups that the faculty must inevitably encounter, which will accuse it of being pro-capitalist, pro-socialist, anti-worker, anti-business, nationalistic, internationalistic, secularizing, clericalizing and so forth? Is thought given, finally, to the strange predicament of the faculty in working in a Province where it is considered normal (and rightly so) to consider as lawyers only those who have completed legal studies, and as doctors only

those who have graduated from medical school, but where so many improvisers may instantly be declared "eminent sociologists" and thereby claim the right to make authoritative judgments on those who have specialized in the field?[46]

Once again, precise arguments, along with Lévesque's firmness and his influential friends in Rome, prevailed with the church authorities. In a decision that represented a major victory for the faculty and for socially oriented Catholicism, the Congregation on Seminaries and Universities determined that there was nothing heretical in the teaching of the social sciences at Laval.[47] Although, unfortunately, the conflict was not yet over, the critics could no longer claim that Lévesque and his faculty were suspected of heresy. The decision marked an important transition in Quebec society, towards an intellectual climate that was more democratic, pluralistic, and secular than before. Jean-Charles Falardeau described in 1959 the exhilarating and challenging experience that the faculty's first generation of students and graduates had enjoyed:

> In our meetings together, we were learning to say exactly what we thought and to say it well. We were learning to allow others to speak, to respect their opinions, and to have unrestrained discussions. We were learning how to use cogent reasoning on a given question, and that social life — any more than human life itself — was not marked out by a definite line that could never be cut. Little by little, we formed *a new intellectual attitude*, which was also a moral position. We learned to accord principles their proper place, but also to realize that it was easier to enunciate them than to apply them to the realities of a human society that had its own laws and logic.[48]

This new attitude had an immediate effect on the research interests of members of the faculty. At the Centre for Social Research, founded in 1943, the professors undertook a systematic analysis of French Canadian society. This endeavour was made possible, according to Falardeau, by "a disengagement from the kind of thinking which had hitherto been bound up with moral and ideological interpretations."[49] The description was not quite accurate, for in reality the first generation of social scientists had its own moral perspective — social Catholicism — and its own, liberal, ideology. It was exactly this novel approach to social-economic questions that brought about a new battle with the traditional elites, this time at the level of politics.

The Social Passion

The dualistic approach to the social sciences, like a double-edged sword, could cut both ways. It had been useful for soothing conservative opposition inside and outside the university. Ironically, though, it was the same approach that drove the dean and his faculty on to formulate a philosophy of social and political action. "The process of gaining knowledge about society," wrote Falardeau later, "must not be allowed to prevent the opening up of a practical approach: to know society and to wish to transform it are two faces of the same mountain."[50] Any systematic analysis of socio-economic and political structures, or of the values and norms of Quebec society, was bound to place the faculty and its professors, in the words of Léon Dion, "outside of the hallowed conventions of nationalism, outside of the traditional ideology of the church, and outside of the prevailing political and electoral mythologies."[51]

In June 1951 Lévesque addressed a joint session of the Canadian Historical Association and the Canadian Political Science Association on the relationship between humanism and social science. Modern humanism, he declared, demanded much more of social scientists than mere scholarly competence: "It demands that they put the results of their research at the disposal of the people and that, whenever possible, they carry their scientific knowledge forward into social action, by entering into conflicts over questions of truth and justice and by bringing their intellect and judgment to bear on the practical issues of the moment. For these days, sciences that do not put themselves at the service of humanity are inevitably turning themselves against it."[52]

Lévesque and his colleagues thus saw themselves as social reformers faced with the great challenge of redefining the traditional values and institutions of Quebec society. Using the weapons of knowledge and methodology of the social sciences, they would be in the forefront of social change.[53] In a sense, they were the social gospellers of French Canada. They had a "social passion," and they were convinced that the Catholic universities had a duty to produce a new elite consisting of social engineers who would become leaders of government, unions, and business. The church would thereby contribute to the development of a more just and democratic society, of the true *cité libre*. For Lévesque, the eventual goal was to create "among men driven by fear and frequently oppressed by injustice, but nevertheless capable of hope and brotherly love, a renewed society bearing on its body and soul the imprint of man regenerated by love, which can only be achieved through a political humanism attaining its true nobility through thought and action."[54] Only through a social Catholicism dedicated to solving the practical problems of the working class, the dean and his professors believed, could the church remain a vital force in the everyday life of French Canadians.

Many members of the traditional francophone elites feared this combination of two new ideological forces, liberal social Catholicism and the social sciences. The political elites of the Union Nationale were apprehensive at the prospect of more militant social and political action by union leaders, social workers, and by the co-operative movement. With the encouragement of some of the bishops, the Duplessis government sent a report to Rome alleging that Lévesque and his faculty were exercising "undue political influence." The report went on to assert that the dean, professors, and graduates of the faculty were creating a political movement aimed at destroying the only Roman Catholic government in North America! Monsignor Montini, however, church Secretary of State for Internal Affairs, rejected the accusations for lack of evidence.[55] If the Duplessis regime had intervened in 1945, it would have had a much better chance of success. By 1952 Lévesque and the faculty enjoyed a high reputation and growing public support. This support existed at all levels of the church, as well as among lay intellectuals associated with *Le Devoir* and *Cité libre* and in the co-operative and trade-union movements. Had Lévesque been forced to resign, in the climate of suspicion recently created by the transfer of Bishop Charbonneau out of Quebec following his intervention in the Asbestos strike, many Catholic Québécois would have concluded that the church in Quebec was under government control. The hierarchy wished to avoid giving any such impression, and this accounted in part for the decision to defend Father Lévesque, at least in the corridors of power in Rome.[56]

The Decline of the Dualistic Approach to Social Science

The hostility between the Duplessis government and the Faculty of Social Sciences was enough to convince Lévesque and his colleagues that Laval must find an alternative source of funding. They believed that they could find a patron in the federal government. In 1949 Prime Minister St Laurent had named Lévesque a member of the Massey Commission on national development in the arts, letters, and sciences. Influenced by the arguments of his colleague the economist Maurice Lamontagne, Lévesque believed that Quebec must pursue "a clear-sighted integration into a new Canadian federalism" so as to ensure survival and the modernization of the traditional and obsolete institutions of French Canadian society.[57] Lévesque convinced his fellow-commissioners that francophone universities in Quebec would support a system of federal subsidies to universities, and the commission recommended accordingly in its report in 1951. In July of that year the St Laurent government decided to put $7.1 million at the disposal of the universities.[58] Quebec nationalists were furious. Gérard Filion, editor of *Le Devoir*, and the neo-nationalist historian Michel Brunet denounced the scheme and portrayed Lévesque and his colleagues as naïve and misguided idealists.[59] The nationalists of the right, such as François-Albert Angers, were even more harsh. The faculty of social sciences prided itself, according to Angers, that, "in the name of a pretended objectivity, it refused to consider seriously our sociological problems from the vantage point of the French Canadian fact, which is nevertheless an objective reality. [It is] a faculty which can only see objectivity in a centralizing and socializing Canadianism, and which never ceases to bubble over with centralist solutions, especially to our social problems. [It is] a faculty which is currently leading an entire generation of young people towards national apostasy."[60] In sum, for Angers, Lévesque and his colleagues were a "fifth column . . . a gang of traitors and *vendus* . . . who do not believe in the cultural ideals" of French Canadians.[61]

The nationalist attack was ferocious, and would create many difficulties within the faculty. It was, ironically enough, these internal disputes that were largely responsible for the decline of the "social passion" and of the dualist approach to the social sciences. The conflicts began in the early 1950s with the arrival of a second generation of social scientists, such as Léon Dion, Guy Rocher, Gérard Bergeron, and Fernand Dumont. Doris Lussier, Lévesque's secretary, precipitated a crisis in the faculty in 1952 when he circulated a Faculty Manifesto signed by all of the first generation of professors. According to Léon Dion, the Manifesto appealed to professors to be faithful to Catholic social doctrine and to Thomist philosophy. Secondly, the Manifesto declared that social-science teaching must be ideologically neutral and must not advance the interests of a Quebec-centred French Canadian nationalism.[62] Father Lévesque acknowledged the existence of the Manifesto but maintained that its chief purpose was to ascertain whether the professors wished to publish a collective response to the article of Angers in *l'Action nationale*, which he and some of his colleagues regarded as defamatory. His impression was that the second generation of professors refused to sign the Manifesto because they thought that such a collective response would constitute a political action on the part of the faculty. They wanted to make it very clear to the public that their dean's public speeches and action did not reflect the official position of the faculty and its staff.[63]

In reality, the professors of the second generation had three reasons for opposing the Manifesto. First, they rejected the dualist approach to social science because it implied teaching "normative" courses on the social doctrine of the church and on the philosophy of Aquinas. This they considered a waste of time. Committed to the objectivity of the social sciences, they disputed the validity of a Catholic sociology. As modern intellectuals they saw their first task as being to wage war on moralists and theologians who sought "to put sociology at the service of the establishment of a Christian society, which would be inspired largely by medieval civilization."[64] These professors gave first priority to their respective disciplines, at least for the time being, and if they had a common goal, it was the development of an entirely secular and liberal university.

Their second reason for rejecting the Manifesto was rooted in their concept of the role of universities in society. The campaign for liberal social Catholicism and a new social order was not to their taste. Direct political action, they believed, should be left to those outside the university. The real responsibilities of a university social scientist lay in research, teaching, and publication.[65]

The third reason, never openly discussed, was that the second generation of professors did not accept the pan-Canadian version of French Canadian nationalism preached by Lévesque and by Maurice Lamontagne. Neither did they subscribe to the traditional nationalism as represented by Angers. Rather, these professors would participate very actively during the 1950s and 1960s in the development of a new québécois nationalism. Stressing cultural evolution and the socio-economic maturing of the francophone majority in Quebec and of the state, they would come to regard this neo-nationalism as a new key to the survival and modernization of the secular, urban, and industrial francophone nationality.

By 1954 the results of this internal crisis were evident. The crusade of Lévesque and his early colleagues to prompt reform in Quebec society following the principles of liberal social Catholicism and of "clearsighted integration into a new Canadian federalism" had virtually disappeared. The "normative" courses had disappeared from the faculty's program of studies, and the new professors were pursuing the "objective" social sciences. The Department of Political Science was established in 1954, and in 1955 the faculty received a second grant from the Carnegie Foundation for research on francophone society in Quebec. The retirement of Father Lévesque in 1955 and the departure of Maurice Lamontagne for Ottawa marked the end of the era of the reformist "social passion" that from the beginning had been characteristic of the development of the social sciences at Laval.[66]

Conclusion

This study has shown how ideological factors prompted Father Lévesque and the first generation of social-science professors at Laval to establish and expand the disciplines and the methodologies of secular social science. Without the "social passion" that originated in a liberal interpretation of Catholic social doctrine, and the "jesuitical" concept of the dualistic approach to social science, Lévesque would never have been able to convince the leading ecclesiastics — at Laval itself, or outside — that the social sciences should have an important role at a modern Catholic university. The struggles that took place did have to do with immediate objectives such as obtaining recognition in society and attaining the institutionalization of the social sciences. Nevertheless, it is the ideological aspirations of Lévesque and his colleagues that largely explain the intensity of the debates and the battles that took place among professors, ecclesiastics, and politicians.

The dean and the first generation of professors believed that the flowering of social science would set in motion among French Canadians a more rational and worldly approach to the discussion of old and new problems that needed to be faced. They believed that the result would be a move towards, in the words of Maurice Lamontagne, "clear-sighted integration into a new Canadian federalism." This view, however, was rejected by the second generation of professors, who could not accept the implication of Lévesque's strategy of renewed "sacralization" of worldly institutions: that the Catholic church would continue to dominate university education. For these younger scholars the purpose of developing the social sciences in Quebec was to offer the Québécois, through economic, social, cultural, and political studies, a wider and deeper appreciation of the strengths and weaknesses of Quebec society.[67]

Contrary to the belief entertained by Lévesque and his early colleagues, the development of the social sciences did not lead to convergence of anglophone and francophone nationalisms in Canada. Rather, it contributed to the rediscovery and redefinition of Quebec's collective image, to the preaching of a neo-nationalism that would form the ideological basis for the Quiet Revolution of the 1960s and 1970s.

NOTES

1. Georges-Henri Lévesque to Radio-Canada, 5 May 1952, in Robert Parisé, *Georges-Henri Lévesque: père de la renaissance québécoise* (Montréal: Alain Stanké 1976), 44. See also G.-H. Lévesque, *Souvenance I* (Montreal: La Presse 1983).
2. Yves Roby, *Les Québécois et les investissements américains* (Québec: Les Presses de l'Université Laval 1976).
3. Marcel Fournier, "L'Institutionnalisation des sciences sociales au Québec," *Sociologie et sociétés* 5, no. 1 (1973): 55.
4. See Kenneth McRoberts and Dale Posgate, *Quebec: Social Change and Political Crisis* (Toronto: McClelland and Stewart 1980), chaps. 3 and 4.
5. Cyrias Ouellet, *La Vie des sciences au Canada français* (Québec: Ministère des affaires culturelles 1964); Pierre Dansereau, "Science in French Canada," *Scientific Monthly* 59 (1944): 261-72.
6. J.-C. Falardeau, "Antécédents, débuts et croissance de la sociologie au Québec," *Recherches sociographiques* (hereafter *RS*) 15 (1974): 142.
7. See Lionel Groulx, *Mes mémoires* (Montréal: Fides 1970), 1:216.
8. École des sciences sociales, politiques et économiques, *Organisation et programme des cours, 1938* (Québec: Université Laval 1938), 3-14.
9. Fournier, "L'Institutionnalisation des sciences sociales au Québec," 31-2; Maurice Tremblay and Albert Faucher, "L'Enseignement des sciences sociales au Canada de langue française," in *Les Arts, lettres et sciences au Canada, 1949-1951; recueil d'études spéciales* (Ottawa: King's Printer 1951), 193-4, 196-7.
10. See Marcel Clément, *Sciences sociales et catholicisme* (Montréal: École sociale populaire, no. 423, 1949), 5-18.
11. Robert Rumilly, *Histoire de la province de Québec* (Montréal: B. Valiquette 1961), 33, 164.
12. G.-H. Lévesque, "La 'Co-opérative Commonwealth Federation,'" in *Pour la restauration sociale au Canada* (Montréal: École sociale populaire, nos. 232-3, 1933), 21.
13. Ibid., 36. For a critical analysis of Lévesque's study, see Gregory Baum, *Catholics and Canadian Socialism* (Toronto: James Lorimer 1980), 97-118. Baum believes that Lévesque and his colleagues misinterpreted the encyclical *Quadragesimo anno* and the program of the CCF, and that the Catholic church should never have condemned the CCF.

14. Interview with Father G.-H. Lévesque, 9 May 1973; Georges-Henri Lévesque, "Itinéraires sociologiques," *RS* 15 (1974): 203–8; Baum, *Catholics and Canadian Socialism*, 100, 118, 128–9.

15. École des sciences sociales, politiques et économiques, *Annuaire de l'Université Laval, 1938–1939* (Québec: Université Laval, nd), 51.

16. Gonzalve Poulin, "L'Enseignement des sciences sociales dans les universités canadiennes," *Culture* 2 (1941): 12.

17. See G.-H. Lévesque, "Action catholique et action sociale," *Cahiers de l'École des sciences sociales de l'Université Laval* 1, no. 4 (1942): 12.

18. Lévesque, "Itinéraires sociologiques," 208. Lévesque's first choice of location for the Faculty of Social Science was Montreal, financial and industrial metropolis of Quebec and Canada, but the presence of Edouard Montpetit and the structure of the University of Montreal — somewhat more autonomous and secular than Laval — forced Lévesque and Cardinal Villeneuve to establish it at Laval.

19. Falardeau, "Antécédents, débuts et croissance," 144.

20. Interviews with Father G.-H. Lévesque, 9 May and 3 September 1976. See also Fournier, "L'Institutionnalisation des sciences sociales au Québec," 37. Professor Everett Hughes was partly responsible for the creation of a true faculty in 1943. Before leaving for Chicago, he had suggested such a course of action in order to stimulate a large-scale program of research. See E.C. Hughes, "Programme de recherches sociales pour le Québec," *Cahiers de l'École des sciences sociales* 2, no. 4 (1943).

21. J.-C. Falardeau, "Itinéraires sociologiques," *RS* 15 (1974): 221–2, 224. Falardeau describes the difficulties he encountered in finding a course on the history of Canada and of Quebec. His decision to choose sociology was prompted by "the need to understand what was in the process of developing in Quebec society." Ibid., 220.

22. Interview with Father G.-H. Lévesque, 9 May 1973.

23. Léon Dion, "Itinéraires sociologiques," *RS* 15 (1974): 229–31; Gérard Bergeron, ibid., 233–7. Interviews with Léon Dion and Gérard Bergeron, 1 Sept. and 31 Aug. 1976.

24. Guy Rocher, "Itinéraires sociologiques," *RS* 15 (1974): 244–5; Fernand Dumont, ibid., 256–7.

25. See McRoberts and Posgate, *Quebec: Social Change and Political Crisis*, chap. 5.

26. Léon Dion, "Aspects de la condition du professeur d'université dans la société canadienne-française," *Cité libre* 25 (July 1958): 13.

27. See Jean-Charles Falardeau, ed., *Essais sur le Québec contemporain* (Québec: Les Presses de l'Universite Laval 1952), for studies of the social repercussions of the industrialization of Quebec that are severely critical of the elites and institutions existing at that time.

28. See Michael D. Behiels, *Prelude to Quebec's Quiet Revolution: Liberalism versus Neo-Nationalism, 1945–1960* (Kingston and Montreal: McGill-Queen's University Press 1985), chap. 4.

29. Interview with Father G.-H. Lévesque, 9 May 1973.

30. Georges-Henri Lévesque, "L'individualisme: source de communisme," lecture given at Laval University in 1934. I thank Father Lévesque for providing a copy of this presentation and other documents from the Lévesque Foundation.

31. Various numbers of *Ensemble*, 1939–44. See also Doris Lussier, "La Faculté des sciences sociales," *Revue de l'Université Laval* 6 (1951): 233–90.

32. Ibid., 278–81.

33. See *Cahiers de l'École des sciences sociales*, 1941–45; *Cahiers du Service extérieur d'éducation sociale*, 1945–49.

34. Interview with Father G.-H. Lévesque, 9 May 1973; Lussier, "La Faculté des sciences sociales," 284–5.

35. G.-H. Lévesque, "Service social et charité," in *Cahiers de la Faculté des sciences sociales* 4 (1944): 3–20; Lévesque, "Integrating the Social Work Curriculum into the Social Sciences," *Social Work Journal* (Apr. 1951): 63–9.

36. G.-H. Lévesque, "L'Université et les relations industrielles," in Congrès des relations industrielles, *Rapport*, 1946 (Québec: Les Presses de l'Université Laval 1947); Gérard Dion, "L'Université et les relations industrielles," *Revue de l'Université Laval* 3 (1948): 56–9; Dion, "Notre département des relations industrielles," *Ad Usum Sacerdotum* 5, no. 7 (1950): 73.

37. The two articles written by Lévesque for *Ensemble* can be found in his pamphlet *La Non-confessionalité des coopératives* (Québec: le Conseil supérieur de la coopération 1946), 26. See also Parisé, *Lévesque*, 82–110.

38. Interview with Father G.-H. Lévesque, 9 May 1973. See also P.-M. Gaudrault, *Neutralité, non-confessionalité et École sociale populaire* (Montreal 1946). Cardinal Villeneuve, in a letter to Lévesque of 17 Aug. 1946, was severely critical of Father Gaudrault for having made

his accusation public and of Archbishop Charbonneau of Montreal for having given it his imprimatur. See Groulx, *Mes mémoires*, 4:263.

39. Interviews with Father G.-H. Lévesque, 9 May 1973 and 3 Sept. 1976.

40. G.-H. Lévesque, "Principles and Facts in the Teaching of Social Sciences," *Canadian Journal of Economics and Political Science* (hereafter *CJEPS*) 13 (1947): 501–6. The French-language version was entitled "Sciences sociales et progrès humain," *Revue de l'Université Laval* 3 (1948): 37–41. G.-H. Lévesque, *L'Enseignement de la doctrine sociale de l'Église et la Faculté des Sciences sociales de Laval* (Québec: Université Laval 1947), mimeo, 10 pp., fondation Lévesque, fonds Lévesque. The abbé Gérard Dion reproduced this work in *Ad Usum Sacerdotum* 4, no. 2 (1948): supp. 1–13. This journal was produced for members of the Catholic church in Quebec, but circulated much more widely.

41. Lévesque, "Sciences sociales et progrès humain," 39. Gérard Dion mentioned the same point in "L'Université et les relations industrielles," 57–8.

42. J.-C. Falardeau, "Qu'est-ce que la croissance de la sociologie au Québec?" *Culture* 10 (1949): 250–61; Falardeau, "Antécédents, débuts et croissance," 146.

43. Clément, *Sciences sociales et catholicisme*, 18–31.

44. Lévesque, "Sciences sociales et progrès humain," 40; Falardeau, "Itinéraires sociologiques," 223.

45. Lévesque, *L'Enseignement de la doctrine sociale de l'Église*, 1–6.

46. Ibid., 9.

47. Interview with Father G.-H. Lévesque, 9 May 1973. See also Blair Fraser, "The Fright over Father Lévesque," *Maclean's*, 1 July 1952. This journalist maintains that Bishop Courchesnes of Rimouski, the same who had undertaken to confront Archbishop Charbonneau after the Asbestos strike, was responsible for the two actions brought against Lévesque.

48. J.-C. Falardeau, "Lettre à mes etudiants," *Cité libre* 23 (May 1959): 7.

49. See J.-C. Falardeau, *L'Essor des sciences sociales au Canada français* (Québec: Ministère des affaires culturelles 1964), 47, 50–1; Université Laval, *Faculté des Sciences sociales, Annuaires 1951–52* (Québec: les Presses de l'Université Laval 1951), 40–2, has a description of the work of the Centre for Social Research.

50. J.-C. Falardeau, "Itinéraires sociologiques," 224. He writes: "The Duplessis régime forced all those who were concerned with social progress to repudiate the negative rhetoric and the immobilism which was once again masking the real problems. We of the social sciences at Laval and Montreal, like some of those at Radio-Canada and many others, were engaged in a sort of politics of resistance. It was necessary to participate in the great leap forward." See also Falardeau, "Antécédents, débuts et croissance," 156.

51. Dion, "Aspects de la condition du professeur d'université," 14.

52. G.-H. Lévesque, "Humanisme et sciences sociales," *CJEPS* 18 (1952): 268. Jean-Charles Falardeau maintains that Father Lévesque was above all a determined man of action. He never limited himself to the theoretical side of things. Father Lévesque was a social animator seeking to disseminate a liberal social Catholicism, just as Father Joseph-Papin Archambault worked for l'École sociale populaire and the ideology of Christian corporatism. Interview with J.-C. Falardeau, 1 Sept. 1976.

53. Falardeau, *L'Essor des sciences sociales au Canada français*, 48; Falardeau, "Lettre à mes étudiants," 14.

54. Lévesque, "Humanisme et sciences sociales," 268. Jean-Charles Falardeau, confirming this idealism, recalls that the pervasive atmosphere of the faculty was that of a social crusade: "I had the feeling of being drawn into sociology in the same way as one says one is drawn into religion. This kind of intellectual life was not for me a labour: it was rather a series of passions, highlighted by periodic resurrections." Falardeau, "Itinéraires sociologiques," 223.

55. Interview with Father G.-H. Lévesque, 9 May 1973.

56. Ibid. See also Fraser, "The Fight over Father Lévesque," 52; and Roger Lemelin, "The Silent Struggle at Laval," *Maclean's*, 1 Aug. 1952, 36. Robert Rumilly mentions the two Jesuit attempts against Father Lévesque and his faculty but makes no mention of an attack by the Duplessis government. Rumilly, *Maurice Duplessis et son temps* (Montréal: Fides 1973), 2:311, 350–1.

57. Maurice Lamontagne expresses his ideas in his book *Le Fédéralisme canadien: evolution et problèmes* (Québec: les Presses de l'Université Laval 1954), 295.

58. Behiels, *Prelude to Quebec's Quiet Revolution*, chap. 9.

59. Gérard Filion, "L'Ingérence du fédéral dans l'enseignement supérieur," *Le Devoir*, 7 June 1951; Michel Brunet, "Le Rapport Massey: réflexions et observations," *L'Action universitaire* 18, no. 2 (1952): 39–41.

60. F.-H. Angers, "Deux modèles d'inconscience: le Premier Saint-Laurent et le commissaire Lévesque," *L'Action nationale 38*, no. 3 (1951): 206.
61. F.-A. Angers, "Les Solutions du Rapport Massey III — À qui la faute?" *L'Action nationale* 39, no. 4 (1952): 267–72.
62. Interview with Léon Dion, 1 Sept. 1976.
63. Interview with Father G.-H. Lévesque, 3 Sept. 1976.
64. Guy Rocher, "Itinéraires sociologiques," *RS* 15 (1974): 247.
65. Interview with Léon Dion, 1 Sept. 1976. See also Dion, "Aspects de la condition du professeur d'université," 15–16.
66. Interview with Jean-Charles Falardeau, 1 Sept. 1976.
67. See Fernand Dumont and Yves Martin, *Situation de la recherche sur le Canada français* (Québec: les Presses de l'Université Laval 1969), 296.

Triple Jeopardy: Assessing Life Experiences of Black Nova Scotian Women from a Social Work and Historical Perspective

WANDA THOMAS BERNARD, LYDIA LUCAS-WHITE, and DOROTHY E. MOORE

The case that racism and sexism combine their effects to produce a double negative status for visible minority women was suggested by us in 1981, at a Canadian Association of Schools of Social Work conference (Bernard et al., 1981). That paper was only an attempt; at the time, little attention had been paid to this topic, and we could find very few written sources to substantiate our perceptions. Those we did find were mostly written by Black or Asian women. The topic has since attracted increasing attention, from women in particular. Some have expanded the theme to focus on multiple disadvantages such as race, gender, class, location, and immigrant status. In updating our perspective, we have chosen to discuss the first three as they affect indigenous Black women in Nova Scotia. Race, gender, and class are important structural elements which profoundly affect the situation of users of social services, before their individual needs can be assessed by social workers.

Throughout North America, when a group of people of low socio-economic status is also non-White, it is usually oppressed by racist treatment in addition to poverty, to varying degrees. If non-White poor people are also female, they suffer not only the inequalities which have afflicted all women, but some additional problems with Whites of the same gender

SOURCE: "Triple Jeopardy: Assessing Life Experiences of Black Nova Scotian Women from a Social Work Perspective," *Canadian Social Work Review* 10, no. 2 (Summer 1993): 256–74. Reprinted with permission of the Canadian Association of Schools of Social Work, Ottawa.

and with men of their own race. Class, race, and gender may be intricately linked and compounding the effects of each other, creating a triple jeopardy for Black women. Associated with each variable is a pervasive powerlessness relative to those who are better off, the White or male dominant group. This situation of triple jeopardy affects the life chances of the individuals or groups afflicted by all three sources of oppression at once. Further, class and race have been closely associated historically and continue to be so; these factors have affected both genders differentially.

Our goal is to show that discrimination and poverty have been the lot of Black Nova Scotian women historically, and that they have also suffered the disadvantages of all women. Our secondary goal is to examine the strengths and strategies of these Black women to survive, struggle against, and even overcome their disadvantages today. As social workers and educators, our final goal must be to suggest ways in which we can work to help achieve social justice for them.

Black History in Nova Scotia

A brief sketch of Black history in Nova Scotia shows all Blacks placed firmly at the bottom of the socio-economic hierarchy, in a province that is part of a chronically underdeveloped and disadvantaged region. It cannot be argued, as it is for some immigrant groups, that their disadvantage stems from late arrival: Nova Scotia has the longest history of European contact and settlement in Canada, and Black people were present either as slaves or free from 1604 onwards (Moore, 1979). Black labour was used in building fortifications and in road-building when Halifax was founded in 1749, and Yankee settlers brought Black domestic servants when they occupied lands vacated by the Acadians expelled in 1755. Several thousand free Blacks arrived with the Loyalists in the 1780s, Maroon prisoners (descendants of runaway slaves in Jamaica) were brought in 1792, and a wave of Black refugees arrived after the War of 1812. Not all of these groups stayed in Nova Scotia; some took an opportunity to emigrate to Sierra Leone. However, many who might have left were obliged to stay because they were bound either as slaves or as "servants for life" — a form of indefinite indenture, which some had been tricked into accepting in order to find employment. Officially slavery in Canada ended in 1834, although it became increasingly difficult to retain slaves after 1800.

Conditions of abject poverty for the Black population in Nova Scotia continued throughout the nineteenth century. Blacks were mostly located in small rural settlements on poor land near the outskirts of towns. Even those who had been promised land grants on their arrival, as were the Black Loyalists, received very little or none at all, and they had great difficulty in obtaining deeds even for house lots. When free to work for wages, they were paid for day-labour at a quarter of the wages paid to Whites. As more poor White immigrants (Irish, Scottish) arrived, cheap labour became more abundant and Whites were hired preferentially, so that jobs for Blacks became extremely scarce. Clearly, then, from the beginning, Blacks in Nova Scotia have been oppressed, exploited, sharply discriminated against, and, to a great extent, segregated. They were allocated a position at the bottom of the ethnic and class hierarchy which was developing in the province (and, indeed, in the region) and this position was reinforced by their subsequent treatment. Only the Aboriginal people were treated as harshly.

In the nineteenth century, Black communities tried to improve their lot by education. They were aided by the Society for the Propagation of the Gospel to set up schools, but, since a community had to provide the first 50 pounds to qualify, this was an impossible sum for many to achieve. Discriminatory Education Acts sanctioned separate schools for Blacks, and the last mention of race disappeared from education legislation only in 1954. One segregated school — the Nelson Whynder Elementary School — still survives in the remote end of Preston, near Halifax. In the late nineteenth century, many Nova Scotian Blacks emigrated to the United States, where they found greater opportunities in employment and education (Boyd, 1975).

Early in the twentieth century, the last major group of Black immigrants was recruited in the Caribbean, especially in Barbados, to work in the expanding steel industry in Sydney, Cape Breton. Many of these people had achieved a better level of education under direct British colonial administration (Beaton, 1988); when they discovered the extent of racial discrimination in Nova Scotia, they tried to maintain a difference by continuing to identify themselves as "West Indians" (Carrington, 1988). In recent decades, a small number of West Indian and African Blacks have settled in the province. Since they must meet Canadian Immigration criteria, they tend to be people with a superior level of education. Some have been hired in government jobs where they are said to represent Black Nova Scotians. All are counted together in census figures (Jabbra & Cosper, 1988). The demonstration by recent Black newcomers of the value of education has verified for the indigenous Black people that their long-held aspiration was a valid one, though few had managed to achieve it. Education was always seen as the passport to better jobs and incomes, but in the meantime they had to survive with very little help from the White population and a great deal of rejection.

Ironically, this rejection provided Blacks with a positive resource in that they were gathered together in segregated communities, where they could support and rely on each other. Black churches arose out of exclusion from White churches, and they became the hearts, leaders, and protectors of the Black communities. The communities themselves were composed of families, usually extended families, trying to provide for each other's needs and to equip the next generation for survival.

As previously mentioned, these communities were usually close to White towns, on poor land which supported few crops. Nevertheless, they used whatever the land offered to earn an income. Many walked miles to town and back to sell berries, mayflowers, firewood, Christmas wreaths — whatever the season provided. Men did casual labouring jobs — usually the hardest and dirtiest — when they were available. Many had to travel to other places to look for work. Women worked as cleaners, maids, and child-carers in White homes for long hours, then made their way home to care for their own families.

More or less segregated Black communities still exist in Nova Scotia, but in recent decades many Blacks have moved into the larger urban centres in search of employment, although usually maintaining their links with relatives left behind. Thus the frequently used term "the Black community" tends to apply collectively to Black citizens in general as well as the geographical communities. One might assume that urban migration and greater mobility would now offer the means for the Black population to improve its position. However, today's circumstances tend to perpetuate history's legacy of disadvantage with respect to class, race, and gender.

Class

It is generally agreed that, in Western societies, including Canada, one's place in the class hierarchy is mainly determined by socioeconomic status comprised of the associated variables of education, income, and employment. Here, we shall rely especially on the study by Jabbra & Cosper (1988), who surveyed ethnic groups in Atlantic Canada using 1986 Census data.

First, we should note that Nova Scotia's Blacks have always formed a large proportion of Canada's total Black population; precisely what proportion has been difficult to estimate, since it is acknowledged that they were undercounted in successive Census data collections. The latest data in 1986 counted 15,665, but the Black United Front, a provincial "umbrella" organization, has consistently claimed that their present population in Nova Scotia is from 30,000 to 35,000 (or approximately 4%) of the population. Jabbra & Cosper refer in their analysis to this group as Afro-Canadians, a term which is becoming preferred among leading members of the Black community.

EDUCATION

Jabbra & Cosper found that, as a whole, Afro-Canadians had a little better level of education than either Aboriginal people or the region's French population, although all three groups rank well below average. Rural location is said to affect educational attainment, but, with respect to Afro-Canadians, Jabbra & Cosper noted a rapid trend to urbanization by 1986.

The process of "streaming" in our high schools left Black females doubly disadvantaged. They were streamed away from male occupations, which would afford them decision-making authority, while Blacks in general were often streamed into general or commercial courses, which provided few marketable skills and left them without prerequisites for university entrance. Streaming now occurs within our elementary grades where students are streamed or separated into groups which carry out school work at different levels.

The high school drop-out rate for Black youth has been fairly high. There are unquestionably a number of reasons for this, but one relates to the curriculum in our schools. Black children are taught little or nothing about their history as people. They are usually taught that they are descended from slaves; they learn little or nothing of the many and varied accomplishments and contributions of their forebears. They learn little of their heritage of which they can be proud.

Blacks are still underrepresented in Nova Scotia universities. The Transition Year Program (TYP) was established at Dalhousie University in 1969 to help bridge the gap for Black and Native students who lacked the academic qualifications or financial means to enter university. In its seventh year, it was noted that more males than females had entered the TYP, but more females had actually graduated (Pachai, 1991, p. 218).

There are currently many Black female teachers in Nova Scotia, but few have attained positions of authority in the system, especially at the secondary level. The provincial government study of the Women's Directorate (1990) confirms this, noting "while women continue to hold the majority of teaching positions in Nova Scotian schools, they represent only a small minority of department heads, vice-principals and principals" (p. 65). Of course, Black women are even more underrepresented.

It is also interesting to look at the placement of Black teachers in our current system. In one central Halifax school in which a large percentage of students are Black, there is only one full-time Black teacher. There is no shortage of indigenous Black teachers; in fact, many have had to find work outside Nova Scotia. In 1987 in North Preston, a Black community, the Nelson Whynder School had four White and four Black full-time teachers, and three White and two Black special teachers. There is no good reason why a majority of Black teachers should not be employed in an all-Black school (Pachai, 1991, pp. 258–259).

The Black Educators' Association (BEA) has compiled informative data on the numbers and distribution of Black students and teachers in Nova Scotia. The BEA has had a broad focus since its formation in 1971. It is committed to advancing the quality of education as well as access to equal opportunities for Black Nova Scotians and other minorities. Until the education system and all other systems in the province provide equally and justly for all Nova Scotians, the BEA has an important function to perform (Pachai, 1991, pp. 258, 269).

Some members of both the Black and White communities have called for immediate revolutionary methods to bring about improvements. For example, after racial incidents involving Black and White students at Cole Harbour District High School in Halifax County in January 1989, the Parent Student Association of Preston called for judicial inquiries to determine the causes and extent of racism in the Nova Scotian school system. This echoed an older inquiry, that of the Graham Commission on Education, Public Services, and Provincial–Municipal Relations, whose recommendations in 1971 pointed to inequalities in the school system and referred to the impact of these inequalities on the Black population. Some issues addressed included the need for more Black teachers, for race relations education for all teachers, and for a review of the curriculum to introduce more Black history. Since similar recommendations are still being made, it would seem that few changes have actually occurred.

INCOME AND EMPLOYMENT

Education levels were not analyzed according to gender by Jabbra and Cosper, but income statistics were. The data were for employed people of 15 years or older, as shown in Table 1. It should be noted here that Afro-Canadian men, while considerably below the average and the British-Canadian men in incomes, still earn considerably more than do women of British background. Afro-Canadian women's incomes are not much less than those of British-Canadian women; this is probably due to the much lower incomes for all women regardless of ethnicity (approximately 56% of men's incomes). Afro-Canadian men's incomes are much more sharply below those for all men, a pattern repeated elsewhere in the Western world (Bruegel, 1989). Only Aboriginal earnings are below those of Afro-Canadians, for both genders.

These incomes only apply to those with employment. Outside the paid sector were 30 and 44 per cent of Afro-Canadian men and women respectively. The men's rate was exceeded only by Aboriginal men, at 39 per cent. In their study, Jabbra & Cosper claim that the percentage of a group without an occupation can be taken as an indicator of the rate of unemployment. Therefore, Table 2 may be understood to refer to those employed in the various occupations.

The only category in which both male and female Afro-Canadians are overrepresented is that of Service Industries. Within these, men are especially overrepresented as janitors and security personnel, and women as cleaners and domestics. At first glance, Afro-Canadians appear to be quite well represented in Managerial and Professional jobs, but within

TABLE 1   Average Incomes of Employed Afro-Canadians in Atlantic Canada in 1986*

Ethnic origin	Males	Females
Afro-Canadian	$14,033	$9,847
Aboriginal	$9,860	$7,326
British	$19,134	$10,541
All origins	$19,075	$10,488

*Census data extracted from Jabbra & Cosper (1988).

TABLE 2   Percentage of Afro-Canadians in Each Category of Occupation, Compared with Percentage of Total Population in Each Category, by Gender, Atlantic Canada, 1986

Group	Gov't., admin., managerial, professional	Service industries	Resource industries	Manufacturing, transport, construction, other	No occupation	Total
Afro-Canadian males	10.5	26.3	2.8	29.9	29.9	100%
Total male population	15.5	18.3	9.2	33.2	23.9	100%
Afro-Canadian females	13.6	39.0	0	3.3	43.7	100%
Total female population	14.4	32.2	1.4	6.4	45.7	100%

these they are overrepresented in specific occupations. For men, this is in teaching, social work, and especially as hospital attendants within health; for women, it is in social work and especially as nurses and nurses' aides within health. Within the Manufacturing, Transport, and Construction category, the only job in which Afro-Canadian men are not underrepresented is construction, where many work as labourers on road-repair and heavy construction. Both men and women are severely underrepresented in the Resource Industries of farming, fishing, forestry, and mining, and also in arts and crafts. This study showed no one in law, but there have been a few indigenous Black lawyers in Nova Scotia, one of whom was recently appointed the first Black female judge in the province. Jabbra & Cosper conclude from their statistics that some upward mobility seems evident for Afro-Canadians. This indicates how marginal the position of Blacks has been in the past.

The census study also found that higher education levels were not perfectly translated into higher incomes, suggesting that institutional discrimination affects income to an extent. This agrees with the national figures for 1986 in which higher educational levels for women did not translate into higher occupation distribution (Status of Women Canada, 1990, p. 144). We must also remember that these statistics include the more affluent and highly trained immigrants from Africa and the West Indies; without them, the data for Black Nova Scotians might appear less promising.

Another phenomenon not addressed in the data is that unemployment soars in the Black community at times of recession, being documented in recent years at over 60 per cent among men in the larger Preston area. Many of their jobs have little security and they often vanish when the economy shrinks and lay-offs occur. Many women's service jobs (domestic or cleaning work) are in large institutions or businesses, or in the homes of the well-to-do, so cutbacks tend to have a smaller effect. The film, *In Service* (written by Black writer Maxine Tynes and directed by Lulu Beating, National Film Board, 1991), vividly portrays the recurrent pattern of Black women's domestic work.

Overall, these figures convey a marked undervaluing and underpayment of women's work within a region where all incomes are relatively low and greater numbers of people are without paid employment. The small gap between incomes of Black and British-Canadian women is very similar to that for visible minority women nationally, but the regional incomes are less than half of the national ones (Status of Women Canada, 1990, p. 145). This is in line with the 1990 findings of the Women's Directorate (p. 95). Blacks are still underrepresented in both provincial and federal government employment and are concentrated in lower occupation levels. Of 172 Black women currently employed by the provincial Civil Service, a total of 116 (or 67%) are in clerical or domestic jobs at the lower end of the job categories and hence at the lower end of the pay scale. In contrast, only 13 (8%) are in management positions.

Overall, these data concerning education, income, and employment do indicate that a much lower socio-economic status for Afro-Canadians in Atlantic Canada (and hence in Nova Scotia where the overwhelming majority of this group lives) has persisted into the present. Only the Aboriginal people rank lower on all indicators, though the French (Acadians) do on some.

Race

Of the many aspects of race and racism, the area most relevant here concerns the relationship between Black and White women in Nova Scotia. From the data above, we note that more Black women are in paid employment, at wages quite close to those of White women, in a region where jobs are hard to find. But since Black women are a very small minority, they are unlikely to be viewed as a competitive threat as a group, at least as long as institutional discrimination is still entrenched, although individuals do encounter such views. White women have been pressing for affirmative action to redress the inequalities suffered by women in general. But only in recent years have they paid any attention to the situation of women from visible minorities — a situation similar to their own, but worse. These are obvious grounds for women to join forces, and we must consider what has caused a less than sisterly relationship between Black and White women, and also the repeated claim by Black women that race is more important than gender in their oppression.

Some visible minority women have been present in the Canadian women's movement since its beginning, though they were often paid little attention or treated as tokens (Adamson et al., 1988, pp. 83–85). Women's organizations within specific ethnic groups also existed, but because they often addressed issues which feminists did not see as specifically women's issues, they were not viewed as part of the women's movement. Visible minority women could scarcely be blamed for not wishing to join a movement which did not understand their different oppressions. Many of them have also pointed out that racism is deeply embedded in Canadian society and so is frequently implemented by White women as well as men. A more positive development emerged in the 1980s with the greater participation of visible minority women in the women's movement and a growing awareness of racism and concern to confront it among both groups. In 1983, this trend was given impetus by the formation in Toronto of the Visible Minority Women's Coalition, the first consciously political "umbrella" group (Adamson et al., 1988, p. 84). The Coalition shared in planning events for the 1986 International Women's Day and in doing so challenged the whole decision-making process by revealing some of the ways in which White women unconsciously reproduce racism. Needless to say, many White women are frightened by the anger minority women feel towards them, as it challenges their definition of feminism in a profound way.

Black women have not experienced the feminist movement as one which addresses their needs. Collins suggests that White women's inability to acknowledge their own racism, especially how it privileges them, is another outcome of the differential relationship that White and Black women have to White women's power (Hill Collins, 1990). White women are not taught to recognize White privilege, just as White men are not taught to recognize male privilege. To be truly reflective of and responsive to Black women, the feminist movement must first acknowledge the racism which is part of our society and hence a part of our reality, and then challenge that racism.

Another issue to which the women's movement is paying increased attention is class — a topic long neglected in Canada in view of the popular impression that almost everyone is middle-class. As the employment and income statistics given here show, there are enormous inequalities of wealth, power, and privilege, which leave more than one in five women living below the poverty line (Hill Collins, 1990, pp. 102–104). Lack of choice and access to resources keeps these women poor and powerless in a patriarchal society, and the "feminization of poverty" is increasing.

The difficult concept of "class" allows us to see the differences between groups of women based on differences in power, resources, and choice. Class also underlines the shared experiences and interests of groups of women. The majority of women in Canada have limited power, resources, and choice, and so have a common basis for organizing to confront these inequalities. In Nova Scotia, it is obvious that most women in paid employment are poor, particularly if they are single wage-earners with dependents. With higher unemployment rates in the area, it is likely that many of the women not in the labour force are also poor. Blacks and Whites alike suffer from these conditions; this provides both groups of women with a strong reason to work together, but it can also bring women and men together in common struggles just as race can.

Gender

The relationships between Black women and Black men have been adversely affected by the history of racism and oppression (Bernard et al., 1981). Black women have assumed the role of matriarch, and their strength has facilitated survival of the Black family and hence the Black community.

Many Black men have been denied access to good education and jobs in Nova Scotia, as is apparent also in the United States and in Britain, with similar results. Amina Mama (1989) writes in a British journal:

> I would argue that dependence on individual men was never a feasible option for the majority of Black women, because of the marginalization of Black men from the waged economy. . . . By far the majority of Black women are waged workers, as they have always been, and those who are not have not usually been able to depend on financial support from a man. Like growing numbers of working class men, many of Britain's Black men have not been able to fulfil the breadwinner role because their wages are too low. (p. 36)

Black men are products of a male-dominated society which states that men should provide for their families and should head their households. How do these expectations affect the self-esteem of the Black man who is unable to meet these unattainable goals? Audre Lorde (1982) asks, if society ascribes roles to Black men which they are not allowed to fulfil, is it society that needs changing? Many of these men are unable to fulfil their prescribed roles, for example, that of parenting.

Many Black women are parenting on their own. Ten years ago we noted that there were a large number of female-headed, single-parent families in our Black communities. In 1991, a needs assessment of the

Black community in Dartmouth, completed by Patrice LaFleur, indicated that the number of Black, female-headed, single-parent families is increasing. This research identified many problems associated with this emerging trend, including poverty, lack of affordable housing and child care, and lack of supports.

The issue of Black female/Black male relationships was also discussed during this research project. This issue is debated by many scholars as well as lay persons. Hill Collins (1990) states that "exploring the tensions between African-American men and women has been a longstanding theme in Black feminist thought." The research conducted by LaFleur (1991) for the Association of Black Social Workers was a participatory research process. The researcher met with several focus groups comprised of females and males, ranging in age from 13 to 80 years. Each of the focus groups identified the tension between Black women and Black men as a major issue which must be addressed by the community. Some women identified feelings of hurt and anger regarding their perception of the relationships between Black women and men. These groups reported that Black males tend to have more respect for White women than Black women and treat them better in relationships. Respondents also expressed the view that Black males tend to become aggressive due to the oppression with which they must contend. Many identified the need to challenge and condemn the oppressive behaviour of Black males towards Black females. Hill Collins (1990) states that Black male admiration for White women is seen as a rejection of Black women and as an acceptance of Eurocentric gender ideology and aesthetics (p. 183).

LaFleur's (1991) study also reported many positive experiences between Black women and Black men. There appears to be a direct correlation between the availability of suitable employment for Black males, the degree of job satisfaction, and the quality of the relationship between Black men and Black women.

Black females, like those in the larger society, are socialized to be good wives, mothers, and homemakers. For the most part, Black women share not only the socialization patterns of the dominant society but also the sexual stereotypes. Black women are caught between White prejudice, class prejudice, male power, and the burden of history. The plight of women in general is certainly magnified for the Black woman who, to survive, must become independent, assertive, and ambitious.

Experiencing Triple Jeopardy

Bell Hooks (1988) says:

> It has been a political struggle for me to hold to the belief that here is much which we — Black people — must speak about, much that is private that must be openly shared if we are to heal our wounds (hurts caused by domination

and exploitation and oppression), if we are to recover and realize ourselves. (pp. 2–3)

We understand Hooks' comment about privacy and share her belief about the need to now speak openly.

As Black Nova Scotian women, our personal experiences have been very challenging. We previously shared some of our experiences as Black social workers (Bernard et al., 1981). As we reflect on these and our experiences of the past 10 years, we realize that little has changed. We must still work twice as hard to build our credibility, to prove our competence, to attain whatever goal we have in sight, and then to hold onto it. We are still in positions where we are the only permanent Black social workers on staff. The expectation, usually unspoken, is that we are representing our race and our community, that we are the experts and must have all the answers on issues relating to the Black community.

Each of us has had the opportunity to achieve some mobility in our careers; one is now working in a management position and one is a social work educator. Our accomplishments have both positive and negative connotations. On a positive note, we are role models for Black social workers and youth and other racially visible people. On a negative note, we have each experienced some professional jealousy. We have had our credentials questioned, as well as the quality of the programs in which we are working. For example, when he heard about the academic appointment of one of the authors, a White male commented, "It can't be much of a program, if you're teaching in it." Feeling the need to prove our competency to our colleagues and the world in general adds another negative aspect to our reality.

We both experience racism on many levels. Our success in our respective careers does not change the fact that we are frequently faced with racist incidents. For example, when one of us facilitated a workshop on racism awareness for a group of junior high school students, their teacher sat with her back to the speaker throughout the presentation. One of us has overheard colleagues make derogatory comments about other minority groups such as "What would you expect from an Arab?" What comments are made about Blacks when we are not within earshot?

We have both taught and supervised male as well as female students. One of us supervises a group of professional social workers which includes several males, and one of us facilitates a male therapy group. We have found that Black women in positions of authority are not always readily accepted or taken seriously — by either their peers or subordinates — though this is not commonly acknowledged. The reality is that many males have difficulty relating to any woman in a position of authority. Having dealt with these experiences, we are now empowered to challenge racism and sexism.

What impact does work-related stress have on family life? The struggle for survival is also present in marriage. Developing and maintaining a positive relationship with a Black male partner must include methods and strategies for dealing with sexism on an individual level and the institutional racism faced by both partners. For one of us this has meant helping the partner understand the system in order to survive in it. Maintaining a positive family life is in itself a full-time job, requiring extra energy and effort. Our situations are not unique; they are the experiences of many Black Nova Scotian women.

Strategies and Strengths

WOMEN'S ROLE AND THE BLACK COMMUNITY

The three variables of gender, race, and class can all place Black women in jeopardy, but they can also provide opportunities for sharing and building alliances to overcome disadvantage. We have already touched on many of the strategies and strengths of Black Nova Scotians to survive and overcome their continuing disadvantages and oppression, including their efforts to improve education and the close-knit homogeneous nature of the Black communities. Throughout, Black women have played a central role in their community's cohesion.

The recent film *Black Mother Black Daughter* (National Film Board, 1989) poignantly expresses the importance and interdependence of family, church, and community in the lives of Black Nova Scotians. Sylvia Hamilton, one of the film's Black directors, notes that Black women in particular patiently fostered and nurtured the survival of the province's Black culture and community. These strategies for survival have persisted into the present. Today, the family in the Black community may be a traditional two-parent nuclear family, a single parent, usually female-headed family, or an extended family. Grandparents who frequently help with child-rearing and household management are often part of extended families. Regardless of its structure, the Black family has played an essential role in providing its members the support, encouragement, and sense of value which is sorely lacking for them outside the boundaries of the family and Black community.

In spite of the bleak realities of day-to-day existence, Black women continue to have high aspirations for themselves, their mates, their children, and their communities. The Black woman's role has included advocating changes for the Black community, within the church and other organizations, and holding the family together. They also have primary responsibility for maintaining their households, including budgeting, child-rearing, and providing discipline as required. Black women have viewed the family household as an arena of solidarity and resistance against racism, as described also in the United States and Britain (Nain, 1991).

At this point, we can ask if there have been dramatic changes in Black women's roles over the past 10 years. We would say "yes" in the sense that Black women are now more conscious of the importance of some of their roles and their impact on Black families. In particular, the parenting role, while a significant one for all mothers, is especially so for Black mothers. For Nova Scotian Blacks to survive as they have and to continue to survive, Black children must be taught survival skills — how to cope in an unfriendly society.

Black women must foster within their children a sense of pride — for self and race — a sense of community and a positive sense of their history in terms of accomplishments. Black mothers have been extremely important in fostering their children's development into adults who can survive the injustices in our society, and who will advocate change without undue bitterness or anger. In *Black Mother Black Daughter*, Dr. Marie Hamilton states that, if we put energy into being angry, it will stop us from getting ahead — from making real progress. Although we cannot change the past, we can help to change the future. But to do this, Black women must struggle on many fronts, even when they have made some real progress themselves.

THE BLACK CHURCH

Black churches were the first organizations to bring the Black populace together. In the nineteenth century, when the church was the only medium articulating the grievances and aspirations of Blacks, it was already functioning as a vehicle for political change, asking for more and better land, titles to land, more and better schools, more jobs, and a greater measure of recognition of the contribution of Blacks to the development of the province (Pachai, 1991, pp. 60–63).

Women were late in becoming actively involved in the African United Baptist Association (AUBA), but made up for this within a few short years with their innovative work. Women's groups were formed and specific tasks undertaken. Black women organized themselves within the AUBA in a way which had no counterpart at the time among the male membership.

The church remains the primary focus of most Black Nova Scotian communities today. It has been more than a religious organization: it has been a training ground for generations of Black leaders and followers, preachers and teachers, politicians and professionals.

OTHER ORGANIZATIONS

Secular Black organizations were needed to complement the work of the church and its various committees. The Nova Scotia Association for the Advancement of Coloured People (NSAACP), formed in 1945, sought relief for Blacks in the areas of housing and employment. Its first success was in reversing the refusal of nurse's training to a young Black woman;

Black women have since taken advantage of this improved access, but many were able to become only nurses' aides.

Since 1968, when the Nova Scotia Human Rights Commission was established, a number of Black organizations have formed to promote specific issues. The Black United Front (BUF) was intended to be a provincial "umbrella" organization. Professional organizations include the Black Educators' Association, the Black Professional Women's Group, the Congress of Black Women, and the Association of Black Social Workers (ABSW). The Black Cultural Society and the Black Cultural Centre have inspired many Blacks to take a renewed interest in their culture, which the broader society repeatedly told them had been lost.

The roles of Black women have figured prominently in the development and the work of these organizations. However, leadership in these groups has largely been a male preserve. The BUF, for example, has had eight directors (including one interim director) since 1969; only one has been female (Pachai, 1991, p. 258). In general, leadership and decision-making roles within Black organizations still tend to be male-dominated, with the exception of the Black Cultural Society and the ABSW, in which there is a more equal distribution of roles.

The ABSW is a volunteer group of Black social workers and human service workers who offer solidarity and mutual support to colleagues who would otherwise be isolated in their workplaces. It is empowered to act as a collective voice to advocate on behalf of the Black community on critical issues. For Black social work graduates, the ABSW has served as a referral source for potential employment, as well as an advocate to assist in securing social work positions. The ABSW has also been a leader in developing anti-racist social work training at the Maritime School of Social Work and in the professional community. It also runs racism awareness workshops on request for a variety of organizations, businesses, and professions.

The fact that there are enough trained Black social workers in Nova Scotia to support an active association must be credited largely to the outreach recruitment efforts of the Maritime School of Social Work. The school's affirmative action efforts began in 1973. While it encountered many problems along the way, the school has effectively attracted and welcomed many Black students as well as other minorities (Aboriginal and Acadian). In Nova Scotia, social work is now one of the few professional areas in which Blacks have increased their representation significantly.

OTHER STRATEGIES

Education and training are still viewed as the most promising solutions to Black poverty, but many schools are still discouraging Black students' ambitions by informal streaming and advice, which sidelines them from further training. Black history is still absent from the curriculum of most schools. There is still a higher than average dropout rate, especially for Black males. In an effort to counter subsequent unemployment, many Blacks have taken all the employment centre courses available to them, usually without obtaining a job at the end.

Black people have tried to resist discrimination through the services of the Human Rights Commission, but this requires a lengthy process and specific proof of a grievance, which is often difficult to secure unequivocally. They have also made good use of affirmative action programs where these have been available, both in education and employment.

All of these strategies have produced a modest improvement in the situation of Blacks, but it is only now being recognized that Black men are lagging behind Black women in their recent achievements. The data in this paper suggest a number of reasons for this. In addition, however, the frustrations of Black men and their rage about blatant racist treatment have erupted in public protests and demonstrations in Halifax, drawing increased recognition that other strategies are not really available to them. Black men are also highly overrepresented in correctional institutions, for a variety of criminal activities including violence against women, pimping, and drug-related offences. Such problems have been widely recognized elsewhere as indicating a lack of access to more socially positive empowerment. However, the specific problems of Black men are only just beginning to be documented, much less addressed.

Conclusion

It is clear that the experiences of Black Nova Scotian women still include many negative features of racism, sexism, and poverty. These characteristics of oppression have disempowered Black women and could have overwhelmed them. Yet, despite these adversities, the Black communities of Nova Scotia have produced many strong women who have contributed much to the survival of the group. It is apparent that they still must struggle for equality in every aspect of their lives. Two of the negative features may be turned into positive opportunities, at least in some work settings. Under the Employment Equity legislation of 1986 with respect to Crown Corporations and Federal Contracts, and also under some Affirmative Action programs, employing a Black woman could be seen as increasing the number of women and visible minority persons at the same time. Black women, then, may seem to have another employment advantage over Black men. There are already more Black women than Black men at higher levels of education, although the exact numbers have not been documented; women are therefore increasingly likely to benefit from such opportunities. Will this sharpen the tensions between Black women and men, or can they tackle the problem together?

When White women see a Black woman hired, will they suspect preferential treatment by the employer to boost a program's numbers? Or can the recent developments in understanding each other's oppressions, within the women's movement and among minority women, avert such charges? Disastrously, the Employment Equity Act provided only one enforcement mechanism — mandatory employers' reports; reluctant or disinterested employers could easily resort to double counting (Din, 1989). While Black and other minority women might receive more jobs, it could be a mixed blessing if they are continually forced to show that success was based on merit and not on preferential hiring. Women from all groups need more opportunities to address the divisive effects of racism, such as that provided recently in Toronto by the Canadian Research Institute for the Advancement of Women (CRIAW, 1992).

Genuine affirmative action programs, which aim to redress systemic discrimination and to provide really equal opportunities for everyone, are sorely needed. Schools of social work have a critical role to play in promoting such efforts, not only within their programs but also within the whole field of social work. Recently the Canadian Association of Schools of Social Work has recognized this; in 1991, a task force made recommendations to facilitate the expansion of appropriate anti-racist and intercultural education in all schools and to entrench this as a priority in the CASSW accreditation standards. This timely development parallels similar initiatives in other disciplines. However, the experiences of Black Nova Scotian female social workers should remind us of the need to contribute on a broader front, through social work in general, through social policies and political action, and through community activity, to the achievement of social justice over oppressions and inequalities. None of this can be accomplished, however, without directly confronting the racism entrenched in our social institutions and our relationships.

REFERENCES

Adamson, N., L. Briskin, & M. McPhail (1988). *Feminist Organizing for Change.* Toronto: Oxford University Press.

Beaton, E. (1988). "Religious Affiliation and Ethnic Identity of West Indians in Whitney Pier." *Canadian Ethnic Studies* 20, no. 3.

Bernard, W.T., L. Lucas-White, & D.E. Moore (1981). "Two Hands Tied Behind Her Back: The Dual Negative Status of Minority Group Women." Paper presented at the CASSW conference, Halifax.

Boyd, F.S., Jr. (1975). *McKerrow: A Brief History of Blacks in Nova Scotia, 1783-1895.* Dartmouth, N.S.: Afro-Nova Scotian Enterprises.

Bruegel, I. (1989, Summer). "Sex and Race in Labour Market." *Feminist Review* no. 32.

Canadian Research Institute for the Advancement of Women (1992, November 13-15). *Anti-Racism and Feminism: Making the Links.* Sixteenth annual conference, Toronto.

Carrigan, D.O. (1988). "The Immigrant Experience in Halifax, 1881-1931." *Canadian Ethnic Studies* 20, no. 3.

Din, R. (1989, September). "The Inequality Behind the Law." *Women's Education* 7, no. 3. Special issue on the economics of inequality, published by the Canadian Congress of Learning Opportunities for Women (CCLOW).

Hill Collins, P. (1990). *Black Feminist Thought*. Boston: Unwin Hyman.

Hooks, B. (1988). *Talking Back, Thinking Feminist, Thinking Black*. Toronto: Between the Lines.

Jabbra, N.W., & R.L. Cosper (1988). "Ethnicity in Atlantic Canada: A Survey." *Canadian Ethnic Studies* 20, no. 3.

LaFleur, P. (1991). "Black Community Needs Assessment." MSW student project, Dalhousie University.

Lorde, A. (1982). *A New Spelling of My Name*. Trumansberg, N.Y.: The Crossing Press.

Mama, A. (1989). "Violence Against Black Women: Gender, Race and State Responses." *Feminist Review* no. 32.

Moore, D.E. (1979). *Multiculturalism: Ideology or Social Reality?* PhD dissertation, Boston University.

Nain, G.T. (1991). "Black Women, Sexism and Racism: Black or Anti-Racist Feminism?" *Feminist Review* no. 37.

Pachai, B. (1991). *Beneath the Clouds of the Promised Land: The Survival of Nova Scotia's Blacks*, Vol. 2: 1800–1989. Hantsport, N.S.: The Black Educators Association, Lancelot Press Ltd.

Status of Women Canada (1990, January). *Forward-Looking Strategies for the Advancement of Women: Issues and the Canadian Situation*. Ottawa: Status of Women Canada, Fact Sheets Update.

Women's Directorate (1990). *Women in Nova Scotia: A Statistical Handbook*. Halifax: Women's Directorate.

Part Four

The Turbulent Sixties and Seventies

By one important measure, what made the twin decades of the 1960s and 1970s "turbulent" is simple — people, a lot more people than ever before, through a dramatic rise in the birthrate and increased immigration. Historians and demographers differ over the precise dates of the postwar baby boom, but none denies its enormous effects and implications. In 1937, Canada's gross birthrate was at its lowest — some 20.1 live births per 1000 population. By war's end, that figure had jumped to 24.3, and by 1946 it was 27.2, where it roughly remained until the end of the 1950s. The result was a lot more Canadians, many of whom were "coming of age" themselves in the 1960s and 1970s. At the same time, immigration increased dramatically beginning in the mid-1960s, with the figures a decade later rivalling those of the heady years of the 1950s. Both the short- and long-term implications of more and more people fuelled much of the social and economic tumult of these two decades. In raw terms, Canada's population grew from 18.2 million in 1961 to some 24.3 million in 1981.

The 1960s marked a collision of old and new values. At the national level, it seemed that the old colonial connections were being cast aside. Canada got a new flag in 1965; showed, through the Auto Pact of the same year, that it could be both independent and an integral part of a close trading alliance; and generally paraded and feted its bicultural accomplishments before an approving world at Montreal's Expo 67. The sixties also saw the launching of a new, apparently zestful, socialist party, the old CCF (Co-operative Commonwealth Federation) reborn as the NDP (New Democratic Party). The welfare state embraced medicare; the national government considered, through Royal Commissions, the new roles of women and biculturalism and bilingualism; and at last, through a bulky, some thought aptly named, White Paper, seriously looked at the problems of Native peoples. All of these events were accompanied by energetic debate and discussion, much of which came from the thriving universities that were stuffed with questioning baby boomers.

The enthusiasm soured in 1970 with the October Crisis of that year, which introduced an intensity into Canada's perpetual French–English language and cultural debates that has not subsided since. Canadians seemed to become obsessed with constitutional matters, especially after the election of a pro-separatist government in Quebec in 1976. Regional issues became generally important, with the Maritimes feeling isolated and deprived and the economically powerful West feeling alienated. But even these political issues were swept aside by larger matters — all part of international rather than national trends. Chief among them was the "liberation of women," inexorably linked with the baby boomers, and the emergence of Native peoples as a kind of "third force" in Canadian polity and society, again a factor linked to the baby boom. A larger, better-educated, more skilled, and more diverse group than ever before, Canadians were reluctant to accept the political and economic bromides offered them by established authorities. The strength of the boomers' reforming convictions, however, would be sorely tested, not least by themselves, in the 1980s, when they were handed the reins of influence.

Perhaps no one exemplified Canadian consensus more than Liberal prime minister Lester Pearson. Pearson struggled to link old traditions with new, attaining more success abroad than at home. An excerpt from John English's masterful biography of Pearson shows the complexity of the man and the measure of his achievements, while at the same time illustrating his domestic short-sightedness and naïvete. A very different view of Canada invigorated the celebrated book-length essay *A Lament for a Nation*, by philosopher George Grant. William Christian's article reveals the dangers of such popular clarion calls, especially of the nationalistic variety: Grant was as much misunderstood as understood, and in both cases too frequently by those who had not actually read his book at all.

Protest in Canada doubtless reached its peak in 1970 with the kidnappings of British diplomat James Cross and Quebec cabinet minister Pierre Laporte by the FLQ. In a short recollection reprinted in this section, Cross describes his ordeal and explains something of the philosophy of his kidnappers, a luxury not afforded the murdered Laporte.

The 1960s and 1970s were particularly marked by what many saw as the relentless and intrusive presence of big government. The implications of this presence are described in the last two readings in Part Four in very different ways. The first of the two, by Ruth Fawcett, deals with the seemingly technical subject of science policy, but is actually an analysis of the Canadian government's reluctance to foster the links among research, technology, and industrial development. It is worth comparing this chapter with the earlier science subjects discussed by John Polanyi and Barry Came in Part One. The last reading in this section, by historian Darlene Abreu Ferreira, shows how the needs of a modern economy perhaps inevitably collide with those of aboriginal societies. The article is particularly effective in charting how the policies of Canada's federal and provincial governments have meandered over the past century — to the evident detriment of all but big business.

Further Reading

Constance Backhouse and David Flaherty, eds., *Challenging Times: The Women's Movement in Canada and the United States*. Kingston/Montreal: McGill-Queen's University Press, 1992.

Thomas Berger, *Fragile Freedoms: Human Rights and Dissent in Canada*. Toronto: Clarke, Irwin, 1981.

Andre Blais, "Reading Trudeau." *Queen's Quarterly* 100, no. 4 (1993): 853-58.

Robert Bothwell, Ian Drummond, and John English, *Canada since 1945: Power, Politics, and Provincialism*, rev. ed. Toronto: University of Toronto Press, 1989.

Ronald Crelinsten, "The Internal Dynamics of the FLQ during the October Crisis of 1970." *The Journal of Strategic Studies* 10, no. 4 (December 1987): 59-89.

William Kilbourn, ed., *Canada: A Guide to the Peaceable Kingdom*. Toronto: Macmillan, 1970.

Alison Prentice et al., *Canadian Women: A History*, 2nd ed. Toronto: Harcourt Brace, 1996.

Denis Smith, *Bleeding Hearts . . . Bleeding Country: Canada and the Quebec Crisis*. Edmonton: Hurtig, 1971.

Mark Winfield, "The Ultimate Horizontal Issue: The Environmental Policy Experiences of Alberta and Ontario, 1971-1993." *Canadian Journal of Political Science* 27, no. 1 (1994): 129-53.

The Liberal Hour: Lester Pearson's Road to Government, 1959–1963

JOHN ENGLISH

On the sun-washed morning of April 22, 1963, Lester Bowles Pearson, riding in a borrowed blue Buick and dressed in a well-worn morning coat, drove up to the front door of Government House to be sworn into office. When he drove away again . . . he turned for a moment to his press secretary, Richard O'Hagan, and said . . . "You know, Dick, somehow I feel like myself again."
— Peter Newman, *The Distemper of Our Times*[1]

SOURCE: Excerpted from *The Life of Lester Pearson*, Volume 2, *The Worldly Years, 1949-1972* (Toronto: Alfred A. Knopf Canada, 1992), pp. 213-52. Used with permission.

John Diefenbaker's government began to crumble in 1960. Two years after it had received the largest mandate in Canadian electoral history, the Conservative government, which had seemed so fresh and vigorous, suddenly appeared unable to make decisions or to keep in step with the times. Just as its triumphs were so much the product of John Diefenbaker's political skills, so its disintegration was, to a large extent, the result of his own weaknesses. Prominent among these was a personal enmity that he directed towards those he believed were denying him the fruits of his victory. By 1960, he had come to resent Lester Pearson.

It was not always so. Diefenbaker had been the Conservatives' external affairs critic in the 1950s, and he contributed to the bipartisan foreign policy identified with Pearson. Their personal and professional relationship was good. Pearson, for example, responded to Diefenbaker's best wishes on his 1955 Soviet trip with a short note that expressed regret that Diefenbaker could not join the party in Moscow.

In the 1957 and 1958 campaigns, Diefenbaker's sarcasm and invective were reserved for Jack Pickersgill, C.D. Howe, and his longtime Saskatchewan rival, Jimmy Gardiner. So decisive was his victory in 1958 that he could afford to be generous to Pearson, and his private letters to his wife and confidante, Olive, reflected such generosity and, perhaps, sympathy.[2] But the mood quickly changed, as the Liberals in the House of Commons opposed his policies with increasing effectiveness. Their effectiveness derived partly from the remarkable parliamentary skills of Pickersgill, Paul Martin, Lionel Chevrier, and, after 1958, Paul Hellyer, and partly from the difficulties that beset the Tories in 1959 and 1960. The government document that predicted an economic downturn, and that Diefenbaker used so effectively to ridicule Pearson's non-confidence motion in 1958, had proved to be accurate. The long post-war boom that had provided the foundation for stability reached its end in 1959–60, and so did the relative harmony between John Diefenbaker and Lester Pearson.

Between 1960 and 1967, the personal enmity that marked the relationship between these two Canadians poisoned the political atmosphere. Although Diefenbaker and Pearson "made up" in their memoirs and claimed that the public animosity was merely a partisan covering that concealed respect, their protests are unconvincing. In private, Diefenbaker mocked Pearson and reserved his harshest barbs for him. Pearson, his confidante Mary Macdonald recalls, had difficulty believing anyone was fundamentally evil, "with the possible exception of John Diefenbaker." Others close to Pearson largely share her view. As always, Maryon [Pearson's wife] was bluntest. She referred to Diefenbaker as simply "that horrid man from Prince Albert."[3]

Their enmity was probably inevitable. Although Diefenbaker, like Pearson, was born in Ontario of British-German Protestant stock in the 1890s, his experience led him to different conclusions about Canada and different approaches to politics. In his memoirs, Pearson analysed their differences:

> My background of official and diplomatic duty, along with my own nature, tended to make me more interested in issues, in finding solutions to problems, and in trying, rather to convince doubters that my answers were right than to make sure they were politically feasible as well as right in themselves. . . . I might have been more effective had I been a politician from the beginning, working my way up from the backbenches, learning on the way to curb my weakness to find something worth supporting in nearly every proposal of an adversary, and remembering that in party politics all is black and white. . . .[4]

He might have been more effective as a politician, but he would not have been Mike Pearson and he would not have been prime minister.

What drew so many different people to Pearson were those qualities that seemed to make him not a politician, but someone who listened directly to them. He had "something," his political opponent Grattan O'Leary wrote:

> I never knew what it was — a kind of instant receptiveness increasingly professional over the years backed up by real and decent concern. He always gave the impression of being genuinely interested. His fault as a politician, if it was a fault, was his ability to place himself in the other person's position: he had all the tricks of a negotiator. Finding out how one side felt, then playing it back to the other side.[5]

In fact, this receptiveness was "professional," acquired by years of diplomatic experience where sensitivity to "the other" was fundamental to his achievement. It was effective, but in time it could create misunderstandings, as receptiveness was mistaken for agreement.

Diefenbaker's schooling came not in London's clubs over aged claret or in U.N. corridors where different tongues and ways compelled a cosmopolitan manner, but in the country stores, fishing parties, and bitter politics of Saskatchewan, a province whose promised future never came and where, as its socialist premier Tommy Douglas said, "the only protection the Tories had in the [1920s and 1930s] were the game laws. . . ."[6] Tories rarely won anything in Saskatchewan — government contracts, judicial appointments, or elections. Diefenbaker lost federal elections in 1925 and 1926, provincial elections in 1929 and 1938, the Prince Albert mayoralty in 1933, and Conservative leadership contests in 1942 and 1948. He was sensitive to his German name, carrying a letter from professors during the First World War certifying that he was of "Canadian birth," and later he never hesitated to proclaim his loyalty to the British crown. To reach his goal he worked ceaselessly, shunned social life, and vacationed rarely. He seemed different and an outsider, not only in Ottawa in the forties when western Tories were rare, but even in the 1920s in Prince Albert, when, as an austere young lawyer, "tall, stiff [and] formally dressed," he strode to his Prince Albert law office along an unpaved street, passing trappers, bush pilots, farmers, Cree Indians, and gold miners.[7] An introvert like so many politicians, Diefenbaker was incapable of being "genuinely interested," which Pearson appeared to be. He needed crowds and the life he gave them he fully shared. But, as Basil Robinson, Diefenbaker's assistant and most perceptive analyst, has observed, he had "little feel for team play."[8]

The styles, then, were different. Diefenbaker was a populist; Pearson distrusted the irrationality of populism. Reading through their papers, one is struck immediately by how different their worlds were and how much the experience of an "Ottawa man" like Pearson differed from that of a prairie lawyer whose world was that of the small town, with its service clubs, its fears about next year's crop, and its sometimes stifling pressures to conform. Even in Ottawa, Diefenbaker had few friends, and in opposition, as he was from 1940 to 1957, his tendencies to stand alone were not constrained. He knew few insiders, could not travel to London, New York, or even Toronto or Montreal and find welcome in their private clubs, and was distant not only from the so-called Liberal establishment but also from what he derisively and rightly called the "Bay Street Boys" who were so influential in the Conservative party under George Drew. The most representative of these was the Toronto businessperson J.M. Macdonnell, who was active in the Canadian Institute of International Affairs and who sat at the head table when the institute honoured Pearson's Nobel Prize.

In 1960, for the first time since the election, the Liberals pulled ahead of the Tories in the Gallup poll, and in September they held a "Study Conference on National Problems" at Kingston. The model was the Liberal summer school organized by Vincent Massey in 1933 against the wishes of Mackenzie King, who, with some justification, thought that Massey was trying to impose upon him a more definite and more liberal platform than he wanted.[9] It is a measure of how different Mike Pearson was from Mackenzie King that he was the main proponent of the Kingston conference and that his hope was for a conference that would bring together independents and Liberals and define, for the party, a more progressive and activist platform. As with Massey's conference, the Kingston conference deliberately invited few members of Parliament, its agenda implicitly rejected the policies of the last Liberal government, and its organizers hoped it would attract new supporters to the party, some of whom might become candidates.

In retrospect, the conference seems to have been a remarkable success. Peter Newman, who attended the conference, later described it as "the most important single source of Lester Pearson's lieutenants and advisers" and pointed out that "of the 196 men and women who attended, 48 were later named to senior appointments in the Liberal administration." J.W. Pickersgill, the only MP to speak at the conference, describes it as "the most important event of 1960" for the Liberals and emphasizes its importance in recruiting candidates and supporters. Others, noting the remarkable similarity between the record of the Pearson government and the policies prescribed by some of the speakers at Kingston, have described the conference as "a forecast of the future." For Pearson himself, it was "the beginning of our comeback."[10] For Jean Chrétien, three decades later, it was a model for a study conference to define Liberalism for the 1990s.

Assessments at the time were much less flattering. Political journalist Harold Greer, who was usually friendly towards Pearson, dubbed it "an unmitigated political disaster" which revealed a party disorganized and divided. Kingston, Greer wrote, "was an egghead conference and Mr. Pearson . . . is something of an egghead himself." The politician, Greer averred, "must think with his liver." There is, accordingly, "a constant quarrel because the intellectual begins by saying he doesn't know, an admission which is fatal for the politician." Greer correctly detected a chasm between the politicians and those who "thought" or who at least wanted the Liberal party to develop a coherent program for the next election. A perceptive assessment of the conference by a young Toronto banker, R.M. MacIntosh, that was widely circulated after the conference, echoed some of Greer's views. The few MPs who were there, apart from Pearson, "seemed not very sympathetic to the purposes of the Conference. . . ." Paul Martin "could almost be heard to mutter, 'Enough of these bloody ideas — let's get back to politics.'" Jack Pickersgill was clearly unhappy in his final luncheon address, not only with the interventionist schemes that were proposed and the criticisms of the United States, but also with the charge, which he most vigorously refuted, that the St. Laurent years had accomplished little.[11] But these objections were mild compared to the bitter attack by Pearson's early and fervent supporters Bruce Hutchison and Grant Dexter.

The most striking contribution to the Kingston conference was a speech by Tom Kent that challenged Canadian Liberals and was, in MacIntosh's words, "a very well-written case for the broad extension of economic assistance to the underprivileged in the fields of health, education, old age assistance and other fields." So bold was his prescription that Frank Underhill,[12] a founder of the Co-operative Commonwealth Federation who told all who cared to listen that he had voted CCF in 1958 despite Pearson's pleas that he not do so, accused Kent "of importing Manchester Guardian–Fabian socialism to a cold climate and to a fast-changing society where security could not receive so much emphasis." If Kent's recommendations were regarded as too sweeping by a socialist, they appalled Hutchison, Dexter, and Victor Sifton, owner of the *Free Press*, who had Dexter write a critical report on the conference for the paper.

By September 1960, Kent had left the *Free Press* to work in Montreal for Chemcell Limited, and there were bad feelings after his departure. Sifton, Hutchison, and Dexter had first encouraged Kent to work with

Pearson and had urged Pearson to employ Kent's skills, but by 1960 their differences were great and fundamentally ideological. The economist John Deutsch, a close friend of Hutchison and Dexter, had warned them earlier that "Tom" had a "blind spot." He was "thoroughly Liberal" on trade and on "freedom of the individual," but had problems on the question of "expansionism." Deutsch explained this aberration in personal terms: Kent's father had been unemployed for a long period, and "Tom" stopped "thinking with his head, the moment an argument on unemployment, underdevelopment — of expansion versus nonexpansion [begins]." Deutsch, Graham Towers, and others had been "working on him" and would get "tougher." But the lesson did not take, and at Kingston Kent demonstrated how committed he was to a wide-ranging program of social reform and "expansionism."[13] The problem, it now seemed, was that Kent had convinced Pearson.

Pearson was aware of this problem. He wrote to the highly influential Hutchison after the conference ended and deprecated the "gross" misrepresentations by the press of what had happened at Kingston. Of course there was controversy, but what was the point of a conference "of this kind, especially one designed for 'liberals' if we cannot receive, discuss, support or destroy proposals and ideas?" He shared Hutchison's concerns "about the trend of things in this country which reflects itself in the extension of government action, with all that that implies. . . . " Any increase of government authority "is only and always the extension of the area of individual freedom and of a realization of its true meaning." There must be change, for "sound reform is preservative rather than revolutionary. . . . " The letter did not convince Hutchison, whose liberalism was different from Pearson's and Kent's. He told Dexter that Mike's thinking had a "woolly quality" to it and wondered what would "come from it" at the National Liberal Rally from January 11 to 14, 1961.[14]

C.D. Howe, the symbol of 1950s *laissez-faire* Liberalism, died before the conference. He had been "distressed" over what had happened at Kingston, where he thought "left-wing intellectuals" were too prevalent, notably Tom Kent, whom he "heartily disliked."[15] Walter Gordon, whom Howe had snubbed for some time after 1957, was the rally's policy chairman. The resolutions called for, among other things, health insurance, regional development funds, urban renewal, a national scholarship plan, greater unemployment assistance, pension reform, increased social investment, limits on foreign control of the Canadian economy, complete processing of raw materials in Canada, and a Canadian flag. Tom Kent, who had written the most trenchant critiques of Gordon's royal commission, and Gordon had "made up" at Kingston and worked together closely for the Ottawa rally. Kent had wanted his remarks at Kingston to be "off the record" and was annoyed when Pearson allowed the press to hear them. It was Gordon who overcame Kent's reluctance and convinced him he should participate in shaping policy resolutions for Ottawa, which, of course, would make Kent's commitment public and his influence obvious. Gordon wrote to Kent after the rally (which he termed a "great success") and told him, with much validity, that "it would have been a ghastly failure without all the preliminary work that went into the policy issues, in which you played the biggest part."[16]

That part deeply disturbed Hutchison and his friends, who saw that their kind of western-Canadian Liberalism had lost the sympathy of Pearson. The convention's support of deficit financing was appalling but expected:

> What I didn't expect was that Mike should so casually destroy that whole image of Responsibility which he has tried so painfully to construct, and which he has encouraged us to build up for him. Nor did I expect that he would assure you (as I understand from Victor) that there would be no plan for a general tax cut and, within a week, would endorse such a plan with enthusiasm. That shakes me. Mike has had three great tests (1) the famous vote-of-confidence resolution in which he fell on his face; (2) the tax holiday of the 1958 election . . . and (3) the present party platform. He has failed every one of them.

Hutchison said he was "blowing off steam" to Dexter and no one else:

> I keep a stiff upper lip. But I am disgusted, not with social reform, or even public spending but with the sheer cynicism and wild idiocy of imitating the Tories and deceiving the public about taxes. This just shocks my moral sense, or what's left of it. What happened to Mike's head and morals? Well, they may be right about these things politically. The Canadian public may be crazy and debauched enough to believe them. We may be fighting history and not a mere Rally of the Grass Roots statesmen. If so, God help us.

Business people would never support the party, "unless Mike finds a way to repudiate or reinterpret this poisonous heresy. And even if he does, who is running the party anyway? Gordon, Lamontagne and Tom Kent, I would guess. Cry havoc."[17]

Havoc or not, Hutchison's guess was not wrong, so far as party policy and organization was concerned. In 1960 Gordon and Pearson reached an agreement whereby Gordon would head the reorganization of the Liberal Party and chair the policy committee for the National Rally. Gordon's demands were clear and bluntly expressed. They included agreement with Gordon's views on economic policy, particularly those on "modest steps to counteract" the U.S. "takeover" of Canada's economy. He also made it clear that he expected the Finance portfolio after a Liberal victory and a commitment from Pearson that, if Gordon entered politics, Pearson would not leave for some "international position." In July 1960, Gordon had sent Pearson some of his policy proposals, and, according to Gordon's record, "she agreed *completely* [italics in original] with my ideas." Gordon then committed himself to assist financially, organizationally, and electorally.[18] At the Kingston conference, Pearson's speech had a major section on foreign investment that drew directly from Gordon's memoranda. The deal, it seemed, was done.

But why was it done? After Kingston and the policy rally, Pearson faced criticism not only from Hutchison and his group, but also from business people who distrusted Gordon's and Kent's plans, and from some of his parliamentary caucus, who worried about the influence Mike had granted to Gordon and Kent. Indeed, in his history of "the road back to government," Jack Pickersgill has only two references to Tom Kent, one trivial, the other critical.[19] In Pickersgill's account of how the Liberal Party travelled the road back to power, no credit is given to Kent and his work. Mary Macdonald also told Mike, especially after Kingston, that he should not rely so much on Gordon and Kent. Between the Kingston conference and the National Rally, the Pearsons spent a winter vacation with the Towerses, and Graham undoubtedly let Mike know how little he thought of Gordon's economic notions — as he continued to do until Gordon finally failed. And we know how C.D. Howe and his friends grumbled in their ample armchairs in the Mount Royal Club that winter before Howe died.[20]

One can suggest several motives to explain Pearson's actions. First, the parliamentary session of 1958–59 convinced Pearson that the Liberals, though few, could be effective in exposing Diefenbaker's weaknesses. On the first anniversary of the 1958 "day of national madness," Mike wrote to Landon and Geoffrey [his daughter-in-law and son] that the "present session of Parliament has shown that the liquidation [of the Liberal Party] has not been effective. . . ." He was "more comfortable" than before because he knew that they could not be humiliated in the House so long as the Liberals had Martin, Pickersgill, and others. He need not worry about their competence or their loyalty. It was an advantage that John Turner, Robert Stanfield, Joe Clark, and even John Diefenbaker did not have, and it permitted Pearson to give Gordon and Kent the latitude he did.[21] Secondly, he had no alternative to Gordon. In his letter to Landon and Geoffrey, he mentioned that the Liberals were gaining in the country, but not because of any organizational work the Liberals themselves had done. He told Hutchison that he had wanted Dave Sim, a former deputy minister, to be his national organizer but it did not work out. He asked Toronto businessperson Bruce Matthews to be party president and treasurer, but Matthews failed to raise sufficient funds and his political outlook was, in Mike's words, "conservative."[22] Intellectually, Mike believed the party should move left, and Matthews would not be enthusiastic about this movement, however strong his "Liberalism by tradition." In 1958, Mike "was idealistic enough to hope that our expenses, including a substantial part of our campaign costs, could be met from membership dues and annual donations from the party faithful." Such hopes, as always, were futile. Gordon's demands were great, his tone a trifle patronizing;[23] but his fundraising abilities were proven. He was, moreover, a *rara avis*, a businessman who wanted a "leftist" and "progressive" party and, perhaps most important, enjoyed people with ideas, like Tom Kent. After Gordon committed himself, $200,000 came in quickly, as did new faces, an "action plan," a "Leader's Advisory Committee," and an attempt to discover who and where Liberals were. Gordon, Keith Davey later recalled, came to their daily meetings with a long, detailed agenda and made decisions quickly. Pearson, whom Davey met twice a week, had no agenda. He would start a meeting by opening the desk drawer and twirling a Dad's cookie at Davey, and seldom answered a question with a yes or no. Instead he left Davey to interpret such comments as, "Well, Keith, if that is really something you feel you must do . . . " as the "no" it was.[24] Gordon filled many gaps created in the Liberal Party by the cyclone of 1958 and the choice of a leader who found "politics" difficult.

Finally, Pearson came to rely on Tom Kent after 1960 because he sensed that this recent arrival in Canada could see more clearly than others what the future would bring and how the Liberal Party and Mike Pearson might become part of that future rather than being overwhelmed by it. Not only the Liberal Party but also the Cooperative Commonwealth Federation had been shattered. The CCF began to rebuild through a formal alliance with Canadian labour and its transformation into the New Democratic Party (NDP). More important, the New Democrats brought Tommy Douglas to Ottawa to be their leader. He had governed Saskatchewan since 1944 and had just given it the medicare the federal Liberals had promised since 1919 but had never delivered. While Hutchison and others were startled by the "leftist" character of the Kingston conference and the National Rally, some on the left declared that they had heard it all before in the Liberal platform of 1919 and in the King government's Green Book proposals of 1945. Why were the 2,000 delegates brought to Ottawa, and what was all the cheering for? asked Ramsay Cook, a young historian attracted to the NDP then taking form and to John Kennedy's challenges to young Americans: "The Liberals now have a guide for the future which is no more radical than Mr. Diefenbaker's promises, and less in tune with twentieth century Liberalism than the program which John Kennedy offered. . . . Clearly the new Pearson is but the old King — with a dash of Walter Gordon." Cook had mockingly entitled his article "Not Right, Not Left, But Forward," a remark Mike made when a hostile reporter suggested that the new party program was "leftist." He had given Cook and others an easy target.[25]

Kent made the target more difficult to hit. Why Pearson came to rely upon this young Englishman whom Mike's old friends disliked so much, who insisted on so much of his time, who challenged him constantly, and who aroused so much suspicion among the caucus becomes clearer when one looks at what Kent gave him. In June 1960, Kent sent on to Pearson a letter about Canada he had sent to "his old friend Jo Grimond . . . ," a "delightful privateer in British politics" who had become Liberal Party leader. It was just after Kennedy had won the historic West Virginia primary, the Soviets had shot down Francis Gary Powers' U-2, Eisenhower had lied, Khrushchev had exploded, and the fresh winds of careful embrace between East and West had turned acrid. Kent's letter is a remarkably prescient document that captures the political emotions that animated North Americans in the sixties:

There are now, I think, many signs that the submerged nine-tenths of the conservative iceberg in North America is melting rapidly. We will soon be in a new reformist phase — which will, one may hope, be reflected in the display of less doctrine and more understanding in U.S. relations with the rest of the world.

In U.S. domestic affairs, the basic fact is that the conservative phase produced no move back towards laissez-faire; despite all the talk, what its opponents call "creeping socialism" was not arrested. The next reformist phase is therefore likely to take even the United States a considerable way further in the creation of what I like to call a welfare economy — which means (as opposed to socialism) an enlargement of the public sphere not in production as such but in consumption — larger public expenditures on education, health, housing and other services.

Our task in Canada is to implement these desirable trends while meeting the considerable structural economic difficulties that are replacing our boom times of the '40s and '50s. Because of those difficulties, there are ways in which our Canadian problems in the '60s may have much more in common with Britain's than they had in the past. In any event, they provide, I think, a most significant challenge to a twentieth-century liberalism; our response could be of considerable significance far outside Canada.

If we can get a Liberal government with Mike Pearson as Prime Minister, I would have few fears about the adequacy of the response. The danger is that this, like so many political issues, will be pre-determined: we will never have the chance to do the big thing adequately unless we plan imaginatively for it now, as a small opposition and a disorganized party. Any real chance of success depends, I think, on Mike taking the crucial, ideological initiative before the end of this year.

It's urgent to get a new image of the party before the public, and to reinvigorate its organization — which depends partly on personalities but also on clarifying a political attitude to fight for. With a good many conservative forces still operating inside the party, that's far from easy. But it badly needs to be done, preferably in the form of a personal political testament by Mike — a statement of his philosophy and general policy which would provide a rallying-point for all the people who want to be liberal reformers but have little guidance as to what that means in the 1960s.

In Canada it is necessary to explain why the Liberal today, without being any less concerned about freedom, would much extend public expenditures on education, health (including medical insurance and sickness benefits), housing and urban renewal. This has to be combined with a national policy for securing more equality among our still very diverse regions. There have to be sound policies for broadening the economy and raising employment levels; for increasing our trade and improving our payments balance; and for giving Canadian defence and foreign policy a satisfactory role in the world.

Primarily, I would say that Liberals need to shift the emphasis of their thinking a good many notches (in our case) towards egalitarianism. That's essential if we really want to regain the radical role that, in Britain, Socialism has muffed and that here is at the moment hopelessly spread among individuals rather than parties. We have to show that we really do want to create a much more equal society. And I would emphasize, too, a more skilful society (more "educated" having rather an odour to it) — which is not only of obvious importance but can have, I think, considerable political appeal. Indeed, the emphasis on the need for greater human skills, for the maximum use of our brainpower, perhaps helps as much as anything to clear away our nineteenth-century hangover about economic liberalism and gladly accept the more collectivist framework of contemporary economics and administration; the Liberal policy is not to wring our hands over the way that science and universal education are taking the world, but to insist that this necessary collectivist framework can and should be fashioned in such a way as to broaden, not narrow, the individual initiative and responsibility that will be more rewarding to individuals who are more skilful, who have more security and who live in a more equal society.

Kent had forecast a future that he enthusiastically looked forward to shaping.[26] The enthusiasm was infectious, and Mike caught it.

The die for a Pearson government was cast in 1960 and 1961, and Pearson's principal task thereafter was to keep those who found other shapes more comely from wandering too far from their old political mate. Pearson called on Hutchison just after the rally whose resolutions had caused Hutchison to have "nervous indigestion," to use Jack Pickersgill's description of the effect of the event on some Liberals.[27] Hutchison was prepared to confront him and had him to dinner with the crusty Jack Clyne, "our largest tycoon." The confrontation misfired: "[Pearson] is so charming . . . and so honest that I find it hard to quarrel with him." Hutchison, who had his own self-deprecating charm, told Dexter that really it was not an argument with Mike "but with a tide of history, the wave of the future. A new generation has taken over in Washington and, at the Liberal convention, in Canada and it won't listen to the mutterings of an old man like me. We now belong to the ages." But, Hutchison wrote in his cottage outside Victoria with the vines in bloom, "it's spring here, flowers everywhere, April temperatures and now I shall repair to the garden where there is peace and no deficit finance. Nature is always in surplus, thank God."[28]

Mike himself, as Gordon feared, was tempted to retreat to the more fragrant orchards of international diplomacy where he had so long flourished. With the assistance of John Holmes, who left External in 1960, he tried to write a major work on "the world in 1960," but too many current events on the international scene and political exigencies in Canada prevented its publication.[29] His letters to Geoffrey reveal how much he yearned for what lay behind him. He wrote to Geoffrey just after the 1960 summit between Khrushchev and Eisenhower had collapsed in the wake of the U-2 incident and told him that he had written an article for *Foreign Affairs* and would be writing another for the *New York Times* "on assignment": "All of this takes up time, of course, that should be devoted to attacking the government in the Commons on the price of eggs." But there was not a word about the price of eggs or other domestic matters. Instead, he talked about "an interesting week" he had spent in Chicago at a conference on world tensions, "another flight from domestic politics." At the conference, a decision was made to create an "International Council on World Tensions," which would be funded by prominent individuals and foundations to undertake a five-year program, and which would concentrate on Asia and Africa in an effort to find means to reduce "tensions." The organizers "pressed him hard" to become the council's first president and offered him a large salary. He admitted to Geoffrey that he was "very tempted." His first concern was whether "this kind of job" could make a contribution. His second concern was justifying to his friends his abandonment of Canadian politics.[30] He did not accept the offer of the position, although he remained wistful about the world he had lost and weary about the "politics" that were now his lot. He told Geoffrey in early 1961 that he wanted an election soon: "Then I would know. Either new and inescapable responsibility as head of a government or freedom from politics. Either prospect would be satisfactory — especially the latter." Certainly his private letters reflect neither interest nor joy in the doings of Ottawa or his political tasks. This indifference contrasts strongly with the obvious excitement that he derived from another "World Tensions" conference, this time at Geoffrey's former college, New College, Oxford. It was all "vastly instructive and interesting" for Mike, as he learned about Asia and Africa from their politicians and intellectuals. The "new, young black leaders," like Kenneth Kaunda, impressed him as "speakers and persons." The experience and, of course, Oxford made him "nostalgic and sentimental."[31] "In the kind of life I lead now," he told Geoffrey and Landon, "with domestic politics and party preoccupations pressing one hard — and I'm not enamoured of these pressures as you know though I do my best to disguise this. With this kind of life, I don't seem to find time for the more important things in life — such as telling Landon and you how very proud I am of what you have both done in your work and your lives." Landon and Geoffrey were then in Mexico City, where Geoffrey was first secretary at the Canadian Embassy. "I wish," Mike concluded, "my own present career gave me as much contentment, shall I call it 'inner cleanliness' as yours does."[32]

The carapace he donned to conceal his discomfort in the political world was sometimes transparent, and his pain as he carried out his political tasks was too obvious. One senses in these remarks Pearson's fear of entrapment, of losing his freedom, of making commitments that he would rather not make. After the Ottawa rally, he did not contact Gordon for more than two months, to Gordon's annoyance and puzzlement. Did he worry about becoming ensnared in policies he did not favour and in commitments he would rather not have made?

The evidence is circumstantial, but we do know that Pearson found opposition extremely uncomfortable and that Gordon asked for commitments that were exceedingly broad in scope. The section of Pearson's Kingston conference speech on economics and trade does not reflect what he said publicly and privately about such subjects before and after the conference. It is true that he was concerned that a too-large percentage of foreign investment in Canada and Canadian export trade was American, but his response — and, for that matter, Liberal policy — was to diversify and seek a broad "Atlantic" trading area. He criticized the Diefenbaker government's trade-diversion policy and its opposition to British entry into the Common Market. He urged the Canadian government to embrace a British "free trade" proposal first made in 1957 and repeated in 1960 as a "first step" in the creation of an "Atlantic Economic Community." Any "narrow" or "protectionist policy" would be out of step with history."[33]

In fact, Mike was not marching in step with history, for the evidence now suggests that his vision of an "Atlantic Economic Community" was almost certainly chimerical, especially after the French rejection of Britain's membership in the Common Market in early 1963 because French president General Charles de Gaulle believed that Britain would be an American "Trojan Horse" within the community.[34] Nevertheless, Mike's statements reveal the difference in emphasis on trade and economic matters between Gordon and himself. His knowledge of and interest in such affairs were, by his own admission, not great. He was therefore less committed to economic policies than he was to policies in areas where his expertise was greater. Still, he must have been uncomfortable, and it must have shown.

After Mike finally contacted Gordon in April 1961 after the National Rally, events moved quickly, partly because of Gordon's determination and partly because an election was likely within a year.[35] Gordon secured Keith Davey as national director in May 1961, and organized a policy committee to draft an election platform. He began, with the assistance of Davey and Toronto lawyer Dan Lang, to seek candidates, and formed a Leader's Advisory Committee, which Pearson chaired and Gordon vice-chaired. Later, Gordon became not only chair of the National Campaign Committee but also a candidate for Davenport riding in Toronto. Davey proved indefatigable in his efforts to restructure, reinvigorate, and centralize party operations. Davey and Gordon paid close attention to provincial wings and broke with precedent by having the provincial campaign chairs appointed by the national leader. Provincial feudal structures, particularly in Joey Smallwood's Newfoundland, successfully resisted these attempts to limit their suzerainty, but there were successes — as in Quebec, where the central campaign assisted the young Montreal lawyer John Turner in gaining a party nomination. More important, Quebec Liberals embraced the practice of nominating conventions and thus abandoned the old "bosses" who normally chose candidates themselves. Turner was helped, but he had to win a democratic nominating meeting.[36]

Quebec, in this respect at least, became a province more like the others.

For a biographer of Pearson, these details of party transformation present a problem. As political scientist Joseph Wearing notes: "Davey's letters and memoranda to Pearson are fascinating, cogent documents; but party organization was not a subject that greatly interested Pearson and it is difficult to judge how much importance he attached to them." Nevertheless, Pearson liked Davey, a sports fan whose affection for the hated Yankees[37] Pearson forgave, and gave him a remarkably free hand.[38] What affected and interested Pearson more than details of party reorganization was the presentation of the party leader in the election campaign. What Davey and Gordon wanted to present was not what Canadians saw when they looked at Pearson in 1961.

Canadians, public-opinion polls seemed to suggest, did not like Lester Pearson as a politician as much as Pearson's advisers had hoped. It was discouraging, for he had performed well in the House in 1961, especially in the so-called Coyne affair. James Coyne, the governor of the Bank of Canada, had followed a restrictive monetary policy and had made controversial public speeches that conflicted with government policy. Finance minister Donald Fleming and Diefenbaker finally decided to fire Coyne. The pretext was a change in the pension to be awarded a retired governor that raised the amount of the pension to $25,000. Fleming informed Coyne that his contract would not be renewed when it expired in December 1961, and the government began to try to undo the pension, which it alleged had been improperly increased. Professor Granatstein, who has most ably chronicled this affair, points out that though the pension was large there was no impropriety. The charge of impropriety naturally outraged Coyne and forced him to defend his integrity. In June the government presented its bill to remove Coyne from office, but made the error of preventing the bill from going to a House committee.[39]

The Liberals were careful to distance themselves from Coyne's policies, which, at a time of high unemployment, seemed restrictive in the view of most academic economists. Indeed, on January 20, 1961, Pearson had endorsed an economic program that was expansionary, featuring tax cuts, lower interest rates, and accelerated depreciation.[40] Pearson denounced the bill because it denied Coyne a hearing and because it made Coyne a scapegoat for the Tories' economic mismanagement. Through the bill, Pearson claimed, "the executive is seeking to make the elected representatives of the people rubber stamps, because they are being asked to take action without information. . . ." Diefenbaker, who directed Conservative strategy, hated Coyne, considering him "an unregenerate Grit" who was being manipulated by his old Winnipeg friend Jack Pickersgill.[41] Coyne, Diefenbaker sarcastically declared, "sat, knew, listened and took" when $25,000 was dangled before him. He was going to "line up" the

Grits with Mr. Coyne's thinking and annihilate them. This time, however, his threats rang hollow, for Pearson deftly persuaded the Senate banking and commerce committee to hear Coyne's case.[42]

They heard his case — and much more. Coyne released a flood of documents that revealed a government uncertain of its economic path, clumsy in its operations, and vindictive in its relations with the governor. It was a sorry tale, but its telling helped the Liberals. Sixty per cent of the 76 per cent of Canadians who had heard of the controversy sided with Coyne; only 9 per cent supported the government's case.[43] The Liberals had battled Diefenbaker and, for the first time since 1958, had decisively won.

★ ★ ★

When Peter Regenstreif later wrote *The Diefenbaker Interlude*, an electoral history of the period 1957 to 1963, a major theme was the deterioration of Pearson's personal support in the opposition years. Regenstreif found that Diefenbaker's "personality and qualities" attracted people to him. "In contrast, Pearson's support was strongly party identified." People chose Pearson because they preferred the party, not because they favoured its leader. When asked why they voted Conservative, 32 per cent in 1962 and 30 per cent in 1963 answered "Diefenbaker." When asked why they voted Liberal, an astonishingly low 3 per cent answered "Pearson" in 1962 and only 6 per cent in 1963.[44] Pearson, bow tie or not, had remarkably little appeal to those who had no regular party affiliation. Even Liberal supporters felt uncomfortable. Regenstreif, who was rumoured to be a Liberal sympathizer, used anecdotal evidence drawn from interviews to support his point. He quoted a Kitchener, Ontario, salesman who intended to vote Liberal as saying "Pearson leaves me out in middle field somewhere. It's like a wonderful singer with a good voice singing trashy songs."[45] Mike probably felt the same way himself.

Successful or not, the remaking of Mike Pearson was one of many Canadian reactions to the election of John Kennedy in 1960. Coming at a moment in Canadian national life when anti-Americanism wafted through the air, the creation of Camelot on the Potomac quickly captured Canada's eye. It immediately disturbed John Diefenbaker, who had liked "Ike," the Kansas farm boy who became a war hero and who shared with Diefenbaker a taste for simple foods, fishing, and complicated syntax. The "new frontier," with its resident intellectuals, youthful glamour, cosmopolitan sophistication, and too-quick assumptions about what America meant and must do, had boundaries that Diefenbaker could never cross. Suddenly, his evangelical fervour, so electric in 1958, seemed as outdated as a crystal radio in the stereophonic age, especially to the young, the intellectuals, the fashionable, and the urban. Apart from the style, itself exceedingly important, the substance of Kennedy's appeal signalled a reinvigoration of the liberal tradition. Just as William Lyon

Mackenzie had responded to the remarkable effervescence of Jacksonian democracy in the 1830s, and his grandson had clasped to his bosom the aura, if not the substance, of Roosevelt's New Deal a century later, Canada's liberals looked southward again for the breath of new life. Ramsay Cook had said that the intellectual content of the Kingston conference and the policy rally could be found in the book *The Affluent Society*, by Kennedy confidant and erstwhile Canadian John Kenneth Galbraith. Cook, a New Democrat, could have said the same of his own party's founding convention. In one of those fundamental shifts in American history between reform and retreat that Arthur Schlesinger, Jr., Kennedy's friend and biographer, has argued are the salient feature of American history, the liberal hour had once again struck, and the sound reverberated in Ottawa as loudly as in Washington.[46]

When Diefenbaker called the election on April 18, 1962, for June 18, his advisers correctly predicted that the Liberals would take the "Kennedy" approach, stressing the need to "get the country moving again." The Liberals led in the polls; Donald Fleming had brought forward a budget with a large deficit; and on May 2 the government pegged the dollar at 92.5 cents.[47] The mood in the House had been foul before the election, with Diefenbaker claiming that Pearson had not stood up to Communist imperialism. The reference was to Pearson's remark in an interview with Pierre Berton that if the choice were death or Communism, he would choose Communism because he could live to fight it. It quickly became "better red than dead" and brought a stream of protest. A Quebec Liberal member, Lucien Cardin, exploded in the House, charging that "From the first day [Pearson] was chosen head of the Liberal party, the Prime Minister by his cynical attitude, words and disparaging remarks about [Pearson] has revealed that in the deep recesses of his soul there burn the envious fires of the little green-eyed monster."[48] The campaign was not much better, particularly when the Tories got off to a bad start. By late April, the Liberals had moved into a significant lead (45 per cent to 38 per cent) in the Gallup poll. Mike, whose restrained language of 1958 had vanished, felt confident enough to challenge Diefenbaker to a debate, which Diefenbaker refused.[49]

The Liberal campaign, based on Harris's surveys, concentrated on Ontario, which Davey and Gordon knew so well, and on Quebec, where Jean Lesage's provincial Liberal government was very popular. The west and the Maritimes were not so well known, but there were hopes for British Columbia. There was also grumbling. Liberal Federation president John Connally expressed his strong suspicions of the influence of Tom Kent and Gordon on Pearson, but Diefenbaker's policies and personalities and Mike's ability to conciliate those who were discontented kept his diverse party together.[50] It was his greatest achievement in the 1962 campaign.

For a while it appeared that the Liberals would win at least a minority government, as Diefenbaker ran his worst campaign and the Liberals ran an innovative and often ingenious one. The "Diefenbuck," a "dollar" with "92½¢" and Diefenbaker's wrinkled jowls upon it, was especially effective. Gordon sent out regular warnings to candidates, however, that they should avoid attacking Diefenbaker, whose personal popularity remained great in many quarters.[51] Perhaps too many attacks had already occurred, for in the final weeks of the campaign, the Liberals began to slip, as the Tories and Social Credit began to rise. In Quebec, Social Credit's Réal Caouette, an unknown car dealer and a firebrand orator, set aflame those rural areas that were suspicious of the changes so quickly occurring around them; and in doing so, he destroyed Lester Pearson's hopes of forming a government.

The election-night photograph shows Mike and Maryon slouched and sad watching the results at the Château Laurier Hotel. There would be no northern Camelot. He won his own Algoma East seat, doubling his margin of victory. The Liberals won 100 seats, but the Tories had 116, even though the parties had an almost identical popular vote. Social Credit won 30 seats, 26 of them in Quebec, and the New Democrats won 19. It was a Conservative minority government, but for Diefenbaker, who had won 208 seats only four years earlier, it was a tremendous defeat. Mike felt much better when he fully realized what had happened, and his resolve to defeat Diefenbaker stiffened.

[His son] Geoffrey had written to him before the election to tell him that he had finally paid his debt to the party and could be his "own man." Mike agreed: he had now "paid [his] debt and now I am on my own."

> But "my own" keeps me here — where I am — for the present — as the work is only half-completed. If the next round is within 12 months — I'll go through it all again — hard though it is. If, however — and this is unlikely — [Diefenbaker] works out a coalition arrangement with [Social Credit] and hangs in for 3 or 4 years — then — after one session — I withdraw — if not with much honour at least without scars.
>
> If it were not for SC in Quebec — our complacent party managers muffed that one[52] — we would now be forming a minority government. And that would be a real headache — in present circumstances. Imagine — with a combination of Dief and Caouette in opposition against you — with a combined majority! . . .
>
> The campaign was very ragged and exhausting — but I am in good condition. Your mother was magnificent — especially as it doesn't come easy for her. But she was a real trouper and I was proud.[53]

Both Pearsons were prepared to fight another day.

One who did not see the next day was Mike's mother, Annie, who died in 1962. On election night, she had talked with Mike after it was clear that the Liberals had lost. As she had since Mike's childhood, she gently chided and challenged him while consoling:[54]

Well, I've been watching the campaign and there seems to have been an awful lot of talk about the dollar and financial matters and all that kind of thing, and I notice you've been taking part in these discussions and I was thinking, you know, that perhaps you haven't been asked to take on the Prime Minister's job at this time because you were never very good at arithmetic.

Mike's own sense of humour obviously came from Annie — and so much else. She had been, most likely, the greatest influence on his life.

Arithmetic also was the government's problem. Shortly after the election it became clear that devaluation of the dollar had not halted the financial crisis. It was an indicator of the bad relationship between Diefenbaker and Pearson that, on June 21, Diefenbaker sent Bank of Canada governor Louis Rasminsky, rather than calling upon Pearson himself, to explain the emergency measures that the Canadian government had to take to prevent further deterioration of Canada's Exchange Reserve Fund. Rasminsky expressed to Mike the hope that "the Liberal Party would forget Politics" and give its support for these emergency measures, which the government had to take. Pearson said that he would give that support at a moment of crisis provided that he was made aware of what specific actions the government proposed to announce on June 24. Pearson called Gordon, who immediately reacted strongly because he believed that Diefenbaker and Donald Fleming were using Rasminsky. Gordon feared that Pearson would accept proposals from "a senior civil servant" that he would reject from politicians. He also charged, most inaccurately according to Louis Rasminsky, that the measures had been proposed to Canada by the International Monetary Fund (IMF) and that their acceptance meant a significant loss of Canadian sovereignty. In any event, no copy of a speech arrived before Diefenbaker gave it, and Pearson did not hesitate to suggest that the measures were the product of government mismanagement, although he did express support on "national grounds." His "political" comment annoyed Rasminsky, but his support for the measures upset Gordon, who cast a cold eye on what he believed — erroneously, it seems — was the IMF's baneful influence.[55]

In fact, the finance minister and the Bank of Canada had adopted policies that would soon lead to a stronger Canadian economy. Their success, however, was clouded by the abundant confusion and contradiction that accompanied decision in Diefenbaker's minority government. By June Mike had come to believe that the Diefenbaker government could not survive long, even if the economy recovered. As he studied the details of the 1962 election results, Mike was pleased that the "Kennedy" approach had attracted to the Liberals in Canada the type of people who were drawn to Kennedy in the United States. Analysing the results, one finds Liberal strength among the young, the urban, the university-educated, professionals, the well-to-do, labour, Catholics, and ethnic groups. These were the sectors that the Liberals had hoped to woo because they believed they influenced others more than the rural and the older Canadians who still followed John Diefenbaker. In metropolitan Toronto, which the Liberals had lost in St. Laurent's heyday, the Liberals had taken fifteen seats, the Tories only six.[56] The Canada of the future seemed to be moving to the Liberal side. It seemed mere months before an issue arose that would precipitate a crisis that would cause an election.

If Kennedy's image perhaps illuminated a path for the Canadian Liberals, his policies soon helped them too. Although Diefenbaker had liked Eisenhower, there were serious differences in policy that arose between Canada and the United States in the Eisenhower years. Some were economic, especially in the area of disposal of surplus agricultural products, but most concerned the Canadian–American defence relationship. In February 1959, the Diefenbaker government announced the cancellation of the Avro Arrow and the acquisition of American Bomarc missiles for Canadian defence. The Americans had refused to buy the Arrow, which, without such purchases, was much too expensive to produce. Bomarcs were cheaper, but, as Diefenbaker said on February 20, 1959, the Bomarc's "full potential" was achieved only if it was armed with nuclear weapons. He pointed out that Canadian forces in Europe were already being equipped with "short range nuclear weapons," the ironically named Honest John missiles. Such weapons were also to be available for the F-104 aircraft, which the Canadians purchased as a strike weapon for their European forces in 1959. The "bombs" would be held by the Americans for Canadian usage under a shared-control system, but the agreement had not been negotiated at the time the Arrow announcement was made; and it never was.

Sidney Smith, the External Affairs minister who took part in these decisions, died on March 17, 1959, and was replaced three weeks later by Howard Green, a veteran British Columbia MP who had been Pearson's most virulent critic at the time of the Suez Crisis. Diefenbaker, who had long suspected that the "Pearsonalities" in External Affairs were feeding information to their friends in the opposition, chose a loyalist who had no background in External Affairs but who had firm views — especially on nuclear weapons, which Green abhorred.

He was not alone. In the later 1950s the doctrine of "massive retaliation," fashioned in the early Eisenhower years, seemed recklessly dangerous as the Soviets and Americans tested hydrogen bombs thousands of times more powerful than those that had incinerated the cities of Hiroshima and Nagasaki. Moreover, the launching of Sputnik in 1957 and the clear evidence that Soviet intercontinental ballistic missiles could rain their warheads upon North America while tanks rolled through Europe, as they had through Hungary in 1956, "unhinged" the pillars upon which NATO doctrine stood. Tactical nuclear weapons such as the Honest John could halt the Soviet advance, but the costs would be unacceptably high. By the end of the 1950s, Theodore Draper comments, "the dilemma was excruciatingly acute — the next war could not be a conventional war and it could not be a nuclear war."[57]

Mike Pearson's lack of interest in economic questions contrasts strongly with his intense interest in the shifting sands of international politics and nuclear diplomacy in the late 1950s and early 1960s. No topic occupied more of his time, and his knowledge was great, his thinking sophisticated, his fears profound. In 1959, Harvard University Press published a series of lectures that he had given at the élite Fletcher School of Law and Diplomacy. John Kennedy, then a Massachusetts senator, reviewed the book, *Diplomacy in the Nuclear Age*, in the *Saturday Review* and pointed to Pearson's concern about "the dangerous ambiguities of a military policy grounded merely in nuclear deterrence." Nevertheless, Kennedy (or his amanuensis, perhaps) stressed that Pearson's major emphasis was on the need to strengthen instruments of negotiation and mediation and to assure that diplomacy furthered the reduction of international tensions. Kennedy noted Pearson's belief that NATO must have more effective "machinery for policy-making," but did not indicate whether he agreed with that belief.[58]

Deeply influenced by the arguments of Henry Kissinger in *Nuclear Weapons and Foreign Policy* and Herbert Kahn in *On Thermonuclear War* — arguments that Stanley Kubrick brilliantly satirized in *Dr. Strangelove, or How I Learned to Stop Worrying and Love the Bomb* — political scientist James Eayrs told the Kingston conference that Liberals should face the terror of nuclear weapons directly. For Canadians there could be no choice: geography dictated that it was "in Canada's interest to do everything in its power to make the Great Deterrent under United States control increasingly effective." To that end Canada should, in Eayr's "realistic" view, open Canada's territory, including its waters, to "United States retaliatory missiles"; acquire American anti-missile and anti-aircraft defences; and allow the atomic warheads that alone would make defence credible.[59]

Others recoiled from such analyses, including the National Liberal Rally, which left Liberal policy ambiguous and in Eayrs's view, silly.[60] Maryon Pearson was one who recoiled (so was Eayrs later), and she let others know how absurd she found the nuclear world of 1960. She and Patsy joined the Voice of Women in 1960. Denounced by some as a "communistic" organization, the Voice of Women, Maryon declared, was not subversive simply because it talked of peace. Women had a special role, because "men are so used to war. . . . This is why it's so important for women to bind together and take a stand." "The present world situation," she told another reporter, "is dreadful. It's got to be stopped. I don't understand how men have allowed such conditions to arise." In direct rebuke to those who urged Canadians to look realistically at nuclear weapons and to consider fallout shelters, Maryon said: "Men get casual and used to talking about piles of bombs here and piles of bombs there."

Women were more inclined to peace because "they produce life and want to see their children live."[61]

Although Mrs. Howard Green would not endorse the Voice of Women's views, her husband's views were, perhaps, closer to Maryon's than Mike's and Geoffrey's were. Geoffrey, who was with NATO at this time, shared James Eayrs's views on the need for Canada to accept the implications of its geography and its membership in NATO and NORAD. After the Ottawa rally, which as we have seen did little to clarify Liberal defence policy, Geoffrey suggested that his father emphasize "NATO control" of nuclear weapons as a "way out," a course that Mike subsequently followed. The trouble was, of course, that NATO control was an elusive concept that never became a reality. Neither did the build-up of NATO conventional forces, which, logically, was the best method of reducing reliance on the bomb. In this situation, the Liberals and the government took refuge in ambiguity. There was, however, a fundamental difference. In 1959, Diefenbaker indicated that nuclear weapons would be obtained, and the Americans took him at his word. Subsequently, his government retreated from this statement. Although Mike had agreed that nuclear weapons could be accepted "under NATO collective control," he had not publicly — or privately in answer to Geoffrey's arguments — agreed that Canadian forces should accept nuclear weapons in Canada or Europe if those weapons were U.S. controlled, and he had not made public commitments as a head of government. He told a peace activist who wrote to him in April 1962: [62] "There has been no full scale debate on defence policy in this present Parliament which would give the Opposition Parties any real idea of all the factors involved in formulating a nuclear defence policy for the space age. So it is hard for the Opposition to be too dogmatic. In the light of the facts at our disposal, we believe that as a nation Canada should stay out of the nuclear club." Later that year the "facts" at his disposal changed.

On the morning of October 16, "Mac" Bundy came to John Kennedy's bedchamber in the White House to tell the president, still in his nightshirt, that the Central Intelligence Agency had proof that Soviet missiles were in Cuba. Kennedy, whom Khrushchev had tested before, reacted angrily: Khrushchev "can't do this to me."[63] The thirteen days that followed brought the world within an eye's blink of a nuclear catastrophe. For John Diefenbaker, it was a political catastrophe.

By October 1962, Diefenbaker's distrust of John Kennedy was profound — with good reason. Several times Kennedy had made it clear that he much preferred Mike Pearson to Diefenbaker. On his first visit to Ottawa in May 1961, at a dinner party at American ambassador Livingston Merchant's residence, Kennedy talked and joked with Pearson and ignored Diefenbaker.[64] A senior American aide later recalled that the president was "absolutely discourteous" towards Diefenbaker.[65] In

April 1962, during the 1962 election campaign, Kennedy, whose loathing of Diefenbaker was now widely known, invited Pearson to a White House dinner. The invitation had been sent before the election was called, but this subtlety was lost upon Diefenbaker, especially when Kennedy paid conspicuous attention to Pearson. Livingston Merchant called on Diefenbaker shortly after the dinner and endured a tirade about the Pearson invitation and a threat by Diefenbaker that he would reveal the memorandum Kennedy had left behind. When Kennedy heard what had happened from Merchant, he called it "blackmail." It was, and it was badly done. Kennedy said he would never speak to or see Diefenbaker again.[66]

When Kennedy decided to blockade Cuba, he called Macmillan of Britain personally and well in advance, but sent Livingston Merchant to inform Diefenbaker only two hours before his historic television speech. The judicious Diefenbaker aide Basil Robinson, who admits the many faults of Diefenbaker, points out that in this case "Diefenbaker's upset was understandable." The blockade was "after all, a very important development for the defence of North America, and it was [Diefenbaker] who had entered into the NORAD agreement five years before," an agreement that provided for the "fullest possible coordination" in North American defence.[67] Diefenbaker's anger, coupled with his confusion over an External Affairs recommendation (made before Kennedy spoke) that the matter be referred to the U.N., made him appear to question Kennedy's decision and words. He briefed Pearson, but then borrowed Pearson's words for his own speech in the House, confirming for Pearson that Diefenbaker could not be trusted.[68] What followed would have been comical had the stakes not been so high. Diefenbaker refused to place Canadian forces under a NORAD alert known as "Defcon 3," and Defence minister Harkness defied him by ordering them on alert despite Diefenbaker's stand. Diefenbaker refused again the following day, by which time his reluctance was noted by a Canadian public overwhelmingly behind Kennedy's stand. Mike told Geoffrey [Pearson] that the House was in a foul temper, but Diefenbaker's end was near.[69]

The Cuban Missile Crisis was a chilling moment in the Cold War that stiffened Canadian spines, including some in Diefenbaker's cabinet. For Kennedy, Diefenbaker was now a marked man. For Diefenbaker, Kennedy was a sworn enemy. Other allies had also been appalled by Kennedy's failure to consult. The Dutch foreign minister, Joseph Luns, for example, opposed Kennedy's action and hesitated to act. The hesitations and objections of The Netherlands and others were forgotten.[70] Diefenbaker's behaviour, however, was neither forgotten nor forgiven, because in American eyes it fitted a pattern that could be identified as anti-American. It also troubled many Canadians and many Conservatives.

Mike was in the midst of reviewing Canadian defence policy when the crisis occurred. He had, as indicated earlier, met with James Eayrs and John Gellner in 1959 to discuss the problems of nuclear weapons. Both men were identified with the view that Canadian defence policy was wrong and that Canada had an obligation to fulfil its alliance commitment to accept nuclear weapons. Eayrs expressed the view at the Kingston conference; Gellner established a close relationship with Liberal Defence critic Paul Hellyer and tried to influence him. Hellyer had toured military bases in the United States and Europe in August 1961 and November 1962. He returned from both tours convinced that defence requirements, quite apart from the question of commitments, demanded that Canada accept nuclear weapons. "The military people at SHAPE [Supreme Headquarters, Allied Powers in Europe]," Hellyer reported in November, "are very concerned about the indecision of the Canadian government." They had not brought "the matter into the international political arena" but, if there were no decision, might not be able to avoid doing so.[71]

Hellyer's prediction proved accurate when retiring NATO commander General Lauris Norstad passed through Ottawa on January 3, 1963. Confronted by reporter Charles Lynch, Norstad said that Canada had made a commitment to provide its F-104s in Europe with nuclear weapons. Air Marshal Frank Miller, who was standing nearby, publicly agreed with Norstad, who had had a private chat with Hellyer in November. The effect was devastating and disastrous for the government. Mike, like Defence minister Harkness, had already concluded that Norstad's view was correct, and 54 per cent of the Canadian public agreed with them.[72]

During 1962, an obviously troubled Pearson had surveyed old friends, colleagues, and others on the subject. At the 1961 policy rally, the party had taken a stand against nuclear weapons for Canada's NORAD forces. They would contemplate such weapons for the European forces only if they were subject to NATO control and requested by the NATO council. Early in 1962, Pearson had tried to write a defence pamphlet to counter Diefenbaker's "ludicrous" stand, but told his former External Affairs colleague Douglas LePan that he found the task difficult. It was, he told another old friend, "in some ways the most agonizing problem" he had faced, because of Canada's "obligations for collective defence" and its other obligations "to prevent the spread of nuclear weapons." No defence pamphlet was forthcoming, but even before the Cuban Missile Crisis, Mike had called for the establishment of a select committee to determine the issue.[73]

After Cuba, he told another old friend, University of Toronto history professor George Brown, that he still believed that Canada could play a "full part" in the Atlantic alliance without nuclear weapons, but he did see a problem in the "commitments" Diefenbaker had made. If elected, Pearson claimed, he would work to negotiate an effective non-nuclear role for Canada in the alliance.[74] Gellner and Hellyer, however, had decided that was not good enough. Hellyer, with Mike's approval, asked Gellner to prepare a draft of a Liberal defence policy, which he did by December 21, 1962. Gellner recommended that Canada "should make good on our commitments to NORAD and NATO until we can change them through negotiation."[75] Pearson sent this paper to several people, asking for their comments. Walter Gordon took the paper with him on a trip to the west coast while he met with Liberal candidate David Groos, a defence expert.[76] Endorsements of the proposed policy came from Gordon's brother-in-law, "Bud" Drury, who had already urged such a policy on Pearson, Hellyer, Mitchell Sharp, Pickersgill, Groos, and others.[77] After Norstad's remarks, Mike himself went to New York for the Council on World Tensions and, at the Sheraton-East Hotel, between Broadway plays and council meetings, drafted and redrafted a statement on nuclear weapons for Canada. On landing at Toronto on his return he immediately and without consultation announced: "As a Canadian I am ashamed if we accept commitments and then refuse to discharge them."

Canada, he declared, "should end at once its evasion of responsibility, and put itself in a position to discharge the commitments it has already accepted for Canada." The Liberals, he argued, had opposed the acquisition of most weapons that required nuclear warheads and would seek, therefore, to renegotiate with the United States and NATO "a more effective and realistic role for Canada" in collective and continental defence. It was hypocritical to invoke "moral grounds," for Canada accepted the protection of the nuclear deterrent in U.S. hands and exported uranium for military purposes. (He did not add that much of that uranium came from Elliot Lake, in his constituency.) Fulfilling the commitments was "the only honourable course for any government representing the Canadian people."[78]

Comments came quickly. A young Winnipeg Liberal, Lloyd Axworthy, wrote to say "how very disappointed and saddened" he was "to see a man renege on past principles, and deny the very policies upon which so much admiration and respect have been built." Axworthy declared that he could no longer be active in the Liberal Party. Two other future Liberal cabinet ministers who had been considering standing as Liberal candidates denounced Pearson. Pierre Trudeau labelled him the "unfrocked priest of peace" and claimed that "les hipsters" of Camelot had intrigued with Pearson to destroy Diefenbaker. Jean Marchand said he would not run because of Pearson's stand.[79] Conservative Defence minister Douglas Harkness, however, welcomed the speech and saw in Pearson's stand an escape for the beleaguered Diefenbaker government. He did not recognize how stubborn Diefenbaker would be, and how strongly Howard Green and his deputy, Norman Robertson, felt about the issue.

Diefenbaker did give a speech in the House of Commons to defend his position. He claimed that, at the recent Nassau conference between

Macmillan and Kennedy to which he had invited himself (to their dismay), Macmillan and Kennedy had agreed that increasing conventional forces was more important than deploying nuclear weapons more widely. He also revealed some details of confidential talks with the Americans. The Americans were livid; Harkness issued, without consultation, his own "clarification"; and Diefenbaker faced a crumbling government.

On January 30, 1963, the U.S. State Department issued an astonishing press release calling John Diefenbaker a liar. Even Mike thought that the Americans had gone too far.[80] They had; but so had John Diefenbaker. Harkness resigned on February 4, 1963, and that afternoon Mike moved a no-confidence motion. The New Democrats had condemned Pearson's nuclear stand, but they and Social Credit were willing to support a motion condemning the "indecision" and "lack of leadership" of the government. On the cold Ottawa evening of February 5, 1963, John Diefenbaker's government was finally put out of its misery.[81]

NOTES

1. Peter Newman, *The Distemper of Our Times: Canadian Politics in Transition* (Toronto: McClelland and Stewart, 1990; original ed., 1968), 27. This valuable journalistic study was based on excellent Liberal contacts, particularly Maurice Sauvé, whom his colleagues suspected of "leaking" to Newman. Walter Gordon also seems to have spoken quite freely with Newman.

2. Interview with Professor Denis Smith.

3. Interviews with Mary Macdonald, Patricia Pearson Hannah, and Landon Pearson. Maryon Pearson to "Issy" Chester, no date [Nov. 1965] (correspondence in possession of Patricia Pearson Hannah). Pearson's favourable comments are found in L.B. Pearson, *Mike: Memoirs of the Right Honourable Lester B. Pearson. Volume III: 1957-1968* (Toronto: University of Toronto Press, 1975), 42-4.

4. Pearson, *Mike, III:* 45.

5. Grattan O'Leary, *Recollection of People, Press, and Politics* (Toronto: Macmillan, 1977), 137.

6. Peter Stursberg, *Diefenbaker: Leadership Gained, 1956-1962* (Toronto: University of Toronto Press, 1975), 26.

7. Garrett Wilson and Kevin Wilson, *Diefenbaker for the Defence* (Toronto: Lorimer, 1988), 66-7.

8. Ibid.; and Basil Robinson, *Diefenbaker's World: A Populist in Foreign Affairs* (Toronto: University of Toronto Press, 1989), 314. I interviewed John Diefenbaker twice in 1978 for another project and observed personally his tendency not to listen to questions. He was very witty, with a quick mind, but was unable to focus on the questions I asked. He was especially friendly because my grandmother had asked me to get an autographed photograph. She had it above her bed until the day she died and, until that day, pointed it out to every visitor.

9. As King travelled to Alice and Vincent Massey's home in Port Hope, he had a dream in which "curiously enough [I] saw first one snake in the grass come out of a marshy ground — a little one — and a little later a larger one. . . . concluded it was a warning to be careful — I wondered if it could mean that by any chance my hosts were not to be trusted." Mackenzie King Diary, Sept. 3, 1933 (NAC).

10. Newman, *Distemper of Our Times*, 102-3; J.W. Pickersgill, *The Road Back, by a Liberal in Opposition* (Toronto: University of Toronto Press, 1986), 96-9; Robert Bothwell, Ian Drummond, and John English, *Canada since 1945: Power, Politics, and Provincialism* (Toronto: University of Toronto Press, 1981), 260; Joseph Wearing, *The L-Shaped Party: The Liberal Party of Canada, 1958-1980* (Toronto: McGraw-Hill Ryerson, 1981), 19-20; and Pearson, *Mike, III:* 52.

11. *Toronto Daily Star*, Sept. 14, 1960; and R. Macintosh, " The Kingston Conference," Kent Papers, Box 6/8 (Queen's University Archives). Interviews with Mary Macdonald and Michael Mackenzie.

12. Underhill had published a collection of his essays in 1960 entitled *In Search of Canadian Liberalism*, which he dedicated to his former colleague at the University of Toronto, Mike Pearson. Pearson, who was fond of Underhill, corresponded with him after becoming Liberal leader. Underhill recommended in January 1958 that Mike should start some summer conferences "as Vincent Massey did years ago at Port Hope." He urged Pearson to listen to "intellectual and educated people." In his reply Pearson said that the letter "persuaded me to bring Tom Kent" to Ottawa to advise him and that he agreed with the direction the party must go. Underhill to Pearson, Jan. 20, 1958; and Pearson to Underhill, Feb. 11, 1958, Underhill Papers, v. 13 (NAC).

13. Grant Dexter to Victor Sifton, Nov. 18, 1968, Dexter Papers, TC747 (Queen's University Archives).

14. LBP to Hutchison, Sept. 14, 1960; and Hutchison to Dexter, Jan. 2, 1961, Hutchison Papers (University of Calgary Library).

15. Robert Bothwell and William Kilbourn, *C.D. Howe: A Biography* (Toronto: McClelland and Stewart, 1979), 346. See the correspondence with Mitchell Sharp in Howe Papers, v. 197 (NAC).

16. Gordon to Kent, Jan. 16, 1961, Kent Papers, Box 6/8 (Queen's University Archives). Tom Kent, *A Public Purpose: An Experience of Liberal Opposition and Canadian Government* (Kingston and Montreal: McGill-Queen's University Press, 1988), 82–94.

17. Hutchison to Dexter, Jan. 17, 1961, Hutchison Papers (University of Calgary Library). Interview with Bruce Hutchison.

18. The relevant documents are found, in their entirety, in Denis Smith, *Gentle Patriot: A Political Biography of Walter Gordon* (Edmonton: Hurtig, 1973), 64–70. Gordon's own memory of the arrangement is found in a memorandum of Dec. 5, 1965, in Walter Gordon Papers, MG32 B44, v. 16 (NAC).

19. Pickersgill describes a parliamentary debate when Diefenbaker ridiculed the Kingston and Ottawa conferences and Tom Kent, "the leader of the leader." When Pearson referred to John Fisher on Diefenbaker's staff and said, "Body by Fisher," Diefenbaker quickly retorted: "Body by Fisher is a great deal better than Brains by Kent." Pickersgill makes no further comment. J.W. Pickersgill, *The Road Back by a Liberal in Opposition* (Toronto: University of Toronto Press, 1986), 150.

20. Interviews with Mary Macdonald, J.W. Pickersgill, Paul Martin, and Fraser Bruce.

21. LBP to Landon and Geoffrey Pearson, Mar. 31, 1959 (PPP).

22. Pearson, *Mike, III:* 53–4.

23. "Further to my letter of yesterday, I have now arranged for John Gellner and Jim Eayrs to meet you at my house at 6:30 p.m. on Sunday, March 1. Gellner, Eayrs and you are to talk about defence." Gordon to Pearson, Feb. 20, 1959, Pearson Papers (NAC).

24. Keith Davey, *The Rainmaker: A Passion for Politics* (Toronto: Stoddart, 1986), 35–6. Also, Wearing, *The L-Shaped Party*, 19–30; and Smith, *Gentle Patriot*, 65–92.

25. Ramsay Cook, "Not Right, Not Left, But Forward," *Canadian Forum* (Feb. 1962), 241–2. See also J.T. Saywell, ed., *The Canadian Annual Review for 1961* (Toronto: University of Toronto Press, 1962), 74–8.

26. Kent to Pearson, June 13, 1960, MG26 N2, v. 127 (NAC). See Kent's own reflections on this document in *A Public Purpose*, 76–7.

27. See Kent, *A Public Purpose*, 100.

28. Hutchison to Dexter, Feb. 8, 1961, Hutchison Papers (University of Calgary Library).

29. John Holmes gave me his copy of the manuscript. He drafted the chapters after a discussion with Pearson, and Pearson revised. It was the same pattern that Arnold Smith used in drafting *Democracy and World Politics*. Pearson had drafted many speeches for others and found it easy to have others draft them for him. Mr. Smith's copy of another Pearson work is inscribed with a note indicating that in that book, it was "my own words."

30. LBP to Geoffrey Pearson (GP), May 25, 1960 (PPP).

31. LBP to GP, Feb. 11, 1961 (PPP).

32. LBP to GP, Sept. 11, 1961 (PPP).

33. See, for example, LBP to James Duncan, Aug. 29, 1962, MG26 N2, v. 53 (NAC); House of Commons, *Debates*, Feb. 28, 1961; "Trade," MG26 N2, v. 96 (NAC); and Peter Stursberg, *Lester Pearson and the Dream of Unity* (Toronto: Doubleday, 1978), 65–6.

34. Walter Laqueur, *Europe in Our Time: A History, 1945-1992* (New York: Viking, 1992), 323ff.

See also an important study by Bruce Muirhead, *The Development of Postwar Canadian Trade Policy* (Montreal: McGill-Queen's University Press, 1992), which illustrates how reluctant Europe was to enter into trading arrangements with Canada in the 1950s.

35. Gordon's annoyance with the delay in making contact is recorded in his memorandum of Dec. 5, 1965, Gordon Papers, MG32 B44, v. 16 (NAC). In this memorandum, Gordon indicates he was "ignored by Mike" for three or four months. Smith, in *Gentle Patriot* (81), says it was "more than two months." Gordon indicated to Tom Kent that "Mike" had visited with him on Mar. 10, 1961. That suggests that he was "ignored" for a shorter time. Gordon to Kent, Mar. 14, 1961, Kent Papers, Box 6/8 (Queen's University Archives). See also Pearson, *Mike, III:* 54ff.

36. On Turner, see the file "John de B. Payne" in Liberal Party of Canada Papers, v. 742 (NAC). Also, see Wearing, *The L-Shaped Party*, 27-8.

37. When Gordon, Pearson, and Davey met, the discussion began with Pearson and Davey dissecting last night's box scores, to the great annoyance of Gordon.

38. Wearing, *ibid.*, 25-6; and Davey, *The Rainmaker*, ch. 3.

39. See J.L. Granatstein, *Canada 1957-1967: The Years of Uncertainty and Innovation* (Toronto: McClelland and Stewart, 1986), 74ff.; and House of Commons, *Debates*, June 14, 1961. The account here follows Granatstein's excellent, detailed treatment of the topic.

40. House of Commons, *Debates*, Jan. 20, 1961; David Smith and David Slater, "The Economic Proposals of the Governor of the Bank of Canada," *Queen's Quarterly* (Spring 1961), 196-211; and Bothwell et al., *Canada since 1945*, 222.

41. They were close friends, and Pickersgill did speak with him and assist him during this period; but Coyne's anger was his own and needed no direction. After the death of Pickersgill's first wife, Coyne had been an "emotional rock" for Pickersgill, who never forgot the many kindnesses at that time. This emotional link undoubtedly intensified the anger in Pickersgill's attack on the government's action. Interview with J.W. Pickersgill.

42. House of Commons, *Debates*, July 7, 1961.

43. Saywell, ed., *Canadian Annual Review for 1961*, 19.

44. Peter Regenstreif, *The Diefenbaker Interlude: Parties and Voting in Canada* (Don Mills, Ont.: Longman, 1965), 72-6. See also Regenstreif, "Group Perceptions and the Vote: Some Avenues of Opinion Formation in the 1962 Campaign," in John Meisel, ed., *Papers on the 1962 Election* (Toronto: University of Toronto Press, 1964), 235-52.

45. Regenstreif, *The Diefenbaker Interlude*, 72-6.

46. Cook, "Not Right, Not Left," *passim*; and Bothwell et al., *Canada since 1945*, ch. 25.

47. See Granatstein, *Canada 1957-1967*, 89.

48. House of Commons, *Debates*, Feb. 22, 1962.

49. *Globe and Mail*, Apr. 26, 1962. He had told Geoffrey earlier that he had given some "slam-bang" speeches and said he was trying to cling "to my higher plane but my grip is slipping." LBP to GP, Jan. 29, 1962 (PPP).

50. Connally told Bruce Hutchison that Kent had been appointed without his knowledge and that he threatened resignation. He blamed Gordon. Hutchison to Dexter, Oct. 1, 1961, Hutchison Papers (University of Calgary Library).

51. *Mike, III:* 58-9; and Gordon to Candidates, June 7, 1962, Liberal Party of Canada Papers, v. 689 (NAC); and Walter Gordon, *A Political Memoir* (Toronto: McClelland and Stewart, 1977), 97-9.

52. The party manager in the Quebec region, the political veteran C.G. "Chubby" Power, was baffled by the Social Credit phenomenon and did not take it seriously until it was too late. Power to Bruce Hutchison, May 29, 1962, Power Papers, v. 6 (Queen's University Archives).

53. LBP to GP, June 26, 1962 (PPP). Quoted in full in Pearson, *Mike, III:* 65.

54. Peason, *Mike, III:* 64.

55. *Ibid.*, 61-3; Smith, *Gentle Patriot*, 107ff.; Rasminsky memorandum on *Gentle Patriot* account of crisis (given to me by Mr. Rasminsky); Donald M. Fleming, *So Very Near: The Political Memoirs of the Honourable Donald M. Fleming. Volume 2: The Summit Years* (Toronto: McClelland and Stewart, 1985), ch. 93; and Granatstein, *Canada 1957-1967*, 98-100, which shows that the plan was drafted by officials on June 12. See also the comments criticizing *Gentle Patriot*'s presentation of Gordon's interpretation in A.F.W. Plumptre, *Three Decades of Decision: Canada and the World Monetary System, 1944-1975* (Toronto: McClelland and Stewart, 1977), 170, 180 n. 27.

56. Regenstreif, *The Diefenbaker Interlude*, 37, 157. Catholic support for Liberals was, of course, traditional.

57. Theodore Draper, *Present History* (New York: Vintage, 1984), 112. The defence crisis is covered in Granatstein, *Canada 1957–1967.*
58. John F. Kennedy, "The Terrain of Today's Statecraft," *Saturday Review of Literature* (Aug. 1, 1959), 19–20. See also L.B. Pearson, *Diplomacy in the Nuclear Age* (Cambridge, Mass.: Harvard University Press, 1959).
59. James Eayrs, *Northern Approaches: Canada and the Search for Peace* (Toronto: Macmillan, 1961), 40–56.
60. The rally called for Canadian interceptors to confine their activities to "identification" of Soviet intruders, with the actual shooting left to Americans. "The proposed policy," Eayrs wrote, "has wittily been dubbed a 'policy for bird watchers,' but bird watchers have more strength and stamina." James Eayrs, *Northern Approaches: Canada and the Search for Peace* (Toronto: Macmillan, 1961), 43.
61. *Calgary Herald*, Sept. 26, 1961; and *Vancouver Sun*, Sept. 20, 1961. Interview with Jo Davis, founder of the Voice of Women.
62. LBP to Mrs. Walter Lee, Apr. 5, 1962, MG26 N2, v. 50 (NAC:); LBP to F.M. Kelly, Oct. 24, 1961, *ibid.*; LBP to GP, Feb. 11, 1961 (PPP). GP to LBP, Feb. 4, 1961; and Paul Hellyer to LBP, Aug. 3, 1961, MG26 N2, v. 55 (NAC).
63. Michael Beschloss, *The Crisis Years: Kennedy and Khruschev, 1960–1963* (New York: Edward Burlingame Books, 1991), 4–5.
64. See Knowlton Nash, *Kennedy and Diefenbaker: Fear and Loathing across the Undefended Border* (Toronto: McClelland and Stewart, 1990), 128. Interview with Willis Armstrong.
65. It was on that visit that Kennedy dropped a memorandum entitled "What We Want from Ottawa Trip." Diefenbaker had it in a vault, took great umbrage at its contents, and claimed that Kennedy had scrawled SOB in the margin. Kennedy, upon learning this, told his friend Ben Bradlee that he "didn't think Diefenbaker was a son of a bitch. . . . I thought he was a prick." Bradlee, *Conversations with Kennedy* (New York: Norton, 1975), 183.
66. See Nash, *Kennedy and Diefenbaker*, 161–2.
67. Robinson, *Diefenbaker's World*, 285.
68. Interview with Mary Macdonald.
69. Granatstein, *Canada 1957–1967*; LBP to GP, Oct. 1962 (PPP).
70. Cees Wiebes and Bert Zeeman, "Political Consultation during International Crises: Small Powers in NATO," in Lawrence Kaplan, S.V. Papacsma, Mark Rubin, and Ruth Young, eds., *NATO after Forty Years* (Wilmington, Del.: Scholarly Resources, 1990), 94–5.
71. Hellyer to LBP, Nov. 25, 1962, MG26 N2, v. 55 (NAC). Hellyer's account is found in his memoirs, *Damn the Torpedoes: My Fight to Unify Canada's Armed Forces* (Toronto: McClelland and Stewart, 1990), 24–5.
72. *Toronto Daily Star*, Jan. 7, 1962 (Gallup poll). Liberals led Conservatives by 47% to 32% in the January Gallup poll.
73. LBP to Douglas LePan, Feb. 28, 1962, MG26 N2, v. 49 (NAC); and LBP to Geoffrey Andrew, Dec. 7, 1961, *ibid.*, v. 50.
74. LBP to George Brown, Nov. 19, 1962, *ibid.* (NAC).
75. John Gellner to Paul Hellyer, Dec. 21, 1962, *ibid.*, v. 49 (NAC).
76. Gordon's later statement that he was caught by surprise and did not support the change seems odd, in light of the fact that he had the Gellner document and even served as its interpreter. See Denis Smith, *Gentle Patriot: A Political Biography of Walter Gordon* (Edmonton: Hurtig, 1973), 119–20.
77. These letters are in MG26 N2, v. 49 (NAC).
78. "On Canadian Defence Policy," Jan. 12, 1963, in Lester Pearson, *Words and Occasions* (Toronto: University of Toronto Press, 1970), 194–206.
79. Lloyd Axworthy to Pearson, n.d., MG26 N2, v. 50 (NAC); and Bothwell et al., *Canada since 1945*, 266.
80. The best account is in Nash, *Kennedy and Diefenbaker*, 239ff. House of Commons, *Debates*, Jan. 31, 1963.
81. John Saywell, ed., *The Canadian Annual Review for 1963* (Toronto: University of Toronto Press, 1964), 13.

George Grant's Lament

WILLIAM CHRISTIAN

As often as he could stand it, George Grant would get into his old car and drive north on Highway 6 from his home in Dundas to Guelph, past the campus of the Agricultural College to the stately grounds of the Homewood Sanatorium, where John Diefenbaker's first wife had also been a patient. By now his mother, Maude, no longer knew who he was; if she recognized him at all, she mistook him for the man who had always been the most important figure in her life, her father, Sir George Parkin. By the beginning of 1963 she was fading, and George Grant stood by his mother's bed in tears, begging her, "let go, mother; let go." On 3 February her struggle was finally over; she died of pneumonia at 82. Maude's funeral took place against a political backdrop that would make her son a national figure.

Grant's uncle, long-time Conservative politician Jim Macdonnell, had served briefly in the Diefenbaker cabinet before standing aside for a younger colleague, and through him George kept in touch with the tensions within the party. In the 1962 election Diefenbaker was reduced to a minority position in the House of Commons. Criticism of his leadership, which was suppressed when he commanded a massive majority, quickly surfaced when it became clear that he might now be an electoral liability. By the time of Maude's death, as many as half the cabinet members wanted a new leader.

The issue that had become central was the matter of nuclear weapons for Canadian troops, both at home and abroad, a principle the government appeared to have accepted in 1959 when it acquired weapons designed with a nuclear capacity. By 1961, however, the government's views had changed, and it increasingly saw its role as that of mediator in nuclear disarmament negotiations. Most of the cabinet wanted to go ahead with the acquisition, but Howard Green, the secretary of state for External Affairs, supported by Diefenbaker, hesitated.

After intense maneuvering within the cabinet, and an acrimonious debate in the House, the Liberals, under Lester Pearson, the New Democrats, and the Social Credit Party combined to defeat the government on 6 February, three days after Maude's death, forcing a general election for 8 April 1963.[1]

Grant knew at once where he stood in this crisis. He wrote almost immediately to express his support and admiration for Diefenbaker's

SOURCE: "George Grant's Lament," *Queen's Quarterly* 100, no. 1 (Spring 1993): 199–214. Reprinted with permission.

speech, defending his government's actions, delivered in the Commons prior to dissolution. He also decided that this event marked the end of his brief association with the NDP. He had liked the party because it supported social measures he thought were intrinsically good — such as state medicine — but he was enraged "that they were voting Diefenbaker out in the name of a servant of the United States like Lester Pearson."[2] The NDP, he concluded, were a "kind of vacuous extension of the Liberals," and he heartily regretted having had anything to do with them. "The last years have cleared my head greatly and I am now an unequivocal anti-progressive." He followed up this change in political allegiance quickly with public support for the Conservatives, even going so far as to help organize coffee parties for the local candidate.

He also took his attack to the media. At the end of July 1963 he was on CBC's *Viewpoint*, delivering a talk about the nuclear test ban treaty between the USA and the USSR; this was a matter, he said, that should be cause for rejoicing for nearly everyone in Canada. Only those with a "hidden love of death" could oppose it. Both superpowers had decided it was necessary to stop the spread of weapons except to "minor satellites such as Canada."

Over the winter he began his most important response, an article about the meaning of the recent events. He had started, he wrote to Rhonda and Doug Hall in January 1964, a "long piece called 'A Lament for a Country' which is just about Canada becoming part of the universal and homogeneous state. It is finally true that one's hope must lie in the transcendent — but what a business it is putting off one's finite hopes." Soon the long piece had grown into a small book. It had required, he explained to his sister Charity, great concentration in the midst of his teaching responsibilities, but he found it therapeutic, "in the sense that understanding tragedy is the way to meet it." It also apparently required support of a more immediate kind. His daughter Kate gave her mother, Sheila Grant, a note: "Please! Please! Make a Siniman Scrudal cake. It will give daddy energy for the book."

More or less written, he had to find somewhere to publish what he now called *A Lament for a Nation*. As he explained to Gaston Laurion, whose French translation was published in 1987, he took the title from William Dunbar's incomparable Scots poem, "Lament for the Makaris [makers]," an appropriate source, he thought, considering the conquest of the Highland Scots by the English at Culloden.[3] Its refrain, *Timor mortis conturbat me* ("The fear of death overwhelms me"), comes from the Office of the Dead,[4] and the poem reminds us to understand the temptations of this world in the light of our mortality. "Our pleasure here is all vain glory,/ This false world is but transitory,/ The flesh is frail, the Fiend is sly; *Timor mortis conturbat me*." Politician and professor alike are equally subject to death's sway. "He spares no lord for his piscence [power];/ Nor clerk for his intelligence;/ His awful strike may no man flee;/ *Timor mortis conturbat me.*" Since everyone must eventually face death, we must live in contemplation of God. "Since for the dead remedy is none,/ Best is that we for death prepare,/ After our death that live may we;/ *Timor mortis conturbat me.*"

*   *   *

On 18 February 1964, Grant wrote to the editor of the *Queen's Quarterly*, to see if the journal might be interested in publishing his pamphlet. Albert Fell replied that although the description had aroused his curiosity, at 25,000 words it was too long for the *QQ*. He suggested Grant try the University of Toronto Press. Although Grant was prepared to consider this, because he preferred his work be published in Canada rather than the US, he was rather sceptical of anything to do with the University of Toronto. Indeed his letter to Frances Halpenny seems bent on persuading her not to publish it.

> Its content may be such as to exclude it from your press, because it is the Canadian established classes (particularly the Liberal party) who are considered most responsible in what I consider Canada's demise. Diefenbaker is criticized, but not from within Liberal assumptions. Neither will it be favourably received by any socialist as it does not presume the world is getting better and better.

On the same day that he wrote to U of T Press, after consulting a colleague in history, he sent a letter to historian Ramsay Cook, seeking advice as to a publisher. He described his book as "very ruthless about the Liberal party's responsibility for the destruction of our independence vis-a-vis the United States; it is hard to think that it would be published in certain quarters." Cook replied promptly, suggesting McClelland & Stewart, or, if that did not prove possible, that Grant write a short piece for the *Canadian Forum*. In the meantime Paul Clifford, a colleague at McMaster, had been in touch with Dent's.

At the beginning of March 1964 Grant wrote to them, indicating that his book would be finished by the end of the month. It would not, he explained, be a gossipy book, but a

> closely written book and full of passion and regret about Canada. It starts with a lot of factual material about Canadian history, but ends with a logic which is deeper, about the age of progress. Its conclusions are, therefore, not likely to appeal to many people. I say all this not, I hope, to scare you off, but to say that although I would be obviously willing to change wordings, etc., I would not be willing to turn it into a popular book, either in style or content.

Toward the end of June, Grant felt his work was almost completed, and he wrote to his old Oxford chum, Derek Bedson, to ask if he might dedicate the work to him and to Judith Robinson, the journalist he so much admired and had met through the Civil Liberties Association, "Two Lovers of their Country, One Living and One Dead." They were, he said, the two people most important in shaping his political opinions.

Bedson had been a close Diefenbaker advisor before he joined the Manitoba civil service. Robinson had died in a car crash in December 1961, and Grant always remembered the discussions he had with her at the end of the war. He described her as one of his greatest teachers about politics: more than anyone else she had made him aware of the fragility of Canadian nationhood on a continent shared with the United States.

Lament was in Dent's hands at the beginning of the summer, and on 29 July John Campsie, an editor from Dent's, wrote to say that it had been "read and highly praised by two or three people here" and that there would be no difficulty getting a decision to publish *Lament*. However their publishing schedule prevented early publication, and if George still wanted that, it would be best to try elsewhere. Now Grant took Cook's advice and sent it to McClelland & Stewart. Like many authors, he felt his work had fallen into a black hole, and at the beginning of September he was writing to Jack McClelland to see if he had reached a decision.

McClelland had in fact acted with dispatch, as publishing goes, and sent the manuscript to James M. Minnifie, a Canadian journalist working in Washington. Minnifie's report was positive, and McClelland & Stewart agreed to publish the book, though by the end of October Grant was again writing to urge them on. "I am sorry to keep bothering you, but I wonder when we could meet about the manuscript on Canadian affairs. I am a slow worker and would like to get going at any changes you suggest, as well as some changes I have in mind." The contract to publish was not signed until 13 January 1965.

On the recommendation of Claire Pratt, the in-house editor, McClelland & Stewart assigned the manuscript to one of their top editors, freelancer John Robert Colombo. Colombo edited about three pages of text, and then arranged to meet Grant in a restaurant in East York for coffee. He was amazed when, in the absence of a spoon, Grant took off his glasses and used one of the arms to stir his coffee. If Colombo thought he might be dealing with a crazy eccentric, Grant worried that the Establishment had set a Liberal on his work, with a mission to emasculate it. However, by the next time Colombo saw the book, they could both relax. It had been transformed. Grant had strengthened the arguments and taken some of Colombo's editorial suggestions; Sheila had polished the style and helped heighten the impact with effective quotations. Now the text, in Colombo's word, "sang."

* * *

Masterpiece is not a word that should be lightly used, but *Lament for a Nation* merits it. In 97 pages Grant had distilled his years of study of theology and philosophy, together with his knowledge of history and his acute attention to the daily passage of political events. The former adult educator had put it all into a book that was instantly accessible to the broad reading public, but rewarded repeated reading by academic philosophers.

What alchemy produced it? We clearly must first mention the proximate cause, the fall of the Diefenbaker government on the nuclear arms question. As he said in an interview in 1973, "my motive for writing that book was rage, just rage, that they'd brought atomic weapons into Canada" (*This Country in the Morning*, 10 October 1973).

Except for the period following his decision to join the British Merchant Marine, Grant was a pacifist, but he distinguished between two sorts. There was pacifism as a moral stance, adopted in the full knowledge of the practical consequences. At the beginning of the war, his best friend at Balliol had been imprisoned for refusing his call-up, and Grant himself had been refused the position of Warden of Hart House because of his own pacifism. Christ and Gandhi, who both died violent deaths, had shown how high the price might be. The other pacifist stance might be known as "tactical pacifism," or better, internationalism. This view said that negotiation and diplomacy must be pursued as far as they could, and further. Force must only be used with the greatest reluctance, and in the very last resort. This was not only morally correct; it would prove an effective policy.

What sort was Grant? He had always been an internationalist, but now the existence of nuclear weapons tipped the balance back towards a more absolute pacifism.

> For years I was immobilized after the war by the fact that I saw my pacifism had been wrong, but there was no feasible alternative. Catholic doctrine on the just war had convinced me, but now most Catholic theologians are saying that the use of modern weapons is "intrinsically wicked" for the Christian. The upshot of this is that one hopes for disengagement from the [NATO] alliance. (letter to Derek Bedson, undated)

The Christian pacifism provided the moral outrage; the rejection of internationalism intensified it. "Diefenbaker's and Green's nationalism was taking the form of a new kind of neutralism, a simple refusal to accept any demand from the present imperialism" (23). Diefenbaker himself was "no pacifist, no unilateralist, nor was he sentimental about Communism. If nuclear arms were necessary for North-American defence, Canada would take them" (31). What so distressed Grant was that there seemed to be an alternative for Canada to accepting these hideous manifestations of technological destructiveness, but that no one other than Diefenbaker and Howard Green seemed to see the significance of the choice. "Green's appeal to a gentler tradition of international morality had little attraction for the new Canada, outside of such unimportant groups as the Voice of Women" (31).

The second force behind Grant's passionate conviction at this time was the death of his mother. In one of his most memorable metaphors, he spoke of the disappearance in Canada of the dream of building a more ordered and more stable society than the United States. This hope was now extinguished. "We find ourselves like fish left on the shores of a drying lake. The element necessary to our existence had passed away." And he talked about the character of a lament, "to cry out at the death or at the dying of something loved" (2). Once, when he was talking with his friend George Wallace, the McMaster artist, Wallace said that after the death of each of his parents he had produced a sculpture that was for him part of his grieving. Grant replied, "I did too; I wrote *Lament for a Nation* under the same circumstances."[5]

For Grant, the passing of his mother involved the loss of his last direct, powerful tie with a past in which family and imperial politics were intertwined. Grandfather Parkin had not been just a sentimental anglophile; he was a tub-thumping charismatic evangelist, an activist and organizer carrying the good news of Imperial Federation not just across Canada but throughout the Empire. Here was a man who thought that the values of British civilization mattered, and who had devoted his life to that belief. George's paternal grandfather, G.M. Grant, the legendary principal of Queen's, also stood and was counted when the time came. In politics he had always distrusted his local MP, Sir John A. Macdonald, a man he held responsible for much of the corruption in Canadian political life. But when free trade, or Commercial Union, was proposed by the Liberals in the 1891 election, he was side by side with Sir John against it. He believed Commercial Union inevitably brought political union in its train. It is therefore not thoughtlessly that Grant lamented the passing of Canada as a "celebration of memory"; in this case, the "memory of that tenuous hope that was the principle of my ancestors" (5–6).

The coincidence of his mother's death and the fall of Diefenbaker's government were, of course, not causally related; it was their accidental conjunction that allowed him to see clearly that the dream of sustaining in Canada any sort of alternative to American civilization was irrevocably extinguished. It also helps explain the intensity of his response: his philosophic imagination transformed his personal grief into political passion.

The third ingredient was the Right Honourable John George Diefenbaker himself. That Diefenbaker responded positively to the book there can be little doubt. He subsequently asked Grant to write speeches for him and prepare background papers. When he went to New York for a visit to the United Nations, he took Grant along. He even paid Grant the highest compliment possible, short of inviting him on a fishing expedition: he asked him to write his biography. He could never quite understand or forgive Grant for declining this offer. I can think of only one reason why someone so prickly about criticism would react to *Lament* in this way. Reviews portrayed it as a pro-Diefenbaker book; it is hard to believe he actually read it through.

Lament is a systematic indictment of Diefenbaker's government. His administration, according to Grant, was confused and inconsistent, his response to the Canadian predicament bewildered (5). Diefenbaker confused rhetoric with policy, and stuck with the rhetoric even when it failed to work (11). His vision of Canada floundered, because he was never specific about what Canada should be. A prairie populist, he appointed the epitome of Toronto Toryism, Donald Fleming, his finance minister (13); his own small town, free-enterprise ideology was "entirely inadequate" to come to terms with the society that had arisen in central Canada since the war. His inept response to economic difficulties lost the support of the ordinary people of Ontario, and associated the Conservatives again with unemployment and recession (14–15). His relations with the civil service, though flawed on both sides, invited "the writing of a picaresque novel" (18). He even forgot that the CBC had been created by R.B. Bennett's Conservative government to prevent the use of the airwaves for private gain, and attacked this central national institution (19). And, in spite of his electoral success in Quebec, he was unwilling to recognize the rights of French Canadians as a community (21). For those who missed the point of the book, Grant summed it up during a CBC discussion on the future of Canadian nationhood on 27 June 1965:

> My book is not a defence of Mr. Diefenbaker. There is a whole chapter saying that he had no constructive nationalist legislation when he was in. . . . Before the Defence Crisis I saw nothing in his favour, just nothing. I thought he had a very poor regime. If that wasn't implied in the book, then I must write very unclearly. Over the Defence Crisis, I see the hero of this book as Mr. Green, not as Mr. Diefenbaker . . .

Without the defence crisis of 1962–63, Diefenbaker would have shown himself to be nothing more than "a romantic demagogue yearning for recognition" (25). But the events of this crisis revealed a "deeply held principle for which he would fight with great courage." "Nothing in Diefenbaker's ministry was as noble as his leaving of it" (25). Yet in Diefenbaker, Grant saw a nationalism similar to his own. Before he had turned to philosophy, he had written pamphlets in 1943 and 1945, *Canada: An Introduction to a Nation* and *The Empire: Yes or No?*, that explored the means by which Canada could preserve its independent identity in North America. On this issue he had agreed with his grandfathers, George Parkin and Principal Grant, that only by maintaining a strong imperial connection could Canada survive the destructive pull of the United States. To be independent, Canada must also be British. He repeated this in *Lament*.

> Growing up in Ontario the generation of the 1920s took it for granted that they belonged to a nation. The character of the country was self-evident. To say it was British was not to deny it was North American. To be a Canadian was to be a unique species of North American. (3)

★ ★ ★

Grant gave Diefenbaker partial absolution for his failures because there were so few successful alternatives. De Gaulle was Grant's favourite contemporary politician, but he did not think that the Gaullism he had encountered during his visit to Paris in 1963 was possible in Canada because we lacked the depth of tradition (47). The other possibility, "leftist" nationalism, was possible only in less-developed countries whose people wanted industrialism but feared they were being thwarted by the American empire. This was not the case in Canada. The large corporations, where real power lay, knew nothing of loyalty, only interest. That directed them south.

His father, Queen's historian and UCC principal William Grant, had been deeply sympathetic to French Canada, and his mother's connection with McGill (where she had served as warden at Royal Victoria College from 1937 until 1940) had led him to spend time and make friends in Quebec. It was a place he knew and loved. This encounter was the fourth element in the mix. He had experienced French Catholicism when he was young, and it had made a powerful impression on him. In other circumstances its oppressiveness would have made him its enemy, but now Grant saw it, *faute de mieux*, as the only sustaining bulwark against the inroads of the universal and homogeneous state. Catholicism might not be pretty, but it was tough. "To Catholics who remain Catholics, whatever their level of sophistication, virtue must be prior to freedom."

But Grant feared that, eventually, even it would not prove tough enough. The concept of the universal and homogenous state, which he had absorbed in his reading of the philosophic controversy between Alexandre Kojève and Leo Strauss,[6] he now used with brilliant effect to analyse the world-wide expansion of American capitalism, "a dynamic empire spearheading the age of progress" (66). Nothing could stand in its way; conservatism was impossible. The belief that science should lead to the conquest of nature was ubiquitous. Conservatives could delay, but not prevent, its triumph; they would fail because, in their hearts, they too thought it was right.

There were, by contrast, those for whom the universal and homogenous state was the proper object of human striving. For them the disappearance of Canada was not just inevitable, it was good because it was a step on the road to total human liberation (37). The Liberal Party's accomplishment was not that it caused the development — it had too little power for that — but that it managed it with a minimum of fuss. They were to politics what Deweyites were to education; they made people comfortable with necessity.

Why did Grant always speak of this process as necessary? The final element that constituted *Lament* was his reading of political philosophy. Grant turned to a work by Leo Strauss, *Natural Right and History*. This helped him see that the apparent conflicts of his contemporary world — progress/reaction, liberalism/conservatism, socialism/capitalism — were ultimately unimportant. They were rival interpretations of the same thing: the freedom to change any order that stands in the way of technological advance (73). No modern western regime could survive if it took seriously the possibility that there was an eternal order by which we were measured and defined.

G.M. Grant had seen the Great Republic as an aggressive predator, and he warned his countrymen to be vigilant about their independence. He put it in language that was somewhat earthy for a clergyman. "Our position under the protection of the United States would be precisely similar [to that of a kept woman]. I wish no such harlot's independence for my country." Canada, in his grandson's view, had done worse. A kept woman at least got money; we had simply been seduced. Over the years Canada's independence had been eroded, not so much by the actions of the Americans, as by Canadians coming to accept the attractiveness of modernity. In a footnote he cited the example of Frank Underhill who, according to Grant, turned away from the Left and expressed in his seventies his belief that liberal hope lay with the corporations and not with doctrinaire socialism (92). Grant himself could testify to the beguiling allure of modernity. He had experienced its theoretical power in the writings of Sartre, Hegel, and Kojève. He knew its practical force every time Sheila washed the clothes in her machine, or the doctor gave antibiotics to one of their sick children. "Those who criticize our age must at the same time contemplate pain, infant mortality, crop failures in isolated areas, and the sixteen hour day" (94). How could he persuade his compatriots to turn away from the science of mastery, particularly if they no longer understood the significance of redemptive suffering?

Yet it might be possible that the assumptions of the age of progress were false. Modern science had led not just to penicillin but to nuclear weapons. And the assumptions of modernity were just that, the postulates of particular men in particular settings, who believed they had preserved what was true from antiquity, while correcting its errors. Plato and Aristotle had not seen their own work in that light, as preparation for a future in which they would be superseded. They thought that the mark of a philosopher was to present a complete teaching that was valid for everyone everywhere (95). To judge that claim would move beyond political philosophy, beyond Strauss, to the metaphysical assertion that "changes in the world take place within an eternal order that is not affected by them." It was at this key point that Grant acknowledged the present limits that he had reached philosophically: he could not yet see how it was possible to preserve freedom without accepting the modern view that it was man's essence, nor how science could be other than the conquest of nature.

Canada's independence no longer served anything the world thought good. Formal annexation by the United States would eventually come, and when it did it would make little practical difference. It was fated because most North Americans accepted the modern understanding of what was good for human beings. Yet these secular developments did not settle the issue. William Dunbar, in fifteenth-century Scotland, reminded us to heed the inevitability of death, and turn to God for comfort. In the Latin quotation that concludes *Lament*, Virgil describes the souls longing for the afterlife. Even though the philosopher might have difficulty in explaining it, the religious man had been told that "process is not all" (97).

★   ★   ★

Was Grant a pessimist? It was an epithet that intensely annoyed him. It was always open to any human being at any time or place to orient his soul to God; God's love and God's grace were always sufficient: the fear of death need not perturb anyone. The pessimist denied the ever-present possibility of salvation; this was foolish and a sin. Others went to the contrary extreme and imagined that God might directly and decisively intervene in the working out of earthly affairs; this possibility Grant rejected as inconsistent with his understanding of the divine. Still others thought that nuclear war might erupt, and its fell consequences would convince its miserable survivors to reconsider the assumptions that had led to it. This solution was too horrible to contemplate. The only genuine possibility was that "enough human beings might wake up and see that technique was destroying them spiritually and try and move against it."[7] Even if this were to happen, it is impossible to say when it might begin and how long, even how many centuries, it would take. To those who thought he was trying to provoke a nationalist response in a last ditch effort to save Canada, he replied firmly:

> Because people quite rightly want finite hopes, people have read a little book I wrote [*Lament for a Nation*] wrongly. I was talking about the *end* of Canadian nationalism. I was saying that this is over and people read it as if I was making an appeal for Canadian nationalism. I think that is just nonsense. I think they just read it wrongly.[8]

However, in the immediate future and on the practical level we would be better off if we retarded the process of integration; residual nationhood was better than none: "I think it a dreadful loss for human beings when they have to lose taking part in the practical life of their society. My *Lament* was also a lament for the loss of the possibility of taking part in politics."[9] It was just that he thought the misfortune had already irrevocably come to pass.

Lament was published on 27 March 1965, and the immediate reaction from Grant's friends was mixed. James Doull thought it "as exasperating as it is brilliant," and accused him of giving up the battle before it had been fought. Jim Aitchison told him that it would shake a lot of people out of their complacency, but did not find the full argument "anywhere near convincing."

However, author Farley Mowat praised it as a:

> veritable masterpiece . . . I have never before read, and never expect to read, a more succinct, accurate and damning appraisal of the "Canadian" decline. . . . I find it a bitter thought that it should have come too late to make any difference. . . . Your book is a tremendous tour-de-force and I admire both it and you very much indeed.

Hugh McLennan, whose cottage was close to that of George's Uncle Raleigh, wrote in a similar vein:

> I have spent the last two nights not so much re-reading *Lament* as studying it. The book is so closely written that one reading is quite insufficient. It is also beautifully written, and one of the most civilized (in the cosmopolitan sense) books on the destiny of this country I have ever read. No political scientist could possibly have written such a book. It is a noble one.

Maude's old friend from McGill, Eugene Forsey, also wrote in admiration:

> I can't claim to understand all of it (I shouldn't have expected to, for I don't move on your intellectual level), and I am dubious about some parts; nor am I quite so ready to lament what may not be so irretrievably lost as you believe; there is still some fight in me, as I am sure there is in you; in fact there is probably a great deal more in you. But it's a powerful work.

Grant took this mixture of praise and criticism from his friends in good part; he reacted more sharply to a correspondent from Edmonton:

> Thank you very much for your letter and poem. The poem is indeed insulting, as it accuses me of lack of courage, and what is worse, valetudinarianism. I do not think I lack hope, because in the Christian sense I interpret hope as a supernatural virtue, and courage is what is necessary in the world.

When Frank Underhill sent a copy of a review in which he had attacked the book and defended Canadian liberalism, George archly replied that there were two points with which he would take exception.

> (a) When you state that I was annoyed with yourself. I tried to state your position as fairly as you tried to state mine. (b) I really think there is a lot of snobbery of an unpleasant kind in many intellectuals' approach to Diefenbaker. Perhaps I should look at the mote in my own eye because I feel the same snobbery about the ambitious little bureaucrat who is your leader.

★ ★ ★

Another critic was closer to home and not so easy to dismiss. Jim Macdonnell, who had been more than anyone Grant's mentor in practical politics, wrote to express his regret about certain features of the book. He was impressed, he allowed, with his nephew's knowledge of political philosophy, less so with his understanding of the "personalities of men active in public life today." He told his nephew that he had criticized the civil service and Queen's unfairly, and warned him that he appeared in danger of treating any successful businessman as a public enemy. As for his general attitude towards the Conservatives, Macdonnell said with dignity: "I think we have played a not unworthy part in this last twenty-year period of anxiety and confusion." Here, at least, was someone who did not mistake it for a pro-Conservative book. At a cocktail party at the Macdonnells', someone asked Grant about his new book. Aunt Marjorie changed the topic firmly: "The less said about that, the better."

NOTES

1. I have followed George Perlin's excellent account in *The Tory Syndrome* (Montreal, 1980), ch. 4.
2. GPG interview with David Cayley, 1985.
3. George always sympathized with the losers at Culloden. Once, though, at a party at McMaster in honour of a visiting Scottish theologian, he was expounding Leo Strauss' view that Culloden marked a turning point in European history. After a while the Scottish divine became annoyed and interrupted: "The Grants fought at Culloden all right, but they were spies for the English, and they fled the minute the battle started." George was crushed.
4. The full passage is: "Since I have been sinning daily and repenting not, the fear of death distresses me. Since in hell there is no redemption, have pity on me, God, and save me."
5. Interview with George Wallace, April 1991.
6. See his article "Tyranny and Wisdom" in *Technology and Empire: Perspectives on North America* (Toronto, 1969), pp. 79–109.
7. From "The Future of Canadian Nationhood," CBC's *Venture*, 27 June 1965.
8. "An Interview with George Grant," by Larry Schmidt, *Grail* 1 Issue 1 (March 1985), p. 36.
9. GPG interview with David Cayley, 1985.

CORRESPONDENCE

GPG to Rhonda and Doug Hall, 24 January 1964.
GPG to Charity Grant, 9 March 1964.
Catherine Grant to Sheila Grant, undated.
GPG to Gaston Laurion, early 1988?
Albert Fell, editor, *Queen's Quarterly*, to GPG, 21 February 1964.
GPG to Frances Halpenny, University of Toronto Press, 25 February 1964.
GPG to Ramsay Cook, 25 February 1964.
GPG to J.S. Campsie, editor, Dent & Sons, 3 March 1964.
GPG to Derek Bedson (Bedson Private Papers, Province of Manitoba Archives), received 2 July 1964.
John Campsie, Dent & Sons, to GPG, 29 July 1964.
James M. Minnifie to GPG, 7 September 1965.
GPG to Mr. Totten, McClelland & Stewart, 29 October 1964.
GPG to Derek Bedson (Bedson Private Papers, Province of Manitoba Archives), undated.
James Doull to GPG, 26 April 1965.
Jim Aitchison to GPG, 30 June 1965.
Farley Mowat to GPG, 30 June 1965.
Hugh McLennan to GPG, 1 July 1965.
Eugene Forsey to GPG, 8 August 1965.
GPG to R.D. Matthews, Edmonton, Alberta, 14 July 1965.
GPG to F.H. Underhill, 18 October 1965.
J.M. Macdonnell to GPG, 18 May 1965.

Kidnapping in Canada — 1970

J.R. CROSS

The fifth of October 1970 dawned as a bright crisp day, typical of the Canadian fall. At 8.00 A.M. I was in our bedroom at 1297, Redpath Crescent in Montreal, the house which my wife and I occupied whilst I was serving as the Senior British Trade Commissioner (Consul General) in the Province of Quebec, when there was a ring at the doorbell. I was walking between the bedroom and the adjoining bathroom, talking to my wife about our programme for the day. The ring puzzled me so early in the morning, but in a minute or two I heard our maid Analia answer the door. I heard voices below, and thought no more about it. A minute later I was walking back into the bathroom, clad only in shirt and underpants, when I was confronted by a young man who had entered the bathroom from my dressing-room beyond. He was holding a pistol in his hand. "Get down on the floor or you'll be fucking dead," he said. I backed through the door into the bedroom and lay down. He made me turn over on my face, told me to put my hands behind my back and clapped a pair of handcuffs on me. My wife was still in bed and our Dalmation dog, who had jumped on the bed, began to growl. "Keep that dog still, or I'll shoot it." He then called for an accomplice who, armed with a machine pistol, appeared shepherding the maid and her small daughter in front of him. This man took me into the dressing-room, still handcuffed, put on my trousers and shoes, and threw a jacket over my shoulders, and brought me back into the bedroom. The other man then tore the telephone out of its socket, informed my wife that they were the FLQ (Front de la Libération du Québec), but that she must not communicate with the police for at least an hour. She said, "At least let me say goodbye to my husband," and they let her come over to kiss me. I was then taken out through the front door, down the steps and into a taxi driven by a fourth man. I was forced down on to the floor in the back of the taxi, and covered with a rug. We drove for ten or fifteen minutes and stopped in a garage or workshop, where I was dragged out of the taxi and made to stand against the wall with my eyes closed, while a gas mask with the eye pieces blacked out was pulled over my head. I was then bundled into another car, again on the floor in the back, and driven for about fifteen or twenty minutes. I believe the driver of this car to have been a woman. We drove into an underground garage. I was taken out of the car and led up some

SOURCE: "Kidnapping in Canada — 1970," *British Journal of Canadian Studies* 5, no. 2 (1990): 269–74. Reprinted with permission.

stairs into a room where I was to spend the next fifty-nine days. Preparations for my arrival included boarding up the windows and nailing bolts to the floor to which I could be manacled. I was made to lie on a mattress in the middle of the floor, the handcuffs were transferred to the front, and the gas mask was removed, to be replaced by a cloth mask.

I asked my captors what they wanted, and was told to wait and see. However, I had a pretty good idea, having heard them declare themselves to my wife as being members of the FLQ. Earlier that year a diplomatic colleague, the American Consul, Harrison Burgess, had been the subject of a foiled kidnap attempt by this organisation.

About mid-morning, news began to come through on the radio of my kidnapping, and one of them read me the demands which were to be made through a communiqué which they had arranged to be left on a university campus. These included:

1. The publication of a political manifesto that they had prepared, listing all their grievances.
2. The liberation of twenty-three so-called "political" prisoners in Quebec.
3. These prisoners then to be placed aboard an aircraft to Cuba or Algeria.
4. The Canadian Post Office to reinstate a number of truck drivers who had been sacked in an industrial dispute.
5. Payment of a "voluntary tax" of $500,000 in gold to be placed aboard the aircraft carrying the released prisoners.
6. Identification of the informer who had betrayed the Burgess kidnapping (above).
7. Immediate cessation of all police activity in the hunt for the kidnapped diplomat.

Failure to meet all these demands would result in my "execution" within forty-eight hours. On hearing this, all I could say was, "In that case, I must compose myself for death."

For the next few days I remained lying on the mattress, handcuffed and with the mask on. In the evening I was allowed to lift the mask slightly, in such a way that I could see the television, but not my captors. These I now estimated to be five in number — four men and one woman. After three or four days I was transferred to a chair facing the corner of the room where the TV was, and my handcuffs were removed.

The radio and TV were on all the time, and every report and bulletin about the case was followed with the keenest interest. For the first few days the hesitation of the Government response gave the impression that they were not sure that this was a serious threat. On the third day, Wednesday, I was allowed to write a short letter to my wife, and forced to write a message to the authorities, dictated by my captors. The deadline was extended by twenty-four hours, and then extended again. In the middle of the week the Government agreed to the reading on television of the FLQ's so-called "manifesto," and one had the spectacle of a straight-faced announcer telling Canadians that their Prime Minister was a homosexual, and that the whole of the political establishment were crooks.

On the Friday, the Quebec Minister of Justice, seeking to establish that I was still alive, asked for a message containing a provided sentence. This was done that evening, the kidnappers themselves adding a warning that this would be their final communication.

On Saturday, 10 October, the Federal and Provincial governments finally decided to reject all the kidnappers' demands, and at 5.30 P.M. that evening the Quebec Minister of Justice, M. Choquette, went on television to announce this, but at the same time offered to review the cases of the twenty-three prisoners, and to guarantee safe conduct out of the country for my kidnappers, if I was released unharmed. Immediately I asked my captors what they intended to do. They replied that they intended to hold me for a while to taunt the police. However, within minutes the whole situation changed, as news came over the radio that Pierre Laporte, the Quebec Minister of Labour, had been kidnapped outside his home. Apparently, he had been playing football with a nephew outside the house when a car drew up. Four armed men got out, forced him into the car, and drove off. A week after my kidnapping, no protection had been provided for provincial ministers! With the kidnapping of Pierre Laporte — by a different cell of the FLQ from the one that was holding me — the situation changed completely. While I was a foreign diplomat, merely a name to Canadians, he was one of the leading political figures in Quebec, and had been a candidate for the leadership of the ruling Liberal Party in the province. Accordingly, over the next week, attention centred on him, and I became very much a spectator. The next week was occupied by a series of negotiations between a government lawyer and a lawyer regarded as acceptable by the FLQ, while on the sidelines a series of communiqués were issued, mainly from the group holding Laporte and reinforcing their demands.

At the same time, a number of organisations in Montreal who had support among students and labour groups were holding public meetings advocating the political and social demands of the FLQ. At this point, the Federal Government decided to act firmly. In the early hours of Friday 16 October, they proclaimed the War Measures Act, which placed Canada on a wartime footing. Troops moved into the province to aid the police and guard public buildings and personages. Some two hundred and fifty people were arrested and held without charge.

That evening Prime Minister Trudeau went on television to reject, as he put it, "the attempt of a small group to force its will on the majority by terrorism." My own future looked bleak at that moment.

The following day, Saturday 17 October, was quiet for me, with no particular activity, until towards midnight, news came in on radio and television that there was believed to be a body in the trunk of a car at the St. Hubert airfield near Montreal. The Bomb Squad was called, and when they blew open the trunk, inside it they found the body of Pierre Laporte. Then followed what I sincerely trust will remain the worst night of my life, for reports began to come in that my body had also been found, and I dreaded that my wife might be watching. It was not until 9.00 A.M. that I was allowed to write her a note to reassure her that I was still alive. She received it about 1.00 P.M. The death of M. Laporte still remains something of a mystery. His kidnappers (later caught and convicted), while refusing to give details, claim that he was accidentally strangled while being restrained after an unsuccessful escape attempt.

For me, the next weeks sank into a dreary routine. Meanwhile, the police continued their activities. My captors released a photograph of me in which they described me as "sitting on a box of dynamite"; allowed me to write one letter to my wife; and forced me to write a public appeal.

Finally, on the evening of 2 December, events started to move. I had noticed during the day that there did not seem to be so many people in the apartment. About 10.00 P.M. when I was as usual watching television, the handcuffs were put on me again for the first time for many weeks. I asked what was happening, and was told that the police knew where I was, that two of them, having gone out earlier, had not returned, and they assumed they had been arrested. About two o'clock in the morning the electricity was turned off and so they knew the police were closing in. They then took me into the corridor and handcuffed me to a doorknob facing the entrance, where I remained in great discomfort for about five hours. When dawn broke, it was clear that we were completely surrounded by a large force of police and troops. About nine o'clock, a lawyer came to the apartment to act as a negotiator — a M. Mergler who had previously acted for some FLQ defendants. After some discussion it was agreed that the three remaining terrorists with M. Mergler and myself would proceed to the old Expo '67 site in the St. Lawrence river, where one of the pavilions would be designated as part of the Cuban Consulate. There they would be joined by the two under arrest, and from there they would all proceed to Cuba in a Canadian Air Force plane, while I remained in the charge of the Cuban Consul. As soon as they reached Cuba I would go free.

So towards 1.00 P.M. I went down the stairs to the garage and climbed into a decrepit old car. I was placed on the back seat, on one side of me was the television set (did they hope to take this symbol of N. American affluence to Cuba with them, I wondered!), on the other an old FLQ man, Jacques Lanctot, heavily armed with dynamite strapped around his waist. In the front were two other members of the group and M. Mergler. Slowly the car backed out of the garage, and I saw the sun for the first time in nearly nine weeks. Then started an incredible car ride through streets lined with police and troops, and behind them crowds of staring spectators. The back door of the car was rather insecure and every time we went round a corner, Lanctot was in danger of falling out. Knowing he was carrying dynamite, I hung on to him, not wanting to end this exploit in some accidental explosion. Finally we drove across the causeway on to St. Helen's Island — the exposition site. We drew up in front of the building now temporarily the Cuban Consulate, and got out. I was greeted by a colleague from my office and went into the building. I turned left, the kidnappers turned right, and I never saw them again. Later that day they flew to Cuba, and as soon as they arrived there, I was again a free man.

FLQ

The Front de la Libération du Québec emerged in the early 1960s as the active arm of a number of groups seeking the separation of Quebec from the Canadian Confederation. It is interesting that in spite of the very close-knit nature of most Quebec political groups, two of the leaders of the FLQ were foreigners — George Schoeters, from Belgium, and Francois Schirm, originally from Hungary. Throughout the 1960s, there were sporadic campaigns of violence — armed robberies, thefts of firearms, placing of bombs in public places. A number of FLQ members were convicted for these offences and were still in prison in 1970 — these were the prisoners whose release was demanded in the communiqué issued the day I was kidnapped.

The first sign that kidnapping, already popular in South America, was to be used by the FLQ came in early 1970, when plots to kidnap an Israeli consul and possibly a Greek consul were foiled. In June 1970 the police raided a cottage in the Laurentian mountains and found all the preparations — arms, explosives and ransom demands — for kidnapping the American consul in Montreal, Harrison Burgess. These demands were exactly the same as those later to be made in my case, except that in my case there was an extra demand, that of the name of the informer who had betrayed the June operation.

The operational strength of the FLQ is difficult to assess. The best estimate is that in 1970 there were about thirty-five active members prepared to carry out operations, with between one hundred and two hundred supporters who would carry messages, lend money, provide safe houses, etc.

The mode of operation was to reach a general decision on a course of action. One group, or "cell," would be given a "mandate" to carry out the particular exercise, and would then withdraw from all contact from the other groups until the operation had been completed. Thus security was preserved. Certain supporters seem to have been used as channels for information or finance.

FLQ Philosophy

The FLQ group holding me talked glibly about being "Marxists" or "Anarchists" but I did not get the impression that they had studied these movements in any depth. The two main influences I could discover were:

1. Franz Fanon's *Les Damnes de la Terre* with its advocacy of violence as the only means of cleansing a colonised people of their problems, whether psychological, political or economic.
2. The French-Canadian writer, Pierre Vallières, who had been very active in the FLQ in the mid-1970s. His book *Les Nègres Blancs d'Amérique* has two main themes — the oppression that Quebeckers have suffered through their "colonial" past, and the general alienation of workers in highly organised societies (whether capitalist or state communist). On the latter theme, he stresses the work of Georges Lukacs, Karl Korsch and the younger Marx. Therefore, he argues, Quebeckers can only be truly independent people when they have freed themselves, not only from the political bonds of being a minority in Canada, but also from the oppression of a capitalist system.

Both these influences led them to regard violence as not only a means to an end, but also an end in itself. To quote one other FLQ supporter when in prison: "The aim of violence is the liberation of man. Violence is a form of love for man."

The Intense Neutron Generator and the Development of Science Policy in Canada

RUTH FAWCETT

In September 1968, the newly-elected Liberal government of Pierre Elliot Trudeau announced the cancellation of the Intense Neutron Generator project. Proposed by scientists from the Chalk River Nuclear Laboratories,

SOURCE: "The Intense Neutron Generator and the Development of Science Policy in Canada," *Queen's Quarterly* 98, no. 2 (Summer 1991): 409–23. Reprinted with permission.

the Intense Neutron Generator (ING) was an attempt to maintain "Big Science" as a fundamental part of the Canadian scientific agenda. Its $155 million price-tag, combined with an estimated annual operating cost of $15 million, made it the most expensive research facility ever proposed for construction in Canada. The enormous costs involved contributed heavily to its 1968 cancellation, but in the five-year period preceding that cancellation the controversy over ING stirred up the Canadian scientific community. That debate concerning Canadian science policy had been brewing since early in the decade, and it found a focus in ING. This paper will examine the background to the ING proposal, its effect on the Canadian scientific community, and its place in the wider national debate over science policy in Canada.

★ ★ ★

The proposal to build an Intense Neutron Generator grew out of a re-examination in the early 1960s of the future direction of the Chalk River Nuclear Laboratories. Established during WWII as part of the Anglo-American atomic collaboration, Chalk River thrived in the post-war years. Its high-flux research reactors provided the necessary tools for pure research in nuclear and condensed-matter (solid-state) science, for the applied research required to develop a power reactor programme, and for isotope production. These programmes were proceeding in a very satisfactory way, but the Chalk River scientists considered that some new initiative would be needed if the laboratories were to remain in the forefront of future research in nuclear science and engineering.

The question of the future of Chalk River prompted Wilfrid Bennett Lewis to convene a Future Systems Committee in the fall of 1963. In his position as Vice-president of Research and Development at Chalk River, Lewis was responsible for the scientific activities at the labs. Educated at the Cavendish laboratories of Cambridge University in the 1930s, Lewis had studied and worked with many famous physicists, including Ernest Rutherford, James Chadwick, and John Cockcroft. During WWII he participated in the development of air-force radar, becoming Chief Superintendent of the radar establishment in 1945. A year later the Canadian authorities in charge of Chalk River, acting upon British advice, asked Lewis if he would come to Canada to head the atomic research establishment. Lewis agreed and quickly became a formidable force behind atomic energy research and the development of nuclear-power reactors.

The Future Systems Committee examined possible future projects in light of their feasibility and their ability to utilize the strengths of Chalk River. Study groups examined a number of different topics, but the search was biased in favour of a high-flux neutron facility based on a proton accelerator — a topic favoured by Lewis. By December 1963 it was evident that the high-flux facility was also favoured by the committee. It would be, they recorded, a "versatile machine" and "full utilization of all its research possibilities would require a very large supporting staff on the scale of Chalk River services for experimental work" (CRNL Records, 1615/F1 Vols. 2 & 3).

This decision was communicated to a receptive Lewis. The accelerator would generate protons with an energy of one billion electron volts, which would be stopped in a molten target of a lead-bismuth alloy. When the protons struck the target, fast neutrons would be produced. These neutrons would then be slowed down in a surrounding volume of heavy water, collected in beam tubes, and very high fluxes of neutrons would result.

There were many aspects to this project that appealed to Lewis. It was a project on a grand scale, which would easily place Chalk River at the forefront of experimental physics. The intense flux produced would be many times greater than that available at other leading institutions. Irradiation-type experiments could be performed in the tank while other experiments exploited the neutron beams. Apart from the neutrons, ING would provide physicists with high-energy protons and many secondary particles, such as mesons. Finally, and most importantly, by using this method of producing neutrons, instead of fission, a minimal amount of heat would be released. Unlike a fission reactor, where a great deal of effort is put towards getting rid of excess heat, ING would only need a simple heat transport system (Elliot 4).

It was up to Lewis to ensure that the proposed new facility enjoyed the backing of his superiors. In May 1964, Lewis made a detailed presentation of the project to the board of directors of Atomic Energy of Canada Limited. Chalk River needed a new focus, he argued. Once the large power reactors were in place, there would be little left for the scientists at Chalk River to do. They had considered trying to increase the flux of NRU, a research reactor, but this did not seem to be practicable. However, a different reaction — spallation — was capable of producing many neutrons, but with minimal output of heat. Lewis reviewed the history of this idea, in particular noting American interest in it as a way of producing fissionable isotopes. The Americans had hoped to use the abundant supply of neutrons to produce plutonium and uranium-233 from supplies of natural uranium and thorium. Lewis noted that their 1953 calculations for the cost of plutonium produced were quite high but added that subsequent advances in technology had probably reduced the price by 25 per cent. This price was still high, but Lewis expected plutonium prices to rise in the next decade. Further, he argued, revenue would be brought in through isotope production (CRNL Records 9226-1-4).

It is interesting that Lewis's case for the new project as presented to the board was based almost exclusively on its revenue-making potential. Clearly, it was important to stress to the board that this extremely expensive project might be able to pay for itself. Lewis's knowledge and understanding of economics, however, was limited, and many of the arguments he put forward were based upon uncertain price projections. He also noted the profound effect the project might have on Canadian industry; it would open new fields where much money was already being spent around the world. Finally, Lewis stressed that it would help Chalk River remain a leading research laboratory (CRNL Records 9226-1-4).

At the time of this presentation Lewis was not asking for large budget increases, so the board of directors of Chalk River's parent company, Atomic Energy of Canada Limited (AECL), agreed that studies of the facility could continue. However, Lewis still had to convince some of his colleagues that the project was worth pursuing. In presenting the project to scientists, Lewis stressed the advance of scientific research as the central reason for building the accelerator. The high neutron flux would make it possible to do advanced research on the structure and dynamics of solids and liquids, properties of atomic nuclei, neutron scattering, and more advanced topics. At the presentation, Lewis repeated many of the arguments he had made to the board of directors: the possibility of producing fissile material and isotopes and the development of high-tech industries. But with his colleagues he particularly emphasized that the new facility would "maintain both the scientific stature of Canada and the leading position in research enjoyed at Chalk River" (CRNL Records 9008-3).

⋆ ⋆ ⋆

Reaction to Lewis's proposed facility was not all positive. Although he felt the project was one Canada could and should afford, AECL president J.L. Gray questioned whether it should be located at Chalk River. He worried about the considerable expansion that would have to take place at Chalk River and suggested that the facility should perhaps replace NRU, the larger research reactor. Other members of the Senior Management Committee did not agree, arguing that Chalk River was the best location for the project. Another location would slow it down, they reasoned, and Chalk River needed to keep up the pace of development in the future (AECL Records).

With the approval of the board, the project would, for the time being, go ahead. In June 1964 Lewis announced a reorganization of the project into three committees — two of which he would chair himself. The policy committee would be concerned with policy and information related to the accelerator at a higher management level. A technical coordinating committee would orchestrate the efforts from working groups and receive reports from various working parties. Finally, a facility study committee would be a forum for verbal reports and discussion among the representatives from various groups (AECL Records). This organizational structure seemed logical and not too large, but it kept the project internal to Chalk River. By August the facility would have a name: the Intense Neutron Generator or ING.

Over the next two years details of ING were worked out. At the same time, Lewis continued to sell the facility to government representatives. Although he noted the importance ING would have as an experimental physics tool, Lewis also stressed its more practical aspects. Isotope production, it was hoped, could help to alleviate the enormous costs of the project. Also, Canadian industry would benefit by participating in the manufacturing of parts for the machine.

Equally important in selling government representatives on ING was the involvement of university scientists in the project. In the spring of 1965 plans were made for a symposium on ING to be held during the summer. University, government, and industry representatives came to Chalk River and attended lectures on different aspects of the facility. It soon became apparent, however, that the universities would not be content to be informed of progress on ING and then asked to lend their support. University scientists insisted that they should be intimately involved not only with every stage of the planning but also with the operation of the new machine. Lewis responded to these concerns in August 1965 by announcing the establishment of an "ING Study Advisory Committee" to act as a regular channel for dealing with ideas from the universities' staff on ING and its users (CRNL Records 9226-2-2-1). In September Lewis sent out invitations to 15 faculty members from universities across the country, as well as to representatives from the National Research Council, the Department of Industry, and the Science Secretariat.

It was clear from the first meeting of the ING Study Advisory Committee that the university community felt it deserved a much stronger voice in decision-making. At the first meeting, committee members voiced a number of concerns. What would the long-term role of the universities be within the project? What kind of collaboration between the universities and AECL was envisaged for the future? Would ING create too much competition for funds? How would the project itself be organized? And finally, where would ING be located — at Chalk River or at a more central location? These valid questions were to plague the project over the next three years.

The committee's paramount concerns were over price and location. University scientists in particular were worried about the high cost of the facility. Noting that there was only so much money to go around, they felt their own research could be harmed if a large proportion of the available funds were allocated to ING. Lewis did not agree. He argued that Canada did not, and should not, have a fixed science budget. Amounts allocated for science would grow, he claimed, and so ING would not use up money meant for university research. But university scientists remained sceptical.

Of equal concern to members of the ING Study Advisory Committee was the location of the project. Lewis believed throughout that the best location for ING would be near Chalk River. Early discussions about ING did not mention a site; presumably at this point a site other than Chalk River was not even considered. However, it became obvious after a few meetings of the Study Advisory Committee that members felt a location other than Chalk River was preferable. They noted the desirability of being near an international centre, perhaps a bicultural location such as Ottawa or Montreal. Chalk River, they argued, was too remote; as one committee member put it, the Chalk River location was an "accident of history" and there was no reason for perpetuating it.

The debate over the location of ING would remain unresolved. Despite a study evaluating the penalty of using a site other than Chalk River, scientists from universities across the country were unconvinced that Chalk River was the best location. This point of contention harmed later attempts to sell the project to the federal government.

In the meantime, costs were mounting steadily. In June 1964, when Lewis had announced a reorganization of the project, he set a limit of $25 million for the accelerator — the big-ticket item. A little over a year later Lewis expressed his hope that the price-tag would be closer to $50 million than $100 million. Twelve months later a more accurate, and larger, estimate had been determined. Assuming a site near Chalk River was used, the cost of the new facility would reach $130 million.

The Liberal government of Lester Pearson was at a loss to decide upon this controversial subject, which was evolving against the backdrop of a larger debate concerning science policy in Canada. In 1963, a Royal Commission chaired by J. Grant Glassco submitted a report on government organization that included a section on scientific research and development. The report concluded that "the whole postwar expansion of government scientific activity has proceeded on a piecemeal basis without adequate coordination" (Royal Commission). In order to correct this situation the report suggested that the "existence of suitable machinery for informing and assisting the Prime Minister and Cabinet with respect to major science policy decisions is of paramount importance" (Royal Commission).

★ ★ ★

Pearson turned to former National Research Council president C.J. Mackenzie for guidance on how to deal with this and other specific recommendations of the Glassco Commission. On the basis of his advice, Pearson announced in April 1964 that a Science Secretariat would be formed as part of the Privy Council Office. Its role would be "to assemble and analyze information about the government's scientific programs and their inter-relation with other scientific activities throughout Canada" (Doern 8-9). Two years later the Science Council was created with a mandate "to assess in a comprehensive manner Canada's scientific and technological resources, requirements and potentialities." The Council would also advise the government on science policy, possible long-term objectives, and the best projects for achieving them. The members sitting on the Council would be a mixture of representatives from the government sector, universities, business, and industry. The main disadvantage of the Science Council was its lack of budgetary control. As was pointed out later during the Senate committee examining science policy in Canada, this made it "analogous to a cabinet meeting without the Minister of Finance. It can very easily agree on all of the projects coming from the various departments" (Senate). Despite this criticism, however, it was hoped that the Science Council could advise the government on the complicated questions of science and technology that kept arising.

Pearson turned to the newly-formed Science Council for advice on ING. The Science Council formed a committee of eight men — drawn from government, universities, and industry — to examine the proposal. Five formal meetings were held and the advice of experts from the United States was sought. The committee examined the ING proposal on the grounds of its scientific, technical, and economic merits. In its report, presented six months later in March 1967 to the Science Council and subsequently endorsed by it, the committee announced that it had found the proposal "well-conceived and imaginative." Its benefits would "extend over a broad range of sciences and technologies" and, in turn, would involve scientists and engineers from government, universities, and industries (Science). The committee acknowledged that the costs of the project were high but argued that, barring sharp escalation, they remained within the bounds possible for the Canadian economy. On one of the more controversial questions of the proposal — that of site — the committee differed from the majority of opinion at Chalk River. Anxious to ensure university and industry involvement, its members recommended that a location with greater accessibility than Chalk River be chosen (Science).

In the end, the Science Council's final recommendation to the government was cautious; a further feasibility study should be undertaken and the project reviewed at the end of it. Provided that costs had not risen excessively and that the goals of the project had not altered significantly, the Council recommended that the project be allowed to proceed.

Despite this recommendation, the government did nothing. As scientists across the country waited for the government to act, controversy mounted. In July 1967, shortly after the Science Council's endorsement of ING was made public, an editorial appeared in the *Globe and Mail* questioning such a large government expenditure on a single project. Noting that estimates stated that ING would cost more than $20 million a year to operate, it pointed out that the same sum would support about

2,000 doctoral research students in universities. The editorial concluded by arguing that the government should consider whether "the well-being of all Canadians would be better served if the money was spread over a much wider area of scientific research" ("Needs").

★ ★ ★

Discussion also continued in the scientific journals. In February 1968 *Science Forum* devoted a large part of its first issue to the ING question. In a five-page, closely argued article, Lewis, with two of his senior colleagues, defended ING against all its detractors. They particularly stressed areas where they had often been attacked. The article argued against the view that the value of ING would be mainly to the nuclear physicists at Chalk River and instead listed a series of subjects — from space technology to oceanography — where the benefits of ING would also be felt. Canada would also gain skills in many areas of high technology, a host of scientific advantages, as well as the prestige of owning and operating a unique and powerful experimental tool. In keeping with Chalk River's original and successful mandate to develop nuclear power, the article pointed out that the machine could be used to develop the next line of power reactors. Finally, in response to the criticisms coming from the universities, the authors argued that with university and technical college enrolment on the increase Canada had to provide work opportunities for the new graduates. In their opinion, the strong interaction that already existed between Chalk River and the university community would only be enhanced by the proposed project (Elliot).

Many scientists and engineers in the university community did not agree. J. Gordon Parr, responding directly to Lewis, wrote that ING was "the wrong thing, in the wrong place, at the wrong time." There was, Parr argued, more important work to be done. Further, too much money was spent on government in-house research already, and more nuclear research was not necessary until the knowledge already gained from it had been utilized. Part of the problem, Parr noted, was that AECL had performed its mandate too well and thereby worked itself out of a job. Parr felt that the academic communities had not been adequately consulted. Other authors echoed this sentiment. Ken McNeill, a physicist at the University of Toronto, wrote that there had not been enough discussion with the university scientists concerning the aims and priorities of ING. As he put it, there was "not enough clearing of the clouds around Olympus" (McNeill).

This final statement summed up the sentiments of many scientists in the academic community. Although ING was likely a viable scientific project for Canada — which would enhance its status in the world, possibly bring benefits to Canadian industry, and further knowledge on many fronts — many Canadian scientists felt that not enough consultation had occurred between them and their counterparts at Chalk River.

As J.G. Parr wrote, they were told about the project after it was well advanced and, upon expressing concern, they were accused of having shown indifference and hostility towards ING ("Generator"). Since the project demanded a massive influx of federal funds, this lack of coordination of scientists on a nation-wide basis was crucial.

Although many other problems with the proposal were pinpointed — the isolated site of Chalk River, the over-emphasis on nuclear science, the huge budget required — the lack of real consultation and involvement with universities on a national basis appears to have been Chalk River's largest strategic error. It was probably this mistake that killed the project.

At the end of 1967, however, the project was still alive. As late as December 1967 the applied physics division at Chalk River received $220,000 for ING development work. But without a positive endorsement from the federal government the future of the project remained in doubt. When Pearson announced his decision to step down as leader of the Liberal party early in 1968, it was clear that a decision on ING would not be made until a new leader was in place.

Controversy continued in the press throughout the summer of 1968. A letter to the editor from members of the National Committee of Deans of Engineering and Applied Science made it clear that many members of the scientific community remained very unhappy with the project. They argued that "if $155 million is to be spent, it would be much better invested in the identification of pressing technological objectives, the establishment of research priorities, and the funding of a number of centres of excellence for the solution of problems that will have a predictable impact upon the Canadian economy" (Letter).

The news that the project was cancelled was no surprise when it came in September 1968. In his announcement to company employees Lewis admitted he was "personally most disappointed" with the decision. He added that Chalk River still retained a research programme in nuclear science; work on ING would, however, be discontinued (CRNL Records 9008-1).

★   ★   ★

There is little doubt that ING was an important episode in the history of science in Canada. It was a bold proposal, challenging scientists, industrialists, and politicians alike to re-examine their views on the future course of Canadian science. Unfortunately these views were numerous and varied. In the end, faced with a lack of consensus in the scientific community and confronted by the enormous expense of ING, the Trudeau government chose to cancel the project.

This was not the only "Big Science" proposal to be cut by the newly-elected Liberal government. Since the early 1960s, a proposal had been in the works for a new astronomical observatory to be located in British Columbia. But as with ING, controversy erupted within the astronomy community over both the price of the new telescope and its proposed location. Confronted with a divided group of scientists, the politicians opted for the easiest route: cancellation.

The abandonment of both these projects can be viewed in the broader context of science in North America. In the postwar years, basic science in Canada and the US received a great deal of financial and popular backing. There existed a widespread belief that support of science would lead to solutions to many of the world's problems. This is perhaps best exemplified by the popular support given to the peaceful uses of atomic energy during the 1950s. That support began to wane during the 1960s. People began to realize that science could not solve all of the world's problems and, in fact, seemed to be creating many of them. As doubts grew, people questioned the massive amount of government money that was funding esoteric science projects with no clear-cut purposes. Reacting to this growing lack of public support, politicians responded by cutting back on expensive basic science projects.[1]

But the cancellation of ING did not stem entirely from a disillusionment with big science. The events surrounding the promotion and subsequent cancellation of ING demonstrated the lack of political acumen of scientists at Chalk River, and in particular of their leader, Lewis. Convinced of the scientific importance of the ING proposal both for Chalk River and for scientists throughout Canada, Lewis and his colleagues did not work hard enough to ensure the support of university scientists and engineers. Those scientists and engineers, angry at the lack of consultation afforded them by Chalk River and afraid that the cost of ING would bite deeply into their own science budgets, opposed the project. The lack of enthusiasm within the university physics community for the proposed project may also have been influenced by the failure a decade earlier of their own "Big Science" proposal to receive approval. In October 1958 the Canadian Association of Physicists submitted a brief to the government requesting funding for a high-energy laboratory for Canada. Six months later the government rejected the proposal. Still smarting from this refusal and concerned about the future of academic physics across the country, it is no surprise that university scientists were doubtful about the more expensive Chalk River facility.

The controversy surrounding both these proposals illustrates the growing resentment felt by academic scientists towards their government colleagues. As one author put it, the "ING affair showed more clearly than ever before the changing balance of power between the academic and governmental sectors of the Canadian scientific community" (Doern 102). The Glassco commission had been the first to argue that government performed too large a proportion of research in Canada. This view would be echoed by the special Senate committee set up in the late 1960s to examine Canadian science policy. Yet the question remained whether a decrease in government-performed research would result in increased support for universities.

The debate over the Intense Neutron Generator highlighted the lack of adequate science-policy machinery in the federal government. In the midst of the ING debate the Senate named a special committee to look into science policy in Canada. Chaired by Senator Maurice Lamontagne, the committee, it was hoped, would pinpoint problems and suggest solutions to ameliorate the confused situation. During its hearings, one witness pointed out that ING was an "excellent case history of how science policy should not be made." After many years of government support and after the government-appointed Science Council had recommended its continuation, the project had been abruptly cancelled for financial reasons. As one senator put it, there was little point in making priorities for decision-making if they were to be disregarded. The government could not simply announce that there was not enough money for ING; it also had to admit that it had decided not to expand the country's science horizons (Senate).

★ ★ ★

The debate over science policy in Canada began in the 1960s, but it continues to the present.

Many questions raised during the debate over the Intense Neutron Generator are still hotly argued today.

NOTES

1. This disillusionment with science in America is discussed in detail in Daniel J. Kevles, *The Physicists* (New York, 1979): 410–60.

WORKS CITED

AECL Records 103-5-8. Vol. 1. Minutes of Senior Management Committee, 15 May 1964.

CRNL Records 1615/F1. Vol. 2. Minutes of Future Systems Committee, 1 October 1963; 1615/F1. Vol. 3. Minutes of Future Systems Committee, 18 December 1963; 9226-1-4. Vol. 2. ING general, Lewis to J.L. Gray and Board of Directors, 28 May 1964; 9008-3. Vol. 1. Minutes of High Neutron Flux Facility Study Committee, 9 June 1964; 9226-2-2-1. Vol. 1. Minutes of ING Policy Committee, 6 August 1965; 9008-1. Vol. 20. Lewis to all members and alternates of AECL, 4 October 1968.

Doern, G. Bruce. *Science and Politics in Canada.* Montreal, 1972.

Elliot, L.G.; Lewis, W.B.; Ward, A.G. "ING: A Vehicle to New Frontiers." *Science Forum* 1 (February 1968): 3–7.

"The Generator That Is Producing Intense Reactions." *Globe and Mail* 20 July 1967.

Letter to the Editor. *Globe and Mail* 28 August 1968.

McNeill, K.G. "ING: A Good Thing — Under Certain Conditions." *Science Forum* 1 (February 1968): 11.

"Needs Before Status." *Globe and Mail* 15 July 1967.

Parr, J. Gordon. "ING: The Wrong Thing, in the Wrong Place, at the Wrong Time." *Science Forum* 1 (February 1968): 8-9.

Royal Commission on Government Organization. *Report*, Vol. 4. Ottawa: 1963.

Science Secretariat, Privy Council Office. "The Proposal for an Intense Neutron Generator: Scientific and Economic Evaluation." Ottawa: 1967.

Senate of Canada. *Proceedings of the Special Committee on Science Policy*. Ottawa: 1968.

Oil and Lubicons Don't Mix: A Land Claim in Northern Alberta in Historical Perspective

DARLENE ABREU FERREIRA

Introduction

All Native groups in Canada have had their land base diminished through the years, while some are still fighting for recognition of their homeland. One such group is the Lubicon Lake Cree Band of Little Buffalo, Alberta. It was 1899, almost one hundred years ago, when a government party visited northern Alberta to make arrangements with the local residents for large land surrenders under Treaty No. 8. Some of these residents were never contacted and continued to live in their traditional manner. With the liquid gold rush of the 1970s, these treaty-less people were overwhelmed with the influx of developers who were equally convinced of their right to use the land. This paper looks at the Lubicon struggle with two levels of government and with developers vying for the oil-rich land which the Lubicon consider theirs. In the process, this study will attempt to provide answers to some fundamental questions relating to the Lubicon: Is there any foundation to their claim? What is there about the Lubicon case that has attracted so much public attention? What makes them a precedent?

There are two primary reasons that attract historians to the Lubicon cause. First, the band provides a contemporary case study of attitudes and processes that have dominated non-Native relations in Canada since the early days of European settlement.[1] Has there been a significant evolution or progression in this area, or are the Lubicon experiencing a common phenomenon encountered by other Native groups? Second, there is a lack of solid academic exploration of Lubicon history. While the band's story was often featured on the front page of major newspapers, these reports were generally done without proper historical reference or

SOURCE: "Oil and Lubicons Don't Mix: A Land Claim in Historical Perspective," *The Canadian Journal of Native Studies* 12, no. 1 (1992): 1-35. Reprinted with permission.

analysis. By explaining the specifics of the Lubicon case within a historical framework of dominant attitudes, the present paper attempts to offer some insight into the development of government–Native relations in Canada.

Treaty No. 8

On 22 May 1899, the Honourable David Laird, Lieutenant-Governor of the Northwest Territories, and a group of his staff, boarded a train in Winnipeg for Edmonton. From there, they loaded thirteen wagons with provisions and travelled north toward Lesser Slave Lake, the predetermined location for their first meeting. Upon their arrival, on 19 June, preparations were made for the eventful occasion, and on the following day Laird addressed the assembled crowd:

> Red Brothers! We have come here to-day, sent by the Great Mother to treat with you, and this is the paper she has given us, and is her commission to us signed with her Seal, to show we have authority to treat with you . . . I have to say, on behalf of the Queen and the Government of Canada, that we have come to make you an offer . . . As white people are coming into your country, we have thought it well to tell you what is required of you . . . The Queen owns the country, but is willing to acknowledge the Indians' claims, and offers them terms as an offset to all of them . . . (Mair, 1908:56–59)

Thus began the ceremonies which led to the signing of Treaty No. 8, Chief Keenooshayo and Chief Moostoos agreeing on behalf of the Crees present. This first step was considered the most important by the treaty party and scrip Commissioners, for the remaining work was seen as merely obtaining "adhesions" to the treaty from other groups in the territory (*Ibid.*:64). The Treaty Commission split into small groups and contacted some Beavers at Fort Dunvegan, the Crees and Beavers at Fort Vermilion and Little Red River, the Crees and Chipewyans at Fort Chipewyan, a group at Great Slave Lake, some Chipewyans at Fond du Lac, other Chipewyans and Crees at Fort McMurray, and some Crees at Wahpooskow. By the end of July the Commissioners had completed their task and headed home. They were aware that not all people were reached, and, accordingly, a second Commission was sent the following summer to meet with those originally missed. This extra trip managed to secure the adhesion of another 1,200 (Mair, 1908:66; and see Madill, 1986:48). Despite these efforts by the Canadian government, however, certain groups living in outlying areas were never visited by treaty officials. Commissioner James A. Macrae noted in his report of 11 December 1900 that

> There yet remains a number of persons leading an Indian life in the country north of Lesser Slave lake, who have not accepted treaty as Indians, or scrip as half-breeds, but this is not so much through indisposition to do so as because

they live at points distant from those visited, and are not pressed by want. The Indians of all parts of the territory who have not yet been paid annuity probably number about 500 . . . (Canada, Treaty No. 8, 1966:21)

Among those were the people of the Lubicon Lake Cree band.

Nearly one hundred years after Laird's initial visit to the Peace region, the Lubicon Lake band has still not "adhered" to Treaty No. 8. According to the band, it attempted contact on several occasions with the Department of Indian Affairs and Northern Development (DIAND), but these early efforts were unsuccessful. Upon their arrival at Whitefish, for example, the Indian Agent put their names on the Whitefish Band list, gave them five dollars each, and sent them off. The agent did not recognize the Lubicon as a separate and distinct group, but at that time they were not too concerned by the miscommunication. In the early part of the 20th century, the Lubicon lived relatively unmolested by outsiders. With the advent of the Great Depression, however, rumours were heard that White people would come in hordes to live in the bush. Fearing that they might lose their land, the Lubicon say that they sent a petition to the federal government in 1933 requesting a land settlement, resulting in a visit from two government officials who recognized the community as a separate band and promised to establish a Reserve. The band also claims that government officials recommended a Reserve of 25.4 square miles, based upon a census count of 127 people present, at one square mile for every five, as stipulated in the terms of Treaty No. 8. The Lubicon selected a portion of land at the western end of Lubicon Lake for their Reserve, a selection that was approved by both levels of government by 1940. Alberta set aside the agreed portion of land for the proposed Reserve, but the federal government had first to conduct a survey of the area before a Reserve could be established. That survey has yet to take place (Lubicon Lake Indian Band Land Claim, 1987:2).

The outbreak of World War II might have disrupted government intentions to deal properly with the Native population, but it did not prevent some bureaucrats from causing further damage. In 1942, for example, Malcolm McCrimmon of Indian Affairs began removing from treaty lists names of those who could not prove their "pure Indian blood." From a list of 154 Lubicons, he removed 90 members at the outset, paying treaty annuity to the remaining 64 only. All others in the group were deemed "non-Indians" or "half breeds" (*Ibid.*; see also Goddard, 1985:73). This move was especially disastrous for the Lubicon because most of their registered members were not added to any membership list until the 1920s and 1930s, and more than half their people had never registered at all. People not registered were ineligible to receive Band funds distributed by DIAND. In 1939, during the government recognition of the Band's existence, all parties were aware that many Lubicon people were not on any membership list. It was also known that many more Lubicons were out in the bush and, therefore, were unable to register at the time the official Band list was created. Officials acknowledged the problem during that visit and made allowances for the "absentees" to be added later to the Band list (Lubicon Lake Indian Band Land Claim, 1987:3). Hence, the department's 1942 policy and decision to trim an already incomplete Lubicon Band membership list was contrary to the 1939 agreement. The government, for its part, acted in response to pressures of rising costs in DIAND administration. Following an internal department study conducted in 1942 on Band lists of the Lesser Slave Lake region, it was found that the number of additions to those Band lists was too extensive. As a result, the department discharged 700 individuals from the treaty lists on the grounds that their parents or grandparents were either White or Métis (Madill, 1986:89).

The Lubicon, and other Bands affected by the removals, protested the government's actions, and DIAND responded by commissioning a study to look into the situation. On 30 June 1943 the report by Judge McKeen was released; it did not applaud the government's stand:

> . . . Your instructions to me . . . say that the facts are relatively simple and will not require any argument of those who are protesting against the removals . . . This may be the opinion of the Department but it is not mine, after reading the Indian Act and Treaty No. 8, then a book "Treaty of Canada with the Indians" by Morris (who was at that time Lt. Gov. of Manitoba and one of the Treaty 8 Commissioners), the Domestic Relations Act of Alberta and the Criminal Code . . . Mr. McCrimmon has . . . followed the principles governing ineligibility . . . signed by Deputy Minister Charles Campbell . . . (however) . . . with all due respect . . . I cannot concur (with the removals) when I study Treaty No. 8 and previous commitments made by various Commissioners appointed by Canada and acting for Canada.[2]

The controversy continued and the government set up a judicial inquiry in 1944. Judge W.A. Macdonald, head of the new inquiry, not only agreed with the previous findings, but recommended that the department reinstate most of the Lubicon Lake Band members struck from membership lists. His judgement reflected an awareness of the complexity of the issue and recommended a more humane treatment of all Native peoples concerned with the controversial Band list removals.

> It is well known that among the aboriginal inhabitants there were many individuals of mixed blood who were not properly speaking Halfbreeds. Persons of mixed blood who became identified with the Indians, lived with them, spoke their language and followed the Indian way of life, were recognized as Indians. The fact that there was white blood in their veins was no bar to their admission into the Indian bands among whom they resided . . .
> When Treaty No. 8 . . . was conducted in 1899, a large proportion of those admitted into treaty at that time were of mixed blood . . . I am quite unable to reconcile this definite pronouncement with the view that individuals of mixed blood who have been in treaty for a great many years can now be removed from the Band rolls and from the Reserve on which their lives have been spent, on the ground that they are not now and never have been Indian.
> It seems to me that the meaning of the word "Indian" is sometimes unduly restricted . . .

Moreover, argued Judge Macdonald, whenever possible, Treaty No. 8 should be interpreted as the Aboriginal people involved understood it:

> An Indian treaty . . . should not be construed according to strict or technical rules of construction. So far as it is reasonably possible, it should be read in the sense in which it is understood by the Indians themselves. When Treaty No. 8 was signed the Indians were well aware that the Government took a broad and liberal view with respect to the class of persons eligible for treaty. Many of them taken into treaty at that time were themselves of mixed blood. They knew that individuals of mixed blood who had adopted the Indian way of life were encouraged to take treaty. They cannot reconcile the removal from the band rolls of a large number of individuals of mixed blood who have been in treaty for many years, with their understanding of the situation as it existed when the treaty was signed.
>
> The Indian Act is loosely drawn and is replete with inconsistencies. I venture to say that flexibility rather than rigidity, and elasticity rather than a strict and narrow view should govern its interpretation.[3]

Of the 294 people which the judge suggested be reinstated to all the Bands affected, the department only accepted 129. Judge Macdonald heard 49 appeals from the Lubicon Lake Band and he recommended the reinstatement of 43. McCrimmon agreed to reinstate 18 (Lubicon Lake Indian Band Land Claim, 1987:5). The stalemate continued until 1952, when, on 17 April, the Director of the Technical Division of Provincial Lands and Forests [Alberta] wrote to DIAND inquiring about the proposed Reserve:

> Due to the fact that there are considerable inquiries regarding the minerals in the (Lubicon Lake) area, and also the fact that there is a request to establish a mission at this point, we are naturally anxious to clear our records of this provisional reserve if the land is not required by this Band of Indians.[4]

This letter re-opened an apparently dormant case within DIAND, for the Departmental Supervisor of Reserves and Trusts was suddenly moved to get the Alberta Regional Supervisor to act:

> You will recall that in 1946 C.D. Brown surveyed six parcels of land . . . for purposes of Indian Reserves . . . On his program for the same year was a survey at Lubicon Lake but it is our understanding that he was not able to undertake this survey during the field season and it was left over until another year. In so far as we can tell from our records, *this proposed reserve seems to have been forgotten* since then and our attention has (now) been drawn to it . . . I shall be pleased if . . . you can advise whether you consider there is (still) a need of a Reserve at this point, for if so, we will give consideration to having it surveyed, possibly this year, and if not, certainly the following year.[5]

The local Indian Agent was thus asked to look into the situation, but he reported that the original site for the Lubicon Lake Band Reserve was too isolated and would be inconvenient to administer. He was then instructed to meet with the Band to select a new location for the Reserve, but the Band refused because the new proposed site was located outside the area traditionally used by them. A second meeting was set up for the same purpose, and the Indian Agent was informed by his supervisor that "Regardless of the result of such a meeting, I certainly recommend the procuring of land (at a more convenient site)."[6] At stake here was the question of mineral rights, which federal officials had not mentioned during talks with the Lubicon. In fact, the Alberta Regional Supervisor indicated the federal government's ambivalence on this matter:

> It is recommended that the twenty-four sections of land set aside for a Reserve at Lubicon Lake be exchanged for (a more convenient site) . . . I interviewed the Deputy Minister of (Provincial) Lands and Forests . . . (and) . . . he stated that he did not have any objections to the transfer though there was no assurance that the mineral rights could be included with (the more convenient site) . . . If this Reserve (at Lubicon Lake) is retained, the Band would have the mineral rights . . . I would recommend the exchange be made even if the mineral rights cannot be guaranteed (at a more convenient site).[7]

Yet another meeting was held between the local Indian Agent and the Band on 4 June 1953, the former's report indicating the impasse: "I explained to Band members present that it would be impossible to administer a Reserve at Lubicon Lake because of the lack of transportation, but the members continued to ask for the Reserve which has been set aside for them by the province of Alberta" (Lubicon Lake Indian Band Land Claim, 1987:8). Later that year, on 22 October 1953, the province requested a clarification of the federal government's position:

> It is some years now since (the Lubicon Lake site was provisionally reserved) . . . (and) . . . it would be appreciated if you would confirm that the proposal to establish this reservation has been abandoned. If no reply is received within 30 days, it would be assumed that the reservation has been struck from the records.[8]

According to the Lubicon, the federal government did not respond to this request. Instead, officials encouraged some Band members to apply for enfranchisement, transferred the names of some Lubicons to other Band membership lists, and questioned the existence of the Band itself (Lubicon Lake Indian Band Land Claim, 1987:10-12). In the meantime, the Alberta Regional Supervisor requested the assistance of the Departmental Regional Supervisor, whose staff was instructed to

> . . . consult the appropriate files and advise whether action was taken by the Department to officially establish (the Lubicon Lake Band) as a Band, for at this time any such action appears rather shortsighted, and if this group was never established as an official band it *will serve our purpose very well at the present time*.[9]

The Lubicon persisted, although, admittedly, they have been affected by numerous setbacks as the Band readily admits:

> We still have no reserve lands. Some of our Band members have never been added to the Treaty list. Others were removed and never reinstated. Some Band members have been enfranchised. And some Band members have had their names transferred to the membership lists of other Bands, in spite of the fact that they were born and raised in our community, in spite of the fact that they have lived all their lives in our community, in spite of the fact that they have never considered themselves to be members of the Bands on whose membership lists their names appear, and in spite of the fact that they have never been considered to be members of those other Bands by the legitimate members of those other Bands. (Lubicon Lake Indian Band Land Claim, 1987:12–13)

Status and Membership in Canada

The Lubicon struggle with authorities who questioned their Band status corresponds with the history of Band definition by the Canadian government. While officials tended to be liberal in defining "band" and "Indian" in the mid-19th century, restrictions were added later, perhaps reflecting a growing sense of limited resources coupled with growing demands for the land. For example, in 1850 an Act was passed in Lower Canada which defined "Indians" as follows:

First — All persons of Indian blood, reputed to belong to the particular Body or Tribe of Indians interested in such lands, and their descendants.

Secondly — All persons intermarried with any such Indians and residing amongst them, and the descendants of all such persons.

Thirdly — All persons residing among such Indians, whose parents on either side were or are Indians of such Body or Tribe, or entitled to be considered as such: And

Fourthly — All persons adopted in infancy by any such Indians, and residing in the Village or upon the lands of such Tribe or Body of Indians, and their descendants (Smith, 1975:40).

This legislation did not define "Body," or "Tribe" or "Band," apparently accepting members "reputed" to belong to such groupings as enough evidence. Also, a relatively broad definition was applied to determine who was an "Indian," including "All persons" intermarried with or adopted by "such Indians." A year later, however, another Act was passed to repeal this earlier legislation, stipulating that people to be considered "Indians" now had to have some "Indian" blood (*Ibid.*:47–48). At this point, all non"Indian" people lost their "Indian" status, except for women marrying "Indian" men and their descendants, whereas before both women and men married to "Indian" persons were also considered "Indian."

These earlier Acts were applicable to a specific territory, namely Lower Canada, but they were to influence later legislation of a federal nature. Following Confederation, politicians grappled with the need for a national "Indian" policy and created "An Act to Amend and Consolidate the Laws Respecting Indians (The *Indian Act*, 1876)." For the first time in the history of the indigenous population in the country, persons of one hundred percent "Indian" blood could be legally considered "non-Indian."

The *Indian Act of 1876* provided a more detailed definition of terminology applied to Native people, starting with the "Band." In order to be considered a "Band" under Canadian law, the group had to have some connection with the federal government, either through the Reserve system or through treaty payments. Autonomous bands, living without government control over their lands, or whose affairs were not "managed by the Government of Canada," were labelled "irregular bands" (*Ibid.*:87). The previous legislation discussed earlier did not apply to groups outside Lower Canada, but the *Indian Act of 1876* specifically stated that the *Act* "shall apply to all the Provinces, and to the North West Territories, including the Territory of Keewatin." In 1880, however, Prime Minister John A. Macdonald said that the "'wild nomads of the North-West' could not be judged on the same basis as the Indians of Ontario" (Ponting and Gibbins, 1980:16; see also Tobias, 1983:45). While that might have been the case in 1880, historians generally agree that the 1876 *Indian Act* set the tone for legislation concerning all Native people in Canada for the next hundred years (Ponting and Gibbins, 1980:8–12; Frideres, 1983:30; Tobias, 1983:44).

In addition to the attempts at defining a "band," the *Indian Act* of 1876 also provided more restrictive designations to determine who was an "Indian," provisions that would greatly affect the make-up of a Band: "The term 'Indian' means . . . Any male person of Indian blood reputed to belong to a particular band . . . Any child of such person . . . Any woman who is or was lawfully married to such person" (Smith, 1975:87–88). With this new legislation siblings of identical ancestry could be divided by the federal government into two categories, "Indian" and "non-Indian," depending on the gender of the individual and the ethnicity or racial category of her/his marital partner. Children born out of wedlock could also be considered "non-Indian" regardless of the "Indianness" of the parents. This legalistic approach toward defining a group of people could reach absurd proportions, as will be seen later with the Lubicon. Suffice to say here that the *Indian Act* and its numerous amendments were bound to cause serious disruptions within existing Bands because their membership was no longer to be determined along community, familial, or traditional ties, but by whether the individual was female or male, and whether the person was born before or after certain legislation. Significantly, the 1876 *Indian Act* also stated that "the term 'person' means an Individual other than an Indian . . . " (*Ibid.*:89).

The 1876 *Indian Act* had numerous revisions and amendments, but these did not change the definitions of "Indian," nor was Band formation clearly addressed. It was not until 1951, with "An Act Respecting Indians

(The *Indian Act*, 1951)," that the government tackled the difficult terminology used for Canadian Indians. The 1951 *Indian Act* indicated that
a "Band" was a body of Indians that had received official recognition
by the Governor in Council (*Ibid.*:154). This same Act also stipulated
that "'member of a band' means a person whose name appears on a
Band List or who is entitled to have his name appear on a Band List."
Thus, for the first time reference was made to a "Band list" in order
to determine who is a member of a recognized Band, a register maintained
by the government (*Ibid.*:156). Furthermore, the Act gives the government
a broad range from whence members might be deleted from a Band
list, including: "Where the name of a male person is included in, omitted
from, added to or deleted from a Band List or a General List, the names
of his wife and his minor children shall also be included, omitted, added
or deleted, as the case may be."

The 1951 *Indian Act* stressed that "Indian" descent was to be determined through the male line, and only as a result of a legitimate relationship. Although an illegitimate child was eligible to be added to
a Band list, the 1951 *Act* indicated that this provision could only apply
"to persons born after the 13th day of August 1956" (*Ibid.*:159).

Not only did the 1951 *Indian Act* stipulate who could be included
on a Band list, it also indicated who was not entitled to be registered,
including "a person born of a marriage entered into after the 4th day
of September 1951 and has attained the age of twenty-one years, whose
mother and whose father's mother are not persons [as described above]"
(*Ibid.*:158). Again, depending on the date of a child's birthday, sisters
and brothers could be legally appropriated a different ethnic stamp. More
importantly, perhaps, families and Bands would lose the corresponding
benefits. Not surprisingly, critics have generally denounced government
attempts to "amend" the *Indian Act*:

> The astonishing feature of the amendments up to 1950 is how little, despite
> their frequency, they sought to accomplish. They were always preoccupied with
> details and never contradicted the basic rationale of the Indian Act, which de-
> manded "civilization" and responsibility from the Indian population while de-
> nying them control over the forces affecting their lives. (Bartlett, 1983)

This perception might also apply to the general policy after 1950,
especially in relation to the wranglings over membership lists. The Lubicon were still struggling with this issue in the 1980s, and their membership problems followed a similar path to that taken by the evolution
of the *Indian Act*. As discussed earlier, upon first contact with government
officials the Lubicon were given fairly liberal assurances regarding their
membership list. Allowances were made for those who were away during
the 1939 census visit and promises were made about their future inclusion
in the official list made at that time. However, the Department did some
reevaluation in the 1940s on Bands and Band lists, at a time when land
was once again in demand following the return of soldiers from fighting

in the Second World War. The 1951 *Indian Act* was the most restrictive legislation to-date dealing with Native people, limiting who was legally "Indian," and, subsequently, who could be registered on a Band list. At that time, as has been shown, officials attempted to question the Lubicon Band's existence. The Lubicon were not officially recognized as a Band until 1973 by Order-in-Council. As far as the Lubicon are concerned, however, they have always been a band. Yet, the "official" number of Lubicons was further reduced by the 1951 *Indian Act*. One member family even had their offspring divided in half. Six who were born prior to the effect of the 1951 legislation were considered "Indians" by the government, while six born after the new policy were treated as "non-Indians," though all twelve children had the same mother and father.[10] Despite the government categories, however, the Lubicon lived together as a community, self-sufficient and relatively unmolested by officialdom. By the 1970s, this, too, would change.

Alberta Policies

Although the Lubicon struggled with the Canadian government at least since 1939, it was not until the 1970s that their battle became more pressing. Prior to that time the Lubicon Lake area was difficult of access and there was little intrusion from outsiders. In 1979, however, the Alberta government completed construction of an all-weather road through the region, which brought an influx of oil companies with their heavy exploration equipment; by 1982 there were 400 oil wells within a fifteen mile radius of the Lubicon Band community. The road provoked an incident with little precedent in Alberta legal history. Fearing the consequences that its construction would entail, the Lubicon and some other affected groups, calling themselves the Alberta Isolated Communities, sought to file a caveat against the Alberta government in 1976. The purpose of this procedure was to halt construction of the road by officially declaring their claim to 33,000 square miles of land in the area, based upon their unextinguished Aboriginal title. The provincial registrar refused the caveat request, forcing the Alberta Isolated Communities to seek court action. The provincial government in turn was granted a postponement on the case until a decision was rendered in a similar case in the Northwest Territories. Although the Aboriginal claimants lost their case in the Northwest Territories, the court indicated that the decision would have favoured the Native claim had the law in the Northwest Territories been written like the one in Alberta and Saskatchewan. The Alberta government took this cue and changed the pertinent legislation, making the changes *retroactive* to a date prior to the date on which the Lubicon filed for caveat. The court case of the Alberta Isolated Communities was dismissed in 1977.

This retroactive legislation caused an uproar. First introduced in the Alberta Legislature on 25 March 1977, the purpose of Bill 29, "The Land Titles Amendment Act, 1977" was "to clarify the interpretation of The Land Titles Act respecting the filing of caveats. It's intended to be consistent with what the government and the legal community have always understood the law to be in this area,"[11] explained Alberta's Attorney General, James L. Foster. He further admitted that the Alberta government was compelled to make this change because of the recent court decision in the Northwest Territories.[12] The opposition reminded the provincial government of public concern over this issue, including an outcry from the Canadian Civil Liberties Association. The Alberta government received a request from the Alberta chapter of this body to make a submission on Bill 29 pointing out their misgivings, but the Attorney General felt that these apprehensions were somewhat misguided.[13] On second reading of Bill 29 the Attorney General indicated once again the nature of the new legislation:

> I should underline and emphasize, perhaps, that it is not the intention or scope of our land registry system to accommodate to the filing of caveats for which no certificate of title has been issued or is in the process of being issued. Indeed we felt it appropriate to clarify the law particularly with respect to Section 136, to ensure that the relationship of the caveator, or the applicant, was tied in some direct sense to the owners of the property or others who have interests in the property. Therefore we intend to make it clear with the amendments in this legislation, and particularly to ensure that no caveat can be registered for which no certificate of title has been issued.[14]

Since the Lubicon Band did not possess a "certificate of title" for their land, they were barred from filing a caveat, but Foster insisted that the notion that Bill 29 denied certain groups their rights was "completely inaccurate." The amendments were related to "fileability," and not to the question of land ownership. Interestingly, though, the Attorney General planned to implement an additional "clarification" in order to alleviate some concerns, "particularly to oil company interests and others" and dispel the doubts expressed "by the legal and the commercial communities."[15]

The opposition declared that the enactment of Bill 29 was tantamount to a "black day" in the history of the province, for the government was showing a "disrespect for civil liberties in Alberta." A Social Credit Member of the Legislature of Alberta (MLA), Walter A. Buck, was also concerned with the priorities in enacting Bill 29 which, he felt, defended the government interests of large groups with political and economic clout. Small groups like the Lubicon Lake Band did not have the resources to defend themselves, and to expect them to use the courts to protect their rights showed "callousness" and "indifference" toward the needs of minorities.[16] Another MLA, New Democrat W. Grant Notley, pointed out some of the possible implications of retroactive legislation:

"What we're really saying . . . is that we have told the native people of Alberta, yes, go to the courts, but only if you lose. If we think we might lose, we'll change the law retroactively."[17] Notley was aware of the difference between a land claim and the filing of a caveat, but he also stressed that there was confusion between the filing of a caveat and a freeze on development, as the government suggested: "Little point in gaining land claims, if development has taken place without any consideration of the possible implications for the people living in the community."[18]

The government responded that the filing of a caveat only aided Aboriginal claims "in a harassing manner," and that the only thing the Native people would have achieved would be to cause "an embarrassment to the government." Furthermore, claimed Conservative MLA Leslie G. Young, to allow the caveat in question to go through would be to "destroy the land title system in this province," for the caveat would affect approximately 5,000 land holdings in the Peace region:

> . . . had this application to caveat been successful . . . every title holder in the town of Peace River would have woken up one morning and found his title was clouded — that he had a caveat against it, couldn't get a mortgage and couldn't sell freely. Now I ask you: in that event, who are the powerless, who are the innocent? What is the nature of the question before us?[19]

The debate over the caveat revealed a real concern for the government: interference with development in northern Alberta. Faced with conflicting interests, the provincial government took a stand for the rights of those who had "some" right to the land. "I'm not concerned about those who want to claim the whole massive area in the north," said Independent MLA Gordon Taylor. In the government's arguments, emphasis was placed on the necessity of facilitating development rather than hindering it. The Lubicon caveat application was seen as a real threat to the land tenure system in the province, which provided for the "orderly transaction of land." Thus, "Bill 29 is intended to prevent abuse of the system of law which is the cornerstone of our society."[20] Nor was the government only worried about hampering development which appeared to benefit only certain groups of Albertans. Sensitive to criticisms of neglecting the Native cause, the provincial government responded that the new legislation was actually for their own good: "By ascension into law of this bill we will be assisting those native people in real need of our support, by indicating that we are prepared to accommodate their objectives under treaty and our obligations. We do not wish to inhibit their individual growth by curtailing total development of the north."[21] The government, however, had its own ideas on what its obligations were to the Native population of the province. As one MLA stated, the purpose of the Alberta treaties was evidently "not to contain the development of the people; its intention was rather to create an orderly and just settlement of all the land."[22] Consequently, the Alberta government had established the Land Tenure Secretariat on 3 June 1975 to provide legal title to eligible people living on public land in northern Alberta, but officials saw a need to encourage "the individuals involved to develop the personal responsibilities inherent in land ownership."[23]

Criticism of the government's position was heard outside the Alberta Legislature. With only four members in the opposition, the Conservatives were confident in the House, but concerns poured in from across the province and the country, including petitions from citizens living in isolated communities, schools, and churches. The Alberta Human Rights Commission feared that the new legislation was discriminatory, and the Canadian Civil Liberties Association held public meetings to discuss the implications of Bill 29, including one meeting on 3 May 1977 at Garneau United Church, Edmonton. It was this gathering that particularly bothered the government of Alberta because some of the guest speakers, including journalist Pierre Berton, were "outsiders" fomenting discord in the province. "I know the civil liberties group from Ontario were in part behind it," said the Attorney General. As a result, Taylor argued, the growing controversy over the legislation could be questioned and even dismissed:

> . . . the Hon. Member for Spirit River mentioned we should be flattered because Pierre Berton came to Alberta to speak about human rights. Personally, I think there's plenty of human rights in the east he could speak against without shoving his nose into our business. The people of Alberta can handle their own affairs without interference from some arrogant radio man from Toronto. I resent him coming. I would wager — maybe I'm wrong — but I'd wager somebody paid his way. I would bet on it. When he pays his own way out here, I might have some reason to listen to what he has to say.[24]

By the time the caveat controversy erupted, the Lubicon had learned that they could no longer ignore the troublesome signs on their horizon. Many Lubicon families moved five miles from their traditional area into Little Buffalo where their children could go to school. They would meet the new challenges with newly-acquired skills. As the Alberta government debated whether or not the Isolated Communities were being influenced by outside rebels, the Lubicon were grooming one of their own to lead them into the uncertain future. In 1978 Bernard Ominayak, 28 years old and with a grade 10 education, was elected to the Lubicon Council; two years later he became Chief of the Band.

Chief Ominayak

Referring to Chief Bernard Ominayak, one journalist said in 1988 that "it is hard to imagine today where the Lubicon Cree would be without him" (Goddard, 1988:43). Ominayak has not resolved the Lubicon dilemma, nor has he diminished the band's troubles, but he changed the character of the struggle. Once a small, unknown group of Native people in northern Alberta on the verge of losing their very identity, the Lubicon surfaced as a force to be reckoned with in the 1980s and in the process have gained worldwide respectability, albeit primarily from non-governmental and perhaps non-powerful groups and individuals. Still, it is almost certain to many observers that whatever happens to the Lubicon, they will not go down quietly. History will not bypass them as it did in 1899. It is difficult to determine whether it was Ominayak's leadership or a new sense of urgency felt by the whole band that gave the Lubicon a spark. Perhaps it was a combination of both. Certainly, the 1980s ushered in new problems for the band that required concerted and deliberate action on the part of the Lubicon. Still, Ominayak is credited with bringing the Lubicon cause to the provincial, national, and even international limelight.

One of the effective strategies picked up by the Lubicon in the early 1980s, under the leadership of Ominayak, was to seek assistance outside the band. They realized that alone, they would be isolated and easily ignored by officials. United with other bands with similar problems, coupled with a broad-based support network, the Lubicon would have a better chance. The Lubicon hired James O'Reilley, a lawyer who negotiated an agreement with the government for the James Bay Cree. Advisers were also sought who had experience dealing with Native issues and the two levels of government. Next came the creation of a coalition of Native, labour, student and church groups across Canada and Europe who helped to raise the public's awareness of the band's plight and who provided support for the band's land claim. The Lubicons became a household name in Alberta, and Peter Big Head of the Blood Band in southern Alberta expressed a common view regarding the Lubicon's position: "The Lubicons are looked upon as the forerunners . . . They've opened the door. Indian people across Canada must stand firm for what belongs to them" (Fisher, 1988). Lawrence Courtoreille, Alberta Vice-President for the Assembly of First Nations, conceded that "People are looking toward Bernard as the new leader who can make changes . . . He is quiet, but he carries the power of his people" (*Ibid.*). With skilful use of political leverage, the band has gained a lot of positive media coverage. Through Ominayak, the Lubicon struggle gained credibility. Soft-spoken and unobtrusive in manner when addressing the public, Ominayak does not forcibly demand anything or attack anyone. Perhaps this is one of the reasons he has succeeded in endearing his people to the Canadian public:

> Unlike the band's lawyer and adviser, he is not given to fancy rhetoric or inflamed, passionate speeches . . . Yet it is Ominayak who controls the situation, which has been growing increasingly volatile as more and more outside supporters arrive to take up the fight. (Darkan, 1988)

Deliberately orchestrated or not, Ominayak is portrayed as the sensible, reasonable leader of a small group of Native people fighting for their very existence. Although he had to fight his own personal battles along the way,[25] he always managed to retain a certain amount of dignity. His lawyer, O'Reilley, and his adviser, Fred Lennarson, are both non-Native. They do the lashing at the government and developers, saying the things that might need to be said but that might make some people feel uncomfortable. The Lubicon are left squeaky clean. Whether this image was a result of a well-crafted plan might not be easily construed, but, either way, it has worked.

One of the ways that Ominayak succeeded in bringing the Lubicon claim to the fore might be his sense of timing. As it will be discussed later, he was able to maximize his opportunities for publicizing the Lubicon cause during the 1988 Winter Olympics, and the federal election in the fall of 1988. The Lubicon also maintained a sense that they went through all the proper channels, exhausted all the available routes to them, and were now at the mercy of the Canadian people. In their press releases, public statements and forums, the band briefly but assiduously recounted the history of the Lubicon, from their being overlooked by the treaty party in 1899 — through no fault of their own, they point out — to the fact that they still have no Reserve while their livelihood has been basically destroyed due to the destruction of the environment by multi-national corporations. At a time when the environment has become a mainstream concern, how can the Lubicon lose the war for public approval?

Soon after he was elected chief, Ominayak was faced with the prospect of his Band losing their Reserve even before they received it. In 1981 the Alberta government proceeded with a plan to turn the region claimed by the Lubicon into a Provincial Hamlet. When the Band protested the move and refused to cooperate with officials, the provincial government demonstrated once again that it was sensitive to "outside" influence in the Lubicon case. Instead of addressing the criticism that surfaced regarding his Land Tenure Program from the Lubicon and other isolated communities, Municipal Affairs Minister Marvin E. Moore pointed out that those who had signed a petition rejecting the program had done so "with the advice of legal counsel from Montreal," and therefore were suspect.[26] Provincial officials insisted that the aim of the Land Tenure Program was not to undermine any land claim put forward by a Native group. "We established it so people who have been legally living as squatters on public land in Alberta in this day and age would have an opportunity to obtain title to that land, title they need for a variety of reasons."[27] Interestingly, though, the government was not moved to provide "title to the land" to residents of the Lubicon area until the early 1980s when oil exploration was booming. Furthermore, the Lubicon resented the label of "squatters" in their own homeland.

The Legal Battle

If attempts to deal directly with the province were discouraging, the legal course proved equally demoralizing for the Lubicon Lake people. The band first approached the courts during the above-mentioned caveat application, which, as has been shown, did not result favourably for the Lubicon. Having failed at the provincial court level, they sought remedy through the federal court system in 1980, but this route also had its pitfalls. First, the band's action was continuously challenged by some of the defendants on procedural grounds. The province and oil companies argued that the federal court had no jurisdiction on what was to them a provincial matter. The court agreed. While the case against the federal government and the crown corporation, Petro-Canada, continued in federal court, a suit against the province and other oil companies was filed in provincial court. In the meantime, oil exploration and development continued in the band's traditional territory. The Lubicon, therefore, sought to obtain an injunction to temporarily halt the disruptive activities in the area pending a settlement of their land claims. This was the fourth court action by the band. The Lubicon filed for an interim injunction on 23 September 1982; the application was not heard until 26 September 1983. On 25 October 1983 lawyers on both sides completed their arguments, and judgement was rendered on 17 November 1983. The Lubicon's application was dismissed.

The crux of the band's argument in seeking the injunction was that "what was being destroyed by development activities was a whole way of life which could never be compensated or replaced with money" (Lubicon Lake Band, 1983:2). In order to prove this point, the Band presented affidavits from Lubicon Chief Bernard Ominayak and from prominent community elders, describing their traditional lands, the history of their people, their hunting and trapping activities, and the effect development had had on their livelihood. Affidavits were also submitted by Joan Ryan, Chairperson of the Department of Anthropology at the University of Calgary, confirming the distinctiveness of the band's traditional way of life and the possible effects to their culture from oil-related activities; another affidavit from Ken Bodden, wildlife biologist with the Boreal Institute at the University of Alberta, described the band's hunting and trapping activities and related this to the economy of the community; an affidavit by Ben Hubert, a zoologist, showed the possible effects of oil-related development on the animals in the band's traditional area; finally, affidavits were read from Gordon Smart, past Director of the Forest and Land Use Branch for the Alberta Department of Energy and Natural Resources, Peter Dranchuk, professor of petroleum geology at the University of Alberta, and Everett Peterson, a forest ecologist. Smart described everything from past, present, and future proposed development in the Lubicon area; Dranchuk discussed the types of development expected in the region; and Peterson gave an assessment of the effects development could have on land-vegetation and biological productivity, including the cumulative effects of development on hunting, trapping and fishing.

Lawyers for the provincial government and oil companies argued that the decrease in wildlife in the area was not due to development activities but to natural cycles of animals, a tick infestation, overtrapping, and decreased trapper effort. The band rejected all these arguments, but especially questioned the theory of ticks and natural cycles for it was not clear to the Lubicon why this phenomenon started only after the oil development, nor why this "natural cycle" was having little effect outside the developed areas (Ibid.:4). The Band's opponents insisted, however, that the idea of a distinctive Native way of life was "nebulous"; that "any aboriginal way of life has already been unalterably affected by the encroachment of modern life"; that "the clock cannot be turned back"; and that "it is impossible to do irreparable damage to something which doesn't exist" (Ibid.). The judge agreed.

In explaining his decision, Judge Gregory Forsyth of the Alberta Court of Queen's Bench concluded that any damages possibly inflicted on the Lubicon Lake Band could be compensated with money:

> . . . to a significant but not complete extent, any damages sustained by the Applicants between the date of the application and the trial of the action were not irreparable but were calculable and could be satisfied by the payment of same by the Respondents. Further, the Respondents had the ability to pay such damages . . . on the basis of the material and evidence before me in this application, adduced by both sides, I am satisfied that damages would be an adequate remedy to the Applicants in the event they were ultimately successful in establishing any of their positions advanced. I have considered very carefully the allegations of irreparable injury or damage not compensable by money and I am simply not satisfied that the Applicants have established in this application such irreparable injury.[28]

The judge did not conclude that the band had not suffered irreparable damage, only that the band had not proven such an allegation. This was of little consolation to an already desperate people, especially when the judge appeared to be much more concerned with financial losses to the oil companies:

> If I was required in this case to consider the factor of adequacy of damages to compensate the Respondents, then I am more than satisfied that the Respondents would suffer large and significant damages if injunctive relief in any of the forms sought by the Applicants were granted. Furthermore, the Respondents would suffer a loss of competitive positions in the industry vis à vis the position of other companies not parties to this action. That loss coupled with the admitted inability of the Applicants to give a meaningful undertaking to the Court as to damages either as individuals, or if authorized to bind the known class, as a class, on which point I have grave doubts, reinforces my decision that injunctive relief in this case is not appropriate.[29]

Not only was the judge concerned with the "significant damages" that the developers would suffer if an injunction was granted, but he also made reference to the point that the band's obvious inability to pay damages if need be at a later date was taken into account. The implication of such a judgment might be that only those who can financially afford the consequences will be granted a court ruling in their favour. Either way, Judge Forsyth's decision gave a clear message which had a historical ring to it: the "nebulous" Native way of life must make way for "inevitable" development by powerful groups.

This court decision had a further twist. The same judge who conceded in the fall of 1983 that the Lubicon did not have a lot of financial security ruled on 6 January 1984 that the band was liable for all costs associated with that case. Judge Forsyth assured the Lubicon that they did not have to pay "forthwith," but the defendants could apply for this payment later on. One Canadian newspaper concluded that the Judge "who went all out to beat the band gets perfect 10,"[30] a feeling shared by the Lubicon's lawyer: "It's not over dramatic . . . to say this is the actual destruction of a people . . . We are presiding at a requiem, and I feel like our learned friends want to take the corpses out of the coffin and stab them again and put them back in the coffin."[31] The Lubicon have striven to convince the public, and Canadian courts, that what the band has lost, and stands to lose if development continues at the rate and extent it has, is something intangible and yet more precious than any amount of money — their way of life:

> Given the choice of returning to the way of life which they enjoyed before the onset of development activity, and which is truly in great jeopardy, or of all becoming oil millionaires living in condominiums in Hawaii, there's absolutely no question whatsoever in the minds of people who know the situation that Band members would immediately choose the return to the way of life they knew in the past . . .
> . . . the Lubicon Lake people have no experience with great sums of money and the alternative lifestyles which such money can buy. What they know of the outside world is more worrisome to them than appealing or attractive. Thus whatever [the judge] might think, the Lubicon Lake people have a great and a genuine and a really quite easily understood concern over the systematic and deliberate destruction of everything they have and know and are as a people. Realistically, the Lubicon Lake people don't have the choice of returning to the way of life they lived before the onset of development activity in their traditional area, and they know it, so they are literally stuck with having to try and figure out how to survive that development activity, how to protect as much as they can of their traditional way of life, and how to best make the clearly unavoidable transition from their familiar traditional economy to some kind of hopefully viable mixed economy. (Lubicon Lake Band, 1985)

The Lubicon appealed the Forsyth decision, but, on 11 January 1985, the Alberta Court of Appeal ruled in favour of the oil companies.

> Seismic activity and exploratory drilling is, in the nature of things, temporary. It is conceded that after it ends the wildlife will return in number. We simply do not know whether new fields have or will be found so we do not know if

there will be a permanent development beyond the existing fields . . . In any event, the timespan here is sufficiently short that the plaintiffs could, if successful at trial, gain through damages sufficient moneys to restore the wilderness and compensate themselves for any interim losses . . . In any event, we agree with [Judge Forsyth] that, on the balance of convenience, the harm done to the respondents would far outweigh any harm done to the appellants during the interval before trial.[32]

It is interesting to note that the Appeal judges also felt that the provincial government and oil companies stood to lose a lot more, or suffer a great deal of inconvenience, if the Lubicon were granted an injunction to halt development pending their Aboriginal claims trial. What is most telling about the judgement, however, is the contention that "sufficient moneys" could "restore the wilderness." The Lubicon appealed the injunction dismissal but the Supreme Court of Canada refused to hear their case. The Lubicon ran out of courts, and began to run out of money as well. The legally recognized band claims that there was a drastic cutback in its operating budget, a consequence the Lubicon believe was in retaliation to their public stance. For example, in 1981, the Band received $104,174 in core and administrative funds. In 1982, they were initially given $76,336, although much lobbying brought an increase to $101,736. In 1983, they received $51,460, though the government insisted "that there was 'no relationship' between (the) legal action and the budget cut-backs" (Lubicon Lake Indian Band Land Claim, 1987:24) . Band records show that the annual income of the average Lubicon trapper dropped by two thirds, from approximately $6,000 in 1982 to $2,000 in 1984, while nearly one million dollars worth of oil was pumped *daily* in the Lubicon area. According to the Lubicon, there is no question of diminishing resources in their region since the arrival of oil developers; in 1979, Band members took 219 moose; in 1981, this number dropped to 110; in 1982, an even more dramatic drop to 37; and in 1983, only 19 were taken. Since then, the annual moose kill has counted in the 20s (Martin, 1984). The provincial government's response to these figures was that the drop was a "countrywide phenomenon" largely due to the anti-fur movement.[33] Provincial Minister responsible for Native Affairs, Milt Pahl, refused to accept the band's allegations that game had disappeared from their land ever since gas and oil exploration began in the area.[34] In addition, the Associate Minister of Public Lands and Wildlife, Don Sparrow, maintained that oil development could actually *help* wildlife because the clearing fires opened up the habitat for the moose, for example, and made hunting easier.[35] The problem, said some government officials, was that the Band had become too dependent on welfare payments, further proof that the Lubicon did not have a traditional way of life worth saving.[36] Ominayak's response was that the province "just wants us to give up or go away" because "we don't fit into any of the little boxes they set up" (Steed, 1984). One report described the onslaught on the community as "ethnocide"; more than genocide, the intrusion from outsiders was tearing "the very fabric of the meaning of life apart."[37] An editorial in a major Canadian newspaper simply stated that "meaner treatment of helpless people could scarcely be imagined."[38]

Continued Conflict

Support for the Lubicon struggle spread to groups outside government agencies, including to the World Council of Churches. Following a visit to the Lubicon Lake area in 1983, the Council observed many abuses "which could have genocidal consequences." Among the Council's findings were instances of provincial officials "deliberately" allowing fires to burn unchecked, destroying thousands of acres of boreal forest in the band's traditional hunting and trapping grounds; turning hunting and trapping trails into private roads for developers with many of the roads fortified with gates, guards, and "no trespassing" signs. Workers employed by the province and oil companies had been instructed to bulldoze traplines and to fire their rifles into the air in order to scare the game away, an activity pursued so enthusiastically that one participant described it as "almost like a competition."[39] This disclosure was followed by the *Penner Report*, as the Standing Committee on Aboriginal Self-Government was known, which described the Lubicon situation as "one of the most distressing problems the Committee encountered" (Canada, 1983). In response to mounting public pressure, the Alberta government conducted an investigation of its own into the band's allegations. For the most part, the Alberta Ombudsman found that "much of what my complainants regard as 'evidence,' I must discount as speculation," although he concurred that it was vital to maintain "an important appearance of fairness" (Alberta, 1984:16; 21). The response from the federal government was no less enthusiastic.

When David Crombie became Minister of Indian Affairs and Northern Development in 1984, his first response to the Lubicon was to appoint a former judge to conduct a study; E. Davie Fulton arrived at the Lubicon site on 9 April 1985. The final *Fulton Report*, which was supportive of most of the Lubicon claims and aspirations, was submitted to Crombie in February, 1986. The updated report was never made public nor responded to by government officials.[40] Crombie, who the Lubicon believe was sympathetic to many of Fulton's recommendations, was named Minister of Multiculturalism in April, 1986. The main stumbling block at this point was still the question of membership. The Lubicon had one figure, the federal government had its own, and Alberta recognized neither (Canada, 1986).

While the two levels of government disputed the membership criteria, and ignored the recommendations of the *Fulton Report*, the Lubicon attempted to deal with their situation on their own. They stopped some developers from entering their territory and even evicted others who "snuck in through the back door," maintaining that "we're acting under our own lawful authority, which is the only lawful authority in our area" (Booth, 1987).

Aware that they were physically incapable of patrolling their entire region, the Lubicon did not oppose most development projects, demanding only that the Band be consulted prior to commencement of operations. They were especially concerned with ensuring protection of particularly sensitive areas, including their nineteen different burial grounds and the proposed Reserve location. As far as the Lubicon are concerned, they own the land. They argue that because they never signed Treaty No. 8, their traditional landbase was never ceded to the federal government, and therefore could not have been transferred to Alberta. The proper cession will take place only when a Reserve is set up, an agreement that must be made between the Canadian government and the Lubicon.[41]

At the same time the Lubicon were involved in another publicity campaign to force the government to come to terms with the band's demands. Since April, 1986, the band had started a boycott of the 1988 Winter Olympic Games to be held in Calgary. From the band's point of view, one of the most ironic and even hypocritical aspects of the Winter Olympics was the proposed Native art display, entitled "Forget Not My Work," to be exhibited at the Glenbow Museum. The exhibition's corporate sponsor, Shell Canada, contributed $1.1 million toward the exhibition, while it also operated a $130 million tar sands plant in the Lubicon claimed traditional territory.[42] "It's an astounding story of injustice and despair, of David against Goliath."[43] Several major museums officially refused to participate in the exhibition in a show of support for the Lubicon claim, withdrawing approximately 200 artifacts from the show,[44] while Joan Ryan, anthropologist and committee member of the exhibition board, resigned in protest against Glenbow Directors having put diplomatic pressure on foreign museums to participate.[45] The controversy led to a Museum Code of Ethics being passed on 4 November 1986 by the General Assembly of Museums, in Buenos Aires, stipulating that "ethnic artifacts should not be used against the ethnic groups who produced them."[46] The name of the Glenbow exhibition also changed to "The Spirit Sings."

Following the completion of the 1988 Winter Olympics in Calgary, the federal government took the offensive by suing the Lubicon Lake Band, asking the court to impose an immediate settlement on the Band. In the fall of that year, the Band responded by withdrawing from all legal actions, declaring that Canadian courts had no jurisdiction on Lubicon territory. Lubicon Lake Band land was not in Canada. The band boldly stated that it never considered decisions by Canadian courts to be binding on the Lubicon; the band retained the option of veto, much as nations do in international courts. In Lubicon land, only Lubicon laws applied.

On 15 October 1988, the Lubicon people intensified the patrol of their borders. Blockades were set up and anyone wishing to enter Lubicon territory had to visit the check points and obey Lubicon laws. People came from across Canada to assist the Lubicon Lake people. At 6:30 A.M., 20 October, this short-lived independent nation was invaded. The Royal Canadian Mounted Police went in with sub-machine guns, sniper rifles and attack dogs, with helicopters flying overhead. Twenty-seven people were arrested but later released. On that same day, the Lubicon received some support from a most unlikely source. The Alberta Premier called Chief Ominayak to set up a meeting. Two days later, the province and the Lubicon reached an agreement.[47]

Continued Inaction

Had the band only been obliged to deal with one level of government, they might have secured a home a long time ago. Traditionally, the provincial government was the most reluctant to acknowledge the band's claim because of pressures from oil developers. The federal government is constitutionally responsible for land claims but it could not proceed without a land transfer from the province. Now that the province settled with the Lubicon, Ottawa had only to act on the proposal. But the fall of 1988 was also the time of a federal election, and other, more pressing business called the attention of the government. When the Lubicon planned to stage demonstrations across the country at every point the electioneering Prime Minister stopped, officials from Ottawa agreed to proceed with negotiations. Soon after the election, on 24 January 1989, talks broke down with Ottawa, federal officials declaring that the Lubicon Alberta agreement was unacceptable, and that the band was "greedy not needy."[48] The Lubicon proceeded with their mandate and released the Treaty of North American Aboriginal Nations, a document modeled after other international treaties, such as NATO or NORAD. This mutual defense pact will ensure that if the Lubicon are ever invaded by outside forces, other groups who have signed the Treaty will come to their support.

Major newspapers across Canada assailed the government's inaction in redressing a case of historical injustice that drags on to the present. Some commentators suggested that the Lubicon dispute was typical of the ill treatment endured by most Native Canadians: "In a way, it is just a routine case of the looting and deceit inflicted on native people by Canadian governments for a century."[49] Others referred to the potential high cost for governments in settling with the Lubicon, but insisted that it was "the price of justice and, whatever it amounts to, it must and will be paid."[50] Still others pointed to the "state of legal limbo" in which the Lubicon were put, and questioned whether it was "possible that more people are harmed by government's inability to make a decision than by their leaders' wrong moves."[51] Some bluntly proposed that "If a scrap of decency exists in Ottawa and Edmonton, the just settlement will be sought immediately."[52]

Government handling of the Lubicon's concerns has been consistent with Canadian reaction to and treatment of its Native population in general. There has been little effort to accommodate Aboriginal needs in the face of White goals. An analysis of the events surrounding the Lubicon struggle reveals a relentless trend that began with first contact in the Americas and persists to the present. Explorers in the 15th and 16th centuries had papal bulls and royal grants to support their territorial claims over those of the original inhabitants of the "New World." Likewise, David Laird approached the Peace region in the late 19th century with a document that informed the local residents of their tenant status. Although he offered the Native people a treaty, he formally stated that "The Queen owns the country." Like his predecessors, Laird did not request permission for white penetration of the area, but rather told the incredulous Natives "What is required of you." One of the groups missed during that initial treaty "negotiation," the Lubicon Lake Cree band, had the audacity to tell government officials what was required of them in order that Lubicon territory be used for non-Aboriginal development. Authorities could only react defensively for the Lubicon stand contradicted the very essence of the Canadian federation: European pre-eminence. When the government met the band on 24 January 1989 federal officials already had a prepared press statement before discussions began.[53]

There is ample documentation showing mismanagement of Native affairs in Canadian history. From the first influx of settlers, expediency was evident in the handling of the Native population, but not all authorities were indifferent to the situation. Native pleas and protests were lost in the clamour of increased settlement and development which the incoming Europeans believed to be necessary and beneficial. In the face of opposing realities and values, the dominant society took precedence, and "authorities viewed the situation with mixed feelings and uncertain loyalties" (Brown and Maguire, 1979:11). On the one hand, there were the needs of the Aborigines; on the other hand there was the urgent call for "progress" by the White settlers. Submission to one group appeared to contravene the goals of the other, and this dilemma continues to plague the Canadian government today. It is fair to conclude that many politicians and well-intentioned officials have tried to resolve the Lubicon situation, but their vision was intrinsically different from that of the Lubicon. This might explain why, despite the numerous meetings between the parties, no agreement has been reached. In the end, however,

it is the Lubicon who are left agonizing over the prospect of their uncertain future.

Europeans had a tendency, from first contact onward, to try to mould
Aboriginal people into something they considered comprehensible
(Upton, 1979:17). The general approach was to help them by changing
them, even to the extent of teaching "natives to be natives" (Brody,
1975:213). The Lubicon, however, did not fit into "the little boxes they
set up." Contemporary officials echoed views that were articulated
throughout Canada's history, for "In each colony . . . the ideal Indian
was the invisible one" (Upton, 1979:136). Indeed, immigration calls for
more settlers in the 19th century insisted that the Natives "were in-
offensive and diminishing yearly . . . now we seldom see a Moose or
an Indian" (*Ibid.*:137). Like the disappearing moose, the demise of the
Native population was considered normal, a passion that was "scientifically" supported by the doctrine of the survival of the fittest (Brody,
1981:58). The Native persistence with their own customs was adverse
to White economic aims. A sneer at a cultural trait might be overlooked,
but an obstacle to financial profits must be eradicated. Thus, the Potlatch
was allowed to make a comeback, but the Native concept of land usage
could never regain a foothold. The question of land was not negotiable.
Natives were to come to their senses or die (Lester, 1988:3). When it
came to the land, Europeans had only one thing to say to Aboriginal
people:"They must yield or perish" (Brody, 1981:58).

To the irritated consternation of such claimants, some indigenous
people refused to do either of the above. The Lubicon, for instance,
were bypassed in 1899 but have fought ever since for a recognition which
they insist is their due. Nor does their fight appear to be weakening.
Like the perennial dandelion, it might be that every attempt to nip the
Lubicon at the bud has led to a persistent rejuvenation of the band's
roots. Like all living things, however, Lubicon roots need some land
in order to survive.

Conclusion

Treaty No. 8 will soon celebrate its centennial. One of the groups the
Treaty Commissioners missed back in 1899, the Lubicon Lake Cree
Band, still does not have a Reserve. While they see their traditional land
bulldozed for oil development, their community joins the welfare ranks,
endures an outbreak of tuberculosis, and experiences the first ever case
of suicide among their people (Goddard, 1988:44–45).

The Lubicon have not been without their supporters. Their claims
were justified by the two first government agents who visited them in
1939; a judicial inquiry in 1944 favoured their position; a statement from
Dr. Anwar Barkat, Director of the Program to Combat Racism, Geneva,

criticized the Canadian government's record on the Lubicon in 1983; the *Report of the Special Committee on Indian Self-Government* ("The Penner Report") agreed in 1983 that conditions facing the Lubicon were critical; church leaders in Canada, led by Archbishop Ted Scott, publicly denounced the treatment accorded to the Lubicon in 1984; the federal government's *Fulton Report* of 1985–86 supported the Lubicon position in all critical areas; a Buffy Sainte-Marie concert sold out in Calgary on 23 October 1987 in support of the Lubicon; after studying the Lubicon case for three years, the United Nations Human Rights Committee concluded in 1987 that the Lubicon Cree had been abused; the North American Indian Support Group took a stand in support of the Lubicon Band on 22 May 1988 (Goddard, 1988:3). Yet the Lubicon remain without a Reserve.

The Lubicon Cree have dealt with numerous officials from the federal government and their provincial counterparts, parliamentary committees, government commissions and studies, federal and provincial negotiators and advisers, various levels of courts, the United Nations, church groups, civil rights groups, museum curators, genealogists, anthropologists and historians, the media and the public at large. Still, the band has no Reserve. Admittedly, the Lubicon could have had a Reserve by now had they accepted the last offer from Ottawa. But the band insists on being compensated for what they consider to be irreparable damage to their way of life. As has been shown, governments, developers, and Canadian courts disagree with this assumption. In the face of such enormous obstacles and incredible odds, what makes the Lubicon hang in? Why have they become a role model for Native groups across Canada? On paper, the Lubicon have not achieved very much, at least not officially. The Lubicon have set a precedent because they have refused to give up. When all else failed, the Lubicon relied on their own sense of justice and fought on. Their response to Alberta's Land Tenure Program was exemplary of the feisty Lubicons. When the province sent property-tax notices to Little Buffalo and threatened those who had built corrals and fences with no provincial authority, the Lubicons trusted their own judgement and ignored Alberta's attempt at usurpation:

> Almost everybody at the settlement . . . cancelled the two-acre deeds, returned tax notices, fought the school proposal, and left the corrals standing, and, when provincial officials arrived to announce the dismantling of four houses deliberately built outside hamlet boundaries, Lubicon hunters strolled into the meeting with loaded rifles, a gesture that so far has kept the province from calling in the bulldozers. (Goddard, 1988:7)

The province could have easily countered the Lubicon with an armed force which the band would have had no chance to overcome. But the province retreated, perhaps knowing that an all-government attack would not be tolerated by Canadians, or maybe because some officials admitted to themselves that the Lubicon had a case. The Lubicon, for their part, could only gain confidence in their struggle with such a show of unified determination. Other groups of the First Nations heard of the incident, and nodded approvingly at the Lubicon display of strength. This same approach was used in October, 1988, when the Lubicon, frustrated by dealings with the provincial and federal government, set up blockades to stop oil trucks from entering their disputed territory. The government forcibly dismantled the blockade, but, for the first time, the provincial government agreed to the Lubicon's proposal for a Reserve. A year later, the federal government had still not come through for the Lubicon, so the band once again took the initiative. On 29 October 1989 the Lubicon gave Petro-Canada a 30-day notice for the crown corporation to obtain band permits and pay royalties for using the band's traditional lands, or else be evicted.[54] If a clash occurs between the Lubicon and federal forces with violent outbreaks, the Lubicon and all their supporters will likely lose. On the other hand, the Lubicon feel that they have already lost a great deal, besides the land disruption around them. Chief Ominayak wonders how long his people will withstand the pressures from without, and hopes that the community will stay intact, otherwise no one will make it. "That is one of the biggest fears I have, all the time — that even if we win, we've lost" (Sniatynski, 1987). Chief Bernard Ominayak feels that the Lubicon already show serious wounds: "People subjected to welfare for eight years, it takes a lot out of people and that can't be resolved overnight . . . Our people survived off our lands for years. To see the destruction right before your eyes hurts in many ways" (Interview with author, 28 June 1989).

NOTES

1. The term band refers to the Lubicon Lake Cree people; the term Band refers to a structure created under and recognized by the *Indian Act* of Canada.
2. As cited in Lubicon Lake Band, "Presentation to the Standing Committee." The report erroneously indicated that Lt. Gov. Morris was present at the Treaty No. 8 negotiations in 1899. Morris died in 1889. Material in parentheses was on the copies provided by the Lubicon.
3. Report by Mr. Justice W.A. Macdonald, of the Supreme Court of Alberta, The Court House, Calgary, Alberta, 7 August 1944. As recorded in Special Joint Committee of the Senate and the House of Commons appointed to continue and complete the Examination and Consideration of the *Indian Act*, Minutes of Proceedings and Evidence, No. 12, Monday, 21 April 1947 (Ottawa: King's Printer, 1947), 557-559. In reaching his decision, Judge Macdonald took into account the report of Commissioner J.A.J. McKenna, dated 31 May 1901, and approved by Order P.C. 1182, in which McKenna states that "I have taken it that everyone, irrespective of the portion of Indian blood which he may have, who enters into treaty, becomes an Indian in the eye of the law and should, therefore, be treated as an Indian both by the Department of the Interior and the Department of Indian Affairs."
4. As cited in Lubicon Lake Band, "Presentation to the Standing Committee," 5-6. Material in parentheses was on the copies provided by the Lubicon.
5. *Ibid.*, 6. Material in parentheses, and emphasis, was on the copies provided by the Lubicon.
6. *Ibid.*, 7. Material in parentheses was on the copies provided by the Lubicon.
7. *Ibid.*, 7-8. Material in parentheses was on the copies provided by the Lubicon.

8. *Ibid.* Material in parentheses was on the copies provided by the Lubicon.

9. *Ibid.*, 12. Material in parentheses, and emphasis, was on the copies provided by the Lubicon.

10. Information provided to author by band adviser, Fred Lennarson, during telephone interview, 1 November 1989.

11. *Alberta Hansard*, 25 March 1977, 483.

12. *Alberta Hansard*, 4 April 1977, 623.

13. *Ibid.*

14. *Alberta Hansard*, 6 May 1977, 1206.

15. *Ibid.*

16. *Alberta Hansard*, 6 May 1977, 1208-1209.

17. *Alberta Hansard*, 6 May 1977, 1210.

18. *Ibid.*

19. *Alberta Hansard*, 6 May 1977, 1211-1212. The Alberta government could not come to terms with the amount of land the Native people were claiming in the province. In 1985, the Minister of Native Affairs, Milt Pahl, made the remark that: "It's like somebody comes along and says: I'm a direct descendant of Christopher Columbus, and I claim all of North America; therefore I want an injunction so that nobody will turn another scoop of dirt until my claim is satisfied." *Alberta Hansard*, 18 April 1985, 460. Pahl would probably have been more astonished to hear that Aboriginal people in the Americas never believed that Columbus had a just claim to their territory.

20. *Alberta Hansard*, 6 May 1977, 1215.

21. *Alberta Hansard*, 6 May 1977, 1216.

22. *Alberta Hansard*, 6 May 1977, 1215.

23. *Alberta Hansard*, 6 May 1977, 1214.

24. *Alberta Hansard*, 6 May 1977, 1218-1219.

25. For example, following the break-up of talks in January, 1989, the federal government announced that some band members were willing to deal with the government on their own. This apparent split within the band and threat to the leadership was seemingly resolved on 31 May 1989 when Chief Ominayak was unanimously reelected. Two months later, however, the federal government agreed to recognize a new band in the region. See *The Edmonton Journal*, 27 July 1989.

26. *Alberta Hansard*, 13 April 1981, 162.

27. *Alberta Hansard*, 29 April 1981, 406.

28. "Reasons for Judgement of the Honourable Mr. Justice Forsyth," copy of the judgement, No. 8201-03713, Lubicon Lake Band records, 9-10.

29. *Ibid.*, 12-13.

30. *The Toronto Star*, 30 January 1984.

31. Statements made by James O'Reilley, legal counsel for the Lubicon Lake Band, as cited in *The Toronto Star*, 30 January 1984. See also, O'Reilley's presentation during Judge Forsyth's hearing on the matter of costs. *Proceedings*, Court of Queen's Bench of Alberta, Judicial District of Calgary, No. 8201-03713, 18-19.

32. *Proceedings*, Court of Appeal of Alberta, Calgary Civil Sittings, Special Hearings for 7-10 January 1985, 16057, 15-16.

33. *Alberta Hansard*, 15 April 1985, 365.

34. *Alberta Hansard*, 15 April 1985, 364-365.

35. *Alberta Hansard*, 15 April 1985, 459.

36. Lubicon Lake Band, "Statement," 10 December 1984, 4. Band records show that while only the Lubicon old and infirm received welfare assistance in the early 1980s, approximately 95 percent of the band is now on welfare.

37. *The New York Times*, 5 June 1984.

38. Editorial, "The helpless abused," *The Globe and Mail*, 7 April 1984.

39. Dr. Anwar M. Barkat, Letter from the Director of the Programme to Combat Racism, World Council of Churches, to the Rt. Honourable Pierre Trudeau, October 1983, 3-6. A copy of this letter is found in the Boreal Institute Collection (Lubicon Lake Indian Band Land Claim).

40. Reporters were able to disclose its contents only after having obtained copies through the *Freedom of Information Act*. See Sniatynski, 1987.

41. Lubicon Lake Band, "Press Statement by Bernard Ominayak, Chief, Lubicon Lake Band," 12 January 1987.

42. *Windspeaker*, 2 May 1986.

43. *Calgary Herald*, 24 May 1986.
44. *Edmonton Journal*, 3 October 1986 and 13 December 1986; Lubicon Lake Band, "Statement," 9 December 1986, 22 January 1987, 26 January 1987.
45. *Edmonton Journal*, 16 November 1986.
46. Lubicon Lake Band, "Statement," 26 January 1987.
47. The province agreed to transfer 76 square miles to the Lubicon, with full surface and sub-surface rights, plus 19 square miles with only surface rights, but the province would not develop this area without Band consent. This information was provided to the author by Fred Lennarson, adviser for the Lubicon, during an interview on 21 June 1989.
48. This was the opinion expressed by government public relations person, Ken Colby, to the news media.
49. Editorial, *Ottawa Citizen*, 2 April 1986.
50. Editorial, *Calgary Herald*, 5 April 1986.
51. Vicki Barnett, "Injustice to Lubicon Indians is national disgrace," *Calgary Herald*, 8 April 1986.
52. Editorial, *Globe and Mail*, 7 April 1984.
53. Lubicon Lake Band, "Statement," 8 March 1989, 1.
54. Don Thomas, "Lubicons threaten to evict Petro-Can," *Edmonton Journal*, 2 November 1989.

REFERENCES

Alberta. 1984. *Special Report of the Ombudsman for Alberta, Re: Complaints of the Lubicon Indian Band*. Edmonton: Province of Alberta.
Bartlett, Richard. 1983. Indian Act of Canada, as cited in James S. Frideres: *Native People in Canada: Contemporary Conflicts*, 2nd Edition. Scarborough, Ontario: Prentice-Hall.
Booth, Karen. 1987. Within Rights to Evict Crews — Lubicon Chief. *Edmonton Journal*, 14 January.
Brody, Hugh. 1981. *Maps and Dreams: Indians and the British Columbia Frontier*. Vancouver: Douglas & McIntyre.
———. 1975. *The People's Land: Whites and the Eastern Arctic*. Markham: Penguin Books.
Brown, George and Ron Maguire. 1979. *Indian Treaties in Historical Perspective*. Ottawa: Department of Indian Affairs and Northern Development.
Canada. 1986. *Lubicon Lake Indian Band — Inquiry Discussion Paper*. Ottawa: Department of Indian Affairs and Northern Development.
———. 1983. *Indian Self-Government: Report of the Special Committee*. Ottawa: Supply and Services Canada.
———. 1966. *Treaty No. 8, Made June 21, 1899 and Adhesions, Reports, Etc*. Ottawa: Queen's Printer.
Darkan, Sean. 1988. The Battle of Little Buffalo. *The Edmonton Sunday Sun*, 23 October.
Fisher, Matthew. 1988. Quiet Persistence Hallmark of Hero. *The Globe and Mail*, 29 October.
Frideres, James S. 1983. *Native People in Canada: Contemporary Conflicts*. 2nd Edition. Scarborough: Prentice Hall.
Goddard, John. 1988. Double-Crossing the Lubicon: How Edmonton and Ottawa Turned Indian Giver. *Saturday Night*, February.
———. 1985. Last Stand of the Lubicon: With No Reserve and No Rights, a Small Band of Northern Indians Battles for Its Ancestral Home. *Equinox* 21.
Lubicon Lake Band. 1983. Lubicon Lake Band Presentation to the Standing Committee on Indian Affairs and Northern Development. 18 May.
Lubicon Lake Indian Band Land Claim. 1987. General Historical Information. February 1987. Boreal Institute Collection, University of Alberta.
Madill, Dennis F.K. 1986. *Treaty Research Report: Treaty Eight*. Ottawa: Department of Indian Affairs and Northern Development.
Mair, Charles. 1908. *Through the Mackenzie Basin: A Narrative of the Athabaska and Peace River Treaty Expedition of 1899*. Toronto: William Briggs.
Martin, Douglas. 1984. Caught Up in an Oil Rush, A Canadian Tribe Reels. *The New York Times*, 5 June.
Ponting, J. Rick, and Roger Gibbons. 1980. *Out of Irrelevance: A Socio-Political Introduction to Indian Affairs in Canada*. Toronto: Butterworths.

Smith, Derek G. 1975. *Canadian Indians and the Law: Selected Documents: 1663-1972*. Toronto: McClelland and Stewart.

Steed, Judy. 1984. The Last Stand of the Lubicon. *The Globe and Mail*, 7 April.

Sniatynski. 1987. Lubicon Disputes: Interview with the author.

Tobias, John L. 1983. Protection, Civilization, Assimilation: An Outline History of Canada's Indian Policy, in A.L. Getty and Antoine S. Lussier (Editors): *As Long as the Sun Shines and Water Flows: A Reader in Canadian Native Studies*. Vancouver: University of British Columbia Press.

Upton, L.F.S. 1979. *Micmacs and Colonists: Indian-White Relations in the Maritimes, 1713-1867*. Vancouver: University of British Columbia Press.

Part Five

Foreign Policy and National Security

War has been an important factor in determining Canadian foreign policy. During the nineteenth century, Canadians were often concerned about the possibilities of an American invasion, but by the First World War they had come to regard the United States as a benevolent ally and protector. This new relationship developed in a climate of world politics dominated by the threat of total war, and, after 1945, under the spectre of a potential nuclear holocaust.

Canada's relationship with the United States since the Second World War was strongly influenced by U.S. hostility toward the Soviet Union. This confrontation often placed Canada in a difficult position, particularly in its attempts to reconcile international obligations to the United Nations, or the Commonwealth, with its military commitments to the United States. Canada's usual strategy in such situations was one of "quiet diplomacy": providing steadfast support for American foreign policy in international forums such as the United Nations, while voicing its criticism and concern to U.S. officials behind the public scene. On occasion, however, some Canadian diplomats, politicians, and scholars have demanded that a more independent and internationalist foreign policy be adopted in keeping with Canada's status as an important middle power.

During the Second World War, Canada and the United States co-operated in the defence of North America through the Permanent Joint Board on Defence. After 1945, fear of the onset of a new war brought renewed co-operation, and by the late 1950s the threat of a Soviet nuclear attack became more ominous because of the development of intercontinental missiles. The North American Air (Aerospace) Defence Agreement of 1958 offered one solution to this problem; another solution was bilateral and multilateral disarmament and arms-control negotiations.

Canadian and American defence and foreign policy relations were severely tested by the 1962 Cuban Missile Crisis, by U.S. military involvement in Vietnam (1965–75), and by the militaristic rhetoric of the Reagan government during the early 1980s. Many Canadians were also critical of American policies toward various Latin American countries (especially Cuba and El Salvador), and deplored the United States' ideologically biased refugee policy. The 1990 Gulf War created another set of concerns and raised serious questions about whether the United States would, as the world's only remaining superpower, use its authority wisely.

As Canada developed closer ties with the United States, the nature of its involvement with the Commonwealth changed substantially. At the same time, Canadian diplomats performed a creative role in trying to sustain the Commonwealth, accommodating its multiracial character, and making it an important bridge between the developed and the under-developed regions of the world. Canada's international commitments and humanitarian aid have, however, been primarily channelled through the various agencies of the United Nations, most notably the World Health Organization, the World Bank, and the United Nations Educational, Scientific and Cultural Organization. Canadians have also been a major participant in U.N. peacekeeping efforts throughout the world.

The end of the Cold War brought some relief from the trauma of living under the threat of nuclear war and internal anti-communist witch hunts. Although Canada escaped many of the excesses of U.S. "McCarthyism," inquiries into the operations of the Royal Canadian Mounted Police and the Canadian Security Agency during the 1980s and 1990s demonstrated that Canada had developed its own internal security state.

During 1994, a special joint committee of the House of Commons analyzed past and future foreign policy priorities. While emphasis was placed on Canada's traditional commitments to the United Nations, NATO, and NORAD, there was also a call for greater commitment to development assistance, global environmental protection, safeguarding of human rights, and cultural interchange. The committee called upon Canadians to recognize "that the most important global requirements for the 90s and beyond are for shared security, shared prosperity and shared custody of the environment" (*Canada's Foreign Policy: Principles and Priorities for the Future* [Ottawa, November 1994], p. 2).

The articles in Part Five respond to these challenges and deal with various aspects of Canadian foreign policy and national security. The late John Holmes, a highly respected diplomat and scholar, provides a sensitive and insightful portrayal of the United Nations and why its con-tinued existence is crucial. Jocelyn Ghent-Mallet and Don Munton crit-ically assess the response of the Diefenbaker government to the Cuban Missile Crisis of 1962, and how this crisis affected Canada's relations with the United States. Canada's involvement in U.N. peacekeeping dur-ing the past 50 years is the focus of J.L. Granatstein's article. Granatstein poses two important questions: Did Canada make a difference? And what difference did peacekeeping make to Canada? Another dimension of Can-ada's international role is explored by T.A. Keenleyside in his analysis of how Canada has attempted to balance human rights and trade con-siderations when providing development assistance to Third World countries.

Although the articles deal with specific aspects of Canada's foreign policies, they should be considered in terms of broader issues and questions. Why did Canada become so involved with the United Nations when its role in the League of Nations had been so limited? How did Canada reconcile its commitment to international co-operation with its membership in U.S.-dominated security alliances? What impact did McCarthyism have on Canada? Was the Cuban Missile Crisis an isolated example of divergent Canada–United States foreign policy priorities? How important have human rights concerns been in determining Canada's development assistance to Third World countries? Do Canadian refugee and immigration policies meet the demands of the 1990s?

Further Reading

Robert Bothwell and J.L. Granatstein, *Pirouette: Pierre Trudeau and Canadian Foreign Policy*. Toronto: University of Toronto Press, 1990.

Roger Bowen, *Innocence Is Not Enough: The Life and Death of Herbert Norman*. Armonk, NY: M.E. Sharpe, 1986.

Gerald Dirks, *Canada's Refugee Policy: Indifference or Opportunism?* Montreal/Kingston: McGill-Queen's University Press, 1977.

James Eayrs, *In Defence of Canada*, vol. 3, *Growing Up Allied*. Toronto: University of Toronto Press, 1980.

John English, *Shadow of Heaven: The Life of Lester B. Pearson*, vol. 1, *1897-1948*. Toronto: Lester & Orpen Dennys, 1989.

John Holmes, *The Shaping of the Peace: Canada and the Search for World Order, 1943-1957*. 2 vols. Toronto: University of Toronto Press, 1979.

George Ignatieff, *The Making of a Peacemonger*. Toronto: Penguin, 1985.

Joseph Jockel, *No Boundaries Upstairs: Canada, the United States, and the Origins of North American Air Defence, 1945-1958*. Vancouver: University of British Columbia Press, 1987.

Anthony Richmond, *Global Apartheid: Refugees, Racism, and the New World Order*. Toronto: Oxford University Press, 1994.

Douglas Ross, *In the Interests of Peace: Canada and Vietnam, 1945-1973*. Toronto: University of Toronto Press, 1985.

Donald Savage, "Keeping Professors Out: The Immigration Department and the Idea of Academic Freedom, 1945-90," *Dalhousie Review* 69, no. 4 (Winter 1989-90): 499-524.

Denis Smith, *Diplomacy of Fear: Canada and the Cold War, 1941-1948*. Toronto: University of Toronto Press, 1988.

C.P. Stacey, *Canada and the Age of Conflict*, vol. 2, *1921–1948: The Mackenzie King Era*. Toronto: University of Toronto Press, 1981.

Denis Stairs, *The Diplomacy of Constraint, the Korean War, and the United States*. Toronto: University of Toronto Press, 1974.

Reg Whitaker, *Double Standard: The Secret History of Canadian Immigration*. Toronto: Lester & Orpen Dennys, 1987.

The United Nations in Perspective

JOHN W. HOLMES

Writing from Geneva in 1938, Canada's representative to the League of Nations, Hume Wrong, noted that what was at stake on the eve of the Second World War was the very habit of international co-operation. It was not then just a matter of saving the League, and it is not now just a matter of saving the United Nations. The habits of international co-operation have been widely, perhaps extravagantly, institutionalized in the past half century, but a mood of rejection is on us again. A rejection of specific institutions, or of customs or actions of one body or another, is healthy, provided it is discriminating, but a cynical approach to international commitments, weariness of seeking consensus, short-sighted pursuit of national advantage, and an inclination for nations to act unilaterally in response to domestic pressures are reasons for concern. Contemporary criticism too often implies that international institutions are dispensable or replaceable.

International law, in the making since the Dark Ages, is at stake. Keeping the basic structure of the United Nations alive and growing is exceedingly important, but it is a mistake to think that the habit of international institutions began only in 1945 or even in 1919 with the League. As Robert Cox has written: "International organization can be thought of as a historical process rather than as a given set of institutions . . . Historically, international organization has not been a unidirectional, cumulative process. It has moved at times towards greater regulation and fuller institutionalization, at times towards lesser."[1] It is hard to say which of those stages we are now in. Perhaps the drive towards institutionalization went too far, and we are experiencing a reaction similar to that against the "intervention" of national governments in domestic affairs: those who want to break loose from regulation cry

SOURCE: "The United Nations in Perspective," *Behind the Headlines* (October 1986): 1–24. Reprinted with permission of the Canadian Institute of International Affairs.

out for the restraint of others. As regulation gets too complex, nostalgia for a free and self-regulated world economy grows stronger. At the same time, the requirement for stable communications and the threat to the environment and the planet itself increase pressures for greater regulation and control.

There is, of course, a bias in my perspective. I was present at the creation of the United Nations as a notetaker for some of the wisest of the founding fathers, from whom I learned invaluable lessons which I have adjusted to changing circumstances but have not forgotten. Having experienced the travail of its birth, I am not disposed to go on about how much better it would have been without the veto, with weighted voting in the Assembly, an Economic and Social Council (ECOSOC) that could manage the world economy, a secretary-general with powers like a United States president, and membership restricted to those who would speak nicely. A United Nations with those utopian provisions would never have come into existence. It is not an expression of the divine will. It is an organization of us, poor sinners that we are, an exercise in self-discipline. Far from being ingenuous about the prospects for great-power harmony after the war, the founders knew they had to commit the powers to a new world organization before the compulsion to collaborate was dissolved by defeat of the common enemy. To get that basic agreement some lovely ideas had to be dropped.

What I presume to offer here are reflections on present problems in their historic setting. In this spirit it is important not just to look critically at what is wrong with the United Nations, or rather with what we are making of it, but also to look at what is not wrong with it.

Conceptions and Misconceptions

The Charter was constructed by a very large committee and was therefore ungainly. But it was flexible, capable of organic growth and adaptation. Its greatest virtue may be its ambiguity. After it became clear, for example, that its provisions for a United Nations force for collective security were not for this world, we were able, nevertheless, to meet a present need with the intermediary United Nations role of peacekeeping — certainly not the enforcement body the founders had hoped for but a useful way to get a ceasefire. It is of limited application, of course, but keeping the peace requires diverse instrumentalities of limited scope. The initial approach was somewhat too holistic.

I would like to dissociate myself from those whose hearts were left in San Francisco, those who perpetuate the legend that a group of saintly statesmen composed in the California sun of 1945 a beautiful world government the ideals of which have since been betrayed by governments concerned for their wretched sovereignty. Recollecting their words and behaviour, I would suggest that the percentage of saints and sinners was not all that different from the present crop. The same saints steered us a few years later and with good reason into different approaches to international security, such as the North Atlantic Treaty Organization (NATO). At San Francisco they were planning for the future; later they were dealing with the present. It was a limited group at San Francisco, furthermore. The present leaders are much more representative of the peoples of the globe. The agenda they have to deal with is a great deal longer and more complex than the founders were able to foresee. We have learned much more about the dimensions of the problems of uniting the nations than Churchill, Roosevelt, or Stalin could comprehend. Nevertheless, it is advisable to understand tolerantly the state of the world they had to cope with.

That they were better orators in those days is part of the trouble today. All those ringing speeches full of "one world" rhetoric were to some extent responsible for beguiling people into believing that a world government with supranational powers had been created which would act with commanding authority. Much of the present cynicism about the United Nations is based on the misconception that it is a failed world government. But "the god that failed" was not that kind of god at all and ought not to be accused of that kind of failure. The United Nations was created as an association of sovereign states, as an instrument for more effective multilateral diplomacy. It can do only what its members find a consensus to do. It is a fact of life that that consensus requires at least the passive acceptance of the great powers. If apartheid has not ended, the war between Iran and Iraq stopped, the Russians been driven out of Afghanistan or the Americans and Cubans out of Nicaragua, it is idle to blame the United Nations. Its members have to work towards agreement and devise tactics by which Russians or South Africans can be persuaded, cajoled, blandished, bullied, bribed, or blackmailed. If the United Nations is to "make countries behave" it must call not on a mythological army but Canadian boys in blue and white berets to parachute into Kabul or Johannesburg.

In some respects the Assembly's power of persuasion is greater than that of the Security Council because it can muster a more impressive majority — as it did, for example, in condemning the Soviet invasion of Afghanistan and the Iranian treatment of American diplomats. Such resolutions did not, of course, immediately liberate Afghanistan or the United States embassy in Tehran. Assembly actions did, however, make the Russians pay dearly in loss of support from the Third World, which denounces Soviet action in the Assembly each year with increasing majorities, and contributed to the ultimate backing down of the Ayatollah by destroying the Iranian legal and moral position. Utopians tend to throw up their hands and do nothing because the United Nations cannot force countries to behave. Functionalists want to use the various instrumentalities of the United Nations to do whatever can be done in a discordant world.

The Charter, in the words of the leading historian of its creation, Ruth Russell, "provided merely the skeleton of authority and principle, of machinery and procedures, whereby governments could resolve their difference through the organization; but it left the use of those means almost wholly on a voluntary basis."[2] It was the resistance, often raucous, of the Australians, Canadians, Brazilians, among others, that prevented the great powers from creating a centralized, hierarchically organized United Nations which would not have worked. Central world government would have to be totalitarian and very brittle whereas its wide membership gives the United Nations resilience. Roosevelt, Churchill, and Stalin were good at winning wars, but their kind of United Nations, run by a "world council" dominated by themselves, would have collapsed in no time. The British Foreign Office was relieved when Mackenzie King and other Commonwealth leaders derailed Churchill's weird scheme for a world run in improbable regions.

The word veto does not appear in the Charter. The special status of the five "great powers" in the Security Council was regarded as conferring not privilege but rather primary responsibility for managing peace by pressure and persuasion and, if necessary, by economic or military sanctions. Unless they acted in concert, however, action would not be possible. Looked at upside down, that is what the veto amounts to. Accepting it was not a concession to the great powers by default, or a surrender to Soviet intransigence at Yalta. The veto was a rational acceptance of the facts of life in a world in which there was no way an international organization could command forces adequate to subdue a great power. If that was not entirely clear in the spring of 1945 in San Francisco, it was all too clear after Hiroshima in August. Atomic power was a feature of the brave new world of which very few planners had been aware.

The endeavour for what were beginning to be recognized as middle powers was to limit the use of the veto and to see that it did not apply in ECOSOC or other United Nations bodies. They did not want a council of the great powers as a kind of executive committee for the vast United Nations network. The Security Council would have no authority over the Assembly, of which all countries would be members and in which there were provisions for majority voting. ECOSOC would have equal status with the Security Council. In practice the great powers, because of their economic clout, would be more or less permanent members by custom, but there would be no veto. Even lesser powers conceived of ECOSOC as a body with considerable control over the various non-political institutions. The great specialized agencies like the International Labour Organization, already some 25 years old, and such new or reconstituted bodies as the World Health Organization or the International Civil Aviation Organization (ICAO) were on their feet before the Security

Council or Assembly had even met. There was no way they would submit to the rule of bureaucracy in New York, even though their membership largely paralleled that of the United Nations as a whole.

Decentralization and Functionalism

To accept this kind of decentralized United Nations as a good thing may seem like simple rationalization, but there is much to be said for accepting what has to be and finding virtue in it — the essence of the functionalist approach. A weak and loose system had space to grow as a network of agencies that could respond to various missions and memberships. The first agency, the United Nations Relief and Rehabilitation Administration, had to be set up quickly to deal with urgent issues at the end of the war and then be dissolved. It was over the council of UNRRA that Canada fought the battle for "functional representation," that is, that agencies should be run not just by the great powers but by countries with special interests in the particular topic. In this case, Canada would be one of the largest contributors to relief. Neither the Russians nor the Americans liked this idea, but the functional principle has in fact played a larger part in the membership of thousands of United Nations bodies than is usually recognized. Because Canada collaborated with the United Kingdom and the United States in wartime research on atomic power it became a permanent member of the United Nations Atomic Energy Commission while the ILO maintained its tripartite constituencies of labour, business, and government to fit its peculiar mission. It is too often forgotten by those who insist on weighted voting in the United Nations that the International Monetary Fund, designed for the urgent function of stabilizing currencies, was established with power in the hands of those countries which contributed most to its funds. That the Russians did not want to join a body with a non-Marxist view of finance did not prevent those who did want an IMF from establishing it.

The United Nations has proved constantly adaptable. New bodies have been created in response to changing requirements, as for instance a United Nations High Commissioner for Refugees or, when the Third World felt the need of an agency to deal with its special needs, the United Nations Conference on Trade and Development. The industrialized powers could create the Organization for Economic Co-operation and Development to deal with not only their wants but their responsibilities. It would not have been easy to set up the OECD under the aegis of the United Nations because of the Third World majority in the Assembly, but it does not much matter that the OECD is outside the United Nations family so long as it sees itself as a responsible member of the community. Many of the specialized agencies, such as the World Meteorological Organization (WMO) or the Universal Postal Union, work so successfully that their importance to life on the planet is forgotten. If a body such as UNESCO (United Nations Educational, Scientific and Cultural Organization) is in trouble, members can abandon it without having to withdraw from the United Nations itself. Nevertheless, when such major powers as the United States and the United Kingdom fight UNESCO from outside rather than as constructive participants, and in a mood of cynicism about international institutions in general, the fabric is weakened.

Proliferation of institutions to meet felt needs has on the whole been a sign of vitality, but there can be too much of a good thing. Committees, commissions, subcommittees, conferences which meet too often by the blissful waters of Lac Leman or the Blue Danube or just two kilometers from Broadway threaten to choke the healthy growth. The phenomenon of creating a new commission or agency when agreement on policy cannot be reached discredits the system and is exploited by those opposed to the United Nations. It is, of course, a kind of jet age corruption by no means confined to non-free enterprises. The cost per annum of such proliferation would probably not buy a jet-fighter, but too much fat, too much duplication of activity, and too little coordination cannot be ignored, even by those who argue the virtues of looseness. The secretary-general, however, cannot run a tight ship when the members, to whom he is responsible, keep setting up commissions and protest vehemently when any of their nationals are trimmed from the establishment. One result of the financial squeeze from big contributors is that it strengthens the secretary-general's hand in resisting expenditures for which he has no money.

Collective Security, Disarmament, and Collective Defence

Although economic and social questions are by far its greatest preoccupation, the United Nations tends to be judged by its success or lack thereof in preventing wars and conflicts. There has not been a great world war since it was founded, but there have been too many others. If the record does not seem impressive one has to bear in mind that wars that do not take place do not appear on television. By no means all potential wars were prevented by specific acts of the Security Council or Assembly, but far more than we realize were frustrated or prevented from spreading by the continuous intercourse in the United Nations corridors of peace-loving diplomats and politicians who may on instructions scream at each other in public sessions but try to strike a deal in the delegates' lounge. My most vivid recollections of the United Nations are of 1950, 1956, and 1958 when we feared that the world would go up in flames over Korea, the Suez Canal or Hungary, or Lebanon. But the representatives of all sides flew into New York. That could not happen in 1914 or 1939. Those who could recall those grim dates were reassured at seeing the Russians, Americans, and the people in conflict at head-quarters huddling in the lounge or in secluded corners.

The founders of the United Nations obviously wanted above all to prevent what had happened when the two great wars broke out. Twice grand coalitions had been formed after years of bitter fighting. In future they should be ready to discourage the aggressor from attacking. The basis of the United Nations was to be a perpetuation of the wartime alliance, the "United Nations" as founded in 1942 after the Soviet Union, the United States, and China had become involved. The approach, how-ever, was obscured by the rhetoric of universal collective security, a high-minded but impractical philosophy tacitly discarded after the one effort to apply it, in Korea in 1950, almost ended in disaster. The idea of uni-versal collective security was that all United Nations members would pledge in advance to join forces to resist aggression so that no one would dare misbehave. It was too logical. The Nazis and the Japanese had made aggression look so clear cut by their classical attacks on Poland, Hawaii, and Singapore. We have since found that getting agreement on aggression is exceedingly difficult in a divided world and that in most conflicts there is some right on each side. Countries are caught in historic predicaments. Who is the aggressor, pure and simple, in the Middle East?

Disarmament received scant attention in the Charter. The prevailing belief was that disarmament of the democracies in the 'thirties had been the prelude to armed aggression. Too many countries, including Canada, failed to realize, however, that there were national military requirements for collective security. When the test came in Korea in 1950 Canada had no force to spare. For economic and social reasons the Western powers had disarmed speedily. Although it was not stated frankly, American possession of the atom bomb was seen as a last resort deterrent of the armed might of the Soviet Union, whose exact strength was unknown. However, a few months after San Francisco, the bomb turned attention to disarmament, or at least to what came to be known as arms control. Thinking on international control became much more radical because of the fear of this dread thing on the loose — a dread thing which none-theless might also provide the energy to transform all the continents. For both purposes strict control would be required. There was a gallant effort by the United Nations Atomic Energy Commission, in which all great and some lesser powers participated, to design a tight international control agency. It failed, not, I think, because of Soviet or American insincerity, as often charged, but because it was not practical. Until the Russians had bombs of their own, there was no hope of a system based on mutual deterrence. Canada was all for international control in prin-ciple but balked at the idea that the agency would own or control the uranium in the ground — Canadian ground that is.

Not since then have we essayed such a bold assignment of national sovereignty to an international authority, but it is possible that a dire and widely perceived threat to the planetary environment or, on the other hand, a comprehensive programme for disarmament might force us to look that way again. The utopians were dismayed, but the functionalists did not give up because so much can and has been achieved through the consensus of sovereign governments on such significant matters as nuclear proliferation or laws for the sea and air and outer space. The relationship of conventional to atomic disarmament had become apparent in the imbalance of forces on the East and West, and the struggle for consensus on disarmament and arms control became a priority on the United Nations agenda from then on. It is habitual to attribute the failures to suspicion, insincerity, duplicity, and what is tiresomely called the "lack of political will" — charges that are not entirely unfounded — but the central question, "the political will to do what?" cannot be ignored. The problems of disarmament are intrinsically difficult, and the toiling negotiators in Geneva or Vienna cannot be written off as insincere.

As for universal collective security, its irrelevance in an atomic world soon became apparent. It was too grandiose an expectation when there was so little agreement in the Security Council. So we turned to collective defence, that is, the association of those countries willing to defend themselves collectively against aggression from outside, not because of the certainty of a Russian military thrust but because of a lack of certainty. Reporting from Moscow after the USSR inaugurated the Berlin blockade in 1948 one felt acutely the perpetual dilemma of East–West confrontation. It would be dangerous to underestimate the threat in the enigmatic position of the Russians, but it could be dangerous also to provoke the kind of panic fear in the West that would lead to actions that would in turn provoke the paranoid Soviet leaders to desperate measures. In this inflammatory atmosphere the North Atlantic countries got together in 1948–9 to create NATO. This was not an American scheme into which the Canadians and West Europeans were drawn. The initiative lay more with the British and Canadians and reflected the European anxiety to get from the United States Senate a commitment to back them with force if necessary and in any case with promises to do so. Some people wanted to drive the USSR out of the United Nations and make it a "free world" organization better able to provide military security. The view prevailed, however, that the United Nations must be preserved as the one universal body.

NATO, as collective defence, was specifically related to article 51 of the Charter which provides for self-defence. It stretched that article's original intention, but it seemed better to do so than to scrap the great experiment before it got off the ground. The official Canadian view has always been that NATO and the United Nations are complementary. NATO relieved the United Nations of a military responsibility that would have dragged it down. In 1945 the thinking was that a stronger League might have prevented World War II, but the only institution that could have staved off war in the late 'thirties would have been something like NATO which linked Europe and North America in credible commitments. If the Americans had joined in tougher sanctions over Ethiopia, Mussolini might have been deterred, but the lesson of Manchuria was surely that there was no way the League, even with the Americans, could enforce collective security in Asia. If collective security was an illusion, there was much to be said nevertheless for collective defence arrangements within the Charter provided they were formed by members of the United Nations who would recognize the requirements of the Charter to work for peaceful settlement. Alliances can provide the sense of security that makes countries more prudent.

I was at the United Nations in June 1950 when the North Koreans crossed the border with tanks and will testify to the almost universal feeling that the United Nations would go under if it could not respond more effectively than the League had done over Manchuria and Ethiopia. When the North Koreans refused to heed the Security Council and withdraw, the United States sent in troops with the blessing of the United Nations. It did not seem then, as it has to some historians in the post-Vietnam period, that the United States was just getting United Nations cover for an imperial venture. Virtually all members, including such non-aligned countries as India, Egypt, and Yugoslavia, wanted United Nations action, even though their public support was cautious. The council, with the USSR absent, made a United Nations Command out of what had to be in fact a United States Command. Faced with a desperate military situation, it was all too obvious that a successful campaign could never be waged by a multinational headquarters in New York. United Nations authority was used to restrain some of the more aggressive Americans from turning the campaign against China. Many countries eventually sent forces to the United Nations Command. Canada was one of the last to do so because it had to recruit troops for the purpose. The fighting in Korea ended largely where it had started, but the aggressors had been denied their gains.

The theory of collective security did not survive this first effort to implement it by military means. It had nearly met defeat in the early stages and we were haunted by the fear that aggression might have to be dealt with in various parts of the world at the same time. The Security Council did not give up, however, but turned its attention to what it could hope to do: forestall conflict, stop fighting and prevent it from spreading. There have been successes and failures, but mostly partial successes and partial failures. In the Middle East, at the time of the Suez crisis in 1956 and on other occasions, conflict has been curbed even if there has been no final settlement. Sometimes the superpowers have quietly acted to put the lid on when the area becomes too inflammatory, as in 1973. Whether these agreements, or rather mute understandings, have been reached in a United Nations chamber, a Washington bar, a Geneva hotel, or during a walk in the woods is of no great consequence. The Charter enjoined the great powers to prevent war by influence and pressure. It was never expected that this kind of rough diplomacy would be conducted openly in five languages in the Council. Agreements could be blessed if possible in United Nations sessions after they had been reached behind the scenes, thereby strengthening their authority. A notable example was the unanimous Security Council resolution of 1968 on the terms for an Arab–Israeli settlement, which still provides guidelines to which East and West are committed.

After the Warsaw Treaty Organization was established and the powers eventually searched for stability in mutual deterrence and détente the two alliances came together at the negotiating tables in Geneva and Vienna and later in the CSCE (Conference on Security and Co-operation in Europe), a more formal association including members of the two pacts and European neutrals. So the hostile alliances have paradoxically created a structure for the maintenance of military balance which is in accord with United Nations principles. It is a triumph of the functional as distinct from the utopian approach, for it is hardly a philosopher's dream of international governance. United Nations bodies still play an essential role in maintaining pressure for the control of arms, but negotiations are best delegated to those with the arms, face to face, with third parties to assist in exploring possible grounds for agreement. Any agreement reached can then be legitimized by a United Nations body.

This may appear to gloss over the rows, the propaganda assaults, the North–South as well as East–West dimensions of disarmament, and, above all, the discouraging results of all this dialogue. Here historical perspective may help. Twenty-five years ago the fact that these countries would talk about their mutual interest in curbing the arms race was almost too much to hope for. The concepts of mutual deterrence and détente are far from utopian, but the recognition that the antagonist must feel secure of his capacity for a second strike so that he will not start a war in panic marks a giant step over the traditional view of defence as simply superiority of armed force which was still being taken for granted in the 'fifties. The stability of deterrence is precarious. A better way must be found, but we cannot ignore the requirements of transition from the age of no confidence. In assessing somewhat favourably the structures, I am suggesting that the problems are with the agenda rather than the institutions. The structures are far from perfect and adaptation must continue, but the problems will not be mastered simply by playing with the institutions or by subverting them because they have not brought instant peace.

Economic and Social Concepts

It is easy to judge the United Nations primarily in terms of security issues. That was the preoccupation just after the slaughter, although the determination for a strong ECOSOC was greater than in 1918. Canada had opposed League pretensions to lay down rules about immigration or racial discrimination in the domestic work force. It was widely assumed in 1945 that economic stagnation in the 'thirties had contributed to the rise of fascism and Japanese expansionism. Many ingenuously assumed that politics could now be kept out of economics, but that illusion did not last, and ECOSOC soon lost its way in confrontational politics. Even though conflicts over economics were inevitably political, there is legitimate concern about obstructing the work of functional agencies by introducing into their operations differences over the Middle East and southern Africa, which are not directly relevant to the activities of the agencies. The United States and other Western powers have made this "politicization" a major charge against the United Nations in general. They might, in humility, recognize that they set unfortunate precedents by the exclusion of mainland China from all United Nations bodies for their own political reasons.

Where vision was lacking in 1945 was over the problems of what came to be called the Third World. We were not so much callous as ignorant. The media had not begun to explore for the public benefit the state of affairs in Africa or Latin America and there was no television to show the face of famine. There were few African representatives at the United Nations, and the Latin Americans there did not look at all impoverished. The preoccupation was with the rehabilitation of war-devastated Europe, and the immemorial problems of other continents would have to wait. The United States Congress and the Canadian Parliament were unwilling to take on Africa and Asia when they were worried that Europe would remain permanently on the dole. Most of the Third World, furthermore, was still within the writ of imperial powers who did not welcome intervention from do-gooders. Besides, there was an unsophisticated confidence in the trickle-down theory: if the channels of trade and finance of the industrial countries could be freed, the benefits would surely be felt by the producers of cocoa and sugar.

The now familiar idea of aid and development assistance on a global scale did not emerge until the early 'fifties when, inspired by the success of the Marshall Plan in Europe, President Truman presented his so-called Point Four proposal for technical assistance, and the Commonwealth brought forth the Colombo Plan. As acting permanent representative at the United Nations when the first pledging conference for technical assistance took place in 1951, I vividly recall how difficult it was to get even the liberal-minded members of the Canadian Cabinet to grasp this concept. Until the eve of the meeting it looked as if Canada was going to be the only major Western country to offer nothing. At the last minute, however, the older members of Cabinet were persuaded to avoid this humiliation by voting modest offerings to the United Nations programme and the Colombo Plan.

Mistakes were made. In hindsight questions can be raised about the effort put into the giant Warsak Dam in Pakistan and, more particularly, the nuclear reactor provided to India in the hope, still strong at the time, that nuclear power was the answer to the challenge of mass poverty. Those who assign failure to the pioneers in aid and development might credit inexperience rather than simple ideological obsession or selfishness. As in other areas of international policies, there are mixed motives. It is as wrong to say that the sole motive is calculating self-interest as it is to pretend that it is entirely humanitarian. There can even be mutual interests served.

I would point out also that United Nations programmes were diverted largely to aid and development before the developing countries had become anything like a majority. Although Third World representatives were few in number, their voices were powerful. Whatever the provisions of the Charter, India under Nehru was a great power, more influential in the Assembly and other bodies than either Britain or France. The legend that in those days the United Nations was run by the West (if not just by the United States) distorts reality. What is not noted by those who point to the success of the Americans in getting resolutions passed is that those resolutions were usually modified considerably to suit the wishes of those who might not otherwise agree to co-sponsor or vote in favour. Canada was certainly not "controlled" by the Americans although it often agreed with them and sometimes (but not often), if it could not change their minds, went along with them to maintain alliance solidarity.

The limits of American "domination" may be illustrated in the case of the acceptance of new members in 1955. Entry had been stalemated for years by great-power confrontation, and Paul Martin of Canada demonstrated the power of a skilled and experienced middle-power leader, backed by a coalition of other lesser powers, to overcome the fierce opposition of John Foster Dulles. It was by no means an inconsequential action as it strengthened the concept of universality. Membership then expanded steadily as the European empires dissolved into independent states. There are those who believe this assisted in the gradual decline of the United Nations. While the membership of mini-states of which we had never heard was certainly not envisaged, clearly membership could not have been held to the very selective collection of 1955. Problems with the Third World would not have been avoided by keeping them out of the General Assembly or ECOSOC.

These shifts in the nature of hegemony have, to say the least, been unsettling. They account to a considerable extent for the doubts and uncertainties about international institutions, especially the United Nations, and the assumption that it is in a time of unique crisis. We live in a perpetual state of crisis, and there is no formula for perfect peace; it will always have to be managed in an atmosphere of alarms and challenges, claims and grievances, rivalries and jealousies. That is why blaming the structures for present conflict is dangerously misleading — blaming the ship for the storm, as Hammarskjöld called it. Nevertheless, we have to keep our eyes on shifting forces in the international scene which condition the work of the United Nations because it always reflects that scene. Some particular changes in the past decade or two contribute to the present malaise about international institutions.

The United States and the United Nations

Most important of all perhaps is the change in the role of the United States and the consequent alterations in American attitudes to institutions in general and to the United Nations in particular. The role of the United States in the United Nations, past and present, is *sui generis* and requires tolerant understanding. It is clear from statements by the Canadian prime minister, the secretary of state for external affairs, and the report of the Special Joint Committee on Canada's International Relations in 1986 that Ottawa's view of the United Nations remains in the Canadian tradition and differs considerably from prevailing views in Washington. These views have wisely been stated in positive rather than confrontational terms. Lesser powers always feel the need of international institutions and international law and regulation more acutely than stronger powers. Canada saw the United Nations in the first place as a guarantor of the weak against the great. Being more dependent on trade, Canada is more dependent on the rules of the General Agreement on Tariffs and Trade (GATT). Having an enormous coast and fishing grounds it needs a United Nations law of the sea. Even in dealing with its neighbours, it has had to have recourse to the International Court of Justice for a settlement of the disputed east coast maritime boundary, and may have to go the same way for its other coasts. It is through international institutions furthermore, that lesser powers can, by consolidating their interests with those of other countries, hope to have some impact on the great powers.

Being a responsible middle power is not easy, but the responsibilities placed on a superpower, especially one like the United States whose decisions often have decisive consequences for others, are burdensome and frustrating. That is the price they pay for a predominant role in making or shaping policies. They must also suffer more than their share of blame for what they do and do not do. They have been goaded by malevolent denunciation as well as legitimate criticism from Third World critics, irresponsibly backed by the Soviet bloc in spite of its lamentable failure of constructive participation in United Nations activities. We must bear this in mind even when their peevish behaviour in the Assembly and their virtual contracting out of its politics are counterproductive and unworthy of the American tradition.

Because the United States, unlike the USSR, has been a positive and constructive force of great consequence, its defection is particularly alarming. From the days of the Hot Springs conference the United States had worked in tandem with the United Nations, seeking to strengthen it as a system, even when its actions were not always what the United States wanted. The ominous difference now is that powerful elements in the administration and prosperous agencies of public opinion treat the United Nations as hostile. This throws the whole system out of kilter. No United Nations body runs on automatic pilot; member states have to programme it. Without input from the most powerful democracy it becomes dangerously lopsided and ineffectual. The paradox is that Americans are magnanimous and zealous in good causes, but they like to run the show because they know best. The United States Senate is so jealous of its sovereignty that it will not let the State Department or the administration commit it. The division of powers makes it almost impossible for Americans to be part of the collective policy-making process that is the essence of international institutions.

Acting collectively was a new experience for Americans in 1945. In our small-power efforts to create a more democratic United Nations the Russians were, of course, the major opposition. The British were the most tolerant. Having been bullied so long by Australians and Canadians wanting to make their own foreign policies, they reluctantly accepted the futility of trying to make the little ones accept parental guidance. The Americans, bemused by the messianic complex from which they have suffered for several centuries, responded with great good will. Since they would be part of the governing body and would have everyone's interests at heart — unlike the old imperialist powers — there was nothing to worry about. That self-confidence has been considerably shaken, but it is an offensive and unacceptable note which crops up as a theme in the present régime de nostalgie.

Nonetheless, the great difference between the United Nations and the League is that the Americans are on board. Although they threw their weight around in an exasperating fashion, they did accept the burdens when the United Nations was struggling to its feet. If the United Nations could not do something that needed doing, such as launching aid and development programmes or acting as a United Nations force in Korea, the United States often acted as a kind of surrogate. If the Americans have acted unilaterally while requiring "loyal" support from their friends it is to a considerable extent because those friends encouraged them to provide leadership. Now the United States is weaker in deployable power and in the will to provide that leadership. Its unsurpassed nuclear capacity is of little use in dealing with terrorism, apartheid, or even the war in the Persian Gulf. While it remains reluctant to share policy-making the rest of us remain reluctant to share the burdens. When the United States assumes the right or the obligation to intervene in the conflicts of dangerous areas like the Middle East we do not object if they come up with helpful initiatives — such as Camp David. Indeed, they are often chided for failing to straighten things out in Cyprus or the Philippines or southern Africa, as if they were God's appointed peacekeeper. Confidence in their infinite wisdom has not been strengthened by their ambivalent postures of late in the Middle East, Central America, or on strategic arms, and the allies have been more anxious than ever to use both the United Nations and NATO to restrain them. Specific policies of the Reagan administration, with which the allies are by no means in total disagreement, are not the only worry. More serious is the volatility of policies made and unmade by Congress and the various competing powers in Washington at a time when fine tuning is necessary to maintain international stability and to deal with a more monolithic superpower.

The actions of the United States administration are not always as perverse as they sound. However antagonistic their speeches about international organization, they still turn to the IMF when they are faced with a banking collapse, and they are now the chief advocates of a strengthened GATT. They have no intention of resigning from such essential services as ICAO or the WMO. Like many critics, they tend to mean the General Assembly or the General Assembly and the Security Council when they talk about the misbehaviour of the "United Nations." But the Assembly is not the United Nations. It is only one of its major organs, with a specific role — raising problems, debating them, giving an indication of forces in the world, recommending solutions, and keeping an eye on what other organs are doing. It is valuable for letting off steam, but whether polemical resolutions promote conciliation or conflict is a question. The answer probably is that some do one and some the other. Most Assembly recommendations are, in fact, passed by consensus. The idea that the Assembly is a reckless legislature, dominated by a malevolent majority from the Third World, forcing everyone to pay for extravagant projects or to believe that Zionism is racist is nonsense. It is not a legislature and cannot force its members to pay for projects they do not like. Paradoxically the utopian idea that the United Nations is an incipient world government is exploited by those who do not like it and want to make it look like a menace.

The rebellion of the United States against the wilder speeches and the profligacy of the Assembly has not been entirely unhealthy. It has up to a point been supported by other Western countries and, more discreetly, by sober statesmen from non-aligned countries. Inevitably, Americans, weary of being called imperialist exploiters, have decided to discriminate as to which United Nations activities they will pay for. The danger is that the sobering effect American toughness has had on the politics of the United Nations may be forfeited if the United States remains aloof. There is increasing realization in the Assembly and in other bodies that passing resolutions with large majorities serves only to alienate. In the Security Council votes are avoided if there is hope of getting agreement of a more helpful kind. There are many reasonable and astute Third World diplomats who seek consensus by compromise, by endeavors to bring parties together on the basis of minimum agreement. In the fortieth Assembly, for example, they produced noncontroversial resolutions on the Falklands and Central America designed only to conciliate. Such good intentions did not, however, meet with an encouraging response from the British and Americans in self-righteous isolation. Indeed, United States delegations are now bound by such rigid regulations that they find themselves too often voting in solitary disapproval.

Nor is it a case of the First World against the ferocious Third. In the 1985 Assembly, for example, such firm allies as Canada, Germany, Australia, and the Netherlands were in the same column as the United States on arms control issues in only some 50 of 71 votes. That the Third World is a bloc which closes ranks only against the United States is a gross exaggeration. Each year an increasing majority in the Assembly vehemently denounces Soviet action in Afghanistan. In December 1985 the Assembly passed for the first time a unanimous resolution condemning terrorism, and the Security Council, also unanimously, condemned hostage-taking. Neither action is going to stop terrorism by itself, but both promote the co-operative mobilization of the resources of all states against a common threat. It should also be noted, in criticizing the intransigence of the Americans, that the Soviet Union is more often found on the winning side because it is less conscientious. To court the favour of the Third World it will vote for resolutions, on disarmament for example, which it does not like any more than does the United States. It is wrong, however, to describe this phenomenon as Third World support for the Soviet bloc; it is the other way around.

The danger is that American denigration of the United Nations has gone too far to be easily reversed. It has induced amongst the public not only hostility but, even worse, an inclination not to take the United Nations seriously, to disregard it as a factor in world politics. The United Nations could be scorned to death. United States withdrawal from UNESCO, its rejection of the authority of the International Court of Justice over Nicaragua's complaint, withholding of funds for programmes Congress dislikes (behaviour the United States bitterly opposed when the USSR and France refused in the 'sixties to pay for peacekeeping operations they did not like), the rough assertion of the right to take offensive action in Grenada, Libya, and Nicaragua without seeking the agreement of any of the international organizations involved have undoubtedly undermined the faith in international action built up over centuries. Each action may have its own justification, but defiant unilateralism is cause for concern.

Shifts in Power

These changes can be traced not only to the election of a Republican administration in the United States and more conservative governments in other Western countries, but also to shifts in the balance and nature of power, both military and economic. They reflect also a more discriminating assessment of the ways in which power, especially that of the superpowers, can be effectively applied. The long postwar period of American hegemony, a kind of pax Americana or, in some ways, a pax Russo-Americana, provided stability, but the American share of the world's product has diminished considerably and the United States could not, even if it wanted, play the same kind of constructive role it once played. There are too many other centres of powers: Japan, China, the European Communities (EC), not to mention the political force of the Third World, whether or not it acts in unison.

Far from the United Nations presenting a menacing threat of hegemony from the Third World instigated by Moscow, the problem is that there is no stable hegemony. The Third World, with or without the collusion of Moscow, is not an "it." Since the Third World countries in the early 'sixties began to mobilize for common action through what is still called the Group of 77 although its membership is now much larger, they have been able to command majorities in the Assembly and in many economic and social bodies where voting is not weighted. They lack the power, however, to carry out agreed policies. They are by no means without influence, even if theirs is only the power to frustrate. So, with the Western countries in a negative mood, there is a vacuum of effective leadership.

At the same time as international governance is weak, so is the capacity of national governments to rule. As we have not a world government but a league of sovereign nations seeking to act by as wide a consensus as is obtainable, only national governments can carry out the wishes of the international community. National governments, however, are finding it increasingly difficult to cope with the complex economic and social problems that face them, many of which require transnational action. Even, for example, with the degree of consensus that exists on terrorism and the drug traffic, expressed in overwhelming majorities in the United Nations and other international bodies, the problems seem to get further out of hand. This is not a defeatist argument;

it is an argument for identifying the nature of the problem, which can too easily be attributed to the failure of international structures. Problems are so complex and conflict so endemic that it is tempting to look for a deus ex machina, but that is not what the United Nations is. It is a self-help agency.

Means and Ends

It would be helpful if the public would think about means as well as ends. Strong denunciation, for example, is not always the most effective way to ease confrontation or extinguish sin — nor is wailing and gnashing of teeth. Dag Hammarskjöld and Lester Pearson did not waste time in 1956 bemoaning the decision of the British and French to intervene in Suez. What was done was done; the problem was how to redeem the error. That is what diplomats have to do, cope with the forces in play, including those of which they disapprove, and the United Nations is what diplomats can make of it. Diplomats often become the scapegoats, but they are the dedicated peacemongers who sit through night after night of persuasion, a more strenuous, frustrating, and exhausting exercise than delivering noble denunciations from the rostrum. And breaking diplomatic relations with an offending state is, for example, usually a way of shooting oneself in the foot. The offender is happy to get rid of a hostile embassy. But without an embassy not just a listening post is lost; so is any ability to influence.

In the promotion of human rights it is particularly necessary to recognize that the identification of a wrong is only the first step. There is no one way to right a wrong. Exposure, especially as practised objectively by a non-governmental body like Amnesty International, is effective, but there are often cases in which subtle deals among diplomats or politicians are more likely to free "warm bodies." Demanding that our leaders take these matters up on visits to Moscow, Beijing, or Seoul might work in a particular case but in general terms it can simply harden resistance.

The role of the Assembly and the various United Nations bodies concerned with human rights is important in establishing what is not acceptable behaviour. Gradually the conscience of the world has been raised. The record of member states is uneven, but many totalitarian states have curbed the excesses of forty years ago. Having to be on the defensive in international bodies has a chastening effect. The change in the international climate meant that Canada could not denounce apartheid and chase the South Africans out of the Commonwealth while discriminating on the basis of race in its immigration policies. When the Charter was drawn up, article 2(7), which forbids interference in internal affairs, was seen as necessary to protect weaker powers from the kind of intervention practised by the fascist states. There were doubts too about the ability of an international organization to agree sufficiently on principles, given the variety of cultures and religions involved. For Canada an additional problem was that most human rights came under provincial jurisdiction. Maintaining sovereignty over domestic policies is still a concern in the international community and most countries can be accused of inconsistency in the sins they choose to denounce, but the pressure of majority opinion on racism has been such that the constitutional restraint of article 2(7) has been largely brushed aside.

One useful function of the United Nations is to produce formulae acceptable to contending parties. The British and French used the disingenuous argument in 1956 that they were intervening in Suez to stop the fighting between Israelis and Egyptians along the Canal. The Assembly agreed that fighting should be stopped but saw that as a job for a United Nations force. In the face of heavy internal and external pressure to withdraw, Britain could use this as an excuse to pull out. But before that position was reached there had to be delicate diplomacy between, among others, the Canadians and the British. Quietly disentangling a fight without passing judgment can be called hypocritical, but surely the end can justify the means. On this Brian Urquhart has some wise words: "In a time when nuclear weapons make the very notion of an actual clash between the nuclear powers a higher form of lunacy, braking mechanisms, safety nets, time-gaining procedures and face saving devices are absolutely essential. Of course no one likes to admit to this in their memoirs, which is perhaps one of the reasons why the role of the Secretary-General and the Security Council are seldom recalled at any great length in retrospect. Who, after all, remembers U Thant's efforts as the honest broker in the Cuban missile crisis? Who remembers Ralph Bunche's long, difficult and successful negotiations over the disputed future of Bahrein?"[3] Recent diplomatic history, one might add, has been written largely from the archives of the great powers, and the helpful, if resented, assistance of lesser powers and mediators is rarely mentioned.

Secret diplomacy can be sinister, but the mindless prejudice against it in general rather than specific terms, induced by muddled thinkers like Woodrow Wilson, ignores the advantages of quiet and bloodless settlement of conflict. Raucous diplomacy gives the United Nations its bad name, but quiet diplomacy has prevented many conflagrations. In the face of such events as the Soviet invasion of Afghanistan there was little to be done except majority condemnation. The secretary-general, nevertheless, quite properly seeks to assist an agreement between Pakistan and Afghanistan which might provide a formula for Soviet withdrawal if it should sometime calculate that is in its interest to do so.

Many people think the Assembly should likewise condemn United States action in Central America. Whether or not it twists arms, the intimidating power of the United States discourages anti-American resolutions, although the extent of American "pressure" is often exaggerated. To pass such resolutions would harden hearts in Washington and strengthen the arguments of those who denigrate the United Nations. Tactful intimations of doubt about United States policy from allies in NATO or the Organization of American States are more likely to make some headway. The difficulty of getting a country to change its ways, even with the entire international community against it, is only too well illustrated by the case of South Africa. The simple assumption that economic sanctions would do the trick if everyone joined in is based more on a conviction that something must be done than on a realistic calculation of their effect on a stubborn people.

A most important function of the United Nations is legitimization. The role of the Security Council and Assembly in particular and most of the system in general is more surveillance than governing. Members keep an eye on the varied activities of all United Nations bodies and the vast number of non-governmental bodies, criticize or approve them, recommend further action, or simply draw attention. They do not need any specified authority over the system to do so, and they can be ignored or heeded. If and when agreement can be hammered out in direct diplomacy, in regional bodies, or under the table, the appropriate United Nations body can give it much wider and stronger authority by enclosing it in a resolution or endorsing it by consensus without voting. The United States successfully used the Assembly, the Security Council, and the International Court of Justice to legitimize its case against the Iranians for violation of diplomatic immunity. Such a seal of approval will be necessary if a settlement can ever be hammered out between Israel and the Arab states because without the assent of all the great powers and the major players of the Third World it would be promptly subverted. If the Contadora should come up with a workable formula for Nicaragua, Security Council approval would undoubtedly be sought. Needless to say, such hopes require patience, but circumstances and governments do change.

Role of Middle Powers

The argument for concerted action by the "middle powers" must be put forward but with prudence because it has been too often overstated, formalized unsubtly as "mediator," whereas it should be a matter of doing what comes naturally. Middle powers have been of particular value in the United Nations because conflict resolution or peacekeeping missions are best left to countries not too directly involved. They can be aligned or non-aligned in the Cold War, provided they can be reasonably objective in the specific quarrel. A cautious, prudent, and sensible temperament — a quality for which Canadians are notorious — best qualifies countries or people for intermediary tasks. Middlepowermanship came to sound like a divine mission for Canada, well-intended but somewhat sanctimonious. Too many debates dealt with Canada's role rather than its policies. Mr Trudeau took a sour view of this "helpful fixing" and tried to turn Canadian attention to closer pursuit of the national interest. This was to some extent healthy, but as Mr Trudeau soon found, there is a continuous need for helpful fixers of Canada's consequence and its not too rigid alignment, preferably able also to deploy a little money and some peaceful soldiers. The United Nations and the Commonwealth invented this role for Canada, Mr Trudeau soon took it on with élan, and Messrs Mulroney and Clark seem to have accepted it without resistance.

In the Assembly, in UNESCO, and in the World Bank and IMF of late a dedication to the preservation and reform of the institutions, along with an ability to understand if not share the American distemper, has led Canada into what might be called a "damage limitation" role. In close association with its traditional "middle power" friends, the Scandinavians, with Australia and other Commonwealth partners, with Japan, the Netherlands, Spain, Ireland, Italy, and often West Germany, Canada has been trying to curb the anti-American sentiments provoked by the disdainful approach of the American delegates. These powers have also been trying to find solutions to the financial crisis posed by the United States policy of withdrawing funds from selected programmes. Since they have the most to gain from the United Nations as a stabilizing force, they must try to fill the gap in leadership, even if it means that their citizens will have to pay more than Americans do. And it is a mistake to picture the United Nations galaxy as perpetually divided between East and West, North and South. The middle power coalitions with which Canada works ad hoc are by no means confined to Western countries. In the law of the sea negotiations Canada was aligned on many issues with such other coastal states as India or Brazil, and very often in opposition to those great naval powers, the United States and the USSR. One might cite also the exercise in helpful fixing of twelve food exporting countries, including Australia, Argentina, Indonesia, and Hungary, who met in Bangkok in July 1986 to try to work out, before the next GATT round, a compromise in the bitter dispute among the United States, the EC, and Japan over food subsidies.

Alternatives

There is always lurking in the assumptions of those who dismiss the United Nations the implication that there is a better alternative. The utopians see the answer in Charter review, getting rid of the veto or establishing weighted voting. But the process of changing the Charter is so daunting that it must be ruled out. The veto cannot be legislated out of existence when it exists in the power structure of the world. No system of weighted voting in the Assembly could get the approval of a majority. It exists in such bodies as the IMF and de facto in many other United Nations bodies because those who are required to pay have to agree to pay. If the Assembly were a legislature, then voting would matter, but no one active in the United Nations believes that the vote of Sierra Leone has the consequence of that of the United States or of India.

The United Nations cannot be exorcised. It is rooted in the expectations of mankind, and, like it or not, it remains a unique and important factor in international relations. If the United States should persist in a policy of abstention, the United Nations would not go away, but merely drift further from United States' interests. The Soviet Union would be in a stronger position to play a cynical game. There are now voices on the Right in Washington arguing that abstention has been a mistake, that the United States should renew an active role and play "hard ball." That would at least mean that they were taking the United Nations seriously. Unilateral action may appeal to some Americans, feeling tall and impatient of the restraints of partnership, but they cannot enforce a pax Americana against a rising tide of resistance without forfeiting those qualities that made American leadership acceptable. A more likely possibility would be a kind of tacit Soviet–American condominium, which might well appeal to Russians as well as Americans. But the ability of the superpowers to manage the economic, social, and political life of the world grows less each year. Indeed a common cause of much of the rest of the world, both aligned and non-aligned, is, through the United Nations, to keep the Cold War out of Africa, the Middle East, and the Caribbean.

Strengthening the fabric certainly does not mean stubbornly maintaining the inflated United Nations galaxy. A house cleaning is needed but it cannot be accomplished with a broad broom. Criticism of extravagance and confrontational rhetoric, such as that delivered by Joe Clark to the 1986 General Assembly, is all to the good when delivered in constructive terms. The growing habit of picking and choosing which programmes to support financially is as bad for the system as the refusal of citizens to pay taxes for projects of which they do not approve. Neither the United States nor the USSR is likely to desist at this stage, however. The United States is bound by congressional stipulations. The only way to change the American mood would seem to be a less reckless disposition on the part of the United Nations majorities in proposing expenditures. It would be a denial of the principles of the Charter to move to a system in which those who pay make the decisions and the receivers can only complain, but everyone would profit from a more sensitive awareness of the dilemma. This is where middle powers can be helpful. The problem has often been met by setting up bodies of limited scope and membership, both inside and outside the United Nations system, to do things on which there cannot be wide consent. In principle such efforts to get around the United Nations are objectionable, but in practice many of them work and do, in fact, serve the broader purpose.

We can worry less than the purists about things done "outside the UN." There is far too much going on in the world for the United Nations to manage it all. We need IGOs (intergovernmental organizations), NGOs (non-governmental international organizations) and QUANGOs (quasi-non-governmental international organizations) such as, for example, the banking consortia set up to deal with the debt problems of individual countries. NGOs like the International Committee of the Red Cross and the International Council of Scientific Unions can operate through the Curtains more easily than IGOs and can, among other things, pursue agreements which could then be ratified by a United Nations body. ICSU, for example, has sponsored the International Geosphere-Biosphere Programme, a remarkable project to study changes in the habitability of the earth which involves among others the scientific academies of China, the USSR, and the United States. International law and regulation are obeyed not because they can be policed but because of the fundamental interest of peoples in having them. Even the much criticized multinational corporations have their own interests in stability, in getting uniform regulations about pollution at sea, for example. In 1974 the oil companies themselves took on the rationing of very short supplies. Accepting this diversity and learning how to use it is the challenge, not pulling the structure up by the roots or running away from it.[4]

While constantly trying to rationalize this sprawling system, we must accept diversity and not make symmetry an end in itself. Building an international order should be a lapidary process, stone upon stone, but the end will not be Westminster Abbey or the Great Wall of China. It is not a finite project. Our natural instinct for hierarchy must be restrained. United Nations bodies have specific functions, and there is no need to say that one function takes priority over another. To say, for instance, that security is more important than economic and social concerns is to ignore the lesson of the past few decades, that they are inextricable one from another. That the Assembly looks like a legislature and the Security Council looks like an executive committee is misleading. The secretary-general is neither a president nor a prime minister, but an international civil servant, inhibited by the will of member governments but nevertheless with a unique status and right of initiative because the United Nations has no government. That it has no government and can have no government is one of the hardest concepts for citizens to accept.

The United Nations system has been described as a cobweb because of the unsymmetrical yet functional pattern of its connections. Cobwebs are fragile, but if they are damaged they are quickly rewoven — unless the spider is killed. Just as the United Nations has the same basic structure as the League, a new United Nations, if we could possibly build one, could not be very different in shape from the present one. In the meantime, however, the alternative would be anarchy, the naked clash of national wills, without institutions or rules in place to avert conflict. That was the situation that the great Hague peace conferences at the beginning of the century were intended to correct. The efforts at The Hague came too late to prevent the disaster of 1914, but the lesson was learned. Out of the First World War came the first try. Although the League was regarded as a failure, it was taken for granted throughout the Second World War that we would try again. The second effort is broader and deeper and has already lasted twice as long. There is no fast track to peace; it requires constant vigilance and invention. Salvador de Madariaga, who had argued that the problem of disarmament was not the problem of disarmament but the problem of world order, wrote in 1929: "no institution, no co-operation; no co-operation, no peace."[5]

NOTES

1. Robert W. Cox, "The crisis of world order and the problem of international organization in the 1980s," *International Journal* 35 (spring 1980), 374–5.
2. Ruth B. Russell, "The United Nations at thirty-five," *ibid*, 227.
3. Brian Urquhart, "Role of the United Nations in maintaining and improving international security," Alastair Buchan Memorial Lecture, International Institute for Strategic Studies, 20 March 1986, 6.
4. This is the sensible approach taken by the Special Joint Committee of the Senate and the House of Commons on Canada's International Relations, and its report, *Independence and Internationalism*, contains a number of practical proposals for consideration rather than plumping for a new heaven on earth.
5. Salvador de Madariaga, *Disarmament* (New York: Coward-McCann 1929), 363.

Confronting Kennedy and the Missiles in Cuba, 1962

JOCELYN GHENT-MALLET and DON MUNTON

The international crisis that developed in October 1962 over the deployment of Soviet nuclear missiles to Cuba was both the most serious superpower confrontation in the postwar period and a major turning point in the Cold War. It was also a crisis for the Canadian government, but

SOURCE: "Confronting Kennedy and the Missiles in Cuba, 1962," in Don Munton and John Kirton, eds., *Canadian Foreign Policy: Selected Cases* (Scarborough, ON: Prentice-Hall, 1992), pp. 78–100. Reprinted with permission of Prentice-Hall Canada, Inc.

at least as much one in its relations with the United States as a Cold War crisis. And it precipitated domestic crises of different sorts in both Canada and the United States.

For decades before the Cuban revolution brought Fidel Castro to power and began the process of turning Cuba into a Soviet ally and military outpost in the Caribbean, Canadian governments, though no less firmly opposed to Soviet expansionism, had taken a view of the struggle with Communism somewhat at variance with that prevalent in the United States. Canadian officials, even in the early postwar period, did not perceive an aggressive ideological element in the Soviet threat to the same extent as most of their American counterparts. Many, but not all, also had misgivings about what they saw as an excessively ideological and emotional drive to policies of the leader of the western forces.[1] Canadian governments supported containment of the USSR but preferred moderation to needless confrontation, military or diplomatic. This wariness, however, was seldom publicly articulated. The differences in approach were there, however, but largely behind the scenes during the Korean War in the early 1950s.[2] It was perhaps thus almost inevitable that Ottawa and Washington would not see eye to eye when the Kennedy administration decided it would respond firmly to the discovery of Soviet nuclear missile sites secretly under construction in Cuba.

Further complicating Canadian–American harmony were clear and public differences over policies toward Castro's Cuba. Beyond the simple fact of geography — Cuba lies not ninety but well over a thousand miles from Canada — Canadians have not shared in the long history of American military and political involvement in Cuban affairs. Where the United States owned eighty percent of the utilities and ninety percent of the mining wealth in pre-1959 Cuba, Canadian investments were small and were not jeopardized by the Castro revolution.

Although generally sharing the American antipathy towards communism, the majority of Canadians did not agree with the United States on the tactics of dealing with communist governments. Living in a nation more dependent on trade than most, they had little use for economic sanctions as a weapon of statecraft and held the view that maintaining normal relations did not signify approval of a particular regime. In Cuba's case, it was widely believed that isolating Castro from western trade and diplomatic contact could not bring about his downfall, but would instead drive him to further reliance on less desirable associations.[3]

Trade relations, moreover, represented one area of foreign policy formulation in which Canadians believed they could and should, if necessary, exercise judgement independent of the United States. In trade relations with Cuba, Canada's normal sensitivity to any interference with its foreign policy was intensified; some Canadians felt that they shared with Cuba the status of economic satellite to American industry. A large part of Castro's offence had been in expropriating the properties of American corporations. If policies should be adopted someday which were displeasing to the American owners of Canadian industries, would Canada too become the target of a United States boycott? This possibility, however remote, was not absent from Canadian minds.[4]

The Kennedy administration inherited not only the problem of Castro's Cuba from its predecessor, but also the plan which eventually resulted in the Bay of Pigs fiasco. Even before the ill-fated Bay of Pigs invasion, "US policy toward Cuba was widely thought to be mistaken and both Prime Minister Diefenbaker and External Affairs Minister Howard Green certainly subscribed to that view."[5] Many Canadians regarded the Central Intelligence Agency's sponsorship of the invasion as irresponsible behavior and deplored the presumed American right to forceful intervention as a means of blocking "Communist penetration" of the hemisphere.[6]

Despite these misgivings, the Prime Minister made a personal effort to offset public and parliamentary criticism. With the President due to visit Ottawa in a month's time, Diefenbaker apparently had no wish to discomfit further the already embarrassed Kennedy administration. On April 19, 1961 — two days after the invasion had been launched — the Prime Minister spoke to the House of Commons. Cuba, he said, had become "the focal point" in an ideological contest which was spreading into every corner of the world. He was following events with "much anxiety and deep concern."[7] Diefenbaker's expression of solicitude, and especially his accompanying characterization of Cuba as "a bridgehead of international communism threatening the Hemisphere, a danger to which Canada could not be indifferent," was gladly recorded by the State Department. The President was informed that the Prime Minister's statement had been his own idea, had been expressed "contrary to the advice of External Affairs," and had been "undertaken at some political risk."[8] While his motivation for offering this political support is not clear, it is now known that Diefenbaker also privately voiced to American officials his hope that, given his "difficult domestic political situation," he would be informed of any future plans "involving drastic action with respect to Cuba."[9] This hope was to be dashed.

While Diefenbaker had expressed misgivings about Kennedy's inexperience and rashness before and during the 1960 presidential election campaign, there was no apparent personal antagonism at this point. Indeed, the meeting with Kennedy in February went well. But the relationship between the two men soon soured. Through 1961 Diefenbaker, by nature suspicious and prone to harbouring slights, "formed an irrational prejudice against Kennedy and Rusk."[10] The animosity was soon reciprocated.

Of considerable irritation to the Americans in May 1961 was a public suggestion by Howard Green that Canada might effectively mediate the Cuba–United States dispute.[11] According to a State Department communication, President Kennedy was "concerned" over Green's statements; in the American view, they reflected a "distressing lack [of] awareness of [the] facts of [the] Cuban situation."[12] The problem was not lack of facts. Nor was the difference of views solely with Howard Green. Officials in External Affairs shared with their minister grave concerns about "the American tendency to go off half-cocked."[13] Nevertheless, the government subsequently denied that Canada had any intention of playing the role of mediator.[14]

Canada had been cooperating with the United States, since late 1960, to the extent of banning the export of strategic materials to Cuba, as well as the re-export of American products covered by the United States embargo. American officials correctly recognized, however, that Canada "probably would not comply with a US request to impose a total embargo on Canadian goods."[15] And with Canada so "extremely sensitive to U.S. public display of our right to control subsidiaries," US policy makers considered it inadvisable to try to pressure Canada by invoking the Trading With the Enemy Act with respect to goods exported to Cuba by Canadian branches of United States corporations.[16]

In spite of continued Canadian assurances that no bootlegged or strategic goods were being exported, criticism from various sources in the United States intensified during 1962. By this time, the US had orchestrated the expulsion of Cuba from the Organization of American States, cut off Cuba's foreign exchange, and extended economic sanctions to include all Cuban imports. Emotions were also running high over the fate of the Bay of Pigs prisoners. In the press, Canada was widely accused of pursuing a "fast buck" policy.[17]

Relations with Cuba, moreover, were not the only issue on which Canada and the United States were at odds in the latter half of 1962. There was, for one thing, Ottawa's reluctance to accept American nuclear weapons, an issue then moving rapidly to the open, public dispute it became in early 1963. And there was External Affairs Minister Howard Green's continuing efforts to promote nuclear disarmament and, in particular, a ban on nuclear testing. Only days before the crisis over the missiles in Cuba broke, President Kennedy had taken the unusual step of signing a personal letter to Diefenbaker in which he expressed his "distress" over Canada's apparent intention to support an upcoming UN resolution calling for an unverified moratorium on nuclear tests. The Canadian vote, Kennedy wrote, "will be tantamount to Canada's abandoning the Western position" and "will be seen by the Soviet Union as a successful breach" of Western solidarity. Thus, if the Canadians did not reconsider their vote, they would "damage, and damage seriously, the Western position on an essential issue of Western security."[18]

These differences were all consequential factors behind the events which unfolded in Canada during and after the Cuban missile crisis, a crisis which forced to a head in Canada the nuclear weapons controversy, which in turn led to the fall of the Diefenbaker government.

Prelude to Crisis

Growing American concern with the Russian buildup of Cuban military power was expressed by President Kennedy on September 4, 1962 and reiterated in a second statement on September 13. Noting the presence of anti-aircraft defence missiles, Soviet-made torpedo boats and Russian military technicians, Kennedy stated that there was no immediate evidence of a "significant offensive capability." Were this to change, however, the United States would "do whatever must be done to protect its own security and that of its allies."[19]

Kennedy's warning did not succeed, and was arguably too late. Khrushchev had decided, likely in May, to deploy the medium and intermediate-range ballistic missiles and their nuclear warheads. The first shipment of missiles had already left the USSR by the time of the President's speech; they arrived in Cuba on September 15.[20] The objectives behind Khrushchev's decision are still a matter of much debate. One likely goal, and the one long favoured by strategic analysts, was that Krushchev was attempting to narrow the substantial American advantage in long-range nuclear weaponry by moving shorter-range missiles close enough that they could reach targets in the United States. Another possibility, as Krushchev himself claimed after the crisis broke, was that the missiles would help defend Cuba against an American invasion. Kennedy advisers at the time and most American analysts since have dismissed this claim, in part because in the US view the missiles were offensive not defensive in nature and in part because such an action by the US was so implausible that Krushchev's claim seemed to be a rather lame, *ex post facto* excuse. Scholars currently give this concern greater credence.[21] It is now known that there was a covert operations campaign against Castro's Cuba organized by the CIA (code named "Mongoose"), there had been "Pin-prick" raids by exile groups against Havana harbour and other targets (four of them in the weeks preceding the missile crisis), there had been large-scale US naval manoeuvres in the Caribbean, and there were, in fact, contingency plans for such an invasion under continuous review.[22] The Soviets, however, were not alone in their perception of the danger of an American invasion. Presidential adviser Arthur Schlesinger reported after a European trip in mid-1961 that a number of those he spoke with "believe . . . an American invasion of Cuba is a distinct and imminent possibility."[23]

Since the Soviet buildup on Cuba had been acknowledged to be of a purely defensive nature, Canadians tended to view Americans' fears as yet another exaggeration of the potential Cuban threat. Calls for an invasion of Cuba, such as those from Senators Homer Capehart and Strom Thurmond seemed too reminiscent of the Bay of Pigs. It was also widely believed in Ottawa that Washington was being pushed into a more extreme position by Republicans campaigning in the off-year elections. Richard Nixon, then involved in an ultimately unsuccessful campaign for the California governorship, accused Kennedy of appeasement and, along with Senator Barry Goldwater, suggested a blockade to stop the movement of armaments to Cuba.[24] There was, in short, "a major partisan fight going on, and a struggle over public opinion," a Kennedy administration official has acknowledged. "The Republicans were really heating Cuba up as the November elections drew closer . . . Things in Congress were getting out of hand. An extreme resolution was even introduced which called for military action against Cuba."[25] A Canadian diplomat posted to the American capital found that the crisis took on an all-consuming, single-minded quality reminiscent of a capital at war. "I was struck," Basil Robinson wrote, "by the extraordinary force of Washington's preoccupation with Cuba and the arch-villain, Fidel Castro."[26]

The *Financial Post* typified the reaction of many Canadians to such statements by terming the demands for invasion a case of "irresponsibility rampant," and by commenting that "emotional anti-Castro jingoists in the U.S. press and the Congress" did enormous harm in deflecting the focus away from Berlin, which was the real Cold War front.[27] Prime Minister Diefenbaker was one of those more worried about an impending confrontation in Berlin than about one in Cuba. As late as October 16, he warned the House of Commons that there were some indications the Russians might soon precipitate a new crisis in that city. Concerning Cuba, he commented that the United Nations was providing "an opportunity to ensure that all possible steps are taken to arrive at a peaceful solution," and that the Canadian government would not fail to do "everything within its power to achieve this objective."[28]

The Crisis Breaks

On the morning of the same day that Diefenbaker made this statement, President Kennedy was informed by his national security adviser, McGeorge Bundy, of the presence of nuclear ballistic missiles in Cuba. Aerial reconnaissance photographs, taken on October 14, revealed that the Russians were in the process of completing launching sites for both medium- and intermediate-range ballistic missiles (MRBM's and IRBM's), capable of reaching targets in Canada as well as the United States and Latin America. The President asked Bundy to assemble in absolute secrecy a group of select advisers who came to be known as ExCom, the Executive Committee of the National Security Council.

The ExCom, in an intensive series of meetings over the next six days, explored the pros and cons of a range of possible American responses, from diplomatic approaches to Khrushchev or Castro to an air strike against the missile sites or a full-scale invasion of Cuba. Both diplomacy ("talking 'em out," as one participant later labelled it) and military force ("taking 'em out") had their proponents amongst the advisers. Ultimately, the President decided that attacking the missile sites was too likely to escalate the crisis, and thus was too dangerous, at least as a first step. On the other hand, diplomacy by itself was unlikely to be productive and, equally important, was certain to be seen by critics of the administration as a weak, insufficient response. The decision was made to establish a naval blockade of Cuba to prevent the shipment of further missiles and nuclear warheads and to demand that the Soviets dismantle the sites already under construction and withdraw the existing missiles.[29]

There is no question that the President and his advisers were very much aware of the risk of nuclear war and much concerned with Soviet objectives and possible responses. At the same time, they were very mindful of American public opinion and its receptivity to the kind of hawkish arguments being made by right-wing congressmen and Republican candidates such as former Vice-President Richard Nixon. As one of the President's closest advisers put the matter at an early ExCom meeting: "I'll be quite frank. I don't think there is a military problem here . . . This, this is a domestic, political problem . . . we said we'd *act*."[30]

Although students of the Cuban Missile Crisis tended initially to emphasize its strategic and foreign policy implications, increasing attention has been paid recently to the domestic side. "The President felt he had to take decisive military action if his Presidency was not to be severely challenged and his political credibility undermined," one analyst has written. "While the risks of escalation pushed the decision down the ladder to the blockade, the President's domestic political interests favored military action over diplomacy. . . . From a domestic political standpoint, the blockade was a less risky course of action."[31]

On Saturday October 20, the group acquiesced in the draft of a blockade speech, although Kennedy did give some last-minute reconsideration to an air strike in a meeting with USAF bombing experts on Sunday morning. With Kennedy scheduled to deliver the public address Monday at 7 P.M., the American government then proceeded to notify the allies. Dean Acheson was dispatched to Paris to brief President De Gaulle and to assist in explaining the situation to the North Atlantic Council. Personal messages from the President were also conveyed to Chancellor Adenauer of Germany and Premier Fanfani of Italy.

Prime Minister Harold Macmillan had already been advised on October 19 that a crisis was imminent in Cuba through David Ormsby-Gore, British ambassador to the United States and a close friend of John Kennedy.[32] In a personal message on Sunday October 21, Kennedy told the Prime Minister that while the American ambassador in London would brief him more fully the next day, he wanted him "to have this message tonight, so that you may have as much time as possible to consider the dangers we will now have to face together." Kennedy explained that he had found it "absolutely essential in the interests of security and speed to make my first decision on my own responsibility," but from that point on he and Macmillan would "have to act most closely together." In a subsequent message, Kennedy added, "I wanted you to be the first to be informed of this grave development, in order that we should have the opportunity should you wish it, to discuss the situation between ourselves by means of our private channel of communication."[33] Immediately after the televised broadcast, the President telephoned Macmillan, the first of many such calls through the duration of the crisis.

Although the missiles were, in the British Prime Minister's words, "A pistol pointed at America and Canada," no such offers of consultation were made to the Canadian Prime Minister. Canada was treated like the other allies, and was deliberately not informed until shortly before the President made his public statement. In a message delivered to Diefenbaker an hour and a half before his address, Kennedy said only that "we should all keep in close touch with each other," and that "I will do all I can to keep you fully informed of developments as I see them."[34] To Macmillan, on the other hand, Kennedy wrote that "it is a source of great personal satisfaction to me that you and I can keep in close touch with each other," and that "I intend to keep you fully informed of my thinking as the situation evolves."[35]

Canadian Responses

The emissary chosen to deliver the message to Diefenbaker was the distinguished former ambassador to Canada, Livingstone Merchant. Accompanied by the American Embassy's Charge d'Affaires and two intelligence officers, Merchant met with the Prime Minister, External Affairs Minister Howard Green and Defence Minister Harkness around 5:30 P.M. on Monday October 22. Merchant thought that Diefenbaker behaved rather coolly towards him, possibly because of his being "tired, harassed and wrapped up in other things,"[36] but possibly also because of the stern letter Diefenbaker had received from Kennedy only days before. In the message now handed to him by Merchant, Kennedy said first of all that the United States had "clear evidence," to be explained by the ambassador, "that the Soviets have secretly installed offensive nuclear weapons in Cuba, and that some of them may already be operational." The situation called for "certain quarantine measures whose object is to prevent the introduction into Cuba of further nuclear weapons, and to lead to the elimination of the missiles that are already in place." Kennedy noted that a personal communication was being sent to Khrushchev, making it clear that the actions in Cuba constituted "an unacceptable threat to the security of this hemisphere" but expressing "the hope that we can resume that path of peaceful negotiation." The longest part of the presidential communication, however, dealt with a proposal to be placed before the United Nations:

> I am also requesting an urgent meeting of the United Nations Security Council. I have asked Ambassador Stevenson to present on behalf of the United States a resolution calling for the withdrawal of missile bases and other offensive weapons in Cuba under the supervision of United Nations observers. This would make it possible for the United States to lift the quarantine.

Kennedy then specifically asked the Prime Minister to "instruct your representative in New York to work actively with us and speak forthrightly in support of the above program in the United Nations."[37]

This paragraph in the President's message was identical to one sent to Macmillan, but it was not preceded as in Macmillan's case by a lengthy exposition on the dangers of the crisis or by offers of private discussion.[38] In the much shorter message to Diefenbaker, therefore, the President appears to be placing a greater emphasis on a solution through the United Nations. Since turning to the UN was the traditional Canadian instinct in time of crisis, this undoubtedly struck a chord with the Canadians.

After Diefenbaker had read the message from Kennedy, the ambassador showed the ministers the photographic evidence, outlined to them the American actions, and read them the text of the President's speech.[39] The Prime Minister asked that one sentence from the speech — a sentence characterizing Soviet Foreign Minister Gromyko in unflattering terms — be deleted. Merchant telephoned Washington and, reaching Dean Rusk, told him that he agreed with Diefenbaker's objection. The offending phrase was removed. Merchant brought no specific requests for Canadian government action, aside from the matter of supporting the US initiative in the UN. After the Americans departed, the Prime Minister went home for dinner and watched Kennedy's address on television.

Opposition Leader Pearson, after conferring with House Conservatives, telephoned the Prime Minister to ask him to make a statement, in view of the Kennedy announcement, when the House of Commons resumed sitting at 8 P.M. Mr. Diefenbaker agreed. Indicative perhaps of the little time he had been given to think about this important statement, the Prime Minister said that it was "impossible to say much" in response, but characterized Kennedy's address as a "sombre and challenging one." Noting that the "construction of bases for the launching of offensive weapons" constituted a threat to most of North America, "including our major cities in Canada," the Prime Minister urged calmness and the avoidance of panic. "Our duty as I see it," he said, "is not to fan the flames of fear but to do our part to bring about relief from the tensions, the great tensions of the hour."[40]

The Prime Minister made no comment on the blockade and, of the other measures announced by Kennedy, noted only the call for a resolution to be placed before an emergency session of the Security Council, the step which had been emphasized in the personal presidential letter to him. "The determination of Canadians," the Prime Minister stated, "will be that the United Nations should be charged at the earliest possible moment with this serious problem." He went on to suggest how the United Nations might help:

> I think what people all over the world want tonight and will want is a full and complete understanding of what is taking place in Cuba. What can be done? Naturally there has been little time to give consideration to positive action that might be taken. But . . . if a group of nations, perhaps the eight nations comprising the unaligned members of the 18 nation disarmament committee be given the opportunity of making an on-site inspection in Cuba to ascertain what the facts are, a major step forward would be taken.[41]

Diefenbaker then asked for the views of, and possible suggestions from, the leaders of the other parties. Lester Pearson, a former External Affairs Minister and now the Liberal leader, noting that the matter was being brought before the OAS as well as the UN, concurred with the Prime Minister that "international organizations should be used for the purpose of verifying what is going on." Like the Prime Minister, he offered no comment on the blockade. Neither did the spokesmen for the two minor parties.[42] The national leader of the New Democrats expressed some skepticism ("we have only the statements of the Americans") but then pointed to precisely the point that Kennedy and his advisers wanted to avoid. "Before we get too excited," he said, "we should remember that for fifteen years the Western powers have been ringing the Soviet Union with missile and air bases."[43]

To turn to the United Nations for assurance was not only consistent with Diefenbaker's own position before the crisis broke but also a typical Canadian response. Canada had consistently supported the UN, Canadian statesmen had played a major role in strengthening it, and the UN was one area of world politics where the Canadians believed they could exert some influence.[44] Canadian doubts, latent or implied, about the wisdom of American actions were a reflection of perceptions of the Cuban–American issue. Some Canadians, their suspicions raised by the original American denials of involvement in the Bay of Pigs operation, may have had doubts about US claims as to the existence of an offensive base. Many, including some Canadian officials, feared that the United States might once more be overreacting. The close circle of advisers around Kennedy, of course, did not see the matter this way. Preoccupied with hawks within ExCom pressing for an attack on the missile sites and worried about right-wing critics in Congress pressing for an all-out invasion, they regarded themselves justifiably as moderates trying to prevent a military escalation of the crisis.[45]

In any case, skepticism was not a uniquely Canadian reaction. Others in the United States and abroad, while accepting the existence of the offensive missiles, questioned the appropriateness of the response. Former President Eisenhower, for example, suspected that Kennedy might perhaps "be playing politics with Cuba" on the eve of the off-year elections.[46] Harold Macmillan, Kennedy's staunchest ally at the time, later wrote in his memoirs that one "had to remember that the people of Europe and the people of Britain had lived in close proximity to Soviet missiles for several years."[47]

The Alert

Meanwhile, a request to raise the alert status for the Canadian component of NORAD — the North American Air Defense Command — had been received through military channels after the President's speech. Merchant had provided no warning that such a request would be made. Air Chief Marshall Frank Miller, the Chairman of the Canadian Chiefs of Staff Committee, arrived at Defence Minister Harkness's home to inform him that the entire military apparatus of the United States had gone on "Defcon 3" alert.[48] Canadian units in NORAD, Miller advised, should be brought to the same state of readiness. At the time NORAD was established, an informal "agreed procedure" had been adopted whereby, in the event of an alert, the President and the Prime Minister would consult about the "risks and repercussions" of recommended joint military proposals.[49] But Harkness had attended the Merchant briefing and knew that Kennedy had not even informed Diefenbaker of the proposed alert, let alone consulted him. Nevertheless, the Defence Minister was in no doubt that some action would have to be taken. He asked Air Chief Marshall Miller to call an immediate meeting of the Chiefs of Staff committee.[50] There were, it emerged, two questions: first, what procedure should be followed when US forces had been put on a Defcon 3 alert and, second, who was the appropriate authority to order it?

Although the first question of what procedure should have been followed would become a contentious one politically, Harkness and his senior military advisers came to a quick agreement on the necessity for an alert. The degree of military integration between the United States and Canada and communality of interest demanded, in their view, that the Canadian forces in NORAD be brought to equivalent status immediately.[51]

The second question of who had the appropriate authority to implement an alert proved more difficult. Initially, the Chairman of the Chiefs thought he had the authority, because the alert was "low-level," equivalent to those he had approved during NORAD exercises.[52] Harkness, however, was not so sure. On checking the Canadian War Books, they found themselves in a complete hiatus. The old War Books, which were no longer in use, gave the authority to the Prime Minister and the cabinet. The new War Books, not yet approved by the cabinet, gave it to the Defence Minister. Harkness decided therefore that he must consult Diefenbaker. Telling the Chiefs to "get ready," he left to confer with the Prime Minister, completely confident that the matter was a mere formality.

Diefenbaker disagreed. He refused to give his permission for an alert until the cabinet could meet and discuss the situation the next morning. Harkness, believing that he had no other choice, returned to the Chiefs of Staff meeting and, in effect, authorized the alert on his own. Apart from a few minor details, such as official announcement of the alert and the recall of men on leave which would, of course, have attracted the attention of both the public and the Prime Minister, all of the requirements were met.[53] The Canadian army, although not involved in NORAD, was also authorized to take whatever steps it could "without putting the country in turmoil." The Canadian navy was a special case. Ships are not as easily dispersed as aircraft, and they must not be caught in harbor. The Chief of Naval Staff, therefore, having received information through his own channels, acted on personal initiative and ordered the Atlantic fleet based in Halifax to get ready for sea. In this case, it was necessary to recall men on shore leave, but further actions were specifically not taken for fear of creating public alarm.[54] The naval alert was approved some hours later by the Defence Minister.[55]

While the close cooperation of the Canadian and American air forces under the aegis of NORAD is well known, the extent of naval coordination under the cover of NATO is not. The integration of the Canadian Atlantic fleet into NATO's SACLANT (Supreme Allied Command Atlantic), headed by an American admiral, meant that the Canadian navy played a key and active role in the Cuban missile crisis, a role that has been either ignored or misstated in all existing accounts of this crisis.[56] The deployment took the covering form of repeating a major SACLANT exercise of a month before, which had simulated a situation very much like the actual Cuban crisis. "In effect," Canadian Admiral Dyer has stated, "we went to our war stations." According to newly released US documents, a "submarine barrier" was established "south of Newfoundland" by October 27, and there seems little doubt that the ships on this "barrier" were Canadian.[57] The purpose was the detection and tracking of Russian submarines, but a close eye was also kept on the Russian fishing fleet which was known to possess communication abilities. The Canadian Navy deployment permitted units of the American navy to move south into the blockade zone.

Given the central role of the United States Navy in the missile crisis, this Canadian contribution was arguably a more significant measure of military support than the alert of Canadian forces in NORAD.[58] Canada was the only ally to order its forces into active duty to aid the Americans. By contrast, Harold Macmillan, who offered the most forthright political support of all the allies, refused to order an alert of British forces.[59]

When the cabinet met to discuss the situation the next morning, Prime Minister Diefenbaker and his colleagues, with one exception, were under the impression that the decision to support or not support the United States militarily still rested in their hands. The debate was pitched. Although they met twice on October 23 and again on the 24th, no formal decision about the alert ever emerged. The government, however, on its own initiative, did officially inform the Soviet embassy in Ottawa Tuesday morning that it was withdrawing landing rights for Soviet planes using Gander as a stopover en route to Cuba.

Although some accounts of this crisis have blamed the lack of a cabinet decision on Prime Minister Diefenbaker and to a lesser extent on External Affairs Minister Green, there was, in fact, a substantial cabinet split. One group within the cabinet agreed immediately with Harkness that, given Canada's NORAD commitment and an apparent Russian threat to the entire continent, the nation's security interests could best be served by declaring an alert. A second group, which included three other ministers (Alvin Hamilton, J. Waldo Monteith, and Richard Bell), as well as Diefenbaker and Green, felt those interests would be better served by avoiding any action that might appear provocative to the Soviet Union. Between these two groups lay approximately half the cabinet, who were at first uncertain as to how to proceed. Although these ministers came eventually to support Harkness, their varying degrees of resentment over the United States' failure to consult Canada initially strengthened the position taken by Diefenbaker and Green. A majority of ministers resented the American failure to consult and the lack of recognition of Canadian sovereignty.

When the ministers gathered together on the morning of October 23, most knew only what they had seen on television or read in the newspapers. None of them, except the three ministers who had been briefed by Merchant, had seen the photographic evidence. Thus they were being asked to reach a decision concerning the advisability of supporting the Americans on the basis of essentially second-hand information. This information had to be fitted, moreover, into existing images of the Cuba–United States issue, images which centered on the belief that the Americans had been overestimating and overreacting to the Cuban threat. Additional information from Washington through open channels of political communication might have revised negative attitudes, but the President never followed through on his implied promise of further contact. It now appears that the two leaders did talk once on the telephone, but it is not clear who initiated the call or what was discussed.[60]

Although little new information was being received from the United States, the Prime Minister was not without trusted sources of advice. Diefenbaker telephoned Harold Macmillan who told him that the United Kingdom had not gone on alert and would not, at this stage, since additional mobilization could easily be interpreted as a provocative measure by the Russians. This was, moreover, not the first time the two prime ministers had discussed this very problem. At a meeting in 1959, Diefenbaker himself had expressed to Macmillan his own similar misgivings about the US Strategic Air Command being placed on increased readiness at times of tension, in the context of a discussion of the Berlin issue.[61]

Macmillan's caution was an important consideration and it bolstered some Canadian predispositions. Actions taken now also had implications for the government's nuclear dilemma. Approval of the alert could have meant that the United States would request the movement of nuclear-equipped interceptors to their bases in Canada, an action that might both appear provocative and compromise the decision on deploying nuclear weapons on Canadian soil. Given the uncertain status of his minority government, voter approval was certainly one of Diefenbaker's concerns if not the rest of the cabinet's. The Prime Minister was sure that the majority of the electorate would not approve of Kennedy's action or want to be militarily involved in the Cuban affair. He was, on this score, quite wrong.[62]

The Crisis Continues

As the cabinet debate wore on, international tension heightened. On October 23, the OAS approved the quarantine with only three countries abstaining from that section of the resolution which authorized OAS members to use force against Cuba. Early on Wednesday October 24, the naval blockade went into effect. Russian ships continued to advance steadily towards Cuba. By the end of the third cabinet meeting in Ottawa on the morning of the 24th, three-fourths of the ministers had set other considerations aside and supported the Harkness position. As one former minister initially sympathetic to a non-alert stated: "We had reason to resent the lack of consultation, but it would have been foolish not to temper it with an understanding of the situation."[63]

During the afternoon of the 24th, Harkness received "a lot of intelligence on Russian preparations." He also learned that certain elements of the United States forces had moved from a "Defcon 3" to a "Defcon 2" alert, indicating full-war footing, just one step removed from actual hostilities.[64] The Defence Minister tried once more to get the political authorization he wanted. This time he succeeded. Diefenbaker was convinced that Canada's security was now gravely endangered by the reported preparations of the Soviet Union.[65] Diefenbaker still delayed formal proclamation of the alert until the next day, Thursday October 25.

During parliamentary question periods on the previous two days, government spokesmen had adroitly circumvented any lengthy discussion of Canadian response to the crisis. Harkness later admitted that he had "very carefully" phrased his answers to opposition queries. When asked by the Liberal defence critic on October 23 if Canadian units assigned to NORAD had been alerted, or if "special orders" had been transmitted to naval units, Harkness replied that "by and large the answer to that question is no."[66] The Defence Minister also denied on October 24 that Canada was taking any part in the quarantine. These answers were of course misleading, but technically correct. No alert had been proclaimed. Naval units were not actually blockading Russian ships — they were merely repeating a NATO exercise. On the other hand, when asked if Canada had defaulted on its NORAD agreement, Harkness could truthfully say "emphatically no, we have not defaulted."

Opposition members had also pressed the Prime Minister for information. One plea for assurance that the government was "doing everything possible to halt this race toward international suicide" was ruled out of order, but to other requests for information, Diefenbaker responded by asking for restraint. "Were we to place before the House various matters that might be spoken of at this time," he suggested, it would not benefit Canada's security situation, " . . . and might indeed be provocative." The theme of non-provocation runs through all of Diefenbaker's statements during the crisis. It was also a constant in the responses of External Affairs Minister Green during a half-hour television interview on the evening of October 24. "We're going to do everything we can to get this crisis settled," he said; "we don't want a nuclear war."[67]

In proclaiming the alert to the Commons on October 25, the Prime Minister's choice of words revealed the differing perceptions of Canada's national security interests which had plagued two days of cabinet discussion. Now conceding the arguments of the Harkness group, he accused the Soviet Union of reaching out across the Atlantic "to challenge the right of free men to live in peace in this hemisphere." He declared the weapons in Cuba "a direct and immediate menace to Canada . . . and indeed to all the free world, whose security depends to such an extent upon the strategic strength of the United States." In light of the "new and immediate threat" posed by the Soviet Union to the security of the continent, Diefenbaker dismissed arguments over the legality of the quarantine as "largely sterile and irrelevant. We have a situation to face," he emphasized. In order to deal with that situation, he announced that "all Canadian military forces have taken precautionary measures," and that NORAD's Canadian component had "been placed upon the same level of readiness" as the forces of the United States. It was later made clear, however, that the same level of readiness did not mean that Canada's weapons systems had been nuclear-armed.

Observing then the arguments of that group in the cabinet who had opposed the alert, the Prime Minister made the following statement:

> It has been necessary and will always remain necessary to weigh the risks of both action and inaction in such circumstances. . . . Canadians stand by their allies and their undertakings, and we intend in the present crisis to do the same. On the other hand, we shall not fail to do everything possible to seek solutions to these problems without war. We shall seek to avoid provocative action. Our purpose will be to do everything to reduce tension.

Taking encouragement from the fact that some Soviet ships had turned back from Cuba, Diefenbaker still cautioned that "it would be dangerously premature to assume that the critical phase" had passed. Returning to the basic theme of his statement on October 22, he stated that the "greatest hope" of finding a peaceful solution lay in the United Nations. While avoiding any expression of personal confidence in American leadership, Diefenbaker praised U Thant both for the way in which he was discharging his responsibilities, and for his proposal of a standstill which would permit time for negotiation.[68]

Opposition Leader Pearson spoke even more intensely of a debt to the United Nations ("the world organization . . . stands between humanity and destruction") and was less supportive than Diefenbaker had been of the quarantine as a security measure. Backing the United States, he suggested, did not necessarily mean that "all the details of that action are to be approved without qualification." Pearson also put forth the idea of a UN naval inspection force to guard against possible Russian evasion of a standstill resolution. The New Democratic Party leader expressed disdain for the "fetish that Canadians must never rock the boat of United States foreign policy," and voiced the belief that the present American course "is likely to land us on the rock of international suicide." He was also sharply critical of the American failure to consult Canada, NATO or the UN before taking unilateral action.

The Superpowers Deal

Quite oblivious to the turn of events in Ottawa, the crisis was entering a new, even more dangerous phase. The same day as Ottawa's halfhearted support was offered, President Kennedy ordered the loading of nuclear weapons on US aircraft in Europe and the open preparation of US troops for the invasion of Cuba many Americans were calling for. The Kremlin meanwhile had ordered work on the missile sites in Cuba to be stepped up. On Friday, October 26, a letter from Khrushchev arrived in Washington that appeared to be offering to withdraw the missiles in return for a US pledge not to invade Cuba. The following day, however, another, tougher message arrived demanding that the United States agree to withdraw its Jupiter missiles in Turkey as well. The same day an American U2 spy plane was shot down over Cuba by a Soviet anti-aircraft surface-to-air missile.

Although Kennedy had said he would retaliate if any US planes were shot down, faced with a mounting crisis, he chose not to do so. The ExCom decided to pursue the terms of the first Khrushchev letter and the President sent his brother to meet secretly with Soviet Ambassador Anatoly Dobrynin. Robert Kennedy told Dobrynin that the United States was prepared to agree formally to the non-invasion guarantee, warned of the mounting pressure on the White House for direct military action and insisted on a response from Moscow by the following day. He also suggested pointedly that, while the President could not now undertake publicly to withdraw the Jupiter missiles from Turkey, he was prepared to remove them in the near future in return for the Soviet missiles being removed immediately. The next morning, in an extraordinary broadcast over Radio Moscow, Khrushchev agreed to remove his missiles from Cuba. The deal was done.[69]

Recent evidence suggests that John Kennedy may have been willing by the 27th to accept a *public* trade of the Jupiters for the Soviet missiles, but only as the alternative to a military escalation such as an attack on the missile sites. The President told the ExCom on 26 October that the Americans could get the missiles out of Cuba only by an invasion or by trading.[70] The strong preference though, for political reasons, was not to link publicly the American missiles in Turkey with those the USSR had been deploying in Cuba. To one of the president's closest advisers, Defence Secretary Robert McNamara, publicly "buying 'em out" was so politically dangerous it was "not much different" from allowing the Soviet missiles to stay in Cuba, at least in the sense that "people would have interpreted this as caving in . . . including a lot of congressmen and our allies."[71]

It is clear from this perspective and mounting other evidence that a dominant concern, if not *the* dominant concern, of the President and his closest advisers was the domestic political reaction in the United States itself. The extent to which the Soviet buildup in Cuba had become a congressional election issue was no doubt a major factor in this preoccupation. A failure to deal forcefully with the missiles, coupled with the 1961 disaster at the Bay of Pigs, would have allowed opponents to brand Kennedy convincingly as a weak and ineffective president, and thus would have dealt him a personal political blow from which he might not have been able ever to recover.[72]

In October 1962, John F. Kennedy appeared victorious. Bold headlines announced Khrushchev had "backed down." Force had, apparently, won the day. The Canadian government's concerns about escalation and provocation appeared, by contrast, weak and inadequate. Across Canada, the censure was widespread and even included important elements within the Conservative Party. External Affairs Minister Green's television appearance on October 24 provoked the first outcry. Both Green and Diefenbaker had been pleased with the interview, but prominent Conservatives across Canada expressed disappointment and anger at what had seemed a confusing and evasive performance. The Young Progressive Conservatives of Manitoba sent the Prime Minister a telegram denouncing the government's position and urging open support for the quarantine.[73] In the afterglow of the successful conclusion of the crisis, disapproval within the party grew and criticism in the nation's press intensified. The Associate Minister of Defence later wrote in his memoirs that the government's behaviour "led a great many staunch Conservatives to doubt Diefenbaker's ability to lead the nation in the event of an international crisis."[74] Much of the censure focused on Canada's alleged delay in backing the United States militarily. One report claimed that Canada had "flunked" its first major NORAD test.[75] Another charged that American defence officials were "furious" over Canada's "sluggish reaction."[76] Various accounts accused the cabinet of refusing the United States request to move nuclear-equipped interceptors into Canada, to allow more US bomber flights over Canada, and to arm the squadrons at American bases in Labrador and Newfoundland with nuclear weapons.[77] Defence Minister Harkness has since said that the request was not in any event specific, but was more in the nature of a "feeler," and that the crisis was over before a decision became necessary.[78] There is also some question whether any such requests were, in fact, authorized by the American political leadership, which was at the time doing much to avoid provocative military moves, or stemmed solely from the American military, which was not displaying the same level of concern.

Given the extent of the military support offered by Canadian forces in NATO and NORAD, however, the Americans had few grounds for complaint. Although government spokesmen in the United States immediately voiced their complete satisfaction with Canadian cooperation during the missile crisis, those in the Kennedy administration who noticed Ottawa's political response were probably disappointed by it.[79] But the Canadian rhetoric, or lack of it, had exposed no weakness and posed no threat to national security interests. The Americans may also have realized that they too were vulnerable to criticism. Under the NORAD agreement, the "agreed procedure" was that the President and the Prime Minister were supposed to consult about the "risks and repercussions" of recommended joint military proposals during a crisis. This, of course, had not been followed in the case of the Cuban alert.

In his first response to the critics within his party and the press, the Prime Minister took aim at this failure:

> Canada and the United States are members of NORAD . . . As I look back on the Cuban crisis I believe that it emphasized more than ever before the necessity of there being full consultation before any action is taken or policies executed that might lead to war . . . Consultation is a prerequisite to joint and contemporaneous action being taken for it could never have been intended that either of the nations would automatically follow whatever stand the other might take.[80]

Diefenbaker's criticism was echoed not only in the press[81] but also by the Liberal leader. "Cuba," Pearson stated, "re-emphasizes the danger of one ally acting alone without consultation with others, though those others are bound to be involved in any results from the decision taken."[82] A formal memorandum written shortly after the crisis by the Under-Secretary of State for External Affairs, Norman Robertson, similarly argues that the provisions of the NORAD agreement, as Canada understood them, had not been followed by the US.[83]

Conclusion

The Cuban missile crisis was not John Diefenbaker's finest hour. But it was also not as thoroughly wrong-headed and lamentable a performance as has been portrayed. His critics have suggested Diefenbaker misjudged the seriousness of the crisis, misunderstood the strategic threat presented by the missiles, misread the concerns of Washington, and misconceived Canadian policy. On all of these points some reassessment is required by the new evidence now available. Diefenbaker cannot be criticized for Canada being slow to put forces on alert (since they were, in effect, on alert virtually from the beginning), for not providing military support (since Canada played an active role in the naval operations), and for not providing an official statement of support, given that this expression was eventually forthcoming. To be sure, it did not come forth immediately or enthusiastically, but it came.

It is also now clear that those Canadians, including Diefenbaker, who worried about American emotionalism over Cuba were quite justified in doing so. Washington's adoption of the blockade option was necessitated not just by the international situation created by the Soviet deployment but also, and perhaps even more, by the internal political situation in the United States. The dangerous state of American public and elite feelings about Cuba made the discovery of the missiles at least as much a domestic political crisis for the Kennedy administration as an international crisis for the superpowers.

Though it is doubtful how much John Diefenbaker thought through the strategic implications, it is clear he had misgivings about the wisdom of Kennedy's publicly announced course of action. It is also arguable that these were justifiable misgivings. The missile crisis did not come to a peaceful conclusion through the resolute coercive action which had worried the Canadian government. Though the blockade forced the issue of the missiles, the crisis was peacefully concluded ultimately by flexible diplomacy. In the end, Kennedy, fearful of escalation and the dangers inherent in the unfolding events he and Khrushchev had precipitated, not only accepted but offered the Soviets the sort of deal he and his advisors had soundly rejected a few days before. The misgivings about the course of action pursued initially by Washington were thus not only to be found in Ottawa.

The missiles in Cuba precipitated more than an east–west crisis and a domestic political crisis for the President. Canadians found themselves at the brink without consent — or even consultation. While the Kennedy administration was very much concerned about the views of the OAS, the views of Canada aroused little interest or attention.[84] The required measure of cooperation seems to have been simply assumed. The realization of this situation in Ottawa created an acute crisis in Canadian–American relations inextricably linked to the broader international crisis.

Canada, the only NATO ally to back the United States militarily, yet ironically criticized for insufficient support, would suffer other repercussions as a result of the missile crisis. In the next months, the government was subjected to increasing pressures, both from domestic sources and from outside Canada, to come to a decision on the acquisition of nuclear arms for the Canadian military. The impotence of Canada's weapons systems during the crisis came as a shock to the many Canadians who had not previously focused on the nuclear issue. The crisis also seriously damaged the credibility of Diefenbaker's promise that nuclear warheads, while shunned in peacetime, would be made quickly available in time of war.[85] Within the cabinet, the nuclear split hardened and became more sharply defined. At the same time, with the world having come so close to nuclear catastrophe, those who opposed nuclear arms were more than ever determined to keep them out of Canada. The major political crisis of the Diefenbaker era was now brewing.

NOTES

1. See Don Page and Don Munton, "Canadian Images of the Cold War, 1946-7" *International Journal*, Vol. XXXII, No. 3, Summer 1977, pp. 577 604.
2. See Chapter 4 in Don Munton and John Kirton, *Canadian Foreign Policty: Selected Cases* (Scarborough, ON: Prentice-Hall, 1991).
3. See, for example, (Toronto) *Globe and Mail*, December 10, 1960; *Toronto Telegram*, February 5, 1962; Denis Stairs, "Confronting Uncle Sam, Cuba and Korea," *An Independent Foreign Policy for Canada?* ed. Stephen Clarkson (Toronto: McClelland and Stewart 1968), p. 62. These differences in views and the pressures brought to bear against Canada by US officials were evident, for example, at the July 1960 closed-door meeting of the Canada–US Ministerial Committee on Joint Defence. See H. Basil Robinson, *Diefenbaker's World: A Populist in Foreign Affairs* (Toronto: University of Toronto Press, 1989), p. 146.
4. See "Why We Won't Join the Blockade to Starve Castro Out of Cuba," *Maclean's*, LXXV (April 21, 1962), p. 2. A similar comment was offered by John Holmes, "Canada and the United States in World Politics," *Foreign Affairs*, XL (October, 1961), p. 107. "A small country," Holmes said, "somewhat concerned itself with the overweening power of the United States has a certain sympathy with aspects of Castroism."
5. Robinson, *Diefenbaker's World*, p. 147. In mid-1961 Diefenbaker remarked to Robinson on "the acute nervousness of the US administration on Cuba" (p. 196).
6. Richard Preston, *Canada in World Affairs, 1959-1961* (Toronto: Oxford University Press, 1965), p. 181.

7. *House of Commons Debates*, April 19, 1961, p. 3795.
8. "The Cuban Situation," May 12, 1961, POF: Countries: Canada Security, JFK Trip to Ottawa, 5/16-8/61, folder (B), Kennedy Papers, John F. Kennedy Library. (Hereafter cited as Kennedy Papers.)
9. "The Cuban Situation," May 12, 1961, POF: Countries: Canada Security, JFK Trip to Ottawa, 5/16-18/61, folder (B), Kennedy Papers.
10. Robinson, *Diefenbaker's World*, pp. 166, 168.
11. *Washington Post*, May 12, 1961, clipping included with briefing papers, POF: Countries: Canada Security, JFK Trip to Ottawa, 5/16-18/61, folder (D), Kennedy Papers. Canada was also involved at this time to a certain degree in what have been described by the Prime Minister's foreign policy advisor as "low key attempts" with Brazil and Mexico to reduce the growing tensions between Washington and Havana. (Robinson, *Diefenbaker's World*, p. 146.)
12. Department of State Telegram from Acting Secretary Chester Bowles to Secretary Rusk, American Consulate Geneva, May 12, 1961, POF: Countries, Canada Security, JFK Trip to Ottawa, 5/16-18/61, folder (D), Kennedy Papers.
13. Canada's senior diplomat at the time, Norman Robertson, was very much of this view. See J.L. Granatstein, *A Man of Influence* (Ottawa: Deneau Publishers, 1981), pp. 343, 345.
14. *Debates*, May 19, 1961, p. 5039.
15. "Trends in Canadian Foreign Policy," National Intelligence Estimate Number 99-61, May 2, 1961, POF: Countries: Canada Security, JFK Trip to Ottawa, 5/16-18/61, folder (D), Kennedy Papers.
16. "Cuban Situation," May 12, 1961, POF: Countries: Canada Security, JFK Trip to Ottawa, 5/16-18/61, Folder (B) Kennedy Papers.
17. John T. Saywell (ed.), *Canadian Annual Review for 1962* (Toronto, 1963), p. 81. In an article entitled "How Canada Helps Keep Castro Going," *U.S. News and World Report* asserted that "food, machinery, aircraft engines and other goods from Canada — even explosives — are being used by Cuba's Communist masters to stave off any internal crisis that might spark an uprising." LII (February 26, 1962), p. 6.
18. Department of State Telegram to American Embassy in Ottawa, "Text of Letter from President to Prime Minister," October 19, 1962, POF: Countries: Canada Security, 1961-1963, Kennedy Papers.
19. *American Foreign Policy, Current Documents 1962* (Washington, 1966), pp. 369, 374.
20. James G. Blight and David A. Welch, *On the Brink: Americans and Soviets Reexamine the Cuban Missile Crisis* (New York: Noonday, 1990), pp. 407, 409.
21. See Graham T. Allison, *The Essence of Decision* (Boston: Little Brown, 1971) and Blight and Welch, *On the Brink*.
22. Various material, Cuba General, 4/63-11/63, Kennedy Papers. See also Blight and Welch, *On the Brink*, and Raymond L. Garthoff, *Reflections on the Cuban Missile Crisis* (Washington, D.C.: Brookings, 1987), pp. 17, 78-9. Although the hard evidence is not conclusive, some recently available materials suggest the possibility that the Kennedy administration was "moving toward a military attack on Cuba in the fall of 1962, even before it discovered the Soviet strategic missiles." See James G. Hershberg, "Before 'The Missiles of October': Did Kennedy Plan a Military Strike against Cuba?" *Diplomatic History*, Spring, 1991.
23. Memorandum to the President, "Reactions to Cuba in Western Europe," May 3, 1961, Cuba Security — 1961, Kennedy Papers.
24. On the role of Congressional critics, see Robert A. Divine (ed.), *The Cuban Missile Crisis* (Chicago, 1971), pp. 7, 9, 14; Louise Fitzsimmons, *The Kennedy Doctrine* (New York, 1972), pp. 129-39.
25. Abram Chayes in Blight and Welch, *On the Brink*, p. 40.
26. Robinson, *Diefenbaker's World*, p. 283.
27. September 22, 1962.
28. *Debates*, October 26, 1962, p. 567.
29. These deliberations have been described by various participants, including Robert F. Kennedy, *Thirteen Days; A Memoir of the Cuban Missile Crisis* (New York: Norton, 1969); Theodore C. Sorenson, *Kennedy* (New York: Harper and Row, 1965); and analyzed at length by Allison, *Essence of Decision*, pp. 185-210. Unknown to most of the participants, however, the ExCom meetings (and numerous other White House meetings of this period) were secretly tape-recorded. Transcriptions of these tapes are now available at the John F. Kennedy Library in Boston, and have been excerpted. See "White House Tapes and Minutes of the Cuban

Missile Crisis," *International Security*, Vol. 10, No. 1, Summer 1985, pp. 164–203, and "October 27, 1962: Transcripts of the Meetings of the ExCom," *International Security*, Vol. 12, No. 3, Winter 1987–88, pp. 30–92.

30. Robert McNamara in "White House Tapes . . .," *International Security*, pp. 164–203. A confidential memorandum to the President from Lou Harris, his political pollster, focusing on the election campaign and drafted only days before the missile crisis developed warned Kennedy that while he was doing well on some other issues such as the racial problem, the balance of American public opinion on his policies toward Cuba was overwhelmingly negative. Over 80% in some key states were in favour of a blockade. The domestic political message was presumably clear. (Memorandum to the President from Louis Harris, "Subject: The New Shape of this Campaign," 4 October 1962, POF, Polls, General, Kennedy Papers). Former President Eisenhower suspected that domestic politics might be involved. See Elie Abel, *The Missile Crisis* (New York: Bantam, 1966), p. 64. So did some Canadians; "There was a nagging worry here which no one put into words publicly but which some responsible people expressed privately . . . that the American reaction . . . may not be completely separate from the American election campaign." *Montreal Star*, October 23.

31. Fen Osler Hampson, "The Divided Decision-Maker: American Domestic Politics and the Cuban Crises," *International Security*, Vol. 9, No. 3, Winter 1984-5, pp. 141, 149.

32. The Ormsby-Gore-Kennedy friendship has been described as a "unique relationship between an Ambassador and a President with no parallel in modern times." David Nunnerley, *President Kennedy and Britain* (New York, 1972), p. 43.

33. Harold Macmillan, *At the End of the Day, 1961–1963* (London, 1973), pp. 182, 186.

34. Message from President Kennedy to Prime Minister Diefenbaker, October 22, 1962, POF: Countries: Canada Security, 1961–1963, Kennedy Papers.

35. Macmillan, *End of the Day*, p. 186.

36. Interview with the Hon. Livingston Merchant, June 18, 1974.

37. JFK message to Diefenbaker, October 22, 1962, POF: Countries: Canada Security, 1961–1963, Kennedy Papers.

38. Macmillan, *End of the Day*, pp. 185–87.

39. Although Merchant thought that the Prime Minister had probably been briefed by his own military on the activity in Cuba, Diefenbaker gave no sign he knew anything at all. It appears, however, that Diefenbaker, in fact, did know by Sunday, 21 October, the day before the Merchant visit and the Kennedy speech, that a serious crisis over Cuba was brewing and that it concerned Soviet missile installations. (Robinson, *Diefenbaker's World*, p. 285.) He almost certainly knew no details, however.

40. *Debates*, October 22, 1962, pp. 805–06.

41. This proposal, contained in a memorandum drafted before the US photo-reconnaissance evidence had been revealed, came from the Under-Secretary of External Affairs, Norman Robertson. This document also drew an explicit analogy with the Suez siuation, which, as Diefenbaker was well aware, had led to Lester Pearson's receipt of the Nobel Peace Prize (Robinson, *Diefenbaker's World*, p. 288). Although Diefenbaker was subsequently much criticized for this proposal, the US State Department was at this time working on a UN-centred plan for the withdrawal of the missiles which would have involved an "observer corps" of inspectors in Cuba and UN-supervised inspection of all nuclear missile sites. Secretary of State Dean Rusk presented these plans to the ExCom on Friday 26 October.

42. The above quotations are all from *Debates*, October 22, 1962, pp. 806–07.

43. Saywell, *Review 1962*, p. 128.

44. This concern for working within the UN is very much evident in such cases as the Korean War and the Suez crisis. See Chapters 4 and 5 of Munton and Kirton, *Canadian Foreign Policy*.

45. This asymmetry of perceptions is one of the most common observations of research on perceptions that members of one group tend to perceive those of another group as like-minded even when they are not. The moderation of the Kennedy administration was recognized by officials in the Canadian embassy in Washington, but not initially by their political masters in Ottawa.

46. Abel, *The Missile Crisis*, p. 64.

47. Macmillan, *End of the Day*, p. 187.

48. Defense Condition 3 indicates very serious international tension. Defcon 5 is normal; Defcon 1 is war.

49. Charles Foulkes, "The Complications of Continental Defence," *Neighbors Taken for Granted*, ed. Livingston Merchant (New York, 1966), p. 121.

50. Except where notes indicate otherwise, the account of this meeting, which lasted until approximately 2 A.M. on October 23, has been put together from interviews with Harkness, Miller, Dunlap and an interview with General G. Walsh (Chief of General Staff), October 25, 1974.

51. As a briefing memorandum prepared for President Kennedy in 1961 had stated, "loss or dimunition of U.S. use of Canadian air space and real estate and the contributions of the Canadian military, particularly the RCAF and Royal Canadian Navy, would be intolerable in time of crisis." Memorandum for the President, February 17, 1961, POF: Countries: Canada Security, 1961–1963, Kennedy Papers.

52. Miller interview, October 31, 1974.

53. NORAD headquarters announced on January 1, 1963, that Canadian units had been on alert since the beginning of the crisis. *Globe and Mail*, January 2, 1963.

54. For example, the recall of men on longer leave and evacuations. Interview with Rear Admiral Kenneth Dyer, October 28, 1974.

55. Harkness interview, July 22, 1974.

56. None of the accounts written from the US point of view mention it. Of Canadian accounts only Peyton Lyon and Robert Reford comment. Lyon states that "The movement of RCN ships out of Halifax freed ships of the U.S. Navy to take up positions further south in the quarantine area." (*Canada in World Affairs, 1961-63* [Toronto: Canadian Institute of International Affairs, Oxford, 1968], p. 42.) Reford makes a similar statement but neither source deals with the NATO implications. (*Canada and Three Crises* [Toronto: Canadian Institute of International Affairs], p. 213.)

57. Blight and Welch, *On the Brink*, p. 61. Rear Admiral Kenneth Dyer, who held the "triple-hatted" position of Atlantic Maritime Commander responsible for the Chairman of the Chief of Staff, Atlantic Flag Officer responsible to the Naval Chief, and most importantly, Canadian Atlantic Area Commander responsible to SACLANT's Admiral Wright in Norfolk, proudly notes in his career résumé that "a major operational test of our effectiveness was achieved during the Cuban missile crisis when all available maritime forces were deployed at short notice in accordance with NATO plans." (Résumé copy provided by Admiral Dyer.)

58. It can be argued that the NORAD contribution mattered far less. One critic of Canadian participation in NORAD, writing under the impression that there had been no alert until the 24th, poses the following question: "Did this hesitancy expose the United States to a possible devastating nuclear attack and did it make the Strategic Air Command vulnerable? The answer is clearly, 'no.' If the Russians had launched a nuclear attack, missiles would have been launched first, and there "was and still is no defence against missiles." SAC missiles were alerted; SAC bombers — not under NORAD control — were dispersed. "The deterrent was protected as well as it could have been." John W. Warnock, *Partner to Behemoth: The Military Policy of a Satellite Canada* (Toronto: New Press, 1970), p. 176.

59. Macmillan recorded in his diary conversations he had with General Lauris Norstad, NATO's Supreme Allied Commander in Europe, on October 22, in which Norstad agreed that NATO forces ought not go on alert. See Macmillan, *End of the Day*, pp. 190, 195.

60. Diefenbaker's memoirs make reference to a phone call with Kennedy on Monday, 22 October, but most other sources contradict this claim. Basil Robinson, citing Diefenbaker's secretary as the source, states there was a "bad-tempered" call with the President on Tuesday, 23 October. (Robinson, *Diefenbaker's World*.)

61. Robinson, *Diefenbaker's World*, p. 176.

62. A poll taken in the first two weeks of November showed that 79% of Canadians approved of Kennedy's action. *Globe and Mail*, November 23, 1962. At the same time, in the US, approval of Kennedy's presidential performance climbed to "nearly 80%." Robert A. Divine (ed.), *The Cuban Missile Crisis* (Chicago, 1971), p. 58.

63. Interview with the Hon. E. Davie Fulton, July 11, 1974.

64. Canadian apprehensions about American tendencies to provoke the Soviets would not have been allayed had they known that the chief of the US Strategic Air Command had deliberately and without authorization sent the order to move to Defcon 2 status (imminent enemy attack expected) "in the clear," rather than in secret, precisely to ensure the Russians would know about it. This was, incidentally, the highest alert level *ever* of American forces. (Blight and Welch, *On the Brink*, pp. 3, 75).

65. Although the source of this intelligence about Soviet preparations is not known, it is now clear that it was false, or at least greatly exaggerated. The Soviet military were not at any point during the crisis put on heightened alert. See Marc Trachtenberg, "The Influence

of Nuclear Weapons in the Cuban Missile Crisis," *International Security*, Vol. 10, No. 1 (Summer 1985), pp. 137-63. It is unclear whether or not Diefenbaker, in fact, knew that Harkness had already, in effect, put the Canadian forces on alert. Although Diefenbaker himself consistently denied he did, a former senior staffer suspects he did know. "Not much," he says, "escaped the Diefenbaker antennae." (Robinson, *Diefenbaker's World*, p. 288.)

66. These and following comments are from *Debates*, October 23 and 24, 1962, pp. 822, 883, 884-5.

67. From a transcript provided by the Canadian Broadcasting Corporation, Green interview, July 9, 1974. A good part of the questioning in the interview was an attempt to elicit a satisfactory response as to the degree of support Canada was offering the United States, but Green avoided any endorsement of Kennedy's blockade. He stated that he didn't know what history would say about the President's action, "but that action has been taken now, and I think the important fact is what's done from now on."

68. For these and following comments, see *Debates*, October 25, 1962, pp. 911-17.

69. None of the early accounts of the missile crisis, including those by Robert Kennedy, *Thirteen Days*, and White House aide Ted Sorenson, *Kennedy*, portray the withdrawal of the Jupiter missiles as an explicit provision of the agreement which ended the crisis.

70. Blight and Welch, *On the Brink*, pp. 102, 108, 190; "White House Tapes," p. 195.

71. Blight and Welch, *On the Brink*, p. 190.

72. This point is reinforced in a number of ways. Blight and Welch, for example, argue that a basic cause of the crisis was Khrushchev's lack of understanding of the potency of American public opinion on both Cuba *per se* and the extent of increasing Soviet influence there. (Blight and Welch, *On the Brink*, p. 303.)

73. Green interview, July 9, 1974.

74. Pierre Sevigny, *This Game of Politics* (Toronto, 1966), p. 253.

75. Warner Troyer, "We Flunked the NORAD Test," *Commentator*, VI (December 1962), 6-7. It might be noted here that the text of the agreement itself stresses the "fullest possible consultation . . . on all matters affecting the joint defence of North America," but formally left open the question of whether such consultation was a prerequisite during an emergency or only during the stage of contingency planning. *Canada Treaty Series*, No. 9.

76. *The Financial Post*, November 3, 1962.

77. "Canada: Defensive Gap," *Time*, LXXX (November 9, 1962), 41. For Harkness's response to a similar report see *Debates*, November 2, 1962, p. 1218.

78. Harkness interview, July 22, 1974. According to Harkness, some confusion arose because the Americans did request extra flights, but not during the crisis. An increase above the usual number was requested for the month of November, and this was approved by Harkness.

79. *Globe and Mail*, November 5, 1962. Theodore Sorenson refers to "some wavering by Canada" (*Kennedy*, p. 705).

80. Canadian Institute of International Affairs Library: Canada–Foreign Relations — Cuba. Notes for Diefenbaker Address to Zionist Organization of Canada, Toronto, November 5, 1962.

81. See the *Globe and Mail*, November 7, 1962, and *Toronto Star*, November 1, 1962, quoted in Saywell, *Review 1962*, pp. 134-35.

82. *The Nation's Business*, October 31, 1962, quoted in Reford, *Three Crises*, p. 210.

83. Department of External Affairs, file 50309-40, NAR to Minister, 7 November 1962, cited in Granatstein, *A Man of Influence*, p. 353.

84. A summary of the foreign press response to the blockade, found in President Kennedy's office files, makes it clear that a differing perception was not expected from the Canadians. The nine-page résumé covers the press reaction of Europe, Latin America, Asia, Africa and the Middle East but does not mention a single Canadian newspaper. USIA Summary of Foreign Press, October 23, 1962, POF: Countries: Cuba 1962, Kennedy Papers.

85. Lyon, *Canada in World Affairs, 1961-63*, p. 119. As one Ottawa commentator wrote on October 27, the crisis "laid at rest for all time the government's theory that the time to acquire nuclear weapons is on the eve of actual hostilities." Quoted in Saywell, *Review 1962*, p. 135.

Peacekeeping: Did Canada Make a Difference? And What Difference Did Peacekeeping Make to Canada?

J.L. GRANATSTEIN

If there is any one area of foreign and defence policy in which Canada did unquestionably make a difference, it is surely in the area of peacekeeping. Lester Pearson's role during the Suez Crisis of 1956 and his subsequent Nobel Peace Prize fixed Canadian — and global — attention on the idea of interposing troops from many nations between warring armies. Before 1956, U.N. and other peacekeeping operations were modest efforts, of limited success, and carried out by relatively modest groups of observers; after 1956, peacekeeping was often a large-scale operation, regrettably also of limited success, and carried out by infantry, armoured reconnaissance, and service troops, as well as air force personnel, sometimes in combat roles. The difference was marked, and much of the change had occurred because of Pearson's initiative, diplomatic skill, and assessment of the need at Suez. Later crises in the Congo, Cyprus, the Middle East, Vietnam, the Iran-Iraq borderlands, Latin America, and the Sahara built on the experience of 1956, and in every case Canadian service personnel and peacekeeping expertise played an important part. More to the point, Canada tried hard to ready its armed forces for peacekeeping and to spread its hard-won knowledge to other nations. The designation of a stand-by infantry battalion and of army and air force peacekeeping specialists was one sign of Canada's initiative. A military peacekeeping conference for like-minded nations held in Ottawa in the mid-1960s was another. Repeated efforts to improve the U.N.'s creaky organizational machinery and stabilize its financing of peacekeeping operations were still others. We have done our part and paid our dues in this area, and the world is likely a better place for our efforts.

Has Canada made a difference? There can be no doubt that, in peacekeeping, we have. But to ask only that question is to overlook other, more important ones. Why were Canadians so attracted to the idea of peacekeeping? What was the attitude of the bureaucracy and the armed forces to the concept? Has that attitude changed? And, if so, why and how? And, finally, has the idea of peacekeeping now come to play too large a role, taking precedence in the Canadian mind? Has the support

SOURCE: "Peacekeeping: Did Canada Make a Difference? And What Difference Did Peacekeeping Make to Canada?" in John English and Norman Hillmer, eds., *Making a Difference?: Canada's Foreign Policy in a Changing World Order* (Toronto: Lester Publishing, 1992), pp. 222–36.

for peacekeeping begun to affect policies in other areas? This brief essay examines these questions.

* * *

"Ours is not a divine mission to mediate," military historian John Holmes wrote in 1984. "Our hand is strengthened by acknowledged success," he went on shrewdly, "but it is weakened if planting the maple leaf becomes the priority."[1] Too often Canada's participation in peacekeeping operations (PKOs) has had some of this "planting the flag" idea about it, a sense that we must maintain our record as the country that has served on more PKOs than any other — whether or not those operations made sense, had much chance of success, or exposed our servicemen and servicewomen to unnecessary risks in an unstable area of the world.

Where did the idea of Canada as peacekeeper *par excellence* originate? Certainly it is not inherent in Canada's origins, which were as violent as those of any nation. The litany of our aboriginal wars, rebellions, bloody strikes, and participation in wars, large and small, is too well known to need reiteration here, and we should accept that violence has been, and might be in the future, as Canadian as apple pie. Probably the idea emerged out of the missionary strain in Canadian Protestantism and Roman Catholicism that saw Canadian men and women go abroad in substantial numbers in the nineteenth and twentieth centuries to bring the word of God to India, Africa, and China. Virtually every church in English and French Canada had a missionary family or religious order in its prayers and as the recipient of its contributions, and letters from the mission fields were staples of Sunday services and church bulletins. Missionaries nowadays do not command good press, the Christian preachers of those simple days before the Second World War more often being painted as despoilers of cultures than as saviours of souls and healers of the sick. But the "do-good" impulse that they represented was a powerful one, and it had its strong resonances in the Department of External Affairs.

So many of External's diplomats were sons of missionaries or of the manse. Some were born in China or in other mission fields; others followed clergyman fathers from parish to parish, imbibing the idealism of the social gospel along with their Bible studies. J.S. Woodsworth exhibited this kind of idealism in political life, and it was not insignificant that one of his sons joined External. Lester Pearson, of course, was another whose Methodist upbringing undoubtedly shaped him profoundly.

But so, too, did Pearson's experiences — and those of his entire generation — in the Great War. The shattering cataclysm of the slaughter on the Western Front cannot be underestimated, especially as it was followed within twenty years by another and even more horrific war. The Great War had sprung from obscure troubles in the Balkans; the

1939 war arose from Hitler's expansionist aims, focused in the summer of 1939 on the Polish Corridor. Small patches of land of relative insignificance, in other words, could lead to global catastrophe. Surely there had to be a better way, and the United Nations was summoned forth in 1945 as an attempt to create a collective security organization with enough teeth to keep aggressor states in check.

Canada had played its part in resisting the aggressors during the world wars, and it had learned something from those two experiences. The most important lesson was that isolation was no guarantee of safety in the modern world and that isolationism as a doctrine was equivalent to fool's gold. Another lesson was that it was sometimes very difficult to get along with your friends. Canadian prime ministers from Macdonald on had realized that about the British, who were certain always that they knew best and that the colonial's duty was to contribute to England's defences and coffers.[2] In the Second World War, however, Canada for the first time cast its lot with that of the United States, and while Ottawa's men got on better with the Americans on a personal basis than they ever had with the British, there were perils, nonetheless. The new superpower was as arrogant in its conviction of rectitude as Britain had ever been, as convinced that God was on Washington's side, and that Ottawa's role was to follow dutifully in its wake. Canadian policy in the postwar world would try to maintain a careful balance between cooperation with the United States and independent action. This was especially true at the United Nations.[3] And peacekeeping, while it often served U.S. interests, to be sure, nonetheless had about it a powerful aura of independence and the implicit sense that it served higher interests than simply those of the United States, or even the West.

The coming of the Cold War paralyzed most of the functions of the U.N., but peacekeeping, initially by observer forces in areas of the world that were either of little importance to the Great Powers or else too dangerous to be allowed to fester, somehow survived.[4] We have now forgotten that Canada initially was not enthusiastic about the idea of participation in U.N. peacekeeping operations. At the 1945 San Francisco United Nations Conference on International Organization, at a time when the focus was on large U.N. military forces to crush aggression, Mackenzie King's Canada inevitably worried about being forced to join in wars without a say in the decisions that led up to them. The United Nations could not become a larger and more powerful replacement for Downing Street and Whitehall, against which Sir Wilfrid Laurier and Mackenzie King had fought for a half-century. The plans of the U.N.'s Military Staff Committee went a-glimmering with the Cold War, but our continuing caution was evident when the U.N. set up observer missions around the borders of the new states of Israel and in the flashpoint state of Kashmir, strategically located between India and Pakistan. Requests for officer-observers in 1948 were treated very coldly by the Department of National Defence in Ottawa. The army was understrength and not very well trained; no one could be spared; and there might be difficulties with Jewish Canadians or with Commonwealth partners. "Ask someone else, please," was the message.

But, in fact, likely because Pearson had just become secretary of state for External Affairs and because Canada was on the Security Council at the time of the creation of the U.N. Military Observer Group in India–Pakistan, Canada did reluctantly agree to send four observers from the reserve army early in 1949. That number was increased to eight later that year, and, in 1950, the regular force took over the commitment. Canadian participation in the U.N. Truce Supervisory Organization (UNTSO) in the Middle East did not begin until 1954, when four officers were seconded for duty there. Before the end of the year, Major-General E.L.M. Burns, a corps commander during the Italian campaign and a senior bureaucrat as the deputy minister of Veterans' Affairs, became UNTSO's commander.[5] Burns's appointment was to have important consequences in shaping Canada's first major peacekeeping contribution.

The same year, Canada found itself unexpectedly asked to participate in a peacekeeping venture outside the ambit of the United Nations. The Geneva Conference, called to wind up the Korean War and provide a cover for France's extrication from the swamp it had made for itself in Indo-China, asked Canada, Poland, and India to create an International Control Commission (ICC) in each of the three successor states of French Indo-China. Canada was a Western democracy and the least objectionable of them to China; Poland was a Soviet satellite, but was deemed acceptable to the West; and India was anti-colonialist, neutral, and a Commonwealth member. Surprised by the request, Ottawa again was genuinely reluctant to participate, not least because the legal basis of the Geneva agreements was hazy and because the Americans were dissociating themselves from them before the ink had dried. Would participating involve us in continuing trouble with Washington? Another reason for Ottawa's reluctance was that the commitment was relatively large; officers, almost all of whom had to be bilingual, were needed, and the armed forces, as usual, were short of such individuals. But Canada found that it could not say no — "If . . . by participating . . . Canada can assist in establishing . . . security and stability in Southeast Asia," the government's press release put it, "we will be serving our own country as well as the cause of peace" — and accepted the commitment. Approximately 150 military personnel and External Affairs diplomats proceeded to Laos, Cambodia, and Vietnam, a group that included three major-generals, eighty army officers, a sprinkling of naval and RCAF officers, and a handful of enlisted men. That was a serious drain on limited resources, one that was resented by National Defence Headquarters at a time when the country's commitments to NATO were large and taken very seriously indeed.

The Indo-China commitment was wearing and wearying. The Indians maintained an air of biased impartiality; the Poles were openly partisan; and the Canadians, after trying to be judicious, soon found that fairness was unfair to the anti-communist elements in all three of the new countries. For the next nineteen years, the ICCs limped along in the midst of war; their presence in Indo-China "radicalized" a generation of military officers and diplomats, in the sense that their experience strengthened their conviction that the communists, Vietnamese and Polish, were totally unscrupulous.[6] On the other hand, Canada's ICC commitment turned out to be a blessing in disguise when the United States became militarily involved in a major way in Vietnam. U.S. allies around the world were pressured to contribute troops to the war, but Canada, sheltering behind its ICC role, was able to deflect Washington's demands. Still, Canadian servicemen and diplomats gathered information for the Americans in North Vietnam and delivered messages from Washington to the leadership in Hanoi. It was obviously sometimes hard to separate the peacekeeper's duty from that of the anti-communist ally.

Canada's military commitment to peacekeeping would soon increase substantially, in 1956, when the Suez Crisis erupted with the Anglo–French–Israeli collusion and attack on Egypt. Prime ministers Louis St. Laurent and Anthony Eden exchanged heated telegrams as the Canadian fumed over the lies despatched from Downing Street.[7] The "supermen of Europe," St. Laurent said in Parliament, had had their day. So it seemed, and especially so when the militarily weak British and French had to cut their attacks short, brought to heel by U.S. pressure on the pound sterling and the franc, and by outrage at the U.N.

Meanwhile, because General Burns was already on the scene at UNTSO, he was tapped to be the commander of the new United Nations Emergency Force (UNEF), created at New York by Pearson and Secretary General Dag Hammarskjöld. And because Burns was there, he was able to step into the problem caused by President Nasser's objection to having Canadian infantry as part of the UNEF. They marched under the same flag as the British invaders, they wore the same uniforms, and the name of the regiment selected for UNEF duty, the Queen's Own Rifles of Canada, was almost literally a red flag to the Egyptian leader, who feared that incidents between his people and the Canadians might cause serious difficulties. The simple truth is that Nasser was right. Burns found the way out of an increasingly embarrassing situation for the Liberals in Ottawa by suggesting that almost any country could provide infantry, and that what UNEF really needed were logistics personnel, which scarcely any of the potential eligible contributors, other than Canada, could provide.[8] In fact, that was precisely correct. Other than the Great Powers and a few of the Dominions (some of whom, like Australia, had taken too much of a pro-British position in the crisis to be even remotely acceptable to the Egyptians), very few nations had skilled military specialists or an air-transport capability. Canada did, because its military had always been prepared for overseas service and, in the 1950s, was relatively well equipped for its NATO role on the Central European front. The irony is clear: Canada's role as a Cold Warrior had given us the types of military forces that were most useful for peacekeeping. In the end, some one thousand Canadians in the various essential services (and including an armoured reconnaissance squadron to assuage Canada's military ardour) duly went to UNEF duty, where they remained until Nasser ordered them out of Egypt in the run-up to the 1967 Arab–Israeli War. That expulsion caused a traumatic shock to Canadian public opinion, dealing peacekeeping one of its very few blows here in the third of a century after 1956.

The impression persists that Nasser's objections to Canada in 1956 and 1967 came as a great surprise to Pearson and the country. Canadians (or English-speaking ones, at least), while still British in their outlook when the UNEF was established, were not used to having their bona fides questioned, and Pearson's initial idea in the heart of the crisis was that the British and French invaders might lay down the Union Jack and the *tricolore* for the blue flag of the United Nations. The invaders, in other words, could become the peacekeepers. It took almost no time for the Canadian to realize that this was simply not on in the atmosphere of the General Assembly at the end of October 1956, but it was nonetheless revealing that the anglocentric Pearson thought, however briefly, that it might be.[9] The Suez Crisis had made it clear, as it had not been before, that our British connections might not always be an asset in the world.[10]

What made all this even more difficult for the government was that the Progressive Conservative Opposition had had a field-day charging that Canada had sold out Britain and France, its mother countries and historic allies, and had slavishly followed a course laid down by Washington. Peacekeeping, in other words, was not going to be a bed of roses, and if Pearson soon won his well-deserved Nobel Peace Prize and the Liberal leadership, John Diefenbaker and the Conservatives won the general election of 1957. Most accounts agree that Canada's UNEF role cut little ice with the electors, more of them seeming to turn against the Liberals for their "betrayal" of Britain than voting for them for Pearson's U.N. role.[11] In 1967, Canada's expulsion from Egypt apparently had little political weight, probably because Pearson, then prime minister, seemed to know what he was about and because the war that engulfed the region (and that caused death and injury to other nations' peacekeeping troops still in the Sinai) followed so quickly on the departure of Canadian troops. The prevailing mood here was simply relief.

In 1958, however, once the Liberals had been driven from office, virtually everyone in Canada had basked in the glow of Pearson's Nobel Prize. This was widely interpreted a sign of Canada's new maturity in the world, and in a curious way that is extraordinarily difficult to trace, peacekeeping became Canada's *métier*. So much so, in fact, that when John Diefenbaker and his Department of National Defence showed little desire to participate in the U.N. operation in the Congo in 1960 (ONUC), public opinion literally forced the government's hand. It was not that Diefenbaker was against peacekeeping or the U.N. While he had been unhappy with Pearson's role at the U.N. during the Suez affair, he was not backward in claiming that he was the first to advance the very idea of peacekeeping forces;[12] moreover, his government was the first to put an infantry battalion on stand-by for U.N. service in 1958, and he sent peacekeepers to Lebanon in the same year. But in 1960, the army, as always hampered by the demands of its NATO commitments, by tight budgets, and by a genuine shortage of signals personnel, now had to provide a squadron of the Royal Canadian Corps of Signals and other units, including RCAF transport aircraft and crews, for the new U.N. force. Once again, there were few other acceptable contributors to ONUC who could possibly provide such technicians. Soon after their arrival in the chaos of a suddenly liberated colonial state, Canadians were attacked and beaten by mobs of soldiery, apparently in the mistaken belief that they were Belgian paratroopers. Later still, Canadian units came under fire on a number of occasions as the U.N. force became involved in open war with separatist Congolese elements. While they did their tasks well in these difficult situations, it might well be questioned whether Diefenbaker's initial response was not the correct one.

At least the Congo operation ended within a measurable time frame. The next major peacekeeping operation, that in Cyprus, did not. The Mediterranean island, divided between Greek- and Turkish-speaking Cypriots, was in turmoil in 1964. The Greek majority wanted *enosis*, political union with Greece; the Turks (and Turkey) adamantly resisted any such thing, and there was fighting in the streets and in the hills.

What made this crisis unusual was that Cyprus was a Commonwealth state (the British continued to maintain bases on the island), and that Greece and Turkey were both NATO allies. The other NATO partners, not least the United States, looked with dismay on the prospect of fighting between the Greeks and Turks, and contemplated the imminent collapse of NATO's southern flank with horror. It was inevitable that efforts to install a peacekeeping force should proceed with urgency, but neither NATO nor the Commonwealth was able to get President Makarios of Cyprus to agree to receive forces raised by them. It had to be a U.N. force, Makarios maintained.

Canada had been tapped to provide troops for Cyprus by both the Commonwealth and NATO, and it was asked once more by the U.N. For a time, indeed, despite their government's concerns about the way the force was being organized, financed, and administered, the Canadian infantry battalion was the only force the U.N. had on the island, other than the British, who were exceedingly uncomfortable in their role. Then secretary of state for External Affairs, Paul Martin, began to work the telephones, creating a force out of nothing. The Americans were duly impressed at the way Canada had rescued the situation, President Lyndon Johnson asking Prime Minister Pearson what he could do for him in return. "Nothing at the moment, Mr. President," Pearson replied, noting carefully that he had some credit in the bank of American goodwill.[13]

Canada's concerns about the Cyprus force were more than justified. The commitment begun in 1964, supposedly for a term of six months, has continued to the present, and promises to go on for the foreseeable future. The U.N. force has survived Turkish invasion, rioting, ennui, and the appalling inefficiencies of the U.N.'s administration,[14] and some Canadian servicemen of long service have put in six, seven, or eight six-month tours of duty on the island. Cyprus was and is an object lesson that peacekeeping is not sufficient and that peacemaking has to be part of every U.N. mandate. The irony of the situation is that the Canadian military, once unhappy about the Cyprus commitment that took a battalion away from training to fight the Soviets in Germany, now look at the role very differently. With the end of the Cold War, the liberation of Eastern Europe, the dissolution of the Soviet Union, and the coming drastic reduction in Canada's NATO commitment, Cyprus is the only continuing locale for small-unit training in a near-combat situation. The once-dreary duty has become the army's main active role, hailed for its training value; with Canada's other commitments to PKOs, it is now the best argument the Department of National Defence can muster for continuing to maintain any credible forces at all in a world of *détente*.

★   ★   ★

My account thus far has lightly traced several of the early peacekeeping operations. There is little point in continuing to chronicle the operations and the Canadian role in them. But it is important to remember that Canadians were not asked to participate in any of the PKOs for their inherent neutralism or because our soldiers and airmen were the equivalent of a gendarmerie. Far from it. We were wanted in Cyprus primarily because we were a NATO power; we were needed in the Suez because, as a NATO ally with a tradition of overseas service in two world wars, we had sophisticated technical capabilities; and we were a natural choice for the ICCs because we were a *Western* democracy. Neutralism or military weakness, in other words, had nothing at all to do with our acceptability as a peacekeeper.

And yet, somehow, Canadians came to believe that they did. Partly, this belief came about because peacekeeping was a role that made us noticeably different from the Americans. The Yanks fought wars, Canadians said, pointing at Vietnam, Grenada, and Panama, while Johnny Canuck kept the peace. In an era in which the military called the shots around the world and defence spending ate up superpower budgets, Canada's main claim to fame was its peacekeeping, its *anti-military* military role. In an era of increasing continentalism, at a time when Canada's independence was seemingly under assault from foreign investors and the all-pervasive force of American culture, such simple myth-making was probably understandable, and perhaps even necessary. All the better, then, that peacekeeping was one of the few roles for our armed forces that could unite all Canadians. New Democrats who disliked NATO, NORAD, and Washington could burst with pride over Canada's U.N. efforts; Quebeckers, historically averse to overseas commitments, beamed at the exploits of the Vandoos in Cyprus or the gallant efforts of French-speaking officers in the Congo. Liberals and Tories vied with each other in urging more and more peacekeeping on the government. After all, were we not maintaining order among the fractious nations and peoples of the world? What could be more Canadian than that?

And so we sent a force to Vietnam once more in 1973, our decision aided by strong pressure from Washington, though sensibly, this time, the Trudeau government slapped some tough conditions in place and followed what it called an "open mouth" policy of telling the truth about violations of the truce. More to the point, when the new ICC could not carry out its role with any chance of success, Canada pulled out its forces. There was little criticism of that, however, probably because all Canadians recognized the intractability of the Vietnamese problem. "Canada would act for peace," two historians suggested, "but not in a charade."[15] It remains only to say that the United States was most unhappy at Canada's withdrawal; likely Washington's unhappiness helped mute any criticism that might have fallen on Ottawa from peacekeeping's Canadian supporters.

And those supporters were legion. Let me, in my anecdotage, give one personal example of the support peacekeeping had come to muster. In August 1988 the United Nations authorized the establishment of UNIIMOG, the U.N. Iran–Iraq Military Observer Group, set up to oversee the cease-fire that brought the eight-year-long war between Iran and Iraq to its end. Canada was asked to participate, once again with a signals unit. I was called by the *Globe and Mail* and asked my opinion of the nation's participation in UNIIMOG, and I suggested that it was a mistake to put Canadian troops into a situation in which they would be at the mercy of what I called "two lunatic governments." That quote, which the next day ended up on page one as the lead story — and which literally made me fall out of bed as I read the newspaper with my coffee — produced some fifteen telephone calls from radio and TV stations and newspapers within three hours, almost all of them vehemently critical of me for daring to suggest that Canada ought not to participate. Both the Iranian and Iraqi governments *were* lunatic, of course, though happily we suffered no casualties in filling our role, probably because exhaustion had temporarily made peace seem to be in the combatants' best interests.

The point I made to the *Globe and Mail*, obviously, was that Canada had to pick its spots and ought not to feel obliged to participate automatically in every peacekeeping operation. We should insist on conditions, there should be a clear mandate, and the financing ought to be levied on all U.N. member states and not, as has all too often been the case, only on those who feel like contributing. Moreover, since the Canadian government is responsible to the public for the lives of its men and women in uniform, we ought not to put them in a position where their safety is at risk — as it undoubtedly was in UNIIMOG.

None of this mattered, however, to those who had made participation the *sine qua non* of Canadian nationalism. Peacekeeping was so popular, I had to conclude, because it was useful, to be sure, but primarily because it was something we could do and the Americans could not.[16] In other words, peacekeeping made us different from our friends and neighbours. And while that was a good thing, it also had about it something of the anti-Americanism that is part and parcel of our identity.

This became all the more obvious to me when Iraq invaded Kuwait in as clear an act of undoubted aggression as the world has witnessed since 1945. The United States mobilized a vast military coalition; Canada took part, though rather more hesitantly than I would have wished; and, in what I have no hesitation in characterizing as a just war under every canonical and legal definition, Iraq was driven from Kuwait at terrible cost to its military and people. This was not a peacekeeping operation, though it was authorized by the United Nations and was, indeed, a throwback to the kind of collective security envisaged by the drafters of the U.N. Charter in 1945 and practised only once before, in Korea.[17]

Canadian public opinion was sorely divided over the war, but in the end healthy majorities supported Canada's role in it. The Liberals and the New Democrats in Parliament went through conniptions trying to oppose the war while simultaneously supporting our servicemen and -women in the Gulf. The government, one eye fixed on public opinion, gave the troops different and progressively more aggressive mandates several times during the struggle. One of the predominant trends in the public discourse, acerbically characterized by Charlotte Gray in the Canadian Institute for International Peace and Security's magazine as a mixture of "idealism, legalism, internationalism and knee-jerk anti-Americanism," was that by participating in the Americans' war Canada was destroying its hard-won credibility as a peacekeeper.[18] There was unquestionably an element of anti-Americanism about all this, not least in the Opposition's stances in Parliament, in much of the media coverage, and in the positions taken by peace groups. And peacekeeping, because it was Canada's particular skill, became one of the main vehicles for expressing it.

The critics who charged that the government had sacrificed Canada's peacekeeping role on the altar of Washington's war over Kuwait and oil were proven wrong almost at once. Within weeks of the end of the Gulf war, Canada was asked to participate — with seven hundred soldiers and the force commander — in a peacekeeping operation (MINURSO) being set up in the Sahara to supervise a referendum designed to end the long war between Polisario guerrillas and Morocco.[19] The country was also expected to participate in a U.N. force in Cambodia. Our role in Kuwait, in other words, proved to have no immediate effect at all on our ability to operate as peacekeepers. Nor should it have been expected to. We were, as I have suggested repeatedly herein, wanted as peacekeepers because of our military capabilities as much as or more than for our national attributes. Participation in a war in no way altered that, except perhaps to demonstrate that our pilots and ships' crews were as genuinely efficient in combat as in patrolling the Green Line in Nicosia. It must also be said that, if Canada cuts its armed forces down to nothing, as many of the supporters of a virtually disarmed Canada urge, and if it takes away the military's versatility, our future capacity to act in peacekeeping roles will be severely constrained, if not ended.[20]

The point of all this is that for too many Canadians peaceeeping has become a substitute for policy and thought.[21] Some countries (but no longer our budget-strapped nation) try to deal with problems by throwing money at them; our people and, to some substantial extent, our governments try to deal with the world's problems by sending peacekeepers. This is not an ignoble impulse, but it is one that has to be checked with realism. Canada was right to participate with its allies in the war against Saddam Hussein, and those who objected to our role, whether out of misguided anti-Americanism or concern for our future as a peacekeeper, were wrong. We have also been right to participate in most of the peacekeeping operations in which we have served. But let us, at the very least, retain and enhance our right to consider which PKOs we shall participate in, just as we have the right to consider which wars we shall fight. Governments, like individuals, are supposed to be capable of rational decision making. And automatic responses — whether "My country right or wrong" or "Send in the Canadian peacekeepers" — are no substitutes for thought.

NOTES

1. J.W. Holmes, "Most Safely in the Middle," *International Journal* 39 (Spring 1984): 384.
2. See J.L. Granatstein, *How Britain's Weakness Forced Canada into the Arms of the United States* (Toronto, 1989), chap. 2.
3. See, e.g., J.L. Granatstein and Norman Hillmer, *For Better or For Worse: Canada and the United States to the 1990s* (Toronto, 1991), chaps. 5–6.
4. See J.L. Granatstein, "Canada and Peacekeeping: Image and Reality," *Canadian Forum* 54 (August 1974).

5. See J.L. Granatstein, "Canada: Peacekeeper," in Alastair Taylor et al., *Peacekeeping: International Challenge and Canadian Response* (Toronto, 1968), pp. 100ff., 116–17.
6. The best study of Canada's experience is Douglas Ross, *In the Interests of Peace: Canada and Vietnam, 1954–73* (Toronto, 1984). See also Ramesh Thakur, *Peacekeeping in Vietnam: Canada, India, Poland and the International Commission* (Edmonton, 1984).
7. See the account in L.B. Pearson's memoirs, *Mike: The Memoirs of the Rt. Hon. Lester B. Pearson,* Vol. II: *1948–1957* (Toronto, 1973), chap. 10.
8. Burns's account is in his *Between Arab and Israeli* (Toronto, 1962), pp. 208ff.
9. Cited in J.L. Granatstein, "The Anglocentrism of Canadian Diplomacy," in Andrew Cooper, ed., *Canadian Culture: International Dimensions* (Waterloo, 1985), p. 37.
10. Pearson later suggested that his decision to give Canada a flag of its own had its genesis in the Suez Crisis and the troubles over the Canadian contingent. Interview, October 21, 1971.
11. John Meisel, *The Canadian General Election of 1957* (Toronto, 1962), pp. 254–55.
12. See John Diefenbaker, *One Canada: Memoirs of the Rt. Hon. John G. Diefenbaker,* Vol. I: *The Crusading Years, 1895–1956* (Toronto, 1975), p. 280.
13. L.B. Pearson, *Mike: The Memoirs of the Rt. Hon. L.B. Pearson,* Vol. III: *1957–1968* (Toronto, 1975), pp. 134–35.
14. On U.N. administration of peacekeeping, see E.H. Bowman and J.E. Fanning, "The Logistics Problems of a UN Military Force," *International Organization* 17 (1963).
15. See J.L. Granatstein and Robert Bothwell, *Pirouette: Pierre Trudeau and Canadian Foreign Policy* (Toronto, 1990), pp. 55ff.
16. Of course, even this was not true, though not one Canadian in a thousand realized it. The United States participated in the U.N. Truce Supervisory Organization from its organization in 1948 and in the Multilateral Force of Observers (MFO) set up in the Sinai as one condition of the peace brokered by President Carter between Egypt and Israel. Eventually Canada would serve on the MFO as well. One might add that there is an irony in the way Japan is struggling with the problems posed for its constitution by the possibility of participating in peacekeeping. There, engaging in peacekeeping is largely seen by public and politicians as being obliged to accede to the Americans' wishes; here, the exact opposite is true.
17. See Kim Nossal, "Coalition-Building's Darker Side: Australia and Canada in the Gulf Conflict," a paper presented at the Australasian Political Studies Assn., 1991.
18. Charlotte Gray, "Home Grown Skirmishes. Canada and the War," *Peace & Security,* Autumn 1991, p. 8. See also Don Munton, "From Paardeberg to the Gulf: Canadians' Opinions About Canada's Wars," ibid., Spring 1991, p. 16.
19. See Richard Brûlé, "Western Sahara: A Settlement in Sight," *Peace & Security,* Autumn 1991, p. 15.
20. When the armed forces were unified in 1968, critics charged that Defence minister Paul Hellyer aimed to create a military that could only do peacekeeping, not fulfil a range of mandates. Ironically, a quarter-century later, defence cuts and the virtual end of Canada's NATO role may lead precisely to that result. The point, however, is that without many capabilities even peacekeeping will not be able to be performed well. On unification, see J.L. Granatstein, *Canada, 1957–1967* (Toronto, 1986), chap. 9.
21. See Desmond Morton's comment: "Peacekeeping is the great [Canadian] morale builder. It is the only thing the public think the military are any good for. It is a distraction from the military role, but it is unfortunately the one that everybody out there will put as priority one, and one has to respect that political reality": "What Is to Be Done? Canada's Military Security in the 1990s," *Peace & Security,* Summer 1990, p. 5.

Development Assistance

T.A. KEENLEYSIDE

It seems appropriate in any analysis of the role of human rights in the conduct of Canada's bilateral relations to examine its place in Canadian development assistance policy. First, many of the globe's worst human rights offenders are developing countries; while Canada may have little influence on their behaviour, its aid programme — as one of the most important dimensions of Canada's relations with these states — is at least a potential instrument for that purpose. Second, aid (unlike withdrawal of commercial services, trade sanctions, and so on) is flexible; it need not be confined to disciplinary use to punish gross violators (by the cessation of aid, for example) but can, with sensitivity and imagination in project selection, advance observance. Third, and most important, as Bernard Wood, director of the North-South Institute said recently: "All aid is or should be about human rights," since "it is supposedly an instrument for the promotion of economic and social rights and the basic standards of a minimum decent existence for those who do not have access to them."[1]

In their more enlightened moments, officials of the Canadian government have acknowledged this intrinsic relation between development in the Third World and human rights: they have sometimes perceived development as advancement of the whole person, embracing his or her economic, social, and, indeed, political well-being. In an eloquent statement in 1976, for instance, Paul Gérin-Lajoie, then president of the Canadian International Development Agency (CIDA), wrote: "There . . . remains a single central objective . . . which has first claim on our attention. It is an objective which supposes on the part of governments and individuals a concrete will to have as the focus of their activities the human person . . . This central objective is the total liberation of man." Liberation meant meeting basic needs by freeing human beings from hunger, disease, illiteracy, unemployment, and chronic underemployment. At the same time, however, if deprivations in these areas prevented the enjoyment of fundamental rights, "the same must also be said of the use of force to silence dissenters, systematic recourse to political imprisonment, and the torture of prisoners."[2] It is, then, appropriate in examining the role of human rights in Canadian bilateral relations to focus on Canadian development assistance: it is a policy

SOURCE: Excerpted from "Development Assistance," in Robert Matthews and Cranford Pratt, eds., *Human Rights in Canadian Foreign Policy* (Montreal/Kingston: McGill-Queen's University Press, 1988), pp. 187–208. Reprinted with permission of McGill-Queen's University Press.

instrument aimed, rhetorically at least, at improving the human condition in all its aspects.

Taking human rights into consideration in the making of Canadian aid decisions emerged as a matter of discussion in the mid-1970s, prompted, in part, by the US Carter administration's severing of assistance to several gross violators. Parliament was one of the earliest loci of the debate. In March 1977, and again in March 1978, a private member's bill was introduced to prohibit aid, Export Development Corporation (EDC) credits, or tariff concessions to any consistent and gross violator of human rights.[3] Later, in 1982, the parliamentary Sub-Committee on Canada's Relations with Latin America and the Caribbean recommended in its final report that "Canadian development assistance be substantially reduced, terminated, or not commenced in cases where gross and systematic violations of human rights make it impossible to promote the central objective of helping the poor." In June 1986, this position was reaffirmed in the report of the Special Joint Committee of Parliament on Canada's International Relations. Finally, in May 1987, the report of the House of Commons Standing Committee on External Affairs and International Trade on aid policies and programs proposed the adoption by CIDA of a four-tier country classification grid for Canadian aid recipients that would "provide incentives for good behaviour as well as penalties for poor human rights performance."[4]

A number of Canadian experts in international relations and development have, since the late 1970s, supported linking aid to rights observance.[5] A 1983 study commissioned by CIDA from Martin Rudner of Carleton University was also significant. After carefully examining the issue of linkage, Rudner proposed "explicitly, coherently and functionally" integrating human rights "within the broader framework of foreign policy," including development assistance.[6] Certain interest groups and/or those writing under their imprimatur, including the North-South Institute, Energy Probe, and various church groups, have also called for greater attention to human rights in aid decisions.[7] Finally, in the press there has been support recently for tying aid to observance, with the *Globe and Mail*, in particular, frequently appealing for "more boldness in External Affairs and CIDA" on this subject.[8]

Since the late 1970s, then, pressure has been mounting from a variety of sectors for attaching higher priority to human rights in development assistance policy.

Nominally at least, human rights have had a place in government aid policy for some time. In the Trudeau government's 1970 review, social justice was adopted as one of the six basic themes of Canadian foreign policy, committing Canada to advance human welfare globally both by supporting economic development in the Third World and by encouraging respect for basic rights. These two sub-themes seemed linked in the review: development assistance was to be concentrated in countries with governments that pursued external and internal policies broadly consistent with Canadian values and attitudes.[9] However, until the late 1970s, Ottawa generally reacted negatively to suggestions that provision of aid be made conditional on satisfactory observance of rights, as reflected in Trudeau's 1977 statement in Parliament that Canada had "not made it a condition of our assistance to starving people in the third world that their governments be above reproach."[10] Nevertheless, increased parliamentary preoccupation with this issue in the 1970s led the government to set out a somewhat different position.

In October 1978, Secretary of State for External Affairs Don Jamieson reiterated that Canadian aid is "designed to help meet the basic human needs of the poorest people in the poorest countries" (and by inference should not normally be affected by human rights criteria). He declared, however, that "human-rights considerations are, nonetheless, a factor in determining levels of aid and the orientation of programs . . . On a few occasions when the human-rights situation in a country has deteriorated to a stage where the effective implementation of the aid program is made extremely difficult, Canadian assistance has been suspended or not renewed."[11] During the Clark government, a similar position was outlined in a brief review of foreign aid policy undertaken by CIDA, and countries were cited where aid had either been suspended or not renewed because of problems of implementation, namely Equatorial Guinea, Kampuchea, Uganda, and Vietnam.[12] With the return of the Liberals to power in 1980, this policy was maintained, with aid curtailed to El Salvador and Guatemala as well, because "gross violations of human rights or conditions of conflict" made "the provision of an aid program impossible."[13] A new element was soon added. Speaking in the House of Commons on 16 June 1981, Secretary of State for External Affairs Mark MacGuigan stated: "We believe that it would be inappropriate for our foreign policy to reward adventurism and interference. Countries of the Third World face desperate and formidable challenges. It is for this reason that we have withdrawn aid programs from those countries whose scarce resources are diverted to war and conquest." The following month he said that aid had earlier been withdrawn from Vietnam and Cuba because of their "imperialist adventures."[14]

Under the Mulroney government the central thrust of policy has remained the same — action only in extreme cases, principally (although not all statements have been explicit on this point) when breakdown in order renders an aid program ineffectual.[15] There have been only vague references to other criteria: "Canada does . . . take account of broad human rights considerations when we determine to which countries Canadian aid will be directed," and "the nature and extent of our programme" is affected by "the human rights records of development partners."[16]

This chapter first examines the advantages and disadvantages of linking development assistance to human rights observance; second, taking these arguments into account, it proposes a strategy for the future; and third, it explores and analyses the history of Canadian linked action, evaluating its appropriateness in the context of both stated government policy and the suggested strategy.

Linkage: Pros and Cons

One of the principal arguments proffered in favour of linking aid and human rights is that all states are responsible for ensuring global respect for human rights: "Today there is near universal international agreement, at least in theory, although often not in practice, that certain things simply cannot legitimately be done to human beings,"[17] including torture, arbitrary arrest and detention, summary execution, and wilful imposition of malnutrition or starvation. Application of rights criteria to aid then becomes appropriate for donor countries because it demonstrates that they recognize a responsibility to enhance respect for universally cherished rights without which no individual is able to lead a life of dignity and worth.[18]

A second, more pragmatic argument is that aid provided to states that abuse basic rights — economic, social, and political — is unlikely to be effective, because meaningful development depends on respect for the individual and his or her basic rights. This point of view is well expressed by Robert Carty and Virginia Smith:

> Human rights must be a central criterion for selecting aid partners and determining aid effectiveness because they are an integral part of the development process . . . The abuse of civil and political rights is not only a direct violation of the integrity of the person but an additional impediment to integral development, because the political participation of individuals and groups in society is restricted. In the same way, the abuse of economic, social and cultural rights makes the full realization of political and civil rights impossible because the economic and social participation of different social classes is grossly unequal.[19]

Even well-intentioned and appropriate aid is unlikely to reach the needy if régimes are not committed to rights; it is likely to be diverted to perpetuate the status of existing élites and to facilitate their repression of the impoverished majority. Attaching conditions to aid may help to ensure that assistance promotes equitable, non-discriminatory development that benefits the least privileged; the net effect may be to strengthen developing countries' "resolve to make progress in the implementation of human rights."[20]

A third argument is that it is in Canada's enlightened national interest to take rights into account in development assistance, because repression often leads to civil unrest and revolution that may be damaging to global security and, hence, to Canadian strategic interests, especially if "friendly" but authoritarian régimes are overthrown. Further, stable Third World states with relatively egalitarian development will in the long run make better trade and investment partners for Canada than countries where persisting violations perpetuate underdevelopment, inequality, and political uncertainty.[21]

The fourth and final argument is that taking human rights into account in aid policy is in accord with the concerns of the Canadian public. In his report for CIDA, Rudner reminded the agency that "those groups in Canadian society that are most pronounced in their support for international development co-operation are also those which place high value on human rights."[22] Regard for human rights may, therefore, help to preserve a constituency supportive of the agency's endeavours. Others have asserted that basic rights reflect values central to the Canadian community which, if neglected in foreign policy, may atrophy internally.[23]

A wider range of arguments has been proffered in opposition to linking aid to human rights, but it is the contention of this chapter that, while many of them have merit, collectively they constitute a case not so much for discounting rights in aid policy as for acting cautiously — for formulating a carefully considered strategy that emphasizes positive rather than punitive initiatives.

First, state sovereignty and non-intervention in the internal affairs of other countries are a central ordering principle of the international system; some argue that linking aid to human rights performance violates that concept. It need be stated here only that donor states "can quite properly manage their economic relations as they see fit,"[24] deciding when, where, and how to expend their own aid funds without fairly being accused of intervention.

Second, a more vigorous stand may provoke reciprocal attacks by developing countries on rights violations in Canada, including charges of racism and ill treatment of certain groups, like native peoples and new immigrants. Rather than being an argument against linkage, however, this serves as a reminder that Canada must vigorously pursue human rights at home while giving this issue greater attention in its foreign policy. It also suggests the wisdom of confining punitive action (that is, cessation of aid) to extreme cases, where comparisons with the Canadian situation would be inapposite.

Third, the ability of Canada acting on its own to influence rights behaviour through its aid program is perhaps limited, because aid from Canada is rarely critical to the recipient. However, this argument merely points to the wisdom of acting in concert with other states wherever possible rather than being a justification for doing nothing.[25] Yet unilateral action should not be discounted, since carefully considered initiatives may induce like responses from other states or even achieve modest results on their own.

Fourth, Canada has a range of interests in its bilateral relations with developing countries, and thus to give attention to human rights in aid policy might well conflict with the realization of other interests, principally of a security and commercial nature.[26] While the centrality of strategic/security considerations must be recognized, Canada's interests in this respect are generally best served by promoting observance of political, economic, social, and cultural rights and, hence, stability in developing countries. Likewise Canadian commercial interests are best advanced by serious attention to rights and creation of conditions of equity and stability in the Third World. To argue in favour of taking rights into account is, then, not to discount Canada's acting on the basis of national interest, but rather to suggest that in most instances such an approach is likely to be in Canada's enlightened interest.

Fifth, there is potential for inconsistency in the application of the aid instrument, especially given that many developing countries violate human rights. For example, initiatives might be taken only where Canada has no significant interests at stake while grosser violations in other countries are ignored because of political/security or commercial interests.[27] The decision to act might also be heavily influenced by media attention to a country and related public attitudes rather than by the severity of violations. Further, there are problems in reaching a consensus on what constitute the most basic rights and on the meaning of "consistent pattern of gross violations," as well as in determining the reliability of evidence, all of which may lead to inconsistent application.[28] Finally, Canada's response probably *should* vary from state to state: countries are at different stages in their respect for human rights, and Canada's expectations may legitimately vary from country to country.[29] In general, for example, human rights observance is much higher in the Commonwealth Caribbean than in Central America. A realistic policy must take that into account and shape Canada's responses so as to reflect awareness of each country's past and its current stage of political and social evolution. These very real difficulties suggest a strategy which, to be consistent, does not ignore serious violations anywhere but is flexible enough to enable varying responses, depending on circumstances. A policy that merely stops aid in selected gross cases subject to media exposure and where no particular Canadian interests are involved would thus be insufficient.

Sixth, a related difficulty is the double standard if Canada uses aid to influence developing countries, where the presence of a program offers that option, but fails to take other forms of action with states — developed and developing alike — that are equally guilty but where the aid instrument is not available. Indeed, reliance exclusively on aid as a tool could be seen as a form of racial discrimination, with Canada treating violations more harshly in non-white, developing countries than elsewhere.[30] An appropriate strategy would thus have to embrace alternative measures for non-aid recipients equally guilty of violations.

Seventh, and the argument most emphasized by the government in opposing anything more than a limited rights orientation, is the effect of such an approach on Canada's ability to meet the needs of the poorest people in developing countries, the alleged focus of the aid program. To place strictures on aid going to those already suffering under repression may be to punish them a second time for the transgressions of their governments.[31] This argument suggests a strategy with initiatives other than termination of assistance, so long as Canadian aid is truly meeting basic needs of the poorest.

Eighth, in a recent article, Martin Rudner refers to increasing calls to use aid as a political instrument to achieve a range of policy goals, of which human rights observance is only one. "Such demands," he argues, "for a more politicized approach would treat development assistance expressly as an instrument for the promotion of politically determined objectives, and reinforce the movement away from the earlier poverty-focused strategy."[32] Linking aid and human rights as part of a general broadening of the acceptable objectives of Canadian aid is hardly compatible with the intentions of most human rights advocates. Again, this potential problem reinforces the notion that Canada's aid–human rights strategy should be "poverty focused." To the extent that aid directly helps the neediest, it fosters basic rights; under such circumstances, aid termination (as opposed to reshaping) is probably unwarranted, even if there are violations within a recipient country.

History

PUNITIVE ACTION

Although there is some evidence of increased government attention to relating of development assistance to human rights performance, Canadian action has been both halting and inconsistent.[33] This has been so since the first apparent case of linkage — that of Indonesia. Starting in the 1964-5 fiscal year, Canadian food aid was terminated for a two-year period in response to Indonesia's confrontation with Malaysia. Further, no new capital projects or commodity shipments to Indonesia were undertaken in 1965-6.[34] Although Canada never explained the withdrawal, it was apparently due to Indonesia's unprovoked attacks against its neighbour in violation of territorial sovereignty and the self-determination of peoples and to parliamentary criticism over aid to a state diverting its resources from development to finance external aggression.[35]

This early incident is particularly revealing in light of subsequent policy toward Indonesia. Canadian aid to Indonesia in the 1960s had been extremely limited and confined largely to food. Indeed, relations in general had been insignificant; the Sukarno government's anti-Western orientation and chaotic management of the economy had rendered Indonesia neither politically nor commercially attractive to Canada and the West in general. However, following Sukarno's fall in 1965 and the gradual reorientation of Indonesia toward the West under President Suharto, the country took on new political and economic importance to Canada, reflected in the decision announced in 1970 "to concentrate more funds for development programmes" in Indonesia.[36] Since that time Indonesia has been a core recipient, with $367 million disbursed bilaterally between 1970-1 and 1985-6.[37] Based on country-to-country aid disbursements over the past three years, it currently ranks fourth as a Canadian aid recipient and, apart from Pakistan, is the largest one outside the Commonwealth.

Yet Indonesia's human rights record has remained bleak throughout this period. Thousands were arrested and detained without trial for many years for purported involvement in the 1965 coup, and as late as 1984 Amnesty International reported that approximately 200 of these people were still held, while those released under a program initiated in 1976 were subject to a variety of restraints.[38] Since 1965 thousands more have been arrested and detained on suspicion of belonging to groups opposed to the government, and there have been "persistent reports of the torture and ill-treatment" of these detainees as well as extrajudicial killings of ordinary criminal suspects.[39] More appalling still has been Indonesia's treatment of the former Portuguese colony of East Timor, which it invaded and occupied in 1975. Since then, it is estimated that 250,000 East Timorese, approximately one-third of the population, have perished as a result of starvation and indiscriminate killings by the occupying Indonesian army. According to Amnesty International, Indonesian forces "systematically tortured and killed people in East Timor" after the invasion. In 1983, there was a new wave of disappearances and death in custody as an operation was launched to eliminate supporters of FRETILIN, the organization that in 1975 had declared East Timor's independence from Portugal; there were even reported killings of prisoners who surrendered after being promised amnesty.[40]

From 1976 to 1980 Canada abstained on UN resolutions deploring the Indonesian invasion and calling on all states to respect the right of the East Timorese to self-determination, and it has cast negative votes on resolutions regarding East Timor since 1980. At the same time, it has maintained a major aid program entailing sizeable capital equipment purchases and support for large-scale infrastructural projects,[41] forms of aid inappropriate for a régime with a long history of political repression. The decision to maintain aid without strictures in the face of the invasion of East Timor is strikingly inconsistent with the posture adopted in the face of the far less destructive assault on Malaysia in the mid-1960s. It also makes a mockery of the government's assertion in 1981 about withdrawing "aid programs from those countries whose scarce resources are diverted to war and conquest."[42]

The reason for the inconsistency seems transparent. In the 1960s Indonesia counted for little in Canadian foreign policy. In the 1970s and 1980s, however, it has been deemed strategically important, especially since the fall of South Vietnam and the communist ascendancy throughout Indochina. Together with its fellow members of the Association of South East Asian Nations, it has been viewed by Canada as "the last bulwark against communism in this part of the world."[43] With its great wealth in natural resources, Indonesia also has "great potential as a locus for Canadian exports and investments," so that Canadian corporate interests have "certainly militated against withholding aid on a human rights basis."[44] The government, however, rationalizes the current high level of Canadian aid on the grounds of the régime's genuine commitment to development.[45] It resists using aid to induce the enhanced respect for human rights that is, in fact, necessary to establish a climate in which equitable development can occur and in which Canada's long-term strategic and commercial interests can be secured.

Canadian development assistance to the brutally repressive Pol Pot régime in Kampuchea — responsible for the deaths by torture, murder, and starvation of from one to three million people — was terminated in 1977. However, as in the Indonesian situation in the mid-1960s, aid had been minimal and the government never stated that its decision was a result of human rights violations.

In response to the Vietnamese invasion of Kampuchea, which led to the fall of Pol Pot, all new Canadian bilateral aid to Vietnam, including food assistance, was cut off, in accordance with the policy of not countenancing external aggression. The persecution of the ethnic Chinese in Vietnam was, according to officials, a secondary factor in cessation of this program, which once more had been limited. Vietnam was treated particularly harshly: in October 1979, Canada, together with the United States, requested at a meeting of the governing body of the World Food Program that WFP assistance to Vietnam be postponed. When the WFP failed to act, due to resistance from other members, Canada and the United States specified that their own WFP contributions not be sent to Vietnam.[46] Canadian policy in the Vietnam case hardly seems consistent with the approach taken toward Indonesian aggression in the 1970s. Nor is it consistent with maintenance of aid to meet the needs of the most disadvantaged even in cases of serious violations — a position that most officials claim to support and, indeed, many use to justify assistance to other violators where Canada is loath to take punitive action.

Finally, following the Soviet invasion of Afghanistan, Canada decided in January 1980 not to recognize the new puppet régime and to suspend all aid. In this decision, according to officials, political and security reasons were interwoven with human rights considerations.

In sum, in the Asian cases we can see inconsistency and lack of explicitness with respect to the role of human rights in the withdrawal decisions. In all instances where action was taken, the régimes were either communist or strongly anti-Western, aid was limited, and Canada had few vested interests at stake. By contrast, Ottawa seems loath to consider linkage in Asian states with long records of abuse if the countries are major aid recipients and have other important ties with Canada. These include — in addition to Indonesia — Bangladesh and Pakistan, the first- and second-ranking Canadian aid recipients worldwide, where violations are certainly of such an order as to require careful shaping of the Canadian programs to discourage abuses and make a constructive contribution to the achievement of social justice.

In Africa, the principal instance of action has been Uganda: "Virtually all CIDA projects . . . were suspended due to a lack of commitment to development shown by the Amin régime." Only the scholarship program for training Ugandans in Canada was allowed to run its course, without renewal.[47] While the human rights situation was appalling and the Amin régime had been universally condemned, aid was suspended not specifically because of the human rights situation, but because the chaotic internal situation, together with lack of local personnel and other support services, had rendered aid ineffective and placed Canadian lives at risk.[48] The human rights argument was thus largely a post facto justification offered in the face of growing pressure in Canada for curtailment of aid to repressive régimes.[49]

Following the overthrow of Amin in April 1979 and restoration of Milton Obote to power the following year, there were grounds for hoping that human rights would improve. In December 1979, the UN general assembly asked the international community to contribute generously to rehabilitation and development, and Canada responded with bilateral aid for the purchase of spare parts and materials needed in reconstruction and with $2 million in emergency food aid.[50] By early 1981, however, Amnesty International had found evidence of arrests by the Ugandan army without legal authority, ill-treatment of prisoners, torture, disappearances, and murders, and the situation continued to deteriorate thereafter. Canadian aid was not again suspended, although it has remained limited and been designed largely to reach those most in need.

In Equatorial Guinea, a one-party state and absolute dictatorship was established in 1970 by Macias Nguena, who forced one-third of the population into exile and slaughtered some 35–50,000 political detainees during his 11-year rule.[51] In August 1979 he was overthrown in a bloodless coup and replaced by a military junta, which improved respect for human rights.[52] Throughout the period of repression, Canada offered no development assistance, but it has provided only nominal aid since that time, which suggests that relations were not constrained by the earlier human rights situation.

While it is difficult to quarrel with Canadian policy in these two African situations, action was not taken explicitly for reasons of violations and both countries had only limited development and commercial relations with Canada.

With regard to Latin America, the first instance of Canadian action was the quiet withdrawal of government-to-government aid to Chile following the 1973 coup that toppled the democratically elected Allende government, replacing it with the repressive Pinochet régime, which has since violated a wide range of security, political, and civil rights. However, yet again, no apparent effort was made to use this decision politically to encourage change. Indeed, the Canadian government seems to have acted reluctantly and only because of its perception of public opposition to aid to Chile. Thus a confidential cabinet document in 1974 asserted that "the attention which the churches and various Canadian groups have focused on the Chilean Government's use of repression against its opponents has led to an unfavourable reaction among the Canadian public — a reaction which will not permit any significant increase in Canadian aid to this country."[53]

In this situation, too, Canadian bilateral aid had been extremely limited, with disbursements varying between $740,000 and $2.4 million between 1970-1 and 1973-4. Had Canada wished to signal its displeasure at Chilean repression, other measures were called for, including termination of Export Development Corporation (EDC) activity. Yet no such action was taken. Indeed, EDC involvement in Chile increased, with Canadian concessional loans over the period 1974–86 amounting to $89.5 million and insurance to exporters to $109.3 million.[54] Further, EDC activity has arguably served to help sustain this universally condemned régime. For instance, the corporation extended a $5-million loan to Chile shortly after the overthrow of Allende to finance the purchase of Twin Otter aircraft; their short-take-off-and-landing capability makes them potentially useful for counter-insurgency.[55] In 1980, the EDC financed a $6.1-million sale of Buffalo aircraft and spare parts by de Havilland Aircraft of Canada to the Chilean air force. The Buffalo, a military support transport plane, can handle troops and equipment. Canadian action toward Chile has thus been inconsistent and hardly constitutes an effective response to persistent repression.

In 1978, CIDA's bilateral aid to Cuba, launched in 1975, was terminated. The ostensible reason was Cuba's military involvement in Angola, indicating that it had "no more need for Canadian aid, given its new priorities,"[56] but this was probably a post facto rationalization designed "to make political mileage" in the face of Canadian parliamentary "criticism of Cuba's military involvement in Africa"; in fact, the aid program had probably "run its course without Cuba's request for renewal."[57] Whatever the reason, action on aid was not supplemented with strictures in other areas, for EDC support for exports to Cuba continued, with, for example, $128.3 million of EDC insurance made available between 1978 and 1986. Certainly, Canada has not communicated a consistent signal to the Castro régime.

It would be possible, officials acknowledge, to identify viable projects in Cuba that would have a real development impact. In accordance with the strategy outlined earlier, Cuba (like Vietnam) remains a legitimate target for carefully structured aid directed at basic economic needs, but Ottawa is unwilling to consider such a program. Indeed, Canada does not even offer mission-administered funds to Cuba, although such a program exists even in South Africa, the most widely reviled human rights violator.[58] The reason seems to be, as stated by one official, that "the regime is hard-Marxist-Leninist, worse than some Eastern European states" and remains heavily committed to overseas military expenditures. Cuba and Vietnam, contrasted with Indonesia, thus suggest that Canada has a different view of "foreign adventurism" depending on whether a régime is communist or pro-Western.

Two of the most widely publicized Canadian punitive actions were the decisions taken in March 1981 to suspend planning for new bilateral projects in El Salvador and to allow the program in Guatemala, begun following the 1976 earthquake, to run out.[59] Though these were later sometimes characterized by the government as motivated by human rights offences, the administrative impossibility of carrying out the program and the risks to Canadian personnel were the key factors. The CIDA annual report of 1981-2 stated: "Political turmoil and civil strife, with an inability of governments to guarantee the protection of development workers, led to the suspension of CIDA bilateral programs in El Salvador and Guatemala.[60]

That human rights was not the motivating factor is apparent also in that in both instances Canada had been providing assistance for some time despite evidence of escalating repression. In El Salvador, from the election of General Carlos Humberto Romero as president in 1977, "the power of the military could no longer be realistically challenged by peaceful legislative, administrative, or judicial means" and "political repression had become institutionalized,"[61] yet Canadian aid roughly doubled each fiscal year between 1977-8 and 1980-1 and then almost tripled in 1981-2, before the suspension came into effect. Once again, suspension did not entail a clear message about human rights.[62]

On 3 December 1984, Joe Clark announced resumption of direct assistance to El Salvador, initially in the form of an $8-million line of credit for purchase of agricultural-sector products. Out of the counterpart funds generated by the line of credit, Canada intended to establish "basic needs" projects, including aid to those displaced by civil war, to be administered largely by NGOs. It justified the reversal of policy by the improved situation in El Salvador, including contraction of human rights abuses.[63]

Resumption of aid to El Salvador has been controversial. America's Watch reported an improved rights situation in 1984: death squad killings and disappearances dropped sharply; but they increased again in 1985, leading the organization to state that there has been no general improvement in the human rights situation, which remains "terrible."[64] Further, there are serious doubts about the Duarte government's will and capacity to surmount the entrenched military and economic establishment and introduce the reforms necessary to ensure that Canadian aid will, in fact, help the long-suffering peasantry. Unfortunately, a line of credit, in effect balance-of-payments support for the government, implies approval of the régime itself. Also, the government controls the use of counterpart funds generated by the line of credit, giving it the potential at least to use them to advance its political goals.[65]

Ottawa's view of Guatemala prior to 1987, when bilateral aid recommenced, was that "the terrifying human rights situation" continued "to rule out any consideration of a resumption of Canadian government-to-government assistance"[66] (although other forms of aid were made available). Despite this firm position (bilateral aid in any event was always limited), Canada offered confused signals, not curbing EDC activity, with loans and insurance amounting to $45.9 million between 1981 and 1986. One observer remarked: "Canadian–Guatemalan relations have been almost humorously Byzantine in the desire to balance commercial and human rights issues."[67]

In 1983, Canada terminated a very small program in Suriname because of the repression that followed the 1982 coup, leading to liquidation of much of the political opposition. In this instance, human rights violations seem to have been the principal motivation, although aid was so limited that this initiative constituted merely a symbolic gesture.

By contrast with Canadian measures with respect to these Latin American states, the government has not curtailed aid to Honduras, the largest recipient of Canadian aid to Central America over the last three years. Yet many observers have noted significant deterioration in human rights observance there and have called for limitations on assistance.[68] Honduras has served as a base for the covert war against Nicaragua waged by the anti-Sandinista contras, yet, inconsistent with its position regarding Cuba, Vietnam, and Indonesia in the 1960s, Ottawa has not seen fit to sanction Honduras for its foreign intervention.[69]

In sum, then, in instances in Asia, Africa, and Latin America where Canada has taken punitive action, aid and other relationships were limited (and no significant Canadian interests were jeopardized),[70] the role of rights violations was ambiguous, and Ottawa was inconsistent in treating different states. In the words of Bernard Wood: "If you try to chart the scales of violations against the scales of sanctions in our past policies, it is not possible to find any systematic pattern."[71]

SELECTIVE ACTION

With regard to filtering out harmful projects in countries where abuses have been marked, but less gross or persistent, only two clear instances have been identified. In November 1980, the government removed newsprint from the list of commodities eligible for purchase under a line of credit to Guyana when it became clear that newsprint was not reaching the opposition press.[72] In 1985, Canada placed on indefinite hold its contribution to Sri Lanka's massive Mahaweli River dam and irrigation scheme, the world's largest foreign aid project. Saudi Arabia had withdrawn from its portion of the scheme (due to Sri Lanka's increasing relationship with Israel), thus affecting the project's financial viability. However, Ottawa also made clear its unhappiness with racial discrimination in Sri Lanka's resettlement plans for the affected area. It would provide no further funding beyond current commitments until financing had been resolved and until it was clear that Tamils as well as Sinhalese would benefit significantly from the project.

The Sri Lankan government apparently intended to resettle some 1.5 million Sinhalese in the 250,000 acres of scrub forest that would be turned into arable land by the project, thus diluting the concentration of Tamils in the Eastern province and concomitantly weakening the Tamil secessionist movement that had evolved into a violent guerrilla campaign in the north and east. This is an interesting first instance of the application of human rights criteria to aid a major recipient. In the Canadian government's view, given Sri Lanka's generally good human rights record until the recent ethnic conflict, termination of assistance was not called for, but rather insistence that Canadian aid be channeled impartially to both communities. However, given the absence of project proposals related to Tamil areas, aid to Sri Lanka was declining significantly by 1985–6.[73]

CREATIVE ACTION

In terms of positive shaping of aid to support equitable development of all groups, CIDA has made the most significant progress in the area of women in development. The agency has established an Integration of Women in Development section, and every CIDA project is reportedly now monitored from its inception to ensure that it encompasses women as well as men and that both sexes benefit. CIDA has also exposed its officer staff to a short course to sensitize them to the vital role played by women in the development process.[74] The Women in Development approach could be applied by CIDA more generally to ensure that broad-based human rights criteria are taken into account in establishing and evaluating all Canadian programs and projects.

Other creative endeavours to encourage rights observance have included use of mission-administered funds to provide legal materials for the Supreme Court library in Guyana and for the Guyana Human Rights Commission. Recently, the Canadian government indicated its willingness to assist Third World countries in developing institutions necessary to achieve effective observance of human rights, through such means as providing legal assistance and assisting in development of procedures for democratic elections and in establishment of human rights ombudsmen. Ottawa is exploring the mechanics of establishing an institute, separate from CIDA, to administer initiatives of this nature.

There has been only limited Canadian involvement in police and military training, essentially in the Commonwealth Caribbean. In 1984, for example, Ottawa began to assist restructuring of Grenada's police force, entailing provision of equipment as well as an advisory service for police training and curriculum planning.[75] Aid of this nature must, of course, be approached with extreme caution. It is unlikely to be welcome where it is most needed, and it might be used for unintended purposes and aid a state's application of repression. Nevertheless, Canadian police forces have well-established programs for disciplined, apolitical training of personnel in procedures of arrest, interrogation, and detention, and the Canadian armed forces have an exemplary record in peacekeeping abroad, which requires restraint, tact, and sensitivity, often under intense provocation. Canada may, therefore, be well suited to assist certain developing countries in achieving conditions of law and order, thereby helping them to establish just environments in which economic, social, and political development can take place.

In sum, action by Canada relating to human rights has been largely punitive in nature and directed at "worst-case" situations. Only now is some support emerging for applying human rights criteria more broadly to all country programs and reshaping them so as to avoid projects that detract from observance and support those that can enhance it. Officers sensitive to human rights may be subjecting projects to a form of human rights filter, but there is no institutionalized project-by-project assessment, applying a broad range of criteria, including political participation. Thus the human rights dimension, beyond perhaps women in development, tends, in the words of one officer, to get "lost" as other traditional criteria are applied in evaluating projects.

MEETING BASIC NEEDS

Finally, an analysis of Canadian aid from a human rights perspective requires a brief assessment of its efficacy in meeting the basic economic and social needs of the most underprivileged. The proportion of Canada's assistance directed to the least developed countries, as classified by the United Nations, has increased substantially since the early 1970s. Measured in terms of country-to-country disbursements, it stood at 26 to 28 per cent of the total over the years 1983-4 to 1985-6. However, of the top 20 Canadian aid recipients since 1983-4, only 5 (Bangladesh, Ethiopia, Niger, Sudan, and Tanzania) are among the 36 least developed countries.[76] Further, Canada has concentrated more aid on some relatively prosperous developing countries as it has sought commercial gains from its development assistance program in an intensely competitive international trading environment. Thus, of the top 20 aid recipients 1983-6, 2 countries, Jamaica and Peru, have per capita GNPs of roughly $1,000, while 4 (Cameroon, Indonesia, Thailand, and Zimbabwe) have figures over $500. Increased Canadian aid has focused on "the higher-growth low-income countries, some of which qualify as 'middle income' by World Bank standards, countries in which the incidence of poverty, economic performance and commercial opportunities seem to come together especially propitiously."[77]

In part because of this growing interest in developing countries with commercial promise, and more obviously because of the resistance for reasons of diplomacy to eliminating countries from the aid program (especially francophone and Commonwealth partners), Canada continues to disburse aid to an inordinately large number of countries. In the 1985-6 fiscal year, for example, at least 120 states received aid from Canada. Apart from reducing aid for the neediest states, this policy harms Canada's development effort. CIDA's capacity to select carefully appropriate development projects, to evaluate effectiveness of implementation, and to ensure that local administration is honest and efficient and that recipient régimes are committed to egalitarian development is seriously hampered by a cumbersome aid program dispersed over so many countries. More specifically, CIDA cannot familiarize itself adequately with the situation in each country and so cannot assess the human rights implications of each project. It would thus be highly desirable to focus on a much smaller number of needy states seriously committed to grassroots, economically redistributive development.[78]

The problem of dispersion is compounded by tight strictures on CIDA's administrative costs, which have resulted in inadequate numbers of trained agency personnel, especially in the field. This situation also hampers project identification, implementation, and evaluation and leads to selection of schemes where large sums of money can be disbursed with minimal overhead costs, for small-scale "basic needs" projects tend to require substantial administrative resources.

If the focus is to be assisting the poorest, there must be significant "untying" of Canadian aid. With 80 per cent of bilateral assistance tied to the provision of Canadian goods and services, Canada operates the second most tightly controlled program among countries of the Organization for Economic Co-operation and Development, with numerous harmful consequences. Because of generally higher Canadian costs, tied aid reduces the value of Canadian assistance by roughly 20 per cent. As a result of complex procurement procedures, tied aid also increases administrative costs and retards disbursements. Still more seriously, tied aid distorts the development priorities of recipient countries toward projects for which Canada can furnish goods and services and leads to reliance on imported rather than local inputs or those from other developing countries.[79]

Finally, tied aid is incompatible with giving priority to the needs of the rural disadvantaged for increased agricultural output, health care, education, and so on. Such projects need untied funds for largely local purchases rather than requiring Canadian equipment and services. Tying, therefore, means that "much foreign aid is finding its way 'to rich people in poor countries,'"[80] so that despite CIDA's intention, as set out in its 1975-80 strategy — and reaffirmed in 1981 — to focus more attention on the neediest in developing countries,[81] there has been no dramatic reorientation; rather, many traditional forms of infrastructural aid, such as electrical power generation and distribution and transport, have been simply reclassified as aid to the agricultural and rural sectors.[82]

Of particular concern has been the tendency in the 1980s to place still higher priority on potential commercial benefits to Canada. In 1978, for instance, an Industrial Cooperation Program was established, enabling CIDA to finance feasibility and starter studies by Canadian investors in the Third World. At about the same time, CIDA also initiated parallel financing: developing countries receive two separate credits for a project — a loan from the EDC and a low-interest loan or grant from CIDA.[83] The resulting attractive financial package induces the developing country to purchase goods from Canada rather than a competitor country. According to a study published in 1987, "Since 1978, CIDA and the EDC have engaged in associated financing for twenty-three projects, which had a total value of $1.5 billion in procurements of Canadian goods and services."[84] Such co-financing increases the emphasis on developing countries with commercial promise for Canada, at the expense of the neediest, and on capital as opposed to "basic needs" projects.[85]

In light of this growing preoccupation with commercial spin-offs, it is particularly discouraging that no significant constituency within the government appears to recognize that meeting basic economic and social needs is central to the program's sensitivity to human rights. The foreign policy establishment seems generally to believe that aid is and should be a broad policy instrument to promote not only development but also the government's political and commercial goals.[86] There is, indeed, a naïve faith that Canadian interests in the latter areas can be met without sacrificing the developmental quality of Canadian aid. Thus at least until recently there has not been much evidence of support for major reforms to allow aid to contribute significantly to the realization of global social justice.

Conclusion

In the last few years there has been increasing attention in Canada on human rights considerations in the context of official development assistance. There are, however, both positive and potentially negative factors to be borne in mind in linking aid disbursements to human rights observance. It is important, therefore, that Canada carefully construct a framework for action flexible enough to fit the circumstances of each case and encompassing not just punitive measures but — especially in cases of serious but not extreme abuses — creative initiatives that will encourage improved respect for human rights.

To date, Canadian action has been largely punitive and has focused on perceived extreme cases. In the most publicized instances, aid was suspended only when violations hindered implementation of programs and placed Canadian personnel in jeopardy. Such action did not deliver a message to offending régimes to alter their behaviour. In other, less well-known instances, there has usually been ambiguity about the role of human rights in precipitating Canadian action. Further, with this essentially negative approach, involving suspension of non-renewal, Canada has confined itself to only a few cases, lest the aid program be seriously disrupted. It has given little attention, apart from the specific area of women in development, to shaping the aid effort in all recipient countries so as to nurture respect for human rights in all their dimensions — security, political, civil, economic, and social. Further, action has been inconsistent and selective. States guilty of similar offences have been treated radically differently, and initiatives have been confined largely to countries where Canada's development and other relations have been minimal. Thus Canada has sustained assistance, unrestricted as to amount or form, to some repressive states on the dubious assumption that that fosters Canadian commercial and security interests.

Finally, the program's usefulness in helping bring about equitable development in countries seriously committed to social justice is in doubt because of the intrusion of political and, more particularly, commercial consideration into decision-making. In the final analysis, Canada's commitment to human rights in the aid program can be measured by the extent to which aid is directed at the basic needs of the world's most underprivileged. Government rhetoric to the contrary, only a modest proportion of assistance is so targeted.

For all these reasons, Canada is still a long way from fulfilling the goal, once so eloquently stated, of making the human condition the locus of its development activities and the liberation of humankind the central objective.

NOTES

I wish to thank Margaret Beddoe for her invaluable research assistance in connection with portions of this chapter.

1. Bernard Wood, in *Proceedings of the Eighth Annual Conference on Human Rights and Canadian Foreign Policy*, Canadian Human Rights Foundation, Ottawa, 29 March 1985, 126.

2. Paul Gérin-Lajoie, *The Longest Journey* (Ottawa: CIDA 1976), 15, 17, 22.

3. Canada, House of Commons, *Debates*, 3 March 1977, 3610, and 21 March 1978, 3989-96.

4. Final Report of the Sub-Committee on Canada's Relations with Latin America and the Caribbean, in Standing Committee on External Affairs and National Defence, *Minutes of Proceedings and Evidence*, 32nd Parl., 1st sess., no. 78, 23 Nov. 1982, 14-15; *Independence and Internationalism: Report of the Special Joint Committee on Canada's International Relations* (Ottawa: Supply and Services Canada 1986), 102-3; *For Whose Benefit? Report of the Standing Committee on External Affairs and International Trade on Canada's Official Development Assistance Policies and Programs* (Ottawa: Supply and Services Canada 1978), 27-30. For a fuller discussion of Parliament's consideration of human rights in context of development assistance policy, see Cathal Nolan, "The Influence of Parliament on Human Rights in Canadian Foreign Policy," *Human Rights Quarterly* 7 (Aug 1985), 380-5.

5. See, in particular, Robert Matthews and Cranford Pratt, "Human Rights and Foreign Policy: Principles and Canadian Practice," *Human Rights Quarterly* 7 (May 1985), 186. See also Geoffrey Pearson, "Emergency of Human Rights in International Relations," *International Perspectives* (July/Aug 1978), 11; Douglas Roche, "Towards a Foreign Policy for Canada in the 1980's," *International Perspectives* (May/June, July/Aug 1979), 6; Robert Carty and Virginia Smith, *Perpetuating Poverty: The Political Economy of Canadian Foreign Aid* (Toronto: Between the Lines 1981), 176; Robert Carty, "Giving for Gain — Foreign Aid and CIDA," in Robert Clarke and Richard Swift, eds., *Ties That Bind: Canada and the Third World* (Toronto: Between the Lines 1982), 202; M.W. Conley, "Development Aid and Human Rights: The Canadian Position," address to the Sixth Annual Conference on Human Rights and Canadian Foreign Policy, Canadian Human Rights Foundation, Ottawa, 22 April 1983, 5-6; Sheldon E. Gordon, "The Canadian Government and Human Rights Abroad," *International Perspectives* (Nov/Dec 1983), 9; and Irving Brecher, "Foreign Aid and Human Rights," *International Perspectives* (Sept/Oct 1985), 23-6.

6. Martin Rudner, *Human Rights Conditionality and International Development Co-Operation*, study prepared for CIDA under contract 82-433/C335, project 083/00009 (Ottawa: CIDA 1983), 71.

7. See *North–South Relations, 1980–85: Priorities for Canadian Policy*, a discussion paper prepared for the Special Committee of the House of Commons on North–South Relations (Ottawa: North-South Institute 1980), 65; E. Philip English, *Canadian Development Assistance to Haiti: An Independent Study* (Ottawa: North-South Institute 1984), 155, 162; Patricia Adams and Lawrence Solomon, *In the Name of Progress: The Underside of Foreign Aid* (Toronto: Energy Probe Research Foundation 1985), 160; "Public Statement of the Canadian Churches on Government Policy and the Crisis in Central America," 31 March 1982, cited in Rudner, *Conditionality*, 57; Inter-Church Committee on Human Rights in Latin America (ICCHRLA), "Canadian Policy on Central America: A Brief Presented to the Honourable Allan MacEachen on 11 October 1983," 17. A number of individuals and groups also made representations before the special joint committee in 1985 and 1986 and before the standing committee on External Affairs and International Trade in 1986 and 1987 in support of an aid–rights link.

8. *Globe and Mail* (Toronto) 20 Aug 1984. See also 18 Nov 1982, 11 Jan 1983, 3 April 1984, 2 May, 27 May, and 12 July 1985.

9. White paper, *Foreign Policy for Canadians*, International Development booklet (Ottawa: Information Canada 1970), 12.

10. *Debates*, 2 March 1977, 3574.

11. Canada, Department of External Affairs, Statements and Speeches 78/13, 26 Oct 1978, 6.

12. "Canada in a Changing World — Part II: Canadian Aid Policy," in Canada, House of Commons, *Minutes of Proceedings and Evidence of the Standing Committee on External Affairs and National Defence*, no. 3, 10 June 1980, 176.

13. External Affairs, Statements and Speeches 83/6, 22 April 1983, 4.

14. Debates, 16 June 1981, 10654; External Affairs Statements and Speeches 81/21, 29 July 1981, 3.

15. See, for example, External Affairs Statements and Speeches 85/16, 18 Oct 1985, 6.

16. Ibid., 81.7, 27 March 1981, 5; and CIDA, *Elements of Canada's Official Development Assistance Strategy* (Ottawa: CIDA 1984), 36.

17. Jack Donnelly, "Cultural Relativism and Universal Human Rights," *Human Rights Quarterly* 6 (Nov 1984), 404.

18. For articulate statements of this argument, see, inter alia, Peter L. Berger, "Are Human Rights Universal?" *Commentary* 64 (1977), 62; Evan Luard, "Human Rights and Foreign

Policy," *International Affairs* 56 (autumn 1980), 592–3; Rhoda Howard, *Is There an African Concept of Human Rights?* Working Paper no. A 8 (Toronto: Development Studies Programme, University of Toronto); Rudner, *Conditionality*, 18, 59–60; Matthews and Pratt, "Human Rights and Foreign Policy," 163.

19. Carty and Smith, *Perpetuating Poverty*, 176.
20. Rudner, *Conditionality*, 64–5.
21. For arguments based on national interest, see ibid., 67, and Matthews and Pratt, "Human Rights and Foreign Policy," 164.
22. Rudner, *Conditionality*, 57.
23. Matthews and Pratt, "Human Rights and Foreign Policy," 163–4. As the Trudeau government in effect stated in the 1970 foreign policy review, basic Canadian values constitute a component of the national interest, so that if Canadians aspire to a foreign policy that gives expression to humanitarian goals, then these goals require a place in its foreign policy. See *Foreign Policy for Canadians*, booklet 1, 10–11, 34. For a development of this idea, see James E. Hyndman, "National Interest and the New Look," *International Journal* 26 (winter 1970–1), 9–10.
24. Robert Matthews and Cranford Pratt, "Human Rights and Canada's Foreign Aid Policy," paper presented at the annual meeting of the Canadian Political Science Association, University of Guelph, 11 June 1984, 11.
25. Even multilateral action may, of course, be ineffective. Yet it may still be desirable to take an initiative on principle to avoid complicity in a state's repression.
26. This line of reasoning is particularly stressed by government officials and formed a central point in the Liberal government's opposition to the Foreign Aid Prohibition Bill of 1978, which, it was argued, would make Canadian development assistance policy a "hostage to only one factor." *Debates*, 21 March 1978, 3992. A CIDA policy document for the period 1982-3 to 1986-7 asserted that "the selection of countries of concentration for Canadian development co-operation assistance reflects" a "blend of humanitarian, developmental, political and commercial considerations"; human rights conditionality could be seen as conflicting with this goal of placing development "within a broader context of foreign policy objectives, governed by an overarching concept of the national interest." Rudner, *Conditionality*, 39.
27. See, for example, Margaret Doxey, "Human Rights and Canadian Foreign Policy," *Behind the Headlines* 37 (June 1979), 16; Rudner, *Conditionality*, 45.
28. See *Debates*, 21 March 1978, 3993. The problems in this regard are already apparent in the frequent differences of opinion expressed in Parliament about those countries where aid should be curtailed.
29. This argument was emphasized by some officials in interviews. See also Doxey, "Human Rights," 16.
30. Wood, in *Proceedings of Conference*, March 1985, 127.
31. See External Affairs, Statements and Speeches 78/13, 6; 81/7, 5; 82/23, 5; 83/6, 4; 84/4, 7; 85/16, 6; *Elements of Canada's Strategy*, 35.
32. Martin Rudner, "The Evolving Framework of Canadian Development Assistance Policy," in Brian W. Tomlin and Maureen Molot, eds., *Canada among Nations, 1984: A Time of Transition* (Toronto: Lorimer 1985), 127.
33. In interviews, some officials have admitted this, while pointing out that only over the last few years has the government been developing a policy.
34. See Theodore Cohn, "Politics of Canadian Food Aid: The Case of South and Southeast Asia," in Theodore Cohn, Geoffrey Hainsworth, and Lorne Kavic, eds., *Canada and Southeast Asia: Perspectives and Evolution of Public Policies* (Coquitlam, BC: Kaen Publishers c. 1980), 43.
35. See, for example, *Debates*, 19 Nov 1964, 10301–2.
36. *Foreign Policy for Canadians*, Pacific booklet, 20.
37. Calculated from CIDA's annual reports, 1970–71 to 1985–6.
38. In the mid-1970s, the estimated number of detainees was over 55,000: *Indonesia: An Amnesty International Report* (London: Amnesty International Publications 1977), 43; *Amnesty International Report 1985* (London: Amnesty International Publications 1985), 215.
39. See *Torture in the Eighties* (London: Amnesty International Publications 1984), 189–91.
40. The Center for Defense Information in Washington ranks the East Timor conflict as the most violent in the world relative to population size: Derek Rasmussen, "East Timor: A Tragedy Ignored," *Globe and Mail* 7 Dec 1985. For further details of the situation in East

Timor see *Amnesty International: East Timor Violations of Human Rights* (London: Amnesty International Publications 1985).

41. See Martin Rudner, "Advantages of Trading with Indonesia," *Canadian Business Review*, 11 (spring 1984), 26.
42. External Affairs, Statement and Speeches 81/16, 16 June 1981, 2.
43. Allan MacEachen, as reported in the Toronto *Star* 30 Sept 1976.
44. Cohn, "Politics of Canadian Food Aid," 49. For similar perspectives, see also Kim R. Nossal, "Les droits de la personne et la politique étrangère canadienne: le cas de l'Indonesie," *Etudes internationales* 11 (June 1980), 223–38; Lorne Kavic, "Innocents Abroad? A Review of Canadian Policies and Postures in Southeast Asia," and David Preston, "The Canada–Southeast Asia Aid and Trade Relationship: Evolution and Future Directions," in Cohn et al., eds., *Canada and Southeast Asia*, 28, 36–8; David Van Praagh, "Canada and Southeast Asia," in Peyton Lyon and Tareq Ismael, eds., *Canada and the Third World* (Toronto: Macmillan 1976), 334–5.
45. Interviews with the author.
46. Cohn, "Politics of Canadian Food Aid," 48.
47. *Country Profile: Uganda* (Ottawa: CIDA 1982), 2.
48. This was acknowledged by officials in interviews.
49. See, for example, *Debates*, 21 March 1978, 3991.
50. *Yearbook of the United Nations, 1979* XXXIII (New York: UN Department of Public Information 1982), 259; *Canadians in the Third World: CIDA's Year in Review, 1980–81* (Ottawa: CIDA 1982), 21–2.
51. For more details, see, for example, Simon Baynham, "Equatorial Guinea: The Terror and the Coup," *World Today* 36 (Feb 1980), 65–71.
52. *Amnesty International Report 1981* (London: Amnesty International Publication 1981), 39.
53. *A Review of Canadian Development Assistance Policy in the Western Hemisphere* (Ottawa: CIDA 1974), 40–3, 43–7, as quoted in Carty and Smith, *Perpetuating Poverty*, 66.
54. Calculated from the EDC's annual reports, 1974–84, and from data provided to the author by the EDC for 1977–9 and 1985–6.
55. See Virginia Smith, "What's Good for Business," *Last Post* 6 (June/July 1977), 11.
56. External Affairs, Statements and Speeches 82/12, 31 March 1982, 3.
57. Carty and Smith, *Perpetuating Poverty*, 67.
58. Such funds, directed at improving the economic lot of poor black South Africans, have been disbursed since 1982–3. In April 1984, Canada also announced a contribution of $1.5 million over five years toward a scholarship program for non-white South African students: "International Canada: The Events of April and May 1984," supplement to *International Perspectives* (July/Aug 1984), 11.
59. *Debates*, 9 March 1981, 8034.
60. *Canadians in the Third World: CIDA's Year in Review, 1981–82* (Ottawa: CIDA 1983), 26. See also Margaret Catley-Carlson, in *Minutes of Proceedings and Evidence of the Standing Committee on External Affairs and National Defence*, 33rd Parl., 1st sess., no. 22, 16 May 1985, 6. In interviews, officials acknowledged that the human rights rationale for these two suspensions was post facto.
61. James Guy, "El Salvador: Revolution without Change," *Behind the Headlines* 39 (October 1981), 4.
62. Indeed, in announcing the suspensions, the external affairs secretary praised the Duarte government for its efforts to bring order to the country and described it as a victim of violence by forces on the extreme left and right, while Duarte himself was seen as favouring reforms: *Debates*, 9 March 1981, 8034.
63. "International Canada: The Events of December 1984 and January 1985," supplement to *International Perspectives* (March/April 1985), 10; *Globe and Mail* 12 June and 10 July 1985; John Graham, "The Caribbean Basin: Whose Calypso?" notes for a speech by John Graham, director general, Caribbean and Central America Bureau, External Affairs, to the Canadian Institute of International Affairs, Foreign Policy Conference, 4 May 1985, 9.
64. *Globe and Mail* 1 April and 18 Dec 1985.
65. See Memorandum of Understanding between the Government of El Salvador and the Government of Canada, 2 April 1986. See also Meyer Brownstone, "Canadian Aid to El Salvador Gone Askew?" *Globe and Mail* 16 June 1986.
66. Graham, "The Caribbean Basin," 10.

67. Edgar J. Dosman, "Hemispheric Relations in the 1980's: Perspective from Canada," *Journal of Canadian Studies* 19 (winter 1984-5), 57.
68. Ibid., 55; ICCHRLA, "Canadian Policy on Central America," 6-7; Cecilio J. Morales, "A Canadian Role in Central America," *International Perspectives* (Jan/Feb 1985), 12; Matthews and Pratt, "Human Rights and Foreign Policy," 179-80.
69. One encouraging exception to this general pattern of treating pro-Western and Communist states differently is Nicaragua. Despite the political orientation of the Sandinista régime (and charges of violations of political and civil rights in particular), Canada continues to maintain a significant assistance program, justified on the grounds of its effective developmental impact at the grassroots level.
70. In interviews, some officials acknowledged this phenomenon and noted the difficulty of "taking on" countries where Canada has sizeable development programs and other important relationships.
71. Wood, in *Proceedings of Conference*, March 1985, 132-3.
72. Ottawa views human rights violations in Guyana as bad by Commonwealth Caribbean standards but not in global terms.
73. Information regarding aid to Sri Lanka has been obtained principally from interviews with officials in Ottawa.
74. *Globe and Mail* 29 Aug 1985, 12 June 1986.
75. "International Canada: The Events of October and November 1984," supplement to *International Perspectives* (Jan/Feb 1985), 8.
76. Compiled from CIDA annual reports, 1983-4, 1984-5, 1985-6.
77. Rudner, "The Evolving Framework," 134-5. See also *In the Canadian Interest? Third World Development in the 1980's* (Ottawa: North-South Institute 1980), 11, 56; Roger Young, *Canadian Foreign Aid Policies: Objectives, Influences and Consequences*, Working Paper no. A 10 (Toronto: Development Studies Programme, University of Toronto 1984), 9.
78. This problem is explored in Wyse, *Canadian Foreign Aid*, especially 47-69. See also *North-South Encounter: The Third World and Canadian Performance* (Ottawa: North-South Institute 1977), 122.
79. For a good recent account of the problems of tied aid, see G.K. Helleiner, "Canada, the Developing Countries and International Economy: What Next?" *Journal of Canadian Studies* 19 (winter 1984-5), 18-19. See also English, *Assistance to Haiti*; Roger Erhardt, *Canadian Development Assistance to Bangladesh: An Independent Study* (Ottawa: North-South Institute 1983); Roger Young, *Canadian Development Assistance to Tanzania: An Independent Study* (Ottawa: North-South Institute 1983).
80. *North-South Relations, 1980-85*, 53.
81. *Strategy for International Development Co-operation, 1975-80* (Ottawa: CIDA 1975), 9, 23-5; External Affairs, Statements and Speeches 81/7, 5; 81/16, 3-4; 81/25, 3-5.
82. Carty, "Giving for Gain," 194; Young, "Canadian Foreign Aid," 34.
83. In April 1986, CIDA adopted an all-grant program.
84. Martin Rudner, "Trade cum Aid in Canada's Official Development Assistance Strategy," in Brian W. Tomlin and Maureen Appel Molot, eds., *Canada among Nations, 1986: Talking Trade* (Toronto: Lorimer 1987), 136.
85. *The Mulroney Program and the Third World* (Ottawa: North-South Institute 1985), 8; *Globe and Mail* 7 Oct and 2 Dec 1985; Rudner, "The Evolving Framework," 137-44. This proposed scheme was, however, shelved as a result of the expenditure cuts announced in the February 1986 budget.
86. *Competitiveness and Security: Directions for Canada's International Relations* (Ottawa: Supply and Services Canada 1985), 9.

Part Six

Contemporary Issues and Debates

Just when is "contemporary?" That is a little like asking "When is history?" — the question with which we started this book.

It seems that certain issues have remained naggingly "contemporary" throughout Canadian history. We are as concerned today as we have ever been with the division of this country between French and English. We seem, as ever, transfixed by the roles that Native people, immigrants, and the environment play in shaping who we are and what we do. It seems that our contemporary interests are simply variations on long-standing themes, issues that merely resonate to current stimuli. But this view is simplistic and invites a kind of impoverished historicism to the interpretation of the world in which we now live. Those traditional issues, if they have not gone away, have been augmented by new and arguably much more interesting historical questions and pursuits.

Those new questions and pursuits are not frequently demarcated by national boundaries. The study of women's history, or Native history, or intellectual history *can* be fashioned within political boundaries, as we have done in this compilation, but they can as profitably be studied in an international context. Indeed, it is this internationalism that marks contemporary Canada more than any other feature. The era that began with the Second World War dragged Canada onto the international stage, and half a century later there can be no turning back.

It is the pluralism of contemporary Canadian society that is its most distinguishing feature, and it is perhaps not surprising that it is frequently difficult to find much unity in all this social diversity. But then we come back to politics — that most despised of contemporary scholarly interests. Politics remains the most conspicuous filter through which social, economic, and cultural change must pass. The Cold War may be officially over, but Canadians are searching for their new international role as much as any liberated state of the old Soviet Union. We are now inexorably linked to the United States (and, indeed, to Mexico) through NAFTA, but we remain uncertain of how we should fit together. We assert with smug confidence that we are very different from Americans and, to prove it, point at our social programs. We might just as well point at our burgeoning national debt — certainly a conspicuous distinguishing feature as well. And we proclaim ourselves proudly multicultural but haven't calculated the social and emotional costs of such "equality" beyond the political rhetoric. These and other issues are raised in our final section of readings.

The failure of the Meech Lake accord raised an important point: the ongoing strength of symbolic as opposed to actual conflict in our discussion of Canadian constitutional issues. Daniel Latouche touches on this idea in a chapter that dares to dream about the values of a formally regionalized Canada. Quebec, one might conclude, certainly is not "a province like the others," but perhaps, if one lets the constitutional dust settle a bit, one might see that "the others" are not like the others either.

Doubtless there will be a great deal more social, political, and economic "dust" descending as the formative and influential baby boomers age. The implications can begin to be seen in Robert Evans and his colleagues' chapter on health expenditures, which compares the Canadian and American health-care systems in terms of their structures and costs. As medical science becomes more sophisticated, it becomes more expensive. As the baby boomers age, the challenge will be to pay for the increased costs from a smaller tax base.

It is not difficult to uncover when "multiculturalism" became part of the Canadian political mantra. Cynics might say government multicultural policy has always been pure opportunism, a vote-getting expedition among impressionable ethnic groups. Others see it as yet another way of dealing with what they call "the problem" of Quebec. If everyone is ethnic, then there is no case to be made for special rights for the old *Canadien* collective. The chapter by V. Seymour Wilson on multiculturalism reminds us of the political implications of our culturally mixed society, especially, as he puts it, "the dynamic interplay between cultural pluralism, racial pluralism and liberalism and what such changes portend politically as dusk settles on this century."

Probably no activity has occupied more time and money at the national level than our devotion to defining ourselves through constitutional means and machinery. This singular pastime reached a kind of frenzy during the Trudeau and Mulroney years, culminating in the frantic efforts to reach agreement through adoption of the Meech Lake and Charlottetown accords. The role of the mass media in these events is analyzed by David Taras in the second-last article. He shows how the nature of media reports may well have changed the negotiation process and how differing reporting traditions in French and English Canada contributed to challenges and misunderstandings. Television's particular need to simplify often distorts important issues — and most of us get our "news" through television.

Finally, historian and former editor of *The Canadian Forum* John Hutcheson turns to another of our perpetual challenges, the nature and implications of our relationship with the United States, specifically in terms of Canadian culture and national identity. He reminds us that trade agreements have cultural connections that we ignore at our peril.

Further Reading

Rosalie Abella, *Equality in Employment: Royal Commission Report*. Ottawa: Minister of Supply and Services, 1984.

Michael Bliss, "Rewriting Medical History: Charles Best and the Banting and Best Myth." *The Journal of the History of Medicine and Allied Sciences* 48, no. 3 (1993): 253–74.

Raymond Breton, *Why Meech Failed: Lessons for Canadian Constitution-making*. Toronto: C.D. Howe Institute, no. 35, 1993.

Sandra Burt, "Women's Issues and the Women's Movement in Canada since 1970." In Alan Cairns and Cynthia Williams, eds., *The Politics of Gender, Ethnicity and Language in Canada*, 111–70. Toronto: University of Toronto Press, 1986.

David Charters, "From October to Oka: Peacekeeping in Canada, 1970–1990." In Marc Milner, ed., *Canadian Military History: Selected Readings*, 368–93. Toronto: Copp Clark, 1993.

Evelyn Kallen and Lawrence Lam, "Target for Hate: The Impact of the Zundel and Keegstra Trials on a Jewish-Canadian Audience." *Canadian Ethnic Studies* 25, no. 1 (1993): 9–24.

Meg Luxton, "Two Hands for the Clock: Changing Patterns in the Gendered Division of Labour in the Home." *Studies in Political Economy* 12 (1983): 27–44.

J.R. Miller, *Skyscrapers Hide the Heavens: A History of Indian-White Relations in Canada*, 2nd ed. Toronto: University of Toronto Press, 1991.

Vivienne Walters, "The Politics of Occupational Health and Safety: Interviews with Workers' Health and Safety Representatives and Company Doctors." *Canadian Review of Sociology and Anthropology* 22, no. 1 (1985): 57–79.

Robert A. Young, *The Secession of Quebec and the Future of Canada*. Montreal/Kingston: McGill-Queen's University Press, 1995.

Canada: The New Country from Within the Old Dominion

DANIEL LATOUCHE

This essay will leap freely from a vision of a "Canada-outside-Québec" to one of "Canada-without-Québec," realizing full well that the two are not equivalent and that the time has not yet come when one can talk freely of such unknowns. English Canada, as we are told, does not exist! Thus an essay about its future is but a loss of energy, and no amount of wishful thinking can escape this stubborn fact. But to engage in such rough play with reality is what an essay is all about, at least in French, where the word *essai* is both a literary genre and a football play (*troisième essai et dix verges à franchir*). And as far as Canada is concerned, this is certainly a "third-down" situation. This late in the game, Quebecers and Canadians alike can no longer afford to reject such illegal tactics.

Innis Revisited

But what does this English-Canadian *refus d'exister* mean exactly? Can it be taken at something else than its face value? True, one of the major stumbling blocks to any serious political reform in Canada has been the impossibility, for a large segment of the Canadian population and an even larger share of the Canadian political and economic élite, of envisaging seriously their existence as a nation. Examples of similar non-nationalism are rare and usually follow attempts to impose an artificial sense of nationhood. The case of East Germany immediately comes to mind. Even in the United Kingdom the existence of distinct nations is fully recognized, including the right to field competing football teams in international tournaments, a not-so-inconsequential compromise, considering the place of football in the social structure of the British Isles. Of course, by refusing their own nationhood, English Canadians have managed to avoid any serious discussion of a bi-national reconstruction of the country. That much is known. But now that the country is falling apart in front of their own eyes, this reluctance takes on a new meaning. There must be more to this self-refusal than mere strategy?

Quebecers of course have no such difficulty, and to some extent their own insistence that the behavior of their fellow Canadians can best be

SOURCE: "Canada: The New Country from Within the Old Dominion," *Queen's Quarterly* 98, no. 2 (Summer 1991): 319-37. Reprinted with permission.

explained by their status as English Canadians surely represents the other major stumbling block to a political overhaul of the country.

It is indeed a curious sight to witness the two "founding peoples" trying to convince one another that they are not what the other would like them very much to become: English Canadians on the one hand and Canadians "first-and-foremost" on the other. For a country that has produced two of this century's most important thinkers on communications — Harold Innis and Marshall McLuhan — this is a welcome paradox. Innis could certainly not have imagined a political empire based on such communication confusion, while McLuhan would have been hard pressed to explain a context where the two messengers pretend they are communicating while refusing to acknowledge each other's existence.

For Quebecers, the unanimity and the insistence with which those Canadians who use English as their lingua franca deny their collective existence is not only suspicious but also a confirmation of the thesis that English Canada does indeed exist. When one hears a Prince Edward Islander emphasizing the difference separating him from his Nova Scotian neighbour, only to be told later (with similar arguments) that an Albertan is not to be confused with a Manitoban (not to mention an Ontarian), it is very difficult not to see the invisible hand of a collective identity behind such an orchestration. These differences — regional, ethnic, and geographic — are almost too good and too profound to be true. On this issue at least, English Canadians all seem to think along the same lines. There must be a "national will" behind this strategy.

One cannot help but find it paradoxical that English Canadians spend so much energy denying they are a nation while acting very much like one, while most Québécois would be upset at the mere suggestion they are not such a nation, yet find it difficult locating the consequences of their widely proclaimed nationality. An outside observer would most certainly conclude that the two deserve one another.

Your insistence at establishing your own specificity from the Americans further confirms that you understand the importance of nationhood and shared symbols as the basis of political autonomy. Your success at doing so testifies to your ability at getting your political act together. Throughout the land, you lament the threat to your distinctiveness posed by the Free Trade Agreement. Quebecers do not always understand the sincerity of this plea, nor do they much sympathize with it, but they nevertheless realize that it constitutes an important bond among all English Canadians. In the eyes of this author, you are all, New Brunswickers and British Columbians alike, equally un-, if not anti-, American. The reasons given vary little from Victoria to Saint John's and are apparently shared by English Canadians of all possible ethnic and religious backgrounds.

Many Quebecers will recognize their own anti-(Parisian)French feelings in your attitude. From Gaspé to Arvida, they will draw up a similar list of reasons explaining why they should not be confused with the French (or with English Canadians for that matter). In our case as in yours, there must be a nation somewhere in the back to support such a widely held feeling of "us–them."

What makes matters worse is that Quebecers spend an inordinate amount of energy glossing over their own very real internal differences in order to present a common front: *Le Québec* and *Les Québécois* abound in their discourse (which includes this essay) and any attempt to break the family apart is always looked upon as a dangerous ploy. Of course, few Quebecers question the deep differences existing among the provinces, the regions, and the ethnic backgrounds of their fellow Canadians. But such differences are not deemed to contradict a more profound sense of community. On the contrary, such differences feed your own sense of unity. The Québécois in general do not know much about English Canada, and you are right in pointing out the dangers as well as the patronizing character of such ignorance. Nevertheless, give us credit for knowing that all English Canadians are not Anglo-Saxons. When we refer to "English Canada," we do not assume that your ethnic, religious, or even linguistic backgrounds are similar. We know they are not. We also know that outside of Québec, the worlds of the arts, business, politics, religion, and sport all operate in English, and, more importantly, all contribute to the definition of a common world. At repeated interludes, we have become the targets, for better or worse, of your shared world vision, as when you decided *en masse* that immersion schools were the best way to show your appreciation for our presence in this land of yours. We know — believe me, we *do* know — how effective you can be in hiding behind your collective non-identity: during the Meech Lake debate, for instance, or when you decided to blame the Québec tribal vote for imposing Free Trade on a reluctant English-Canadian princess.

On this last point, allow me a digression. It has to do with an incidental casualty of the Meech Lake ordeal. I am referring here to the demise of political civility which, in the words of my only true mentor, the late Donald Smiley, is the backbone of any pretense at political nationality. The fact that three premiers have either reconsidered or rescinded the signatures of their predecessors is one thing. But that so few voices were raised to object to this despicable behavior is another. Up until the end, we hoped for an opponent of Meech Lake to come forward and announce that such tactics were indeed unacceptable and would not be condoned. Alas!

For Quebecers, it is very difficult to understand that a common language — be it French, Portuguese, or Russian — is only a collection of shared linguistic symbols allowing individuals to communicate more rapidly than with sign language. On this matter, English Canadians think surprisingly like those very Americans from whom they strive so hard to differ. Over the years, Quebecers have come to believe that you are what you speak and that a community whose members can invent new words to describe new realities, be it a *dépanneur* or a *logiciel*, shares more than a communication space. Somewhere, some place, English must mean something to English Canada. And if it does not, then it should, just as it did to the Irish. If English is as "nationally neutral" as is often proclaimed, then why this insistence by so many that it occupy all of the space on *Corn Flakes* boxes? On this matter, we are both past the point of possible reconciliation. For us, a commercial sign is necessarily part of a culture; for you, it is the manifestation of free enterprise.

The ethnic physiognomy of Québec is changing. But these changes, as puzzling as they are, only serve to reinforce the importance of language as the ultimate Québec common denominator. Cultural pluralism is everywhere in Montréal, and many feel uncomfortable with this new diversity. But when this diversity expresses itself in French, one finds that it is more easily accepted. The integrative power of their own minority language makes it even more difficult for Quebecers to understand English Canadians when they claimed that their own increasing ethnic and racial diversity makes it unthinkable to talk of English Canada as a community. Is it not the case that in the rest of the country, English and the culture that comes with it carries a similar integrative power? How do you expect to hold your part of the country together if not by language and culture?

Of course, such questions are not completely disinterested on our part. The rise of radical chic multiculturalism in English Canada would be just another reason to express puzzlement at the English-Canadian habit of jumping on the bandwagon once it has gone by (similar to Québec's habit of staying forever on the train after having finally caught it), were it not for the impact of your passion for multiculturalism on Québec itself. We are already paying a heavy price for your linguistic nonchalance. We can only plead with you to take the issue of language back from the hands of the bigots who seem to have monopolized it. We understand your reluctance to interfere in linguistic matters, but, in the end, the character of a community is determined by the quality of its interventions in such delicate matters, not by the extent of its benign neglect.

As it is now officially expressed, the Canadian politics of multiculturalism within a framework of official bilingualism makes little sense anywhere in Canada, especially west of the Ottawa River. Does anyone really believe that Italians from Toronto or Chinese from Vancouver will ever express their ethnicity and their different way of "being Canadians" in French? I have not looked at the figures recently, but the rate of assimilation to French of second-generation Polish immigrants in Edmonton must fall well within the margin of error.

This is not the trivial matter you seem to think. Can we not assume instead that, one day, the majority of English Canadians from a non-English origin will insist on obtaining some form of recognition for their own language? English-Canadian élites assumed too easily that all who make use of English as the day-to-day language of communication share in their casual, almost benevolent, attitude towards language. How long can Canada-outside-Québec resist attempts at a linguistic reconstruction of the country in line with a more realistic assessment of the linguistic landscape? In order to placate non-French groups, the federal government has promoted a multicultural policy that is bound to clash with its presumably more important objective of promoting French-speaking rights outside of Québec. Unfortunately, these two unreal visions do not neutralize one another. They only serve to compound the problem.

As irrational as it might be, this bilingual–multicultural stand cannot but find support among Québec's own cultural communities, since it facilitates their mobility across the country. Since succeeding Québec governments, of the PQ or Liberal variety, have all proclaimed that bilingual multiculturalism was a non-starter in Québec, one can easily see the potential clashes that will come as a result of your own linguistic free trade. Of course, if you believe that such a mobility is to be encouraged — since it prevents Québec from becoming too French a province and deprives the West of labourers from East Montréal, then it is another matter altogether.

In the end, we do not understand what is so terribly wrong with being an English Canadian. Why claim that your regional, ethnic, or religious diversity does not contribute to your very own national identity? Why insist on incorporating the Quebecers in an identity game that you can play by yourselves? Why insist that English Canada and Québec both be made to disappear in order to create an identity for which we have very little use and which, I would claim, has long ceased to be profitable even to you?

Clearly, the answers to these questions belong to English Canada and I can only plead naïveté for speculating on the future of English Canada. Naïveté? Certainly, but with a portion of political realism also. The Free-Trade debate, the Meech Lake events, and — before that — the 1982 Constitutional ordeal all seem to indicate that English Canada will find it increasingly difficult to escape from its own reality and its own destiny. More difficult and more costly, I might add.

Of course, it makes a big difference if the coming of age of English Canada is achieved against a sovereign Québec or in tandem with a parting of the ways (perhaps even an amicable one). This is where the future comes in. As Québec moves closer, centimetre by centimetre, to sovereign status, it slowly comes to terms with the idea that its fate is intricately linked with that of the other non-American North Americans. Québec can probably survive outside of Canada and federalism. But can it do so if Canada itself ceases to exist and English Canada maintains to the end its *refus d'exister*?

The Status Quo Scenario

When all Canadian political leaders agree that the constitutional status quo is a non-viable option, one has to begin wondering if it is not both the most likely outcome and the most appropriate solution. Cynicism is not even the major justification for such a surprising conclusion. The status quo is not only a viable option for the short range but also one of the few options whose conditions are familiar to everyone: maintenance of the present constitutional framework (with the 1982 modifications) and preservation of the essential rules of the Canadian game (equality of all provinces and the predominance of Ottawa as the country's senior government).

Québec, of course, is the Achilles heel of the status quo scenario. A convincing case can indeed be made for Québec refusing to accommodate itself to even a revised form of status quo. The *independentist* forces, whether they made up 30 or 60 per cent of the population, will never agree to such a position. As for the rest, both the non-*independentist* nationalists and the non-nationalist federalists, Meech Lake has dealt a near-fatal blow to their hopes and aspirations. They are now convinced that something major has to happen on the constitutional front in order to prevent them from moving to a position of tacit acceptance of sovereignty. If these are the facts, at least as perceived by Québec protagonists, then clearly the case for the status quo is an open-and-shut one.

But a closer look at this much-maligned option will reveal that it has a rational calculus of its own and should not be discarded simply because it is presently a political orphan. As untenable as it may look, the status quo scenario contains the germs of its acceptability; after only a few months in the post–Meech Lake period, some are already apparent.

It is now clear that for both the Parti Québécois and the Québec Liberal Party the status quo is the second-best choice to their preferred option, since it keeps open the possibility of reviving either the *independentist* or the federalist drive. Without federalism or independence, the two parties cannot hold together their respective coalitions. The roles of the State, social welfare, economic development, energy policies, and the environment have created internal divisions that the two parties are barely able to contain. This is especially the case within the Parti Québécois, which is at peace with itself only when the dream is allowed to live on. As for the Liberal Party, the status quo is clearly preferable both for tactical and ideological reasons. Any attempt to significantly redefine a non–status quo position will clearly split the party and move some of its members toward either the Parti Québécois or the Equality Party.

In the rest of the country, the status quo is even more appealing. After all, the 1982 Constitution did go a long way to satisfy, at least partially, some of the pressing demands of the most vocal constituencies. The multicultural character of the country was recognized as a fundamental feature of Canadian society, and the collective rights of Native People received constitutional status, as did the paramount role of the central government in the area of economic regulation. The provincial priority over natural resources and the right of the poorer provinces to receive transfer payments are now part of the Canadian framework. And, of course, there is the Charter of Rights. Protection of minorities (including that segment of the English-Canadian majority that lives in Québec) has been so firmly entrenched that recent rulings of the Courts — notwithstanding the famous clause — have made it clear that any attempt to modify the linguistic framework is unacceptable under the principles of democracy. As a result, the bilingual nature of Québec society has now been made an integral part of the Canadian constitutional order.

Allow me a second digression, again on the same lines. When the Supreme Court verdict came down — arguing as it did that Bill 101 was indeed dictatorial and undemocratic in nature — no English-Canadian voice was raised deploring this flagrant hijacking of democratic principles. No political leader was heard declaring that this task was the sole responsibility of the elected officials of the country. All preferred to hide behind the Court and thus preserve their own electoral future. Is it then surprising that Quebecers see little use in an elected federal parliament, or a reconstituted senate, to protect their own specificity? If the Courts are to decide on everything that is controversial, how can we expect political parties to fulfill their brokerage role?

When one talks of the status quo, one is actually talking of the new situation created by the 1982 reform. Few countries in the world benefit from such a "recent" status quo. Indeed, the Canadian political and constitutional status quo has yet to give its full measure. It is still an underdeveloped status quo, a most uncomfortable situation for any such situation! As a result, this status quo is still changing before our very eyes.

Although few Quebecers will admit to it, the 1982 constitutional reform is nothing less than a striking accomplishment — assuming we disregard the Québec situation for a moment — and one on which we should all reflect. One cannot understand Meech Lake and speculate intelligently on the post–Meech Lake era without taking into account the lessons of 1982. It was, if I might be allowed to say so, English Canada at its finest constitutional hour.

The 1982 constitutional package was both a respectable and a sensible one. I happen to believe that the decision to incorporate the American principle of a Bill of Rights was a serious error, but one cannot help but admire the elegance with which it was achieved. It shows that not only can a partly-written and partly-unwritten constitution be modified — no small feat in itself — but that such a modification can be achieved according to the rules of the art. Compared to the French, who are still struggling to come to terms with their 1958 constitutional upheaval, the transition from the First to the Second Canadian Constitutional Order was an especially smooth one.

It should all be clear by now: the major reason why Meech Lake failed has little to do with the idiosyncrasies of the Newfoundland Premier or the congenital bad faith of English Canada. Meech Lake failed because it ran against everything that had just been constitutionalized and had been proven to work relatively well. Compared to Meech Lake, the 1982 reform was the result of a long and public process. Although there were confidential bargaining sessions, sometimes late into the night, premiers had the chance to publicly air their positions and to talk, if only for posturing reasons, of what the "people of Manitoba" or the "fishermen of Nova Scotia" really wanted. In 1982, there was no unique provincial agenda and certainly not a Québec-based one; the participants could avoid having to resort to the artifice of a second round, thereby saving the susceptibilities of those whose issues are often relegated to "further considerations." In 1982, everything that was being discussed was on the table and no one — except perhaps the Native People — felt that this was not their round. The 1982 agenda was not only an inter-provincial one, it also had a Canadian component. In the end, the central government could also claim that it had gained some new powers and that its role as the senior government, the government of all Canadians, had been reinforced. This was not the case with Meech. Except for Québec, and more precisely the Québec Liberal government of Robert Bourassa, Meech Lake had no constituency and no prospective client who could stand up and defend the deal.

Clearly, the 1982 deal proves that it is possible for Canada-outside-Québec (COQ) to get its act together, to adjudicate its internal differences, and to come up with a constitutional package that reflects the values, the aspirations, and the *rapports de force* as they exist in COQ. This suggests that it is indeed possible to "constitutionalize" the agenda of COQ; Canada-without-Québec (CWQ) could eventually undergo a similar process. How can anyone pretend that English Canada does not exist beyond its provincial incarnations? You are more than the sum of your parts.

Québec was not part of the 1982 deal. Much has been made of the intentionality and the legitimacy of such an exclusion. Was Québec a bona fide participant in the negotiation, or was the obvious lack of good faith of a separatist Québec delegation sufficient reason to exclude it from the final settlement? As all the participants publish their memoirs, we can get a clearer picture of their states of mind at the time. But the important lessons of that fateful conference lie elsewhere. None of the provincial actors felt obliged to conclude that the absence of Québec, whatever the government in place, was sufficient reason to call off the whole deal. The participation of Québec in the constitutional process was judged with a different set of criteria than that of the other provinces. Furthermore, the fact that a deal was eventually struck also indicates that the absence of Québec does not destroy the natural equilibriums (East versus West, centre versus periphery, original charter provinces versus "new" provinces) that are often said to constitute the foundations of the Canadian federal experience. Once Québec was excluded, all the pieces of the Canadian constitutional puzzle fell rapidly in place, almost by magic. If Québec had not been present throughout the 1980–82 negotiations, would the final deal have been significantly different from the one finally struck in November 1981? To ask the question is to answer it. The particular chemistry of the 1982 agreement, including the famous infamous clause, had little to do with Québec. Of course, this confirms what we had known all along: the sole objective of the English-speaking provinces of Canada is not to make life miserable — constitutionally speaking, that is — for its French-speaking province. The 1982 Constitution was not a conspiracy but an act of state-making and nation-building. For Quebecers, this is particularly difficult to admit, since it implies that they are not necessarily the centre of Canadian existence. As an afterthought, one can only speculate as to how much "better," and more representative, the 1982 Act could have been if Québec had been left outside from the beginning.

This rehabilitation, however suspect, of the 1982 Constitutional Act should at the very least convince a reluctant observer that the present constitutional set-up is not an accidental one or the mere result of an "adhocratic" process of muddling through. It is here to stay, one might be tempted to conclude, were it not for Québec, of course, and for this unfortunate "status quo" label. The fact that even the insignificant proposals contained in the Meech Lake Accord were deemed to be dangerous to the future health of the 1982 Act only testifies to the delicate craftsmanship that went into its creation. Can we not conclude, then, that English Canada has finally given itself, if not its first constitution, at least the general outlines of where its constitutional future lies?

This status quo can and will probably suffer numerous accommodations. The Meech Lake Accord provided one set of them, which was rejected because it moved the entire document in the wrong direction. Other packages can be imagined with more attention being paid to the Senate and Native Peoples.

The present and all possible future *status quos* defined along the 1982 lines are clearly unacceptable to Québec. But as in the past — in 1760, 1840, or 1982 — the status quo is not detrimental to the point of imposing a final process of "normalization." The resurgence of the *independentist* sentiment between 1982 and 1987, well before the agony of Meech Lake, only confirms that "political nights" never last for very long in Québec. In fact, since 1760, such periods have tended to be shorter and shorter, the last one lasting fewer than 50 months.

More important still, and certainly more controversial, is the fact that such a status quo would also be detrimental to English Canada. True, the preservation of the status quo provides English Canada with more breathing room, since it does not have to face the question of its own cultural and political existence. But there are costs to such a holding action. A strong sense of one's cultural identity, firmly grounded in traditions, language, geography, and mythologies of all kinds, will come to play an increasingly important role in the emergent world system. English Canada needs this sense of self; it no longer can expect the traditional instruments of Canadian nationalism — Via Rail or the CBC — to play this role. The Canadian state can no longer do the job. Society has to take over. In this world of global competition and commercial warfare, culture is the ultimate non-tariff barrier, one that you cannot do without. Will you find it patronizing if I conclude that you are almost there?

The Independence Scenario

Let us assume that the constitutional continuity of Canada has been broken and that Québec has become a sovereign state. Such an assumption immediately raises a number of interesting questions concerning how such a break would occur and what sort of Canada–Québec relationships would emerge in its aftermath. Would there be a referendum in Québec? Would the federal government and the other provinces have to acquiesce in this process? Would sovereignty be part of an association deal? What about Canadian territorial claims in Northern Québec? The list of questions is almost infinite and only serves to indicate that the extrication process would be a long and complex one. Any attempt by a "separatist" Québécois to depict the post-sovereignty world of Canada–Québec relations is necessarily suspect. To speculate positively on the internal arrangements of Canada after the Big Bang raises even more eyebrows. No one likes to be told, "Come on. You can do it." But silence, however respectful, is no solution either.

Attention so far has been directed at the costs of such a constitutional break-away and at the likely reaction of the rest of Canada. To assume, as many do, that COQ would never negotiate or would have no other choice but to negotiate its transformation into a CWQ is a somewhat futile exercise. More often than not it rests on a misguided vision of why, when, where, and how nations negotiate.

There are only two alternatives to a direct Canada–Québec negotiation following a decision by the latter to achieve a sovereign status. One is the use of economic and legal sanctions against the "secessionist" province, backed up by the threat or the actual use of military force. However unpleasant, this eventuality should be evaluated more seriously than it has been in the past. Sanctions and force do not necessarily entail a full-fledged civil war on the Biafran scale. Nor should we conclude that they would not succeed in their objective, that is, to preserve the territorial and political integrity of Canada. Force does indeed work, as the 1968 Prague spring should remind us. For 20 years thereafter, Russian troops did not have to intervene.

The choice of such a brutal alternative to negotiation with an aspiring sovereign Québec is not unthinkable. But to succeed, it would require Canada to find the necessary consensus, the leadership, and the resources to embark on such a course. What would the objectives of such a declaration of political war be? To restore federalism? To abolish the Québec National Assembly? To install a more "sensible" provincial government? Would it indeed be in Canada's self-interest to exact as high a price as possible before acquiescing to Québec's sovereignty? Would Canada benefit from a poor, unstable, and recriminatory neighbour? Would Western Canada increase its position within the reconstituted federation if the latter "welcomed" with open arms the Montréal West Island? Nations often act irrationally, but they usually do so to defend what they believe to be their interests. They rarely do so to get even or to make a point.

While the outcome described above requires the existence of a strong national will in the rest of the country, one could also imagine another scenario: the total absence of such a will, so that Québec would find nobody to talk to, as provinces and regions sought to profit from Québec's departure while the central government sat powerless, without the legitimacy or the will-power to regroup the federation. Thus, we are back to discussing English Canada. The disintegration hypothesis has a number of variants, all centred on whether or not some or all of the provinces decide to cast their lot with the U.S. Until now no provincial or federal political party has advocated such a union, but there is no doubt that logical reasoning as well as a conjuncture of events could lead Canadians to accept and even seek such a union. Nevertheless, it is difficult to imagine that Québec's departure would have such cataclysmic consequences. To make it come true, one has to assume that Québec is such a necessary component of Canada — politically, economically or psychologically — that its departure would make it impossible for Canadians to want to live together or make the annexation hypothesis suddenly more attractive. Nothing in recent Canadian history suggests that Québec is so indispensable. Of course, Canada without Québec would be a very different kind of country, but it still could be a country.

Would such a CWQ be a workable one? With Ontario occupying a pivotal position, with 49 per cent of the population and 54 per cent of the GNP, the new Canada will undoubtedly have to be reorganized to prevent this imbalance from paralyzing the country. The creation of new provinces in the North, the partition of Ontario itself, and the regionalization of the West and Atlantic Canada are possible ways of correcting this imbalance. But by itself, an Ontario-dominated Canada is not an unworkable outcome and would not necessarily exacerbate the regional frustrations coming out of the West and East, tensions that owe much of their acrimony to the perturbing impact of a "Québec Problem," which always seems to monopolize attention. Of all the provinces, Ontario is probably the one with the most to lose — economically and psychologically speaking, that is — if Québec decides to opt out. Its position within the new CWQ will surely reflect this fact.

Undoubtedly, the exit of Québec would affect Canada's international standing, notably as an already fringe member of the select "Group of Most Industrialized Countries." It would nevertheless remain in its present standing as the seventh member of the Club. Its reputation as an oasis of peace and harmony and as the land where complex problems are always resolved through even more complex solutions would also suffer. But even on this front, Canada has been living off its old capital for some time, and the new geography of world politics calls for more imaginative positioning than that of honest broker or middle power. Though harsh for Canadians, such a penalty would barely be noticed in today's turbulent international environment.

Why assume, as so many do, that this new Canada would necessarily have a weak central government and, as a consequence, a higher level of provincial balkanization? True, culture and geography have made it increasingly difficult to rule Canada from the centre. But its demography and traditions will continue to make it equally difficult for the parts to ignore one another. Left on their own, provinces have been able to achieve substantial harmonization, whether in the areas of trucking deregulation, lotteries, forest management, professional certification, or even financial services. Rarely has the involvement of the federal government enhanced this process. The degree of policy transfer and imitation across provincial barriers has remained strong, and it is in those areas where balkanization seems to have hit the hardest that Canadian successes have been greatest: the arts and culture, welfare, and — more recently — financial deregulation. In the areas of university education and scientific research, to name only two, only the presence of Québec has prevented the other governments from moving more effectively towards the establishment of truly national policies. Canada needs a national university and a national network of research centres. Even in Québec, we know that much, although we cannot afford to say so.

In this vision of a new regional Canada, one could also expect a move to consolidate many parallel policies among neighbouring units. One can already envisage an amalgamation process through which the institutional and policy differences between Nova Scotia and Alberta might increase (for example, in the fisheries and agricultural areas), but where similar differences between Alberta and Saskatchewan, on the one hand, and Nova Scotia and New Brunswick, on the other, might be considerably attenuated as each region attempts to pool its resources. Policy and political differences are no threat by themselves. They become so when they have no other foundations than administrative mimetism.

Paradoxically, a regionalized Canada would be more likely to achieve a higher degree of interdependence than the present provincially-based format. In many cases, the nine remaining provinces will ask for such harmonization and will be willing to provide the central government with the authority to create it. Larger regional units will have a more diversified economic base and thus will be able to engage in a full spectrum of exchanges with their neighbours. For example, economic relations between Saskatchewan and Ontario, which until now have been largely antinomic because of the weak economic base of the prairie province, would certainly grow in complexity and interdependence as Saskatchewan is slowly incorporated into a larger and more diversified regional unit. In short, an increase in the scale of the confederal sub-units would likely reduce the probability of deviation from centre-of-the-road policies.

What kind of political life would characterize this new Canada? Would any of the three major parties cease to exist because of the loss of its Québec partisan base? The creation and the rise of the *Bloc Québécois* in Ottawa and its likely success at the next federal election is most likely to put all three federal parties on the same footing *vis-à-vis* Québec. One can also expect a reduction in the autonomy of the present provincial and municipal party systems. With Québec out, the three major Canadian party traditions will find it easier to achieve a higher level of integration across system levels, thereby providing further policy and personnel integration.

To what extent can we expect the various regions to follow divergent political orientations? Again, geography and demography can provide preliminary answers to this perplexing question. With the existing framework of 10 provinces, there are on average three provincial or federal elections a year and one turnover. With regional governments taking over some of the present provincial responsibilities, turnovers would necessarily be less numerous, and they would carry fewer consequences. In the past, non-traditional parties, either of the left or right variety, have tended to emerge in the smaller provinces, notably in the West. The amalgamation of the existing provinces in larger constituencies would make such deviations more difficult to achieve and less extreme if and when they ever took place. In no way does this "Australiation" of Canadian politics threaten its democratic foundations.

What about the situation of the French-speaking minority in this scenario? The rationale for its eventual downfall is well known. But there is a danger in looking at the future through the lenses of the past 20 years. Indeed, if one assumes that these minorities owe much of their survival to the vigorous policies of the central government and to a desire to keep Québec within Canada by providing the basic linguistic requirements for French minorities across Canada, then one is forced to conclude that Québec's accession would indeed bring doom and gloom to these minorities. Official bilingualism will no doubt be one of the first victims of a CWQ. If indeed Western Canada becomes a politically recognized region within the new arrangement, there is little doubt that bilinguism will not receive the same level of support as it presently does.

But has official bilingualism been so good to the French minorities? And what of the English minorities in Québec? Could we not argue that the drive towards two unilingual entities has little to do with the existence of government programmes and official support? One could also claim that, considering the financial position of the Canadian government, it makes little difference whether or not it seeks to play an active role on the minority front: it no longer has the resources to do so. Outside of Ontario, New Brunswick, and possibly Manitoba, French simply does not have the necessary demographic strength, immersion or no immersion, to maintain a livable cultural base. The same argument would apply to English in the Mauricie or Beauce regions of Québec.

But this debate is a sterile one. It raises few new ideas. It has been going on for a generation, and both sides of the argument share equally in the hypocrisy of appearing to care for minorities while waiting for the verdict of history. Eventually the verdict will come, and after an initial we-told-you-so reaction Québec nationalists will be forced, for the first time, to address the question of the French-speaking minorities outside of Québec. Indeed, one may even predict a dramatic change of attitude on the part of Quebecers. Until now, French-speaking minorities have been caught between Ottawa's desire to prove that you could indeed live in French in Moose Jaw and Québec's own assertion that only in Québec could a French culture survive. It was the perfect non-zero-sum game. There will be little need for such demonstrations in a post-sovereignty scenario.

It can also be argued that the geo-political conditions under which the two distinct nations would then operate would create a radically new situation — one likely to have a more lasting impact on the situation of the two minorities than the old ones. Both Canada and Québec (especially Québec) will be forced or will find it to their advantage to offer a satisfactory deal to their respective minorities. This possibility has little to do with generosity and open-mindedness, but rests entirely on a geopolitical calculus. Curiously, the anglophone minority of Québec is most likely to benefit from this new era. Of course, it will likely lose more of its members, and it cannot hope to come back to the pre-Bill 101 days. But even within these constraints, its margin of maneuvering could increase. It no longer controls the economic or commercial levers of the province and, as such, there is little fear that it could be made an ethnic scapegoat along the lines of the Asian enclave minorities in East Africa. One cannot expect English to ever reach in Québec the snobbish status it has attained in France. Even in the best of worlds, certain things remain out of reach. Nevertheless, English and the language issue are bound to play a less pivotal role in the internal debates of a sovereign Québec, if only because there will be more important issues around which to rally.

But I am getting dangerously close to speculations about an independent Québec. My intention was to talk exclusively about your Canada. We all knew I could probably not succeed in this task. A lack of practice, I suppose. I can only hope that this short and meandering excursion into territory that is not mine will not have shocked you (not too much, anyway). You should consider it as a first attempt to see beyond the Québec problem.

Controlling Health Expenditures — Canada and the United States

ROBERT G. EVANS, JONATHAN LOMAS, MORRIS L. BARER, ROBERTA J. LABELLE, CATHERINE FOOKS, GREGORY L. STODDART, GEOFFREY M. ANDERSON, DAVID FEENY, AMIRAM GAFNI, GEORGE W. TORRANCE, and WILLIAM G. THOLL

American interest in the Canadian health care system appears to be on the rise, as evidenced in a recent three-part article by Iglehart[1-3] in the *Journal*. Such interest has been intermittent in the past, depending in part on the position of national health insurance on the U.S. political agenda. In the early 1970s, the most recent period during which national health insurance seemed imminent, Americans paid considerable attention to the structure, logic, and history of the Canadian system.[4] At the time, that system had just been established in its entirety. Although its origins and organization were documented, there had been little experience with universal, public coverage, and data were not yet available on its performance. Universal hospital coverage was a decade or more old (in Saskatchewan, a quarter century), but the extension of insurance

SOURCE: "Controlling Health Expenditures — The Canadian Reality," *The New England Journal of Medicine* 320, no. 9 (March 2, 1989): 571–77. Reprinted by permission of The New England Journal of Medicine. Copyright 1989, Massachusetts Medical Society.

to cover physicians' services was very new. Then the moment passed, national health insurance moved off the American agenda, and after a variety of attempts to regulate the health care system at arm's length, competition and the marketplace became the dominant ideas of the 1980s. In this context the Canadian experience was of little relevance.

So far, however, market forces, at least as applied in practice, have been even less successful in containing the growth of health care expenditures than were the regulatory efforts of the 1970s.[5,6] The one major success in this field, prospective payment and diagnosis-related groups, is virtually a pure type of regulatory intervention, despite its being occasionally clothed in market rhetoric. At the same time, the proportion of the American population with no insurance coverage or grossly inadequate coverage is believed to be both large and growing,[7,8] and there is increasing uneasiness about the effect of market forces in health care on the interests of both patients and providers.[9-11] In this context, the radically different Canadian approach to funding may deserve a second look — not as a panacea, but as evidence that perhaps things could be different. By now that system has generated nearly two decades of experience that can be compared with the American record.

To an American audience, the most striking feature of the Canadian experience may be the association of universal coverage with substantially lower expenditures for health services. Despite (or, as many Canadians would argue, because of) universal access on equal terms and conditions, overall costs in Canada have risen more or less in line with the growth of national income, rather than eating up a steadily increasing share of it, as in the United States.

Before 1971, when the Canadian funding system was more similar to the American one, health care costs consumed a share of national income that was virtually identical in both countries and was rising steadily. In 1971 it reached 7.4 percent in Canada, as compared with 7.6 percent in the United States. After 1971, however, the Canadian share remained stable, whereas in the United States it continued to rise.[5,12-14] By 1981 their spending shares were 7.7 and 9.2 percent, respectively. In the 1982 recession, the share of expenditures for health care rose sharply in both countries, to 8.6 and 10.2 percent.[12,14] In both systems, health care escaped the effects of the recession — an interesting and unstudied observation. But the Canadian share stabilized at its new level; preliminary estimates for 1987 show it still at 8.6 percent. In contrast, the United States share continued to rise. Estimates for 1987 are in excess of 11 percent.[5,15]

The large and growing gap between the United States and Canada drives home the point that, for good or ill, the form of funding adopted by Canada does permit a society to control its overall outlays on health care. Furthermore, it is unnecessary to impose financial barriers to access in the process. In this paper we sketch some of the basic institutional and statistical facts of that process, and their implications for physicians in particular.

Cost control, although successful in general, can be a bruising political process, producing much sound and fury. External observers who rely on newspaper reports may not always get a clear picture, either of the critical issues in dispute or of the distinction between facts and rhetoric. Further confusion arises from casual interpretations of the comparative data, such as that by Feder et al.[16] Looking at the period from 1970 to 1984, they noted that health spending in Canada rose faster than in the United States, but that the gross national product (GNP) rose faster still. They concluded that the apparent success of the Canadian system with cost control was illusory, and that the stability of the share of the GNP applied to health care was simply the result of rapid economic growth. A more detailed look at the data shows this conclusion to be incorrect.

National Income and Health Expenditures in Canada and the United States

Table 1 provides the relevant data for Canada and the United States over the period referred to by Feder et al. The Canadian GNP does in fact outpace the American by 2 percent per year. But after adjustment for the more rapid rate of inflation in Canada, our advantage shrinks to 0.7 percent. When adjusted further for the slightly faster growth of the Canadian population, the difference in real per capita growth rates is less than half a percent per year — respectable enough over the long term, but not enough to account for the divergence in the shares of the GNP spent on health. The oversight of confusing nominal with real rates of GNP growth leads Feder et al. to their erroneous conclusion.

The relevant base year for examining the effect of national health insurance on health spending is not 1970, however, but 1971. Quebec, the second-largest province, with about a quarter of the Canadian population, adopted its health plan in October 1970, and New Brunswick began its plan on January 1, 1971. Correspondingly there was a substantial jump, from 7.1 to 7.4 percent, in the share of the GNP applied to health care for all of Canada.

Table 2 shows the annual rates of increase in total health spending in Canada and the United States since the completion of universal Medicare coverage in Canada. Spending in nominal dollars did rise somewhat faster in Canada, by 0.7 percent per year. But when account is taken of the more rapid rate of general inflation in Canada and the slightly faster rate of population growth, health spending in constant dollars per capita rose more slowly in Canada, by 1.6 percent per year.

TABLE 1 **Average Annual Percentage Increases in Gross National Product (GNP), 1970 to 1984***

Measures of GNP	Canada	United States	Difference**
Current dollars	12.1	9.8	2.0
Constant dollars	3.4	2.7	0.7
Constant dollars per capita	2.2	1.7	0.4

*Data for the United States are from the Health Care Financing Administration[5] and the Bureau of Economic Analysis;[17] data for Canada are from the Department of Finance.[18,19]
**Differences in annual growth rates must be calculated geometrically, not by subtraction $[d=(1+r_1)/(1+r_2)-1]$. Rates have been rounded after calculation.

TABLE 2 **Average Annual Percentage Increases in Total Expenditures for Health Care, 1971 to 1985***

Measures of health expenditures	Canada	United States	Difference**
Current dollars	13.1	12.3	0.7
Constant dollars***	4.3	5.8	-1.4
Constant dollars per capita***	3.1	4.8	-1.6

*Data for the United States are from the Health Care Financing Administration,[5] Gibson et al.,[14] and the Department of Commerce;[17] data for Canada are from Health and Welfare Canada[12,13] and the Department of Finance.[18,19]
**Differences in annual growth rates must be calculated geometrically, not by subtraction $[d=(1+r_1)/(1+r_2)-1]$. Rates have been rounded after calculation.
***These constant-dollar measures are not real output measures for the health sector; they have not been adjusted by price indexes specific to the health sector. Rather, they are adjusted for changes in the general level of prices, economy-wide, as reflected in price indexes based on gross national expenditures, and they therefore reflect the increase in generalized purchasing power that is absorbed by the health care sector, in the form of either increased resource inputs or health sector-specific inflation.

To put this more concretely, in 1985 Americans spent an average of $1,710 each on health care.[5] If their rate of cost escalation since 1971, in real terms, had been the same as that in Canada, they would have spent only $1,362, or 20 percent less. Preliminary estimates for 1987 show Americans spending just under $2,000 each for health care. Detailed Canadian data are not yet available, but the spending gap is clearly continuing to widen. One may estimate conservatively that if the Canadian rates of escalation in real cost since 1971 had prevailed in the United States, health spending would by 1987 be about $450 less, on average, for every person in the country, or at least $100 billion less in all.

The Process of Cost Control in Canada

How such control has been achieved, and with what effects, continues to form a major part of the agenda for research in health services in

Canada.[20] As Iglehart pointed out,[2] virtually the entire difference between Canada and the United States in the share of GNP that is spent on health is accounted for by three components: insurance overhead, or costs of prepayment and administration; payments to hospitals; and payments for physicians' services. In 1985, these three items took up 0.59, 4.18, and 2.07 percent, respectively, of the U.S. GNP, and 0.11, 3.48, and 1.35 percent of the Canadian GNP.

Relative to the expenditures that might have been generated by a system comparable to Canada's, in 1985 Americans spent about $20 billion more for insurance and prepayment costs, and just under $30 billion more for each of physicians' services and hospital costs.

ADMINISTRATION AND PREPAYMENT EXPENSES

In relative terms, the most extraordinary difference between Canadian and American spending is in the area of administration and prepayment expenses. In 1985 the overhead component of health insurance — the share of premiums that goes not to the reimbursement of physicians, hospitals, and other providers, but to paying for the handling of the flow of paper and dollars — cost Americans $95 each, out of their overall $1,710. Canadians spent $21 — and those were Canadian dollars. Indeed, Canadians spent less per capita to administer universal comprehensive coverage than Americans spent to administer Medicare and Medicaid alone (about $26 U.S. per capita[5]).

A universal, tax-financed system can simply be much less costly to administer, at all levels, and the Canadian system is. On the revenue side, once a tax system is in place, as it is in all modern societies — with income tax, sales tax, and everything else — the additional cost of raising more funds is minimal. (Some Canadian provinces continue to collect premiums, which are taxes in all but name. They are related to family size, but not to risk status; they cover only a portion of the total plan outlays; they are compulsory for most of the population; and most important, coverage is not conditional on payment.)

On the expense side, all the costs of determining coverage and eligibility are avoided — everyone is eligible, and for the same benefits. Patients drop out of the payment system entirely, and reimbursement takes place between the public insurer and the provider. There are no marketing expenses, costs of estimating risk status in order to set differential premiums or decide whom to cover, and no allocations for shareholder profits; the process of claims payment, although not free of costs, is greatly simplified and much cheaper. In this area it is obvious that the public sector is more efficient and less costly than the private sector,[21] a fact that was recognized early on in Canada. The 1964 Royal Commission on Health Services, which drew up the blueprint for Canada's universal system, described the private administration of insurance as "an uneconomic use of . . . limited resources."[22] This "uneconomic use" accounts for nearly one quarter of the difference in cost for health insurance between Canada and the United States.

Nor is that the end of the story. Himmelstein and Woolhandler[23] calculate that in the United States, the provider-borne overheads for hospitals, nursing homes, and doctors' offices (the accounting costs of complying with the requirements for documentation by a multiplicity of insurers, as well as coping with the determination of eligibility, direct billing of patients, and collections) amounted to $62.1 billion in 1983. They estimate that shifting to a national health insurance system could save $21.4 billion in the administrative costs of hospitals and physicians' offices. This would be 6 percent of total health care costs, or 0.63 percent of the GNP in 1983 — leading to the startling conclusion that the costs of running the American payment system itself, independent of the costs of patient care, may account for more than half the difference in cost between the Canadian and the U.S. systems.

For the Canadian physician, differences in the costs of insurance administration show up as a lower overhead for practice. The problems of determining insurance status and managing the collections process disappear, along with the problem of uncollectable accounts. The costs of compliance with the requirements of the health care reimbursement system also show up outside the area of health expenditures as it is normally defined, particularly in the budgets of the social welfare services, and to no inconsiderable degree in the monetary and nonmonetary costs borne by individual patients and their families. Furthermore, the considerable research, legal, and regulatory efforts required to put the complex and varied reporting and compliance requirements in place are not without cost, but will be counted as outside the health care system.

There is private insurance for some forms of health care in Canada. But for hospital and medical care, such coverage is prohibited for services that are included in the public plans. The original intent was quite explicit — to prevent private firms from skimming off the good risks, supporting the development of multiclass service, or both. But the restriction also has the very important effect of making provincial governments to all intents and purposes the sole funders of hospital and medical care, and of creating a bilateral bargaining situation as the foundation for cost control in these sectors.

THE EFFECT ON HOSPITALS

In Canada, controlling hospital costs is a two-part process. Operating budgets are approved, and funded almost entirely, by the Ministry of Health in each province, but they include no allowance for capital expenditures. New facilities, equipment, major renovations, and the like are funded from a variety of sources, but they require the approval of the same provincial agency, which generally also contributes the major share of financing. This process of centralized approval prohibits hospitals from accessing private capital markets, and has historically limited their efforts to support expansions of capacity from community sources. So far, it has been relatively successful in limiting such expansion,[24] but somewhat less successful in managing the diffusion of major equipment.[25,26]

Centralized control over operating costs is more complete. Annual global budgets are negotiated between ministries and individual hospitals. Although political pressures have often forced governments to pick up the deficits of hospitals that are unable or unwilling to stay within these budgets, this process has resulted in a significantly less rapid rise in hospital expenditures in Canada than in the United States.[27,28]

The more rapid rate of escalation of hospital costs in the United States since 1971 has been shown to result from major differences in the growth in hospital costs per patient day at constant hospital input prices, or intensity of servicing.[29-30] This measure increases in response to increases in the number of nursing hours or drugs, or in the use of operating rooms, magnetic resonance imaging, and other such complex technology, per day of inpatient care. In the case of particular technologies that are embodied in specifically countable items like machines, capacities available per capita have tended to increase less rapidly in Canada. On the other hand, changes in the intensity of servicing in hospitals also include relative increases in internal administrative costs. Therefore, some portion of the apparent relative increase in servicing intensity simply reflects the increasing administrative intensity of the American hospital system.

But the different trends in servicing intensity also reflect quite different patterns in the use of beds in acute care hospitals. In Canada, a growing share of such beds has been occupied by patients over 65 years of age, whose stays exceed 60 days and whose daily care requirements are well below average. These patients prevent physicians from using the beds in question to treat short-term patients.[31]

Thus, Canada can have higher rates of hospitalization and greater average lengths of stay than the United States, yet also have lower per capita hospital expenditures.[32] Even if such expenditures, in terms of the cost of hospital care, are less different than is usually believed (because so much of the U.S. expenditure is for administrative activity), it does appear that the resulting mix of hospital activities favors intensive, high-technology services in the United States and long-term, chronic care in Canada. Nor should this come as a surprise, given the history of cost and procedural reimbursement in the United States, and of global budget-constrained funding in Canada. Which is preferable, in terms of value for money or benefits to patients, is harder to say. Possibly, each system generates its own forms of overuse and underuse.

One product that is clearly generated by the Canadian system, structured as it is to place the sole responsibility for control of hospital resources on the provincial governments, is intense, continuing public debate. The rhetoric of underfunding, shortages, excessive waiting lists, and so on is an important part of the process by which providers negotiate their share of public resources — including their own incomes.[33] Furthermore, there are reasons for the noticeable recent increase in such rhetoric. Increases in the supply of physicians per capita, in the face of a relatively constant supply of beds, have resulted in steady reductions in the number of short-term hospital beds available to each physician since 1971.[27] As bed availability and operating budgets have undergone increasing scrutiny, hospital administrators responded first (in the mid-1970s) by rationalizing administrative operations, and more recently by joining physicians in stepped-up rhetoric and pressure about underfunding.[34]

The difficulty for health policy and funding is that, since the boy always cries wolf (and must do so, given the political system of funding), one does not know if the wolf is really there. The political dramatics should not mislead external observers into believing that the wolf is always at hand. What varies most between the two nations in the method of establishing total hospital expenditures is the centralized, overtly political process in Canada, in contrast to the largely decentralized, institution-centered, and only implicitly political process in the United States. The Canadian controls on hospital expenditures impinge on individual physicians by limiting the complementary resources that are available to them. In this way, the environment of medical practice is changed, and practice patterns change in response. But individual physicians are not subject to any substantial direct intervention by hospital management or third parties. In this sense, Canadian physicians are actually much more autonomous than their American counterparts.

THE EFFECT ON PHYSICIANS

From 1971 to 1985, the share of the American GNP going to physicians has risen by over 40 percent. By contrast, Canadian physicians had an increase of only 10 percent. The stories that U.S. physicians hear about disaffected Canadian physicians, outmigration, underfunding, and occasional strikes correspond to an underlying reality of less generous funding. Despite the rhetoric, however, there has been no mass bailout of physicians from Canada. The supply of physicians per capita has risen throughout the period, is currently growing at between 1.5 and 2 percent per year, and is projected to continue its growth for the foreseeable future.[35] At the end of 1985 there were about 490 people per physician in Canada — very similar to the U.S. ratio. As in the United States, the policy concern is with surpluses, not shortages.[36] There may be some loss of superstars to the United States, but that is hard to document — individual anecdotes do not make a trend. In any case, there is always some leakage of stars in any field from countries with small populations to populous neighbors (the Gretzky effect).

The main explanation for the difference in outlays to physicians is that real fees have increased much faster in the United States than in Canada.[27,37] This difference, in turn, has resulted from the effect of universal public coverage on the process of fee determination. Increases in the general levels of fees and rules of payment are negotiated periodically between provincial medical associations and Ministries of Health. Over the long term, this complex negotiation process has had a major impact on the overall rate of escalation of fees.[37] Ironically, for a society that believes in the influence of competitive markets, the increasing supply of physicians in the United States seems to be associated with an acceleration in fee increases. In 1986, the rise in fees relative to the overall Consumer Price Index was one of the largest on record.[5]

Two other related issues have been particularly contentious for Canadian physicians — billing at rates above those reimbursed by the provincial plans ("extra billing") and the growth in the use of services per physician. Since 1971 these factors have become increasingly prominent in the political negotiating process, although the first one may at last have been pushed off center stage.[4]

With the passage of the Canada Health Act in 1984,[38] the right to "extra bill" was removed in all provinces in which such billing had previously occurred. This act, passed unanimously by the House of Commons, was a response to public perceptions that extra billing was undermining the fundamental principle of universal access on uniform terms and conditions. The termination of extra billing was met with intense opposition from physicians in some provinces, however, culminating in a lengthy strike in Ontario.[2,39] Physicians argued that the threat of widespread extra billing was a safety valve, protecting them against overly aggressive bargaining by the Ministries of Health and helping to push up public reimbursement rates. Although relatively few physicians engaged in extra billing, the majority strongly supported the option. They were unable to mobilize any sizable public support, however.

The extreme distress among physicians in Ontario appears to have been based largely on symbolic considerations. The right of ultimate access to the patient's economic resources seems to have had a meaning difficult for nonphysicians to understand. In fact, no change has occurred in the prevailing pattern of private, fee-for-service practice with reimbursement at uniform, negotiated rates. But Canadian physicians do have real concerns about the future, which have been linked to the extra-billing issue.

Once governments have achieved control over fee levels by ensuring that the public reimbursement rates represent payment in full, it is feared that the next step in cost control will be to restrict the amount or type of care provided, or at least the number and mix of services for which reimbursement will be made. This is particularly likely if physicians increase their delivery of services to compensate for the loss of extra billing, for a stagnant fee structure, or both.

The latter possibility has been an important consideration in recent American discussions of physicians' reimbursement under Medicare.[40,41] Analyses of the U.S. experience with fee freezes in the early 1970s clearly demonstrated that increased billing occurred as a response.[42,43] Billing activity per physician has risen faster in Canada than in the United States since 1971, in a manner consistent with this concern, although in Canada fee controls have clearly moderated the rate of escalation of expenditures for physicians' services, not just that of fees. Until recently, the provincial governments have been willing to accept an additional rise in expenditures (increases in physicians' productivity or more creative billing, depending on one's point of view) over and above increases in fees and numbers of physicians. Nationally, this has averaged 1 to 2 percent per year since 1971.[37]

The exception was Quebec, where over a four-year period of unchanged fees (1971 to 1975) the increase became so large as to create a fiscal problem.[37,44] Starting in 1976, Quebec introduced modifications to the reimbursement process that limited its liability for increases in services, billings, or both (per practitioner and in the aggregate) that exceeded preset target levels. From a billing standpoint, 26 office-based diagnostic and therapeutic procedures were bundled into the office visit. These procedures had been billable separately, in addition to the basic visit fee, and during the early 1970s their number and cost per office visit had risen rapidly. Their consolidation into the office-visit fee removed one of the principal mechanisms by which Quebec physicians had been able to stem some of the erosion in their real incomes during the period of unchanged fees.[37]

In addition, there are ceilings on the quarterly gross billings of individual practitioners, above which physicians are reimbursed at only 25 percent of the allowable fee. For the profession as a whole, negotiated fee increases are implemented in steps, conditional on the rate of increase in use. If the rate of use per physician (i.e., average gross receipts) rises faster than a predetermined percentage, subsequent fee increases are scaled down or eliminated.

None of these measures impinge directly on the autonomy of individual physicians in their practices, however. Specific clinical decisions are not reviewed by the reimbursement agency, nor are therapeutic protocols established. If the aggregated bill for all clinical decisions exceeds the limits. then fees to either the individual or the group as a whole will be scaled down, but physicians remain free to determine their own practice patterns.

Committees to review patterns of practice have existed for years in each province, under various names. But they were established to monitor a very small number of practitioners whose patterns deviated radically from those of their peers, and to look for fraud or incompetence. Such committees have neither the mandate nor the resources to go beyond statistical outliers in their investigations; even in this role, a recent commentary suggests that they are not very aggressive or effective.[45]

Since 1985, British Columbia, Alberta, Saskatchewan, Manitoba, and Ontario have all negotiated contracts setting limits on aggregate billings. British Columbia attempted to go further, by restricting the numbers of new physicians entitled to reimbursement by the provincial plan and controlling their locations of practice.[46] This policy, however, was successfully challenged on constitutional grounds. It was sustained at the provincial court, but overturned on appeal, and leave to appeal further was denied by the Supreme Court of Canada.

The absence of intrusion by any of these measures into the autonomy of individual practice contrasts markedly with the situation in the United States, where managed care systems and prospective payment, designed to alter individual physicians' care of individual patients, have become the principal tools for the control of expenditures for physicians' services. In the absence of a centralized bargaining mechanism between physicians and payers — a single-source payer — there is no way to limit the overall levels of billings. Hence the leap from constraints on capacity (as by a certificate of need) straight to the level of minute scrutiny of the behavior of individual physicians or the treatment of specific diseases.

Thus, many Americans already feel the threats to clinical freedom that Canadian physicians fear for the future. Whether such fears actually materialize will probably depend in large part on whether the provincial governments can continue to contain overall expenditures. What is disturbing, however, is that the current aggregate approaches to control of the use of services leave unexplored the cost-effectiveness, and even the efficacy, of the actual services provided. Such concerns, if left unaddressed by the profession itself, may become the catalysts for more detailed scrutiny of the use of services within the fee-negotiation process in Canada. To date, we see little evidence of this, but a decade ago there was little sign of the now widespread practice of bargaining over aggregate use along with fees. The context of policy decisions changes more slowly in Canada than in the United States, but it does move forward.

ORCHESTRATED OUTRAGE VERSUS DIFFUSE DISTRESS

Thus, the major difference between the two countries with respect to health expenditures lies in the degree of centralization of the cost-control process. In the United States the battles are fought in a myriad of private struggles between physicians and their employers, or their hospitals (or their competitors). When the struggle becomes public, as in the call by Minnesota physicians for unionization,[47] it takes the form of a series of isolated and localized incidents. The general pattern is obscured. In Canada, by contrast, the struggle over shares of income between physicians and the rest of the society is played out as large-scale public theater, with all the rhetorical threats and flourishes that political clashes require.[48] Physicians in Canada, and perhaps also in the United States, may perceive the Canadian conflicts as more severe and as arising from the presence of a universal public-payment system. That system serves to focus and channel such conflicts and to bring them into the headlines, but it has also afforded Canadian physicians a greater degree of professional autonomy.

Whatever the liabilities of such an overt and at times rancorous process, the Canadian approach has controlled health care costs more effectively. In the end, this may be the root of the sense of unease among Canadian physicians, who face a problem common to physicians in every country with a rapidly rising supply, including the United States. In such circumstances, every community of physicians must struggle for an ever-increasing share of national income or accept falling personal incomes. In the process, they must urge on the rest of society the benefits of buying the additional services that the additional numbers of physicians make possible (some would say inevitable) — and of doing so at fees that will sustain their own incomes. Whether such benefits are real or illusory is important from the standpoint of health policy, but irrelevant to the needs of the medical community.

The rest of society, or at least a sector of it, attempts to resist this expansion under the banner of cost control. When such resistance is organized collectively through public insurance, it is relatively successful. When it is disorganized and fragmented, an inconsistent and contradictory mix of strategies, as in the United States, it has so far been unsuccessful. Again, that observation is logically independent of whether the lack of success in the United States reflects waste, or whether the Canadian success leads to "underfunding."

In such an environment the pressure on physicians can only grow. To the extent that they resist such pressures successfully and continue to expand their share of the national income, as in the United States, the public and private responses to cost escalation will become increasingly radical. Major institutional changes are already transforming the

American health care system to an extent much greater than has been the case in the more conservative Canadian environment. Fears and anecdotes about the erosion of professional autonomy, and even of incomes, are becoming increasingly widespread. In the United States, corporate competitors or employers may turn out to be more ruthless than public regulators.

Such are the costs of economic success. The Canadian environment is more stable and predictable precisely because its cost-control processes work relatively well. But in Canada, whatever has happened or may happen can be blamed on government and on the evils of "socialized medicine." Anxiety and dissatisfaction are easily, if not always accurately, focused and channeled collectively through the process of public negotiation. In the United States, it is harder for individual practitioners to find the villains, and still harder to identify an effective response.

At the same time, it is easier to misinterpret the experience of other countries with more visible bargaining processes.

NOTE

We are indebted to Sidney Lee, Theodore R. Marmor, and Uwe E. Reinhardt for helpful discussions.

REFERENCES

1. Iglehart JK. Canada's health care system. N Engl J Med 1986; 315:202-8.
2. *Idem*. Canada's health care system. N Engl J Med 1986; 315:778-84.
3. *Idem*. Canada's health care system: addressing the problem of physician supply. N Engl J Med 1986; 315:1623-8.
4. Andreopoulos S, ed. National health insurance: can we learn from Canada? New York: John Wiley, 1975.
5. Division of National Cost Estimates, Health Care Financing Administration. National health expenditures, 1986-2000. Health Care Financ Rev 1987; 8(4):1-35.
6. Fein R. Medical care, medical costs: the search for a health insurance policy. Cambridge, Mass.: Harvard University Press, 1986.
7. Wilensky GR. Viable strategies for dealing with the uninsured. Health Aff (Millwood) 1987; 6(1):33-46.
8. Library of Congress, Congressional Research Service. Health insurance and the uninsured: background data and analysis. Washington, D.C.: Government Printing Office, 1988.
9. Fuchs VR. The "competition revolution" in health care. Health Aff (Millwood) 1988; 7(3):5-24.
10. Brook RH, Kosecoff JB. Competition and quality. Health Aff (Millwood) 1988; 7(3):150-61.
11. Gray BH, ed. for the Institute of Medicine. For-profit enterprise in health care. Washington, D.C.: National Academy Press, 1986.
12. Canada, Health and Welfare Canada. National health expenditures in Canada, 1975-1987. Ottawa: Health and Welfare Canada, 1985.
13. *Idem*. National health expenditures in Canada, 1970-1982. Ottawa: Health and Welfare Canada, 1985.
14. Gibson R, Levit K, Lazenby H, Waldo D. National health expenditures, 1983. Health Care Financ Rev 1984; 6(2):1-29.
15. Ginzberg E. A hard look at cost containment. N Engl J Med 1987; 316:1151-4.
16. Feder J, Scanlon W, Clark J. Canada's health care system. N Engl J Med 1987; 317:320.

17. Department of Commerce, Bureau of Economic Analysis. Survey of Current Business, September 1987; 67(9).
18. Canada, Department of Finance. Quarterly economic review: annual reference tables, June 1987. Ottawa: Department of Finance, 1987.
19. *Idem.* Economic review April, 1985. Ottawa Department of Finance, 1985.
20. Evans RG. Finding the levers, finding the courage: lessons from cost containment in North America. J Health Polit Policy Law 1986; 11:585-615.
21. Reinhardt UE. On the B-factor in American health care. Washington Post. August 9, 1988:20.
22. Canada, Royal Commission on Health Services (Hall Commission). Report Vol. 1. Ottawa: Queen's Printer, 1964:745.
23. Himmelstein DU, Woolhandler S. Cost without benefit: administrative waste in U.S. health care. N Engl J Med 1986; 314:441-5.
24. Bellerose P-P, Tholl W. Capital spending in the health sector. Presented at the Annual Meeting of the Canadian Health Economics Research Association, Halifax, Canada, June 8, 1987.
25. Feeny D, Guyan G, Tugwell P. Health care technology: effectiveness, efficiency and public policy. Montreal: Institute for Research in Public Policy, 1986.
26. Deber RB, Leatt P. Technology acquisition in Ontario hospitals: you can lead a hospital to policy, but can you make it stick? In: Horne JM, ed. Proceedings of the Third Canadian Conference on Health Economics. Winnipeg: University of Manitoba, 1987:259-77.
27. Barer ML, Evans RG. Riding north on a south-bound horse? Expenditures, prices, utilization and incomes in the Canadian health care system. In: Evans RG, Stoddart GL, eds. Medicare at maturity: achievements, lessons and challenges. Calgary: University of Calgary Press, 1986:53-163.
28. Detsky AS, Stacey SR, Bombardier C. The effectiveness of a regulatory strategy in containing hospital costs: the Ontario experience, 1967-1981. N Engl J Med 1983; 309:151-9.
29. Barer M, Evans RG. Prices, proxies and productivity: an historical analysis of hospital and medical care in Canada. In: Diewert E, Montmarquette C, eds. Price level measurement. Ottawa: Statistics Canada, 1983:705-77.
30. Detsky A., Abrams HB, Ladha L, Stacey SR. Global budgeting and the teaching hospital in Ontario. Med Care 1986; 24:89-94.
31. Evans RG, Barer ML, Hertzman C, Anderson GM, Pulcins IR, Lomas J. The long goodbye: the great transformation of the British Columbia hospital system. Health Serv Res (in press).
32. Newhouse JP, Anderson GM, Roos LL. What accounts for differences in hospital spending between the United States and Canada: a first look. Health Aff (Millwood) 1988; 7(5):6-16.
33. Reinhardt UE. Resource allocation in health care: the allocation of lifestyles to providers. Milbank Q 1987; 65:153-76.
34. Murray VV, Jick TD, Bradshaw P. Hospital funding constraints: strategic and tactical decision responses to sustained moderate levels of crisis in six Canadian hospitals. Soc Sci Med 1984; 18:211-9.
35. Barer ML, Gafni A, Lomas J. Accommodating rapid growth in physician supply: lessons from Israel, warnings for Canada. Int J Health Serv 1989; 19:95-115.
36. Lomas J, Barer ML, Stoddart GL. Physician manpower planning: lessons from the MacDonald Report. Toronto: Ontario Economic Council, 1985.
37. Barer ML, Evans RG, Labelle RJ. Fee controls as cost control: tales from the frozen north. Milbank Q 1988; 66:1-64.
38. Heiber S, Deber R. Banning extra-billing in Canada: just what the doctor didn't order. Can Public Policy 1987; 13:62-74.
39. Barer ML, Antioch K. Bill 94 and the Ontario physicians' strike: lobbying as professional emasculation. Vancouver: University of British Columbia, 1987.
40. United States Congress, Office of Technology Assessment. Payment for physician services: strategies for Medicare. Washington, D.C.: Government Printing Office, 1986:146-50.
41. United States Congress, Congressional Budget Office. Physician reimbursement under Medicare: options for change. Washington, D.C.: Government Printing Office, 1986:10-12.
42. Holahan J, Scanlon W. Price controls, physician fees and physician incomes from Medicare and Medicaid. Working paper no. 998-5. Washington, D.C.: Urban Institute, 1978.
43. Gabel JR, Rice TH. Reducing public expenditures for physician services: the price of paying less. J Health Polit Policy Law 1985; 9:595-609.
44. Contandriopoulos A-P. Cost containment through payment mechanisms: the Quebec experience. J Public Health Policy 1986; 7:224-38.

45. Wilson PR, Chappell D, Lincoln R. Policing physician abuse in British Columbia: an analysis of current policies. Can Pubic Policy 1986; 12:236–44.
46. Barer ML. Regulating physician supply: the evolution of British Columbia's Bill 41. J Health Polit Policy Law 1988; 13:1–25.
47. Doctors' dilemma: unionizing. New York Times. July 11, 1987:13, 21.
48. Tuohy CJ. Conflict and accommodation in the Canadian health care system. In: Evans RG, Stoddart GL, eds. Medicare at maturity: achievements, lessons and challenges. Calgary: University of Calgary Press, 1986:393–434.

The Tapestry Vision of Canadian Multiculturalism

V. SEYMOUR WILSON

Cultural pluralism is now thoroughly entangled in our history, it is a rising force in our contemporary life, and it will most assuredly be central to our future destiny as a nation.

— David R. Cameron

There is clearly room enough for all of us in this mythical canoe of Canada, providing we reopen our minds and respect each other's dignity in our diversity.

— Keith Spicer

Introduction

This address centres on a subject which, until very recently, was surprisingly neglected in political science, but which, nevertheless, has resonated in Canadian political life since its inception: the changing dimensions of societal pluralism in our country, particularly the dynamic interplay between cultural pluralism, racial pluralism and liberalism and what such changes portend politically as dusk settles on this century.[1] Its relative neglect in the study of Canadian politics is particularly troubling to me, given my own understanding of political phenomena and how we, as social scientists, approach their study.[2]

As political scientists it seems we have not been particularly comfortable dealing with cultural and racial pluralism and their effects on political life. In this country we approach the study of societal pluralism almost exclusively from our perspective on Quebec nationalism, despite the varied nature of the subject matter.[3] No doubt this may be due to the neglect of the subject in the Western tradition of political thought. As Kenneth McRae has so compellingly, if not comfortably, argued, "Western political thought in general has shown little understanding or respect for the cultural diversity of mankind and has made scant allowance for it as a possible concern of government."[4]

SOURCE: "The Tapestry Vision of Canadian Multiculturalism," *Canadian Journal of Political Science* 26, no. 4 (December 1993): 645–69. (Presidential address to the Canadian Political Science Association, Carleton University, June 1993.) Reprinted with permission.

McRae's general indictment masks a multitude of historic reasons why this relative neglect has been sustained until recently. For some in our discipline cultural and ethnic considerations in politics have either to be relegated to the ragbag of historical curiosities, or at least be subsumed as secondary to class interests. Ethnicity is an "apolitical force" so far as class-based actions are concerned. The primacy of the "economic base" and "class considerations," not ethnicity, have remained the "crucial variables" for the analysis of political life.[5]

Traditionally, sociologists have paid more attention to ethnicity than have we. But even within our sister discipline the study of ethnicity has suffered from a disciplinary mobilization of bias which places too much influence on a form of economic determinism that makes it difficult for us to appreciate the significance of society's symbolic order.[6]

Further, Canadian political science's traditional concentration on the institutional forms of federalism distorts our view of ethnicity by directing our attention to territorially concentrated ethnic/national groups that can be accommodated by provincehood or a third order of government.[7] This bias has led us to pay too little attention to dispersed metropolitan ethnicity, an emerging demographic reality destined to have important implications for Canadian social and political life: for the last two decades, for example, 90 per cent of Canada's heterogeneous influx of immigrants went to the country's eight largest metropolitan areas. To put it in David Cameron's evocative phraseology, this "riotously multicultural" change in Canadian society will continue apace, with important implications for Canadian political life in the coming century.[8]

To the extent that we, as social scientists, study cultural or racial pluralism, we have concentrated on group-centred or ethnocentric theories, whether the group in question be the polis, or the nation, or a collectivity of mythical group conceptions of racial superiority. In the United States this group bias has led to "the melting pot concept." In Canada, while we must avoid such a metaphorical phrase to characterize our ideal society, there is a strongly held belief in some quarters that we should make ourselves into a "smelting pot," that is, two major cultural groupings, English and French, both assuming totemic significance in subsuming all the other cultural and racial groupings comprising the Canadian mosaic. This is the perspective whose evolution I trace and against which I propose to contend.

Since the 1960s these metaphorical conceptions have been under severe criticism in both societies. Black Americans, for example, resented the melting pot metaphor.[9] White Americans did not have to worry about the pot for, after all, they constituted the pot. Black Americans have, however, been in the frying pan, or in the fire, for well over 300 years, with very little relief in sight. The depradations that have been so long visited upon the lives of black people found their reflections, both in the past and the present, in this metaphorical conception and in the historical sleight of hand that limited and even eradicated the histories of a deprived race of people. From this perspective the melting pot concept of an inclusive society has come to be viewed as a mere camouflage for the perpetuation of an exclusive community controlled by and rooted in the assumptions of cultural domination and white patriarchy. Pluralism, or more accurately, E Pluribus Unum, that lip-service celebration of liberal democracy, turns out to be not what its proponents had implicitly assumed, that is, the defence of difference, but its denial. A similar indictment can be levelled against much of the contemporary opposition to the official policy of multiculturalism, both in Quebec and in the rest of Canada, a theme to which I will return later.

Stripped of its rhetoric "the smelting pot" metaphor in Canada has many characteristics of cultural domination, and for the visible minorities in the population, is nothing more than racism and a perpetual inferior status in our country. Canada now has an impending rendezvous with its polyethnic nature — the extent to which the extraordinary ethnic variety of recent flows of immigration has altered, and will continue to alter, the old playing field on which the comfortable conceptions of the two "founding groups" could play itself out, and indeed complacently overlook the real founding peoples conveniently sidelined on reserves.

Culturally distinct groups other than French or English have consistently argued, since the days of the Royal Commission on Bilingualism and Biculturalism in the 1960s, that instead of cultural and ethnic differences being dismissed as incompatible with national goals, they should be endorsed as an integral component of a national mosaic, a reflection of the Canadian ideal, and a source of enrichment and strength in a plural Canadian society. Ralf Dahrendorf expressed this notion in a different context: "The rediscovery of ethnicity was a step forward in the process of civilization. It meant an incipient understanding that common citizenship rights are not in conflict with cultural distinctions, but, on the contrary, give them new scope."[10]

Dahrendorf's statement cannot be dismissed as a somewhat romantic reaction, for it seriously seeks insights into some of the most intractable problems facing mankind. The rediscovery of ethnicity is set against an environmental background which Jean Laponce described almost 33 years ago as "an endless and world-wide struggle among cultures," a Sisyphean search to obtain some "equilibrium among races or languages."[11] Now, after centuries of ebb and flow when cultural homogeneity was idealized if not realized, cultural and racial diversity is approaching near universal proportions.[12] Polyethnicity is the nation-state form of the future, and in Canada we are destined to be more, not less, ethnically and racially diverse than we now are. Gone, it appears, are the days when ethnicity in the democratic capitalist West could be handled by the policies of cultural homogeneity and dominance, exclusion and coercion. As Clifford Geertz so graphically stated, "it seems shatteringly clear [that] . . . the world is coming at each of its local points to look more like a Kuwaiti bazaar than like an English gentleman's club."[13] The management of ethnicity within the practice of universal democracy is going to be a central task of the Canadian state as we enter the twenty-first century.[14]

Within this context political science's role lies in devising and assessing the institutional means to accommodate this management. Earlier I resorted to hyperbole in making my point about the relative neglect of the changing dimensions of societal pluralism in the study of Canadian political life. Two areas of the discipline exonerated of these charges of neglect are immigration and refugee policy and the study of electoral behaviour at all three levels of governance. The works of David Corbett, Freda Hawkins, Reg Whitaker and Gerry Dirks on immigration and refugee policy, Elliot Tepper on ethnodemographic change and the electoral studies of Jerome Black, John Wood, Jean Laponce and Thomas Flanagan, among others, readily come to mind. Another excellent demonstration of that role for political science can be seen in the October 1992 issue of the *International Political Science Review*, which deals exclusively with the resolution of ethnic conflict.[15]

I think most of us would agree with the view that a discipline, at least to the initiated, is known more by the questions it asks than by the answers that it provides: for questions indicate goals or aspirations that answers may not reach. Jean Laponce's earlier work in the 1950s is a classic in this genre, because the fundamental questions posed at the very beginning of the book, and the framework derived as a result of those questions, still remain very germane to political science's interest in, and relevance to, ethnicity.

Laponce's earlier work, and the central themes in Cameron's 1989 Morton Lecture,[16] all have an interesting affinity in that they articulate some fundamental lessons for our discipline, namely, that state tasks are never given for once and for all, that they are constantly evolving, and that cultural lag is always a danger in the conduct of state business. For political science this translates into the danger of disciplinary lag. But lag is not an option we can entertain. Given the nature of the state tasks involved, a responsible community of social scientists should have something to contribute. It means, further, that we cannot escape the obligation to predict, and a function of prediction is to sharpen and to broaden moral choice. This admonition is of particular relevance for us as political scientists as we increasingly turn our attention to cultural and ethnic diversity within our society.

Polyethnicity and Multiculturalism: Reality, Vision and Policy

The concept of multiculturalism is a label for many things in Canada: it describes our polyethnic and racial mosaic; it articulates a vision of cultural pluralism which many feel is suitable for the Canadian reality; and it denotes a policy of the federal government first introduced in

1971.[17] It is, as Kallen indicated, useful to clarify these different shades of meaning although all the various dimensions of the concept cannot be neatly differentiated from each other because they overlap.

That Canada has been, and is increasingly, a more polyethnic and racial mosaic there can be no doubt. The social fabric of this country, from the very beginnings of white settlement, has always been composed of a polyethnic weave. "Other ethnics" have a long history of settlement: German settlers, for example, outnumbered the British among the original United Empire Loyalists in Upper Canada.[18] Black, Chinese, Irish, East Indian and Jewish settlements go back, in some cases, over 200 years. These groups, however, were small in numbers and perceived as marginal to the Canadian mainstream.

At our very beginnings as a nation, Canada's Fathers of Confederation proclaimed a "new nationality." Our political elite visualized it to be a pan-Canadian nationality, or what George-Étienne Cartier called a "deep racial diversity" — a composite, heterogeneous plural society transcending differences of ethnic origins and religion among its citizens. But this idealized vision of a code of ethnic relations was, from the very beginning, leavened by the nation's migration policy which reflected *a dialectic between the desired population increase and the impact of immigration on the racial and ethnocultural composition of the country.*

At first this created no real challenge to the policy-makers. The "preferred" immigrants from northern and western Europe presented no problems in cultural assimilation. As Lupul has observed, these "settlers" were co-opted very quickly by the Anglo-Celtic mainstream of Canadian society. Praised for their parliamentary traditions, their eagerness to give up their mother tongues, their education, literacy, hard work, thrift, cleanliness and temperance, and their Protestant religion, the Nordics were from the outset the weakest advocates of cultural diversity. They blended well and they did not upset the population mix. They put behind them life in the old country very quickly and for most their term as white ethnics was very brief, lasting no more than the first immigrant generation and almost never past the third.[19]

Overriding the dialectic was a further ineluctable fact: the country's population must grow in order to defend its vast habitable spaces in the west and to exploit its bountiful forest and mineral resources — all prerequisites for the development of nationhood and a healthy, prosperous economy. These were the overriding considerations which drove our Canadian gatekeepers to adopt, first, the 1890s policy of peopling "Canada's empty prairies" with the "less preferred stock" of Slavic peoples from the Austro-Hungarian Empire and, second, to institute the post–Second World War controlled immigration policy of the "non-preferred stock" of Portuguese, Greeks and Italians — those brawny immigrants who supplied the engine power for the rapid urbanization of much of southern Ontario in the 1950s.

But the almost insatiable demand for balanced population growth to ensure the needs of economic prosperity and national integrity could not be denied. By the 1960s and 1970s polyethnicity in Canada became much more complicated. Demographic studies began revealing that over the past generation Canada's population has been growing at a steady but decelerating pace from about 19 million in 1961 projecting to about 27 million by 1991. There were two factors in the projections, both of which were disturbing to the political decision-makers and their advisors. One was the rate of natural increase, which accurately indicated a precipitous decline from 26 births per 1,000 population in 1961 to approximately 14 births per 1,000 by 1991. Linked to this decline in the rate of natural increase was the other factor of note — an aging population. Both factors operated to reduce future population size unless countered by immigration. If we depended solely on natural increase, we would be faced with zero population growth or actual decreases in the early years of the twenty-first century. Incremental expansion of the population rests, in part, on net immigration, and that too had been decreasing, particularly from the traditional sources of immigrants.[20] Voluntary and involuntary (refugee) immigrants began increasing from third world countries: what the then minister responsible for multiculturalism, John Munro, called "the real minorities" began emerging as a significant element in the immigration influx.[21] Before 1967, 80 per cent of Canada's immigrants used to come from Europe or from countries of European heritage; by 1991 almost 75 per cent came from Asia, Africa, Latin America and the Caribbean. Currently, Asian-born persons represent almost half of the immigrants who came to Canada between 1981 and 1991.[22] And, to all these immigrants, Canada is not some woebegone spot, some way-station on the route to an economic Valhalla elsewhere: the census reports that 81 per cent of immigrants who were eligible to become Canadian citizens had done so by 1991. Polyethnicity, in all its racial dimensions, has within the past three decades become a "riveting reality" in Canadian life. As one commentator recently put it to me, "We Canadians are creating a 'bouillabaisse society' of the North — a stew rich in ethnic and racial variety."

A "bouillabaisse society," however, need not be multicultural. In many countries throughout the globe polyethnicity is forced to coincide with a dominant cultural homogeneity and cultural and racial diversities are officially denied. Multiculturalism rejects this as a solution to cultural and racial diversity: it calls, first, for the action of societal decision-makers to recognize a social reality (polyethnicity) within their midst, and secondly, to articulate both *a vision* and *a policy* devised to achieve some basis for tolerance and mutual respect. No other basis as a substitute ever lasts, and, as we are all painfully aware, the rendering of accounts is almost always horrifying and is never forgotten.

What is truly revolutionary is this attempt to devise a democratic vision by employing the policy instruments of the nation-state in the reconstruction of the symbolic order and the redistribution of social status among racial and ethnocultural groups in Canadian society.[23] And it is this aspect of multiculturalism which has caught the imagination of onlookers throughout the world. In 1988 the Australian Advisory Council on Languages and Multicultural Education emphatically drew the attention of the Australian government and citizenry to this "fundamental characteristic" as it exuberantly claimed that "multiculturalism is a Canadian creation. Canadians are to enter the twenty-first century as the world's best prepared country enjoying an important advantage over her friends and competitors."[24]

From this point of view, multiculturalism is construed as a doctrine that provides a *political framework* for the official promotion of *social equality* and *cultural differences* as an integral component of the social order. It is government having authority in the realm of the mind and an articulation that its responsibilities there are among the most important it has.[25] Multiculturalism provides a vision for a strategic policy designed to *shape, redefine* and *manage* Canada's racial and ethnic diversity — a purposeful attempt to address the historical and contemporary exclusion of ethnocultural and racial minorities. The policy attempts to grapple with the struggle between integration and pluralism, a struggle accentuated by the problems of migration and settlement created in a country open to immigrants. Abu-Laban and Stasiulis state it well: "Multiculturalism allows for a more inclusionary political discourse than either liberal individualist or two-nations models of Canadian society, providing legitimacy for both the presence and the articulation of concerns of ethnic minority collectivities."[26]

Visualized in this way, multiculturalism is employed to identify aspects and elements of a more harmonious Canadian society and is not confused with the reality which confronts us. For our reality has been a changing and complex one: the Canada of the 1990s is, it is almost trite to say, not the Canada of 40 or 50 years ago. There has certainly been some progress made in the understanding and appreciation of racial and cultural diversity in this country but it is my belief that it is much easier for us to regress than to progress. No law of historicism will be suggested here, no evolution of upward and onward progress is divined in the scheme of things.

History can help us, though, with a few lessons. Having accurate knowledge of our past and present human failings, as well as of our achievements, can foster understandings in appreciating what is at least humanly possible, and in sharpening our moral choices. For such understandings teach us invaluable lessons from our mistakes: how to approach them critically, how to handle them and how to tame our conflicts and use the knowledge thus derived in our struggle for a more open society.[27]

Canada's Pied Pipers and the Policy of Multiculturalism

Canada's ethnocultural policy towards immigrants in the nondominant groups is based on what is known as the "multicultural assumption": that is, that people's confidence in their own individual identity and place in the Canadian mosaic facilitates their acceptance of the rights of members of other groups to have their own place in Canadian society.[28] As outlined by Prime Minister Pierre Trudeau in the House of Commons on October 8, 1971, the policy was to play a critical role in allowing for individual freedom as well as national unity:

> For although there are two official languages, there is no official culture, nor does any ethnic group take precedence over any other. No citizen or group of citizens is other than Canadian, and all should be treated fairly. . . .
> National unity, if it is to mean anything in the deeply personal sense, must be founded on confidence in one's own individual identity; out of this can grow respect for that of others and a willingness to share ideas, attitudes and assumptions. A vigorous policy of multiculturalism will help create this initial confidence.
> (Canada, House of Commons, *Debates*, October 8, 1971, 8545)

For most observers, the 1971 policy ostensibly had three principal objectives derived from the "multicultural assumptions": the promotion of intergroup contact and sharing; the promotion of the maintenance and development of cultural heritage; and the promotion of other-group acceptance and tolerance.[29] The prime minister's heavily symbolic signal about the equality of all cultures and ethnic groups in Canada was overlooked or entirely ignored in the subsequent decade-long debate over multiculturalism which ensued.

An investigation into this period is both revealing and disappointing. Year after year commentators were beside themselves to read in the cultural policy of the government every conceivable intention known to the human imagination. For example, some viewed the policy as a cynical electoral ploy of the Liberals;[30] a policy reinforcing the concept of "symbolic ethnicity" which provides an appearance of democratic pluralism but is in reality a racist policy of assimilation at best and exclusion at worst;[31] as a set of programmes providing legitimacy to the accumulation function of the state, thus befuddling the more fundamental issues of class in Canadian society;[32] as an English-Canadian conspiracy to dilute the Quebec question;[33] and, in a memorable rhetorical flourish of indifference by Gad Horowitz, a dismissal of both the multicultural vision and the policy as that "masochistic celebration of Canadian nothingness."[34] In summary, multiculturalism as a policy was denounced for many of the same reasons assimilationists have always raised against the maintenance of ethnicity. It would breed "double consciousness" — loyalty to more than one country; it would contribute to turning immigrant quarters into permanent ethnic ghettos; it would slow the process of overcoming an ignorance of English and French that made the immigrants exploitable in the past. Part of most ethnic heritages, they claim, is a traditional enmity for some other group. Was the Canadian government intending to contribute to that problem by funding ethnocultural organizations? Among the English-speaking, hostility to multiculturalism ran from the viscerally xenophobic to well-reasoned preference for a laissez-faire approach to liberal meritocracy, and an abhorrence of state intervention in the issue of group status, even if a hierarchy of privilege based on ethnicity and class was obvious in the Canadian economy. Sometimes, of course, the viscerally xenophobic and the apparently reasonable became confused with one another. Former MP and journalist Douglas Fisher told a conference on multiculturalism in 1975: "You and me and our children have enough to do with the basic problem of hyphenated Canadianism, that is the French and English duality, without enshrining the whole world's diversity within our history and our border."[35] Seldom are academics, politicians and social commentators summoned to shoulder responsibility for the false roads down which they have piped so many people.

By 1982, as Knopff and Morton have shown, the Charter of Rights and Freedoms

> struck a balance between Trudeau's concept of dualism and the concerns of third-force Canadians. . . . On the one hand, dualism was constitutionally entrenched in the establishment of English and French as the official languages of Canada, and in the provision of linguistic educational rights to the English minority in Quebec and the French minority elsewhere. On the other hand, section 27 says that the Charter "shall be interpreted in a manner consistent with the preservation and enhancement of the multicultural heritage of Canadians." *In short, the balance between bilingualism and multiculturalism established at the statutory level early in Trudeau's prime ministership was duplicated at the constitutional level in the Charter.*[36]

Placed against this backdrop the entire drift of that part of the constitutional debates involving multiculturalism took on a specific complexion: questions arose concerning the meaning of egalitarianism in a liberal democracy and on Quebec's claims to distinctiveness on the basis of culture. Armed with long memories and the constitutional gains of 1982, these recently enfranchised "Charter Canadians" took our political decision-makers by surprise in serving notice that they were now serious players in the constitutional stakes: the earlier kibitzer's roles assigned to them were no longer acceptable.

It should be remembered that between Trudeau's pronouncement — his first and last parliamentary utterance on the subject — and the *Multicultural Act*, Bill C-93, brought before the House of Commons in Ottawa late in 1987, there had been no enabling legislation of any kind dealing with multiculturalism. *Charter recognition, however, had a dramatic effect in galvanizing not only the "real minorities" but also the aboriginal peoples.*

Under the 1982 legislation aboriginal organizations had secured, for the first time in Canadian history, constitutional entrenchment of aboriginal and treaty rights. *It was Canada's aboriginals, not other ethnic minorities, who were responsible for cracking the "two nations" crucible.* Additionally, their claims to special legal and constitutional status, land and self-government are the most profound challenges to the Canadian "bi-national" state since they anticipate a third order of government, based on ethnicity or race. This area, however, is an extremely large and complex odyssey in Canada's constitutional history, a subject relevant but nevertheless tangential to the main thrust of this address.

It is at this juncture that the inclusionary debate on multiculturalism began to take on new dimensions: the criticisms of the first decade in the life of the policy quickly became secondary to larger concerns. The supposed vast wastage of public funds implied in the often repeated criticism that the policy encouraged "ex-fascists' dances in church cellars" and "bongo drums music festivals" and the dire warnings given to English Canada that "its old familiar British North American culture [was being] half bludgeoned to death by the cast-iron balalaikas of multiculturalism"[37] surely could not be substantiated by the federal spending on multiculturalism. A policy so poorly funded (to the tune of an average of $26 to $27 million a year, two thirds of which was spent on combating the problems of racism in Canadian society), could not be seriously compared to the expenditures on bilingualism (approximately $350 million annual expenditures).

Why then was ethnic pluralism under siege? A small part of it, having nothing to do with ethnocultural policy in particular, centred around the indiscriminate usage of the concept of "rights and freedoms" in our Charter discourse which encourages a level of stridency with no consideration for what limits it is reasonable to attach to rights and freedoms, and how decisions about those limits should be made.

Another part of the furore relates to the fact that the Charter of Rights and Freedoms gave more "pith and substance" to evolving human rights policy in our liberal democracy. Rainer Knopff, for example, argued that this equality of rights initiative, together with anti-discrimination legislation and affirmative action programmes, promote social equality at the cost of undermining private liberty and the democratic political process. Furthermore, this "new war on discrimination," as he calls it, implies an "exercise in social technology," which, despite its rhetoric of human rights, actually deprives the idea of rights of any solid foundation.[38]

I want to concentrate rather briefly on two contributions to this ongoing debate, because both views have received wide dissemination amongst the academic community and the general public, and both have raised equality and ethnocentrism as fundamental issues.

Professor Gilles Paquet, writing in a periodical marvellously entitled the *Journal of Cultural Economics*, noted what this emphasis on equality was all about:

> Changes in the symbolic order often have fundamental impacts on the framing of decisions and on the dynamics of society: the slow process of status enhancing of ethnic minorities in Canada has acquired a logic of its own which has blown away the containment [policies] of the 1970s. . . . *Multiculturalism is redrawing mental maps and redefining levels of aspirations.*[39]

In subsequent writings Paquet continued in this vein: conceding that multiculturalism policy was conceived as "generous in spirit" to Canada's ethnic minorities, he contended, however, that all evidence led to the conclusion that the policy exacerbated jealousies and envy amongst minorities and made no demands on new Canadians to adapt to the reality of a Canadian mainstream.[40] Additionally the policy increased the "degree of cacophony in the forum" and reduced "the degree of effective participation in the national and civil society spheres." This has led to a new ethnocentrism, a new rhetoric of rights and a dangerous drift from unhyphenated Canadianism to ethnic particularism. Paquet's preference is clearly what Lise Bissonette of *Le Devoir* has described as "a gentle ecumenical embrace," an official brand of ethnic pluralism sanctioned by the Quebec government and overwhelmingly supported by the Quebec intelligentsia. This "gentle ecumenical embrace" is "an asymmetrical, moral contract" for the province's cultural minorities "with the degree of asymmetry to be clearly understood": citizenship does not mean egalitarianism. Paquet cautioned: "In a multiethnic and bi-national society meaningful membership may not develop without a sense of hierarchy. Different but equal is an impossible gambit: this antinomy is at the core of a most important double-bind plaguing intercultural relations. Equality denies differences."[41]

This reality had led him to posit a solution stressing differences, separateness and hierarchy. But before this solution of a "new civil theology" is operationalized we must first "slaughter the sacred cow of egalitarianism." That, he concedes, would be no mean task:

> To effect a turn in the direction of separateness and hierarchy in discussions over intercultural relations will require nothing less than a revolution in the mind of liberals: a recasting of the problem of cultural diversity, [and] a critical assessment of the passion for equality that has inspired them. . . . It would be unwise to presume that this revolution will occur overnight. Many sacred cows will have to be slaughtered, and other, less vulnerable sacred cows raised before such a turn can be effected.[42]

I find this line of thought quite startling and disturbing, for there are some definite ideological undertones repugnant to me resonating from Paquet's contribution to the debate on multiculturalism. I find there a view which emphasizes that the world is a study of contrasts and natural inequality, and that these conditions must be accepted as given. There is also a tendency to attach a "devil theory" of politics to "the ethnics" (they being accused of importing jealousies and envies and other forms of ethnocentric behaviour detrimental to Canadian tranquillity). And finally there is the imposition by the state of an ethnic hierarchy of order which, whatever way one cuts it, assigns to those outside the inner circle an inferior and subservient role in society. Others will come to their own conclusions on this line of thought.

However, in April 1987, Keith Spicer, earlier Canada's first Commissioner of Official Languages and later the head of the Citizens' Forum on Canada's Future (the Spicer Commission), unleashed all his formidable powers of expression. Paquet's hierarchical, binational society views and his "devil theory" of politics shared some common ground with Keith Spicer's binationalist conception of the Canadian mosaic. But, while Paquet is no assimilationist, Spicer is. In 1987, Spicer saw the need for assimilation quite clearly: "isn't the time coming to stop making a religion of mosaics altogether and to start fostering a national spirit we can all identify with? With constant intermarriage, for how many generations more must an English — or Ukrainian — Canadian revere his presumed roots?"[43] Spicer went on to accuse the government of "making a virtue of a weakness, a glory of a hindrance to nationhood; we pay people to have foreign roots." Robert Harney, commenting on Spicer's outburst, noted somewhat mischievously that "Only a naif would ask why Spicer did not add French Canadians to his list; that would be to step outside the limits of legitimate discourse."[44]

Two years later, in March 1989, Spicer turned to the themes of ethnocentrism and ethnocentric hatreds. Writing in the *Montreal Gazette*, he caricatured state-funded multiculturalism as a "multicultural zoo" encouraging the creation of "not Canadians but professional ethnics." Then followed a litany replete with racial and ethnic biases. Multiculturalism, he added, was "an anthology of terrors: Balkanization, ethnic politicians siphoning off political protection money, ghetto mentalities, destabilization of Quebec leading to secession, reverse intolerance by immigrants for Canadian culture and institutions, devaluation of the very idea of a common nationality."[45]

But, one may ask, where is the evidence of this anthology of terrors? Where and how have the jealousies, envies and violence manifested themselves amongst Canada's ethnic minorities? For what is particularly disturbing in these charges is how easily the victims of ethnocentrism in Canada's past now stand accused of the practice in Canada's present and future. In short, the victims have now become the accused. This phenomenon is not unlike the common occurrence nowadays of the rapist turning the tables on his victim with accusations of provocation or seduction (the "you asked for it" theory in victimology), or those suffering the deliria of anti-semitism who invent the Jewish menace in an environment where there are no Jews. To employ a mixed metaphor, why do these pied pipers conjure up these demons from the murky deep when there is not a shred of credible evidence that Canada's ethnic minorities are busily invoking malevolent spirits? Is this not obsolete alarmism of a fairly low order? I am reminded of the art critic Robert Hughes's memorable observation about those who saw blood feuds and theocratic hatreds lurking under every bed in America: "They cannot know what demons they are frivolously invoking. If they did they would fall silent in shame."[46]

Why did the Spicer Commission concentrate on thrashing multiculturalism despite the fact that this policy was overall of less concern to participants of the forum than the questions of bilingualism and Quebec, the prime minister's credibility and the state of the Canadian economy? Abu-Laban and Stasiulis supply us with a plausible answer.

> While the final report presents more than the voice of one or all of the Commissioners, its disdainful and dismissive attitude towards multiculturalism policy is nevertheless consistent with Chief Commissioner, Keith Spicer's personal views on multiculturalism. . . . The net effect of trashing multiculturalism policy is to resuscitate a "two founding nations" framework. Indeed this is also implicit in Spicer's own commentary in the Citizens' Forum Report that "Quebec is the heart of the matter."[47]

Putting aside the relatively recent Oka incident and the FLQ episode of the 1970s, it is indeed a curious twist of logic that ethnocentrism should be a charge levelled at Canada's ethnic minorities. For, ethnocentrism in its most perverted manifestation, namely racism, has been in our recent past a fungal growth widely infecting not the minorities, but the Canadian mainstream as such. These racial incidents are telling of a latent and, in some instances, a raging intolerance which is the undercurrent threatening the mythical Canadian canoe, charting a dangerous course for Canadian identity. If these most recent criticisms and recommendations on multiculturalism policy are the bellwether of current Canadian sentiment, then the fundamental question to be addressed is not how much money is spent on "cast-iron balalaikas" and "bongo drum folk festivals," but how Canadians must finally reconcile themselves to the many different and heretofore unrecognized faces in the canoe. Warnings of ethnocentrism among minorities by "mainstream Canadians," coupled with their advice that governments should "let things be" because of "a relatively passive tolerance pact" in the land, therefore appears as so much casuistry. For the first-order concern of the "real minorities," the socially visible Canadians, is to shield themselves from the worst ravages of racism which, as I will briefly discuss, is no stranger to public policy in this land.

In confronting the past, I anticipate a charge that it is totally inappropriate to attack past generations using 1990s standards of judgment, knowing that the situations faced by those generations were very different in structure and resources from those that we have today. In other words, to some people it would seem completely unjustified to review Canadian public policy historically by evaluating it in post-Charter terms.

But is it that simple, really? Recently I read with intense interest what John Stuart Mill had to say about the subject of ethnocentrism when confronted with the morality of the issues involved. In correspondence between himself and the economist Henry George, dated October 23, 1869, Mill declared that the subject matter involved "the most difficult and embarrassing questions of political morality" confronting him at the time.[48] All I can add at this juncture is that if the subject matter involved "the most difficult and embarrassing questions of political morality" for Mill in 1869 then it is so equally for me in 1993. Mill and the ruling elite knew the issues then as you and I know them now. He saw no reason to qualify his moral judgment; nor do I.

But another charge can be laid at my doorstep. In dealing with past historical policies as I do here, some may find that my comments are laced with a tone of official idealization which they might judge to be offensive: that it is, for example, highly inappropriate to adopt a tone of high moral outrage for situations of which mainstream society was, at the time, supposedly unaware. In sum, do I have the right to declare "open season" on Canada's founding groups because of actions taken in yesteryear?

My response is that over the past two and a half years I have been diligently searching the private papers of prime ministers and cabinet colleagues who were relevant to the issues at hand; the official documentation and other archival material of relevant federal departments; enabling legislation of every region of Canada with the exception of the provinces of Prince Edward Island and Newfoundland; relevant parliamentary debates in *Hansard*; and judicial decisions and the reasoning behind those decisions. Additionally, I have been privy to quite a few of the background research papers of the lawyers, psychologists and sociologists commissioned by Nova Scotia's royal commission on the wrongful prosecution, conviction and imprisonment of Donald Marshall, Jr. for murder.[49]

I am therefore faced with an enormous amount of evidence demanding some personal conclusion. And the only conclusion I can, with any sincerity, arrive at is one which states categorically that ethnocentrism of the worst variety, namely racism, was a widespread characteristic in the halls of decision-making in the Canada of yesteryear. This does not condemn everybody, it simply states a fact. For those who find this fact to be unpalatable I urge you not to shoot the messenger because of his message.

Confronting the Past of the Mythical Canoe

The rich imagery we employ to capture the quintessential characteristics of our country speaks volumes about our assumptions. Keith Spicer's mythical canoe imagery which he employs to good effect in the preface to the Citizens' Forum Report is the visionary symbol of the First Nations Confederacy emphasizing mutual respect, harmony and understanding.[50] So, too, is the popular image of Canada as "the peaceable kingdom" — a gentle, tolerant, caring and amiable land free of the grating features characteristic of so many other nations.[51]

Earlier I had used the terms "less preferred stock," "preferred stock" and "non-preferred stock" in describing the categorizations attached to Canada's immigration influx up to the 1950s. These are official designations, euphemisms which both politicians and senior bureaucrats employed to describe Canada's increasingly polyglot population. There were of course other categories. Chinese and East Indian labourers who worked tirelessly and died tragically in droves building our railway system, mining our minerals and harvesting our forests, together with Canada's aboriginal peoples, the Inuit and the Indians, were deemed to be nonpersons. Section 91 (24) "Indians and Land Reserved for the Indians" was mentioned in one sentence in the *British North America Act, 1867* only as a subject of federal jurisdiction. Aboriginal peoples were treated as subjects, not citizens of the new dominion.

For the country's marginal population of "other ethnics" the prognosis for acceptance as citizens remained virtually non-existent. Jews and blacks were deemed to be unassimilable in Canadian society. Our guardians of the immigration gates had some particularly choice commentaries and phrases for potential black immigrants. The more gentle of these argued that blacks were "not of any permanent asset to Canada" and given their "loose sexual habits, laziness and mental deficiencies and diseases" they would, if allowed into the country, "pollute the pure stream of Canadian morals."[52] It is these ethnocentric attitudes and beliefs, this conglomeration of emotions around blood, land, language, religion, traditions and ancestors — this *affective* nationalism or what nationalist Abbé Lionel Groulx has described as the deterministic "incoercible force," which has fed the "Aryan" assumptions of most English-Canadian social and political elites openly manifested well into the 1940s and 1950s, and the introverted racial nationalism of French Canada. In his incisive study of the subject, Carl Berger is unequivocal in his assessment of the phenomenon:

> If Canadian nationalism is to be understood, its meaning must be sought and apprehended not simply in the sphere of political decisions, but also in myths, legends and symbols. . . . For, while some might think that Canadians have happily been immune to the wilder manifestations of the nationalist impulse and rhetoric, it seems that they too have had their utopian dreamers, and that

they are not totally innocent of a tradition of racism and a falsified but glorious past, tendencies which have always been the invariable by-products of nationalism. For by its very nature, nationalism must seize upon objective dissimilarities and tendencies and invest them in the language of religion, mission and destiny.[53]

As "scientific" racism gained credence in the later nineteenth century, much of its conclusions and assumptions crept into Canadian public policy. It was premised on the belief that certain types of humankind were unsuited to the democratic government and to the free institutions established in Canada, and their participation would subvert those institutions and ruin them for everyone else. The attitudinal impact this approach had on public policy at the federal level was first registered in the areas of immigration, military service and the franchise. Soon questions of race assumed critical importance in the jurisdictional contests introduced by Canadian federalism. Because aliens and naturalization were federal matters under the BNA Act, provincial legislatures were required to apply their restrictive policies openly in racial terms to areas such as housing, employment, professional certification (law, pharmacy, medicine) and education. Thus euphemisms were invoked and the federal sphere avoided for fear of the federal power of disallowance. The courts upheld the provinces' right to discriminate on racial grounds, as there existed no protection against it in the Canadian constitution. As Robert J. Sharpe noted:

> There was no constitutional guarantee of equality, and there was nothing to permit a court to strike legislation down as invalid solely on the ground that it was racist in nature. In order to mount a constitutional challenge, one had to show that the legislation fell outside the powers allocated to the provinces in section 92 of the Constitution Act, 1867.[54]

Unfettered by jurisdictional limitations to their legislative powers, the provinces enacted racist laws. Sharpe is scandalized: "The overt racism of the legislation challenged in these cases is shocking. Equally disturbing is the implicit acceptance by many of the judges of the racist assumptions underlying the legislation."[55] The courts rendered decisions that upheld the existing laws and practices as not violating rights or freedoms, or at least as not constituting unreasonable limitations on these rights and freedoms. After a thorough examination of the legislation involved and the court challenges made throughout the decades, I can only conclude that this ethnocentrism will remain a permanent blot on the record of our liberal democratic society.[56] The whole sorry mess probably had its apotheosis in the celebrated case of *Christie v. York*, when the Supreme Court of Canada concluded in December 1939 that racial discrimination was legally enforceable throughout Canada. The Court's decision did not establish racial segregation in Canadian society, but by putting the constitutional seal of approval on the practice it created a major obstacle to the eradication of racism in Canadian institutions. A somewhat misleading editorial note of the *Dominion Law Report*, commenting on the case, claimed that this was the first decision enforcing "coloured" inferiority in Canada.[57] It was by no means the first such case, as legal research is now beginning to reveal, but that it was interpreted in this way was indicative of a new awareness by mainstream Canadians during the Second World War that racial disadvantage was supported by law.[58] By the end of the hostilities in 1945, Canadians found themselves, to paraphrase Alan Cairns, with political, administrative and judicial decisions constituting a cake of custom which threatened to hold subsequent generations in unwilling thralldom in a world they had never made.[59]

What turned things around, forcing us to confront these "most difficult and embarrassing questions of political morality"? By the early 1950s the world knew the full extent of the massive genocide of the Jews and other "undesirable ethnics" — an ethnocentrism which had run rampant like an uncontrolled forest fire throughout Europe. It is to the full credit of our political, judicial and bureaucratic elites that by the 1960s Canada was taking purposeful measures to deal with the systemic problems created by this social disease. But the approach taken has been revealing: speaking at the United Nations in 1948 during the debate on the international convention which declared genocide a crime against all humanity, Lester Pearson *announced, with apparent sincerity, that Canadian policy was and had always been protective of racial equality.* Thereafter successive governments took the position that whenever blatant discrimination was unearthed, the laws of gentle restraint, providing for the enlightenment rather than the punishment of offenders, would be the most effective way to deal with the problems of discrimination.[60] Furthermore, until recently, the position taken was that systemic discrimination, rooted in the body politic, could not be redressed by any corrective policy measures. The policy context of the late 1940s, 1950s and 1960s did not consider compensation to victims of past discrimination, or assistance in facing long-established barriers to their advancement. The problem definition suggested only the removal of "race" as an acknowledged qualification for admission to employment, accommodation or services. The thrust was preventive, not corrective, for the policy process did not recognize a legacy of disadvantage. For a large proportion of Canada's multicultural community, particularly the visible minorities, the problems encountered cannot be compared to the "glass ceiling" analogy so often cited in analyses of female discrimination in societal institutions. Rather, the problem for them remains one of a "plexiglass" character: fully transparent like glass but much more formidable to shatter.

The point in all this is that a tradition of racism and ethnocentrism amongst Canada's founding groups is either seldom acknowledged, often denied, sometimes conveniently ignored, soft-pedalled or suppressed. Coming with the present charges that Canadian ethnic minorities are busily fostering ethnocentrism, this is particularly disturbing. But history denied or ignored can easily lead to history relived. Contemporary critics of multiculturalism, as evidenced in the Citizens' Forum's hearings, were allowed to mouth easily such solipsistic remarks as "tolerance has always been a hallmark of Canadian society" or "there is no real discrimination in this country" or "it can't happen here" without having their veracity seriously challenged.

Are We Beaching the Canoe on an "Archipelago of Envies and Anxieties"?

"The virus of tribalism," says *The Economist*, "risks becoming the AIDS of international politics — lying dormant for years, then flaring up to destroy countries."[61] In the century that lies darkly ahead, ethnic and racial conflict seems to be replacing the conflict of ideologies as the explosive issue of the time. We in Canada have not entirely escaped this viral infection. In the memorable imagery of Keith Spicer we live on "an archipelago of envies and anxieties." Yet many feel that there is still a chance that we can contain the malady. Anxious eyes are tracking our perilous journey, many hoping that ours will be one of the few successful attempts both to shoot the rapids and beach our canoe away from the mythical archipelago. For whether we like it or not, we must all become reconciled to the many other fellow travellers in the canoe, a motley collection of different faces and skin hues. In my view, to deal with one's fellow voyagers on the basis of hierarchy and separateness will exacerbate the envies and jealousies which one seeks to avoid or mitigate in the first place. This leads to the real and present danger of capsizing the canoe at the confluence of our many cultural and racial streams. As Clifford Geertz so admirably stated it: "It is not that we must love one another or die. It is that we must know one another and live with that knowledge or end marooned in a Beckett-world of colliding soliloquy."[62]

Antonine Maillet recently wrote that "Canada is just now discovering that it is a multiplicity. Until now, it thought that meant that its splendours were many and varied; from now on, it will have to understand that such great abundance has a price."[63] Canada does have splendours which are many and varied. It is true that it must still be ranked among the most congenial and civic-minded communities in the world, despite its fair share of demagogues, racists and other malcontents. But it is necessary for Canadians to temper that love of country with a strong dose of realism and skepticism.

Almost 130 years ago, when plans for a Canadian federation were still on the drawing board, our liberal politicians made excessive and illusory comments about the splendours of our plural society. As I have argued, much of this was rhetorical cant, for ethnocentrism in the form of cultural dominance and officially approved racism prevailed until recent times. As we enter the twenty-first century we are all forced to confront a pluralism which must be based on demographic realities and Richard Rorty is right in pointing out that we must reckon with these realities. For a small "l" liberal society that price is: "to take with full seriousness the fact that the ideals of procedural justice and human equality are parochial, recent, eccentric cultural developments, and then to recognize that this does not mean that they are any the less worth fighting for. It urges that ideals may be local and culture bound, and nevertheless be the best hope of the species."[64] In sum, our liberal democratic values call for the acceptance of polyethnicity and the continuous maintenance of free and fair institutions to make daily life in Canada rich, safe and hopeful. *That is the bottom line of equality.*

Keeping this "moralistic, culture bound" admonition in mind we can now revisit the Confederation Debates of 1865. It was, for me, somewhat delightful to read the following proposal from Henri Gustave Joly, a politician from Lotbinière, during the debates in the Legislative Assembly of Canada on the proposed scheme of a British North American Confederation. The date is February 20, 1865, the venue, Quebec City:

> I propose the adoption of the rainbow as our emblem. By the endless variety of its tints the rainbow will give an excellent idea of the diversity of races, religions, sentiments and interest of the different parts of the Confederation. By its slender and elongated form the rainbow would afford a perfect representation of the geographical configuration of the Confederation. . . . An emblem we must have, for every great empire has one; let us adopt the rainbow.[65]

Canadians can rightly claim that we were the first to coin the concept "the rainbow coalition": our American friends have nothing on us on this score. But are Canadians up to the challenge that it implies? The impending rendezvous with Canada's growing cultural and racial diversity will soon supply us in dramatic fashion with the answers to this question.

NOTES

1. I am grateful to my colleagues, Rhadda Jhappan, Sharon Sutherland, John Meisel, O.P. Dwivedi, Alan Cairns, Ted Hodgetts and Yasmeen Abu-Laban for their valuable comments on an earlier version of this manuscript, and I absolve them of responsibility for any errors of fact or interpretation.
2. I have always found Samuel P. Huntington's conception of our approach to the study of political phenomena acceptable, with a few qualifications and caveats added to that understanding: "Political scientists attempt to explain political phenomena. They view politics as a dependent variable, and they naturally look for the explanations of politics in other social processes and institutions. This tendency was reinforced by the Marxian and Freudian intellectual atmosphere of the 1930s and 1940s. Political scientists were themselves concerned with the social, psychological, and economic roots of political behavior. *Consequently social change, personality change, and economic change were, in their view, more fundamental than*

political change. If one could understand and explain the former, one could easily account for the latter" (Samuel P. Huntington, "The Change to Change," in Roy C. Macridis and Bernard E. Brown, eds., *Comparative Politics: Notes and Readings* [4th ed.; Georgetown: Dorsey, 1972], 408, emphasis added). For a partial critique of this pervasive conception of political phenomena, see Alan C. Cairns, "The Governments and Societies of Canadian Federalism," *Canadian Journal of Political Science* 10 (1977), 695-725.

3. Howard Palmer rightfully complained in 1982 that "Political historians and political scientists in Canada have shown very little interest in ethnic relations, other than their concern with the all-pervasive question of conflict and accommodation between English and French" (see H. Palmer, "Canadian Immigration and Ethnic History in the 1970s and 1980s," *Journal of Canadian Studies* 17 [1982], 45). Recently, Abu-Laban and Stasiulis expressed almost the exact sentiment: "While immigration and ethnic diversity have been mainstays of Canadian life, these features have not always found widespread legitimacy among either ruling or popular groups" (Yasmeen Abu-Laban and Daiva Stasiulis, "Ethnic Pluralism under Siege: Popular and Partisan Opposition to Multiculturalism," *Canadian Public Policy* 18 [1992], 365).

4. Kenneth D. McRae, "The Plural Society and the Western Political Tradition," *Canadian Journal of Political Science* 12 (1974), 685. This criticism is tempered by the fact that since the mid-1970s several leading Canadian political scientists, including McRae, have attempted to redress this imbalance through their addresses and writings. The footnotes which follow throughout this piece give testimony to these attempts. See also David J. Elkins, "Facing Our Destiny: Rights and Canadian Distinctiveness," *Canadian Journal of Political Science* 22 (1989), 699-716; "The Sense of Place," in David J. Elkins and Richard Simeon, eds., *Small Worlds* (Toronto: Methuen, 1980), 1-30; "The Horizontal Mosaic: Immigrants and Migrants in the Provincial Political Cultures," in ibid., 106-30; and Charles Taylor, *Multiculturalism and "The Politics of Recognition"* (Princeton: Princeton University Press, 1991).

5. John Cater and Trevor Jones, "Asian Ethnicity, Home-Ownership and Social Reproduction," in Peter Jackson, ed., *Race and Racism* (London: Unwin, 1987) 190-211; and Alan C. Cairns, "Political Science, Ethnicity, and the Canadian Constitution," in Douglas E. Williams, ed., *Disruptions: Constitutional Struggles from the Charter to Meech Lake* (Toronto: McClelland and Stewart, 1991), 169. See also Donald L. Horowitz, *Ethnic Groups in Conflict* (Berkeley: University of California Press, 1985).

6. Raymond Breton, "Multiculturalism and Canadian Nation-Building," in Alan C. Cairns and Cynthia Williams, eds., *The Politics of Gender, Ethnicity and Language in Canada* (Toronto: University of Toronto Press, 1985), 27.

7. Alan C. Cairns, "Political Science, Ethnicity and the Canadian Constitution," 161-80, and "The Past and Future of the Canadian Administrative State," *University of Toronto Law Journal* 40 (1990), 319-61.

8. David R. Cameron, "Lord Durham Then and Now," 1989 Morton Lecture, Trent University, *Journal of Canadian Studies* 25 (1990), 5-23.

9. Arthur M. Schlesinger, Jr., *The Disuniting of America* (New York: W.W. Norton 1992), esp. chap. 2, "History the Weapon," 45-72; and N. Glazer and D.P. Moynihan, *Beyond the Melting Pot* (Cambridge, Mass.: M.I.T. Press, 1963).

10. Ralf Dahrendorf, *The Modern Social Conflict: An Essay on the Politics of Liberty* (London: Weidenfeld and Nicolson, 1988), 309.

11. J.A. Laponce, *The Protection of Minorities* (Berkeley: University of California Press, 1960), 1.

12. Clifford Geertz, "The Uses of Diversity," *Michigan Quarterly Review* 25 (1986), 105-23.

13. Ibid., 121.

14. Cairns, "The Past and Future of the Canadian Administrative State," 358-61.

15. *International Political Science Review* 13, 4 (1992).

16. "I am fond of Ernest Renan's definition of a nation — 'une plébiscite de tous les jours,' a daily plebiscite. For me, it calls to mind the importance of time, and the importance of the affirmation and re-affirmation of a will to perpetuate a common existence. The act of living together one day after another, solving problems, making things work, is after all how most free societies hang together" (Cameron "Lord Durham Then and Now," 22).

17. Evelyn Kallen, "Multiculturalism: Ideology, Policy and Reality," *Journal of Canadian Studies* 17 (1982), 51-63; and J. Burnet, "Multiculturalism," in J.H. March, ed., *The Canadian Encyclopedia*, Vol. 3 (2nd ed.; Edmonton: Hurtig Publications, 1988), 1401.

18. Elliot L. Tepper, "Demographic Change and Pluralism," in O.P. Dwivedi et al., eds., *Canada 2000: Race Relations and Public Policy* (Guelph: Department of Political Studies, 1979), 20–52; and Joan Magee, *Loyalist Mosaic: A Multi-Ethnic Heritage* (Toronto: Dundurn Press, 1984), 25. The foreword to this book by the National President of the United Empire Loyalists Association of Canada made this revealing admission: " . . . the myth that these political and war refugees were English 'blue blood' still persists after 200 years. Almost the exact opposite is true, of course. . . . these exiled Americans were as diverse ethnoculturally as they were in their *faith*, their livelihood and their economic status. *To understand and accept these facts is a basic first step towards grasping the elusive Canadian identity* . . . of the 7000 or so that made up the 'critical mass' that came to the future Ontario there is no question that the English or British element was a minority" (emphasis added).

19. Manoly R. Lupul, "Multiculturalism and Canada's White Ethnics," *Canadian Ethnic Studies* 15 (1983), 103.

20. M.V. George and J. Perreault, *Population Projections for Canada, Provinces and Territories: 1984-2006* (Ottawa: Statistics Canada, 1985); Warren E. Kalback and Wayne W. McVey, *The Demographic Bases of Canadian Society* (2nd ed.; Toronto: McGraw-Hill Ryerson, 1979); and Shirley B. Seward, "Policy Context of Immigration to Canada," in Charles M. Beach and Alan G. Green, eds., *Policy Forum on the Role of Immigration in Canada's Future* (Kingston: Queen's University, 1988). According to these forecasts Canadian population figures are expected to peak at 29 million, then begin a slow decline in the early twenty-first century. In Canada we have never set an official ideal population size although there have been many wishful estimates, the most remarkable cited by Shirley Seward: "In the early years of the Laurier administration, the Minister of the Interior said that by the end of the twentieth century, Canada would have a population of 400 million" (7).

21. See *The Globe and Mail* (Toronto), November 26, 1975.

22. Statistics Canada, *The Daily* (editions of December 8, 1992 and February 22, 1993 on the highlights of the 1991 Census of Canada).

23. Raymond Breton, "The Production and Allocation of Symbolic Resources: An Analysis of the Linguistic and Ethnocultural Fields in Canada," *Canadian Review of Sociology and Anthropology* 21 (1984), 123–44; Daiva K. Stasiulis, "The Symbolic Mosaic Reaffirmed: Multiculturalism Policy," in Katharine A. Graham, ed., *How Ottawa Spends, 1988–89: The Conservatives Heading into the Stretch* (Ottawa: Carleton University Press, 1988), 81-111; and Abu-Laban and Stasiulis, "Ethnic Pluralism under Siege," 366.

24. Quoted in Jean Leonard Elliott and Augie Feras, *Unequal Relations: An Introduction to Race and Ethnic Dynamics in Canada* (Scarborough: Prentice-Hall, 1992).

25. Joseph Tussman, *Government and the Mind* (New York: Oxford University Press, 1977); and Kit R. Christensen, "Multiculturalism and Uniculturalism: A Philosophical View," *American Review of Canadian Studies* 15 (1985), 205-12.

26. Abu-Laban and Stasiulis, "Ethnic Pluralism under Siege," 367.

27. See Karl Popper, *The Open Society and Its Enemies* (Princeton: Princeton University Press, 1950).

28. John W. Berry, Rudolf Kalin and Donald M. Taylor, *Multiculturalism and Ethnic Attitudes in Canada* (Ottawa: Minister of State for Multiculturalism, 1977).

29. J.W. Berry, "Psychology of Acculturation," in J. Berman, ed., *Nebraska Symposium on Motivation*, Vol. 37 (Lincoln: University of Nebraska Press, 1990), 201-34.

30. I. De Faveri, "Janen on Multiculturalism," in *Multiculturalism: Perspectives and Reactions* (Edmonton: Occasional Paper 86-1 of the Department of Educational Foundations, University of Alberta).

31. B. Singh Bolaria and Peter S. Li, *Racial Oppression in Canada* (Toronto: Garamond Press, 1985); Peter S. Li and B. Singh Bolaria, *Racial Minorities in Multicultural Canada* (Toronto: Garamond Press, 1983); and D. Forbes, "Conflicting National Identities among Canadian Youth," in Jon Pammett and M.S. Whittington, eds., *Foundations of Political Culture* (Toronto: Macmillan, 1986), 288-315.

32. Brian M. Bullivant, "Multiculturalism — Pluralist Orthodoxy or Ethnic Hegemony?" *Canadian Ethnic Studies* 13 (1973), 1-22; and Karl Peter, "The Myth of Multiculturalism and Other Political Fables," in Jorgen Dahlie and Tissa Fernando, eds., *Ethnicity, Power and Politics in Canada*, Vol. 8, Canadian Ethnic Studies Association (Toronto: Methuen, 1981), 56-67.

33. "Multiculturalism, really is folklore. It is a 'red Herring.' The notion was devised to obscure 'the Quebec business,' to give an impression that we are all ethnics and do not have to

worry about special status for Quebec" (R. Lévesque, "Education in a Changing Society: A View from Quebec," in A. Chaiton and N. McDonald, eds., *Canadian Schools and Canadian Identity* [Toronto: Gage Educational Publishing, 1977]).

34. Quoted in Reginald W. Bibby, *Mosaic Madness: The Poverty and Potential of Life in Canada* (Toronto: Stoddart, 1990), 176-77.

35. Douglas Fisher, presentation in *Multiculturalism as State Policy* (Ottawa: Minister of State for Multiculturalism, 1976), 15.

36. Rainer Knopff and F.L. Morton, *Charter Politics* (Scarborough: Nelson, 1991), 88 (emphasis added).

37. Quoted in Robert F. Harney, "So Great a Heritage as Ours: Immigration and the Survival of the Canadian Polity," *Daedalus* 117 (1988), 51-97.

38. Rainer Knopff, *Human Rights and Social Technology* (Ottawa: Carleton University Press, 1989).

39. Gilles Paquet, "Multiculturalism as National Policy," *Journal of Cultural Economics* 13 (1989), 24, 25 (emphasis added).

40. Gilles Paquet, "Philosophy of Multiculturalism," paper prepared for the Conference, "Multiculturalism in Canada Today," Queen's University, October 3-6, 1991; and Paul Laurent and Gilles Paquet, "Intercultural Relations: A Myrdal-Tocqueville-Girard Interpretative Scheme," *International Political Science Review* 12 (1991), 171-83.

41. Paquet, "Philosophy of Multiculturalism," 27.

42. Laurent and Paquet, "Intercultural Relations," 181.

43. Quoted in the *Hamilton Spectator*, April 15, 1987, A7.

44. Harney, "So Great a Heritage as Ours," 91.

45. Keith Spicer, "Ottawa Should Stop Money for Multiculturalism," *The Montreal Gazette*, March 9, 1989, B3.

46. As quoted by Alfred Kazin in *The New York Review of Books*, April 22, 1993, 3.

47. Abu-Laban and Stasiulis, "Ethnic Pluralism under Siege " 371.

48. John Stuart Mill to Henry George, quoted in R. Takaki, *Iron Cages: Race and Culture in Nineteenth Century America* (New York: Knopf, 1979), 245.

49. This research on the expressed official attitudes and behaviour on the issue of race and their direct effects on Canadian public policy, the bureaucracy and the judiciary are developed in my unpublished manuscript, "Myths, Symbols and Selective Memories: Canadian Governing Institutions and the Issue of Race to the 1960s." This work is part of a larger study I am undertaking on polyethnicity in Canada.

50. Darlene Johnston, "First Nations and Canadian Citizenship," in William Kaplan, ed., *Belonging: The Meaning and Future of Canadian Citizenship* (Montreal: McGill-Queen's University Press, 1993), 349-67.

51. John Meisel, "Fin de siècle Mutations in English Canada: Has the Peaceable Kingdom Turned Ugly?" in *Être contemporain: mélanges en l'honneur de Gérard Bergeron* (Québec: Presses de l'Université du Québec, 1992), 225-47. For his use of the imagery Meisel explained how William Kilbourn also borrowed it from Northrop Frye for his 1970 anthology, *Canada: A Guide to the Peaceable Kingdom*. Kilbourn explained: "To identify that which is most essentially Canadian in our literature, Frye recalls a painting, *The Peaceable Kingdom* [by Edward Hicks], which depicts a treaty between Indians and Quakers, and a group of animals — lions, bears, oxen — illustrating the prophecy of Isaiah; it is a haunting and serene vision of the reconciliation of man with man and man with nature. Frye suggests the Canadian tradition as revealed in literature might well be called a quest for the peaceable kingdom" (xvii).

52. Wilson, "Myths, Symbols and Selective Memories."

53. Carl Berger, "The True North Strong and Free," in Peter Russell, ed., *Nationalism in Canada* (Toronto: McGraw-Hill, 1966), 24.

54. Robert J. Sharpe, "Citizenship, the Constitution Act, 1867, and the Charter," in Kaplan, ed., *Belonging*, 223-24.

55. Ibid., 229.

56. Wilson, "Myths, Symbols and Selective Memories."

57. *Christie v. York* [1940] 1 D.L.R. 81, and [1941] *Canadian Law Reports*, Supreme Court of Canada, 139.

58. For a most telling exposé of what the fostering of this state of mind meant to the Canadian war effort as this country entered the war, see Norman Hillmer, Bohdan Kordan and Lubomyr Luciuk, *On Guard for Thee: War, Ethnicity, and the Canadian State, 1939-45* (Ottawa: Ministry of Supply and Services, 1988).

59. Alan C. Cairns, "The Living Canadian Constitution," *Queen's Quarterly* 77 (1970), 483–98.
60. James W. St. G. Walker, "Race Policy in Canada: A Retrospective," in Dwivedi et al., eds., *Canada 2000*, 1–19.
61. "War in Europe," *The Economist*, July 6, 1991.
62. Geertz, "The Uses of Diversity," 119–20.
63. Antonine Maillet, "Canada: What's That?" *Queen's Quarterly* 99 (1992), 650.
64. Richard Rorty, "On Ethnocentrism: A Reply to Clifford Geertz," *Michigan Quarterly Review* 25 (1986), 532.
65. Quoted in F.H. Underhill, *In Search of Canadian Liberalism* (Toronto: Macmillan, 1960), frontispiece.

The Mass Media and Political Crisis: Reporting Canada's Constitutional Struggles

DAVID TARAS

The media's coverage of Canada's constitutional crisis has stirred enormous controversy. There have been charges of biased reporting made against the CBC and francophone journalists, questions asked by parliamentary committees about the obligations of news organizations to the country, and investigations by the CBC into its own reporting practices. The prolonged and agonizing constitutional crisis opened many wounds in the journalistic community and provoked an almost unprecedented political debate about the nature and quality of Canadian journalism.[1]

The coverage given to the constitutional struggle may also represent a turning point for academic work on journalism and public affairs in Canada because it raises issues that are of critical importance to scholars. Questions about the effects that modern communications and particularly television have on political behaviour, the mandates and roles of public broadcasters, how journalists see their moral and professional responsibilities, and the problem of how to make difficult and complex stories understandable and compelling to audiences that are increasingly disconnected from political events are prominent features of the debate over media coverage. There is little doubt that the constitutional crisis will be a fertile battleground among contending schools of thought about the responsibilities of journalists and news organizations for years to come.

SOURCE: "The Mass Media and Political Crisis: Reporting Canada's Constitutional Struggles," *Canadian Journal of Communication* 18 (1993): 131–48. Reprinted with permission.

This article will apply a framework of analysis developed by Joshua Meyrowitz (1985) to explain how media coverage may have affected the constitution-making process. In *No Sense of Place*, Meyrowitz argues that the real power of television comes from its capacity to reach into and expose behaviour that was once relegated to "back regions." Television creates a "shared arena" by allowing viewers access to political and social settings that were once shielded from public view. Where political leaders were once distant figures, the mysteries of their power enhanced by their remoteness, today's politicians are followed by TV cameras and a media entourage which relentlessly captures and records their controlled messages as well as their unintended gaffes, their brave words as well as the fear in their eyes. Moreover television transports viewers to other places. The poor can see how the wealthy live, Jews and Moslems can watch how Christmas is celebrated, and Iraqi Generals can watch the U.S. Congress vote on whether or not to go to war.

The article will deal with three issues that are central to the debate over how the constitution was reported. First, using Meyrowitz's framework, I will discuss the extent to which media coverage intruded on and structured the negotiations. It will be argued that the instant and powerful nature of the modern media transformed the bargaining process and created new political routines and rituals that scholars, and indeed politicians, are only beginning to understand. Second, charges of political bias that were leveled against both the CBC and against francophone journalists will be examined. It can be argued that in Meyrowitz's "shared arena," journalistic practices have also been opened up to increased scrutiny. Finally, I will deal with the difficulties that journalists encountered in covering the constitutional crisis.

The focus will be on media reporting during the so-called Meech Lake and Canada Rounds, the period from the launching of the Meech Lake initiative in April 1987 through to the agreement reached by the First Ministers in Charlottetown in August 1992. It will not include coverage of the October 26 referendum. The referendum took place under different conditions, was guided by unique rules and procedures, had an entirely different structure, and is worthy of detailed study as a distinct phenomenon in its own right.

The study is based on interviews conducted in Ottawa and Toronto in July 1992 and December 1993 and on documents obtained by the investigator. Twenty persons were interviewed in all; some of them were interviewed twice. Ten CBC employees and officials were interviewed as were journalists from *Le Devoir*, *The Globe and Mail*, *Maclean's*, CTV, and Southam News. All were protected by an ethics procedure that guaranteed them anonymity unless they themselves agreed that their names could be used. Documents were obtained on a confidential basis and decisions about their disposition remain with the news organizations to whom they belong.

Negotiations in a Shared Arena

Meyrowitz contends that television's shared arena has changed the political environment by placing almost all aspects of the political process under a harsh spotlight. Political leaders are enveloped in a media canopy from which there is no escape or hiding. While Meyrowitz never applied his hypothesis to a particular event or process, the media's coverage of the Canadian constitutional struggle would seem to confirm Meyrowitz's argument. For television was not only the window through which political leaders conveyed messages to their publics but was a vehicle for communication among the parties themselves. The media could be likened to the walls in a squash court (although media scholars might argue that the walls were themselves in motion); negotiating positions would have to be hit against the media walls to keep them in play, test reactions, and give them legitimacy.

The negotiations took place in a shared arena. Participants were expected to state their views after each meeting or event in front of waiting banks of microphones, TV cameras, and scrums of reporters fighting for position. CBC Newsworld was a constant presence. Political leaders were often asked to react instantly, in so-called "real time," to the positions or comments of others, would talk to and see other leaders through television monitors, and frequently used interviews to reveal information for the first time or stake out positions. Occasionally journalists were used as go-betweens, carrying messages between the parties. The media's presence was deeply interwoven into the fabric of events.

The media cocoon that surrounded the negotiations seemed to alter the dynamics considerably during the tense and gruelling negotiations that took place in Ottawa as the Meech Lake deadline approached in June 1990. Each of the first ministers would appear each day to make statements and answer questions in front of a wall of reporters that stretched 60 to 70 feet in length. Some saw it, as Clausewitz might put it, as a continuation of the negotiating process by other means; an additional opportunity to apply pressure on other delegations and rally support for their positions. What was peculiar, however, was that these news briefings seemed to take on a life of their own. They produced an outpouring of pent-up emotions, a platform for threats, explosions of anger and frustration, and the leveling of charges and countercharges. As one senior journalist described what took place,

> It was there that Gary Filmon . . . said that he was being screwed around and shown nothing. It was there that Bourassa announced his refusal to negotiate. It was there that Clyde Wells said a clause was missing and said at other times he couldn't stand the pressure. It was there that Frank McKenna questioned other premiers' sanity, that Don Getty admitted to barring the door, and that Getty said first, there was no will to make a deal, and then that there was. It was there that Mulroney ate shit in front of the whole country about the missing clause.

This entire story was told in those goings in and goings out of uni-mikes and scrums. It was there that his whole bizarre process was stripped bare and exposed for what it was. (Confidential document)

During the dramatic last day before the deadline for approval of the Meech Lake Accord, Newfoundland Premier Clyde Wells, who was ex-pecting a phone call from federal constitution minister Lowell Murray, watched on TV as Murray announced the federal strategy with respect to the pending vote in the Newfoundland House of Assembly. Murray had in turn been reacting to the events in Newfoundland as he had seen them unfold on television. As Chantal Hébert of *Le Devoir* has described the shock produced by this new era of television diplomacy,

> Although in this current round you can see that people have gotten used to the fact that what they say is instantly into someone else's living room or someone else's capital, this had never happened before. You'd never seen Lowell Murray say screw you to Clyde Wells who hadn't gotten a phone call, but who could see Lowell Murray screwing him on TV.

Perhaps no group was better at using this new "frontchannel" method of negotiations than were the Aboriginal delegations. On several occasions during the Canada round, Aboriginal leaders were able to "participate" in the negotiations because their grievances and concerns had received extensive coverage, even when they were excluded from the negotiating table. Having made their case in front of millions of Canadians, it was then impossible for governmental leaders to ignore the Aboriginals' agenda. The natives' power was enhanced considerably, it can be argued, by the fact that they fit the media's "frame" better than did some of the more established players. Their colourful dress, heated rhetoric, and constant availability — not to mention their skillful use of media sources and contacts — had much to do with keeping them in front of the cameras and in the headlines.

Constitutional Minister Joe Clark was also adept at rallying support for his positions via the media. When the deal that he had negotiated with the English-speaking premiers in July 1992 was being blown apart in Cabinet, Clark initiated an interview on CBC Newsworld so that he could regain the high ground and put his opponents on the defensive. His appearance and the media coverage that it generated seemed to strength-en his credibility and might even have given him a few more chips at the table. Graham Fraser, the Ottawa bureau chief for *The Globe and Mail*, de-scribes how instant television coverage has changed the flow of politics:

> There was a time when it was possible to think in terms of the civil servant giving advice, politicians making a decision talking about it or making promises, reporters reported it, it appeared in the paper and people read it — a fairly easy loop. We are now in a really complicated information environment.
>
> Increasingly, people involved in this process have Newsworld in their office — they have the television on all day. When constitutional talks are going on, tele-vision isn't reporting the event, television is the event.

Another factor in the constitutional negotiations was that leaks and plants, the more traditional methods of tilting the news to affect political outcomes, reached almost epidemic proportions. A typical example occurred in late May 1990 when an Ontario government strategy paper was leaked to Southam News (Bryden, 1990). It described plans to "discredit the holdout premiers" and ensure "that the blame for failure falls squarely on the dissident provinces and not on Quebec." Whoever leaked the document intended to foil the strategy and embarrass Premier Peterson.

Sometimes members of the same delegation would leak different messages to reporters. During the hot-house negotiations that took place in Ottawa in June 1990, for instance, the Manitoba delegation was "at war with itself." One source at the CBC has described how members of the Manitoba delegation played both sides of the street, "We had a junior attacking us for accepting federal spin on the deal while another, more senior was giving [Wendy] Mesley all the details (that the federal government was giving us)."

During the Canada Round the leaking of information and documents reached almost comic proportions. One prominent news manager has described the deluge that resulted from so many delegations all leaking at the same time.

> At every session Clark would stand up and review the progress and it would be the same sort of silliness where individual delegations would leak documents, and people would ask Clark (about the documents) and he'd respond. The presumption that everybody made in the process was you couldn't prevent leaks because the Aboriginals were there, and the interest groups were there, so that there was no way the paper would stop, let alone (leaks from) the political strata. . . . It became clear that everything would be transparent on a certain level. The ritual dance was more substantive than it normally is because they knew that within fifteen minutes of a paper being tabled upstairs, there were copies floating downstairs. There were moments of high absurdity . . . there was an air of unreality to the whole thing.

The major delegations also had "spin doctors" eager to explain the various twists and turns to journalists and ensure that their perspective was given prominence in the coverage. Reporters were continually being pressured and cajoled, cultivated, and charmed.

In addition, the reporting of the constitution was almost a classic case of pack journalism. A tight web of relationships developed among journalists and their sources and a collective psychology based on sharing common experiences seemed to take hold among reporters. One senior media manager has described the "pressure cooker" within which journalists had to operate during the Canada Round,

> Essentially they had to put in 70,000 or 80,000 air miles over nine months, travelling from one end of the country to the other, covering one manifestation or another of this. . . . Even the accoutrements were exactly the same — there

was always the same blue curtain, the same guy with the box full of flags, every location was made to look like every other location. The audiovisual technicians were always the same, the wagon-masters were always the same people, and the ministers and their aides were always the same people. Essentially you had a community that pulled up stakes and travelled everywhere together. Over time the linkages that they fanned with each other were quite tight — not in the sense that they became friends, but a banter developed. The ministers knew all the reporters, they understood the thrust of their questions, they prepared for the thrust of the questions, they knew who was going to ask the "what did Quebec get today" questions, who was going to ask the "what was the movement on the Aboriginals" question.

There was an Aboriginal pack of spinners, ministers and reporters. There was a francophone pack. There was an anglophone pack. . . . They found themselves, night after night, going to dinner with each other, talking. At each of these events . . . everybody stood around for hours. . . . People started trading notes. People were trading information — they were comparing stories . . . in some cases they would carry messages between delegations. . . .

It is difficult to know how the media environment that both enveloped and intruded on the constitution-making process affected the outcome. But it is probably fair to say that media coverage made negotiations much more complicated and far more difficult than might otherwise have been the case.

For much of Canadian history, constitutional practice was guided to some degree by unwritten agreements and understandings. One can argue that for many decades Quebec had a special place and special powers not enjoyed by other provinces. The system of "alternance" ensured that English- and French-speaking office holders would alternate in the top government positions; tradition guaranteed three civil law judges on the Supreme Court; Quebec had an enlarged role in areas such as immigration, pensions, communications, and foreign affairs and it had the right to opt out of federal programs and fashion its own. Such careful understandings, however, could not withstand the glare of the media magnifying glass.

The first difficulty was the tendency among journalists, one can say the obsession, to declare winners and losers. During the Meech Lake negotiations, compromise was often depicted as a failure, an act of weakness. Consequently political leaders could not retreat from the positions that they had taken without losing face. Premier Bourassa, for instance, was watched continually by Quebec journalists for any sign that he had abandoned what they saw as Quebec's rights. When he was accused in a taped conversation between Diane Wilhelmy, Quebec's deputy minister of Intergovernmental Affairs, and an unidentified civil servant of having "settled for so little" in negotiating the Charlottetown Accord, Bourassa found himself in a firestorm of media exposure and attacks. In a similar fashion, Alberta Premier Don Getty was hounded by reporters for weeks during the leadup to the Charlottetown deal over whether he had won or lost on a Triple E Senate. Under such conditions face-saving compromises were exceedingly difficult and perhaps in some cases impossible to achieve.

Second, as every province or societal group could see what every other constituency was getting there was pressure to match what others had achieved. It can be argued that as the negotiations became overloaded with too many demands and too many interests, they became more brittle and acrimonious.

How and in which ways media reporting shaped the texture of the negotiations, altered agendas or conditioned or provoked certain kinds of behaviour is likely to be grist for scholarly analysis and debate for years to come. In this regard the constitutional crisis is a prime example of the new kind of politics described by Meyrowitz, one in which media exposure transforms and reconstructs the political arena. At the very least the constitutional struggle provides evidence to support Meyrowitz's contention that political leaders are no longer able to control many of the images that are conveyed to the public.

Caught in the Crossfire: The CBC's Constitutional Wars and Francophone Journalists Under Attack

In *No Sense of Place*, Meyrowitz describes how television's intrusiveness and accessibility have profoundly affected almost all of the major institutions in society. Yet Meyrowitz does not push his analysis further to suggest that media institutions have themselves become vulnerable to increased scrutiny and that the corrosive light that they focus on others can also be turned on them. News organizations can also come under the glare of the political spotlight.

CBC AND THE CONSTITUTIONAL CRISIS

There are few events that the CBC has covered in its long and distinguished history that have challenged its integrity, caused as much soul-searching and brought as much painful criticism as has its coverage of the constitutional crisis. Most of the attacks have centred on the CBC's coverage of the final months of the Meech Lake negotiations but other controversies were ignited and continue to burn.

A number of observers have claimed that during the last months of the Meech Lake negotiations the CBC helped to foster a crisis atmosphere by its sensational reporting, its uncritical acceptance and repetition of the Mulroney government's crisis rhetoric, the sheer magnitude of its coverage, and by its mournful "10 Minutes to Midnight" vision of despair (*On Balance*, July/August 1990). According to Bob Fife, *The Toronto Sun*'s Ottawa bureau chief, "The CBC got in bed with the government . . . they got captured by it, and they got fed at 9:30 every night. . . . It was a good deal, surely that was the thinking [at CBC]. When your views mesh, it's dangerous — you're not able to walk away and say 'look we're being used here' because you believe the overall purpose of getting the deal through is in the public interest." Rick Salutin has described the haunting, foreboding quality of two shows produced by *The Journal* in 1990:

> guests were shot against darkness, and perhaps a single source of light. The many bridging shots were haunting landscapes of a stagnant river, a wave-beaten coast, a lonely lighthouse, a city in fog, all photographed through filters to give the impression of perpetual twilight, plus repeated images of Canadians walking slow motion, perplexed and ghostly, through their cities' streets. (Salutin, 1990)

Michel Vastel, a well-known Quebec journalist, went as far as to claim that there had been "systematic collusion" between the CBC and the Mulroney government during the waning days of the Meech Lake negotiations (Alberta Report, 1991; Salutin, 1991). The CBC has launched a libel action against Vastel.

CBC management argued that the network reacted as a national broadcaster had to during what it thought to be a time of crisis — it opened up its arsenal of weapons; extensive coverage, a large commitment of resources, and its considerable journalistic expertise. During the dramatic week of June 4–10, 1990, the CBC produced 882 minutes of live coverage excluding the time allocated for *The National* and *The Journal*, pre-empting regularly scheduled programs 20 times. This compared to only 528 minutes on CTV (Switzer, 1990). Anchor Peter Mansbridge was brought on location and 25 journalists were assigned to the story. The CBC had enough personnel so that it could mount an around-the-clock vigil to protect its positions opposite the podium where the first ministers came to give their briefings. Consequently Wendy Mesley and Don Newman had the best opportunity to ask questions. Vice-President Trina McQueen has explained that the CBC's ground rules required that no story could go on air unless it had been triple-checked and that information had to be confirmed by sources from at least one delegation that was favourable to the accord and one that was against it (McQueen, 1991). Veteran reporter Jason Moscovitz describes the dilemma that the CBC faced during the Meech Lake negotiations: "You have a prime minister who keeps saying it's the end of the world if this thing doesn't go through. I think that the prime minister deserves to be covered." CBC-TV's Ottawa bureau chief Elly Alboim believes that by treating the Meech Lake talks as so overwhelmingly important, the popular perception was that the network "ended up subscribing to the deadline-world-is-ending thesis of the role of the dice." Alboim doesn't believe that the CBC had subscribed to doomsday forecasts. He is convinced, however, that viewers now look to television to validate their views and that when television does not reflect the attitudes of viewers — in this case by not criticizing an accord that most Canadians no longer supported — then anger is turned against television. As the CBC dominated coverage, it, according to Alboim, became a lightning rod for criticism.

It is interesting to note that polls conducted by Angus Reid in June 1990 in the wake of the CBC's massive constitutional coverage found that 63% of those surveyed viewed the CBC's reporting as having been balanced as against only 17% who saw it as biased. A larger number, 30%, claimed that media reporting in general had been biased and irresponsible (Canadian Broadcasting Corporation, 1990).

The CBC had come under such fierce attack, however, that it established an oversight group made up of network vice-presidents headed by Michael McEwan to monitor its coverage (House of Commons Standing Committee on Communications and Culture, 1992). When the Canada Round began in September 1991, the CBC issued guidelines to its reporters restating the journalistic principles that normally dictate the CBC's political reporting. The guidelines emphasized that those advocating partisan positions had to be presented as such and that a full range of views had to be reflected in the coverage. One paragraph, however, did cause discomfort among some journalists in Quebec newsrooms. The guidelines instructed reporters to "reflect Canada as a nation and evoke the social, economic, cultural and political benefits of nationhood" and to "explore as well the costs and consequences of the changes being proposed" (Canadian Broadcasting Corporation, 1991). Some reporters felt that these were in effect federalist marching orders (Seguin, 1991).

CBC president Veilleux and chairman Patrick Watson were put under close scrutiny when they appeared before the House of Commons Standing Committee on Communications and Culture to explain the network's coverage and journalistic policies. Some MPs were incredulous that the network's guidelines on objectivity and balance did not allow it to do more to promote national unity (House of Commons Standing Committee on Communications and Culture, 1991).

Perhaps the most damaging criticism, however, has come from John Meisel, one of Canada's most distinguished scholars and a former chairman of the CRTC. Reacting to a talk given at an academic conference by CBC-TV's Ottawa bureau chief Elly Alboim in which Alboim argued that the prime minister's "sole motivation" was "to establish that he could do in Quebec what Pierre Trudeau could not" (Alboim, 1988), Meisel (1991) accused the CBC journalist of having undermined Brian Mulroney's efforts during the opening rounds of the Meech Lake negotiations in 1987 by giving play to the deal's critics. According to Meisel, the CBC "contributed to the process that ultimately scuppered constitutional reform by seeking out and encouraging attacks against the Meech Lake project by people who could be expected to attract a lot of public attention." Meisel's charges provoked a firestorm of reactions from leading journalists who either leapt to Alboim's defence or joined in a frenzy of criticism. Alboim argued in turn that it is the role of journalists to seek and present opposing viewpoints rather than "sit in an office and wait for press conferences" (Malloy, 1991).

Rumour had it that when CBC president Gérard Veilleux attempted to dismiss Alboim, considered by many in the profession to be one of Canada's most talented news managers, he apparently faced open rebellion from the networks' leading journalists, including Peter Mansbridge and David Halton. Although an internal CBC investigation cleared Alboim of the allegation that he had manipulated news coverage of the Meech Lake deal, there is speculation that Veilleux demoted Trina McQueen from the position of director of TV News and Current Affairs at least in part as a retaliation for her defence of the bureau chief (Winsor, 1992).

The ramifications of the Alboim incident are quite considerable. There is fear that journalists now feel a "chill" that prevents them from discussing their work at conferences and public forums. This means that journalists may become increasingly distant and even cut off from the audiences and readers to which they are ultimately accountable. Moreover there is also anxiety about whether journalists will be able to continue to exercise their independent judgement in deciding how news stories will be covered. Many see this independence as the cornerstone of professional journalism.

FRANCOPHONE JOURNALISM UNDER THE SPOTLIGHT

The different ways in which English- and French-speaking journalists have reported the constitutional crisis also aroused considerable anger and suspicion. Specifically there are charges that the Quebec media created its own agenda, became a powerful participant in the political process, and exercised extraordinary influence over attitudes in Quebec. Keith Spicer, the chairman of the Canadian Radio-Television and Telecommunications Commission (CRTC) and chairman of the Citizen's Forum on Canada's Future, raised the spectre of media "ayatollahs" who manipulated coverage in order to discredit the constitution-making process (Seguin, 1992). Historian and broadcaster Laurier Lapierre has lamented the existence of the "notables," a journalistic and intellectual elite that is unable to accept the "goodwill, the passage of time and the usual trade-offs that make for a democratic political process" (Lapierre, 1992). Ovide Mercredi, the Grand Chief of the Assembly of First Nations at one point accused all francophone parliamentary reporters in Ottawa of being separatists (Saulnier, 1992).

At a conference sponsored by the Fédération des journalistes professionnelle du Québec held in April 1992, Dorothy Dobbie, the co-chair (with Gerald Beaudoin) of the Special Joint Committee on a Renewed

440 CONTEMPORARY ISSUES AND DEBATES

Canada declared that "journalism and nation building should be the same task." She complained about "members of the media who have no sense of their country" (Off, 1992).

The litany of accusations made against francophone journalists includes charges that excessive and sensational coverage was given to extremist views in English-speaking Canada, that Lucien Bouchard's defection from the Mulroney government was treated as an act of heroism and worthy of celebration, that there was an obsession with finding examples of Quebec's humiliation, regardless of how obscure the incident (for instance, the anger among francophone reporters when the English-language version of the Beaudoin-Dobbie Report was made available 15 minutes before the French version), and that a constant vigilance was maintained over Quebec Premier Robert Bourassa to ensure that he did not betray what journalists saw as being in Quebec's interests. But it was the general tone of the coverage that caused the most concern especially during the Meech Lake Round. It was felt by some that opposition to the Meech Lake Accord by English-speaking politicians or critics was presented too often by Quebec journalists as an attack against Quebec. Quebec's dignity was portrayed continually as always being under assault. As Susan Delacourt of *The Globe and Mail* has described the tone that underlay much of the reporting, "The issue [to Quebeckers] is about whether they feel wanted or not. So they [Quebec journalists] weigh up every story. They think in terms of rejection, acceptance or humiliation."

Meyrowitz has described how television has allowed different groups in society to see each other's back regions. During the Meech Lake negotiations audiences in Quebec could witness for themselves the unleashing of anti-French passions in places like Thunder Bay and Sault St. Marie or at rallies held by the Reform Party.

The coverage that generated the most controversy was the play given on French-language television to the so-called "Brockville incident." A 10-second television clip showing the desecration of the Quebec flag by English-language extremists was shown repeatedly during the closing rounds of the Meech Lake negotiations even though this incident did not reflect the attitudes of English-speaking Canadians.

At least as inflammatory was the coverage given in February 1992 to scenes of an Inuit leader holding up a map of Quebec which showed half of Quebec under native control as a result of proposed land-claims settlements. Although this was clearly an instance of grandstanding, an obvious playing to the cameras, reporters were unable to resist the bait. This dramatic visual became a symbol for Quebec nationalists of the threats supposedly posed by the Aboriginals to Quebec's territorial integrity and the dangers of negotiating Aboriginal self-government.

What may have been the most glaring instance of political agenda-setting by the Quebec media occurred after the Clark proposals which launched the Canada Round were presented in September 1991. Robert

Bourassa found himself surrounded by a scrum of francophone reporters who accused him of betraying Quebec because he did not seem to be insisting on the reinstatement of Quebec's veto over future constitutional changes. According to Bob Fife, "These guys acted like they were the conscience of Quebec. . . . They literally ganged up on him. Why Bourassa would allow himself to be bullied I really don't know." Chantal Hébert saw the event differently, "Robert Bourassa is not complaining about the way the press is working in Quebec. What is the best deal for Quebec? That's where these people start from. Bourassa sets lines in the sand and the media asks what happened to the line in the sand."

Few could doubt the extraordinary influence and prestige that journalists seemed to have in Quebec. Whenever there was an important development, Quebec politicians seemed to wait with considerable suspense to see how journalistic opinion leaders were reacting before they themselves took a position. Perhaps the supreme example was *Le Devoir* publisher Lise Bissonnette's one-word editorial — her famous *"non"* — in response to the conditional agreement reached by Joe Clark and the English-speaking Premiers in June 1992. Her strong statement seemed to harden opposition to the deal and leave the Quebec government with little immediate room for manoeuvre.

Quebec journalists argue that their responsibilities differ from those of English-speaking journalists because they serve readers and audiences that have different needs. As the virtues of confederation are not taken for granted in Quebec, all political options, including sovereignty, must be discussed and evaluated. According to Susan Delacourt, "To francophones the phrase 'national unity' is loaded with connotations and implies a federalist point of view. They have to balance between federalism and sovereignty. They have to offer their readers an informed choice. For us [anglophones] it's do nothing or accept new options — for them they have active choices."

Lance Bennett (1990) among other scholars has suggested that the range of opinions in news reporting and editorials is "indexed" to the range of views that exist among the political elites that are being covered. One avenue for future research would be to analyze whether such indexing could be found in the reporting of the constitution by Quebec journalists. It might explain why Quebec journalists pitched their stories differently from anglophone journalists — as their work reflected the different constellation of views and the fierce debate that was being waged in Quebec.

The Age of Missing Information?

Bill McKibben, in his book *The Age of Missing Information* (1992), argues that despite our heavy television viewing and the fact that television has become virtually a companion to many of us, what we learn from television has a vapid and elusive quality. We get images and sounds of considerable power but presented in packets of information or info-tainment that provide little depth, little sense of how the world actually functions. Television may dominate the "moment" with its commanding presence but it cannot deliver a meaningful learning experience.

While McKibben's criticisms of TV are hardly new to media scholars, the constitutional crisis would seem to suggest once again that there is an astonishing disconnectedness between media reporting and public awareness. The convulsions produced by the failure of the Meech Lake Accord and the almost saturation coverage given to the Meech Lake drama by the country's major news organizations seemed to produce a profound malaise; throughout the Canada Round Canadians seemed to know little about the constitutional crisis and cared even less.

Seventy-three percent of those surveyed in an Environics poll taken in the wake of the Clark proposals in October 1991, found "nothing" in the package that attracted their attention. Only 10% of Quebeckers expressed interest in the provisions on "distinct society" even though they had aroused heated passions and had been portrayed as the symbol of Quebec's acceptance by English-speaking Canada (Environics Research Group, 1991). More perplexing perhaps was a survey conducted in April 1992 by the Centre de Recherches en Opinion Publique which revealed that 31% of respondents believed that a sovereign Quebec would remain part of Canada. An even higher number, 40%, thought that if Quebec were to separate they would remain Canadian citizens (Gagnon, 1992).

There are several explanations about why basic information about the country's political crisis did not seem to reach or interest large numbers of people, did not seem to penetrate a fog of indifference, in-attentiveness, and misperception. First, it can be argued that the prospect of Canada's breakup is so monumental, the issues so painful, that large numbers of people preferred not to think about the consequences. Many Canadians were unprepared psychologically to deal with events that had such dire consequences. A corollary argument was that the public had been "burnt out" by the emotional agony of Meech Lake; news consumers had reached their threshold and were now simply too numb to absorb the details of a new round of bargaining. Undoubtedly the ravages of the recession also took a toll; people may have been too consumed by worries about their economic survival and prospects to pay much attention to constitutional wrangling. Even the journalists who covered the con-stitution sensed and were demoralized by their audience's fatigue. As the CBC's Jason Moscovitz has described the frustrations that he ex-perienced during the Canada Round,

> The difficulty in personal terms of reporting this round — I've been doing this story all my life — and this one time that I had such great difficulty doing it

because I knew that nobody wanted to listen to it. How hard it is to do a story that your audience doesn't care about. . . . The whole world was turned off this story. . . . As a professional, it's just awful, [you get an] awful feeling doing a story that you know that nobody wants to hear.

A second argument is that the constitution was simply too complex to be understandable to the average citizen. Issues pertaining to the amending formula or the notwithstanding clause or the number of E's in a reformed Senate were so abstract that few people had the "handles" necessary for grasping what was being talked about. It was as if the country were treated to a lesson in advanced physics with most people left glassy eyed and wishing for a reprieve.

A third explanation is that the media, particularly television, failed to educate the public, failed to tell the story in the way that it needed to be told. Too much of the constitutional reporting on television was presented as a series of breathless "moments," popping up without explanation, appearing fragmented and out of context. The CBC's *The National* and *The Journal* experimented tirelessly with various methods of engaging and re-engaging the audience. They did in-depth reports, used graphs and charts, did numerous specials, and devoted unprecedented amounts of airtime to covering the constitution. In the end, however, they fell remarkably short in explaining what the constitutional proposals would mean for the country.

The focus was inevitably on the drama of whether or not there would be a deal and on the machinations and strategies of the various players. There were few attempts to explain the motivations that lay behind the politics of the moment. Why a veto for Quebec over future constitutional changes was seen as critical by so many in Quebec, the consequences of not having a strong economic union, the pros and cons of adopting a system of proportional representation for an elected Senate, how Aboriginal government would work, and the reasons why Senate reform was seen as a necessity by some of the small provinces were not dealt with to a sustained or systematic way.

Quite typical was a three-part report done by Joe Schlesinger that appeared on *The National* in June 1992. The report, entitled the "Constitution industry" was supposed to be an inside look at the people and machinery that had become part of the process. Yet Schlesinger said nothing about how much the process had cost Canadians, the size and makeup of Ottawa's constitutional bureaucracy, the small army of advisors and influential experts that appeared at conferences and commented in the media, or the structural problems created by Quebec's "reach out but don't touch anyone" bargaining strategy. Instead Schlesinger merely recounted the events that had taken place; reports that contained shots of the comings and goings of political leaders and of delegates speaking at the constitutional conferences staged by the Beaudoin-Dobbie joint parliamentary committee. Schlesinger's commentary was laced with references to "a bulky, complex and unfinished package," "a mess devoid of philosophy," and a "hodge-podge" without explaining in any concrete way why he had come to these conclusions (Cuff, 1992).

The TV networks may have feared that more detailed reporting would lose viewers at a time when viewers were simply not interested in the constitution and at a time when the struggles over audiences had become especially viperous. But it may also be that TV's inherent limitations, the accepted routines of TV reporting and the constraints of time, budgets, and resources prevented bolder steps from being taken. The CBC's Carol Off put it bluntly, "The current constitutional debate is certainly one of the biggest tests of their trade that Canadian journalists have ever faced. A complex issue often reduced to political optics and thirty second sound bites — or to raw emotion. Unfortunately, no one seemed to have any clear idea how to do things differently" (Off, 1992).

Conclusion

Examining the media's reporting of the Canadian constitutional crisis offers many avenues for research. As the constitutional struggles analyzed in this article took place over a five-year period, many characteristics of media reporting were exposed. Unlike case studies which dwell on the coverage given to a single event or incident: a riot, a trial, a strike, an election — episodes that are fleeting and perhaps idiosyncratic, this case study encompasses an enormous landscape of activity. Issues relating to the differences in coverage by public as against private news organizations, the gulf that separated anglophone and francophone journalists, the interplay between journalists and their sources, the social/political control imposed in the newsroom, and the effects of media reporting on the negotiating process and on public opinion were all illuminated by controversies that erupted during the Meech Lake and Canada Rounds. The many episodes explored in this case study will allow scholars to identify repeated and consistent patterns of behaviour and examine some of the more nagging questions that have plagued Canadian journalism.

Perhaps the critical question that emerges from this study is the degree to which media reporting, and more specifically television coverage, transformed events. Despite hundreds of studies on media agenda-setting, scholars are still perplexed by the potency of television as a political force. Preliminary evidence presented in this article suggests that Meyrowitz's notion of the shared arena may offer scholars a fruitful avenue for future research. There can be little question that the media invaded the negotiating process and influenced the conduct of the negotiations. More work will have to be done to determine the extent to which media coverage altered public perceptions.

Yet this study also encountered evidence that conventional television reporting cannot reach and educate its audience when the issues are too painful or too complex to be easily understood. The dilemma was stated poignantly by Jonathan Schell, who wrote, "Television is powerful because it can dominate the moment. It is weak because it cannot outlast the moment" (Rosen, 1991).

NOTE

1. I am grateful to the Social Sciences and Humanities Research Council of Canada for the funding which made it possible for me to travel to Ottawa to do the interviews that were necessary for this study. All information and quotations not cited were obtained from interviews conducted or documents given to the author.

REFERENCES

Alboim, Elly. (1988). Inside the news story: Meech Lake as viewed by an Ottawa bureau chief. In Roger Gibbins et al. (Eds.), *Meech Lake and Canada: Perspectives from the West* (pp. 235–245). Edmonton: Academic Printing and Publishing.

Alboim, Elly. (1991). Response to "Mirror? Searchlight? Interloper? — The Media and Meech." *Electronic Journal of Communication, 2*(1), 63–68.

Bennett, W. Lance. (1990). Toward a theory of press–state relations in the United States. *Journal of Communication, 40*(2), 103–125.

Bryden, Joan. (1990, May 30). Plot to discredit holdouts. *Calgary Herald,* p. A1.

Canadian Broadcasting Corporation (1991). *Guidelines for Coverage of the Constitutional Debate by CBC/SRC Journalists.* Ottawa: CBC.

Cuff, John Haslett. (1992, August 13). When no news is bad news. *The Globe and Mail,* p. A9.

Dasko, Donna. (1991, December). Presentation on behalf of Environics Research Group to the Renewal of Canada Conference Organizing Committee.

Gagnon, Lysiane. (1992, April 4). Why a large number of Quebeckers are loath to leave the fold. *The Globe and Mail,* p. D3.

House of Commons Standing Committee on Communication and Culture. (1990 January–1992 May). *Proceedings.*

Lapierre, Laurier. (1992, March 21). Meet the notables who dictate what Quebeckers think. *The Globe and Mail,* p. D1.

Malloy, Katie. (1991, May 9). At the centre of the controversy. *The Hill Times,* p.12.

McKibben, Bill. (1992). *The Age of Missing Information.* New York: Random House.

McQueen, Trina. (1991?). How the CBC covered Meech Lake. Newspaper clipping.

Meisel, John. (1991). Mirror? Searchlight? Interloper? — The Media and Meech. In David Smith, Peter MacKinnon, & John Courtney (Eds.), *After Meech Lake: Lessons for the Future* (pp. 147–168). Saskatoon: Fifth House.

Meyrowitz, Joshua. (1985). *No Sense of Place.* New York: Oxford.

Off, Carol. (1992, May). Is the media losing its grip? A seminar on covering the constitutional debate. *Network Conference Reports.*

On Balance. (1990, July/August). Key journalists accuse networks of Meech Lake coverage bias.

Rosen, Jay. (1991). TV as alibi: A response to Michael Schudson. *Tikkun, 5*(2), 52–54, 87.

Salutin, Rick. (1990, November). Brian and the boys. *Saturday Night,* p. 17.

Saunier, Alain. (1992, April 23). Don't blame the media. *The Globe and Mail,* p. A19.

Seguin, Rheal. (1991, September 4). Anti-sovereignty bias exists at CBC, PQ says. *The Globe and Mail,* p. A1.

Seguin, Rheal. (1992, January 21). Spicer assails media "ayatollahs." *The Globe and Mail,* p. A1.

Switzer, Kara. (1990, October 18). CTV research. Interview (telephone).

Winsor, Hugh. (1992, July 1). Cross currents: Broadcasting. The *Globe and Mail,* p. A10.

Culture and Free Trade

JOHN HUTCHESON

Introduction

Free trade talks seem to be about "economics" rather than "culture," but in fact cultural issues are inevitably involved. It might even be said that no other aspect of the free trade talks poses so many questions about the consequences for Canada. Given that cultural policies are crucial for the survival of Canada as an independent nation, it is disturbing that the advocates of a free trade deal between Canada and the United States have paid so little attention to this question.

A "culture" is a way of doing things and a way of reflecting on what we do. A culture is a shared life, because individual experiences can only be shared with others in cultural terms. Much of our culture is so apparently natural and so inherently a part of our lives that it requires no specialized production. It is spontaneously taught and learned — "at our mother's knees," to quote a figure of speech which is full of cultural meaning. But the parts of culture that are reflections on how we live, and on why we live, have to be consciously organized. (Here the fathers have played a larger role.) They can be organized by custom, by convention, by individuals, or by the collectivity. But crucial to our present concerns is the fact that as the world has become industrialized, cultural reflection has increasingly moved from folk product to industrial product. A large proportion of our culture is now, inevitably, the product of "cultural industries."

The way babies are raised, the games children play in the schoolyard, the way people socialize, patterns of courtship and marriage, or non-marriage, are all aspects of behaviour which we frequently experience as intensely personal, but which are at the same time culturally conditioned. These aspects of our culture are not industrially organized, nor are they traded, though they do get modified as a result of contacts between one group of people and another and they do change over time, sometimes as a result of industrial development. The ways in which we work, also a part of our culture, have of course been profoundly changed by industrialization, and continue to change at an almost revolutionary pace. In a like manner, the way in which we reflect on and comment on our actions, whether in the form of gossip or popular comedy, or

SOURCE: "Culture and Free Trade," in Michael D. Henderson, ed., *The Future on the Table: Canada and the Free Trade Issue* (Toronto: Masterpress, 1987), pp. 101–19. Reprinted with permission.

as art or philosophy, has been transformed by industrial development. From the invention of moveable type and the printing press to the direct broadcast satellite, a long list of technical innovations has given rise to industries which produce cultural products.

But cultural industries are not the consequences of technology alone. They are the result of corporate organization for the purposes of the production and distribution of cultural products using the available technology. Such corporate organization can take many forms. Production may be organized as a state monopoly or may take the form of smallscale private enterprise. Distribution can vary from exclusive lists to free broadcasting. Typically, though with some significant exceptions, industrialization has meant more and more aspects of culture have been produced and distributed for profit by commercial enterprises seeking the widest available market.

The impact of any particular cultural enterprise varies greatly. A small theatre performing a play for a limited run will not reach a very large audience, and will thus have a limited cultural impact. It is of course true that the play might have a very large impact on those who actually see it, and it is also true that the play may be performed in other theatres thus creating a larger, and perhaps international, audience. If it achieves the status of a classic it may be repeated for successive generations and thus have a continuing cultural presence. A single television broadcast, on the other hand, can reach an audience of hundreds of millions simultaneously with the transmission, and can also be reproduced endlessly. A school text, handed to a child who has just discovered the excitement of reading or the possibility of uncovering the past through the study of history, may well shape the cultural attitudes of that child.

It is hard to be specific about the impact of any one cultural product but it seems clear that every society needs to be aware of the way in which its cultural values are transformed by new technology. Marshall McLuhan was right to point to the connection between the medium and the message, but the medium is only part of the message. The message is also partly shaped by the owners of systems of production and distribution who have the power to determine what products they will purvey. McLuhan used to speak of the "global village" that would be created by the electronic revolution, but not everyone wants to live in a village in which all the speeches are delivered by the headman in the interests of maintaining his authority, whether the message is advertised as the "traditional" way of doing things or as the "new" way.

Industrialization does to some extent create a homogeneous world, but it is equally important to see that each country has its own industrial history and its own place in the world economy. The best guide to the industrial history of Canada is the work of the economic historian Harold Innis. Innis recognized that at any given time the world economy is characterized by a division between "centre" and "margin." Countries which play the role of centre are those which dominate in the formation of trade patterns, price systems, and capital movements. Countries at the margin play a dependent role in relation to a specific centre. Canada began its modern history at the margin of the European world, with first France and then Britain starring at the centre, but by the late nineteenth century the United States began to take over as the relevant centre to which Canada was marginal. By the mid-twentieth century, the United States was the centre for much of the world economy.

In its growth to superpower status, the United States was initially aided by its highly productive agriculture and manufacturing. In the twentieth century the military role of the United States has become increasingly an indicator of its centre status. Equally important has been the growing international significance of the service sector of the U.S. economy. Examples of trade in services are travel and freight transportation across national boundaries as well as a large number of business transactions such as royalty payments, franchise rights, advertising and financial services. Also included is the trade in films and broadcasting.

In the United States, film and broadcasting are seen as part of the entertainment industry. But they are also cultural industries because they organize the way viewers look at the world and the way that audience reflects upon the world. The cultural values of the United States, packaged as entertainment, have an immense impact on the rest of the world, and Canada has had a maximum exposure to those values.

Free-trade talks between Canada and the United States will inevitably involve cultural industries in which the United States has a very strong interest. Furthermore, the terms of trade in cultural products set the limits within which Canadian cultural policies must operate.

Cultural Industries and Trade Balances

In the conclusion to *Canada's Cultural Industries*, a study of broadcasting, publishing, records and film, Paul Audley writes: "The structure of the domestic production and distribution industries in every case is organized around the supply of imported content to Canadians . . ."[1] The evidence for this conclusion is beyond doubt, and the level of imports of cultural products is so high that it raises serious questions about the cultural viability of Canada. It is of course desirable that Canadians should have access to foreign products, and in the case of cultural products, particularly, consumer choice is an important aspect of a free and open society. But a problem arises when imports dominate the marketplace to the extent that few Canadian alternatives are available. In such a situation, choice is limited and the freedom to subscribe to Canadian cultural values is hampered.

The amount of importing and the way in which products are imported vary from one industry to another. Newspapers, for example, are primarily local, and most newspapers sold in Canada are published in this country, although a considerable portion of the editorial content is purchased from foreign wire services. Magazines, by contrast, tend to be national, but a quick look at any magazine stand quickly establishes the fact that the Canadian market is an international one. In 1979, 46 percent of magazine circulation was accounted for by foreign magazines. A further 25 percent of the total circulation was taken by Canadian editions or adaptations — such as *Reader's Digest* or *TV Guide* — which add a small amount of Canadian content to an essentially foreign product, leaving only 29 percent of total circulation to Canadian-originated magazines.[2] The situation in bookstores is not very different. In 1980, foreign books captured 72.4 percent of total sales, the remaining 27.6 percent going to Canadian-published books.

The print media are not alone in exhibiting this pattern of high import content. In the recording industry in 1980, sales of Canadian content recordings were only 7.6 percent of total industry wholesale revenues.[3]

Canadian film production is subject to more erratic cycles of optimism and pessimism than any of the industries we have so far considered, but whether the industry is in one of its "we've finally arrived" manic phases, or in the more usual state of depression, the number of Canadian films in the theatres is not very high. In 1979, Canadian productions accounted for just 1.8 percent of the theatrical film market in Canada.[4]

There is a common thread in the history of all these media of communications. As new technology has been introduced, the competitive advantage has gone to those producers who could profitably introduce the new technology and offset its cost by producing on an ever larger scale and at the same time creating the necessarily larger distribution network. Mass production, force fed by new technology, requires mass marketing. The Canadian market has as a consequence become an extension of other markets. Primarily it is an extension of the U.S. market for magazines, books, records and films. In the case of newspapers, the advertising copy that they carry is essentially local and thus their market is, in most cases, inherently local. But the other products are sold by advertising to the largest available market. Mass market magazines, paperbacks, records and films produced in the United States are advertised, distributed and sold in Canada in such quantities that many Canadian consumers are barely conscious of the fact that they are foreign products. For many they are just magazines, books, records and films.

Television is both similar and special. It is similar because the same pattern of development characterized the U.S. industry; as programme production levels increased to fill the available capacity of the network distribution systems, a wider market was sought for those programmes beyond the American border. But television is special because it has be-come the most widely marketed cultural product of all time. The number of hours people spend reading, listening to records, or watching films in a theatre, pales into insignificance by comparison with the audience for television.

Television viewing time for Canadians, from infancy on, is an average 22 hours per week.[5] The 1986 Report of the Task Force on Broadcasting Policy, chaired by Gerald Caplan and Florian Sauvageau, tells us that only 28 percent of all the programming available on English television is Canadian. Less than one third of the total time spent watching English language television is devoted to Canadian programming. Anglophone teenagers spend 80 percent of their viewing time watching foreign pro-grammes. Ninety-eight percent of all drama on English-language tele-vision is foreign.[6]

Canadian audiences do in fact watch Canadian programmes to the extent that they exist. But the Canadian television system is to a very great extent a delivery system for programmes made in the U.S.A. The cable television companies make their profits by delivering cost-free American signals to Canadian households. Private broadcasters find it cheaper to buy American programmes than to produce in Canada. The CBC, which in its advertising-free radio networks — with the help of imported recorded music — is able to deliver close to 100 percent Ca-nadian programming, is forced by budget constraints to buy imported programmes for its commercially supported television networks.

The traffic in cultural products across the U.S.–Canadian border is of course immensely profitable. American producers and Canadian dis-tributors, whether they are U.S.-owned branch plants or Canadian-owned companies, are trading on a large scale, and the balance of the trade is always in the same direction. In 1984, Canada's exports to the United States in the film and broadcasting category were worth $23 million. But U.S. exports to Canada were worth $136 million.[7] Given the dif-ference in the size of the populations the cultural imbalance is overwhelming.

Pierre Juneau, President of the CBC, recently asked the question: "what would people think if all our monuments, statues in public squares, our streets, and on the grounds of our legislatures represented mainly United States generals and politicians? If all the portraits in public build-ings, universities and schools featured American scholars and historical figures?" Yet, as Juneau says, "in moving pictures and television imagery this is precisely what is going on in Canada."[8]

Artists and Cultural Integrity

Despite the imbalance in trade in cultural products, the past 25 years have seen a considerable improvement in the state of the arts in Canada.

More publishers are producing more books by Canadian authors. More theatres exist to perform new Canadian work. There is more space in newspapers and magazines for critical writing on the arts.

Some of the evidence of the growth of the arts was presented in the 1986 Report of the Task Force on Funding of the Arts, chaired by Edmund Bovey. The Bovey Task Force looked at the performing arts, museums, art galleries, the visual arts, and creative writing and found that these arts are now a $1.1 billion industry, even before indirect economic effects are taken into account.[9] Thirty thousand Canadians work as painters, sculptors, actors, musicians, dancers or writers. About 35 percent of the Canadian population go to theatres and visit galleries at least once a year. In 1982 the audience for professional performing arts groups totalled 10 million.

Although these figures do not include the higher technology activities of film and broadcasting, they are reassuring to those who are concerned with the cultural identity of Canada. Artists are essential to the process of reflecting on cultural values, recognizing a cultural heritage, and changing cultural values to correspond to new concerns. But a key to understanding this $1.1 billion arts industry is the fact that only a little less than half of its revenues are garnered by commercial activities — theatres, galleries or festivals that receive no government sudsidies. Of almost equal importance to the commercial sector, and of far greater significance artistically, are the non-profit arts organizations that receive government funding. Although audiences have grown, non-profit arts activities receive only 35 percent of their total revenue directly from consumers. Fifty-six percent of their revenue comes from government sources. It should also be noted here that a large hidden subsidy for the arts comes from many of the artists themselves who work for low pay and often in unfavourable working conditions. But federal and provincial government policies have been key actors in the development of the arts in Canada.

There is no question that someone has to act as a patron for the arts once professional artists become central to cultural reflection. With the development of publishing houses and commercial theatres, professional artists who had previously been the servants of a few wealthy noble patrons were able to seek a wider "public" audience, although the work of the artists had first to pass through the hands of the publishers, impressarios and gallery owners. Once the professional artists spoke to the public their work became fundamental to the cultural life of the whole of society, and with that change the question of the cultural freedom of the artists became part of the larger issue of the freedom of all.

Professional artists can work for different kinds of masters and for many different purposes. Artists can enhance freedom or they can reinforce the dominance of those who are already powerful by virtue of their control of other institutions. Which path an artist takes is not just a matter of his or her personal choice but is also conditioned by the opportunities made available by a particular society.

A commercial audience offered the artist freedom from the wealthy patron, but the marketplace imposes its own forms of coercion. The industrialization of artistic production, more complete obviously in some arts than in others, creates mass production which requires a mass audience. Products which are less successful in mass marketing campaigns are relegated to the cultural fringes. The Canadian mass market is an extension of the American market. For most Canadian artists, as for Canadian audiences, that is a limiting, rather than an enabling, factor.

In 1952, in an essay entitled "The Strategy of Culture," Harold Innis explained why the cultural life of English-speaking Canadians had been "subjected to a constant hammering from American commercialism."[10] Innis' explanation, based primarily on the print media, showed how technology, copyright laws and the demands of advertising had transformed the culture of the United States and created a cultural pattern that had overflowed the borders of the United States. The only protection, Innis saw, was to "explore the cultural possibilities of various media and to develop them along lines free from commercialism."[11]

Canada has had a long history of developing various media along lines free from commercialism. From canals, to railroads, to radio and airlines, "public entrepreneurship" — to quote a term coined by Herschel Hardin — has been used to create Canadian networks that would offer an alternative to the ever expanding penetration of the Canadian border by American networks. Canadian nationalism and the patronage of Canadian governments have been necessary to cultural integrity. These forces have never closed the Canadian border, and of course it is not desirable that they should ever do so, but they have been necessary for the maintenance of a cultural freedom of choice. Cultural policy has become a critical weapon in the struggle for survival in which Canadian culture is perennially engaged.

Cultural Policies

In 1941 a group of artists meeting in Kingston formed the Federation of Canadian Artists. Led by Lawren Harris, Sir Ernest Macmillan and sculptor Elizabeth Wyn Wood, the group began the process of lobbying for the formation of an independent, government-financed organization to aid the performing and creative arts. The Massey Commission — the Royal Commission on National Development in the Arts, Letters and Sciences — endorsed the creation of such an arts council, and finally, in 1957, the Canada Council was brought into being by an Act of Parliament. At first funded entirely from the estates of two wealthy financiers, Sir James Dunn and Izaak Walton Killam, the Canada Council began receiving Parliamentary grants in 1967. In 1985–86, the Council allocated $67.5 million in grants to a wide range of artistic activities including dance, music, theatre, visual arts, writing and publishing. There are also provincial arts councils in some provinces, some of which (those of Saskatchewan and Alberta) predated the Canada Council. In the financial year ending 31 March, 1986, the Ontario Arts Council spent $22 million in support of the arts.[12]

But government policies to support Canadian culture involve more than direct subsidies administered by arts councils. Regulations and tax measures are of equal importance and perhaps more subject to change in the reorganization of policy which is accompanying the free-trade negotiations. All the cultural industries in Canada have grown up in a framework of regulation, subsidization and taxation which has determined degrees of foreign ownership, profitability and cultural content.

Broadcasting is, for cultural policy, both a special case because of its immense cultural impact, and a paradigm because it illustrates the complex weave of technological, financial, regulatory and artistic attributes which is characteristic of all cultural industries. Both private and public broadcasting accompanied the early days of radio in Canada. CFCF in Montreal was licensed in 1919, and legendary entrepreneurs such as Roy Thomson and Foster Hewitt were soon making money selling advertising on their own stations. In 1923, Sir Henry Thornton, president of the Canadian National Railways, opened a public broadcasting network as a service for train travellers, hotel guests and employees. As the Caplan-Sauvageau Report puts it, "while nearly all the radio stations were privately owned and were broadcasting mostly American material, the CNR service used Canadian performers for concerts, talks and other programming."[13]

In 1928 Mackenzie King established a Royal Commission on Radio Broadcasting, the first of many attempts to establish the rules for government regulation. The Aird Commission, noting that Canadian listeners wanted Canadian programmes, recommended a public broadcasting system. Private broadcasters, Aird said, could not raise sufficient advertising revenues to pay for Canadian programmes. It was R.B. Bennett, one of two Conservatives who interrupted Mackenzie King's incumbency, who introduced into Parliament the principles that broadcasting should be under national control, that a publicly owned system was necessary, and that the airwaves were a publicly owned natural resource. The Canadian Radio Broadcasting Commission was established by Bennett's government in 1932, and then in 1936 remodelled into the Canadian Broadcasting Corporation by Mackenzie King.

In 1936 the CBC stood at the centre of the national broadcasting system, producing a national radio service and also regulating the private sector. The campaign for public broadcasting, which had been launched by Alan Plaunt and Graham Spry through the Canadian Radio League, appeared to have won the day. The campaign, some of which had been fought in the pages of *The Canadian Forum*, had given rise to Graham Spry's revealing slogan, "The State or the United States." The government had chosen "the State" but the private broadcasters still had an interest in distributing the produce of the States.

Television broadcasting posed many of the same questions but in an even more acute form because the costs of television programming were dramatically higher. U.S. border stations were accessible to many Canadians and a market for American programmes had been created before the CBC went on the air. When the CBC did set up stations in Montreal and Toronto, private stations were licensed as affiliates, and the combination of public and private broadcasting was reaffirmed along with the combination of Canadian and U.S. programme content.

Ottawa wanted a "truly Canadian entity" and the CBC controlled the airwaves. But as Peter Morris[14] has recently pointed out, some of the early technical decisions made by the CBC had momentous consequences. Influenced by Alphonse Ouimet, then an engineer with the CBC, later to be its president, the CBC opted for the 525-line transmission signal used by U.S. broadcasters, and also for Very High Frequency (VHF) rather than Ultra High Frequency (UHF) broadcasting. Canadians, noted Ouimet, would be able to "tune in directly to American stations" and there would also be "the paramount advantage of using American programmes on Canadian stations." Equipment could also be bought from the RCA-NBC conglomerate. CBC television was off to a great start as, to use Morris's term, a "regional affiliate" of the American networks.

The CBC lost its regulatory authority over the private sector with the creation of the Board of Broadcast Governors, and in 1961 the BBG licensed the private CTV network. The 1968 Broadcasting Act, which with amendments still provides the regulatory framework for broadcasting, created a new regulatory body, the Canadian Radio-Television Commission (re-styled the Canadian Radio-television and Telecommunications Commission, in 1976), to control both the CBC and the private sector. The CRTC was mandated to "safeguard, enrich and strengthen the cultural political, social and economic fabric of Canada." But if the CBC had had trouble juggling the unstable mixture of public broadcasting, American technology and American programming, the CRTC was soon to prove hapless with the explosive mixture of private stations plus American technology and American programmes.

The 1968 Broadcast Act had brought cable systems under control as "broadcasting receiving undertakings." The CRTC allowed cable systems to provide the full programme schedules of the American networks. The CRTC is responsible for the Canadian content requirements which accompanied the creation of new stations including the Global network and pay-TV. But the CRTC has also allowed the routine failure of private broadcasters to fulfill those commitments. In *Closed Circuits: The Sellout of Canadian Television*, Herschel Hardin comments on the work of communications economist Robert Babe, author of *Canadian Television Broadcasting Structure, Performance and Regulation*, a study published by the Economic Council of Canada. Hardin writes that "Babe documented how the CRTC had allowed the de facto establishment of private property rights in the public radio spectrum through trading in the profitability of licences, automatic licence renewals, weak enforcement of original licence conditions and the exclusion of competing application."[15]

Notwithstanding this very large gap between the stated aims of broadcast policy and the reality of broadcast performance, the Government of Canada and some provincial governments are responsible for the maintenance of such Canadian programming as there still is, a matter of vital concern to Canadian producers, writers, technicians and performers as well as to those interested in the accessibility of Canadian culture.

The CBC received a parliamentary operating grant, worth $848 million in 1986–87. Private radio and television stations are kept in Canadian hands by legislation requiring Canadian ownership, and their profitability is partly enhanced by the negative policy of allowing them to substitute cheaper American programming for Canadian production. The Caplan-Sauvageau Report suggests that "a general rule of thumb is that it costs ten times as much to produce a Canadian show as it costs to buy an American show."[16] But a positive boost to profitability is given by means of tax incentives for advertisers, regulatory mechanisms and subsidies for production.

Bill C-58 is a 1976 amendment to the Income Tax Act which allows the cost of advertisements directed to Canadian audiences to be deducted as business expenses only if the advertisements are placed on Canadian stations or networks. Expenses incurred by buying advertising on American stations with Canadian audiences cannot be deducted. A corresponding CRTC regulation on simultaneous substitution requires cable companies to substitute the Canadian broadcast and its advertising whenever a local Canadian station and an American station are showing the same programme at the same time. By arranging for simultaneous broadcasting, Canadian private stations are able to increase their audience by including the cable audience for the American station. The Caplan-Sauvageau Task Force estimated that "in 1984 Bill C-58 had the effect of increasing the net revenues of Canadian television stations and networks by $35.8 million to $41.8 million, and simulcast regulations increased them by about $53 million."[17]

The Broadcast Fund, more properly called the Canadian Broadcast Program Development Fund, was established in 1983 as a supplement to the Canadian Film Development Corporation, which became known from that point as Telefilm Canada. The Canadian Film Development

Corporation itself had been set up in 1968 to stimulate the development of a feature film industry in Canada, and had concentrated its efforts on making feature films for release in movie theatres. The Broadcast fund was established to subsidize independent Canadian producers of programmes for the television market. In Canada there is no profitable domestic marketplace for independent producers. The acquisition cost of American programmes determines the license fees that both public and private broadcasters pay for programmes. Because American programmes are available in Canada at a fraction of their cost, Canadian producers are rarely able to earn more than 20 percent of their costs from sales in the Canadian market, unlike British and French producers who can recover costs, or American producers who can make substantial profits in their home markets. The Broadcast Fund, which covers less than one-half of the cost of projects and thus involves arrangements with stations and other financial sources, allocated more than $50 million in 1985 and thus gave production a considerable boost. But the low licence fee structure remains a part of Canadian broadcasting.[18]

The Canadian music recording industry shares with film producers in having an interest in broadcasting regulations. Most recordings played by radio stations are produced by multinational corporations which have little incentive to produce Canadian music in the absence of Canadian broadcasting regulations. For AM radio, 30 percent of the musical content must be Canadian. For FM there are adjustable quotas for various categories of music. For the purpose of this regulation, the CRTC defines a recording as Canadian if it meets at least two of the following criteria: the instrumentation or lyrics were principally performed by a Canadian; the music was composed by a Canadian; the lyrics were written by a Canadian; or the live performance was wholly recorded in Canada. The cost of discs and tapes is determined in the marketplace by the dominance of foreign controlled companies who have access to imported foreign master tapes from which records or tapes are manufactured for the Canadian market. As Paul Audley notes in *Canada's Cultural Industries*, "in what might fairly be considered a form of dumping, almost all foreign master tapes come into Canada valued as though they were blank tapes. The value of the creative performance which is on the tape is ignored . . . "[19] The CRTC broadcast policy is essential for the development of Canadian recordings.

The pattern is repeated in one cultural industry after another. Canadian production holds only a minor share of the market, but what little there is is a consequence of some form of government support, whether subsidy regulation or tax incentive.

The movie screens of the world have been dominated by the products of Hollywood. Canada is no exception in this respect. But Canada was for a long time an exception in having no policy to maintain the domestic production in the face of the Hollywood invasion, and Canada still is an exception in being treated as part of the domestic market by the production and distribution industry of the United States. The Canadian film industry does go back to the years before the First World War. Much of the early production was newsreels and shorts, but there were feature films, and in the 1920s there was an Ontario Government Motion Picture Bureau as well as a Canadian Government Motion Picture Bureau.[20] But for many years until the creation of the Canadian Film Development Corporation in 1968, the Canadian government's film policy was restricted to maintenance of the National Film Board. The only exceptions were some advertising contracts for a small number of private producers and a bizarre agreement to leave the Canadian market open to Hollywood in return for the insertion, where appropriate, in some movies, of plugs for Canadian scenery which might lure American tourists north of the border. (This latter policy is depicted with relish in the at once amusing and distressing film, *Has Anybody Here Seen Canada?*, produced by Kirwan Cox, written by Donald Brittain, and directed by John Kramer for the Great Canadian Motion Picture Company and the National Film Board.)

The National Film Board, created in 1939 by the federal government, has a mandate to "interpret Canada to Canadians and other nations." Though the NFB has played a pioneering role in the development of film technique, its presence has been under-represented in the theatres and much of its work has been restricted to documentary and educational film. It has, however, garnered one international award after another, and despite its limited distribution system has served specialized audiences numbering in the millions annually. The NFB is a major force in the non-theatrical film market, about 65 percent of which is created by the purchase of films, increasingly in videocassette form, by educational institutions. But even in this largely educational market, in which public authorities are the purchasers, Canadian material accounts for only 30–40 percent of sales.[21] In the past few years the NFB, sometimes in co-productions, has registered some notable successes at the box office, but in 1986 its Parliamentary appropriation of $59.4 million was necessary to bridge the large gap between its $73.6 million expenses and its $13.6 million revenues.

When the Canadian Film Development Corporation was established in 1968, its principal mandate was to encourage the development of a Canadian feature film industry. By 1974 the CFDC was able to report considerable success in production, but by then distribution and marketing problems were becoming apparent. Foreign control of distribution was becoming a barrier to domestic production. In 1974 an additional federal government policy arrived in the form of the Capital Cost Allowance Program, a tax-shelter scheme which encouraged a boom in private investment. But the production boom, much of which had little artistic merit, merely widened the gap between production and marketing, and by the early 1980s the film industry was to be no exception to the general economic depression.

The 1983 reorganization, which resulted in the creation of Telefilm Canada and the Broadcast Fund, diverted the focus of film-making from theatres to television and has been successful in stimulating production. It has not, however, resolved the problems of feature film production. Funding of films on a project-by-project basis has left the production sector without well-structured and adequately capitalized production companies. Neither has the new policy resolved the problem of the foreign control of distribution and exhibition. In 1920, Famous Players Lasky, better known as Paramount, entered Canada with the formation of Famous Players Canadian Corporation. They were soon joined by other studios who collectively established a cartel, the Motion Picture Distributors and Exhibitors of Canada. Many of the Canadian-owned theatre chains were eliminated. In 1985, Famous Players, now owned by Gulf Western, a conglomerate with control of production and distribution companies, operated 471 screens in Canada. Its only rival is Odeon-Cineplex which has 472 screens. Together the two take in 60 percent of the more than $1 billion box office receipts.

Cineplex-Odeon was the result of the 1984 purchase by Cineplex of Odeon, a company set up as a British subsidiary in 1941 and bought by Canadians in 1977. Cineplex itself had been founded in 1978 by Garth Drabinsky and Nat Taylor who also launched Pan-Canadian Film Distributors. In 1982 Cineplex had taken a complaint to the Restrictive Film Practices Commission alleging that Odeon and Famous Players had long-term arrangements with the predominantly U.S. distributors which excluded other exhibitors. The complaint resulted in a new bidding system for distribution rights, but ironically the same distributors remain the major suppliers for Famous Players and Cineplex-Odeon. In late 1985 Cineplex sold 50 percent of its ownership to MCA, a U.S. communications conglomerate.[22]

Many of the same ownership and distribution issues characterize the print media. Newspapers, however, are exceptional in requiring no direct subsidies from the government, partly perhaps because long-term policies on Canadian ownership have protected the development of the substantial corporations which now control the majority of newspapers, and partly perhaps because the technology of production has not yet overcome the advantages of local production. Canadian newspapers do, though, benefit from the federal sales tax, a benefit worth $70 million in 1980 according to the 1981 Royal Commission on Newspapers.[23] The Kent commission also estimated that the special postal rate available to newspapers was worth another $27.5 million, and the newspaper industry receives an additional benefit from Bill C-58 which, as with television, encourages advertisers to use Canadian publications.

Canadian magazines are significantly affected by government policies. Many smaller magazines which are published on a not-for-profit basis rely heavily on grants from the Canada Council and provincial arts councils. For the commercially based magazines the provisions of Bill C-58 are central to the advertising revenues which determine their commercial viability. Bill C-58 is a necessary shelter against the combined effects of spillover advertising and the use by advertisers of Canadian editions of U.S. magazines. Spillover advertising — the capacity for U.S. advertisers to reach Canadian audiences through U.S. publications which are widely circulated in Canada — is a significant factor in the competition for magazine advertising dollars. A study done in 1978 for the Department of the Secretary of State (responsible for cultural policy until it was shifted to the Department of Communications in 1980) noted that in 1977 the four U.S. automobile companies spent $91.6 million on magazine advertising in the U.S., while their Canadian subsidiaries spent less than 2 percent of that on magazine advertising in Canada.[24] The Special Senate Committee on Mass Media, chaired by Keith Davey, found that in 1971 — before the tax policy of Bill C-58 was brought in in 1976 — more than half of Canadian magazine advertising was going to the Canadian editions of *Time* and *Reader's Digest*.[25]

Like newspapers, magazines benefit from federal sales tax exemptions and from postal subsidies. The cultural value of these policies has, however, been less clear-cut in the case of magazines than in the case of newspapers because foreign magazines have historically benefitted along with Canadian owned publications. In recent years the postal subsidy has been refined to distinguish between Canadian and foreign magazines, and it is a significant factor in the ability of magazines to maintain sales by subscription.[26] Magazine circulation is also dependent on single copy newsstand sales, and here magazines face some of the same issues as film producers. The dominant companies in national distribution are U.S.-owned and, as with movies, those distributors regard Canada as part of the U.S. market.

Canadian literature has enjoyed a remarkable flowering in recent years and is now perhaps the most self-assured of the arts in Canada. "CanLit" has now established its place in the university calendars. Publishers' lists also contain many more non-fiction titles on Canadian subjects than could be found twenty years ago. But imports still outnumber Canadian books by three to one in the market, and the Canadian market for U.S. books is so large that Canada alone absorbs about half of all U.S. book exports.[27]

For many years book imports were handled by agencies, but by the 1960s many U.S. publishers had cut out the agencies by establishing directly controlled subsidiaries in Canada. As is the case with television programmes and with films, there is a cost advantage for the publisher who imports rather than develops new Canadian books. In the case of publishing, this cost advantage enhances the competitive position of branch-plant publishers who have access to imported books and who typically produce less Canadian work than the Canadian publishers.

As in the case of film, Canadian governments have subsidized the work of writers and have made even substantial contributions to Canadian publishers through a variety of programmes, but have generally drawn back when it comes to the more contentious question of foreign ownership in both the production and distribution aspects of the industry. In July 1985, then Minister of Communications Marcel Masse announced that it was his intention to seek the Canadianization of the publishing industry, but in March 1986 the Cabinet approved the transfer of Prentice-Hall Canada to the new owners of the U.S. parent Prentice-Hall. In the face of very strong lobbying from Gulf-Western, the new owners of the American parent, the Canadian government decided that it could neither use the old Foreign Investment Review Agency provisions which were in force at the time of the acquisition, nor retroactively use its own newly stated policy to deny takeover.

Although the details vary from one sector to another, the pattern which emerges in the cultural industries is remarkably uniform. Government subsidies of one form or another are critical for the maintenance of Canadian production, but Canadian production is very far from having a secure place in its own domestic market. The issue for Canadian culture is not the need to gain access to foreign markets, but to gain access to the Canadian market. That is an issue for producers who want to be able to turn their own visions into art and for consumers who want to see their own society reflected in the arts.

It is hard to give a precise dollar figure to the contribution of governments to the sustenance of Canadian culture. It is not even easy to define precisely what is or is not a cultural policy. The 1985 Annual Report of the National Advisory Committee on Cultural Statistics suggests that overall annual expenditures by the three levels of government for arts and culture were "in the region of $2.9 billion."[28] In addition there are, as we have seen, many policies and regulations that are as important as expenditures. Many of these expenditures and regulations will be of intense interest to U.S. free-trade negotiators who are searching for "level playing fields."

Free Trade and Industrial Policies

The most comprehensive argument in favour of a free trade arrangement with the United States is found in the Report of the Royal Commission on the Economic Union and Development Prospects for Canada — the Macdonald Commission. In that Report, the commissioners say that "trade in service industries will probably figure prominently in any Canada–U.S. trade talks. . . . The removal of existing Canadian restrictions on the entry of U.S. firms in some fields could result in significant penetration of Canadian markets by U.S.-based competitors without conferring comparable benefits in the other direction. Overall, it is likely that the United States has more to gain from the reciprocal reduction in barriers to trade in services than has Canada."[29] The Macdonald Commission also offers a caveat in its passing reference to culture: "Cultural activities may also require special treatment under a general free-trade agreement. Canada provides both import protection and subsidies for cultural activities, because of the widely held view that our domestic market is not large enough to support these activities. Current policies aimed at creating and disseminating more Canadian cultural products, such as the so-called 'Canadian content' rules imposed by the Canadian Radio-television and Telecommunications Commission (CRTC), discriminate against U.S. firms in the cultural industries and might therefore be inconsistent with a general free-trade scheme."[30]

Given these rather substantial warning flags, it is all the more astonishing that in the entire list of the 72 volumes of expensive and time-consuming studies prepared for the commission there is not one single volume, and not even one chapter of a volume, that is specifically devoted to cultural industries. Nor was the Macdonald Commission alone in passing over the cultural questions. Of the original 84 industry profiles prepared by the government for the free-trade talks, not one dealt with a cultural industry, though as David Crane reported in *The Toronto Star*, the U.S. embassy in Ottawa commissioned a study of Canada's cultural industries from Statistics Canada.[31]

In a speech in Chicago on December 4, 1985, Mr. Mulroney said that "our unique cultural identity" was "not at issue in these negotiations." But the series of statements from the major participants on the U.S. side make it clear that the United States has a very different perspective on free-trade negotiations with Canada. At the March 1985 Shamrock Summit meeting between Prime Minister Mulroney and President Reagan, the U.S. president himself raised the subject of royalty payments to U.S. broadcasters by Canadian cable TV operators. Following the meetings, a U.S. official briefing reporters said that both sides understand that there are no preconditions and that nothing is taken off the table. The point has been reiterated by Clayton Yeutter, chief U.S. trade representative, and by Peter Murphy, chief U.S. trade negotiator for the U.S.-Canada talks. Murphy has said that "cultural sovereignty" seems to be "a guise for protectionism." William Merkin, another negotiator, has said that the United States will target key cultural policies such as Bill C-58, foreign investment rules affecting subsidiaries when there is a change in U.S. ownership of a parent company, and Canadian moves to limit U.S. control of film distribution in Canada. In a letter to Senator Packwood, written in the context of softwood lumber disputes and while Packwood was chairman of the U.S. Senate Finance Committee, President Reagan wrote: "During Prime Minister Mulroney's recent visit to this country, he and I agreed that we would attempt to initiate comprehensive bilateral trade negotiations between our two nations on a 'clean launch' basis. We believe it is in the best interest of us all to have everything on the table when the negotiations begin, and to start without preconditions on either side."[32] And when the new Democratic chairman of the same finance committee, Senator Lloyd Bentsen, visited Ottawa in December 1986, he told reporters that among the "difficult" items that would be on the agenda in talks would be "obviously the cultural question, intellectual property rights, the question of what you do in investment . . ."[33]

One cultural industry has already been placed on the table by the Canadian government. In the summer of 1986, in retaliation for a U.S. tariff on Canadian shakes and shingles, Ottawa imposed a 10 percent tariff on U.S. teabags, computers, Christmas trees and books. The irony of this move is increased by the fact that there is already virtually free trade in cultural industries. In a four-part article in *The Toronto Star* in August 1986, David Crane reported that Marcel Masse, while he was still Minister of Communications, had failed in an attempt to get a cabinet agreement to keep cultural policies off the table.[34]

The existing pattern of trade in cultural industries produces a surplus of $1.5 billion for the United States, Masse reported to the cabinet. Twenty-nine subsidiaries of foreign corporations earn 60 percent of publishing revenues, while 173 Canadian-owned companies earn 40 percent. Nineteen subsidiaries earn 67 percent of film distribution revenues in Canada, while 95 Canadian companies earn 33 percent. Twelve foreign-owned subsidiaries in sound recording earn 89 percent of industry profits while 123 Canadian companies earn 11 percent.[35] Cultural trade is on the agenda because it is big business for the Americans. Some of the giant U.S. conglomerates are increasing their holdings in cultural industries. Among them are Coca-Cola with an interest in Columbia Pictures and Tri-Star Pictures; General Electric Corporation with ownership of RCA Corporation and NBC; Gulf and Western Industries which owns Paramount Pictures and publishing companies Prentice-Hall and Simon and Schuster. There are other giants in the same business — Warner Communications, MCA Inc. and Time Inc. They are certainly keeping the U.S. government informed about the stakes in free-trade negotiations.

The United States has long had an interest in gaining access to the cultural markets of the world. Freedom of information is for the U.S bound up with the freedom of U.S. cultural industries to operate without limits. An insistence on "domestic treatment" for multinationals — the doctrine that U.S. companies should be regarded as Canadian when in Toronto or Italian when in Rome — is fought for just as strongly in cultural industries as in the oil industry. The shaping of opinion is part of foreign policy and the battle for the "hearts and minds" of the world is fought on many different kinds of ground.

Canadian culture has always been embattled. Free-trade talks have not changed anything in that respect. But they do open up the possibility of losing what little cultural autonomy we do have and of losing ground with the policies which are essential to our cultural integrity.

From the pre-school years with television programmes, to school textbooks and computer software, to the movies and the continued and pervasive television programming, to novels and theatres and art galleries, a Canadian grows up seeing a large part of the world through American eyes and has to work hard to find a Canadian alternative. The issue is not closing borders — in cultural terms Canada has the most wide-open border in the world — but maintaining a place for Canadian culture in Canada itself.

It is possible, by means of government leverage, to provide some breathing room for Canadian cultural industries. It would be possible to do a lot more than is now being done. A more integrated set of cultural policies, combining the interests of both federal and provincial governments through their powers over broadcasting and education for example, is a possibility. A more active awareness of technological change and its cultural implication should be available to the descendants of Harold Innis. As a British cultural critic, commenting on the British Peacock Report on Broadcasting policy, wrote: "Technologies exercise their influence over society not through their intrinsic possibilities but through the institutions to which they give rise."[36] Part of the process of assuring adequate public services involves the Canadian government in developing the institutions which will both protect and enhance Canadian culture. In that light the opening of free-trade talks with the United States has been a momentous decision. The evidence so far suggests that it might well close some of the windows on our future.

NOTES

1. Paul Audley, *Canada's Cultural Industries*. Canadian Institute for Economic Policy, 1983, p. 321.

2. Ibid., p. 57.

3. Ibid., pp. 147-8.

4. Ibid., p. 221.

5. Pierre Juneau, "The Impact of Cultural Industries on Canadian Identity," a speech at the 28th Annual Canadian-American Seminar, University of Windsor, November 6, 1986.

6. *Report of the Task Force on Broadcasting Policy*, Minister of Supply and Services, Ottawa, 1986, p. 691.

7. *Canada's International Trade in Services*, Statistics Canada, Ottawa, 1986, p. 27.

8. Juneau, op. cit., p. 13.

9. *Funding of the Arts in Canada to the Year 2000*, The Report of the Task Force on Funding of the Arts, Government of Canada, chapter 3.

10. Harold Innis, "The Strategy of Culture," in *Changing Concepts of Time*, University of Toronto Press, 1952, p. 18.

11. Ibid., p. 20.

12. The annual figures for the Canada Council and the Ontario Arts Council are available from the Annual Reports which both organizations publish. On the history of the arts councils, see Arthur Gelber, "The Arts in Canada Come of Age," in *You've Got Ten Minutes to Get That Flag Down* . . . Proceedings of the Halifax Conference: A National Forum on Canadian Cultural Policy, Nova Scotia Coalition on Arts and Culture, 1986.

13. *Report of the Task Force on Broadcasting Policy*, op. cit., p. 6. See also Michael Nolan, *Foundations: Alan Plaunt and the Early Days of CBC Radio*, CBC Enterprises, 1986, and Frank W. Peers, *The Politics of Canadian Broadcasting*, University of Toronto Press, 1969.

14. Peter Morris, "Electronic Free Trade: How the CBC Brought U.S. Television to Canada," *Cinema Canada*, December 1986.

15. Herschel Hardin, *Closed Circuits*, Douglas and McIntyre, 1985, p. 264.

16. *Report of the Task Force on Broadcasting*, op. cit., p. 443.

17. Ibid., p. 460.

18. Ibid., pp. 362-3 and p. 366.

19. Audley, op. cit., p. 158.

20. For the early history of Canadian film, see Peter Morris, *Embattled Shadows: A History of Canadian Cinema, 1895-1939*, and also S. Daniel Lyon and Michael J. Trebilcock, *Public Strategy and Motion Pictures*, Ontario Economic Council, 1982.

21. *The Other Film Industry*, Report of the Non-theatrical Film Industry Task Force, Government of Canada, 1986, pp. iv-vi.

22. On theatrical film distribution, see *Canadian Cinema: A Solid Base*, Report of the Film Industry Task Force, 1985; Paul Audley, op. cit., chapter 6; and the feature on Garth Drabinsky in *Report on Business*, December 1985.

23. Audley, op. cit., p. 42.

24. Ibid., p. 60.

25. Ibid., p. 61.

26. Ibid., p. 75.

27. Ibid., p. 89.

28. *Culture Statistics Programme*, Annual Report of the National Advisory Committee on Culture Statistics, October 1985, p. 13.

29. *Report of the Royal Commission on the Economic Union and Development Prospects for Canada*, Minister of Supply and Services, Canada, 1985, pp. 308-9.

30. Ibid., pp. 309-10.

31. *The Toronto Star*, 2 August, 1986.

32. Duncan Cameron, ed., *The Free Trade Papers*, Lorimer, 1986, p. 44.

33. *The Globe and Mail*, 10 December, 1986.

34. *The Toronto Star*, 4 August, 1986.

35. *The Toronto Star*, 5 August, 1986.

36. Quoted by Bernard Ostry, "After Convergence," a speech to the 17th Annual Conference of the International Institute of Communications, Edinburgh, 12 September, 1986.

Reader Reply Card

We are interested in your reaction to *Coming of Age: Readings in Canadian History since World War II*, by Donald Avery and Roger Hall. You can help us to improve this book in future editions by completing this questionnaire.

1. What was your reason for using this book?

   ☐ university course   ☐ continuing education course   ☐ personal interest
   ☐ college course   ☐ professional development   ☐ other _____

2. If you are a student, please identify your school and the course in which you used this book.

3. Which chapters or parts of this book did you use? Which did you omit?

4. What did you like best about this book?

5. What did you like least about this book?

6. Please identify any topics you think should be added to future editions.

7. Please add any comments or suggestions.

8. May we contact you for further information?

   Name: _____
   Address: _____
   _____
   Phone: _____

(fold here and tape shut)

MAIL ➤ **POSTE**

Canada Post Corporation / Société canadienne des postes

Postage paid
If mailed in Canada

Port payé
si posté au Canada

**Business
Reply**

**Réponse
d'affaires**

0116870399   01

0116870399-M8Z4X6-BR01

Heather McWhinney
Publisher, College Division
HARCOURT BRACE & COMPANY, CANADA
55 HORNER AVENUE
TORONTO, ONTARIO
M8Z 9Z9